DATE DUE

APR 5 1994	
MAY 2 7 1994	FEB 1 6 1999
JUN 1 0 1994	APR 1 4 1999
NOV 2 4 1994	DEC - 8 1999
JAN 2 3 1995	MAR 1 6 2000
JUN - 7 1995	APR 1 9 2000
JUN 2 0 1995 OCT - 4 1995	NOV 1 4 2001
MAR - 7 1996	NOV 2 8 2001
APR 1 5 1996	SEP 2 5 2003
DEC 1 3 1996	DEC - 2 2003
FEB 2 4 1997 MAR 1 2 1997	
MAR 3 1 1997	
Apr 11 APR 2 1 1997	
FEB 2 3 1998 Mar 9	

BRODART   Cat. No. 23-221

Technology and Infertility

Clinical, Psychosocial, Legal, and Ethical Aspects

Machelle M. Seibel
Judith Bernstein
Editors

Ann A. Kiessling
Susan R. Levin

Technology and Infertility

Clinical, Psychosocial, Legal, and Ethical Aspects

With 186 Figures

Springer-Verlag

New York Berlin Heidelberg London Paris
Tokyo Hong Kong Barcelona Budapest

Machelle M. Seibel, M.D.
Harvard Medical School
and
Faulkner Centre for Reproductive
  Medicine
Faulkner Hospital
Boston, MA 02130, USA

Ann A. Kiessling, Ph.D.
Harvard Medical School
and
Faulkner Centre for Reproductive
  Medicine
Faulkner Hospital
Boston, MA 02130, USA

Judith Bernstein, R.N., M.S.
Faulkner Centre for Reproductive
  Medicine
Faulkner Hospital
Boston, MA 02130, USA

Susan R. Levin, LICSW
The Boston Psychoanalytic Society
and
Faulkner Centre for Reproductive
  Medicine
Faulkner Hospital
Boston, MA 02130, USA

Library of Congress Cataloging-in-Publication Data
Technology and infertility: clinical, psychosocial, legal, and ethical
  aspects / [edited by] Machelle Seibel [et al.].
      p.   cm.
    Includes bibliographical references and index.
    ISBN 0-387-97793-7. — ISBN 3-540-97793-7
    1. Infertility—Treatment.   2. Infertility—Psychological aspects.
  3. Human reproductive technology—Moral and ethical aspects.
  4. Human reproductive technology—Social aspects.   I. Seibel,
  Machelle M.
    [DNLM: 1. Ethics, Medical.   2. Infertility—psychology.
  3. Infertility—therapy.   WP 570 T255]
  RC889.T43   1992
  616.6'92—dc20
  DNLM/DLC
  for Library of Congress   92-2180

Printed on acid-free paper.

Production managed by Terry Kornak; manufacturing supervised by Jacqui Ashri.
Typeset by Best-set, Chaiwan, Hong Kong
Printed and bound by Kingsport Press, Kingsport, TN,
Printed in the United States of America.

9 8 7 6 5 4 3 2 1

ISBN 0-387-97793-7 Springer-Verlag New York Berlin Heidelberg
ISBN 3-540-97793-7 Springer-Verlag Berlin Heidelberg New York

Dedication

In January 1990 the Faulkner Centre for Reproductive Medicine (FCRM) was created. Our goal was to provide the highest level of infertility, endocrinology and reproductive technology expertise in a modern and pleasant environment oriented to patient comfort. Our other objectives were to conduct state of the art research and to provide psychological support for our patients. We assembled an outstanding group of psychological, theological, legal, medical, and technical individuals to serve as our ethics advisory committee in order to provide guidance in understanding the complex issues facing infertility teams today. This book is dedicated to FCRM and its staff and consultants, who have allowed those goals to be realized.

Preface

Medicine is changing at a speed never witnessed before in history. With each passing year, medical technology achieves the capacity to provide cures and improve treatments that even a short time before were difficult to conceptualize and impossible to provide. Reproductive technology personifies this concept perhaps better than any other field of medicine. The 1990s have seen an explosion in endoscopic and ambulatory procedures, the application of molecular biology to clinical conditions, and the refinement of assisted reproduction to allow third parties (donors and surrogates) into the process of family building. More than ever before, comprehensive medical care requires a team approach. However, the team comprises not only medical and scientific personnel, but also mental health professionals, lawyers, and ethicists. This integrated and multidisciplinary approach to medical care will become even more necessary as medical capabilities continue to develop faster than society can respond. This book reflects such an approach.

It is based on a Harvard Postgraduate Course in June 1990 entitled Infertility in the 1990s: Technological Advances and Their Psychosocial Implications that was sponsored by the Faulkner Centre for Reproductive Medicine. The first half of the course was directed by Drs. M. Seibel, A. Kiessling, and C. Richards. The second half of the course was directed by Dr. M. Seibel, J. Bernstein, R.N. and S. Levin, LICSW. A renowned group of American and European scientists, physicians, lawyers, clergymen, mental health professionals, and ethicists were assembled to provide a multidisciplinary discussion of infertility treatment. Additional chapters were added by the editors to broaden the scope of the book. The editors would like to thank each of our contributors for their thoughtful and well written chapters. We feel that combining technological advances in infertility with their psychosocial, legal, and ethical implications within one text will help the reader will gain insight into and appreciation of the complexities of modern reproductive medicine.

Contents

Cellular and Molecular Advances

Nonsurgical Advances in Infertility

Alternatives to Reproductive Failure

Psychosocial Aspects

Legal Aspects

Ethical Aspects

Contributors

Eli Y. Adashi, M.D., Professor of Obstetrics and Gynecology, University of Maryland, Baltimore, MD 21201, USA

George Annas, J.D., M.P.H., Professor, Center for Health Law, Boston University Schools of Medicine and Public Health, Boston, MA, USA

Roberta J. Apfel, M.D., Associate Professor of Clinical Psychiatry, Harvard Medical School, Boston, MA 02215, USA

Herbert Benson, M.D., Associate Professor of Medicine, Harvard Medical School, Boston, MA 02215, USA

Judith Bernstein, R.N., M.S., Clinical Nurse Specialist, Reproductive Endocrinology, Faulkner Centre for Reproductive Medicine, Boston, MA 02130, USA

John D. Biggers, Ph.D., Professor of Physiology, Harvard Medical School, Boston, MA 02215, USA

E.G. Blakewood, Department of Animal Science, Louisiana State University, Baton Rouge, LA 70803, USA

Merle Bombadieri, LICSW, Private Practice, Lexington, MA 02173, USA

Mara Brill, M.D., Consultant, Faulkner Center for Reproductive Medicine, and Assistant Clinical Professor of Psychiatry, Tufts New England Medical Center, and Private Practice, Needham, MA 02194 USA

Louis Burke, M.D., Associate Professor of Obstetrics and Gynecology, Harvard Medical School, Boston, MA 02215, USA

Dianne Clapp, R.N., M.S., Resolve, Nurse-Counselor, Private Practice, Lexington, MA 02173, USA

Bruce Cohen, M.D., Resident, Beth Israel Hospital, Harvard Medical School, Boston, MA 02215, USA

Susan Cooper, Ed.D., Psychologist, IVF Australia, Director, Focus Women's Health Center, Boston, MA 02146, USA

Alice D. Domar, Ph.D., Deaconness Hospital Behavioral Medicine Program, Boston, MA 02215, USA

Jean Bernard Dubuisson, M.D., Professor of Obstetrics and Gynecology, Port Royal University, 75014 Paris, France

Gary Ellis, M.D., Director, Health Promotion and Disease Prevention, Institute of Medicine, National Academy of Sciences, Washington, D.C. 20148, USA

Mark L. Fallick, M.D., Boston University School of Medicine, Boston, MA USA

Susan M. Fisher, M.D., Department of Psychiatry, University of Chicago, Pritzker School of Medicine and Psychoanalyst, Private Practice, Chicago, IL, 60615, USA

Herve Foulot, M.D., Assistant Professor of Obstetrics and Gynecology, Port Royal University, 75014 Paris, France

Rochelle Friedman, M.D., Clinical Instructor in Psychiatry, Harvard Medical School and Psychiatrist, Massachusetts Institute of Technology Health Service, Boston, MA 02165, USA

Carol Frost-Vercollone, LICSW, Private Practice Stoneham, MA 02180, USA

Ellen Glazer, LICSW, Private Practice, Newton, MA 02158, USA

Robert A. Godke, Ph.D., Professor of Animal Science, School of Veterinary Medicine, Louisiana State University, Baton Rouge, LA 70803, USA

Donald P. Goldstein, M.D., Assistant Professor of Obstetrics and Gynecology, Harvard Medical School, Boston, MA 02215, USA

Andrew Herzog, M.D., Assistant Professor of Neurology, Harvard Medical School, Boston, MA 02215, USA

Robert Hunt, M.D., Clinical Instructor of Obstetrics and Gynecology, Harvard Medical School, Boston, MA 02215, USA

Ann A. Kiessling, Ph.D., Associate Professor, Harvard Medical School, Boston, Massachusetts, Director of Embryology, Faulkner Centre for Reproductive Medicine, Boston, MA 02130, USA

Susan Levin, LICSW, Director, Continuing Education for Graduates and Student Organizor of the Advanced Training Program in Psychoanalytic Psychotherapy for The Boston Psychoanalytic Society, Director, Mental Health, Faulkner Centre for Reproductive Medicine and Private Practice, Boston, MA 02130, USA

R. Tracy MacNab, Ph.D., Director, Continuing Education, Boston Institute for Psychotherapy, Newton Centre, MA 02159, USA

Barbara Eck Menning, Founder, Resolve; *P.O. Box 430*, Falmouth, MA 02574, USA

James O'Donohoe, J.C.D., Associate Professor of Theological Ethics, Department of Theology, Boston College, Chestnut Hill, MA 02167, USA

Ralph Philosophe, M.D., Consultant, Faulkner Centre for Reproductive Medicine, Boston, MA 02130; and staff physician, Norwood Hospital, Norwood, MA, USA

Joseph Polak, Rabbi, University Chaplain and Director, B'nal B'rith Hillel Foundation, Boston, MA 02115, USA

David H. Porter, M.D., Beth Israel Hospital, Boston, MA 02ll5, USA

Charlotte J. Richards, M.D., Instructor in Radiology, Harvard Medical School, Boston, MA 02215, USA

Zev Rosenwaks, M.D., Professor of Obstetrics and Gynecology, Cornell University, New York, NY 10021, USA

Machelle M. Seibel, M.D., Associate Clinical Professor of Surgery (Gynecology), Harvard Medical School: Director, Faulkner Centre for Reproductive Medicine, Boston, MA 02130, USA

Ricardo Serta, M.D., Obstetrician-Gynecologist, Jardim Botanico, Rio de Janeiro R.J. 22460, Brazil

Sherman Silber, M.D., Urologist, Reproductive Microsurgeon, St. Luke's Hospital, St. Louis, MO 63017, USA

Andrew Singer, M.D., Instructor in Radiology, Harvard Medical School, Boston, MA 02215, USA

Sharon Steinberg, R.N., M.S., Psychiatric Nurse Specialist, Harvard Community Health Plan, Boston, MA 02167, USA

J.K. Thibodeaux, Ph.D., Department of Veterinary Science, Louisiana State University, Baton Rouge, LA 70803, USA

Lyle L. Warner, Ph.D., Private Practice, Boston, MA 21208, USA

1
A Historical Perspective of Obstetrics and Gynecology: A Backdrop for Reproductive Technology

Bruce Cohen and Machelle M. Seibel

Women today are living longer, healthier, more productive lives than did their ancestors. This statement could not have been made by the colonial American any more truthfully than by his or her ancient Roman counterpart, and it is a direct result of the great advancements in technology and science that have occurred during the twentieth century. The technologic explosion of our times is similar to that of other periods of rapid intellectual development throughout history in that it appears to have resulted from a combination of great minds and a ripe political, economic, and cultural climate. However, today's technology can be fully appreciated only through consideration of modern political, economic, and cultural factors and of the historical context from which they emerge. Therefore, before embarking on a detailed discussion of the recent medical advances in reproductive technology and their psychosocial, legal, and ethical implications, it is useful to review briefly the history of medicine, and obstetrics and gynecology in particular, prior to the twentieth century.

Ancient History

Egyptians

Our knowledge of medicine in antiquity begins in Egypt with writings on papyri, sculptures, and tombs dating back to 1500 B.C. The typical Egyptian's life was rigidly controlled by religious doctrine as well as laws of the pharaoh and was largely devoted to preparation for the afterlife. The tremendous emphasis placed on life after death did little to promote

thought concerning the medical problems of the Egyptians' day-to-day life. Moreover, a manifestation of the individual's lack of control over his or her own life was the nearly universal belief that disease was caused and remedied only by the gods.

Nevertheless, the ancient Egyptians did possess a moderate amount of medical knowledge. Particularly noteworthy was their understanding of anatomy, which was a direct result of their practice of mummification. When an individual died, all of the internal organs were removed with the exception of the heart, which was thought to encase the soul. Thus, with ample opportunity for human dissection, impressive knowledge was achieved. With regard to the female reproductive system, the external genitalia, vagina, cervix, and uterus were named and differentiated in the medical papyri. The uterus, however, was erroneously believed to wander about the abdomen like an animal in response to odors or to engulf a man's seed during coitus.

The Egyptians' understanding of conception was less advanced. Although they understood the relationship between sexual intercourse and the production of offspring, the male-dominated society viewed the conceptus to be wholly contained in the man's seed, with the woman as a mere receptacle to house it. They therefore mistakenly believed that a woman could become pregnant after oral sex.

Fertility was of great concern to the Egyptians, as was conception. The 1350 B.C. Berlin Medical Papyrus informs us that wheat and spelt were watered daily with a woman's urine; if both grew she was pregnant. We also learn that mixtures of crocodile dung and honey were introduced into the vagina to provide a mechanical barrier to pregnancy. Fumigation prior to intercourse and a postcoital douche with urine and garlic were also popular methods of contraception.

Suspected to be spread by sexual contact, gonorrhea, which means "running of the seed," was common in ancient Egypt and was thought to be an involuntary passage of sperm. Although the manifestations of the disease were not appreciated, condoms made out of lamb or sheep cecum were devised to protect one from transmitting this affliction.

Hebrews

A civilization that would have greater impact on future medical thought was that of the Hebrews of approximately 1300 B.C. Our source of information with regard to the Jewish people is the Talmud, written during the second through the sixth centuries A.D. The Jewish people, unlike the Egyptians, worshipped one god, whom they viewed as the source of both health and disease. However, whereas most treatment of illness consisted of prayer and animal sacrifice, there was clearly a greater humanism and a less rigid religiosity among the Jews. In Ecclesiastes 38, the sick are advised, "Pray unto the lord, but then give place to the physician; for the lord hath created him and you have need of him." The ancient Hebrews may thus be credited with developing the first human healers, despite their metaphysical beliefs.

The Hebrew civilization introduced several other concepts. They were the first people to practice organized preventive medicine. The laws of Moses placed great emphasis on hygiene. Bathing was required after coitus and menstruation. The menstruating woman was considered unclean and could not participate in religious or sexual activity until 7 days after cessation of the menstrual flow. This delay probably resulted in sexual intercourse occurring around the time of ovulation, with obvious beneficial effects.

Around 1300 B.C. the Jewish people became the first to use a vaginal speculum. A bamboo shoot was customarily used for this purpose.

A piece of cotton passed down the bamboo differentiated uterine from vaginal bleeding. Vaginal bleeding would stain only the bamboo, whereas bleeding from the uterus would stain the cotton as well. Intermenstrual bleeding was recognized first by the Hebrews to be pathologic.

Hebrew writings were the first to mention coitus interruptus as a method of birth control. The Old Testament speaks of the two sons of Judah, Er and Onan. After the death of Er, who had sinned, Judah said to Onan, "'Go into thy brother's wife and marry her and raise up seed to thy brother.' And Onan knew that the seed should not be his; and it came to pass when he went to his brother's wife that he spilled the seed on the ground lest he should give seed to his brother." The Jewish people of this period also introduced the contraceptive sponge from plants growing in their local waters for the purpose of absorbing semen.

The first cesarean section was recorded at this time, although not necessarily by the Hebrews. It was probably performed on a dead mother in an attempt to save the child or to provide a separate burial. There is no record of a cesarean section, as we know it today, on a live woman ever being attempted in antiquity. With regard to the origin of the term "cesarean," clearly, Julius Caesar was not delivered by cesarean section because we know his mother was alive during his adult life. The two most likely possibilities for the origin of the word are that it is derived from the Latin *caedare*, "to cut," or it was taken from the ancient Roman law, the *lex Caesaris*, which stated that a fetus of advanced gestation should surgically be removed from a dead mother to have a separate burial performed by the state.

Greeks

The next civilization of medical historical importance is that of the Greeks during the fourth and fifth centuries B.C. One aspect of this civilization that appeals to the historian is the substantial and outstanding written record offered by Hippocrates during the fourth century B.C. Another interesting aspect is its profound influence on later medical thoughts.

The Greeks worshipped many gods and, like the Egyptians and Hebrews, believed that disease was divinely caused. However, the Greeks were the first to study and write extensively on disease and to hypothesize about the mechanisms of illness. This intellectual process did not emanate from scientific pursuit. Science, as we know it today, did not exist. Instead, this movement was inspired by the schools of philosophy that were emerging at this time.

The most important school of philosophy with regard to medicine arose in the sixth century B.C. and was named the Pythagorean School. This philosophy attempted to explain all worldly phenomena in terms of numbers. The numbers four and seven were particularly important. For example, the length of gestation was established to be 4×70 days, and a child born in the seventh month was thought likely to survive, but one born in the eighth month of gestation would surely die.

Based on the number four, the pythagoreans probably invented the humoral theory of medicine. This theory, although it had no basis in scientific truth, was the mainstay of medical thought and practice for the next 2000 years. It taught that the body is made up of four humors—blood, phlegm, yellow bile, and black bile—which have varying characteristics of heat, coolness, moisture, or dryness. Every individual had his or her own blend of these four characteristics. When the humors became unbalanced in a given person, due, for example, to an offended god, the person became ill. Diagnosis was concerned with determining which humors were distorted and counteracting this imbalance with heat, moisture, various diets, or blood purging.

Although the humoral theory was an advance from the previous ways in which groups of people viewed disease in that it did not merely dismiss disease as a metaphysical phenomenon, it provided little in the way of rational treatment or understanding of bodily processes. Menstruation, for example, continued to be grossly misunderstood. The word menstruation was coined by the Greeks and means "a catharsis." This meaning is the Greeks' extension of the Hebrew belief that the menstrual blood was impure. Pliny wrote, "So pernicious are the properties of the menstrual discharge that if a pregnant women be touched with it, if indeed, she so much as steps over it, she will be liable to miscarry." Many of the humorists believed that menstrual blood was female semen, which mixed with male semen to produce offspring. When a woman became pregnant, the blood became food for the growing fetus so that no menses occurred. After parturition, it was thought to migrate up to the breasts to provide nutrition for the child.

Romans

Roman civilization, which rose from 500 B.C. to 500 A.D., was not a great period of advance in medicine. Intellectual progress in general slowed. One of the contributing factors to the slowing of medical advances was the introduction of certain beliefs associated with the rise of Christianity. The widespread belief in an imminent second coming of Christ and a judgment day, with its resulting end of the here and now, did not encourage concern for man's mundane physical afflictions. Two notable figures lived during this period, however. One was Savanus of Ephesus, who treated uterine prolapse with pessaries and artificially ruptured the fetal membranes to promote delivery in prolonged labors. The other was the great anatomist Galen, who was the first to describe cancerous growth.

Middle Ages

If Roman civilization saw the deceleration of intellectual progress in medicine, the Middle Ages witnessed a virtual halting of medical advance. This was an age of obsessive religiosity in which human dissection and surgery were forbidden, and touching the human body outside of marriage was considered unclean. With no knowledge of anatomy and little interest in academic thought, the Middle Ages fostered an environment in which medical misconception was the order of the day. Multiple births were thought to result from adulterous relations or from sexual intercourse with animals. One set of twins was reported in which one boy looked like the woman's husband and the other twin like her lover. When a woman named Mary Toth claimed that she could give birth to rabbits at will, many paid money to witness the event.

The Renaissance

The Renaissance, from 1,450 to 1,600, saw the rebirth of human intellectual thought and creativity. Three important factors were involved in the progress of medicine. First, the rise in humanism and the decrease in the influence of the Church once again forced interest on the human experience, including health issues. In addition, human dissection was again allowed, without which anatomy could not be understood. The second factor was the invention of printing, which permitted observations, experiences, and ideas to be shared over great distances. Third, the revisitation and appreciation of the classical authors brought back much of the premedieval medical knowledge into common use.

One area of intense study during the Renaissance was anatomy. Leonardo Da Vinci performed human dissections and was the first to describe a unilocular uterus. Galen had reported seven chambers—three for boy infants, three for girl infants, and one that leads to miscarriages. In addition, Leonardo was the first to describe the fetal membranes with any accurate anatomic detail.

The first documented cesarean section on a live woman was performed by Jacob Nuter in the year 1500. Nuter was a swine spayer from Switzerland, who obtained permission from the local officials to cut his wife with a razor after she had labored unsuccessfully for several days. The story states that the baby lived to be 77 years old and Mrs. Nuter delivered five more children (the first reported vaginal delivery after cesarean section without complication). Mortality from cesarean sections during the Renaissance approached 100%, however, despite isolated successes.

Another important development concerned sexually transmitted disease. One version of this story is as follows. In 1495 Charles VII of France was besieging Naples. His army was made up of Frenchmen and some Spanish mercenaries. Many of these mercenaries were reportedly members of Christopher Columbus' crew who had recently returned from the Americas. During the battle they experienced a terrible disease that manifested itself in skin ulcerations, tissue destruction, and death. It was postulated that the disease was contracted from the natives with whom these sailors had come into contact in the New World. Two years later it had spread throughout Europe, killing tens of thousands of people. In France it was called the Neapolitan disease (after the battle of Naples), in England the Spanish disease, and in Italy (also not wanting credit for it) the French disease.

An Italian named Fracastoro in 1530 wrote a poem that depicted Ovid's story of a mythical shepherd named Syphilus. To place the story in a contemporary setting, Fracastoro bestowed the French disease on the shepherd as punishment for cursing the gods. From that time on, the disease has been known as syphilis. It was somewhat different from the condition seen today in that it was frequently fatal, with tertiary symptoms appearing only months after the initial infection. The response in the early 1500s was one of panic. The city fathers of Paris became so alarmed that they evicted everyone affected with syphilis, hanging those who refused to leave. The next year the laws became more stringent, and infected individuals were thrown into the River Seine. By 1497 mercury was discovered to have some therapeutic benefit to sufferers from syphilis, but thousands died, and more suffered from mercury poisoning even into the twentieth century. From a historical perspective, the panic associated with the lack of a cure for a mysterious and lethal disease is not unlike our groping with human immunodeficiency disease today.

During the Renaissance, as it had been in previous centuries, obstetrics was the exclusive practice of the mid-wife (literally, "with-woman"). Midwives were by and large women who had no formal education and who practiced using relics, charms, and incantations. With the advent of printing, some knowledge and experience was spread, but obstetrics was primitive. One anonymous author describes how "Belligerent midwives guarded the lying-in chamber against all medical interference, particularly the male species." According to legend, one Dr. Wirtt of Hamburg was caught at a delivery disguised in a woman's garb and was burned at the stake.

Prior to the seventeenth and eighteenth centuries, the discipline and practice of medicine, and obstetrics and gynecology in particular, were based purely on empiricism and lacked any scientific basis. Obstetrics was the realm of uneducated midwives with their fumigations and incantations. Although many accurate observations concerning gynecology were made, the lack of understanding of physiology precluded effective therapy. The humoral theory of the ancient Greeks was still widely accepted, as was a metaphysical basis of disease.

Modern History

Seventeenth and Eighteenth Centuries

An incredible intellectual outburst began during the seventeenth century in England and reached its summit with such men as Sir Isaac Newton, Francis Bacon, and William Harvey. These men drastically changed the world forever, for it is with them that science was born. Suddenly, higher mathematics and the fields of chemistry, physics, and physiology were developed, and would bring a scientific basis to medical thought.

For the time being, however, medical advance continued at a very slow pace. The major contributions during these centuries were instruments of measurement and the microscope. Galileo invented the thermometer in 1592, and soon after body temperatures were recorded. Watches acquired minute hands in the late seventeenth century, and pulses were measure. Most significant, in 1677 Anton Van Leeuwenhoek introduced his microscope, giving birth to the field of embryology and histology. The world was turned on its ear when, using a microscope, de

Graaf in Holland discovered follicles in the female ovary. The notion that the female bore the seed threatened the Aristotelean notion of the woman's secondary role in conception.

The emergence of the basic sciences and the concepts of scientific inquiry, experiment, and research led during the eighteenth century to the foundation of thousands of institutions of study throughout the world. In the United States, the first medical school, the University of Pennsylvania, was founded by John Morgan, and the first hospital, Pennsylvania Hospital, was founded by Benjamin Franklin and Thomas Bond.

Although obstetrics continued to be practiced on a largely empiric rather than scientific basis, the nature of that practice began to change, due in part to a French family of physicians named the Chamberlens. Beginning in 1598, Peter Chamberlen I, the elder, of Paris began carrying a large wooden box to the homes of laboring women whom the midwives were unable to deliver. For centuries, the only treatment to save women with such an unproductive labor had been craniotomy (crushing the baby's skull with a clamp and removing the infant from the uterus). The Chamberlens advertised a secret means of delivering these babies without killing them. By blindfolding everyone in the birthing room, the Chamberlens kept their secret in the hands of a few practitioners for more than a century. In 1813 a chest containing Peter Chamberlen's instruments was found in Essex, England; the Chamberlens are thus credited with introducing the modern forceps.

One of the major results of the widespread use of the forceps was a change in the practitioners of obstetrics. Now armed with an instrument that could be used to alter the course of labor, men flocked to the birthing rooms for the first time during the late eighteenth century. However, it was still unforgivable for a man to view a woman's private parts during birth. One male obstetrician, William Smellie of London, customarily tied the top bed sheet around his neck. One day, he cut the umbilical cord on the wrong side of the ligature. Realizing what he had done and not wishing to be laughed at by the midwives in attendance, he announced that he was intentionally bleeding the woman to prevent the seizures of toxemia.

The Nineteenth Century

By the end of the eighteenth century the basic sciences were flourishing in new universities and laboratories, but not yet influencing the practice of medicine. Nevertheless, the theory of humoral medicine, which had been the basis of medical theory for two millennia, was quickly found to have no scientific basis and was, for all practical purposes, dead. Disease could no longer be regarded as a metaphysical phenomenon but was explicable by the laws of nature and organic matter. Empiricism had been replaced by scientific inquiry and deduction. Rational and definitive therapy would await only the application of these scientific principles to medicine; this application would begin during the nineteenth century but would come to fruition only during the twentieth century.

One clear example of the new scientific model at work in nineteenth-century obstetrics and gynecology was the demonstration of the infectious nature of puerperal fever. Ignaz Semmelweiss, chief of the obstetrics clinics in Vienna, observed that in one of his clinics there were 406 deaths and that in the other there were only 105 deaths from maternal puerperal fever. The two clinics took care of approximately the same number of deliveries, housed the same types of patients, and were located within the same hospital. The only difference Semmelweiss could find between them was that the one with the greater number of deaths was staffed by medical students who worked there after their anatomy dissection laboratory; the other was staffed by midwives. Semmelweiss hypothesized that the students might be transmitting a lethal agent from the cadavers to the postpartum women. In a beautiful prospective study, he made all the students wash their hands with chlorinated lime after their dissection lab to determine the effect this would have on maternal mortality. Within 1 year the rate of maternal mortality from puerperal infection had fallen to the level of the clinic staffed by midwives. Thus it was proved that puerperal fever was infectious and preventable by hand washing.

Gynecologists of the nineteenth century were notable for their great contributions to the fields of surgery and anesthesia. James Young Simpson, the head of gynecology at the University of Edinburgh, for example, introduced the anesthetic chloroform for widespread use. Nitrous oxide and ether had been used since 1846, but were unpopular in obstetrics since they were clumsy to use and smelled badly. Simpson, searching for a compound to use during labor, was given chloroform by a Liverpool chemist. One night he and his friends inhaled the pleasant-smelling drug and became unconscious. Simpson introduced chloroform as an obstetric anesthetic, and it became the most popular general anesthetic in England for the next 50 years. Of course, not everyone was as happy with the drug as Simpson. The Calvinist Church called chloroform sacrilegious since it had been ordered that "In sorrow shall she bring forth."

No history of gynecology would be complete without mention of Ephraim McDowell's ovariectomy. McDowell was an American gynecologist educated at the University of Edinburgh. He had been practicing in Kentucky for 14 years when he was called to see a Mrs. Crawford whose pregnancy was long past due. He diagnosed an ovarian mass and explained to her that untreated she would certainly die. He said he had never performed such surgery before, since at that time abdominal surgery was essentially a death sentence, but he was willing to try if she wished. Mrs. Crawford rode 60 miles on horseback in the middle of the winter to McDowell's office, where he operated on her on Christmas Day 1809. With no anesthesia, McDowell, who was assisted by his nephew, made a left rectus incision 9 cm long; the patient's intestines promptly fell on the floor. McDowell incised and drained 20 pounds of fluid from her huge ovarian cyst after ligating the fallopian tube. He then incised the tube, which he removed with the sac en masse. The abdominal wound was then sutured with interrupted sutures. The patient chanted psalms throughout the entire procedure.

During the operation, McDowell became aware that an angry mob was gathering outside awaiting the results of his "experiment at butchering a woman." Had she died, those men would have certainly killed the surgeon. Twenty-five days later, Mrs. Crawford returned home on horseback to live a long life.

Success in abdominal surgery by an American gynecologist was news indeed and was called America's greatest contribution to surgery at the time by many. McDowell performed several more ovariectomies, losing only one patient. In so doing he showed that abdominal surgery was possible. The progress in anesthesia, bacteriology, and antiseptic techniques that occurred at the end of the nineteenth century paved the way for the greater developments of surgery as a treatment option in the twentieth century.

The Twentieth Century and Beyond

Reviewing the last 4,000 years of the history of obstetrics and gynecology, it is evident that only very recently have physicians been able to provide women with rational care capable of extending and improving the quality of their lives. One cannot help but wonder why such

TABLE 1.1. Developmental milestones in obstetrics and gynecology.

Decade	Advance	Author
1920	Prenatal care	Ballantyne[1]
	Twilight sleep	Gauss[2]
	Anesthetic agents	Simpson[3]
	Radiation treatment of cancer	Cleaves[4]
	Rubin's test	Rubin[5]
	Semen analysis	Macomber/Sanders[6]
	Prophylactic use of forceps and episiotomy	DeLee[7]
1930	American Board of Obstetrics and Gynecology	Dannreuther[8]
	Basal body temperature	Rubinstein[9]
	Endometrial biopsy	Rock/Bartlett[10]
1940	Treatment of syphilis and gonorrhea	Noeggerath[11]
	Papanicolaou smear	Papanicolaou[12]
1950	Diethylstilbestrol treatment	Smith[13]
	American College of Obstetricians and Gynecologists	Mengert[14]
	Carcinoma in situ	Rubin[15]
	Coagulopathy-fibrinogen	DeLee[16]
		Cohn[17]
		Moloney[18]
	46 chromosomes	Tjio/Levan[19]
	Oxytocin synthesis	DuVigneaud[20]
1960	National Institute of Child Health and Human Development	Ref.[21]
	Psychoprophylaxis	Buxton[22]
	Oral contraceptive	Pincus[23]
	Radioimmunoassay	Yalow/Berson[24]
	Ultrasonography	Donald[25]
	Virus etiology of cancer	Rous[26]
1970	Chemotherapy for gynecological cancer	Hertz[27]
	Hypothalamic releasing factors	Guillemin[28]
		Schally[29]
	In vitro fertilization	Steptoe, Edwards[30]
	Fetal monitoring obstetrics	Larks[31]
		Hon[32]
1980	Fetal surgery	
	Tocolytics	
	Assisted Reproductive Technology	

Modified from Little B. The sin of pride. Research in obstet gynecol. Am J Obstet Gynecol 1989;160:771.

a great amount of time elapsed without significant medical progress, especially when disciplines such as art, agriculture, and architecture reached high levels in antiquity. It is the principles of observation, hypothesis, experimental design, and scientific deduction born in seventeenth-century England that fueled medical advances and provide the foundation for all of today's technology. However, what history has taught us is that real medical progress cannot occur without both science and a setting of broad social support for those advances.

During the twentieth century, advances in obstetrics and gynecology and in reproductive technology in particular are occurring at an explosive rate (Table 1.1).[1-32] "The long slow turn of world time has given way in the human realm to a fantastically speeded up social evolution induced by technology. So fast does this change progress that a growing child strives to master the sociological mores of a culture which might, compared with the pace of past history, compress centuries of change into his lifetime."[33] In 1900 there were practically no tests for the evaluation of infertility. Prior to the development of the Rubin's test[5] in 1920, a major laparotomy was required to assess tubal patency. The association of semen analysis with pregnancy was not appreciated until 1928,[6] and the basal temperature chart and endometrial biopsy were not available prior to 1937.[10]

It is against this backdrop that we observe advances in the diagnosis and treatment of infertility occurring at monthly intervals. The possibilities are limited only by our own imagination. In parallel with our medical predecessors, the twentieth-century physician is struggling to select those treatments that are truly beneficial from an ever-increasing list of therapeutic acronyms. Similarly, the psychosocial, legal, and ethical implications of family building must be viewed within the religious and societal mores in which they were spawned. Therefore, our challenge today, as in antiquity, is to scrutinize carefully each new piece of technology for the scientific proof of its efficacy and safety, while being ever mindful of the potential impact of advances in reproductive technology on the infertile couple, their physician, and the society in which they live.

References

1. Ballantyne JW. Visits to the wards of the pro-maternity hospital: a vision of the twentieth century. Am J Obstet Dis Women Child 1901; 43:593.
2. Gauss CJ. Geburten in Kunstlichem Dammerschlaf. Archiv fur Gynakologie Bd 1906;78:579–631.
3. Simpson JY. Notes on the employment of the inhalation of sulphuric ether in the practice of midwifery. Monthly J Med Sci 1847;2:721–728.
4. Cleaves MA. Radium: with a preliminary note on radium rays in the treatment of cancer. Med Rec 1903;64:601–606.
5. Rubin IC. The nonoperative determination of patency of the fallopian tubes. JAMA 1920; 75:661.
6. Macomber D, Sanders MB. The spermatozoa count: its value in the diagnosis, prognosis and treatment of sterility. N Engl J Med 1928;200: 981.
7. DeLee JB. The prophylactic forceps operation. Am J Obstet Gynecol 1920;1:34–44.
8. Dannreuther WT. The American Board of Obstetrics and Gynecology. Am J Obstet Gynecol 1954;68:15–19.
9. Rubinstein BB. The relation of cyclic changes in human vaginal smears to body temperatures and basal metabolic rate. Am J Physiol 1937; 119:635.
10. Rock J, Bartlett M. Biopsy studies of human endometrium: criteria of dating and information about amenorrhea, menorrhagia, and time of ovulation. JAMA 1937;108:2022.
11. Noegerrath E. Transactions American Gynecological Society 1876;1:268, In: Speert H, ed. Obstetric and gynecologic milestones. New York: Macmillan, 1958;359.
12. Papanicolaou GN. New cancer diagnosis. In: Proceedings of the Third Race Betterment Conference, Jan. 2–6, 1928. Battle Creek, MI.: Race Betterment Foundation, 1928;528–534.
13. Smith OW, Smith GV, Hurwitz D. Increased excretion of pregnanediol in pregnancy from diethylstilbestrol with special reference to late pregnancy accidents. Am J Obstet Gynecol 1946;51:411–415.
14. Mengert WF. History of the American College of Obstetricians and Gynecologists, 1950–1970. Washington, DC: American College of Obstetricians and Gynecologists, 1970.
15. Rubin IC. The pathological diagnosis of incipient carcinoma of the uterus. Am J Obstet 1910;62:668–676.

16. DeLee JB. A case of fatal hemorrhagic diathesis with premature separation of the placenta. Am J Obstet Gynecol 1901;44:785–792.

17. Cohn EJ. Chemical, clinical, and immunological studies on the products of human fractionation. J Clin Invest 1944;23:417–606.

18. Moloney WC, Egan WJ, Gorman AJ. Acquired afibrinogenemia in pregnancy. N Engl J Med 1949;245:596–598.

19. Tjio JH, Levan A. The chromosome number in man. Hereditas (Lund) 1956;42:1–6.

20. DuVigneaud V, Ressler C, Swan JM, Roberts CW, Katsoyannis PG, Gordon S. The synthesis of an octapeptide amide with the hormonal activity of oxytocin. J Am Chem Soc 1953;75:4879–4880.

21. Freedom from handicap. Concerning the establishment of the National Institute of Child Health and Human Development. Baltimore: Harriet Lane Home of the Johns Hopkins Hospital, 1962;1–18.

22. Buxton CI. A study of psychophysical methods for relief of childbirth pain. Philadelphia: WB Saunders, 1962.

23. Pincus G, Borno R, Pean V. Effectiveness of an oral contraceptive. Science 1959;130:81–83.

24. Yalow RS. Radioimmunoassay: a probe for the fine structure of biologic systems. Science 1978;200:1236–1245.

25. Donald I, MacVicar J, Brown TG. Investigation of abdominal masses by pulsed ultrasound. Lancet 1958;1:1188–1194.

26. Rous FP. A transmissible avian neoplasm (sarcoma of the common fowl). J Exp Med 1911;12:696–700.

27. Li MC, Hertz R, Spencer DB. Effect of methotrexate therapy upon choriocarcinoma and chorioadenoma. Proc Soc Exp Biol Med 1956;93:361–366.

28. Guillemin R. Purification, isolation, and primary structure of the hypothalamic luteinizing hormone-releasing factor of ovine origin. Am J Obstet Gynecol 1977;129:214–218.

29. Schally AV, Coy DH, Meyers CA. Hypothalamic regulatory hormones. Annu Rev Biochem 1978;47:89–128.

30. Steptoe PC, Edwards RG. Birth after the reimplantation of a human embryo. Lancet 1978;2:366.

31. Larks SD, Dasgupta K. Fetal electrocardiography with special reference to early pregnancy. Am Heart J 1958;56:701–714.

32. Hon EH. The electronic evaluation of the fetal heart rate. Am J Obstet Gynecol 1958;75:1215–1230.

33. Eiseley L. The freedom of the juggernaut. Mayo Clin Proc 1965;40:7–21.

2
Medical Evaluation and Treatment of the Infertile Couple

Machelle M. Seibel

The desire to reproduce is an intensely motivating human force. It is through children that we have continuity with the past and future; in this respect, children are our immortality. Couples may also experience strong religious, cultural, and societal pressures to conceive. It is therefore understandable that when people experience difficulty conceiving, most perceive their infertility as a major life crisis.

It probably is the determination of such couples to overcome their infertility that has led this area of medicine to evolve more rapidly than almost any other. Certainly, few if any other specialty fields have given rise to so many emotional, ethical, and legal considerations.

The advances in diagnosis and treatment have led many physicians to believe that all infertility must be treated by a subspecialist. This is compounded by the fact that experts themselves disagree on the best management. The literature also has on occasion created confusion, as results of similar trials often are inconsistent, and controls are not always included. Nevertheless, if an obstetrician-gynecologist, family practitioner, or urologist has a clear understanding of the basic principles, there is no reason why he or she cannot carry out a large portion of the diagnosis and treatment.

General Principles of Infertility

Fertility is the ability of a man and a woman to reproduce. Similarly, infertility is an involuntary reduction in the ability to have children; it is a relative term. Sterility, on the other hand, is the absolute inability to reproduce. These medical conditions differ from most others because even normal fertility requires a variable period of time for pregnancy to occur, whereas countless other disorders either are present or they are not. Women who have never achieved a first pregnancy are classified as having primary infertility. Those who have been pregnant at least once before, regardless of the outcome, and who cannot achieve a subsequent pregnancy are defined as having secondary infertility.

Estimates vary as to the actual incidence of infertility. Approximately 53 million women in the United States are in their reproductive years (ages 15–44 years). It was calculated that of the 28 million couples in the United States of reproductive age in the late 1980s, 3.0 million were conclusively sterile, 2.8 million were subfertile, and 1.2 million required a long wait before conception occurred.[1] The sole reliable sources of demographic information about infertility in the United States are national surveys conducted by the National Center for Health Statistics, the last of which was carried out in 1982 (Fig. 2.1). At that time, an estimated 8.5% of married couples in which wives were aged 15 to 44 years were infertile. Remarkably, an additional 38.9% were surgically sterile and only 52.6% were believed potentially able to conceive.[2] Surgical sterilization no doubt masks some individuals who would have been infertile. If one excludes them from the population base, the 2.4 million infertile couples represent 13.9% of the remaining 17.3 million couples. This translates into nearly 2 million office visits for

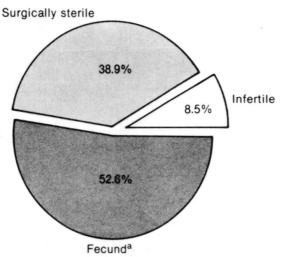

FIGURE 2.1. Prevalence of infertility in the United States, 1982. Married couples, 15–44 years.

aPotentially able to conceive.

SOURCE: Office of Technology Assessment, 1988.

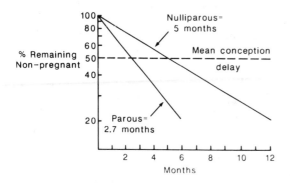

FIGURE 2.2. Timetable of conception rates in unselected populations for nulliparous and parous women. Reprinted, with permission, from ref. 3.

infertility annually to an estimated 45,600 physicians.[2] These physicians include 20,600 obstetrician-gynecologists, 17,500 general or family practitioners, 6,100 urologists, and 1,400 surgeons.

Despite the prevalence of infertility, physicians are cautioned against intervening too early. In unselected populations, half of the nulliparous women will achieve pregnancy within the first 5 months of unprotected intercourse, and half of those who remain nonpregnant at the beginning of each subsequent 5-month period will do so (Fig. 2.2).[3] Therefore, if 1,000 unselected nulliparous women

are followed, 500 will remain nongravid after 5 months, 250 after 10 months, and 125 after 15 months. Women who have already completed one or more pregnancies follow a similarly predictable but more rapid pattern.

These data demonstrate that if treatment is initiated after 5 or even 10 months of inability to conceive, a large number of women will have become pregnant without intervention. Although advancing reproductive age or particular circumstances might encourage prompt initiation of therapy, it is imperative to share this information with couples at their initial interview. It also underscores the need for appropriate controls in all treatment of infertility.[4] Finally, it implies that for any form of treatment to be considered as having had a reasonable trial toward correcting an infertility problem, at least 5 months of therapy are required in most instances.

The Couple

The diagnosis of infertility contrasts with almost all other medical conditions in that it involves two people. Therefore, the physician must view the couple as a unit (Fig. 2.3). This is important in several ways. First, both partners must be evaluated. Since infertility is due

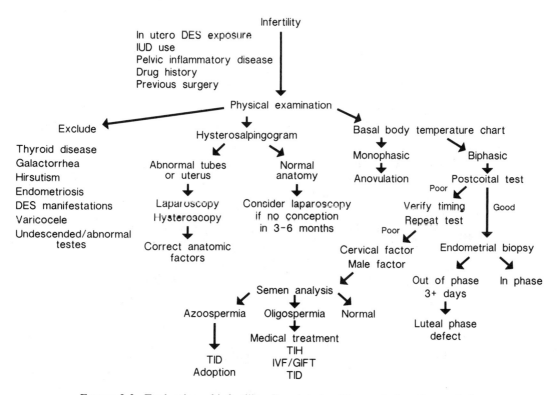

FIGURE 2.3. Evaluation of infertility. Reprinted, with permission, from ref. 4.

to male factors in 40% of instances, female factors in 40%, and both male and female factors in 20%, thorough assessment of both partners is essential. Second, when two physicians are caring for the man and woman separately, treatment must be coordinated. In this fashion the couple's overall fertility can be optimized through the simultaneous enhancement of each individual's fertility.

In my opinion, it is preferable for the couple to be interviewed together for the initial visit, even if each is cared for by a different physician.[4] A detailed emotional, medical, and sexual history should be obtained from the partners together and separately. In this way sensitive information or events that one partner does not want the other to know may be revealed. These include ethanol and drug consumption,[5] previous abortion, venereal disease, impregnating a previous partner, marital discord, sexual dysfunction, and faulty ejaculation. The physician also may determine whether one partner is more upset by or motivated to reverse infertility than the other, or conversely, if one is more resistant or indifferent to the evaluation.[4] On eliciting this information, a more directed fertility investigation is facilitated. Finally, one can evaluate the degree of stress that infertility per se has placed on the couple.[6]

Etiologies of Infertility

Ovulatory Factors

Ovulatory dysfunction accounts for approximately 25% of infertility. Although ovulation can be affected by many conditions, by far the three most common are excessive weight loss or gain, excessive exercise, and extreme emotional stress.[4]

Individuals who are more than 20% above or below their ideal body weight may experience this disorder. The relationship between excess body fat and ovulatory disturbances appears to be stronger for early-onset obesity.[7]

Mechanisms include alterations in androgen, estrogen, insulin/glucose, gonadotropin, and prolactin homeostasis. It is also important to recognize that obese individuals may be protein-deficient and thin ones may have normal protein intake. Therefore, a dietary history must be obtained.

An exercise history usually is easily elicited. Evaluating the degree of stress a couple is experiencing is often more challenging. Many individuals find it necessary to hold more than one job, thus creating a schedule inherently associated with stress. The tension understandably is exacerbated by the need to leave work frequently for infertility testing. A careful history may also uncover the recent death of a parent or loved one, which creates an urgent need to fill the void. This need is felt with increasing frequency, as many couples have moved away from their core families and feel a sense of isolation.[4]

Additional factors that are associated with ovulatory dysfunction include thyroid disease, galactorrhea, and hirsutism. The last must always be asked about directly, as some hirsute women expend considerable effort removing or bleaching unwanted hair, which causes them to appear not to have a problem.[8] A complete medical history is also invaluable, as a wide array of conditions (e.g., seizure disorders, thyroid disease, genetic conditions) may also contribute to ovulatory dysfunction.[9]

Peritoneal Factors

Peritoneal factors, including tubal disease and endometriosis, account for approximately 30 to 40% of reported infertility. They are fairly evenly distributed among the population and are not restricted to any one socioeconomic group. Important historical information includes appendicitis, particularly if the appendix ruptured,[10] abdominal or pelvic surgery, use of an intrauterine device (IUD), and pelvic inflammatory disease (PID).[11] *Neisseria gonorrhoeae* and *Chlamydia trachomatis* are overwhelmingly responsible for the 1 million annual cases of PID.[12] Approximately 50% of all women with tubal infertility and 30% of those who are seropositive for chlamydial

insections report no history of PID. Use of an IUD is associated with as much as a four-fold increased risk of acquiring pelvic adhesions.[11] Premenstrual spotting, dysmenorrhea, and dyspareunia are all associated with endometriosis.[13]

Cervical Factors

Cervical factors are implicated in no more than 5 to 10% of cases of infertility, but because spermatozoa must pass through the cervix for conception to occur, it is important to determine if cervical factors are present. Inadequate cervical mucus and/or cervical stenosis reduce sperm viability and may follow overzealous procedures such as cryosurgery, cautery, and cone biopsy. Cervical factors may also result from prenatal exposure to diethylstilbestrol (DES). It is estimated that between 1945 and 1955 approximately 4 million persons (male and female) in the United States were exposed to DES in utero.[14]

Patients must also be questioned regarding a chronic vaginal discharge or spotting, which may represent chronic cervicitis. Information regarding the use of commercial douches and vaginal lubricants such as K-Y Jelly must be elicited, as these products may be spermicidal.

Uterine Factors

Infertility is caused by uterine factors in approximately 5% of cases. As with the cervix, prenatal exposure to DES can cause uterine anomalies, the most common of which is a T-shaped uterus. Such abnormalities are associated with fetal wastage and increased frequency of obstetric problems.

Müllerian anomalies are congenital uterine malformations that adversely affect reproduction.[15] Also related is a history of a dilation and curettage or therapeutic abortion, both of which could result in intrauterine synechiae and reduced menstrual flow, and intrauterine polyps or fibroids, which could lead to increased menstrual bleeding.

Smoking

The hazardous effect of smoking on reproduction has been discussed widely[16-18] and is an area of increasing investigation.[19] Epidemiologic studies have demonstrated that infertility increases significantly with an increase in the number of cigarettes smoked per day,[20,21] particularly when the consumption is more than 16 cigarettes. Fecundity decreases directly with the number of cigarettes smoked. In women who smoke up to 20 cigarettes per day it is 25% less than that in nonsmokers; in those who smoke more than 20 cigarettes per day it is 57% less.[22] Some of this decrease is due to the adverse effect on the uterine cervix and the fallopian tubes.[21] In addition, ectopic gestations are far more frequent among smokers than among controls.[23]

Mutagenic agents in cigarette smoke have been identified in follicular fluid, cervical mucus, amniotic fluid, breast milk, urine, and seminal plasma.[24–27] Nicotine is 10 times more concentrated in uterine fluid than it is in plasma, which may be why it impairs decidualization in the pseudopregnant rat and causes delays in embryo cleavage from the two- to the four-cell stage, entry of conceptus into the uterus, blastocyst formation, shedding of the zona pellucida, and implantation.[4]

Women who smoke are also at increased risk of menstrual abnormalities and early menopause.[28] These symptoms appear to be most common among those who smoke 20 or more cigarettes per day. Many mechanisms may play a role. Substances such as nicotine may enhance vasopressin centrally, which can diminish luteinizing hormone (LH) levels, or peripherally through reduced aromatase activity in granulosa cells.[29,30]

Cigarette smoking also may adversely affect male reproduction, reducing sperm density by 22% on average. The effects on sperm morphology and motility are less consistent.[19,31] Cigarette smoke, nicotine, and polycyclic aromatic hydrocarbons are capable of producing testicular atrophy, blocking spermatogenesis, and altering sperm morphology in experimental animals.[29] In addition, smokers who have a testicular varicocele are 10 times more likely to have oligospermia than smokers who do not have a varicocele.[32] For all of these reasons, in couples with unexplained infertility or in whom any fertility value is marginal,

cessation of smoking may play a substantive role.

Age

Over the last half-century, the tendency to delay childbearing has increased. Numerous factors contribute to this, including improved methods of birth control, increased numbers of women in the work force, and the choice by more people to delay marriage. The increasing frequency of divorce, with a desire to conceive in a subsequent marriage, also plays a role in the delay. As a result, many couples find that they have a relatively shorter period of time in which to conceive.[33] Even in couples with prolonged unexplained infertility, the age of the woman has been found to be a prognostic factor.[34] This is substantially worsened by the fact that older women experience a progressive increase in the risk of spontaneous abortion, and in congenital anomalies should their pregnancy reach term.[34–36]

Although the primary focus of increasing age has been on women, the absolute frequency of autosomal dominant disease due to new mutations among offspring of fathers 40 years or older is at least 0.3 to 0.5%.[37] Male fecundity also is diminished with advancing age. Men over 40 impregnate their partners within 6 months at one-third the rate of those under age 25. This may be in part due to involution of testicular function, decreased sperm production, and maturation arrest of spermatogenesis, all of which have been associated with advancing age.[38,39]

Fecundity is also reduced with reduced frequency of intercourse,[40] which may occur in older couples. The rate of conception in 6 months is approximately 15% if the frequency of intercourse is below once a week, 30% if it is once a week, and 45% if it is twice a week. Therefore, a sexual history is particularly important among reproductively older patients.

Despite the potential adverse effect of age on reproductive outcome,[41] women over age 40 whose weight is below 67.5 kg and those who are of low parity can expect a healthy infant.[42] Nevertheless, it is advisable to expedite the evaluation and treatment when either patient is reproductively older.

Male Factors

Because 40% of infertility is due to male factors, each evaluation must include a history and physical examination of the man. Prenatal exposure to DES is associated with epididymal cysts, microphallus, and hypertrophy of the prostatic utricles as well as abnormal semen analyses.[43] Reduced semen values have also been identified in association with unilateral or bilateral undescended testes, regardless of when orchipexy was performed.[44] It was further determined that even with a unilateral undescended testis, spermatogenesis is impaired in the descended testis as well.

Testicular trauma and inflammation are recognized causes of hypogonadism.[45] Nearly one-third of adult men who develop mumps have unilateral clinical orchitis. In 10% it is bilateral and substantially impairs fertility. Mumps is rarely accompanied by orchitis before age 10, however.

Reduced seminal volume and azoospermia or oligospermia may be due to bladder neck or prostate surgery. Decreased ejaculate volumes may be a clue to diabetes mellitus. Chemotherapeutic agents, particularly the alkalating agents mustargen, cyclophosphamide, and chlorambucil, can damage the testes.[45] After chemotherapy it may take 4 to 5 years for sperm production to resume, and the quantity is generally reduced when it does.[46]

Careful attention must be given to ethanol and drug consumption,[6,31] as these substances are pervasive in our society. Ethanol is associated with reduced testis size, seminal volume, and sperm morphology, motility, and density.[47,48] Similarly, opiates are associated with abnormal ejaculates and reduced serum testosterone levels.[49] Marijuana appears to affect testosterone biosynthesis in adult males and in fetal males exposed in utero.[50] Several agents, for example, sulfasalazine,[51] cimetidine, and nitrofurantoin, may be gonadotoxic.[4] A new antiinflammatory medication, mesalazine, appears to have substantially fewer gonadotoxic effects.[52] Anabolic steroids are occasionally administered to improve gonadal function, and the number of young athletes taking 17-α-alkyltestosterone anabolic steroid derivatives is increasing at an alarming rate.[4] Because these substances inhibit gonadotropin secretion and may profoundly interfere with normal spermatogenesis, they should be stopped immediately. Although the dosages of steroids used by athletes are frequently so high that controlled clinical studies under similar conditions appear prohibited for ethical reasons, the shorter the duration of use, the more likely it is that sperm production may return to normal.[53,54]

Physical Examination

The woman's head is examined to exclude signs of androgen excess such as temporal balding, acne, or increased facial hair at the angle of the jaw, chin, or upper lip. The thyroid gland and breasts should also be examined carefully. Galactorrhea may not be detected unless an attempt is made to express discharge from the nipples. Presternal hair or acne, hair or acne on the back, an increase in suprapubic hair, and a male escutcheon all point to androgen excess.[4] When androgen excess is extreme, clitoromegaly may also be noted.

Pelvic examination should determine the amount of cervical mucus. Copious amounts are associated with either impending ovulation or a state of estrogen excess such as polycystic ovary disease. If mucus is abundant and coitus has occurred within the last few days, it should be examined for the presence or absence of sperm. Identification of abundant sperm precludes the need for further evaluation of the cervix. The position and size of the uterus and ovaries, and whether or not they are fixed or mobile, should be recorded. A rectovaginal examination should be performed to exclude nodularity, which is frequently associated with endometriosis.[13]

Examination of the male includes observation of general body habitus and limb length to exclude genetic conditions such as Klinefelter's syndrome. Decreased body hair, gynecomastia, and eunuchoid proportions are signs of possible inadequate virilization.[4] The genitalia must be evaluated carefully to be certain that the urethral meatus is normally located for proper placement of the ejaculate, and that the testes are of normal consistency. Testes are measured to the nearest millimeter, or their volume can be determined with an orchidometer. They should be at least 4 cm long and at least 20 ml in volume.[44] Small testicles often are associated with impaired spermatogenesis. A varicocele may be identifiable with the patient standing, although scrotal ultrasound or temperature probes may be required.[55] Varicocele size will increase on performing a Valsalva maneuver and will decrease when the patient is recumbent.

Basic Infertility Tests

The basic infertility workup followed by most specialists has been outlined by the American Fertility Society. Incomplete evaluations, for example performing only one or two tests, or immediately performing a laparoscopy, often do not identify the etiology of infertility. The basic minimum workup usually can be completed within 2 to 3 months.

Postcoital Test

The postcoital test is an assessment of the cervix as a reservoir for sperm survival. Cervical mucus usually is thick and tenacious. With elevated estrogen levels in the periovulatory period, however, its consistency becomes thin and watery like eggwhite. The cervical os also opens, allowing the cervix to act as a passageway for spermatozoa. During this period the sperm should be able to survive for many hours or even days.[4]

The couple is asked to have intercourse the evening before day 12 to 14 of a 28-day cycle, with the postcoital test scheduled the next morning. This allows the physician to determine whether the sperm can live for an extended period of time, thus establishing that the cervix can serve as a reservoir. It also permits the couple to have intercourse in a natural, unhurried manner.[56]

A bivalve speculum lubricated only with warm water is inserted into the vagina. With large dressing forceps and a cotton ball, vaginal secretions are removed from the exocervix. The closed forceps are placed into the cervical canal, opened, rotated 180°, closed tightly, and withdrawn. The mucus that is obtained is placed on a microscope slide and quantified as scant, moderate, or profuse.[4] Its degree of clarity is recorded. Spinnbarkeit is assessed by placing a glass coverslip on the mucus, drawing it slowly from the slide, and noting the number of centimeters the mucus stretches. As ovulation approaches it should stretch 6 to 10 cm.

The slide is then placed under the microscope using a low-power objective, and the cellularity of the mucus is noted. Once a representative field has been identified, the microscope is switched to a high-power objective to count the number of active, sluggishly motile, and nonmotile sperm per high-power field (hpf). A natural assumption would be that the more sperm present the greater the likelihood of pregnancy, but this has not been borne out. The presence of more than 20 sperm per hpf has been correlated with pregnancy. Finding no sperm suggests faulty sperm production, poor coital technique, or destruction of the sperm by antibodies in situ. After the slide is assessed it is dried with an alcohol lamp and the degree of fern formation is noted (Fig. 2.4).

It is important to recognize that many patients personalize a poor outcome and equate it with "failing their love-making test" or a suboptimal interpersonal relationship. Therefore, extreme sensitivity must be used when interpreting the test results to the couple.

Special tests of cervical factor include the capillary tube mucus-penetration test and sperm antibody testing. In the former, mid-cycle cervical mucus is suctioned into a flat capillary tube, with care to ensure that no air bubbles are included. The capillary tube is then placed vertically into a test tube containing 1 ml of the partner's semen, and this tube is placed in a rack. At the end of 1 hour the flat tube is placed under a microscope and the distance the spermatozoa have traveled is measured. These results are compared with sperm

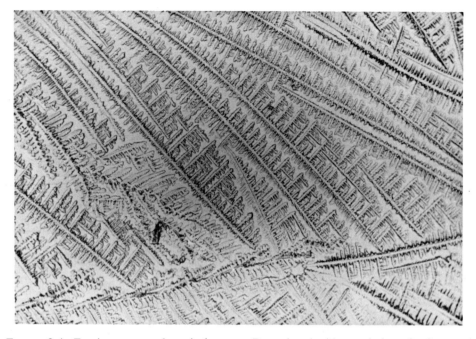

FIGURE 2.4. Ferning pattern of cervical mucus. Reproduced with permission of reference 4.

penetration in bovine cervical mucus already drawn in a flat capillary tube. Failure of sperm to penetrate the column of mucus implies an immune factor. The presence of motile sperm seen throughout the 30-mm column implies normal migration.[4]

Sperm antibody testing should be undertaken when no sperm or predominantly immotile sperm are found on a well-timed postcoital test with copious cervical mucus present. A poor mucus-penetration test, and sperm found shaking in place on a postcoital test, are also indications for immune testing.[57,58]

Tubal Disease

By far the most widely used test for tubal disease is the hysterosalpingogram (HSG) (Fig. 2.5). It is performed in the first half of the menstrual cycle after cessation of menses but before ovulation.[59] The timing prevents inadvertent reflux of menstrual endometrium into the peritoneal cavity, which has been implicated in the pathophysiology of endometriosis. It also prevents the procedure from interfering with an intrauterine conception or

causing an ectopic pregnancy. Patients with a history of PID should receive a prophylactic antibiotic. Oral tetracycline starting the day before and continuing for several days after the procedure is usually adequate. If pelvic tenderness is present before the HSG, the test should be canceled.

With the patient in the dorsolithotomy position, a plastic speculum is introduced into the vagina. A metal speculum will obscure radiologic visualization of the cervix. The vaginal cavity is cleansed with an aseptic solution such as benzalkonium chloride or povidone-iodine. A paracervical block is helpful to diminish discomfort. Prostaglandin inhibitors taken 1 to 2 hours before the procedure are also helpful.[60] Several instruments are available. I prefer to use a Jarcho cannula in association with a tenaculum on the anterior lip of the cervix (Fig. 2.6A,B). Either water-soluble or oil-soluble contrast material can be used.[59] Because the uterine cavity is a potential space of only 4 or 5 ml, slow injection of the contrast medium will prevent uterine distention and cramping. If pain does occur, temporary pausing often relieves it. Care should

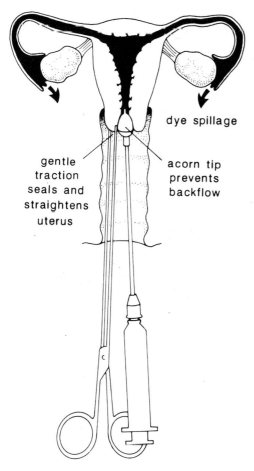

gentle
traction
seals and
straightens
uterus

dye spillage

acorn tip
prevents
backflow

FIGURE 2.5. Schematic drawing depicting hysterosalpingogram. Reprinted, with permission, from ref. 4.

be taken to avoid excessive pressure during instillation to prevent intravasation, which has an associated 1% risk of embolization.[61] Should the spiderweb pattern typical of intravasation be seen, the HSG should be stopped at once.

Ovulation

The presence or absence of ovulation, and the quality of ovulation, are typically assessed by basal body temperature (BBT), endometrial biopsy, and serum progesterone levels. All are dependent on progesterone secretion by the corpus luteum. Rarely the ovary may produce progesterone without releasing an oocyte.[62] The luteinized unruptured follicle cannot be differentiated from normal ovulation using standard evaluation methods.

Basal Body Temperature Chart

Since the BBT chart was first described in 1904, it has been considered the simplest and least expensive method of assessing the presence or absence of ovulation. The normal temperature pattern is biphasic, with a sustained midcycle rise of at least 0.4°F for 12 to 15 days. Prolongation of the rise is typical of pregnancy. Because the chart is only a rough index of ovulation timing, and because several temperature peaks and nadirs may be observed before the sustained rise occurs, intercourse is unwarranted and may only cause stress. Nevertheless, viewing the chart retrospectively does allow the physician to estimate the timing of ovulation for insemination, determine the efficacy of ovulation-inducing agents, and plan treatment of luteal phase deficiency.[4] The BBT chart is also valuable to ensure that fertility testing is performed at the appropriate time in the cycle (Fig. 2.7).

Endometrial Biopsy

The secretory evolution of the endometrium is due to progesterone. The changes produced by the hormone are so predictable that sampling the endometrium can reveal how many days earlier ovulation occurred.[63] The endometrial biopsy is usually performed as close to the menstrual period as possible and even up to 18 hours after the onset of menses (Fig. 2.8). Obtaining a pregnancy test prior to performing the biopsy greatly reduces the potential risk of interrupting a pregnancy. Local anesthesia helps to minimize pain.

The results of the biopsy are interpreted in reference to the subsequent menstrual period. Considering the first day of menses to be day 14 of the luteal phase, the endometrial sample is dated as postovulatory day 1 to 14. Counting backward from day 14 to the day on which the biopsy was performed, the actual postovulatory day can be compared with the apparent postovulatory day as indicated by the biopsy.[4] A discrepancy of 3 or more

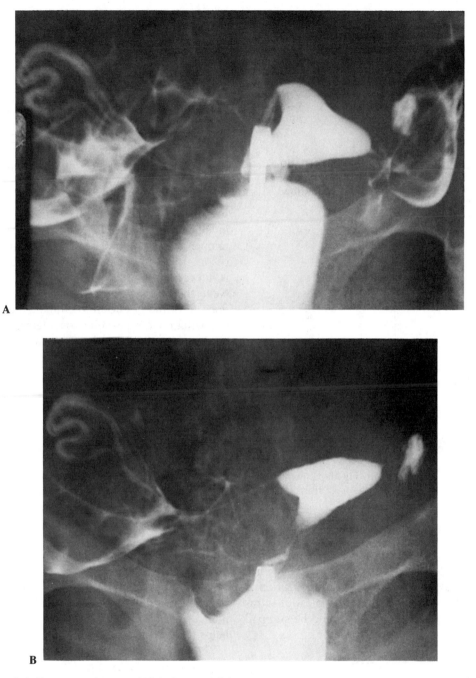

FIGURE 2.6. Retroverted uterus (A) before and (B) after traction is applied to the cervix. Reprinted, with permission, from ref. 4.

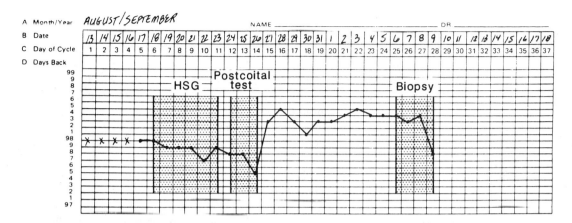

FIGURE 2.7. Basal Body Temperature Chart demonstrates schedule for testing. Reprinted, with permission, from ref. 4.

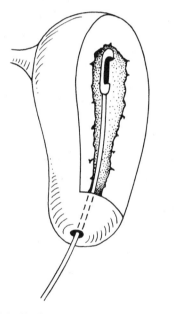

FIGURE 2.8. Endometrial biopsy. Reprinted, with permission, from ref. 4.

days defines a luteal-phase progesterone deficiency.[64]

Progesterone Level

Although a serum progesterone level of 4 ng/ml or greater is evidence that ovulation has occurred, considerable controversy exists as to what value or values constitute an

adequate luteal phase.[64] Due to the marked variability of luteal phase progesterone levels and the lack of a sharp demarcation between values of a normal and deficient luteal phase, I prefer the endometrial biopsy as a marker of luteal phase adequacy.

Semen Analysis

A postcoital test alone is an insufficient evaluation of the male, and at least two semen analyses should be performed. After 48 hours of sexual abstinence, the semen should be collected by masturbation into a clean, wide-mouthed, 1- to 2-ounce ointment jar with a screw-on lid. Larger containers allow the sample to dry out during transportation. If masturbation is objectionable, the semen may be collected during intercourse. Latex condoms without spermicidal agents are commercially available. The specimen should be delivered to the laboratory within 2 to 3 hours and be properly labeled with the names of the man and his partner and the time of collection.

The normal volume in a semen sample is between 2.5 and 8 ml. A smaller amount may reduce cervical insemination. Among men with a history of prostate or bladder neck surgery, if the small ejaculatory volume is oligospermic or azoospermic and also alkaline, a post-ejaculation urine sample should be evaluated to exclude retrograde ejaculation. Semen volumes above 8 ml frequently are associated with a diminished sperm density.

Conventional semen analysis has been performed for 60 years,[65] and laboratories still vary as to what constitutes normal results.[66] Furthermore, normal values have demonstrated seasonal variation, being highest in late winter and early spring and lowest in late summer.[67] General guidelines of a fertile sample include sperm density of 40 million/ml, motility at 6 hours above 60%, and normal morphology in 60%. Values associated with infertility include density below 20 million/ml, motility at 6 hours below 35%, and less than 60% normal forms. Results between these levels indicate a relative infertility problem that deserves to be treated. Nevertheless, it must be remembered that sperm counts below 1 million/ml have been associated with normal pregnancy outcomes.[68] Computerized sperm analyzers capable of providing precise documentation of sperm motility, speed, and motion patterns are available. Although they provide exciting potential for the future, their use has not been associated with a better pregnancy outcome than can be achieved with information obtained from an experienced technician.[69]

Treatment of Female Infertility

The treatment of infertility has evolved dramatically since the 1950s. Safe and effective ovulation-inducing agents were introduced in the 1960s. During the 1970s, refinements in surgical technique and equipment led to the development of microsurgery for tubal disease. Further advances in cell culture and embryology in the 1980s resulted in the widespread availability of in vitro fertilization and related reproductive technologies. It appears almost certain that in the 1990s the diagnosis and treatment of infertility will progress to a subcellular level and molecular biology will move to the forefront. This section highlights the current treatment of infertility and describes those areas that are likely to emerge in the foreseeable future.

Clomiphene Citrate

By far the most prevalent medication for ovulation induction is clomiphene citrate. It is triphenylchloroethylene in which the four hydrogen atoms of the ethylene core have been substituted with three phenyl rings and a chloride anion.[70] The drug can be purchased as a racemic mixture of two stereochemical isomers, the *trans* (62%) and *cis* (38%) isomers. The pharmacologic effect is largely the result of the *cis* isomer. It is available as a 50-mg tablet in the United States. Clomiphene is primarily indicated in normoprolactinemic, anovulatory infertile patients who are well estrogenized as assessed by progestin-induced withdrawal bleeding or the presence of copious cervical mucus. Indiscriminate administration to women who are ovulating normally in hopes of "accentuating" ovulation in order to improve the pregnancy potential has no scientific basis. Rather, clomiphene should be used to restore suboptimal ovulation to normalcy.[71]

The usual starting dosage of clomiphene is 50 mg daily on days 5 to 9 of spontaneous or induced menses, although therapy may be initiated as early as cycle day 3 or as late as day 7.[72] Ovulation is monitored with a basal body temperature chart or serum progesterone level on cycle day 22. If ovulation occurs, the current dose is maintained; otherwise it is increased in a stepwise fashion to 100, 150, 200, and 250 mg daily for 5 days until a therapeutic response is obtained.[73] Ovulation usually occurs 7 to 10 days after the last tablet. The overwhelming majority of the conceptions occur at dosages of 150 mg daily or less, and within six treatment cycles. Anovulatory patients receiving clomiphene who also have elevated levels of dehydroepiandrosterone sulfate (DHEA-S) may benefit from a low dose of dexamethasone or prednisone with the clomiphene citrate. Similarly, in patients who demonstrate ultrasound evidence of follicular development but who do not ovulate, human chorionic gonadotropin (HCG) may be administered to induce ovulation.

Serious side effects with clomiphene citrate administration are rare. Multiple births, most of which are twins, occur in less than 10% of instances. Hot flushes occur in up to 10% of patients; visual and gastrointestinal symptoms are not uncommon and are totally reversible. Although clomiphene has been found to have a direct effect on the ovary,[74,75] there is no evidence that it increases the prevalence of congenital malformations among live births.[76]

Human Menopausal Gonadotropin

Human menopausal gonadotropin (HMG) has been in clinical use for nearly 30 years. It comes as a lyophilized powder containing 75 or 150 IU each of follicle-stimulating hormone (FSH) and LH. The FSH is primarily responsible for follicular recruitment, selection, growth, and ripening. The LH is responsible for the final maturation of the FSH-stimulated follicles, ovulation, and transformation of the follicular remnants into functional corpora lutea.[77] Once follicular growth and development are optimal, HCG, the hormone secreted by the trophoblastic cells, must be injected to simulate the midcycle LH rise and ensure ovulation. HMG is produced primarily by extraction from pooled menopausal urine. Recombinant DNA technology using *Escherichia coli* has produced polypeptides devoid of the requisite carbohydrate chains. In the 1990s, recombinant DNA technology using mammalian cells will probably result in sufficient HMG production for clinical use.

The most common indication for using HMG is anovulation, although it is also used to treat oligoovulation, luteal phase deficiency, and unexplained infertility, as well as in multiple follicular recruitment for in vitro fertilization and related reproductive technologies.[78-80] HMG stimulates the ovary directly and therefore can be used in patients with pituitary stalk transection or those with pituitary adenomas resulting in hyperprolactinemia. Because it is relatively expensive (approximately $40.00/ ampule) and potent, it should not be administered without first performing a thorough infertility evaluation. A screening laparoscopy is not mandated in the presence of a normal HSG and a negative history; however,

laparoscopy should be performed if pregnancy does not occur within four ovulatory cycles.

Seventy-five to 150 IU of HMG are usually initiated between days 4 and 6 of a spontaneous or induced menstrual cycle. After 4 to 6 days of this dosage, careful monitoring of serum estradiol levels and ultrasound measurement of ovarian follicle diameter[81] are initiated and the HMG dosage is increased accordingly. The dosage is maintained when estradiol levels increase by a steady geometric increment and follicle diameter increases 1.5 to 2 mm/day. Ovulation is induced with HCG when one or two follicles have reached a diameter of 16 mm or more and serum estradiol levels are between 500 and 2,000 pg/ml. The cycle is canceled and HCG withheld to prevent multiple births or ovarian overstimulation if poor follicle response is noted after 14 days of medication, if more than three preovulatory follicles are present, or if estradiol levels exceed 2,000 pg/ml.[77] If these guidelines are followed, severe overstimulation occurs in less than 2% of cycles and multiple pregnancies occur in 26% of cycles, 75% of which are twins. In centers where in vitro fertilization and embryo freezing are available, cycles with multiple follicles can be salvaged by aspirating the excessive oocytes after HCG administration, fertilizing them, and cryopreserving them for later in vitro fertilization should conception not occur in vivo.[82]

The overall pregnancy rate with HMG-HCG therapy in hypothalamic–pituitary amenorrheic patients exceeds 80%,[77] but age greatly affects outcome. In patients under age 35 years the rate of pregnancy is more than 95% after six treatment cycles, whereas in those above 35 years it is only 60%.[77] Since the introduction of HMG more than 8,000 patients with ovulatory problems have been treated for more than 22,000 cycles, resulting in 3,120 pregnancies.[77]

Follicle-Stimulating Hormone

In November of 1986 purified FSH became available for clinical use in the United States. A further purification of HMG, FSH is primarily indicated for clomiphene-resistant patients with polycystic ovary disease.[83] Each lyophilized vial contains 75 IU of FSH. As with human menopausal gonadotropins, ovulation induction with FSH must be monitored with measurements of serum estradiol levels and pelvic ultrasound to reduce the potential for multiple births and ovarian overstimulation. Ovulation may occur spontaneously but is much more consistent if an ovulatory trigger of HCG is administered.[84]

Gonadotropin-Releasing Hormone

The decapeptide hormone gonadotropin-releasing hormone (GnRH) is located predominantly in the arcuate nucleus of the medial basal hypothalamus and is responsible for the release of LH and FSH from the pituitary gland. The realization that GnRH is released in a pulsatile fashion paved the way for applying it to clinical medicine.[85] For clinical applications the dose and pulse frequency must be established within certain limits, although there is substantial flexibility in the system.[86] A pulse frequency window of 60 to 120 minutes seems to occur in humans, within which GnRH can be administered at a fixed frequency with normal gonadotropin stimulation, follicular development, release of an LH surge, ovulation, and development of a healthy corpus luteum. Dosages generally range from 2.5 to 20 ug/pulse, and administration may be either subcutaneous or intravenous. Several pulsatile infusion devices are available.[87]

In general, women with hypothalamic amenorrhea respond well to subcutaneous administration, whereas patients with polycystic ovary disease require intravenous administration. Although pulsatile GnRH is theoretically more physiologic and therefore safer than HMG, in my experience the frequency of ovarian overstimulation and multiple pregnancy does not differ markedly between the medications when patients are carefully matched. Other potential side effects include infection at the indwelling catheter site, allergic reactions, and rarely anaphylaxis with the development of anti-GnRH antibodies.[88]

Bromocriptine Mesylate

Bromocriptine (2-bromo-α-ergocriptine) is a semisynthetic product derived from a family of ergot alkaloids. The drug was approved for clinical use in the United States in 1979. The primary indication for bromocriptine is to inhibit prolactin, particularly when associated with pituitary adenomas. Several newer ergot and non-ergot dopamine agonists have recently been developed to treat hyperprolactinemia (Table 2.1). Other indications for bromocriptine include inhibition of physiologic postpartum lactation, acromegaly, and Parkinson's disease, as well as a variety of other endocrine and nonendocrine conditions.[89] The principal administration is by an oral 2.5-mg tablet, although both vaginal and injectable applications are now available.[90,91]

In recent years bromocriptine has been investigated as a treatment for a number of conditions associated with infertility, including polycystic ovary disease.[92,93] Except for its use as the first-line treatment for amenorrhea associated with hyperprolactinemia, however, the literature does not support its application in polycystic ovary syndrome, idiopathic infertility, and normoprolactinemic luteal phase defect.

Surgery

One of the most significant breakthroughs in infertility surgery has been the introduction of magnification and microsurgical techniques.[94] Magnification initially meant the use of loupes attached to a headband or pair of eyeglasses. While loupes remain useful for distal tubal disease, operating microscopes are now standard for tubal reanastomosis and correction of proximal tubal obstruction. The principles of microsurgery include avoiding picking up tissue with either fingers or crushing instruments, repairing raw peritoneum, using fine suture such as 8–0 nylon or 6–0 proline, keeping tissue moist throughout the surgery with irrigation, and paying careful attention to hemostasis.[95] Pregnancy rates after pelvic surgery range between 20 and 75%, depending upon the extent of pelvic adhesions and the presence or absence and location of tubal

TABLE 2.1. Comparison of ergot and non-ergot dopamine agonists in the treatment of hyperprolactinemia.

Drug	Recommended Dosage	Route of Administration	Duration of Action	Response	Common Side Effects
Ergot Parlodel	2.5–10 mg/day (divided)	PO	8 to 12 hrs.	Resolution of symptoms Lowers prolactin Shrinks adenomas	CNS Dizziness, headache, syncope, nasal stuffiness GI vomiting, nausea Cardiovascular Orthostatic hypotension
Parlodel SRO (Sandoz, Basle, Switzerland)	2.5–15 mg once-a-day	PO	24 hrs.	Similar	Similar
Parlodel LA	50–100 mg q-monthly	IM	~28 d	Similar	Similar, milder transient
Parlodel, vaginal route	2.5 mg once-a-day	Vaginal	24 hrs.	Similar	Less GI
Mesulergine	0.25–2.0 mg/day (divided)	PO	~10 hrs.	Similar	Similar more prevalent
Lisuride (Dopergin, Schering AG Germany)	0.2–0.5 mg/day (divided)	PO	8–12 hrs.	Similar	Similar nausea, dizziness drowsiness more prevalent
Teguride	0.25–1.5 mg/day (divided)	PO	<24 hrs.	Similar	Similar transient central more prevalent
Hydergine	6–12 mg/day (divided)	PO	<24 hrs.	Lower	None reported
Pergolide	0.025–0.1 mg once-a-day	PO	24–48 hrs.	Similar	Similar fever, nasal congestion hypotension more common
Dihydroergocriptine (POLI Industria Chimica S.P.A. Milan, Italy)	20–30 mg/day (divided)	PO	<12 hrs.	Similar	Similar, less frequent, less severe
Carbergoline Farmitalia Carlo Erba, Millan, Italy	0.25–1 mg q weekly	PO	7–14 days	Similar	Similar hypotension more common
Non-Ergot CV-205-502 (Sandoz, Basle, Switzerland)	0.075–0.15 mg once-a-day	PO	24 hrs.	Similar to better	Similar, milder transient, less common

Modified from Philosophe R, Seibel MM. Novel approaches to the management of hyperprolactinemia. Current Opinion in Obstet Gynecol 1991; 3:336–342 occlusion. The highest percentages follow correction of proximal tubal occlusion (e.g., tubal ligation reversal, obstructed uterotubal junction), and the lowest percentages reflect correction of distal tubal occlusion with bilateral hydrosalpinges.[96]

In an effort to improve the outcome in patients with distal tubal disease, laparoscopic techniques are being developed to gain access to the tubal lumen prior to surgery in order to evaluate the mucosa of the ampullary segment.[97] By placing a 3-mm salpingoscope into the distal lumen and distending the tube with a warm saline drip, the presence or absence of adhesions between the mucosal folds can be quantified and equated with outcome. Preliminary data suggest that this technique will allow physicians to recommend salpingostomy only for women with mild mucosal lesions and reserve in vitro fertilization for those with more severe tubal disease.

Infertility surgery not requiring microscopic reanastomosis has been revolutionized by the emergence of operative laparoscopy (pelviscopy) and laser laparoscopy.[98–100] Both procedures allow many of the operations that previously required laparotomy to be performed by laparoscopy.[98–100] Examples include lysis of adhesions, salpingostomy, myomectomy, removal of endometriosis, and management of ectopic pregnancy.[101,102]

Similar basic principles are utilized for pelviscopy and laser laparoscopy. The patient is positioned for diagnostic laparoscopy, and prepared and draped in the usual fashion. The laparoscope is placed through a subumbilical incision, and ancillary instruments are inserted through second, third, or even fourth puncture sites along the suprapubic line. In some instances, there is also an operating channel within the laparoscope. Increasingly smaller video cameras have been developed that attach directly to the laparoscope and allow the physician and his or her assistants to visualize the procedure and operate comfortably. Whether pelviscopy or video laseroscopy is chosen, atraumatic grasping forceps are used to stabilize structures and provide optimum exposure. Many types of scissors, biopsy forceps, and coagulation, irrigation, and evaporation equipment have been developed for pelviscopy. The coagulation device is set at 100°C for everting mucosal flaps and 120°C for coagulating adhesions and endometriosis implants. The depth of destruction is approximately 2 mm.

Several endoscopic lasers, including carbon dioxide (CO_2), argon, potassium-titanyl-phosphate (KTP-532), and neodymium: yttrium-aluminum-garnet (Nd:YAG) are also available. Each of these laser lights has a different wavelength and therefore different characteristics when exposed to tissue. In general, however, soft tissue absorbs the energy from the laser and converts it into heat. Water within the tissue is converted to steam, resulting in the production of water vapor, cellular debris, and smoke (the laser plume).[103] Therefore, the tissue is vaporized. The depth of thermal damage below the vaporized tissue is less than 0.5 mm, which provides the experienced surgeon with extreme precision. The laser plume is evacuated through a filtered suction machine. In my opinion, insufficient attention has been given to the observation that intact DNA particles have been identified within the laser plume.[103] For this reason, as well as the potential irritating effect of laser plume on the lungs, careful evacuation of the plume is mandatory for the long-term safety and comfort of operating room personnel.

Since the 1960s, hysteroscopic technology has advanced in parallel with laparoscopy. The three types of hysteroscopes in current use are the contact hysteroscope, the panoramic hysteroscope, and the microcolpohysteroscope.[104] Contact hysteroscopy is performed without uterine distention. The distal lens of the telescope is placed in direct contact with the surface to be observed. Panoramic hysteroscopy is hysteroscopy combined with uterine distention. The most common distention media are CO_2 gas, dextrose 5% in water, and high-molecular-weight dextran. Although all of these are widely used and safe, complications such as gas embolism, hyperglycemia, hyponatremia, transient liver function disturbances, and anaphylaxis have occurred rarely.[105,106] The telescopes are adapted cystoscopes with external diameters between 4 and 6 mm. The microcolpohysteroscope can be used as a panoramic hysteroscope, a contact hysteroscope, or a microscope. Uterine polyps, fibroids, adhesions, and septa may all be surgically removed by hysteroscopy. Simultaneous laparoscopy reduces the risk of uterine perforation.[107]

Treatment of Male Infertility

The treatment of male infertility continues to be a challenge for the clinician. Although most infertile men have oligospermia (reduced sperm number), asthenospermia (poor sperm motility), teratospermia (sperm with abnormal morphology), or a combination of these, the etiology is frequently unknown.

Primary testicular failure is diagnosed by elevated circulating levels of LH and FSH. Whether the condition is due to congenital disorders such as Klinefelter's syndrome or to acquired disorders such as trauma, orchitis, or testicular torsion, these patients usually do not respond to treatment. Conversely, men with hypogonadotropic hypogonadism resulting from inadequate gonadotropin stimulation of the testis respond extremely well to gonadotropin therapy.[108] Although opinions vary as to optimum treatment, most use either HMG or purified FSH, 75 IU intramusculary three times weekly combined with 1,500 to 2,500 IU of HCG once or twice weekly. Alternatively, pulsatile infusions of GnRH, 2 to 8 µg/pulse every 90 to 120 minutes, have also been used successfully unless the hypogonadotropism is due to pituitary stalk transection.[109] Because sperm maturation requires approximately 72 days, several months of treatment are required before sperm are produced. Patients should be treated at least 8 to 12 months before treatment is considered unsuccessful.

In most instances, oligospermia and asthenospermia are found to be idiopathic. Several treatments have been investigated, including the aromatase inhibitor testalactone, clomiphene citrate, tamoxifen, and gonadotropins.[110] Others have used empiric antibiotics, varicocelectomy, and gluco-corticoids. None of these treatments has yielded consistent improvement in idiopathic oligospermia or asthenospermia.

For this reason, attempts have focused on laboratory manipulation of semen samples to increase the concentration of normal motile sperm. Several methods exist for separating motile sperm from the seminal plasma. The specimen may be centrifuged and the sperm that "swim up" from the pellet may be collected, or the specimen may be centrifuged on a Percoll gradient and the desirable sperm collected from a defined layer of the gradient.[111] The latter method is particularly helpful for ejaculates containing increased numbers of white blood cells or immature forms. Approximately 0.3 ml of prepared spermatozoa are then drawn into a tuberculin syringe and the syringe is attached to a catheter. Expected ovulation is predicted by basal body temperature, hormonal analysis, or ovulation-inducing agents (Table 2.2). The catheter is passed into the uterine fundus and the suspension slowly injected (Fig. 2.9).[112] The pregnancy rate for this type of treatment is approximately 19% per couple.[113] The use of ultrasound guidance or of a falloposcope, a flexible and directional fiberoptic scope less than 1 mm in diameter, for transuterine intratubal insemination is under investigation (Fig. 2.10),[113] as are direct intraperitoneal insemination through the posterior cul de sac[113] and intrauterine insemination combined with superovulation.[114] The results obtained with all of these techniques must be compared with untreated background pregnancy rates, which have been reported as 14% (Fig. 2.11).[112]

Among couples with oligospermia or azoospermia who do not or cannot conceive, artificial insemination with donor sperm has evolved as a widely acceptable alternative. The most recent reliable data reveal that in 1986 in the United States there were 25,600 newborn adoptions.[115] During the same period over 30,000 children were conceived using anonymous sperm donors.[116] Pregnancy rates are excellent with donor insemination but, as expected, are reduced when the female has additional fertility factors or is of advanced reproductive age (Fig. 2.12).[117]

TABLE 2.2. Newer methods of timing and predicting ovulation.

Product	Function	Time	Cost ($)	Manufacturer and telephone number
Thermometers				
Terumo	Digital BBT	60 S	32.95	Terumo (301)398-8500
Cue	Oral sensor/vaginal probe measures changes in saliva, vaginal secretions	10 S	300–700 rent 68/mo	Zetek (303)343-2122
Fertil-A-Chron	Computerized digital thermometer with memory	45 S	95	Fertil-A-Chron (516)435-0913
Urine test kits				
First Response	1st morning urine, ovulation 12–24 h	30 min	30	Tambrands Inc (516)437-8800
Ovu Stick	Midafternoon urine, ovulation 24–36 h	30 min	60, 9 day 45, 6 day	Monoclonal Antibodies (800)227-8855
Quidel	Morning urine, repeat throughout day	35 min	30	Quidel (619)450-1533
Ramp	1st morning urine days 7, 8, 9 after LH surge to measure progesterone, quality of ovulation	5 min	115–140	Monoclonal Antibodies (800)227-8855
Clearplan	1st morning urine, ovulation 24–36 h (10-day test)	5 min	30	Whitehall Labs (800)883-EASY

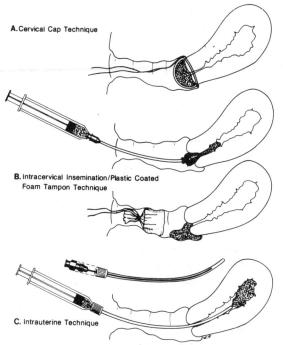

A. Cervical Cap Technique

B. Intracervical Insemination/Plastic Coated Foam Tampon Technique

C. Intrauterine Technique

FIGURE 2.9. Methods of artificial insemination. Reprinted, with permission, from ref. 4.

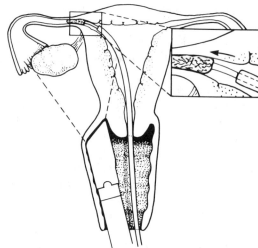

FIGURE 2.10. Ultrasound-guided intratubal insemination. Reprinted, with permission, from ref. 145.

Psychologic support and informed consent of both partners is essential prior to initiating donor insemination. Although legal, ethical, and medical issues are discussed, currently the greatest concern is the inadvertent transmission of disease. Transmission of gonorrhea, hepatitis B, genital herpes, and human immunodeficiency virus type 1 has been documented.[118] For this reason, repetitive screening of donors for a wide variety of infectious diseases has become standard.[119] Further safety is achieved through cryopreservation of donor samples followed by reevaluation of the donors 6

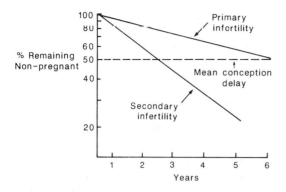

FIGURE 2.11. Timetable of expected pregnancy for patients with unexplained infertility. Reproduced with permission of reference 4.

months later. Negative results at this time virtually ensure safety of the samples.

For some males, surgical intervention is required to overcome infertility. As with females, the use of microsurgical techniques has greatly improved results. Microsurgical vasectomy reversal results in pregnancy in 43 to 82% of cases, depending on the location and extent of the vasectomy.[120] Less common procedures such as testicular autotransplantation for intraabdominal undescended testes and transplantation of the human testis for anorchia have also been developed.[121] A less invasive measure was developed for males with congenital absence of the vas deferens. Sperm aspirated directly from the epididymal tubule have achieved fertilization and resulted in off-spring following transfer of the embryos into the woman's fallopian tubes.[122] Procedures such as these are applicable to relatively few patients. They do, however, demonstrate the potential impact of surgery on male infertility.

Reproductive Technology

Perhaps no other area exemplifies the advances made in infertility treatment as well as the reproductive technologies[123] (Tables 2.3 & 2.4). The best known of these is in vitro fertilization (IVF). In that procedure, pre-ovulatory oocytes are surgically removed from the ovary and inseminated in a Petri dish with the husband's sperm, which have been specially prepared. After 48 to 72 hours of incubation, the fertilized oocytes are drawn into a catheter and transferred into the woman's uterus through the cervix. Indications include tubal disease, endometriosis, immunologic infertility, oligospermia, and unexplained infertility. Gamete intrafallopian transfer (GIFT) differs from IVF in that the spermatozoa and oocytes are placed into the fimbriated end of the fallopian tube when oocyte retrieval is performed (Fig. 2.13A, B). Candidates for this procedure must have at least one patent fallopian tube that appears to be normal. My personal recommendations for deciding which procedure to use are listed in Table 2.4. A report of the United States Registry of in vitro

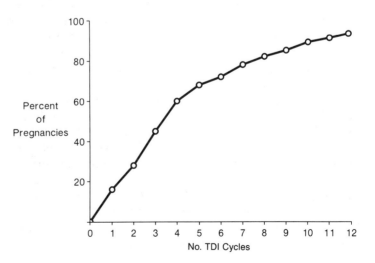

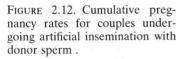

FIGURE 2.12. Cumulative pregnancy rates for couples undergoing artificial insemination with donor sperm.

TABLE 2.3. Common acronyms in reproductive technology.

ART	Assisted reproductive technology
IVF	In vitro fertilization
GIFT	Gamete intrafallopian transfer
PROST	Pronuclear stage tubal transfer
TEST	Tubal embryo stage transfer
ZIFT	Zygote intrafallopian transfer
POST	Peritoneal ovum and sperm transfer
DIPI	Direct intraperitoneal insemination
AIH	Artificial insemination, husband
AID	Artificial insemination, donor
TDI	Therapeutic donor insemination
GUT	Gamete uterine transfer

TABLE 2.4. Choosing the best treatment option for infertile couples.

Clinical situation	Surgery	IVF	GIFT
Tubal implantation	No	Yes	No
Tubocornual anastomosis	Yes	No	No
Tubal reanastomosis (≥3.5 cm tubal length)	Yes	No	No
Tubal reanastomosis (<3.5 cm tubal length)	No	Yes	No
Previous fimbriectomy	No	Yes	No
Salpingostomy	No	Yes	No
Repeat tubal surgery	No	Yes	No
Pelvic adhesions—mild	Yes	Yes	Yes
Pelvic adhesions—severe	No	Yes	No
Previous ectopic pregnancy	Yes	Yes	No
[a] Endometriosis—stages I–II	No	No	No
Endometriosis—stages III–IV	Yes	Yes	No
Age >35, surgical option	No	Yes	Yes
Unexplained infertility <3 yr duration	No	No	No
Unexplained infertility >3 yr duration	No	Yes	Yes

[a] Other treatment options and adequate observation recommended first.

fertilization described the 1989 experience of 163 member clinics performing 24,183 ovarian stimulation cycles.[124] Of 15,392 oocyte retrievals, 4,598 (19%) resulted in a clinical pregnancy and 3,472 (14%) in live births. Ninety-eight percent of the clinics had at least one delivery, and overall a total of 4,736 babies were born. The overall live delivery rate for GIFT was 23% based on 3,652 oocyte retrievals, 26% for both procedures in combination based on 452 retrievals, and 17% for zygote intrafallopian transfer (ZIFT) and related practices based on 908 retrievals.[124] Although results for GIFT appear higher than those for IVF, this is not the case when

identical patient populations are treated. Of those women who do deliver a viable baby, the overwhelming majority will do so within four attempts and more than 80% will do so within two attempts.[125] This information is helpful in counseling couples who require this form of treatment. Early psychosocial development[126] as well as development at the first birthday[127] appears normal.

Advances in IVF and GIFT have resulted in the development of many related techniques for assisted reproduction. Due to space constraints, only two will be mentioned because they have become more common: cryopreservation[128] and embryo donation.[129] Most IVF centers do not transfer more than four or five embryos to reduce the risk of multiple births. Therefore, if excess embryos result, couples may choose to have them cryopreserved for their own use at a later date, or donate them anonymously. The identities of the donor and recipient are kept confidential, and donors are not informed of the outcome. Most recipients of donated embryos are women with premature menopause whose endometrium has been artificially prepared with estrogen and progesterone. Synchronization of the donated embryo with the recipient endometrium is the critical factor for success. With precise timing, success rates may be as high as 30%.

Emotional Aspects of Infertility

The desire to procreate is a powerful force. Because fertility is time-limited, most infertile couples experience their infertility as a crisis. This crisis becomes intensified as infertile couples soon realize that each time they resolve their conflicts and consider discontinuation of treatment, assisted reproductive technology provides new options. Issues surrounding donated gametes are particularly complex.[130] In my opinion, far too little psychologic support is provided for couples being treated for infertility. In one report a stress reduction program for infertile women resulted in a 34% conception rate within 6 months of completing the course.[131] Studies such as this suggest that some form of behavioral therapy and

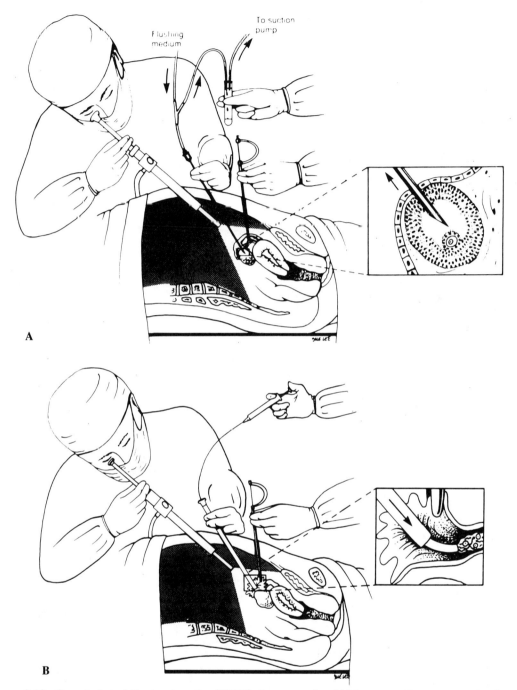

FIGURE 2.13. Gamete intrafallopian transfer (GIFT) demonstrating (A) laparoscopic oocyte retrieval and (B) transfer of sperm into fallopian tube. Reprinted, with permission, from ref. 145.

TABLE 2.5. State laws on infertility insurance coverage.

State	Date enacted	Mandate to cover	Mandate to offer	Diagnosis & treatment incl. IVF	Diagnosis & treatment excl. IVF	IVF Only
Maryland	1985	X				X
Arkansas	1987	X				X[a]
Texas	1987		X			X
Hawaii	1987	X				X[b]
Massachusetts	1987	X		X		
Connecticut	1989		X	X		
Rhode Island	1989	X		X		
California	1989		X		X[c]	
New York	1989	X			X[d]	
Illinois	1991	X		X[e]		

October 1991

[a] Includes a lifetime maximum benefit of not less than $15,000.

[b] Provides a one-time only benefit for all outpatient expenses arising from IVF.

[c] Excludes IVF, but defines IVF as "the laboratory medical procedures involving the actual in vitro fertilization process." Covers gamete intrafallopian transfer (GIFT).

[d] Provides coverage for the "diagnosis and treatment of correctable medical conditions."

[e] Limits first-time attempts to four complete oocyte retrievals. If a child is born, two complete oocyte retrievals for a second birth shall be covered. Excludes businesses with 25 or fewer employees.

Prepared by The American Fertility Society, Office of Government Relations. (202)863-2494/2576.

emotional support should be considered for all couples being treated for infertility.[132]

Ethical and Legal Considerations

Although decisions about whether or when to have children are thought to be a matter of personal, private concern, issues surrounding treatment of infertility have become the subject of extensive ethical and legal consideration, as well as front-page news. Prominent legal issues concern the disposal of cryopreserved embryos, length of storage, posthumous use, inheritance rights, and custody issues in cases of divorce. Other legal issues surround whether or not insurance will be available to cover infertility services (Table 2.5).[133,134] The major ethical considerations include the moral status of an embryo, whether conception that involves the efforts of a third party redefines parenthood, and clarification of when a given treatment is proven and when it is experimental.[2,135] An extensive literature is developing surrounding these and related topics.

A more practical ethical issue involves honesty. People providing infertility services must be adequately trained for the services they provide and truthfully report their success rates.[136,137] Several regulatory agencies have emerged to provide guidelines and standardize reporting.[124,138,139]

Infertility in the Future

The diagnosis and treatment of infertility have changed remarkably in recent years. There is little doubt that these changes will continue. Micromanipulation techniques are now sufficiently refined to allow the microinsemination of an oocyte by a single sperm (Fig. 2.14).[140] These techniques may be of great importance

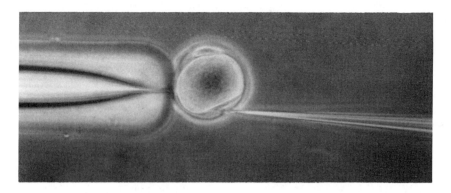

FIGURE 2.14. Micromanipulation of human oocyte.

to oligospermic males. The merging of micromanipulation with molecular biology will also have a great impact on preimplantation genetic diagnosis. Because early embryos are totipotent, a single blastomere may be removed and the remaining embryo will develop fully into an individual.[140] Using DNA probes and DNA amplification techniques,[141] single-gene defects could be diagnosed from the removed blastomere, and even potentially corrected. Sex determination of human pre-implantation embryos has already been achieved.[142] Similarly, DNA analysis of a single sperm or the polar body of an unfertilized oocyte can be performed.[143] The potential applications of these techniques to the diagnosis and treatment of infertility are far-reaching. It is clear that the options available to help infertile couples achieve a healthy baby will continue to increase at a rapid rate. The challenge will be for these technological advances to keep pace with the legal, moral, and ethical environment in which they themselves were conceived.[144]

References

1. Menning BE. The psychology of infertility. In: Aimen J, ed. Infertility: diagnosis and management. New York: Springer-Verlag, 1984;17–29.
2. Infertility: medical and social choices. Congress of the United States, Office of Technology Assessment, May 1988.
3. Fundamental considerations. In: Keller DDW, Strickler RC, Warren JC, eds. Clinical infertility. East Norwalk, CT: Appleton-Century-Crofts, 1984;2.
4. Seibel MM. Work-up of the infertile couple. In: Seibel MM, ed. Infertility: a comprehensive text. East Norwalk, CT: Appleton & Lange, 1990;1–21.
5. Smith CG, Asch RH. Drug abuse and reproduction. Fertil Steril 1987;48:355.
6. Cook EP. Characteristics of the bio-psychosocial crisis of infertility. J Counsel Dev 1987;65:465.
7. Azziz R. Reproductive endocrinologic alterations in female asymptomatic obesity. Fertil Steril 1989;52:703.
8. Talbert LM. Hirsutism: cause and diagnosis. Obstet Gynecol Rep 1988;1:72–83.
9. Herzog A. Neurologic considerations. In: Seibel MM, ed. Infertility: a comprehensive text. East Norwalk, CT: Appleton & Lange, 1990;249–257.
10. Mueller BA, Daling JR. Epidemiology of infertility. In: Soules MR, ed. Controversies in reproductive endocrinology and infertility. New York: Elsevier, 1989;1.
11. Kessel E. Pelvic inflammatory disease with intrauterine device use: a reassessment. Fertil Steril 1989;51:1–11.
12. American College of Obstetricians and Gynecologists. Chlamydial infection. Washington, DC, 1987.
13. Bayer SR, Seibel MM. Endometriosis: pathophysiology and treatment. In: Seibel MM, ed. Infertility: a comprehensive text. East Norwalk, CT: Appleton & Lange, 1990; 111–128.
14. Bibbo M, Haenszel WM, Wied GI, et al. A twenty-five-year follow-up study of women exposed to diethylstilbestrol during pregnancy. N Engl J Med 1978;298:763–767.
15. Golan A, Langer R, Bukovsky I, Caspi E. Congenital anomalies of the mullerian system. Fertil Steril 1989;51:747–755.

16. U.S. Department of Health and Human Services. The health consequences of smoking: a report of the Surgeon General. Washington, DC: U.S. Government Printing Office, 1984.
17. Bos RP, Henderson PT. Genotoxic risk of passive smoking. Rev Environ Health 1984; 4:L161.
18. Fielding JE. Smoking effects and control. N Engl J Med 1985;313:491.
19. Stillman RJ, Rosenberg MJ, Sachs BP. Smoking and reproduction. Fertil Steril 1986; 46:545.
20. Howe G, Westhoff C, Vessey M, Yeates D. Effects of age, cigarette smoking, and other factors on fertility: findings in a large prospective study. Br Med J 1985;290:1697.
21. Baird DD, Wilcox AJ. Cigarette smoking associated with delayed conception. JAMA 1985;253:2979.
22. Phipps WR, Cramer DW, Schiff I, et al. The association between smoking and female infertility as influenced by cause of the infertility. Fertil Steril 1987;48:377.
23. Campbell OM, Gray RH. Smoking and ectopic pregnancy: a multinational case-controlled study. In: Rosenberg MJ, ed. Smoking and reproductive health. Littleton, MA: PSG, 1986.
24. Bos RP, van Heijst CHM, Hollanders HMG, Theuws JLG, Thijssen RFA, Eskes TKAB. Is there influence of smoking on the mutagenicity of follicular fluid? Fertil Steril 1989;52: 774–777.
25. Rivrud GN, Berg K, Anderson D, Blowers S, Bjoro K. Mutagenic effect of amniotic fluid from smoking women at term. Mutat Res 1986;171:71.
26. Holly EA, Petrokis NL, Friend NF, Sarles DL, Lee RE, Flander LB. Mutagenic mucus in the cervix of smokers. J Natl Cancer Inst 1987; 76:983.
27. Rivrud GN, Hagen I, Borresen AL. Mutagenicity testing of human milk from smokers and non-smokers in the salmonella/microsome test. Life Sci 1987;41:2389.
28. Baron JA, Adams P, Ward M. Cigarette smoking and other correlates of cytologic estrogen effect in postmenopausal women. Fertil Steril 1988;50:766–771.
29. Mattison DR. The effects of smoking on fertility from gametogenesis to implantation. Environ Res 1982;28:410.
30. Barbieri RL, McShane PM, Ryan KJ. Constituents of cigarette smoke inhibit granulosa cell aromatase. Fertil Steril 1986;46:232.
31. Marshburn PB, Sloan CS, Hammond MG. Semen quality and association with coffee drinking, cigarette smoking, and ethanol consumption. Fertil Steril 1989;52:162–165.
32. Klaiber EL, Broverman DM, Pokoly TB, et al. Interrelationships of cigarette smoking, testicular varicoceles and seminal fluid indexes. Fertil Steril 1987;47:481.
33. Gindoff PR, Jewelewicz R. Reproductive potential in the older woman. Fertil Steril 1986;46:989.
34. Collins JA, Rowe TC. Age of the female partner is a prognostic factor in prolonged unexplained infertility: a multicenter study. Fertil Steril 1989;52:15–20.
35. Antenatal diagnosis of genetic disorders. ACOG technical bulletin. 108, Sept 1987.
36. Warburton D, Kline J, Stein Z, Strobino B. Cytogenic abnormalities in spontaneous abortions of recognized conceptions. In: Porter IH, Willey A, eds. Perinatal genetics: diagnosis and treatment. New York: Academic Press, 1986;133.
37. Friedman JM. Genetic disease in the offspring of older fathers. Obstet Gynecol 1981; 57:745.
38. Paniagna R, Martin A, Nistal M, Amat P. Testicular involution in elderly men: comparison of histologic quantitative studies with hormone patterns. Fertil Steril 1987;47: 671.
39. Warner BA, Dufau ML, Santen RJ. Effects of aging and illness on the pituitary-testicular axis in men: qualitative as well as quantitative changes in luteinizing hormone. J Clin Endocrinol Metab 1985;60:263.
40. James W. The causes of the decline in fecundability with age. Soc Biol 1979;26:330.
41. Herbert WNP. Pregnancy with maternal age of 35 years or older. In: Cefalo RC, ed. Clinical decisions in obstetrics and gynecology. Rockville, MD: Aspen publishers 1990; 162–165.
42. Spellacy WN, Miller SJ, Winegar A. Pregnancy after 40 years of age. Obstet Gynecol 1986; 68:452.
43. Stillman RJ. In utero exposure to diethylstilbestrol: adverse effects on the reproductive tract and reproductive performance in male and female offspring. Am J Obstet Gynecol 1982;142:905.
44. Lee RL, Lipshultz LI. Evaluation and treatment of male infertility. In: Hammond MG, Talbert LM, eds. Infertility: a practical guide for the physician. 2nd ed. Oradell, NJ: Medical Economics Books, 1985;42–63.
45. Winters SJ. Evaluation and medical management of male infertility. In: Seibel MM, ed. Infertility: a comprehensive text. East Norwalk, CT: Appleton & Lange, 1990; 157–168.
46. Damewood MD, Grochow LB. Prospects for fertility after chemotherapy or radiation for neoplastic disease. Fertil Steril 1986;45:443.

47. Kucheria K, Saxena R, Mohan D. Semen analysis in alcohol dependence syndrome. Andrologia 1987;19:32.

48. Brzek A. Alcohol and male fertility (preliminary report). Andrologia 1985;17:558.

49. Ragni G, DeLauretis L, Gambaro V, et al. Semen evaluation in heroin and methadone addicts. Acta Eur Fertil 1985;16:245.

50. Dalterio SL, de Rooij DG. Maternal cannabinoid exposure: effects on spermatogenesis in male offspring. Int J Androl 1986;9:250.

51. Wu CH, Aitken RJ, Ferguson A. Inflammatory bowel disease and male infertility: effects of sulfasalazone and 5-aminosalicylic acid on sperm-fertilizing capacity and reactive oxygen species generation. Fertil Steril 1989;52:842–845.

52. Rachmilewitz D. Coated mesalazine (5-aminosalicylic acid) versus sulphasalazine in the treatment of active ulcerative colitis: a randomized trial. Br J Med 1989;298:82–86.

53. Knuth UA, Maniera H, Nieschlag E. Anabolic steroids and semen parameters in bodybuilders. Fertil Steril 1989;52:1041–1047.

54. Rogol AD, Yesalis CE. Anabolic-androgenic steroids and athletes: what are the issues? J Clin Endocrinol Metab 1992;74:465.

55. Yamaguchi M, Sakatoku J, Takihara H. The application of intrascrotal deep body temperature measurement for the noninvasive diagnosis of varicoceles. Fertil Steril 1989;52:295–301.

56. Taymor ML, Overstreet JW. Some thoughts on the postcoital test. Fertil Steril 1988;50:702–703.

57. Hellstrom WJG, Samuels SJ, Waits AB, Overstreet JW. A comparison of the usefulness of sperm mar and immunobead tests for the detection of antisperm antibodies. Fertil Steril 1989;52:1027–1031.

58. World Health Organization. WHO laboratory manual for the examination of human semen and semen-cervical mucus interactions. 2nd ed. Cambridge: The Press Syndicate of the University of Cambridge, 1987.

59. Loy RA, Weinstein FG, Seibel MM. Hysterosalpingography in perspective: the predictive value of oil-soluble versus water-soluble media. Fertil Steril 1989;51:170.

60. Owens OM, Schiff I, Kaul AF, Cramer DC, Burt RAP. Reduction of pain following hysterosalpingogram by prior analgesic administration. Fertil Steril 1989;43:146.

61. Nunley WC, Bateman BG, Kitchin JD, Pope TL. Intravasation during hysterosalpingography using oil-base contrast-medium—a second look. Obstet Gynecol 1987;70:309.

62. Katz E. The luteinized unruptured follicle and other ovulatory dysfunctions. Fertil Steril 1988;50:839–850.

63. Noyes RW, Hertig AT, Rock J. Dating the endometrial biopsy. Fertil Steril 1950;1:3.

64. McNeely MJ, Soules MR. The diagnosis of luteal phase deficiency: A critical review. Fertil Steril 1988;50:1–15.

65. Macomber D, Sanders MB. The spermatozoa count. N Engl J Med 1929;200:981.

66. Dunphy BC, Neal LM, Cooke ID. The clinical value of conventional semen analysis. Fertil Steril 1989;51:324–329.

67. Saint Pol P, Beuscart R, Leroy-Martin B, Hermand E, Jablonski W. Circannual rhythms of sperm parameters of fertile men. Fertil Steril 1989;51:1030–1033.

68. Silber SJ. The relationship of abnormal semen values to pregnancy outcome. In: Seibel MM, ed. Infertility: a comprehensive text. East Norwalk, CT: Appleton & Lange, 1990;149–155.

69. Mortimer D, Goel N, Shu MA. Evaluation of the cell soft automated semen analysis system in a routine laboratory setting. Fertil Steril 1988;50:960–968.

70. Adashi EY. Ovulation initiation: clomiphene citrate. In: Seibel MM, ed. Infertility: a comprehensive text. East Norwalk, CT: Appleton & Lange, 1990;303–310.

71. Seibel M, Bayer SR. Complex forms of ovulation induction. In: Soules MR, ed. Controversies in reproductive endocrinology and infertility. New York: Elsevier, 1989;107–134.

72. Wu CH, Winkel CA. The effect of therapy initiation day on clomiphene citrate therapy. Fertil Steril 1989;42:564–568.

73. Shalev J, Goldenberg M, Kukia E, Lewinthal D, Tepper R, Mashiach S, Blankstein J. Comparison of five clomiphene citrate dosage regimens: follicular recruitment and distribution in the human ovary. Fertil Steril 1989;52:560–563.

74. Wrambsy H, Fredga K, Liedholm P. Chromosome analysis of human oocytes recovered from preovulatory follicles in stimulated cycles. N Engl J Med 1987;316:121–126.

75. Seibel MM, Smith DM. The effect of clomiphene citrate on human preovulatory oocyte maturation in vivo. J In Vitro Fert 1989;6:3–7.

76. Harlap S. Ovulation induction and congenital malformations. Lancet 1976;2:961.

77. Lunenfeld B, Lunenfeld E. Ovulation induction: HMG. In: Seibel MM, ed. Infertility: a comprehensive text. East Norwalk, CT: Appleton & Lange, 1990;311–322.

78. Seibel MM. A new era in reproductive technology: in vitro fertilization, gamete intrafallopian tube transfer and donated gametes and embryos. N Engl J Med 1988;318:828–834.

79. Dor J, Itzkovic DJ, Mashiach S, Lunenfeld B, Serr DM. Cumulative conception rates follow-

ing gonadotropin therapy. Am J Obstet Gynecol 1980;136:102–107.

80. Dodson W, Hughes CL, Yancy SE, Haney AF. Clinical characteristics of ovulation induction with human menopausal gonadotropins with and without leuprolide acetate in polycystic ovary syndrome. Fertil Steril 1989; 52:915–918.

81. McArdle CR, Seibel MM, Weinstein FG, Gaymor ML. Induction of ovulation monitored by ultrasound. Radiology 1983;148:809–813.

82. Belaisch-Allart J. L'aspiration ovocytaire: une conduite possible devant l'hyperstimulation. Horm Reprod Metab 1987;4:95–99.

83. Claman P, Seibel MM. Purified human follicle-stimulating hormone for ovulation induction: a critical review. Semin Reprod Endocrinol 1986;4:227–232.

84. Buvat J, Buvat-Herbaut M, Marcolin G, Dehaene JL, Verberg P, Renouard O. Purified follicle-stimulating hormone in polycystic ovary syndrome: slow administration is safer and more effective. Fertil Steril 1989;52: 553–559.

85. Knobil E. The neuroendocrine control of the menstrual cycle. Recent Prog Horm Res 1980;36:53–88.

86. Seibel MM, Claman P. Gonadotropin-releasing hormone and ovulation induction. Obstet Gynecol Report 1988;1:45–57.

87. Chambers GR, Sutherland IA, White S, Mason P, Jacobs HS. A new generation of pulsatile infusion devices. Ups J Med Sci 1984; 89:91–96.

88. Claman P, Elkind-Hirsch K, Oskowitz SP, Seibel MM. Urticaria associated with antigonadotropin-releasing hormone antibody in a female Kallmann's syndrome patient being treated with long-term pulsatile gonadotropin-releasing hormone. Obstet Gynecol 1987; 69:503–506.

89. Vance ML, Evans WS, Thorner MO. Bromocriptine. Ann Intern Med 1984;100: 78–86.

90. Katz E, Adashi EY. Treatment of infertility using bromocriptine mesylate. In: Seibel MM, ed. Infertility: a comprehensive text. East Norwalk, CT: Appleton & Lange, 1990; 351–362.

91. Ciccarelli E, Miola C, Avataneo T, Camanni F, Besser GM, Grossman A. Long-term treatment with a new repeatable injectable form of bromocriptine, Parlodel LAR, in patients with tumerous hyperprolactinemia. Fertil Steril 1989;52:930–935.

92. Seibel MM, Oskowitz ISP, Kamrava M, Taymor ML. Bromocriptine response in normoprolactinemic patients with polycystic ovary disease: a preliminary report. Obstet Gynecol 1984;64:123–127.

93. Ben-David M, Schenker JG. Transient hyperprolactinemia: a correctable cause of idiopathic female infertility. J Clin Endocrinol Metab 1983;57:642–644.

94. Winston RML. Microsurgery of the fallopian tube: from fantasy to reality. Fertil Steril 1989; 34:521–526.

95. Winston RML. Additional aspects of tubal surgery: a British perspective. In: Seibel M, ed. Infertility: a comprehensive text. East Norwalk, CT: Appleton & Lange, 1990; 417–432.

96. Gillett WR, Herbison GP. Tubocornual anastomosis: surgical considerations and coexistent infertility factors in determining the prognosis. Fertil Steril 1989;51:241–246.

97. Bruyne FD, Puttemans P, Boeckx W, Brosens I. The clinical value of salpingoscopy. Fertil Steril 1989;51:339–340.

98. Nezhat C, Crowgey S, Nezhat F. Video-laseroscopy for the treatment of endometriosis associated with infertility. Fertil Steril 1989; 51:237–240.

99. Armar NA, McGarrigle HHG, Honour J, Holownia P, Jacobs HS, Lachelin GCL. Laparoscopic ovarian diathermy in the management of anovulatory infertility in women with polycystic ovaries: endocrine changes and clinical outcome. Fertil Steril 1990;53:45–49.

100. Semm K. History of operative laparoscopy. In: Sanfilippo JS, Levine RL, eds. Operative gynecologic endoscopy. New York: Springer-Verlag, 1989;1–18.

101. Hunt RB. Operative laparoscopy. In: Seibel MM, ed. Infertility: a comprehensive text. East Norwalk, CT: Appleton & Lange, 1990; 377–396.

102. Pouly JL, Mahnes H, Mage G, Canis M, Bruhat MA. Conservative laparoscopic treatment of 321 ectopic pregnancies. Fertil Steril 1986;46:1093–1096.

104. Taylor PJ. Diagnostic and operative hysteroscopy. In: Seibel MM, ed. Infertility: a comprehensive text. East Norwalk, CT: Appleton & Lange, 1990;377–396.

105. Carson SA, Hubert GD, Schnock ED, Buster JE. Hyperglycemia and hyponatremia during operative hysteroscopy with 5% dextrose in water distension. Fertil Steril 1989;51: 341–343.

106. Weinans MJN, Kauer FM, Klompmaker IJ, Wijma J. Transient liver function disturbances after the intraperitoneal use of 32% dextran 70 as adhesion prophylaxis in infertility surgery. Fertil Steril 1990;53:159–161.

107. Sullivan B, Kenny P, Seibel MM. Hysteroscopic resection of fibroid with thermal injury to sigmoid. Obstet Gynecol, In press.

108. Finkel DM, Phillips JL, Snyder PJ. Stimulation of spermatogenesis by gonadotropins in men with hypogonadotropic hypogonadism. N Engl J Med 1985;313:651–654.

109. Finkelstein, JS, Spratt DI, O'Dea LSL, Whitcomb RW, Klibanski A, Schoenfeld DA, Crowley WF. Pulsatile gonadotropin secretion after discontinuation of long term gonadotropin-releasing hormone (GnRH) administration in a subset of GnRH-deficient men. J Clin Endocrinol Metab 1989;69: 377–385.

110. Sokol RZ, Steiner BS, Bustillo M, Petersen G, Swerdloff RS. A controlled comparison of the efficacy of clomiphene citrate in male infertility. Fertil Steril 1988;49:865–869.

111. Berger T, Marrs RP, Meyer D. Comparison of techniques for selection of motile spermatozoa. Fertil Steril 1985;43:268–271.

112. Long RA, Seibel MM. Therapeutic insemination. In: Seibel MM, ed. Infertility: a comprehensive text. East Norwalk, CT: Appleton & Lange, 1990;199–215.

113. Kerin J, Quinn P. Washed intrauterine insemination in the treatment of oligospermic infertility. Semin Reprod Endocrinol 1987; 5:23–28.

114. Dodson WC, Whitesides DB, Hughes CL, Jr, Easley HA III, Haney AF. Superovulation with intrauterine insemination in the treatment of infertility: a possible alternative to gamete intrafallopian transfer and in vitro fertilization. Fertil Steril 1987;48:441–444.

115. Adoption factbook. National Committee for Adoption. Washington, DC, 1989.

116. Artificial insemination practice in the United States: summary of a 1987 survey. Office of Technology Assessment. U.S. Congress. Washington, DC, August 1988.

117. Yeh J, Seibel MM. Artificial insemination with donor sperm: a review of 108 patients. Obstet Gynecol 1987;70:313–317.

118. Chiasson MA, Stoneburner RL, Joseph SC. Human immunodeficiency virus transmission through artificial insemination. J Acquired Imm Defic Syndromes 1990;3:69–72.

119. Silber SJ, Surgical management of male infertility. In: Seibel MM, ed. Infertility: a comprehensive text. East Norwalk, CT: Appleton & Lange, 1990;169–188.

120. Silber SJ. Transplantation of human testis for anorchia. Fertil Steril 1978;30:181–184.

121. Overstreet JW. (ed) Male infertility. Infertility and Reproductive Medicine Clinics of North America. W.B. Saundess, Philadelphia, April 1992.

122. Silber SJ, Ord T, Balmaceda J, Patrizio P, Asch RH. Congenital absence of the vas deferens: studies on the fertilizing capacity of human epididymal sperm. Proceedings of the 45th annual meeting of the American Fertility Society, November 13–16, 1989, San Francisco, S24.

123. Seibel MM. A new era in reproductive technology: in vitro fertilization, gamete intrafallopian transfer, and donated gametes and embryos. N Engl J Med 1988;318:828–834.

124. Medical Research International and the Society for Assisted Reproductive Technology. The American Fertility Society. In vitro fertilization-embryo transfer in the United States: 1988 results from the IVF-ET Registry. Fertil Steril 1990;53:13–20.

125. Seibel MM, Ranoux C, Kearnan M. How much is enough? Knowing when to stop in vitro fertilization. N Engl J Med. 1989;321: 1052–1053.

126. Mushin DN, Barreda-Hanson MC, Spensley JC. In vitro children: early psychosocial development. J In Vitro Fert Embryo Transf 1986; 3:247–252.

127. Yovich JL, Parry TS, French NP, Grauaug AA. Developmental assessment of twenty in vitro fertilization (IVF) infants at their first birthday. J In Vitro Fert Embryo Transf 1986; 3:253–257.

128. Friedler S, Giudice LC, Lamb EJ. Cryopreservation of embryos and ova. Fertil Steril 1988;49:743–764.

129. Rosenwaks Z. Donor eggs: their application in modern reproductive technology. Fertil Steril 1987;47:895–909.

130. Mahlstedt PP, Greenfeld DA. Assisted reproductive technology with donor gametes: the need for patient preparation. Fertil Steril 1989;52:908–914.

131. Domar AD, Seibel MM, Benson H. The mind/body program for infertility: a new behavioral treatment approach for women with infertility. Fertil Steril 1990;53:246–249.

132. Seibel MM, Levin S. A new era in reproductive technology: the emotional stages of in vitro fertilization. J In Vitro Fert Embryo Transf 1987;4:135–140.

133. Robertson JA. Ethical and legal issues in cryopreservation of human embryos. Fertil Steril 1987;47:371–382.

134. Andrews LB, Jaeger AS. Legal aspects of infertility. In: Seibel MM, ed. Infertility: a comprehensive text. East Norwalk, CT: Appleton & Lange, 1990;539–550.

135. The Ethics Committee of the American Fertility Society. Ethical considerations of the new reproductive technologies. Fertil Steril 1986;46(Suppl 1):1S–94S.

136. Seibel MM. In vitro fertilization success rates: a fraction of the truth. Obstet Gynecol 1988; 72:265–266.

137. Blackwell RE, Carr BR, Chang RJ, DeCherney AH, Haney AF, Keye WR, Rebar

RW, Rock JA, Rosenwaks Z, Seibel MM, Soules MR. Are we exploiting the infertile couple? Fertil Steril 1987;48:735–739.

138. The American Fertility Society. Revised minimum standards for in vitro fertilization, gamete intrafallopian transfer, and related procedures. Fertil Steril 1990;53:225–226.

139. United States General Accounting Office. Human embryo laboratories: standards favored to ensure quality. Post Office Box 6015, Gaithersburg, MD 20877, December 1989.

140. Ng S-C, Bongso A, Sathananthan H, Ratnam SS. Micromanipulation: its relevance to in vitro fertilization.

141. Eisenstein BI. The polymerase chain reaction: a new method of using molecular genetics for medical diagnosis. N Engl J Med 1990;232:178–183.

142. Handyside AH, Pattinson JK, Penketh RJ, Delhanty JD, Winston RM, Tuddenham EG. Biopsy of human preimplantation embryos and sexing by DNA amplification. Lancet 1989;1:347–349.

143. Li H, Gyllensten UB, Cui X, Saiku PK, Erlich HA, Arnheim N. Amplification and analysis of DNA sequences in single human sperm and diploid cells. Nature 1988;335:414–417.

144. Anderson WF. Genetics and human malleability. Hastings Center Report 1990;20:21–24.

145. Tan SL, Jacobs HS. Infertility: your questions answered. Singapore: McGraw-Hill, 1991.

3
The Laser and Infertility: Present and Future

Louis Burke

One of the most disturbing things that occurs maybe two to four times a month is a telephone call from the operating room saying that Dr. So-and-so is doing laparotomy or a laparoscopy and wants to know what number to put on the machine, because he wants to use the laser. I'll ask what laser he is going to use, and there is blank silence. Is he using a colored fiber, the neodymium:yttrium-argon-garnet (Nd:YAG), or the carbon dioxide (CO_2)? There is silence.

Although lasers in the past two decades have found a place in the practice of most gynecologists, much misunderstanding still prevails as to their uses and effects. The laser is a surgical instrument. To use it one must understand the basic effects of light on tissue; one must understand that there are different lasers to be used at different times and places. This is especially true in infertility. Lasers have both advantages and limitations. In various areas one might use a variety of techniques other than laser, such as bipolar cautery combined with the use of the laser. In addition, there are several different types of lasers that may be used in the same case.

Laser Light

The laser is a device for converting some form of "pumping energy," such as heat, light, or electricity, into radiant energy of a special kind at one or more discrete wavelengths. The word "laser" is an acronym derived from the first letters of the words "*L*ight *A*mplification by *S*timulated *E*mission of *R*adiation." The laser is a light. Light is an electromagnetic wave generated by atomic processes. The light wave has four characteristics (Fig. 3.1): (1) Wavelength—distance between two successive crests. This determines the color of the light. (2) Frequency—the number of waves passing a given point per second, expressed as cycles per second or hertz. (3) Velocity—the speed of a given number of units passing in a unit of time. (4) Amplitude—the vertical height of the wave. The higher the wave, the more power it contains.

The energy of an atom is determined by the distribution of its electrons in different orbits. Normally atoms will be at their lowest state of energy. However, by the insertion of optical, chemical, or electrical energy, the atoms can be raised from a resting state to a higher energy level. This is known as spontaneous absorption of energy. The excited atom will now quickly return to ground state and give up its excess energy. Planck and Einstein predicted that this excess energy would occur in the form of a light particle called the photon. This process is called spontaneous emission of light (Fig. 3.2). When the atoms release their extra photon of energy, it is of a wavelength determined by the atoms involved. If an excited atom is hit with a photon prior to its spontaneous decay, it will prematurely give up this excess energy. This process is called stimulated emission of light (Fig. 3.3). The photon that is stimulated to be released will be of the same wavelength and will travel in the same direction as that of the photon that hit the excited atom. Thus, one incoming photon has been amplified to two outgoing photons.

The apparatuses that produce lasers are essentially similar (Fig. 3.4). The laser medium is built in an "optical cavity" or resonator

LIGHT IS AN ELECTROMAGNETIC WAVE

C = Speed of Light = 3 x 10^8 Meter/Sec

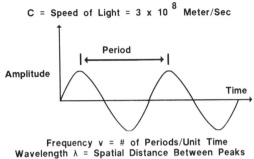

Frequency v = # of Periods/Unit Time
Wavelength λ = Spatial Distance Between Peaks
λv = C

FIGURE 3.1. Diagram of light wave.

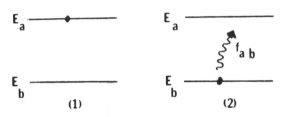

FIGURE 3.2. Spontaneous emission of light. The atom before (1) and after (2) transition. The photon is emitted during transition.

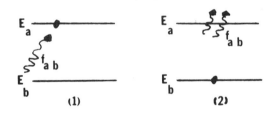

FIGURE 3.3. Stimulated emission of light. The atom before (1) and after (2) stimulated emission.

which is closed at each end by a mirror. Both mirrors have a common optical axis coinciding with the axis of the resonator. The lasing medium can be gas, glass, or crystal; the exciting source can be electrical, chemical, or mechanical. At one end of the resonator the optical mirror has a pinhole through which the light produced exits as the laser light. As the atoms within the resonator are excited by the pump source, they spontaneously give off their photons. The photons are emitted in various directions. A small fraction are emitted

in the direction of the resonator and mirrors. This causes them to pass back and forth many times between the mirrors. On the way, these photons hit other excited atoms, stimulating them to release more photons, all streaming in the same direction and having the same wavelength. The photons then stream out as a beam of light—the laser light. This laser light can be focused by a lens put through a microscope or through a laser fiber down to a finite spot so that its effect can occur.

Laser light is different from ordinary light (Fig. 3.5). Ordinary light is made up of various wavelengths and the light is scattered in many directions. Thus, the light spectrum goes from the infrared to the visible. Laser light is monochromatic, i.e., made up of one wavelength. The photons of laser light are all in special coherence and phase, producing what is called a collimated beam of light. Thus, if we wished to harness the energy of a light bulb with a lens, only a small amount of the energy could be used, whereas with a laser light, almost all of the energy can be used. Lasers can be produced in nearly every region of the electromagnetic light spectrum from the near ultraviolet through the visible to the infrared range (Fig. 3.6). The laser with which most gynecologists have the greatest experience, because it was the one that was first used in gynecology, is the carbon dioxide (CO_2) laser. This is produced in the invisible infrared light spectrum at 10.6 nm. Other lasers, such as the Ruby and Argon lasers, are produced in the visible light range.

The lasers that are commonly used in medicine today are noted in Table 3.1. Each of the lasers has different biological effects and is therefore useful for different applications (Table 3.2). The difference in tissue effects of these lasers depends upon the degree of absorption in biologic tissue, which is primarily water. If one looks at the diagram in Figure 3.7, which shows the absorption of these various lasers in water, one can see that the CO_2 laser (10,600 nm) is almost completely absorbed as soon as it comes in contact with water, whereas the neodymium:yttrium-aluminum-garnet (Nd:YAG) (1,060 nm) and the Argon (564 nm) lasers are absorbed in a

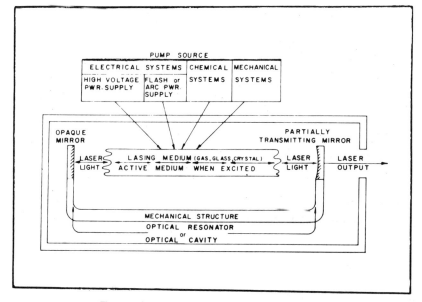

FIGURE 3.4. Components of laser apparatus.

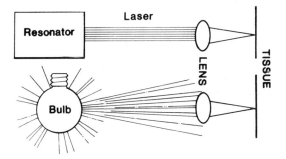

FIGURE 3.5. Laser light and ordinary light.

minor degree. These latter lasers tend to work at a greater depth and their particular actions are primarily coagulative, whereas the CO_2 laser has more of a vaporization effect. Laser light works primarily by causing molecular vibration and therefore the production of heat. The surgical effects of the primary laser systems rely on heat transfer from the beam into the tissue. In addition, the wavelength at which the beam is produced also determines its ability to be transmitted by fiber bundles and also influenced by various colors. Thus, CO_2 laser light is in the invisible light range and cannot be transmitted by fibers but must

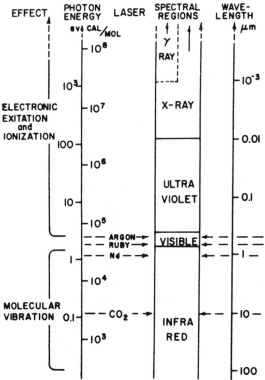

FIGURE 3.6. Portion of the electromagnetic spectrum indicating major effects of radiation on matter and location of principal.

TABLE 3.1. Medical lasers.

Laser	Wavelength (nm)
Carbon dioxide (CO_2)	10 600
Neodymium-ytrium aluminum garnet (Nd:YAG)	1060
Double Nd:YAG (KTP-532)	532
Argon	564–517
Erbium:YAG (Er:YAG)	2900
Holmium:YAG (Ho:YAG)	2100
Tuneable dye	350–1100
Excimer	193–308

depend upon so-called hollow wave guides. On the other hand, the Argon laser is influenced by reds and blues and will be selectively absorbed by these colors. The potassium-titanyl-phosphate (KTP-532) laser, on the other hand, will have a different absorption depending upon coloration. The color of the beam has an important effect on the efficiency of this thermal transfer. The energy of the blue-green beam is absorbed much differently in tissue than that of a laser in the infrared range. Some lasers, such as the Argon, produce more than one color.

To understand the effect of lasers on tissues one must recognize that the amount of heat generated within the tissues varies. The effect of heat on biologic tissue is outlined in Table 3.3. If the tissue is heated to 60°C or less, whatever change occurs will be reversible. Between 60 and 65°C, proteins are denatured in biologic tissue. At 61°C or higher, damage is irreversible. At 70°C, veins and arteries shrink. At 70 to 90°C, coagulation occurs but tissue is not removed. In other words, tissue dehydration occurs. At 100°C, steam forms, vaporization occurs, and tissue disappears. This information helps us to understand how to perform surgery and prevent scarring. Lasers affect three layers of tissue. The first layer has been vaporized and is gone. In the layer below, the temperature has not reached 100°C but is above 61°C. This damage is irreversible, and the width of the layer determines the extent of scarring that will develop. The third area receives some damage but will revert to normal because the temperature is below 60°C.

It is also important to understand that although the laser beam appears to be a circle,

it is not. The distribution of power is Gaussian in shape. Only 86% of the power that comes out is used, because the 7% of power on each side of the beam causes only reversible damage. Therefore, a laser beam can do several things: it can excise tissue, vaporize tissue, and coagulate tissue to achieve hemostasis.

The interaction of all laser light with biologic tissue can be described in terms of reflection, transmission, scattering, and absorption. For any of the medical lasers to exert an effect on tissue, the beam has to be absorbed. If it is reflected from or transmitted through tissue, no effect will occur. If the light is scattered, it will be absorbed over a broader area so that its effects are more diffuse (Figs. 3.8, 3.9). A thorough understanding of these four interactions of light with tissue is necessary before the surgeon can appropriately select the correct laser system for a particular application. Regardless of the laser system used for a surgical application, its effects may be broadly classified as either (A) coagulation, including (1) hemostasis and (2) necrosis or (B) vaporization, including (1) cutting and (2) debulking.

An understanding of the power density of the laser beam is probably the most important factor in the effective use of any laser. The range of the power density determines whether a laser will coagulate, vaporize, or excise living tissue. A lens system directs all the energy of the laser beam to a relatively small spot. The concentration of the energy per surface area of this spot is called its power density, expressed in W/cm^2. The following formula demonstrates the method of determining the approximate power density:

$$\text{Power density} = \frac{\text{Watts} \times 100}{(\text{Spot size})^2} = \text{WATTS/cm}^2$$

The size of the spot varies with the focal length of the lens. The longer the focal length of the lens, the smaller the spot size. If the amount of energy is equally distributed, there will be a greater concentration of energy per surface area in the smaller spot than in the larger spot. That is to say, the power density of the smaller spot is greater than that of the larger spot, given a constant power supply. Low power densities will produce coagulation of tissue and

TABLE 3.2. Advantages and disadvantages of lasers in medicine.

Laser type	Wattage (W)	Wavelength (µm)	Advantages and disadvantages								
			Cutting	Plume	Visible	Coagulation	Through fluids	Protective lenses required	Flexible fibers	Special electrical currents	Water cooling
CO_2	100	10.6	++++	++++	No	+	0	Yes	No	No	No
Argon	20	0.458–0.515	++	++	Yes	++	++	Yes	Yes	Yes	Yes
KTP	20	0.532	++	++	Yes	++	+++	Yes	Yes	Yes	Yes
YAG	20	1.064	+	+	No	++++	++++	Yes	Yes	Yes	Yes

From American College of Obstetrics and Gynecology Technical Bulletin 146 September 1990, with permission.

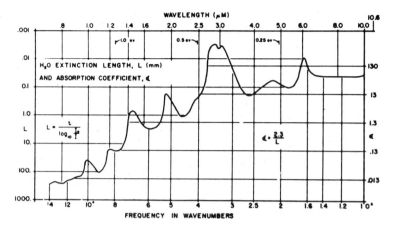

FIGURE 3.7. Water absorption curves of light at different wavelengths. (From Bayly et al., 1963. Courtesy of *Infrared Spectra*, Pergamon Press.)

TABLE 3.3. Effect of heat on biologic tissue.

Temperature	Effect
Below 60°C	Reversible
60–65°C	Protein denatured
	Irreversible damage
65–90°C	Coagulation
	No removal of tissue
Over 100°C	Vaporization
	Tissue removed

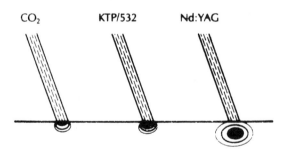

FIGURE 3.8. Scatter of laser in tissue.

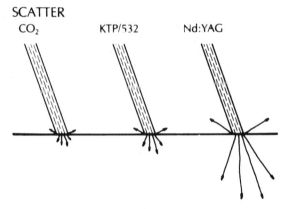

FIGURE 3.9. Thermal pattern of laser in tissue resulting from scatter and absorption.

blood proteins by heat. Higher power densities will produce vaporization so that the tissue may be removed layer by layer. Too high a power density may cut or incise too quickly, so that the depth of destruction will be difficult to control. Higher power densities are used for excision. Lateral heat is minimized with a faster cutting beam and a higher power stroke of the beam. The optimum power density to be used by the operator is the highest value that he or she can safely control in the movement of the beam. It is a matter of hand-eye-foot coordination.

Lasers in Medicine

Carbon Dioxide

The CO_2 laser is the most commonly used laser in gynecology. The beam is highly absorbed by soft tissue, and absorption is independent of the color of the tissue. It is produced in the infrared range of 10,600 nm wavelength; most commercial machines can produce up to 100 W output. The CO_2 laser is considered a precision surgical laser because of its high degree of absorption in soft tissue with limited lateral damage. It is associated with cutting and vaporizing tissue. It does provide some hemostasis, but only against small vessels and capillary-type oozing. The depth of an incision is determined by both the power density and the time of application (how fast the beam is moved). It cannot be put through light bundles but can be utilized using special wave guides.

Neodymium: Yttrium-Aluminum-Garnet (Nd:YAG)

The Nd:YAG laser scatters its energy over a much broader volume of tissue. As a result its heating effect is much less intense than that of the CO_2 laser. The effect is to bring tissue temperature to just under 100°C, thus causing a coagulation and subsequent necrosis of tissue. At higher power densities it may be used to vaporize tissue by heating above 100°C. The Nd:YAG laser causes a deep coagulation of tissue. The effectiveness of this laser is somewhat dependent on the dark coloring of its target, although it is not as color-dependent as the Argon laser. Generally, the darker the tissue, the more readily the light will be absorbed. The Nd:YAG laser is considered a "cooking" laser. It is associated with better hemostasis but less precision than the CO_2 laser, and is used primarily endoscopically. Its use with new types of contact tips makes it an excellent cutting and contact coagulation instrument.

Argon

The Argon laser is also a photocoagulator, but it is much more superficial than the Nd:YAG laser. It is also much more color-sensitive than the Nd:YAG laser. The Argon laser is absorbed by tissues of its opposite color, red, or by black, which contains all colors. Argon produces a blue-green light at 488 and 515 nm. It is particularly useful through the laparoscope in the treatment of endometriosis.

Potassium-Titanyl-Phosphate (Frequency-Doubled Nd:YAG) (KTP-532)

This laser has Argon-like characteristics. A potassium-titanyl-phosphate frequency-doubling crystal is used to change the output of the Nd:YAG laser to 532 nm or green light.

Applications in Infertility

The main applications of lasers in infertility depend on their ability to be used through the laparoscope. Procedures in which the laser may be employed include excision of endometriotic lesions, adhesiolysis, uterosacral ablation, neosalpingostomy, fimbrioplasty, ablation of hydatid cysts, follicle ablation for polycystic ovarian syndrome, and excision of ectopic pregnancies.

Endometriosis

The objective in endometriosis is to remove the tissue implants. In general, the resolution of the CO_2 laser affords more accurate excision of pathologic tissue than is possible with conventional techniques. The margin of the implants can be well delineated, allowing more complete eradication of the disease. The method is hemostatic. The surgeon can operate around vital structures by using the pulse and superpulse modes rather than a continuous mode. This preserves normal tissue. The CO_2 may be brought down directly through the laparoscope or be brought into contact with the lesions utilizing the newer hollow wave guides that can be attached to the operating arm.

The Argon and KTP-532 lasers have a distinct advantage in areas of increased vascularity. Their energy is absorbed by hemoglobin, providing additional hemostasis. On the other hand, the Nd:YAG laser with sapphire tip cause slightly more of a thermal effect, which results in delayed necrosis. For this reason the Nd:YAG laser is not used to ablate lesions over vital structures.

Adhesiolysis

The main benefit of laser surgery for adhesiolysis is more precise excision of adhesions and minimized bleeding due to its hemostatic effects. Fluid in the cul-de-sac absorbs stray radiant energy, preventing injury to normal tissue. Titanium rods can be used to prevent damage to normal tissue beyond the area of infarct. Vascular adhesions consisting of vessels that are greater than 1.5 mm in diameter are usually best treated with KTP or Argon rather than CO_2 laser.

Neosalpingostomy

Neosalpingostomy is performed with the CO_2, Argon, and KTP-532 lasers because their high resolution results in accuracy. The delicate structure of the fallopian tube precludes the use of the Nd:YAG laser because of the greater coagulation it produces. The shorter wavelength and higher energy of the Argon and KTP-532 lasers, in certain circumstances, makes them superior even to the CO_2 laser for maintaining hemostasis.

Hydatid Cyst of Morgagni

Since these benign cysts can be successfully treated with any technique of excision or ablation, there are no technical advantages to use of the laser.

Uterosacral Ablation

In uterosacral ablation the parasympathetic and sympathetic sensory nerve fibers to the uterus and cervix are interrupted. Using the laser the surgeon can create a crater at the attachment of the ligament with greater precision than is possible with any other technique. It is safer than the use of either unipolar or bipolar cauterization.

Polycystic Ovary Syndrome

Using the laser "drilling" technique, an effective simulation of wedge resection can be achieved without inducing postoperative adhesions (Fig. 3.10). A sapphire tip attached to an Nd:YAG laser probe is used to drill a minimum of 15 holes that penetrate the stroma of each ovary. The absence of sutures on the surface of the ovary and of raw bleeding edges results in a decreased formation of adhesions. The CO_2 laser can also be used for this procedure.

Ectopic Pregnancy

The CO_2, Argon, Nd:YAG, and KTP-532 lasers can be used to remove an ectopic pregnancy. Using the laser as a "light scalpel," an incision is made over the antimesenteric site of the unruptured ectopic mass, and the products of conception are released from their attach-

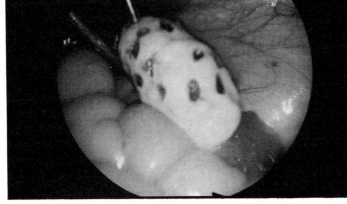

FIGURE 3.10. Polycystic ovaries illustrating "drilling" technique. (Courtesy Machelle M. Seibel, M.D.)

ment by way of a teasing technique with a grasping forceps. If bleeding occurs, the Argon or KTP-532 laser can be used to pinpoint coagulation. If a fiberoptic laser is unavailable, then a bipolar coagulator can be used.

Hysteroscopy

When the laser is combined with the hysteroscope, it can be used to remove adhesions, benign polyps, submucous myomas, or a uterine septum, or to ablate the endometrium for the treatment of metropathia hemorrhagicum.

Since the energy of the CO_2 laser is absorbed by water, it is not suitable for use during hysteroscopy. However, fluid does not disperse the KTP-532, Nd:YAG, or Argon laser wavelengths, which can be introduced into the endometrial cavity by means of fibers. Hysteroscopic removal of submucous fibroids that are up to 2 cm in size may be accomplished with the laser. Larger submucous fibroids may first be treated with gonadotropin-releasing hormone (GnRH) agonist, allowing the fibroid to shrink, and then either shaving it from the uterine cavity or allowing it to slough out.

As for incision of an intrauterine septum, the most difficult problem is deciding how far to proceed with the dissection. Ideally, the laparoscopist should view the procedure from above, continuing the incision until the hysteroscopy light illuminates the fundus. At this point, the septum is usually completely incised.

Laparotomy

Open abdominal operations in which the laser may be of use include removal of endometriotic lesions, neosalpingostomy, fimbrioplasty, ovarian cystectomy, tubal anastomoses, metroplasty, and myomectomy. It can also be employed in open adhesiolysis, wedge resection of the ovary, excision of hydatid cysts, and the open approach to treat ectopic pregnancy. In each procedure the laser acts as a light scalpel, though its advantages and disadvantages should be considered.

Advantages of the Use of Medical Lasers in Infertility

There are a number of potential advantages of medical lasers in infertility: (1) Hemostasis permits reduced operating time. (2) Shorter operating time translates into reduced hospital costs. (3) The CO_2 laser can reach otherwise inaccessible areas through the use of mirrors. (4) Postoperative pain is less than with conventional surgery because of less thermal effect on adjacent normal tissue than cautery and the need for fewer sutures. (5) Cutting can be done more precisely than with a knife. (6) Procedures formerly requiring major inpatient surgery may be shifted to minor, outpatient procedures. These advantages must be weighed against potential disadvantages, such as (1) the cost of the laser, (2) the need for special training, and (3) the potential risk of the laser plume.

Training

The laser is not a technique. It is an instrument which in unskilled hands can be dangerous. The surgeon who lacks technical skills in its use will at best not achieve any better surgical results and may at worst cause damage. Therefore, training combined with supervised, hands-on experience is necessary.

The Future

Newer lasers are on the horizon that are likely to have application for gynecology and infertility in particular. They are more precise, with less laterel heat damage. Therefore, healing, scarring, and adhesion formation are less. Two lasers that are being considered emit beams in the mid-infrared range. Because there is a very strong absorption of mid-infrared radiation by water, strong absorption by biologic tissue will occur. Using these mid-infrared lasers, one can cut tissue leaving only 5 μm of damaged cells at the cut edge. Because of the water absorption curve in the mid-infrared range, there exists a potential for development of systems that can continuously vary the cut-to-coagulate ratio. In general, as the absorption coefficient decreases, the penetration of the laser radiation increases and the amount of coagulation tissue increases. Thus, in using the tuneable laser, that is, a laser whose wavelength can be changed, one could precisely control the width of the damaged zone by tuning up and down the water absorption curve.

The most prominent of these mid-infrared lasers used clinically are termed "solid-state lasers." The major advantages of solid-state lasers are their relatively low cost, small size, high reliability, and low maintenance. The Erbium:YAG (Er:YAG) laser emits laser light in the 2,900-nm range. It leaves a very thin zone of damaged tissue at the edge of the laser cut. The width of the damaged zone varies somewhat from tissue to tissue and correlates with the presence of collagen. In tissue with high collagen content, it leaves about 10 µm of damage. These damaged zones can be decreased to approximately 5 µm in which the laser pulse duration is decreased to 100 ns or less. The Holmium:YAG (Ho:YAG) laser emits at 2,100 nm. However, it typically leaves 500 µm of damaged tissue at the cut edge. The hemostatic ability of the Ho:YAG laser is greater than that of the Er:YAG laser. Tissue healing, however, is not as rapid and scar-free as with the Er:YAG laser. The major advantage of the Ho:YAG laser is that its radiation can be transmitted through a silica fiber, which cannot be done with the Er:YAG laser. Thus, the Ho:YAG laser can be used endoscopically. These two lasers are now being investigated for their application in all fields of neurology, ophthalmology, orthopedics, and cardiology, and certainly will find application in gynecology.

There are increasing reports of complications with the CO_2, Nd:YAG, and KTP-532 lasers. Therefore, one must ask if there is any advantage to using the laser rather than the bipolar cautery needle. It is very difficult to find hard data to prove, for example, that the use of the KTP, CO_2, or Nd:YAG lasers for adhesions in infertility is any better than the use of the bipolar cautery knife. However, lasers may be useful in combination with other instruments. For example, if one is doing an ectopic pregnancy, it is nice to use the CO_2 laser, but the bipolar needle may be necessary to help control the bleeding because the CO_2 laser is a poor coagulator. As stated initially, the laser is a surgical instrument and not a surgical technique. Understanding its advantages and limitations makes it a valuable tool in the treatment of infertility.

Suggested Reading

1. Adamson GD, Subak LL, Pasta DJ, Hurd SJ, von Franque O, Radriguez BD. Comparison of CO_2 laser laparoscopy with laparotomy for treatment of endometriomata. Fertil Sterd 1992; 57:965–973.
2. Burke L, Covell L, Antonioli D. Carbon dioxide laser therapy of cervical neoplasia: analysis of 60 patients. Lasers Surg Med 1980; 1:1–4.
3. Burke L. The use of the carbon dioxide laser in the therapy of cervical intraepithelial neoplasia. Am J Obstet Gynecol 1982;144:337.
4. International lighting vocabulary. Commission International de L'Eclairage (International Commission on Illumination), Paris, Publication CIE 1970; No.17 (E-1.1).
5. Davis TP. The heating of skin by radiant energy. In: Herzfeld CM, ed. Temperature, its measurement and control in science and Industry. Vol 3. Part 3. New York: Reinhold, 1963;149–169.
6. Gabel VP, Birngruber R, Weinberg W, et al. Comparison of temperature measurements and fundus reflectometry in laser coagulation. Mod Prob Ophthalmol 1979;20:169–173.
7. Goldman L, Rockwell RJ. Lasers in medicine. New York: Gordon and Breach, 1971.
8. Gorisch W, Boergen KP. Heat-induced contraction of blood vessels. Lasers Surg Med 1982;2:1–13.
9. Halldorsson T, Rother W, Langerholc J, Frank F. Theorectical and experimental investigations prove Nd:YAG laser treatment to be safe. Lasers Surg Biol 1981;1:253–262.
10. Hillenkamp F. Interaction between laser radiation and biological system. In: Hillenkamp F, Pratesi R, Sacchi CA, eds, Lasers in medicine and biology. New York: Plenum Press, 1980; 37–68.
11. Parrish JA, Anderson RR. Considerations of selectivity in laser therapy. In: Arndt KA, Noe JM, Rosen S, eds. Cutaneous laser therapy—principles and methods. New York: John Wiley and Sons, 1983.

12. Sliney DH, Wolbarsht ML. Safety with lasers and other optical sources. New York: Plenum Press, 1980;65–185.
13. Sliney DH, Trokel SL. Medical Lasers and Their Safe Use. New York: Springer-Verlag, 1992.

14. Choe JK, Baggish MS. Hysteroscopic treatment of septate uterus with Neodymium-YAG laser. Fertil Steril 1992;57:81–84.

4
Operative Laparoscopy: Patient Selection and Instrumentation

Robert Hunt

Operative laparoscopy is replacing laparotomy for the correction of many disease states. With this technique the hospital stay and cost are lower, patient discomfort is reduced, cosmetics are better, the patient returns to work much sooner, and there probably are fewer postoperative adhesions. Some procedures, such as tubal anastomosis, clearly remain in the purview of laparotomy. Others, such as adhesiolysis, can be dealt with effectively by laparoscopy in most instances. The following summarizes some of the basic laparoscopic instrumentation, techniques, and perspectives.

Instrumentation and Personnel

It is essential to obtain the support of the administrative and operating room staff to acquire proper instrumentation and use it optimally. In-house lectures and the use of intraoperative video go far in heightening enthusiasm.

Ergonomics

The surgeon can do much to achieve relative physical comfort for the duration of these often lengthy operations. The following are useful in lessening back stress: place a support over the patient's chest; tilt the operating table toward the surgeon; wear a molded back brace to prevent excessive lateral flexion of the spine; and position a low stand beneath the forward foot, which also serves as a platform for the endocoagulator and bipolar foot controls.

Laparoscope

The choice of a laparoscope depends on many factors. For example, should it have an operating channel for laser use? I prefer a 10-mm (0°) operating and a 10-mm (30°) standard laparoscope. In addition, it is helpful to have a 5-mm (0 or 30°) laparoscope to position through one of the 5-mm accessory cannulas for special tasks, such as extracting large tissue fragments through the 10-mm primary cannula.

Light Source

A bright light source, at least 250 W, is necessary if video is to be used with a beam splitter. If the surgeon wishes to take still photographs through the laparoscope, a strobe flash unit is important. Visual documentation is quite helpful from the legal, educational, and patient-relations standpoints (Fig. 4.1). New advances are being made, such as the ability to obtain images directly off the video equipment.

Primary Cannula

So-called safety cannulas and disposable insufflation needles are available and seem to offer some advantages (Fig. 4.2). The Hassan cannula converts open laparoscopy into a much simpler procedure.

Secondary Cannulas

I prefer the disposable screw design cannula with a self-sealing cap. It serves well and seems to be very safe. I use one lateral to each deep epigastric vascular complex and one in the

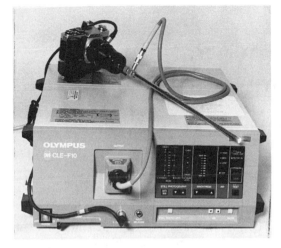

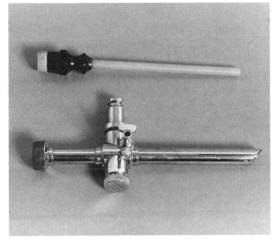

FIGURE 4.1. The Olympus halogen light source with built-in flash unit and associated laparoscope are excellent units. The xenon light source is model CLV-F10 (Olympus Corp., 4 Nevada Drive, Lake Success, NY 11042).

FIGURE 4.2. Top. The open cannula prevents damage to delicate instrument tips inserted through it (order no. 8351.03, Richard Wolf). Bottom. The 11-mm cannula is used for large secondary instruments (order no. 7620-1, WISAP/USA).

midline just cephalad of the urinary bladder in most cases. Open cannulas make tissue removal easier (Fig. 4.2).

Insufflator

This essential device should deliver at least 5 L/minute of gas at a pressure not to exceed 20 mm Hg. Gas should come into the insufflator directly, thus eliminating the need to refill the machine. This "high-flow" insufflator should never be used for hysteroscopy.

Irrigator Aspirator

Like the rapid insufflator, this instrument is required. By moving fluids in and out of the abdomen rapidly, surgery becomes much safer (Fig. 4.3). A properly designed cannula attached to the unit allows the surgeon to perform aquadissection, a useful technique (Fig. 4.4).

Bipolar Coagulator

The bipolar coagulator is invaluable in achieving hemostasis. I prefer the Kleppinger forceps (Fig. 4.5). It is modified in that the paddles are one-half as wide as usual, and insulation is

extended to the paddles. This allows more precise coagulation and lessens the possibility of unintended damage to nearby tissues.

Unipolar Coagulator

This instrument must be used with the utmost care since electrons released from the coagulation tip travel the path of least resistance to the passive plate.

Endocoagulator

This elegant instrument is developed around the general concept of a hot plate (Fig. 4.5). I use it solely for eversion of the mucosal flaps after salpingostomy by laparoscopy. The temperature of the generator is adjusted to 100°C, and the serosa of the flaps is briefly and lightly touched by the point coagulator. Provided the hydrosalpinx is thin-walled, eversion is quick and dramatic.

Lasers

The CO_2, neodymium: yttrium-aluminum-garnet (Nd: YAG), and potassium-titanyl-phosphate (KTP-532) lasers have had extensive use in reproductive surgery with a commend-

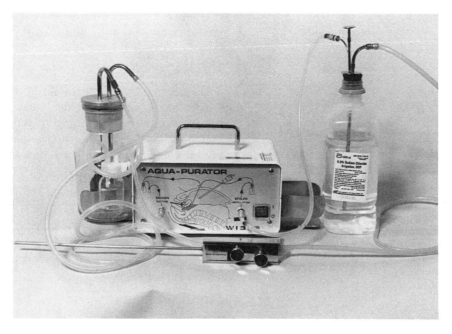

FIGURE 4.3. The Aqua-Purator.

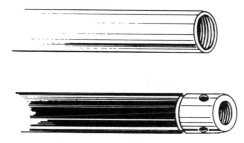

FIGURE 4.4. Top. The suction/irrigation cannula tip for the Aqua-Purator (WISAP/USA). Bottom. A standard suction/irrigation cannula tip (order no. 8384.72, Richard Wolf; order no. 26178 U; Karl Stortz).

able safety record. Although lasers are not ordinarily required for most laparoscopic procedures, their proponents emphasize the shortened operating time and relatively bloodless surgery. Optimally, the surgeon should have at least one of the lasers available and be trained in its use. Different wavelength lasers will become available in the near future.

Scissors

An assortment of scissors should be available, including standard, hook, and straight designs

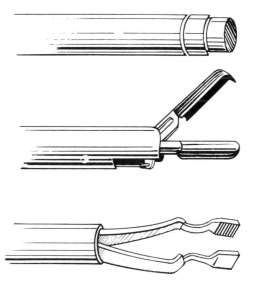

FIGURE 4.5. Top. Point coagulator (order no. 7515, WISAP/USA). Middle. Crocodile forceps (order no. 7510, WISAP/USA). Bottom. Kleppinger bipolar forceps (order no. 8383.24, Richard Wolf).

(Fig. 4.6). When dissecting close to the bowel or ureter, hooked scissors should not be used, as they tend to pull tissue into the jaws. Serrated scissors specifically used for cut-

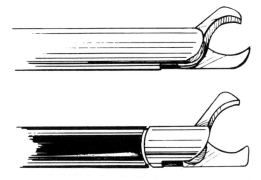

FIGURE 4.6. Top. Hooked scissors are excellent for opening a hydrosalpinx or opening the fallopian tube to remove an ampullary ectopic pregnancy (order no. 7652, WISAP/USA; order no. 26175 EH, Karl Stortz; order no. 8384.02, Richard Wolf; order no. A5264, Olympus Corp; order no. 6614, Reznik Instruments, 7308 N. Monticello, Skokie, IL 60076). Bottom. Standard dissecting scissors (order no. 8381.02, Richard Wolf).

FIGURE 4.7. Serrated scissors are useful for cutting sutures (order no. 26174-PS, Karl Stortz; order no. 7653, WISAP/USA).

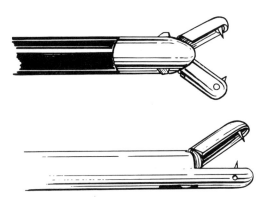

FIGURE 4.8. Top. The double-action biopsy forceps is excellent for removing adhesions as well as performing biopsies of ovaries and peritoneal surfaces (order no. 8383.10, Richard Wolf; order no. 6613, Reznik Instruments; order no. A5261, Olympus).

ting sutures are helpful to prevent operating scissors from becoming dull (Fig. 4.7).

Biopsy Forceps

These are very useful for stabilizing and biopsy purposes. For example, they may be used to support the ovary during resection of an endometrioma. A sterile rubber band placed around the handle of the instrument keeps the jaws from opening passively (Fig. 4.8).

Graspers

Several graspers are available. They facilitate organ inspection and dissection. An assortment of them should be on hand (Fig. 4.9).

Needle Holders

Suturing through the laparoscope is a technique well worth mastering. It can be used when performing a salpingostomy or closing an ovary after removing an ovarian cyst. Figure 4.10 shows two examples.

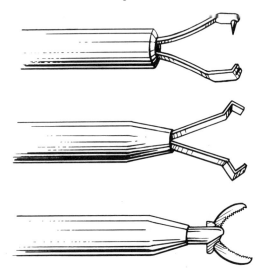

FIGURE 4.9. Top. The toothed grasping forceps is useful in stabilizing the fallopian tube when performing a salpingostomy (order no. 26177G, Karl Stortz). Middle. Ampullary dilator is helpful in dilating a phimotic fimbrial ostium (order no. 7651, WISAP/USA; order no. 8384.14, Richard Wolf). Bottom. The atraumatic grasping forceps is effective for lifting the fallopian tube by its serosa while performing delicate dissection (order no. 7655, WISAP/USA).

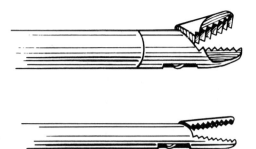

FIGURE 4.10. The 5-mm (top) and 3-mm (bottom) needle carriers are designed for placing intra-abdominal sutures (order no. 7668-1 [5-mm] and 7668 [3-mm], WISAP/USA).

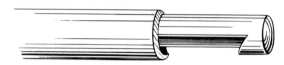

FIGURE 4.11. The tissue punch is used for morcellating large specimens such as a leiomyoma or an ovary (order no. 7674, WISAP/USA).

Morcellator

Occasionally specimens removed by laparoscopy will require morcellation to remove them from the abdomen. A spoon or claw forceps through a second puncture is often necessary to stabilize the specimen during morcellation (Fig. 4.11).

Claw and Spoon Forceps

These instruments (Figs. 4.12, 4.13) allow removal of large tissue specimens from the abdomen.

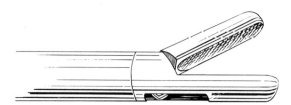

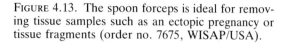

FIGURE 4.13. The spoon forceps is ideal for removing tissue samples such as an ectopic pregnancy or tissue fragments (order no. 7675, WISAP/USA).

Patient Selection

As skills increase, the list of disease processes treated laparoscopically grows longer. Many of the procedures described here will necessarily change as techniques are improved, and consequently, the surgeon's knowledge must be updated continually.

Adhesiolysis

De novo adhesions from laparoscopic surgery are infrequent, and preexisting adhesions that are excised laparoscopically seem to reform less extensively. Most pelvic adhesions can be removed efficiently by laparoscopy, and in my opinion it is the method of choice (Figs. 4.14, 4.15). Adhesions attached to the ovary are coagulated with the point coagulator, being careful not to damage the ovarian cortex.

Fimbrioplasty and Salpingostomy

Most tubal conditions requiring fimbrioplasty or salpingostomy can be managed superbly with operative laparoscopy. In my view, this

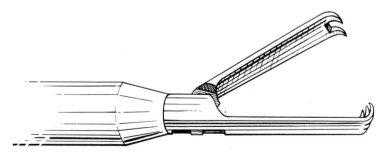

FIGURE 4.12. The claw forceps is an excellent instrument for removing large tissue specimens such as leiomyoma, fallopian tube, or ovary (order no. 7672, WISAP/USA).

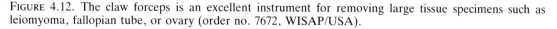

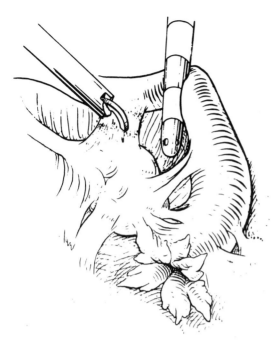

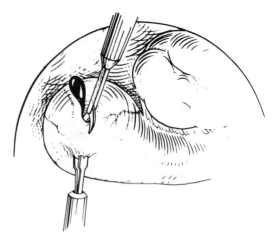

FIGURE 4.16. The distal fallopian tube is incised initially with hooked scissors.

FIGURE 4.14. Broad adhesions are coagulated and cut allowing separation of structures.

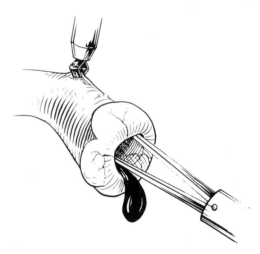

FIGURE 4.17. The tubal ostium is dilated completely using an ampullary dilator.

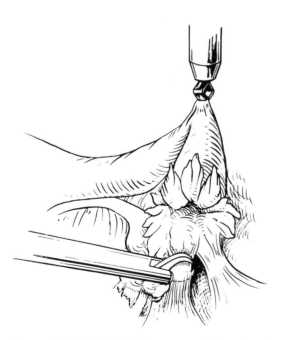

is the treatment of choice for most of these patients (Figs. 4.16–18).

Endometriosis

This disease is frequently a challenging one to treat medically, and surgical management is no different. The invasive characteristics of endometriosis and its tendency to recur add to

FIGURE 4.15. Tubal fimbriae are carefully released by sharp dissection.

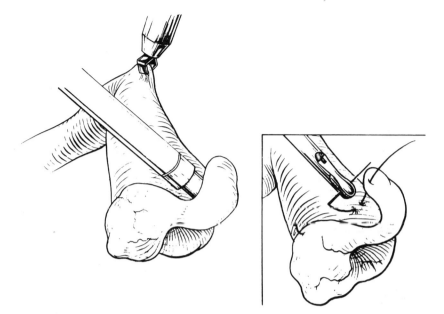

FIGURE 4.18. The salpingostomy is completed by everting the mucosa with the point coagulator at 100°C or suturing with 4–0 polydioxanone (order no. Z-420, Ethicon, Rt. 22 West, Somerville, NJ 08876; 201-524-0400).

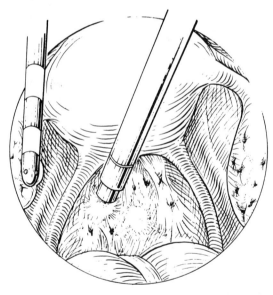

FIGURE 4.19. Cul-de-sac endometriosis is coagulated with a point coagulator at 120°C. The surgeon must be aware of the location of the extraperitoneal rectum and ureters.

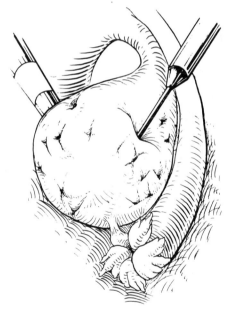

FIGURE 4.20. An endometrioma is partially collapsed by aspiration.

the difficulty of treatment. Most sites involved with pelvic endometriosis can be excised, coagulated, and/or ablated successfully by the surgeon skilled in operative laparoscopy. Disease involving the ureter or bowel wall is excised laparoscopically by some, but such an aggressive approach must still be considered experimental until experience is greater (Fig. 4.19). Endometriomas should be partially collapsed by aspiration (Fig. 4.20), opened by

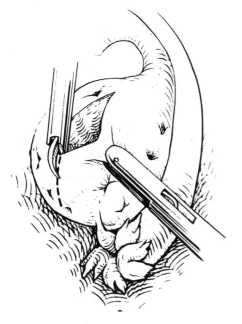

FIGURE 4.21. The endometrioma is opened by scissors.

scissors (Fig. 4.21), and the endometrial cyst wall removed (Fig. 4.22).

Ovarian Cyst

One of the most controversial areas faced by those performing advanced laparoscopic procedures is the treatment of ovarian cysts. Many cysts can be excised laparoscopically, but the problem is not knowing their histology until they have been drained, inspected, biopsied, and/or removed. The proper resolution of this important issue will come as we collect and share our data, and offer them for thoughtful assessment by a recognized group of experts, including gynecologic oncologists and laparoscopists who perform advanced laparoscopic procedures. It is hoped that such efforts will result in the establishment of preoperative criteria for patients with an ovarian cyst.

Myomectomy

Uterine fibroid(s) in patients desiring children often can be removed laparoscopically (Figs. 4.23–27). Submucous myomas may be resected hysteroscopically. Many intramural and subserosal myomas can be excised by laparoscopy, particularly if they are less than 5 cm in diameter and do not involve major vessels or the fallopian tubes. Gonadotropin-releasing hormone (GnRH) analogs, suturing techniques, and improved methods of removing the specimen have increased the number of patients who can be treated by this method.

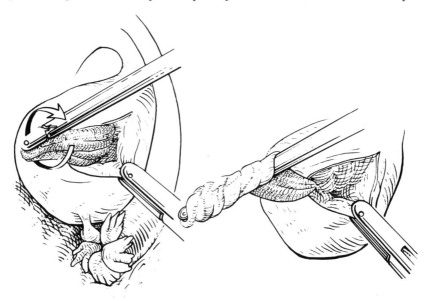

FIGURE 4.22. After visual inspection, the endometrial cyst wall is removed. The gaping ovarian defect can be left open or closed with 4–0 polydioxanone.

Some, however, believe that the patient who requires a myomectomy and desires children should be treated by laparotomy. Probably laparoscopy will emerge as appropriate therapy in carefully selected patients.

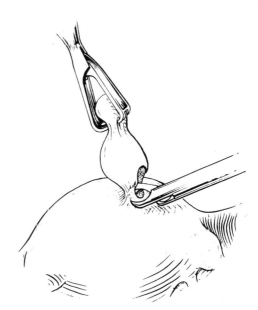

FIGURE 4.25. The uterine serosa is incised.

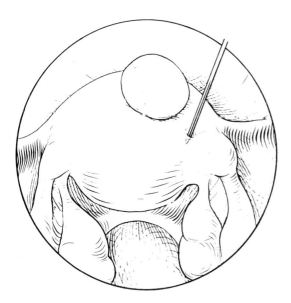

FIGURE 4.23. Dilute Vasopressin 3U is injected into the myometrium with a 4½-inch 22 gauge spinal needle. The vasopressin should be diluted 20 U/ 50 cc of lactated Ringer's solution.

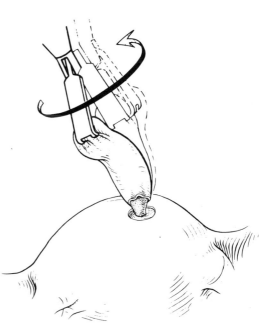

FIGURE 4.26. The leiomyoma is removed by rotating the claw forceps.

Conclusion

Operative laparoscopy is assuming an increasingly important role in the surgical management of women who desire children. Established

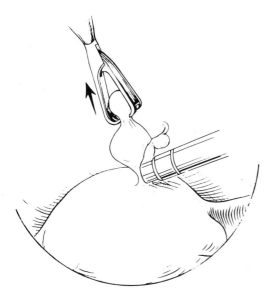

FIGURE 4.24. An 11-mm claw forceps provides excellent traction for coagulation with the point coagulator at 110°C at the base of the fibroid.

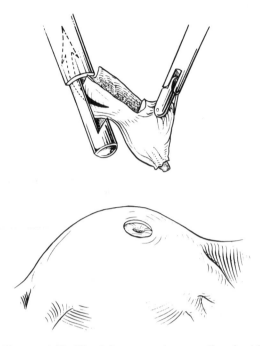

FIGURE 4.27. The leiomyoma is morcellated with the 11-mm tissue punch.

techniques are improving and new ones are being introduced. Courses are offered widely to teach these techniques.

For those of us treating these women, it is essential to become adept in advanced operative laparoscopy or to have such a person available.

Acknowledgment

Figures 4.1 through 4.13 and 4.17 through 4.27 are reproduced from Hunt R. Operative laparoscopy. In: Infertility, edited by Machelle M. Seibel. 1990:377–396. Reproduced with permission of Appleton-Century-Crofts.

Suggested Reading

1. Hunt RB, ed. Atlas of female infertility surgery. 2nd ed. St. Louis: Mosby-Year Book, 1992.
2. Martin DC, ed. Manual of endoscopy. Santa Fe Springs, CA: American Association of Gynecologic Laparoscopists, 1991. [Available by calling the AAGL office at (800) 554-AAGL]
3. Sanfilippo JS, Levine RL, eds. Operative gynecologic endoscopy. New York: Springer-Verlag, 1989.
4. Seibel MM, ed. Infertility: a comprehensive text. East Norwalk, CT: Appleton & Lange, 1990.
5. Semm K. Operative manual for endoscopic abdominal surgery. Chicago: Year Book, 1987.

5
Operative Pelviscopy: Techniques and Results

Jean Bernard Dubuisson

Over the course of the past decade operative laparoscopy has provided one of the major breakthroughs in the practice of gynecology. The major components of these advances have had to do with the development of atraumatic instrumentation, smaller video cameras, and the CO_2 laser. Laparoscopy provides easy access to the pelvis and allows for the diagnosis and treatment of a wide variety of pathologies. In addition, operative laparoscopy has several advantages over laparotomy. The postoperative recovery is much shorter and more comfortable. There is a minimum of postoperative pain, ileus, and venous stasis. Feeding can typically be resumed the same day and women can ambulate normally by the next day. In most instances, the hospital stay is 2 days or less, unless there are complications. These may be avoided in most cases by careful patient selection, use of appropriate instrumentation, and experience in laparoscopic surgery. For best results, the operating room personnel must be correctly trained not only in the techniques of operative laparoscopy but also in the maintenance of the sophisticated and fragile instruments. The majority of procedures can be completed within 1 to 2 hours of general anesthesia. Laparoscopy should always be performed using a 10-mm scope to achieve optimum visualization and lighting. The use of a video camera with a high-resolution monitor allows the surgeon to stand upright which reduces back strain and fatigue and also allows for greater assistance during the procedure. A midline suprapubic incision with a 5-mm sheath and two accessory trochars to the left and right of midline allow adequate instrumentation to accomplish virtually any type of

operative laparoscopy procedure. When the laparoscopic laser is indicated, we prefer the laser to be introduced through the laparoscope for a more direct approach rather than a suprapubic port, although either approach is acceptable.

Ectopic Pregnancy

Ectopic pregnancy continues to be the major cause of maternal mortality associated with pregnancy.[1] The most frequently encountered location of an ectopic pregnancy is in the ampullary portion of the fallopian tube (Fig. 5.1). In this situation, linear salpingostomy is the most frequently employed technique. This method was first introduced in 1974 by Bruhat in France.[2] The hemoperitoneum is aspirated initially and the peritoneal cavity irrigated with warm lactated Ringers solution to obtain clear visualization. The salpingostomy incision is generally 8 to 10 mm in length. We prefer to use the focused laser beam with a power of 20 to 40 watts. A dilute solution of pertressin may be injected on either side of the mesosalpinx for hemostasis although this is not absolutely necessary. Alternatively, bipolar cautery may be used to create an avascular plane on the antimesenteric portion of the fallopian tube. Iris scissors may then be used to incise the tube above the implantation site. Gentle pressure can then be generated to cause the pregnancy to be extruded from the incision. Alternatively an aspirating instrument can be introduced into the salpingostomy incision and the trophoblastic material aspirated. The tube is then copiously irrigated

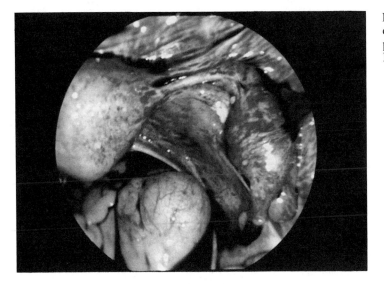

FIGURE 5.1. Fallopian tube demonstrating ampullary ectopic pregnancy (Photo courtesy of Machelle M. Seibel, M.D.).

to ensure hemostasis. It is not necessary to close the tube as the tubal serosa heals spontaneously. This has been confirmed on many occasions by second look laparoscopy.

Ectopic pregnancies located in the interstitial portion of the tube can often be treated conservatively unless rupture has occurred. Under laparoscopic vision salpingostomy is simpler and less hazardous than resecting the interstitial portion of the tube because of the risk of hemorrhage. For these type of cases a second puncture port for the CO_2 laser is recommended as this allows the surgeon to achieve a better access to the ectopic site. Conservative treatment for interstitial ectopic pregnancies may be contraindicated when the tube has been irreversibly damaged by pre-existing chronic salpingitis or by a large trophoblastic implantation site and hematoma formation. In these instances, total salpingectomy is advised.[3] When salpingectomy is indicated, we initiate the procedure using thermocoagulation and transection of the isthmic portion of the tube at its junction with the uterus. Following transection of the tube the mesosalpinx is thermocoagulated and transected in successive bites of 1 to 2 centimeters until the tuboovarian ligament is reached, coagulated, and the entire tube removed (Fig. 5.2).

It is necessary to thermocoagulate all the mesosalpinx to prevent hemorrhage. To re-duce the risk of hemorrhage occurring after the vasopressin wears off, our preference is to never use vasopressin for salpingectomy. After thermocoagulation and transection, the tube is extracted through one of the two suprapubic incisions using a long Palmer forceps. The incision may also be extended and a 10-ml trochar inserted suprapubically which allows removal of the tube through the larger diameter trochar sheath. Alternatively, when the tube is too voluminous after salpingectomy for easy extraction by the suprapubic incision, a salpingostomy can be performed and the products of conception aspirated to reduce the tubal vol-

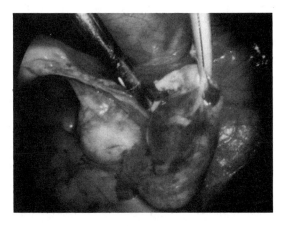

FIGURE 5.2. Ectopic pregnancy demonstrating thermocoagulation and transection in successive bites of the mesosalpinx.

FIGURE 5.3. Scissors are used to lyse adhesions between the ovary and the posterior broad ligament.

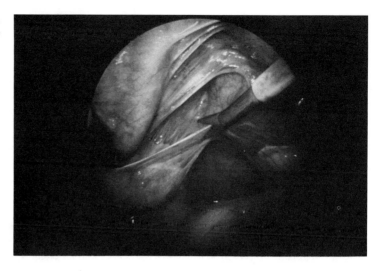

ume before extraction through the suprapubic incision. We have performed 56-second look operations to determine the presence or absence of adhesions and adhesions were never observed. Following salpingectomy, the pouch of Douglas is aspirated to remove blood clots and possible remnants of pregnancy aborted from the tube. The pelvis is washed with warm lactated Ringer to ensure hemostasis. In centers with experienced laparoscopists, 90 to 95% of ectopic pregnancies are treated laparoscopically.

Lysis of Adhesions

Since Palmer first proposed lysis of adhesions nearly 30 years ago, the technique has greatly evolved with the development of fine iris scissors and the CO_2 laser. We perform microsurgical adhesiolysis using scissors without prior coagulation (Fig. 5.3). The adhesions are grasped with an atraumatic forceps to facilitate their dissection. Counteraction reduces the risk of tearing the peritoneum. Thorough irrigation with warm lactated Ringer usually provides immediate hemostasis. For those adhesions near the ovary, laparoscopic techniques in our experience are easier and more effective than microsurgical techniques performed at laparotomy.

The final result following fimbriolysis is comparable to that achieved with microsurgical techniques performed at laparotomy. This is possible in part due to the excellent vision obtained from the operating laparoscope in combination with the video camera. Denser adhesions are sometimes excised using a CO_2 laser. This is especially useful for dense adhesions which glue the ovary to the uterus or the ampullary portion of the tube.

Salpingostomy

Laparoscopic correction of hydrosalpinges was described more than a decade ago by Victor Gomel and Kurt Semm.[4,5] Since then the technique has greatly evolved with the development of thin iris scissors, atraumatic forceps, and the CO_2 laser.

Following transcervical chromohydrotubation, the fimbriated end of the dilated fallopian tube is incised with scissors at the thinnest point in the tubal wall. The incision is then enlarged using scissors (Fig. 5.4). When the tube has been sufficiently opened to create a neoostium, eversion is obtained by retracting the distal serosa using the defocused CO_2 laser beam (Fig. 5.5). Alternatively, the endocoagulator can be used to create this effect or sutures can be placed.[6] At the end of the procedure the peritoneal cavity is irrigated. For this procedure, prophylactic antibiotics are administered systemically and the antibiotic continued for two weeks. Since 1986,

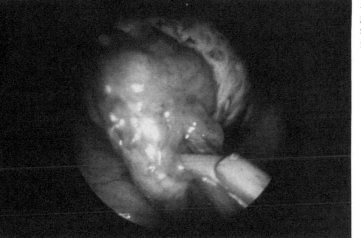

FIGURE 5.4. Laparoscopic salpingostomy showing the use of scissors to enlarge the initial incision.

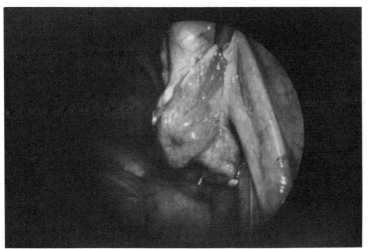

FIGURE 5.5. Neosalpingostomy demonstrating eversion of fimbria.

the laparoscopic technique has increasingly replaced microsurgical salpingostomy by laparotomy.

Ovarian Cystectomy

Ovarian cysts are among the most common entities seen by gynecologists. These must be investigated to determine whether they are functional or organic. Following clinical evaluation, ultrasound examination and blood sampling for suspicion of malignancy may be obtained. Ovarian cysts identified in older patients, particularly if they are postmeno-

pausal, are more suspicious for malignancy. Bilateral cysts, excrescences, ascites, and cancer markers may be additional clues. In such instances laparotomy should be performed following the classic rules of oncologic surgery. However, in most situations the cyst appears to be benign. The technique consists of total removal of the cyst and this may be performed quite well laparoscopically.[7] Intraperitoneal cystectomy involves separation of the cyst wall from the ovarian capsule using traction with two grasping forceps. Afterward the cyst is removed through the abdominal incision created by the trochar. The ovary can be left open if hemostasis is good or the ovary may be closed either using clips or sutures. This technique in general is followed by limited adhesion formation as evidenced on second look laparoscopy.

Oophorectomy may also be performed laparoscopically. The uteroovarian ligament is thermocoagulated and transected. Clips are then placed on the infundibulo pelvic ligament. The ovary is removed through a small "endo-bag" to avoid contact with the abdominal wall. Alternative approaches include morcellation of the ovary when malignancy is clearly not a question or removal of the ovary through an incision in the cul-de-sac. To date we have performed 15 oophorectomies under laparoscopy. Most of these were in patients above the age of 45.

Endometriosis

Endometriosis is among the most common entities treated by laparoscopy. We prefer most often to use CO_2 vaporization of the endometriotic implants rather than electro-coagulation or thermocoagulation.[8] This preference is based on the fact that coagulation is less precise than laser which results in an increased potential risk of damage to the blood vessels or the ureter. If an ovarian endome-trioma is more than 3 cm, vaporization of the lesion is not sufficient. In those instances, we perform a total cystectomy as described above. In those circumstances when the excision of the endometrioma is difficult, we use a technique in which a portion of the cyst is removed by making a circular cut over the protruding portion of the cyst. The residual endometriosis is then vaporized.

Uterine Fibroids

Myomas may be treated using laparoscopy when they are subserosal or interstitial. The first step is to incise the serosa and separate the myoma from the uterus. We do not use vaso-pressin. Myomectomy is performed using a knife and thermocoagulation without opening the uterine cavity or a hook and monopolar current. Uterine incisions are closed by laparoscopy by running 3–0 vicryl sutures. The myoma is then removed through the abdominal wall. When it is of sufficiently large size, it may be necessary to morcellate the fibroid or remove it through the posterior cul-de-sac.

Acute Salpingitis

Operative laparoscopy can be used in cases of acute salpingitis. Tube ovarian abscesses can also be treated laparoscopically. Lysis of adhesions is performed by a hydrodissection technique. To prevent recurrence of adhesions, the lysis of adhesions must be meticulous without any bleeding. After the lysis of adhesions is performed we evacuate the pelvic abscess and thoroughly irrigate the peritoneal cavity. The peritoneal cavity must also be thoroughly irrigated to prevent seeding of the infection.

Second look laparoscopy of patients with tuboovarian abscess treated laparoscopically can result in no adhesion formation between the tubes and the ovaries. The reformation of a hydrosalpinx can cause the patient to experience pelvic pain. If this occurs we per-form a salpingectomy by laparoscopy. Alter-natively, the hydrosalpinx can be open using a salpingostomy technique. In such instances copious irrigation of the ampulla is warranted.

Results of Operative Laparoscopy

The results of laparoscopic salpingostomy for ectopic pregnancy are encouraging. In a series of 118 cases Pouly and Bruhat in France achieved 64% intrauterine pregnancies and 22% repeat ectopics.[9] In our series of 88 cases comparable results were obtained. Following salpingostomy, fertility outcome was poor in patients with a past history of infertility or ectopic pregnancy. Forty-one percent of patients achieved an intrauterine pregnancy and 28% experienced a repeat ectopic preg-nancy. Intrauterine pregnancies were also less frequent in patients with a history of tuboplasty (23%) or with a solitary tube (45%).

In our experience of nearly 300 laparoscopic salpingectomies for ectopic pregnancy, the major indications for salpingectomy was a pathological tube that resulted from an ectopic in which the diameter was >5 cm or a tube in which phimosis was present. Other indications for salpingectomy included rupture of the ectopic, a previous ectopic pregnancy treated by tuboplasty, or an ectopic pregnancy following in vitro fertilization.

Two contraindications to laparoscopic salpingectomy are hemorrhagic shock and severe adhesions around the tube that cannot be excised by laparoscopy. Following laparoscopic salpingectomy for ectopic pregnancy we observed a 33% intrauterine pregnancy rate within 18 months of follow-up.[10] Reproductive outcome depends primarily on the status of the contralateral tube. Forty-six percent of patients with a normal contralateral tube achieve an intrauterine pregnancy whereas only 25% of patients with a patent but pathologic tube have an intrauterine pregnancy.

Following adhesiolysis by laparoscopy using modern methods, the intrauterine pregnancy rate is approximately 50% which is equivalent to the results with microsurgical laparotomy techniques.[11,12] See Table 5.1.

Fertility outcome after laparoscopic salpingostomy varies greatly between authors.[4,13] We have reported 65 cases of distal tuboplasty resulting in a 27% intrauterine pregnancy rate within 18 months of follow-up.[6]

Ovarian cystectomy is another area in which results are now available. Eighty-seven percent of the nonmalignant organic cysts were removed laparoscopically.[7] Among 444 cysts which were removed laparoscopically, 349 were organic and 95 functional. In our series of laparoscopic cystectomies the greatest number were endometriotic followed by benign cystic teratoma and serous cystadenoma.

The fertility outcome after laparoscopic treatment of endometriosis is encouraging. The mean pregnancy rate is 50%.[8] The pregnancy rate is related to the stage of the disease. Laparoscopic treatment of endometriosis is effective in the relief of pain. Forty percent of patients can be expected to have relief of pain and an additional 35% have improvement in pain.

In conclusion, operative laparoscopy has evolved into a major tool in the field of gynecology. It is constantly being refined as new procedures and are developed and new indications are evaluated.

References

1. Rochat RW, Koonin L, Atrash HK, Jewett JF and the Maternal Mortality Collaborative. Maternal Mortality in the United States: Report from the Maternal Collaborative. Obstet Gynecol 1988;72:91.
2. Bruhat MA, Manhes H, Mage G, Pouly JL. Treatment of ectopic pregnancies by means of laparoscopy. Fertil Steril 1980;33:411.
3. Dubuisson JB, Aubriot FX, Cardone V. Laparoscopic salpingectomy for tubal pregnancy. Fertil Steril 1987;47:225.
4. Gomel V. Salpingostomy by laparoscopy. J Reprod Med 1977;18:265.
5. Semm K, Mettler L. Technical progress in pelvic surgery via operative laparoscopy. Am J Obstet Gynecol 1980;138:121.
6. Dubuisson JB, Bouquet de Jolinière J, Aubriot FX, Daraï E, Foulot H, Mandelbrot L. Terminal tuboplasties by laparoscopy: 65 consectutive cases. Fertil Steril 1990;54:401.
7. Mage G, Wattiez A, Canes M, Manhes H, Pouly JL, Bruhat MA. Traitement Coelioscopique des kystes annexiels. Contraception-Fertilité-Sexualité 1990;18:201.
8. Donnez J. CO$_2$ laser laparoscopy in infertile women with endometriosis and women with adnexal adhesions. Fertil Steril 1987;48:390.
9. Pouly JL, Manhes M, Mage G, Canes M, Bruhat MA. Conservative laparoscopic treatment of 321 ectopic pregnancies. Fertil Steril 1986;46:1093.
10. Dubuisson JB, Aubriot FX, Foulot H, Bruel D, Bouquet de Jolinière J, Mandelbrot L. Reproductive outcome after laparoscopic salpingectomy for tubal pregnancy. Fertil Steril 1990;53:1004.
11. Gomel V: Salpingo-ovariolysis by laparoscopy in infertility. Fertil Steril 1983;40:607.
12. Aubriot FX, Dubuisson JB, Bouquet de Jolinière J, Bruel D, Foulot H. Resultats des adhesiolyses pereoelioscopiques. A propos d'une série continue de 49 cas. Contraception-Fertilité-Sexualité, 1990;18:127.
13. Fayez JA. An assessment of the role of operative laparoscopy in tuboplasty. Fertil Steril 1983;39:476.

6
Hysteroscopy in Infertility

Herve Foulot

Hysteroscopy is becoming increasingly more prevalent in the diagnostic workup of the infertile woman. There are two main reasons for this increase. First, hysterosalpingography is less precise in the evaluation of the uterine cavity. Both false negative and false positive results are occasionally reported.[1] In addition, hysterosalpingographic abnormalities can be misinterpreted. Such erroneous diagnoses can be corrected by hysteroscopy. Second, progress in the design of the hysteroscope has reduced the diameter of the instrument, which allows the procedure to be performed on an ambulatory basis while maintaining excellent visualization of the uterine cavity.

Indications for Hysteroscopy

There are several indications for the use of hysteroscopy in infertility (Table 6.1). Hysteroscopy allows for the confirmation of abnormal hysterosalpingographic findings.[2] In patients with unexplained infertility, hysteroscopy should be employed to identify factors that could otherwise be missed in the basic workup. Hysteroscopy may be particularly important in the evaluation of patients experiencing repeated spontaneous abortions.[3]

More recently, there has been an increasing interest in the use of hysteroscopy in protocols related to assisted reproductive technology (ART).[4] In vitro fertilization (IVF) is an expensive and energy-intensive procedure which has been used with increasing frequency. The major cause of failure following IVF is lack of embryo implantation. Because much of the concern revolves around the quality of the embryo, evaluation of the endometrium is often neglected. Hysteroscopy provides valuable information concerning the quality of the endometrium.

In our department we use a Hamou microcolpohysteroscope for this purpose. The instrument is 25 cm long with a 30° foreoblique view providing either a panoramic view (position 1) or a contact view (position 2) at 60× magnification (Fig. 6.1). The small, 4-mm outer diameter usually eliminates the need for prior cervical dilation. Minimal or no anesthesia is required. Because the cervix does not have to be dilated, the discomfort is very minor. The procedure is entirely ambulatory, and most patients do not receive medication. The ideal period for performing the procedure is during the preovulatory phase between days 10 and 12 of a 28-day cycle.

Care must be taken during the introduction of the hysteroscope to prevent bleeding, which could hinder examination of the uterine cavity. While the hysteroscope is passing through the cervical canal, contact vision may be useful as the tip of the hysteroscope slides along the anterior wall. The 30° angle must be taken into consideration while guiding the hysteroscope through the cervical canal and isthmus.

The operator must not push the instrument through the internal cervical os but rather wait for the isthmus to open under CO_2 pressure before entering the uterine cavity. If the uterus is significantly antiflexed, passage through the isthmus can be facilitated by exerting pressure on the abdomen suprapubically. Hysteroscopy can also be used to assess the quantity and quality of cervical mucus, view the endocervical canal, and locate the transformation

TABLE 6.1. Main indications for hysteroscopy in infertility.

Abnormal hysterosalpingogram
Negative infertility workup
Recurrent miscarriages
Uterine septum
Myoma(s)
Removal of intrauterine device
Assisted reproductive technology (ART)
Sterilization

zone within it. The glandular papillae can also be visualized. In cases of atrophy of the cervical canal, only fibrous structures are seen.

The thickness of the endometrium can be evaluated by hysteroscopy. A groove can be created in the uterine mucosa on the posterior wall with the tip of the hysteroscope. Simple and polypoid endometrial hyperplasia can be suspected and polyps can be easily identified. Both tubal ostia can also be explored. Tubal patency can be confirmed by the passage of CO_2 bubbles through the ostium.

Hysteroscopy allows for the diagnosis of specific disorders. Asymptomatic endometritis can be detected. However, this can only be diagnosed in the follicular phase, since endometrial congestion is difficult to interpret in the luteal phase. Marked endometritis appears as a diffuse congestion of the endometrium, which appears bright red. This condition is usually associated with pathological tubes (Fig. 6.2). Mild congestion of the endometrium can also

be visualized. However, the significance of these less serious forms of congestion remains to be demonstrated.

Uterine myomas may be missed by hysterosalpingography or ultrasound. Myomas have a whitish appearance and often have a rich vascularization (Fig. 6.3).

Uterine polyps can also be easily visualized using hysteroscopy. These can be single or multiple. They are usually small and can be depressed by the hysteroscope. Fibromucous polyps are often larger and less motile due to their fibrous component.

The diagnosis and treatment of intrauterine synechiae[5,6] has been greatly improved with the aid of hysteroscopy. The location and type can be determined by direct inspection. Following diagnosis, recent filmy intrauterine adhesions can be resected with the tip of the hysteroscope during the same procedure. Müllerian anomalies are also evaluated and treated with the aid of hysteroscopy.

We have reported upon a series of 100 consecutive hysteroscopies carried out between September 1989 and February 1990 in the outpatient department of Port Royal University Clinic. Among 41 patients the indication was failure to achieve pregnancy with IVF. An additional 35 patients were evaluated prior to IVF. The remaining 24 patients were being evaluated for infertility, eight of whom were found to have an abnormal hysterosalpingogram.

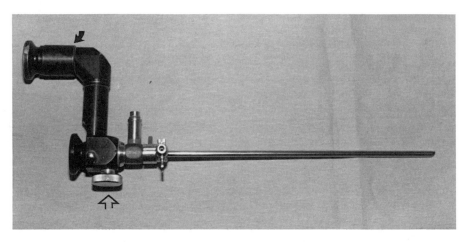

FIGURE 6.1. Hamou microhysteroscope. Open arrow points to knob.

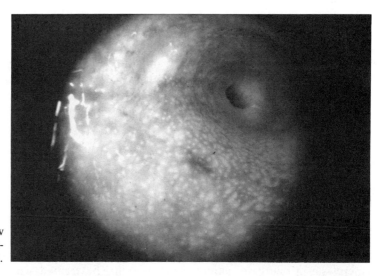

FIGURE 6.2. Hysteroscopic view of tubal ostium. The endometrium displays marked congestion.

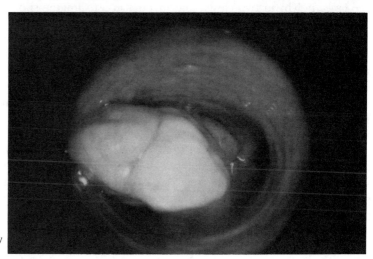

FIGURE 6.3. Hysteroscopic view of uterine myoma.

Among the 41 patients who failed to conceive with IVF, the indications for IVF were tubal factor in 30 cases, male factor in seven cases, and unexplained infertility in four cases. Thirty-seven of the 41 patients had already had one of several previous unsuccessful IVF attempts with easy embryo transfer. In two cases embryo transfer had been traumatic, and in the remaining two cases IVF had not been followed by embryo transfer. Among the IVF patients with atraumatic transfer, an abnormal hysteroscopy was found in 19 cases (51.3%). Anomalies identified included marked diffused congestion in eight cases, mild diffuse congestion in five cases, localized congestion in one case, hyperplasia in one case, polypoid hyperplasia in two cases, and synechia in two cases (one of whom had isthmic synechiae).

Among the eight patients with marked diffuse endometrial congestion, seven had tubal infertility. Four patients had tubal infertility with pathological patent tubes and three had at least one tube distally obstructed. Serological tests for chlamydia were positive in five of the seven patients. One patient had unexplained infertility with a negative serological test for chlamydia. Two other findings suggest that this congestive appearance was related to endometritis. Following antibiotic therapy, a second-look hysteroscopy performed in two patients showed almost complete disappearance of endometrial congestion. IVF was successful following antibiotic therapy in two patients who had previously had three and four IVF failures despite embryo transfer. Among the group who experienced a traumatic embryo transfer, hysteroscopy showed acute isthmic angulation in one patient and isthmic synechiae in the other patient. The latter was treated during the hysteroscopy. Among the pre-IVF patients investigated with hysteroscopy, the hysteroscopy was abnormal in 37% of cases. The following anomalies were detected: marked diffuse congestion in one case, mild diffuse congestion in three cases, localized congestion in three cases, simple endometrial hyperplasia in one case, isthmic synechiae in one case, polyps in two cases, and myoma in one case.

Among the 24 patients undergoing infertility workup, the indications for hysteroscopy were as follows: abnormal hysterosalpingography in eight cases, repeated spontaneous abortions in five cases, abnormal ultrasound in four cases, abnormal uterine bleeding in two cases, negative infertility workup in one case, and other indications in four cases. The other four cases that were indicated included two hysteroscopic procedures performed as part of the infertility workup and two additional cases in which hysteroscopy was performed as a second-look procedure following medical treatment for endometrial hyperplasia and surgical treatment of intrauterine adhesions. Hysteroscopy was abnormal in 18 cases (75%). Marked diffuse congestion was present in three cases, mildly diffused congestion in one case, synechia in four cases, submucous myomas in three cases, polyps in three cases, hyperplasia in one case, atrophy in one case, metaplasia in one case, and a deformed uterine cavity due to an interstitial myoma in one case. Diffused endometrial congestion was found in three of five patients with spontaneous repeated abortions.

These hysteroscopic findings suggest that patients who have previously undergone unsuccessful IVF and candidates considering workups for IVF often have unsuspected abnormalities identified using hysteroscopy. It is our opinion, therefore, that hysteroscopy should be included in the workup of every IVF patient.

Diagnostic hysteroscopy is a simple procedure with a low rate of complications. In our studies, one patient with tubal infertility who had not received prophylactic antibiotics after the procedure contracted pelvic inflammatory disease (PID). Therefore, we suggest that antibiotic treatment be prescribed following hysteroscopy in patients with tubal infertility.

Operative Hysteroscopy

Several abnormalities of the uterine cavity can be treated with operative hysteroscopy. The technique should be carried out under general anesthesia. We prefer to use glycocoll 1.5% as the distension medium because it is nonconductive, electrolyte-free, less viscous than dextran, and washes the uterine cavity well. Complications may arise in the event of massive intravascular injection, which can result in cerebral edema due to hyponatremia and acute renal failure by oxalic acid precipitation.

The risk of intravascular injection can be minimized by using an irrigation pump in which flow is regulated according to intrauterine pressure. Excessive intrauterine pressure can thus be avoided because the irrigation flow will be interrupted if a predetermined pressure is exceeded.

For diagnostic purposes, normal saline (NS) or dextrose 5% (D_5W) can be used. They are readily available and relatively inexpensive. Since blood and mucus are miscible with both NS and D_5W, irrigation is necessary to keep the medium relatively clean. In addition, because NS and D_5W mix with blood, operative procedures are difficult. If electrosurgery is intended NS should not be used. The amount of fluid used should be monitored to prevent fluid overload. Whatever form of distension medium is used, it is important to check that liquid input is equal to output throughout the procedure. A video camera is useful for teaching the process and improves the operator's comfort and performance. It also allows the operator to keep his or her face away from the optics in the event that inadvertent leakage results in the distension medium spraying the face of the operator.

Techniques

Submucous Myomas

Submucous myomas are most readily treated using a resectoscope (Fig. 6.4) with a 3- or 7-mm loop. The choice of loops depends on the diameter of the myoma and on the diameter and flexibility of the cervical os. The myomas are resected in strips until multiple fragments are contained within the uterine cavity. These should be removed before completing the procedure to increase vision and to ensure that the entire fibroid has been removed. The resection of myomas is relatively easy, with the exception of those located near the uterine fundus or near the tubal ostium. The uterine wall is most likely to be perforated in this last location. In such instances, it is helpful to have an assistant visualize the uterine fundus via the laparoscope. It is occasionally easier to see the increasing intensity of the hysteroscopic light source with the laparoscopic light source turned off. Perforation is less likely if the resection is performed when the loop is being moved toward and not away from the surgeon. Should perforation occur, it is essential to

adequately evaluate the pelvic area to assure that there has been no damage to adjacent organs. If laparoscopy cannot ensure this with certainty, laparotomy must be performed. Bowel injury, even if performed with the resectoscope can often be treated by debriding the wound and closing the defect by primary intent.[7]

Uterine Septum

The treatment of a uterine septum is easily addressed with a transverse electrode. The septum should be cut halfway between the anterior and posterior walls of the fundus. Bleeding vessels can be coagulated immediately with the same electrode. The transection should be stopped just below the level of the tubal ostium so that the uterine fundus is not weakened. Scissors may also be used for this purpose. An intrauterine device is ideally suited for insertion into the uterus at the end of the procedure to avoid the formation of synechiae at the point of the transection. Alternatively, a large malecot catheter may also be inserted postoperatively.

Intrauterine Adhesions

The history associated with an intrauterine adhesion is a curettage of a recently pregnant uterus followed by amenorrhea or hypomenor-

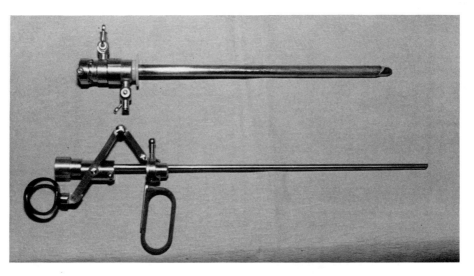

FIGURE 6.4 Resectoscope which can be used for operative hysteroscopy.

rhea. The adhesions can be vertical or oblique columns. Occasionally, crescent-shaped adhesions may obscure the corresponding cornua.[4] Intrauterine synechiae are treated by operative hysteroscopy using scissors or the same transverse electrode as those used for the uterine septum. The aim is reconstruction of a normal uterine cavity using the tubal ostia as a reference point. Difficult cases are best performed in conjunction with laparoscopy to help prevent inadvertent perforation.

Assisted Reproductive Technology

A growing number of centers are using transuterine tubal cannulation for intratubal inseminations and gamete intrafallopian transfer (GIFT). The majority of these have been performed under ultrasound guidance.[8] However, hysteroscopic transfer has also been utilized.[9] As techniques become refined, the ultimate role of hysteroscopy in ART will have to be determined.

In conclusion, diagnostic hysteroscopy has evolved as an important ambulatory procedure which provides valuable diagnostic information pertaining to infertile couples. In addition, in those instances where uterine factors contribute to infertility, the hysteroscope is capable of providing a valuable treatment modality.

References

1. Loy RA, Weinstein FG, Seibel MM. Hysterosalpingography in perspective: the predictive value of oil soluble versus water soluble contrast media. Fertil Steril 1989;51:170.
2. Siegler AM, Lindemann HJ. Hysteroscopy, principles and practice. Philadelphia: Lippincott, 1984.
3. Hamou J. Hystéroscopie et microcolpohystéroscopie: atlas et traité. Paris: Masson, 1986.
4. Taylor PJ. Diagnostic and operative hysteroscopy. In: Seibel MM, ed. Infertility: a comprehensive text. East Norwalk, CT: Appleton & Lange, 1990.
5. Siegler AM, Valle RF, Lindemann HJ, Mencaglia L. Therapeutic hysteroscopy: induction and techniques. St. Louis: CV Mosby, 1990.
6. Schenker J, Margaliath EJ. Intra-uterine adhesions: an updated appraisal. Fertil Steril 1982;37:593.
7. Sullivan B, Kenney P, Seibel MM. Hysteroscopic Resection of fibroid with thermal injury to sigmoid closed by primary repair. Obstet Gynecol 1992;80:546
8. Jansen RPS, Anderson JC, Sutherland PD. Non-operative embryo transfer to the fallopian tube. N Engl J Med 1988;319:288.
9. Gubbini G, Tabanelli C, Guerra B, et al. Inseminazione intratubarica. Fisiopat Rip 1988; 6:80.

7
Surgical Advances for Male Infertility

Sherman Silber

The traditional discussion of surgical correction of male infertility usually involves the merits of varicocelectomy. I plan to dismiss varicocele as a major fertility factor by saying that three well-controlled studies by endocrinologists have demonstrated no difference in pregnancy rates or semen values over prolonged follow-up in couples where the husbands have a varicocele, whether they have undergone varicocelectomy or not.* I recognize that few urologists in the world will agree to this because varicocelectomy is a major form of treatment used by urologists for male factor infertility. All three of these studies, however, failed to prove that the procedure really makes a difference.

Treatment of the male is obviously an integral part of the treatment of the infertile couple, and the major area that is holding us back. Most of the female factor problems are being solved by new technology, and the major barrier to further progress is in dealing with severe male factor problems.

Surgical treatment of male infertility hinges on an old concept that in the testicle the sperm

are nonmotile or very weakly motile and as they pass through the epididymis they become highly active and able to fertilize. Therefore, it was believed that something important must happen during transit through the epididymis.

Our data now suggest that as the sperm come out of the testicle they are not particularly fertile, but they mature over time. They do not require specific secretions in the epididymis. The epididymis is just a tubule that allows the sperm passage, but while they are in there, they undergo intrinsic maturational changes.

The maturation process is not an imaginary phenomenon. We have known since 1973, when Bedford summarized all the data, that although no modification in acrosomal appearance occurs, disulfide bonds and the tail organelles of the sperm are stabilized. Sperm cell surface changes are determined by response to fixatives and the binding of visible markers. There is also migration and shedding of the cytoplasmic droplet. All these clear-cut anatomic phenomena are occurring as the sperm pass through the epididymis. The question is whether these maturational changes occur on their own or whether they require the epididymis. It is important to answer this question because it will have an effect on how we treat obstruction in the male.

Young ligated the epididymis at various levels in guinea pigs and discovered that the distal sperm, the sperm closest to the ligature, had poor or no motility. The sperm that were located most proximally had the greatest motility. This is an inversion of what was found in a nonobstructed epididymis, in which the distal sperm were motile and the proximal

* References:
Nilsson S, Edvinsson A, Nilsson B. Improvement in semen and pregnancy rate after ligation and division of the internal spermatic vein; fact or fiction. Br J Urol 1979;51:591.
Baker HWG, Burger HG, deKretser D, Hudson B, Rennie GC, Straffon WGE. Testicular vein ligation and fertility in men with varicocoeles. Br Med J 1985;291:1687.
Vermeulen A, Vandeweghe M. Improved fertility after varicocoele correction: fact or fiction? Fertil Steril 1984;42:249.

sperm were poorly motile. It was suggested in 1930, on the basis of these guinea pig studies, that sperm mature with time alone and passage through the epididymis is not necessary.

However, many studies since 1930 suggested the opposite. Studies in several animals showed that fertilization did not occur with proximal sperm but did with distal sperm. The fact that the epididymis is really just a long tube that does not provide a magical substance which the sperm need to become fertile was clearly established when it was shown that sperm do not require 11 days to go through the epididymis, as was commonly thought. They go through the epididymis in 2 days or less, many of them in just 1 day.

It should have been obvious to all of us that this was the case. Whenever a urologist operated on a young man for cancer of the testicle or for other reasons and he had a high fertile sperm count, the epididymis was collapsed and contained hardly any sperm. We should have realized that sperm travel through the epididymis immediately, and are not stored there but rather in the ampullary region of the vas. Thus epididymal sperm transit is not necessary for sperm to become fertile.

Drawings from Strassburg from the 1850s show the testicle duct work, the seminiferous tubules, the rete testis, and the vasa efferentia leading into the head of the epididymis, the corpus epididymidis, and the tail. The old concept was that sperm from the vasa efferentia could not fertilize an egg. We are now finding that sperm taken from the rete testis can fertilize an egg if they have had sufficient time to mature on their own.

There are numerous natural causes of obstructive azoospermia, and probably 10% of men with azoospermia have an obstructed epididymis as their cause of infertility. Perhaps the most common cause of epididymal obstruc-

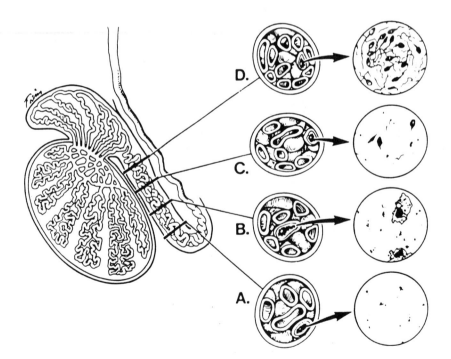

FIGURE 7.1. Stepwise transection of the epididymis, distal to proximal, in the course of determining the site of obstruction. (A) No sperm or cells are seen in the epididymal fluid. (B) Macrophages are visible, signifying that at least one site of epididymal perforation is near. (C) Some sperm heads and debris are seen. (D) The areas of obstruction are passed, as indicated by the multiplicity of normal sperm. Histologic sections between points C and D demonstrate epididymal inflammation, interstitial sperm granuloma, and tubular obstruction. Reprinted, with permission, from Ref. 13.

tion is vasectomy, because when performed in the usual fashion it creates a buildup in pressure which travels down to the epididymis, with secondary blowouts and inspissation and blockage in the epididymis.

We locate the site of blockage in the epididymis surgically. Originally, we would transect proximally until we reached epididymal fluid which did not contain sperm. A few millimeters more proximal it would contain abundant sperm. Our initial approach was to perform the anastomosis at the lowest possible point where sperm were identified, whether they were motile or nonmotile. We now transect as proximal as necessary to find motile sperm. This distance may be substantial, as we want to be certain there are no additional sites of blockage proximal to the anastomosis site.

The basic principles of obstruction are that distal obstruction causes proximal obstruction, and that older senescent sperm are found distally and younger sperm proximally. When we go from distal to proximal, we may see what looks like no sperm at all on light microscopy, just a lot of debris (Fig. 7.1). On electron microscopy we find that the debris actually consists of senescent, dead sperm that have undergone degenerative changes. When we move more proximal, some degenerated sperm are still seen, but not as many. Continuing further proximally, normal spermatozoa are found. Light microscopy reveals fairly vigorously motile sperm, despite the fact that it is often necessary to go to a much more proximal region of the epididymis to find them. Electron microscopy proves that nonmotile sperm are not immature sperm, they are overmature sperm.

It is important to have a phase contrast microscope in the operating room at the time of vasovasostomy because in contrast to the light microscope, a phase contrast microscope usually allows one to see motility when we are beyond all areas of blockage. This is important because the epididymis is one long, coiled, 20-foot tubule. Therefore, when we cut beyond the obstruction we frequently see many cut tubules, most of which are convoluted blind loops. Only one of those cut tubules will be leaking sperm. We perform a specific, end-to-

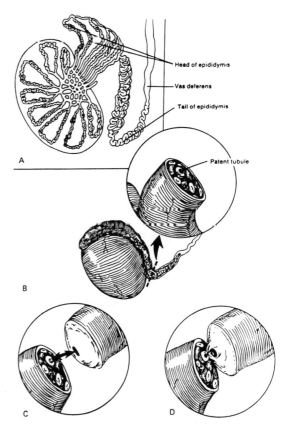

FIGURE 7.2. Diagram of the specific tubule technique for vasoepididymostomy first described in 1978. Reprinted, with permission, from ref. 13.

end anastomosis of the vas to that tubule (Fig. 7.2). All the other cut ends are just discontinuous blind loops, which are left alone. The outer muscularis of the vas is sutured to the epididymal tunic just for support. With experience, the surgeon performing a vasoepididymal anastomosis should be just as sure he has an accurate mucomucosal approximation as for a tubal reanastomosis.

Our original end-to-end anastomosis was a difficult technique, in a sense, because it required freeing up the epididymis so that we could transect serially until we reached a point beyond the blockage (Fig. 7.3). If postanastomotic azoospermia occurs with this technique, it is usually not due to a surgical failure, but rather to a more proximal blockage that was not detected or recognized. This critical point caused us to transect as proximal as needed to find good, vigorously motile sperm.

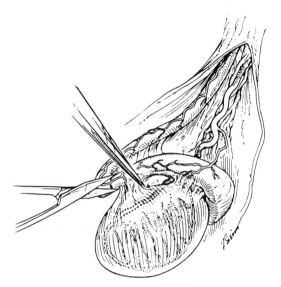

FIGURE 7.3. The epididymis is freed up without damaging the blood supply in preparation for a transverse sectioning before a specific tubule-to-tubule vasoepididymostomy. Reprinted, with permission, from ref. 13.

When we examine pregnancy rates, we find a lack of relation of the postoperative sperm count anywhere along the corpus epididymis to the pregnancy rate. Two of three patients impregnated their wives with postoperative sperm counts of 0 to 1 million/cc. When the postoperative sperm count was 1 to 5 million/cc, five of eight women conceived. When the postoperative sperm count was over 40 million/cc, we had 32 pregnancies out of 43 cases. Therefore, the pregnancy rate was fairly similar in the 60% range, no matter how low the sperm count, as long as the patient was not azoospermic. The overall patency rate was 78%, and the overall pregnancy rate was 56%. However, when we had patency and sperm in the ejaculate, the pregnancy rate was 72%. We also observed that no matter what the postoperative sperm count, there was also no difference in the mean time to pregnancy. This is without reproductive technology such as in vitro fertilization (IVF) or gamete intrafallopian transfer (GIFT).

Our initial pregnancy rates for a patent vasovasostomy, a patent vasoepididymostomy to the corpus epididymidis, and a patent anastomosis to the head of the epididymis were 88, 73, and 43%, respectively. These data originally were evidence to us that we should do the anastomosis as distal as possible. We only went to the head of the epididymis in cases where we found no sperm whatsoever in the distal epididymis. However, what we did not appreciate originally was that those select patients who had vasoepididymostomy to the head of the epididymis had much more extensive damage than those who underwent vasoepididymostomy in the corpus. Our findings now are really far different. If we do all of our anastomoses to the head of the epididymis, there is no significant difference in overall pregnancy rates. The findings have been confirmed by our colleague in Moscow, Dr. Victor Krylov.

Many people attempting to do vasoepididymostomy are still using the microscope at low-power magnification because they find the higher-power magnification uncomfortable, or they have insufficient practice with it. However, to see the lumen well enough to be sure you are getting an accurate anastomosis, 25 or 40× is usually necessary.

We have simplified the procedure not by avoiding high-power magnification but by limiting the amount of dissection we do. When working on a dilated epididymis we do not suggest that it be freed up, transected, and rigorously have all the bleeders stopped. Rather, we suggest simply picking any area where it looks as if there is access to the tubule, which can be seen through the epididymal tunic. Make a little opening in the epididymal tunic and then make a little opening in the tubule along the surface with microscissors. Hemostasis can be achieved easily with microbipolar forceps.

If the tubule is transected, it is unclear on which side to attach the vas because sperm will flow from both above and below the transection. This can be overcome by performing an end-to-side anastomosis. With this technique it is simply a matter of doing a posterior suture of the vas lumen to the side of the epididymal tubule and then going from the 6 o'clock position anteriorly in both directions until finally you have three posterior sutures. Three anterior sutures are then placed, and the anastomosis becomes much easier to perform.

If a creamy yellow or orange fluid is observed in the vas, no sperm will be seen within it. When fluid of this color is seen in the head of the epididymis, however, it is not necessarily a bad sign; it may contain vigorously motile sperm.

The posterior muscularis of the vas is sutured to the opening of the posterior epididymal tunic to fix the vas in place near the opening in the epididymal tubule. We then place a 6 o'clock suture and continue to place sutures moving around the specific tubule anteriorly without ever rotating it, as we would with a vasovasostomy.

Occasionally one has to go directly to the vasa efferentia if no sperm are found anywhere in the epididymis. Blockage distally always causes more proximal blockage because of pressure buildup that causes blowouts and inspissation of the sperm in concretions. Sometimes these concretions are right in the vasa efferentia, and one will not find sperm until nearly the entire caput epididymidis is shaved off.

Bedford showed long ago that macrophages can enter the epididymis only if there is a disruption of the integrity of the ductal epithelium. If one finds macrophages and sperm in the vasa efferentia, it is most certainly due to disruption of the tubule caused by secondary blockages. Sometimes one vas efferens is found with no sperm, and a second one next to it is loaded with sperm. In such cases the specific tubule containing sperm should be picked up delicately and anastomosed directly to the vas lumen. The success of these operations led us to realize that sperm do not have to transit the epididymis to gain maturity and fertilize an egg.

Take the case of a man who had a vasectomy 15 years earlier. No sperm were present in the vas on either side, and he had blowouts all the way up to the vasa efferentia. We did an end-to-end anastomosis on both sides of the vas to the vasa efferentia. At 10 months the motility was only fair, but after 12 months he had 40% motility. His wife became pregnant 1 year, 8 months postoperatively.

What are the causes of vasovasostomy failure? If one is doing a vasectomy reversal and puts the two ends of the vas together, why is success so infrequent? We have found that a low sperm count with poor motility after the vasovasostomy is always caused by obstruction. The obstruction is caused either by a poor vasovasostomy by blockage in the epididymis or the vasa efferentia. Azoospermia is more commonly the problem, but even a low sperm count with poor motility is usually caused by a partial blockage. In the case of a good sperm count and poor motility, we know there is no obstruction, but some damage has occurred to the epididymis, and long-term improvement is the rule.

With a low sperm count and good motility, no obstruction exists. This count is no different than it was before vasectomy. In comparing the count to quantitative evaluations of the testicle biopsy, we found no difference between the predicted and the actual sperm count. Men normally have sperm counts ranging from 1 to 150 million. If motility is good and no pregnancy occurs, no matter what the count, the wife must be evaluated because a female factor will surely be involved (Table 7.1).

What are the problems with vasovasostomy? Many urologists are still doing this procedure without a microscope. The anastomosis is one layer, and one cannot accurately line up the dilated testicular end with the nondilated abdominal end. Leakage occurs, and the sperm may go through a fistula, causing a sperm granuloma with either partial or complete blockage. Also, some urologists use a splint to line up the two ends of the vas, then do the

TABLE 7.1 Correlation between oligospermia and pregnancy.

Motile sperm count (millions/cc)	Pregnancy rate (%)	
	5 Years	12 Years
0.1–1	3.9	8.7
1–5	11.9	26.6
5–10	22.1	34.3
10–15	45.0	58.5
15–20	68.6	82.0

From Schoysman et al.[32]

suturing, and pull the splint out up to 5 days later. This technique can cause blockage.

A large series of men experienced severe oligospermia after this kind of vasovasostomy. They were told by their physicians that sperm antibodies were the cause of their infertility. Many of these men did have elevated sperm antibody titers. However, when vasovasostomy was performed and the former vasovasostomy site excised, a vasogram showed no anastomosis. Rather, sperm reached the other side of the repair by leaking through a scarred, fistulous granuloma. The sperm were so delayed in their process of migration that by the time they reached the other side they were mostly senescent. This underscores the need for an accurate anastomosis of the vas.

If the vas fluid contains no sperm, or poor-quality sperm, epididymal damage has occurred more proximally. That is the most common problem with an accurate vasovasostomy. Unfortunately, the literature in this field is extremely confusing. After having studied 4,000 patients, however, I feel fairly comfortable stating that if the vas fluid contains no sperm preoperatively, the ejaculate will not contain sperm postoperatively.

The presence of only sperm heads or short-tail sperm is also an indication of epididymal damage. These are sperm that have died of old age. The distal portion of the epididymis will contain no sperm, except perhaps some sperm heads, and numerous macrophages. More proximally, the finding generally will be epididymal extravasation or epididymal concretions without extravasation. More proximally still, sperm will be seen in the epididymal tubule.

We have come across some interesting cases of epididymal pathology, including a huge series of smallpox infertility due to obstructive azoospermia. These are mainly men from the Near East and India who had the disease before it was eradicated. It is safe to say that men who survive smallpox as infants are virtually assured of having epididymal blockage.

One of these men had undergone a vaso-epididymostomy by macrotechnique. The attempt failed and microsurgery was performed. Postoperatively he had 8 million sperm with 50% motility, sufficient to impregnate his wife. I point this out to illustrate that these patients all have blockage at the head of the epididymis, and yet they are fertile, despite anastomosis to the proximal head.

Hernia repair in infants may accidently ligate the vas in the region of the sac at the internal ring. For these men, reconnecting the vas requires opening the abdomen. After the anastomosis in the abdominal area, because of secondary epididymal blockage, it is also necessary to do a vasoepididymostomy in the scrotal area because there will be no sperm in the vas. Instead, the sperm will be somewhere in the epididymis at the site of secondary blockage. A proper vasoepididymostomy plus a vasovasostomy in the abdomen should result in an excellent chance of success.

We operated on a man in whom we diagnosed obstructive azoospermia on the basis of a normal testicle biopsy, normal fructose level, and azoospermia. We performed a vasogram as part of the vasoepididymostomy procedure, to make sure that the vas emptied into the ejaculatory duct normally and that there was no ejaculatory duct blockage. The vas on the right side was found to empty into the ureter, which emptied into the pelvic kidney. The man had complete blockage on this side with a normal testicle, and normal sperm in the epididymis that could not get out because they were going into his kidney. The kidney was nonfunctional due to blockage as a result of emptying into his testicle. A vasogram on the other side showed an atrophic testicle, with the vas emptying normally into the ejaculatory duct, seminal vesicles, and bladder the way it should. At that time we chose a conservative approach. We took the vas from the side in which we found some old degenerate sperm and anastomosed it to the vas on the other side. Unfortunately, the man remained azoospermic. He was persistent, however, and we performed a second operation in which we found sperm in the epididymis. We anastomosed the other vas to that epididymis, and now the man is fertile.

Antibodies have little to do with failure to conceive after a vasovasostomy. If good sperm are present in the vas fluid, a vasovasostomy is enough. We reviewed 326 patients who were followed for up to 10 years, and 282 had sperm in the vas fluid. Of the 44 who had no sperm, all were azoospermic after a perfect micro-surgical vasovasostomy. Of the 282 who had sperm in the vas fluid, over a 10-year period 81% eventually impregnated their wives. The sperm count postoperatively did not cor-relate with the pregnancy rate.

In double-blind studies done 10 years ago using the simple Kibrick method and then the simple Isojima method for sperm antibody titers, among men who were not azoospermic postoperatively, there was no difference between those who did and who did not im-pregnate their wives in the frequency of finding either immobilizing or agglutinating anti-bodies. I thought the titers would be different in azoospermic men because they might reflect extravasation in the epididymis; however, we found no relationship. The sperm antibody titer did not indicate epididymal blockage, and it had no effect on the pregnancy rate.

With the more sophisticated immunobead methods, we have videotapes of epididymal sperm that are absolutely clogged with IgG and other antibodies. One would never anticipate these sperm would be able to fertilize, and yet, the fertilization rate with epididymal sperm is absolutely unaffected by the presence or absence, or by the magnitude of the titers, of sperm antibodies of any type. Thus we con-clude that the pregnancy is not related to vari-cocele, sperm antibodies, testicle biopsy findings, or even postoperative sperm counts, as long as there is no partial obstruction. In the absence of secondary epididymal blockage, the pregnancy rate for vasovasostomy is extremely high. The overall pregnancy rate is approxi-mately 55%. However, if we achieve patency, the pregnancy rate is about 73%. The presence or absence of antibodies appears to play no role in pregnancy rates (Fig. 7.4).

What can we do to make vasectomy a more popular method of birth control? Can men not fear it because they might lose their manhood or the prospect of future fertility? Years ago

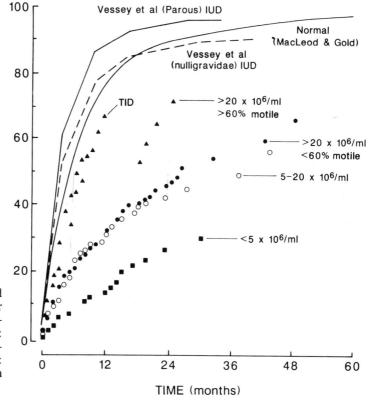

FIGURE 7.4. Pregnancy rates based on sperm counts. From Baker HWG and Burger HG, Male infer-tility in reproductive medicine. In: Steinberger E et al (eds). *Repro-ductive Medicine*, New York: Raven Press, 1986. modified with permission.

we suggested open-ended vasectomy. In this procedure the testicular end is left open and allowed to leak. This was greeted with a tremendous wave of controversy. Sperm antibodies, recanalization, and vasectomy failures were predicted. In fact, none of those fears proved true in more than 4,000 open-ended vasectomies.

One stipulation is in order regarding the procedure. The abdominal end must be sealed very carefully with a cautery needle for 1.5 cm. Sealing it for less than 1.5 cm increases the possibility of recanalization and failure. The reason that open-ended vasectomy is critical is that only 20% of patients requesting a vasectomy reversal have sperm in their vas fluid, and 80% have epididymal blockage.

Few reports about vasovasostomy have appeared in the journals lately. This is because success rates have deteriorated significantly due to the popularity of cautery for sealing the vas. Cautery provides a very tight seal, but sealing the abdominal side and the testicular side results in greater and faster pressure buildup. Our problems now are worse than they were. Not only are we trying to make vasectomy more reversible, we are trying to circumvent a modern trend that is very damaging. That is why we recommend sealing only the abdominal side.

Of those 4,000 patients, 50 came back requesting vasectomy reversal. A comparative group were prospectively studied who had closed-ended vasectomy performed by different urologists in Ottawa and St. Louis. Of these 50 patients operated on following the open-ended technique, 49 (98%) had patency after vasovasostomy. Forty-seven (94%) impregnated their wives. Following the closed-ended technique with cautery, only 15 (37%) were patent and only 5% impregnated their wives due to the epididymal damage caused by the closed-ended cautery technique. We maintain that if in the future vasectomy is going to be easily reversible, urologists must switch to open-ended vasectomy.

The failure rate with open-ended vasectomy is extremely low with the technique described. The success rate with simple vasovasostomy is going down now dramatically because of the popularity of closed-ended cautery. If open-ended vasectomy does not replace closed-ended vasectomy, reversal will require vasoepididymostomy, which is much more difficult and has a notably low success rate.

Suggested Reading

1. Silber SJ. Microscopic technique for reversal of vasectomy. Surg Gynecol Obstet 1976;143:630.
2. Silber SJ. Perfect anatomical reconstruction of vas deferens with a new microscopic surgical technique. Fertil Steril 1977;28:72.
3. Silber SJ, Galle J, Friend D. Microscopic vasovasostomy and spermatogenesis. J Urol 1977;117:299.
4. Silber SJ, Crudop J. Kidney transplantation in inbred rats. Am J Surg 1973;125:551.
5. Silber SJ, Crudop J. A three kidney rat model. Invest Urol 1974;11:466.
6. Silber SJ, Malvin RL. Compensatory and obligatory renal growth in rats. Am J Physiol 1974;226:114.
7. Silber SJ. Growth of baby kidneys transplanted into adults. Arch Surg 1976;111:75.
8. Silber SJ. Transplantation of rat kidneys with acute tubular necrosis into salt loaded and normal recipients. Surgery 1975;77:487.
9. Silber SJ. Successful autotransplantation of an intra-abdominal testicle to the scrotum using microvascular anastomosis. J Urol 1976; 115:452.
10. Silber SJ. Compensatory and obligatory renal growth in babies and adults. Aust NZ J Surg 1974;44:421.
11. Silber SJ. Microscopic vasectomy reversal. Fertil Steril 1977;28:1191.
12. Silber SJ. Vasectomy and vasectomy reversal. Fertil Steril 1978;29:125.
13. Silber SJ. Reproductive microsurgery. Baltimore: Williams & Wilkins, 1984.
14. McLeod J, Gold RZ. The male factor in fertility and infertility. IV. Sperm morphology in fertile and infertile marriage. Fertil Steril 1951;2:394.
15. Silber SJ, Rodriguez-Rigau LJ. Quantitative analysis of testicle biopsy: determination of partial obstruction and prediction of sperm count after surgery for obstruction. Fertil Steril 1981;36:480.
16. Silber SJ. Epididymal extravasation following vasectomy as a cause for failure of vasectomy reversal. Fertil Steril 1979;31:309.
17. Bedford JM. Adaptation of the male reproductive tract and the rate of spermatozoa following vasectomy in the rabbit, rhesus monkey, hamster and rat. Biol Reprod 1976; 14:118.

18. Silber SJ. Microscopic vasoepididymostomy, specific microanastomosis to the epididymal tubule. Fertil Steril 1978;30:565.
19. Silber SJ. Vasoepididymostomy to the head of the epididymis: recovery of normal spermatozoa motility. Fertil Steril 1980;34:149.
20. Silber SJ. Reversal of vasectomy in the treatment of male infertility. J Androl 1980;1:261.
21. Silber SJ. Reversal of vasectomy in the treatment of male infertility: role of microsurgery, vasoepididymostomy, and pressure induced changes of vasectomy. Urol Clin North Am 1981;8:53.
22. Charny CW. Testicular biopsy: its value in male sterility. JAMA 1940;115:1429.
23. Nelson WO. Interpretation of testicular biopsy. JAMA 1953; 151:1449.
24. Mannion RA, Cottrell TLC. Correlation between testicular biopsy and sperm count. J Urol 1961;85:953.
25. Albert A. The mammalian testis. In: Young WC, ed. Sex and internal secretions. Vol 1. 3rd ed. Baltimore: Williams & Wilkins, 1961;305.
26. Heller CG, Clermont Y. Kinetics of the germinal epithelium in man. Recent Prog Horm Res 1964;20:545.
27. Steinberger E, Tjioe DY. A method for quantitative analysis of human seminiferous epithelium. Fertil Steril 1968;19:960.
28. Tjioe DY, Steinberger E, Paulsen CA. A simple method for quantitative analysis of seminiferous epithelium in human testicular biopsies. J Albert Einstein Med Center 1967;15:56.
29. Zuckerman Z, Rodriquez-Rigau LJ, Weiss DB, Chowdhury AK, Smith KD, Steinberger E. Quantitative analysis of the seminiferous epithelium in human testicular biopsies, and the relation of spermatogenesis to sperm density. Fertil Steril 1978;30:448.
30. de Kretser DM, Burger HG, Hudson B. The relationship between germinal cells and serum FSH levels in males with infertility. J Clin Endocrinol Metab 1974;38:787.
31. Schoysman R. Presented at the meeting of the American Fertility Society, Miami Beach, FL, April 1977.
32. Schoysman R, Drouart JM. Progrès récents dans la chirurgie de la sterilité masculine et féminine. Acta Clin Belg 1972;71:261.
33. Amelar RD, Dubin L. Commentary on epididymal vasostomy, vasovasostomy and testicular biopsy. In: Whitehead E. Douglas, ed. Current operative urology. New York: Harper & Row, 1975;1181–1185.
34. Hanley HG. The surgery of male sub-fertility. Ann R Coll Surg 1955;17:159.
35. Hotchkiss RS. Surgical treatment of infertility in the male. In: Campbell MF, Harrison HH, eds. Urology. 3rd ed. Philadelphia: WB Saunders, 1970;671.
36. Silber SJ. Results of microsurgical vasoepididymostomy: role of epididymis in sperm maturation. Hum Reprod 1989;4:298–303.
37. Silber SJ. Apparent fertility of human sperm from the caput epididymis. J Androl 1989; 10:263–269.
38. Gaddum P. Sperm maturation in the male reproductive tract: development of motility. Anat Rec 1969;161:47.
39. Bedford JM. Development of the fertilizing ability of spermatozoa in the epididymis of the rabbit. J Exp Zool 1966;163:312.
40. Orgebin-Crist MC. Sperm maturation in rabbit epididymis. Nature 1967;216:816.
41. Glover TD. Some aspects of function in the epididymis. Experimental occlusion of the epididymis in the rabbit. Int J Fertil 1969;14: 215.
42. Gaddum P, Glover TD. Some reactions of rabbit spermatozoa to ligation of the epididymis. J Reprod Fertil 1965;9:119.
43. Paufler SK, Foote RH. Morphology, motility and fertility in spermatozoa recovered from different areas of ligated rabbit epididymis. J Reprod Fertil 1968;17:125.
44. Orgebin-Crist MC. Studies of the function of the epididymis. Biol Reprod 1969;1:155.
45. Silber SJ. Transurethral resection. New York: Appleton-Century-Crofts, 1977.
46. Porch PP, Jr. Aspermia owing to obstruction of distal ejaculatory duct and treatment by transurethral resection. J Urol 1978;119:141.
47. Silber SJ, Asch R, Ord T, Borrero C, Balmaceda J. New treatment for infertility due to congenital absence of vas deferens. Lancet 1987;2:850.
48. Devroey P, Braeckmans P, Smits J, et al. Pregnancy after translaparoscopic zygote intrafallopian transfer in a patient with sperm antibodies. Lancet 1986;1:1329.
49. Girgis SM, Etriby AN, Ibrahim AA, Kahil SA. Testicular biopsy and azoospermia. A review of the last ten years experiences in over 800 cases. Fertil Steril 1969;20:467.
50. Orgebin-Crist MC. Studies of the function of the epididymis. Biol Reprod 1969;1:155.
51. Levitt SB, Kogan SJ, Engel RM, Weiss RM, Martin DC, Ehrlich RM. The impalpable testis: a rational approach to management. J Urol 1978;120:515.
52. Weiss RM, Glickman MG, Lytton B. Clinical implications of gonadal venography in the management of the non-palpable undescended testis. J Urol 121:745.
53. Clatworthy NW, Hallenbaugh RS, Grossfeld JL. The long-louped vas orchidopexy for the high undescended testis. Am Surg 1972;38:69.
54. Fowler R, Stephens FD. The role of testicular vascular anatomy in the salvage of high undescended testes. In: Stephens FD, ed. Con-

genital malformations of the rectum, anus, and genital urinary tract. London: Livingston, 1963;306–320.

55. Gibbons MD, Cromie WJ, Duckett JW, Jr. Management of the abdominal undescended testicle. J Urol 1979;122:76.

56. Martin DC. The undescended testis: evolving concepts in management. Urol Dig 1977.

57. Cohen R, Silber SJ. Laparoscopy for cryptorchidism. J Urol 1980;124:928.

58. Silber SJ. The intra-abdominal testis: microvascular autotransplantation. J Urol 1981; 125:329.

59. Silber SJ, Kelly J. Successful auto-transplantation of intra-abdominal testis to the scrotum by microvascular technique. J Urol 1976;115:452.

60. Campbell HE. Incidence of malignant growth of the undescended testicle: a critical and statistical study. Arch Surg 1942;44:353.

61. Martin DC, Menck HR. The undescended testis: management after puberty. J Urol 1975;114:77.

62. Atkinson PM, Epstein MT, Rippon AE. Plasma gonadotropins and androgens in the surgically treated cryptorchid patient. J Pediatr Surg 1975;10:27.

63. Altwein JE, Gites RF. Effect of cryptorchidism and castration on FSH and LH levels in the adult rat. Invest Urol 1972;10:167.

64. Hadziselemovic F, Herzag B, Seguchi H. Surgical correction of cryptorchidism at two years: electron microscopic and morphologic investigations. J Pediatr Surg 1975;10:19.

65. Kiesewetter WB, Shull WR, Fetterman GH. Histologic changes in the testis following the anatomically successful orchidopexy. J Pediatr Surg 1969;4:59.

66. Mengel W, et al. Studies on cryptorchidism: a comparison of histologic findings in the germinative epithelium before and after the second year of life. J Pediatr Surg 1974;9: 445.

67. Nelson WO. Mammalian spermatogenesis, effect of experimental cryptorchidism in the rat, and nondescent of the testis in man. Recent Prog Horm Res 1951;6:29.

68. Sohval AR. Testicular dysgenesis as an etiologic factor in cryptorchidism. J Urol 1954;72:693.

69. Britton BJ. Spermatogenesis following bilateral orchidopexy in adult life. Br J Urol 1975;47:464.

70. Comhaire F, Derom F, Vermeulen L. The recovery of spermatogenesis in an azoospermic patient after operation for bilateral undescended testes at age of 25 years. Int J Androl 1978; 1:117.

71. Silber SJ. Recovery of spermatogenesis after testicle autotransplantation in an adult male. Fertil Steril 1982;38:632.

72. Bevan AD. The surgical treatment of undescended testicle: a further contribution. JAMA 41:718–724, 1903.

73. Moschowitz AV. The anatomy and treatment of undescended testes: with special reference to the Bevan operation. Ann Surg 1910;52:821.

74. Mixter EG. Undescended testicle: operative treatment and end results. Surg Gynecol Obstet 1924;39:275.

75. Wagenstein OH. Undescended testes: experimental and clinical study. Arch Surg 1927; 14:653.

76. McCollum DW. Clinical study of spermatogenesis of undescended testicles. Arch Surg 1935;31:290.

77. Silber SJ. Transplantation of human testis for anorchia. Fertil Steril 1978;30:181.

78. Silber SJ. Relationship of abnormal semen values to pregnancy outcome. In: Seibel MM, ed. Infertility: a comprehensive text. East Norwalk, CT: Appleton & Lange, 1990;149–155.

79. Silber SJ. Surgical management of male infertility. In: Seibel MM, ed. Infertility: a comprehensive text. East Norwalk, CT: Appleton & Lange, 1990;169–188.

8
Epididymal Sperm in Obstructive Azoospermia for In Vitro Fertilization

Sherman Silber

In 1967 an article in *Nature* stated that in the rabbit there are virtually no fertile sperm in the caput or proximal corpus epididymis, and that fertilizing ability is acquired when the sperm pass through the distal regions of the corpus epididymis. Most human males with congenital absence of the vas have no or only a rudimentary corpus epididymis. All that are present are the caput, the proximal corpus epididymis, and, in many, a little proximal epididymis. It seemed unlikely that these patients would ever be fertile.

This article has been considered the one establishing that sperm must travel through the epididymis in order to fertilize. In fact, the author was the first to question whether the factors governing the maturation process were intrinsic to the sperm or whether they resided in epididymal secretions. Anywhere from five to 11 vasa efferentia ducts in the human carry sperm out of the rete testis into the caput epididymis. At this level the caput is not just one tubule, but rather multiple compartments that connect through a small epididymal duct near the surface. At the end of the caput it becomes the proximal corpus, and then just one duct. The duct begins very thin and becomes more thick-walled until it reaches the caput epididymis. It once was thought that sperm required 11 days to travel this distance of 20 feet and that the epididymis was a storage depot. Indeed, that is the case in most animals. We now know that in the human, sperm travel rapidly—within a day—through the epididymis. The epididymis does maintain a milieu in which sperm can survive for long periods of time, but in this respect it is no different from the seminal vesicles or the ampullary region of the vas deferens. It is simply an area that keeps the sperm alive where they can mature on their own.

The objectives of our study were twofold: (1) to assess the extent to which human sperm require epididymal transport, as opposed to time alone, to fertilize, and (2) on a more practical level, to evaluate whether results with epididymal sperm aspiration and in vitro fertilization (IVF) or zygote intrafallopian transfer (ZIFT) were sufficiently repeatable to warrant routine use of the procedure in couples in whom the men had congenital absence of the vas.

Before beginning the sperm aspiration, we palpate the scrotum to locate the vas. One does not need a prior surgical exploration to make a diagnosis of congenital absence of the vas. The vas should always be palpable through the scrotal skin. The operating microscope is essential for visualization. Following transection one finds no vas deferens and only small remnants of epididymis. Because it seemed that the more distal portion of the vas would contain the most fertile sperm, we originally opened the epididymal tunic and began aspirating distally and later moved more proximally. This made these early operations extremely tedious. Before one can make an opening in the epididymal tubule, one must cut the loose areolar tissue off the surface of the epididymal tubules with careful microsurgical dissection under 40× magnification. Four or 5 hours are needed to perform a single sperm aspiration because 20 to 30 samples are sent back and forth to the laboratory to assess whether or not motility can be increased with Percoll separation. Consistently, however, good sperm are identified only in the proximal areas. This is surprising, as we thought it would be the reverse.

The experimental design involved an ovulation induction protocol for the women using leuprolide acetate, human menopausal gonadotropin (HMG), and follicle-stimulating hormone (FSH). Our approach from the beginning was different from that taken in IVF without male factor, where there are some benefits to a natural cycle. Our goal was to obtain 30 or 40 eggs. We felt that with sperm of such poor quality it would be better to have the maximum number of eggs to increase the possibility of fertilizing a few.

The sperm aspiration was begun distally and stopped only when sperm motility exceeded 10%. The procedure is relatively painless because no muscle cutting is involved. A Penrose drain was left on both sides to minimize postoperative swelling, and the men were discharged the following morning. Much greater sperm motility was noted proximally. In many cases motility was not found at the proximal head of the epididymis, and it was necessary to attempt aspiration from the vasa efferentia (Fig. 8.1). When the epididymis was squeezed in these cases, we found no fluid flow because everything had already been milked out of the epididymis. However, when the testicle was squeezed, a rapid flow of fluid was obtained. It appeared likely that what was coming out of the vasa efferentia was actually testis fluid that had never been in the epididymis.

A mini-Percoll gradient was developed to separate the motile sperm for insemination because Percoll separation of poor-quality sperm often results in a substantial reduction in the sperm count. Thesefore, instead of 1- or 2-cc columns of 95, 70, and 50% Percoll, 0.3-ml columns of Percoll were used for the 95% bottom, 70% middle, and 50% top layer. The aspirated sperm were contained in a volume of 100 to 500 µl of HEPES-buffered medium which was spun down and concentrated into 0.3 ml of medium, layered on top of the Percoll gradient, and centrifuged at $400\,g$ for 45 minutes. Only the sperm from the 95% Percoll layer area was removed. The Percoll

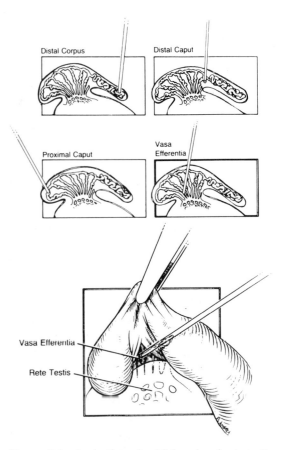

FIGURE 8.1. Aspiration of epididymal and rete testis fluid from the vasa efferentia and other sites.

was washed away from the prepared sperm and placed into a test tube containing 1 cc of culture media to which all the eggs were added. The eggs were obtained in the usual fashion by transvaginal aspiration.

The laboratory approach we employ is simple. There are several ways of maintaining a constant pH in culture medium outside of the CO_2 incubator. One way is to use oil with microdroplets, another is rapid handling of the culture dishes, and a third is to use test tubes. The advantage of a test tube is that with 1 cc of culture medium in the small tubes, the surface-area-to-volume ratio is low. Test tubes can be out of the incubator for 10 minutes without any significant change in the pH and without the need to use oil. In addition, the round bottom of the tube encourages even motile sperm to collect on the bottom over a period of time, and the eggs obviously collect down there. Therefore, this is a simple way of obtaining maximum contact for egg and sperm interaction. Although test tubes are clumsy to use compared to culture dishes, I think they provide the ideal environment for the sperm and egg, especially when the sperm are weak. Well-controlled studies show that the implantation rate per embryo with a tubal transfer for the embryo is about 18% per embryo, whereas in IVF transfer the implantation rate for embryos is about 7 to 8%. Any group that is doing both IVF and ZIFT, with a proper alternation of transfer methods, should find that tubal transfer results in about 2.5 times the implantation rate per embryo, and therefore even a greater multiplication of pregnancy rates. If more than two healthy-looking embryos are transferred to the fallopian tube, there should be a 60% pregnancy rate no matter how bad or good the sperm might be. With uterine transfer of the same number of embryos, however, a 20% pregnancy rate will be considered excellent and will probably result in no more than a 15% live birth rate.

Animal physiologists and veterinarians have known for 15 years that cow embryos can be delicately threaded into the cervix and 20% should result in pregnancy. Following a major surgical operation on anesthetized cows, one can open up the flank, place embryos into a uterine horn, and obtain an 80% pregnancy rate. It has nothing to do with delicacy of the method of transfer; it simply has to do with where the embryos are placed. That is the case in every species that has ever been studied. When the embryo is placed in the uterus the implantation rate is lower.

Among couples with male factor infertility, in which the embryos are extremely precious, we decided to place them in the fallopian tube based upon the animal data. Human data have now borne that out. In this study we had no way of making a comparison, because if we had only one embryo or poor-looking embryos we did not subject the wife to surgery. Instead we put them in the uterus. In the early series we had no pregnancies with uterine transfers, but since then we have had two. Therefore, we cannot compare uterine and

fallopian tube transfers with epididymal sperm aspiration because we selected our worst patients for uterine transfer. In other series of more than 100 cases of male factor, where the placement was alternated randomly, tubal transfer resulted in a higher implantation rate than uterine transfer.

In the initial 32 transfers, the first two patients became pregnant. However, the next 10 women did not conceive. Then we achieved one more pregnancy, but failed with the next six. Then two in a row became pregnant, and the next three did not. Finally, five in a row conceived, but the last three failed the procedure. To summarize these first 32 patient cycles, we obtained 10 pregnancies (31%). Three miscarried and seven women delivered eight live babies (one set of twins) for a 22% live birth rate. We found motile sperm in the corpus epididymis in only three of the 32 patients. In the other 29 patients motile sperm were only found either in the caput or vasa efferentia.

Of 352 mature oocytes, 93 embryos resulted for an overall fertilization rate of 26%, which is rather low, but 21 of the 32 cycles produced at least one embryo. Thus, 66% of the women knew that they were at least able to get one embryo and were encouraged to try again. Only 38% produced more than two embryos. The pregnancy rate per transfer overall was 48%, but the pregnancy rate per tubal transfer of more than two embryos was 75%. If there were more than two good-quality embryos, and we put them in the fallopian tube—in other words, they were good enough embryos that we wanted to put the women through surgery and perform ZIFT—we achieved a 75% pregnancy rate per transfer.

If fewer than 10 eggs were retrieved in the initial group, no pregnancies resulted. If 10 or more eggs were retrieved, pregnancies occurred in 10 of 20 patients.

With respect to sperm motility in those first cases, we considered all kinds of possible cutoff points. When there was less than 10% motility in the sperm that was used for insemination, we had only one pregnancy out of 11 cases. That is a 9% pregnancy rate. For those with greater than 10% motility, we achieved nine pregnancies, for a 43% pregnancy rate.

These numbers do make sense, because the wife is fertile in 95% of infertile couples in which the man is azoospermic. In other words, the women are usually normal. In cases of oligospermic male factor, the women are often subfertile also, or they would have become pregnant. We were dealing with normal women, which is why we were able to obtain so many eggs. It makes sense that if you are able to achieve fertilization because the sperm are adequate, you would have a high pregnancy rate in this group of women.

Four of those first 32 cycles were second attempts in the same patient after an initial failure. Three of those women became pregnant on the second attempt. We found that these cycles could be repeated over and over again until a woman finally did conceive. The man could undergo a number of cycles, possibly up to six, before the scar tissue would create a serious technical problem.

In the most recent follow-up series of 21 cycles, we had five pregnancies (24% pregnancy rate) and four live births (19% success rate). We had 314 mature eggs and 60 embryos, for a 19% fertilization rate. Fourteen (66%) cycles produced at least one embryo. Nine patients (43% of cycles) produced more than two embryos. The pregnancy rate per transfer was 36% overall; that is, five of 14. The pregnancy rate per tubal transfer of greater than two embryos was five (56%) out of nine.

In cases with less than 10% motility, we had 96 eggs and only three embryos, a 3% fertilization rate. When there was greater than 10% motility, we had a 26% fertilization rate. Our total fertilization rate was low, 19%, but it was even lower when motility was less than 10%. In the group with less than 10% motility, we had no pregnancies; when motility was greater than 10%, we had 36% pregnancies. Overall, we can expect a 21% delivery rate. We can expect a 41% pregnancy rate if greater than 10 eggs are retrieved, and 5% if less than 10 eggs are retrieved.

A group in Melbourne, Australia, did sperm aspiration-IVF before we did, and indeed they reported one pregnancy. This was a case of vasectomy reversal failure, and they used distal epididymal sperm. They never went to the proximal epididymis, and they have had no success with congenital absence of the vas. Now they are going to the proximal area of the epididymis to retrieve sperm. They have done five cases of congenital absence of the vas and now have a 43% fertilization rate, which is higher than ours, and they have one pregnancy.

That one pregnancy is actually a fascinating case that demonstrates that gamete intrafallopian transfer (GIFT) may be just as successful as ZIFT in this procedure, particularly if the number of eggs is not large. They had already obtained sperm from the husband. When they did the ultrasound on the wife, they found she had had a premature ovulation. They decided to do a translaparoscopic tubal transfer of the sperm. Fortunately, she was a normal woman, and the fallopian tubes must have picked up the eggs.

What is the role of the epididymis in humans versus other animals? In birds we know testicular sperm fertilize eggs when placed in the fallopian tube, but do not fertilize eggs when placed in the cloaca. This goes along with our findings in humans. The in vitro fertilizing capacity may not be equivalent to in vivo unassisted fertilizing capacity. We know there is an inversion of motility in the obstructed epididymis, so that we find the best motility proximally, which is quite the opposite of what we would see in a nonobstructed epididymis. The reason for this lies in the fact that the more distal sperm are quite senescent, having been there for a longer period of time than the more proximal sperm.

Now we feel we have a potentially desirable clinical approach for achieving pregnancies in congenital absence of the vas. This can obviously be used as a backup for failed vasectomy reversals or vasoepididymostomy. We have conclusive proof that the epididymis is not absolutely necessary for sperm maturation.

One possible approach that may or may not succeed is for patients who have had a failed vasoepididymostomy and want to try again. IVF could be combined with the vasoepididymostomy attempt. There are a number of possible indications. In cases in which oligospermia is so severe we cannot obtain enough sperm for IVF, we are performing a vasectomy on the husband. Six months later we plan to perform sperm aspiration as a method of using the epididymis as a storage organ. We feel fairly certain that the sperm can be kept alive for long periods of time in the epididymis. This would be a way of saving up 6 months worth of sperm that might be more successful than freezing and combining multiple ejaculates. Clearly, the information learned from performing epididymal sperm aspiration has provided new forms of treatment for male infertility, and caused us to rethink our understanding of sperm maturation.

Questions and Answers

Machelle Seibel. Some men with congenital blockage may not have any sperm. Are there any secrets or tricks in anticipating that set of conditions?

Sherman Silber. Well, I think it is important to realize that the testicle biopsy on people with congenital blockage is always normal and is not necessary. You are right, we will not find sperm in all of these patients even if you go right up to the vasa efferentia. In a small number of the patients there will either be no sperm or there will be no motile sperm. Almost half the patients will have less than 10% motility, which is usually not enough to obtain fertilization. We wondered why this occurred. We did a testicle biopsy at the time of the sperm aspiration, to establish a reliable and accurate method for predicting the amount of sperm that should be obtainable in the ejaculate in an unobstructed man from simply quantitating the sperm cells in the testicle biopsy. We found that no sperm, low sperm numbers, or very poor sperm did not correlate at all with what one would have predicted from the testicle biopsy.

In patients presumed to have an extremely poor prognosis, we transected the rete testis and took sections of it. Among those cases we found extravasation, inflammation, and damage in the rete testis. When one obtains poor specimens from the vasa efferentia, there

is no treatment because the entire rete testis has been damaged or destroyed by this long-term blockage.

One thought was that viable sperm could be extracted from testicle biopsy tissue. However, that clearly doesn't work because as soon as the sperm are released from the Sertoli cells they are immediately transferred to the rete testis and the vasa efferentia. It is a very, very quick process. Sperm are rarely found within the seminiferous tubule except those that aren't ready yet and that are still attached to the Sertoli cells. Theoretically, one could solve that problem through Sertoli cell culture, which is very, very complex, and wait for the sperm over the course of many days to be released into culture from the Sertoli cells. We have no solution to the problem of rete testis damage. That does appear to be why in some of these cases one obtained no sperm, not because those people have a problem with sperm production.

Question. Dr. Silber, you emphasize the point that sperm motility is the most important parameter. What would be considered an actual sperm count per cubic centimeter that is borderline or oligospermic?

Sherman Silber. I assume you are asking about a regular semen analysis and not about epididymal sperm. What is male factor, and what isn't? Actually, I wrote a chapter on this in Infertility: A Comprehensive Text, edited by Dr. Seibel (Appleton & Langer, East Norwalk, CT, 1990). I did spend a lot of time trying to discuss that issue because it is really confused in the literature. If you look at men coming in for a vasectomy who have already had kids, and who don't have any indication of infertility in their past, you will find sperm counts ranging anywhere from 1 to 150 million/cc, and actually you will find motility that can be as low as 15% or as high as 90%. There is a wide fluctuation in sperm count in men who you would have no reason to think are infertile because they have already had kids. This causes a great deal of confusion. The American Fertility Society 20 years ago defined oligospermia as below 40 million/cc. About 15 years ago they redefined oligospermia as below 20 million/cc. Today many people define oligospermia as anything below 10 million/cc. No matter what parameters are chosen above 5 million/cc, one can find men who are perfectly fertile. In fact, Ron Swerdloff reported a case of a man with 100,000 sperm/cc and 10% motility who impreganated his wife before they had a chance to be treated. The pregnancy was achieved without assisted reproduction, and they proved that indeed he was the father by red blood cell typing.

There are only a few good studies on this topic. One of the best comes from Gordon Baker and de Kretser's group in Australia. Another good paper comes from Schoupman, who followed people with oligospermia wait-listed for donor insemination. When parameters fall below 20 million/cc, the lower the sperm count and the lower the motility, the lower the pregnancy rate is per cycle when following them for 2, 3, or 4 years. When the sperm count is over 20 million/cc, the pregnancy rate per cycle doesn't get any higher, even if the count is 40 or 50 or 60 or 80 or 100 million/cc. So 20 million/cc is a legitimate cutoff, whereas below that, based on population statistics, one finds a lower pregnancy rate. However, some men that one would think infertile with counts of 3 million/cc and 10% motility have a normal mean time to pregnancy with their wives. Those who are fertile, whose wives do get pregnant in that severely oligospermic group, are really surprised. That is why people develop hamster tests and sperm antibody tests, because they presume the semen analysis is not really an accurate preditor of male fertility. If one evaluates studies comparing couples with male factor infertility, the best are those in which the husband is azoospermic or oligospermic and the couples are undergoing insemination with donor sperm. The pregnancy rate among women whose husbands are azoospermic is much higher per cycle than among those whose husbands are oligospermic. Emperaine in Bordeaux, France, was the first to make that observation. This indicates to me that pregnancy is an interaction between the couple. Therefore, a man who is in an oligospermic range below 20 million/cc may have no difficulty getting a very fertile woman pregnant. He will, however, have trouble getting a women pregnant who also has an infertility problem herself. Similar observations are found when one analyzes the pregnancy rate with donor insemination, which is always higher per cycle when the wife's husband is azoospermic than when he is oligospermic.

Question. John Collins from McMaster University in Canada is very interested in the issue of statistical analysis and the positive and negative predictive values of many of the tests that we embark upon. When the only reason for infertility is oligoteratoasthenospermia, as defined by the World Health Organization, a third of the women are pregnant when they are followed for 3 years.

Elsewhere Dr. Collins published that he has not been able to show a statistical difference in pregnancy rates until the total normal motile count falls below 4 million/cc. The total normal motile count is defined as the product of the sperm density times the percent motile times the percent normal. If it is more than 4 million, he is unable to show any predictive value of fertility versus infertility. If it falls below that number, it has a good positive predictive value for infertility.

Sherman Silber. Collins has done really brilliant work on that. It is very similar to Baker and de Kretser's figure of 20 million. It is just that Baker and de Kretser are being much simpler. They are simply talking about sperm count per cubic centimeter with motility of greater than 20% or less than 20%. Motility tends to correlate with morphology, so when you multiply it all out you find that the cutoff of 4 million that Collins came to is not much different from Baker and de Kretser's cutoff of 20 million. When you get below that cutoff of 4 million, however, pregnancy may still occur. That is the point. They found a 30% pregnancy rate in 3 years, which is about the same number that Baker and de Kretser found in 3 years with men in what you would have to define as a male factor category. In a similar group of infertile couples where the only difference was that the sperm count was over that, the pregnancy rate in 3 years was about 60%. I am fairly convinced now that the semen analysis is probably the best test we have for male factor, and that when it appears that men with low sperm counts are getting their wives pregnant easily it is not because we don't have a good test. It is because a very, very fertile woman can override the impact of oligospermia.

Suggested Reading

1. Orgebin-Christ MC. Sperm maturation in rabbit epididymis. Nature 1967;216:816–818.
2. Orgebin-Christ MC. Studies on the function of the epididymis. Biol Reprod 1969;1(Suppl 1): 155–175.
3. Bedford JM. Development of the fertilizing ability of spermatozoa in the epididymis of the rabbit. J Exp Zool 1966;162:319.
4. Glover TD. Some aspects of function in the epididymis: experimental occlusion of the epididymis in the rabbit. Int J Fertil 1969;14: 216–221.
5. Gaddum PJ. Sperm maturation in the male reproductive tract: development of motility. Anat Rec 1968;161:471–482.
6. Rowley MJ, Teshima F, Heller CG. Duration of transit of spermatozoa through the human male ductular system. Fertil Steril 1970;21:390–396.
7. Johnson L, Varner DD. Effect of daily spermatozoan production but not age on transit time of spermatozoa through the human epididymis. Biol Reprod 1988;39:821–817.
8. Zorn JR, Boyer P, Guichard A. Never on a Sunday: programming for IVF-ET and GIFT. Lancet 1987;1:385–386.
9. Ord T, Marello E, Balmaceda JP, Asch RH. The use of modified Percoll technique in IVF for cases of severe oligoasthenospermia. Presented at International Symposia of Gamete Physiology, Newport Beach, CA, November 6–10, 1988.
10. Yovich JL, Yovich JM, Edirisinghe WR. The relative chance of pregnancy following tubal or uterine transfer procedures. Fertil Steril 1988; 49:858–864.
11. Silber SJ, Ord T, Balmaceda J, Patrizio P, Asch RH. Congenital absence of the vas deferens— the fertilizing capacity of human epididymal sperm. N Engl J Med 1990;323:1788–1792.
12. El-Itreby AA, Girgis SM. Congenital absence of the vas deferens in male sterility. Int J Fertil 1961;6:409–416.
13. Girgis SM, Etriby AA, Ibrahim AA, Kahil SA. Testicular biopsy in azoospermia: a review of the last ten years' experiences of over 800 cases. Fertil Steril 1969;20:467–477.
14. Sakatoku J, Yoshida O, Komatsu Y, Takayama H, Harada T. Congenital aplasia of vas deferens. Hinyokika Kiyo 1967;13:769–784.
15. Schoysman R, Drouart JM. Recent progress in the surgery of male and female sterility. Acta Chir Belg 1972;71:261–280.
16. Anguiano A, Oates RD, Amos JA, et al. Congenital bilateral absence of the vas deferens: A primary genital form of cystic fibrosis. JAMA 1992;267:1794–1797.
17. Vickers MA, Jr. Creation and use of a scrotal sperm bank in aplasia of the vas deferens. J Urol 1975;114:242–245.
18. Jimenez-Cruz JF. Artificial spermatocele. J Urol 1980;123:885–886.
19. Pryor J, Parsons J, Goswamy R, et al. In-vitro fertilization for men with obstructive azoospermia. Lancet 1984;2:762.
20. Temple-Smith PD, Southwick GJ, Yates CA, Trounson AD, de Kretser DM. Human pregnancy by in vitro fertilization (IVF) using sperm aspirated from the epididymis. J In Vitro Fert Embryo Transf 1985;2:119–122.
21. Silber SJ. Results of microsurgical vasoepididymostomy: role of epididymis in sperm maturation. Hum Reprod 1989;4:298–303.
22. Krylov VS, Borovikov AM. Microsurgical method of reuniting ductus epididymis. Fertil Steril 1984;41:418–423.
23. Young WC. The study of the function of the epididymis: functional changes undergone by spermatozoa during their passage through the epididymis and vas deferens in the guinea pig. J Exp Biol 1931;8:151–162.
24. Silber SJ. Apparent fertility of human spermatozoa from the caput epididymidis. J Androl 1989;10:263–9.
25. Silber SJ. Pregnancy caused by sperm from vasa efferentia. Fertil Steril 1988;49:373–375.
26. Bedford JM, Calvin H, Cooper GW. The maturation of spermatozoa in the human epididymis. J Reprod Fertil Suppl 1973;18:199–213.
27. Mooney JK, Jr, Horan AH, Lattimer JK. Motility of spermatozoa in the human epididymis. J Urol 1972;108:443–445.

9
Gamete Intrafallopian Transfer and Ultrasound-Guided Transcervical Fallopian Tube Canalization

Charlotte J. Richards, Mark L. Fallick, and Machelle M. Seibel

Since the birth in 1978 of the first child conceived by in vitro fertilization and embryo transfer (IVF/ET),[1] the technologies that may be used to treat infertility have expanded rapidly. Each new procedure has been developed as a more efficient treatment for specific disorders.[2] The classic gamete intrafallopian tube transfer (GIFT) procedure was seen as an advantage over IVF, as it provided a more natural and physiologic environment for fertilization. However, GIFT did require laparoscopy and general anesthesia, which were neither natural nor physiologic. In contrast to the classic GIFT procedure, transcervical tubal canalization is one of the latest developments in the continuing refinement and simplification of assisted reproductive technology (ART). It can be performed under minimal sedation and therefore has potential application in an outpatient setting.

As with the laparoscopic GIFT procedure, the diagnoses most amenable to transcervical tubal canalization are unexplained infertility, endometriosis, male factor infertility, failed artificial insemination with donor sperm, periadnexal adhesions, and cervical factor. Premature ovarian failure with ovum donation by GIFT was initially thought to yield superior results, but randomized studies have found this not to be the case. This chapter will review the history of GIFT and describe the current status of ultrasound-guided transcervical fallopian tube canalization.

History

The historic perspective of GIFT has been recently reviewed.[3] The first report in the American literature of the successful transfer of human eggs into a patient's fallopian tube occurred in 1979.[4] Ovulation was enhanced with clomiphene citrate, 50 mg daily on days 5 to 9. Artificial insemination was performed on cycle day 12 and a laparotomy performed the following morning to reanastomose the ligated fallopian tubes. Six follicles were aspirated, at least one oocyte was identified, and the collected follicle fluid was equally divided and transferred into each reopened tube. A normal, single-term delivery followed.

The following year Kreitman and Hodgen reported on the reproductive potential of gamete tubal transfer in a primate model.[5] Following tubal ligation, 55 primates were mated prior to the day of anticipated ovulation. Laparoscopic oocyte retrieval was performed within 12 hours of ovulation and the oocyte injected into the ipsilateral fallopian tube proximal to the ligation. The monkeys were again mated and five of 31 (16%) conceived and delivered normal offspring. These studies clearly demonstrated the potential application of gamete transfer following surgical tubal occlusion and paved the way for more clinical application.

The first successful transfer of sperm and oocytes occurred in 1983.[6] Six patients with a

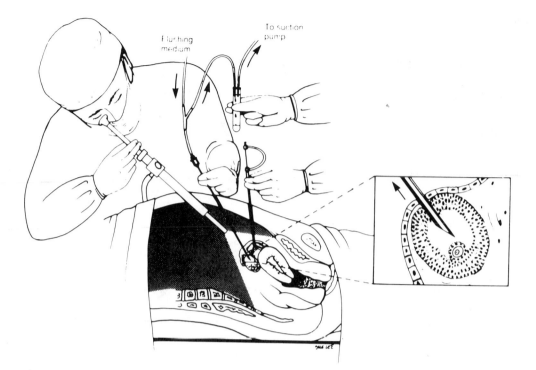

FIGURE 9.1A. Laparoscopic oocyte retrieval. Inset illustrates needle entering a preovulatory follicle. (Courtesy of Machelle M. Seibel, M.D.)

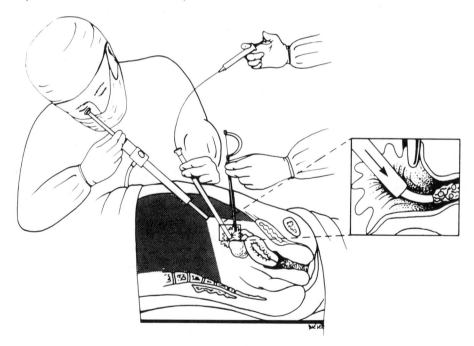

FIGURE 9.1B. Laparoscopic gamete transfer. Inset illustrates transfer of sperm and eggs into a fallopian tube. (Courtesy of Machelle M. Seibel, M.D.)

history of pelvic inflammatory disease underwent ovarian stimulation and microsurgical repair at laparotomy just prior to anticipated ovulation. Following sperm capacitation, the sperm were mixed with the oocytes in a small amount of culture medium and transferred into the repaired fallopian tubes. Of the four women treated, two conceived. One miscarried in the fifth week postoperatively and the second continued to term without complication.

In that same year, the first United States center specializing in low ovum transfer was opened in a Catholic hospital in an attempt to overcome the ethical objections to in vitro fertilization. Couples were instructed to have intercourse 24 and 30 hours following the preovulatory injection of human chorionic gonadotropin (HCG). Laparoscopic oocyte retrieval followed and the oocytes were transferred into the fallopian tubes. Because of poor results, moral theologians at the Pope John XXIII Medical-Moral Research and Education Center allowed semen also to be transferred, provided it was collected in a special perforated silastic sheath so that neither contraception nor masturbation was employed.[7] As with all the procedures described above, the gametes were transferred into blocked fallopian tubes.

Ricardo Asch and colleagues were the first to report the use of gamete transfer in patients with unexplained infertility.[8] The gametes, separated by an air space, were transferred laparoscopically into the fimbriated end of a normal fallopian tube. These same investigators subsequently utilized minilaparotomy for the gamete transfer to assure optimum placement of the gametes. Since this original work, GIFT has evolved to become one of the major ART techniques.

Technique

Ovulation induction for GIFT is achieved by a number of protocols. More mature oocytes yield higher pregnancy rates. Daily monitoring is performed using ultrasound and serum estradiol measurement. HCG 5,000 to 10,000 IU is administered intramuscularly when two or more follicles are at least 16 mm in

diameter and serum estradiol levels exceed 700 pg/ml.

A semen sample is obtained 2.5 to 3 hours before the woman is to undergo GIFT. After it is liquified, the specimen is washed using a swim-up technique in modified Ham's F-10 culture medium. Pooled cord serum is no longer used to enhance medium due to the risk of sexually transmitted diseases. Approximately 100,000 to 200,000 motile sperm/25 μl droplets are allowed to equilibrate at 37°C in a CO_2 environment at pH 7.3.

The woman is taken to the operating suite 36 hours after receiving HCG. Most programs use a laparoscopic technique for ovum retrieval (Fig. 9.1A,B). However, in the original series minilaparotomy was performed in 20% of patients because of concerns that the high CO_2 content of the pneumoperitoneum would alter the pH (Fig. 9.2). Follicles are aspirated and flushed. The intrafollicular contents and flushes are sent immediately to the laboratory for examination with the aid of a microscope. Oocytes are graded and placed in the incubator in organ culture dishes containing the Ham's F-10 plus 5% heat-inactivated patient serum. The most mature ones are selected for transfer after all have been evaluated. If fewer than three oocytes are mature or if unexpected tubal pathology is encountered, some programs prefer to change the procedure to IVF/ET.

Under direct visualization, the fallopian tube is picked up with an atraumatic grasper (Fig. 9.1). The metal outer catheter is placed in the tube. The inner catheter, which has been loaded with two or more oocytes and at least one droplet of sperm in a volume of approximately 50 μl, is advanced into the tube to the ampullary-isthmic junction and the gametes are deposited.[9] The catheter and syringe are filled with a column of medium, thereby reducing air compression and ensuring proper deposition of the gametes. The process may be repeated with the other tube, although four to five oocytes may be transferred into the same tube. There seems to be no loss in efficiency if only one tube is used, and in fact this may result in less tubal damage in the future.[10] In cases of oligoasthenospermia, all the sperm should be loaded in one catheter with all the oocytes.

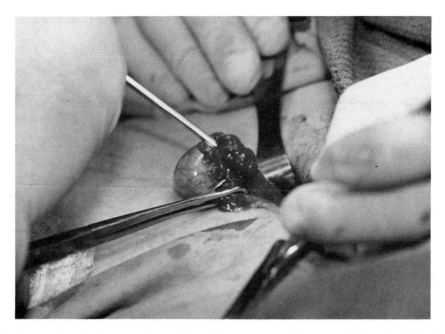

FIGURE 9.2. Gamete transfer being performed by minilaparotomy. (Courtesy of Machelle M. Seibel, M.D.)

In cases of male factor infertility, when the ability of the male sperm to penetrate oocytes is used as an indication for continuing treatment with ART or using donor sperm, or when female sperm antibodies are present, tubal embryo stage transfer (TEST) of two- to eight-cell embryos,[11] pronuclear stage embryo transfer (PROST),[12] and zygote intrafallopian transfer (ZIFT) of a fertilized oocyte[13] have been developed. These newer technologies (and even GIFT in some centers) may involve either transvaginal or transurethral ultrasound-guided ovum retrieval in order to avoid a second laparoscopy. Fertilized oocytes or embryos are transferred to the ampullary isthmic junction of the fallopian tube at a designated time afterward. The conventional method of transfer has heretofore been laparoscopic. However, with the advent of transcervical tubal canalization, it may be accomplished through the cervix using ultrasound guidance, thereby avoiding general anesthesia and exposure of oocytes and embryos to pH alterations secondary to CO_2 pneumoperitoneum.

The overall success with GIFT in the United

TABLE 9.1 Gamete Intrafallopian Transfer Treatment Outcomes by Woman's Age.

Age	Stimulation cycles	Retrievals[1]	Transfer cycles	Clinical pregnancies[2]	Ectopic pregnancies[3]	Spontaneous abortions[4]	Deliveries[5]	Multiple deliveries[5]
<25	23	18 (78)[6]	18	2 (11)	0 (0)	1 (50)	0 (0)	0 (0.0)
25 to 29	228	202 (89)	200	68 (34)	3 (4)	6 (9)	60 (30)	25 (12.5)
30 to 34	737	645 (88)	634	228 (36)	13 (5)	36 (16)	183 (29)	64 (10.0)
35 to 39	659	544 (83)	532	142 (27)	8 (5)	25 (18)	109 (21)	33 (6.2)
40+	315	219 (69)	214	36 (17)	1 (3)	14 (39)	19 (9)	3 (1.4)
Unknown	3	3 (100)	3	0 (0)	0 (0)	0 (0)	0 (0)	0 (0.0)
Total	1,965	1,631 (83)	1,601	476 (30)	25 (5)	82 (17)	371 (23)	125 (7.8)

[1] Retrievals are expressed as a percent of stimulation cycles.
[2] Clinical pregnancy rates are expressed as a percent of transfer cycles.
[3] Ectopic pregnancy rates are expressed as a percent of all pregnancies (clinical and ectopic).
[4] Spontaneous abortion rates are expressed as a percent of clinical pregnancies.
[5] Delivery (live)/multiple delivery rates are expressed as a percent of transfer cycles.
[6] Values in parentheses are percents.

TABLE 9.2 Gamete Intrafallopian Transfer Outcome by Total Number of GIFT Retrievals Performed.

GIFT cycles	No. clinics	Retrievals	Transfer cycles	Clinical pregnancies[1]	Ectopic pregnancies[2]	Spontaneous abortions[3]	All deliveries[4]
<25	95	815	795	204 (25)[5]	7 (3)	48 (24)	154 (19)
25 to 99	31	1,472	1,451	414 (28)	26 (6)	76 (18)	326 (22)
>99	9	1,463	1,446	475 (32)	21 (4)	83 (17)	361 (25)
Total	135	3,750	3,692	1,093 (29)	54 (5)	207 (19)	842 (22)

[1] Clinical pregnancy rates are expressed as a percent of retrievals.
[2] Ectopic pregnancy rates are expressed as a percent of all pregnancies (clinical and ectopic).
[3] Spontaneous abortion rates are expressed as a percent of clinical pregnancies.
[4] Delivery rates (live) are expressed as a percent of retrievals.
[5] Values in parentheses are percents.

TABLE 9.3 Gamete Intrafallopian Transfer Treatment Outcome by Stimulation Protocol.

Stimulation protocol	Stimulation cycles	Retrievals*	Transfer cycles	Clinical pregnancies[†]	Ectopic pregnancies[‡]	Deliveries[§]	Multiple deliveries
HMG alone	94	76 (81)	75	22 (29)	1 (4)	18 (24)	6 (8.0)
HMG, GnRH-a	1,006	884 (88)	886	265 (31)	14 (5)	196 (23)	58 (6.7)
HMG, clomiphene	121	81 (67)	79	20 (25)	1 (5)	14 (18)	6 (7.6)
HMG, FSH	152	112 (75)	110	32 (29)	1 (3)	28 (25)	8 (7.3)
HMG, FSH, GnRH-a	456	361 (79)	356	110 (31)	5 (4)	93 (26)	39 (11.0)
Other combinations	136	117 (86)	115	27 (23)	3 (10)	22 (19)	8 (7.0)
Total	1,965	1,631 (83)	1,601	476 (30)	25 (5)	371 (23)	125 (7.8)

[1] Retrievals are expressed as a percent of stimulation cycles.
[2] Clinical pregnancy rates are expressed as a percent of transfer cycles.
[3] Ectopic pregnancy rates are expressed as a percent of all pregnancies (clinical and ectopic).
[4] Delivery rates (live) are expressed as a percent of transfer cycles.
[5] Multiple delivery rates are expressed as a percent of transfer cycles.
[6] Values in parentheses are percents.

States was 23% live-born infants per retrieval (Tables 9.1, 9.2, 9.3).[14] It should be noted that in 1990 the live-born rate per transfer for patients over age 40 years was 9%, as opposed to 7% for IVF/ET, suggesting that there is little difference in these procedures for biologically older women. The overall multiple pregnancy rate for GIFT was 7.8% versus 4.4% for IVF/ET.

Development of Ultrasound-Guided Transcervical Tubal Canalization

The first report of transcervical tubal canalization was by Platia and Krudy in 1985.[15] During hysterosalpingography, they passed a flexible 0.018-inch guidewire into the cornu of the right fallopian tube in a woman with bilateral cornual occlusion. Recanalization was confirmed by subsequent intrauterine pregnancy. The technique of therapeutic transcervical fallopian tube canalization was improved using special catheters and balloons.[16,17]

Jansen and Anderson[18] have pioneered the ultrasound approach for transcervical tube canalization and intratubal insemination of gametes. Together with the William A. Cook company of Melbourne, Australia, they devised a catheter (K-JITS-1000) consisting of (1) a soft Teflon 3-french open-ended inner catheter 33 cm long, taper to 2-french (0.66 mm) for the distal 3 cm; (2) a firm, but still flexible, opaque Teflon 4.4-french outer cannula 28 cm long, bearing a lateral curve for entering the uterine angle; and (3) a malleable metal obturator, which overrides the outer cannula's laterally directed curve during transit of the cervix. The obturator has a curve in the sagittal plane for negotiation of the endocervical canal.[15] Because the inner catheter was difficult to image, the authors modified it by adding a platinum-tipped guide wire (K-JITS-5000) for easier visualization. Because excessive manipulation was necessary to withdraw the guidewire before loading the embryos, they modified the K-JITS-1000 catheter by adding an expanded bulb to slide easily into the lateral uterine angle.

Technique

First, transvaginal ultrasound-guided ovum retrieval is performed. Oocytes are sent to the laboratory, where semen has already been processed as described. The gametes are left in the incubator while the tubal canalization is accomplished.[18–20]

The metal obturator with the outer cannula is placed into the cervical canal past the internal os and the ultrasound transvaginal transducer is placed into the vagina. Once the tip of the obturator is located, the metal obturator is withdrawn. The outer cannula, which has a laterally directed curve, is advanced to the uterotubal junction and its position confirmed by scanning the lateral angle of the endometrial cavity in the parasagittal plane. When correctly positioned, the patient often describes mild lateralized discomfort in the pelvis.

The patient may again experience mild lateralized discomfort when the inner catheter passes through the uterotubal junction. Because the inner catheter is soft, there is a limit to the force it can exert on tissues. If its passage is obstructed, the catheter will displace the outer cannula away from the obstruction.

The operator usually encounters transient resistance as the catheter passes through the uterotubal junction. To confirm that the catheter is placed correctly, bubbles of 5% CO_2 in air suspended in sterile culture medium from a gamete incubator can be injected down the catheter. Real-time ultrasonography in the coronal plane is usually able to display the moving reflective interfaces. In very experienced hands the average time of placement has been reported to be as short as 7 to 8 minutes per tube, although a more realistic time interval is 30 minutes or longer per tubal canalization.

The gametes are then loaded into a duplicate inner catheter and passed into the fallopian tube. The catheter has been loaded in the same way as for the conventional GIFT procedure catheter, except that the volume of medium containing the gametes is smaller and there is a 10-μl column of medium at the distal end. This medium is used to confirm placement, by ultrasound, of the catheter after the inner cannula has been replaced in the ampullary-isthmic junction. The contents of the inner catheter are gently injected. The inner catheter is withdrawn and examined in the laboratory for gametes. After confirmation that the gametes have been deposited, the outer catheter is withdrawn.[21]

Indications for Ultrasound-Guided Transcervical Canalization

Ultrasound-guided fallopian tube catheterization, or transcervical intrafallopian insemination, provides new options in techniques of artificial insemination (Fig. 9.3). We have called this procedure TIFI, to distinguish it from intratubal insemination performed through the cul-de-sac or by laparoscopy.

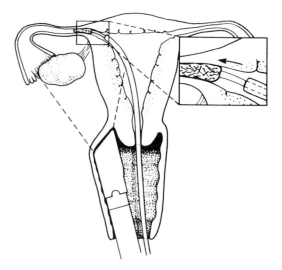

FIGURE 9.3. Technique of transcervical intrafallopian insemination (TIFI). (Courtesy of Machelle M. Seibel, M.D.)

Artificial insemination has been demonstrated to be therapeutic in a variety of conditions such as immune factor, cervical factor, oligoasthenospermia, and idiopathic infertility. Fallopian tube catheterization, especially in the presence of oligoasthenospermia, allows for placement of sperm high into the tube near the ampulla where fertilization takes place. Five continuing pregnancies were reported among 29 women undergoing 46 of 50 (10.9% per procedure) successful canalizations with frozen thawed donor semen. This technique would seem especially applicable in situations where the availability of sperm is limited, such as samples frozen prior to chemotherapy for testicular cancer.

One possible sequence of events might be to perform TIFI in the office before patients undergo transcervical ultrasound GIFT, ZIFT, or TEST. In so doing, the ease of canalization could be evaluated prior to subjecting the patient to the rigors of the operating suite. The best tube for GIFT could be chosen at the time of TIFI. This protocol might shorten operating room scheduling time, and the patient would be sedated for a shorter time intraoperatively when the GIFT, ZIFT, or TEST procedure is performed. In addition, prior knowledge of the uterine, cornual, and tubal architecture could minimize damage to the endometrium at the time of the ART procedure.

Other investigators have explored the use of intrafallopian catheterization guided only by tactile sensation using the Cook K-JIT-1000 and two new devices (Lobotect, Labortechnik, Gottingen, Germany; Baudelocque Black Catheter, BBC Ingenor, Paris, France). Although experience is limited, successes appear comparable to the ultrasound-guided technique, and these devices may prove useful in the future.[22]

Results

As of May 1990, the total number of cases of transcervical assisted reproductive technology procedures was still small, and results varied greatly between centers.

Bustillo and Schulman, using IVF and GIFT failures, obtained two pregnancies in 44 cases for a 4.5% pregnancy rate per procedure (M. Bustillo, personal communication). Of those 44 cases, GIFT was performed on seven occasions (six of which were unilateral), unilateral ZIFT was performed in 19 cycles, and unilateral TEST was performed in 18 cycles. As of March 1990, the cumulative European experience was 387 cycles, of which 85 resulted in conception (22%). Only GIFT cases were reported in this experience (M. Bustillo, personal communication). At the same point in time, Jansen and colleagues obtained five pregnancies in 20 cycles (25%), GIFT was performed in one cycle and ZIFT in the remaining four (R. Woolcott, personal communication). The overall ectopic pregnancy rate with this procedure is between 8 and 14%. Because the total number of cycles is still limited, the benefit of transuterine ultrasound-guided techniques remains to be established.

Technical Difficulties

There are three principal difficulties associated with TIFI: (1) Poor visualization of the catheters. Attempts are continuing to make the catheters easier to visualize to assure fast and atraumatic placement. (2) Failure to canalize. Lateralizing the tip of the outer catheter to the desired cornu is difficult, and perhaps could be improved by increasing the memory of the outer sleeve. (3) Cornual occlusion found at the time of attempted canalization (inability to pass the inner cannula once the outer cannula has been placed). This underlines the need to confirm tubal patency and normalcy prior to initiating such procedures.

In summary, ultrasonic-guided transcervical fallopian tube catheterization with placement of gametes and embryos is a promising technique. It offers the advantages of being an outpatient procedure that does not require administration of general anesthesia. Furthermore, gametes and embryos are not exposed to pH alterations found with laparoscopic procedures, which require pneumoperitoneum. While the technique per se holds great promise, widespread application has not occurred, most likely due to technical difficulties causing fewer successes. The use of this methodology will probably not increase until the development of equipment that allows for more efficient catheter placement into the tubes and more consistent success.

References

1. Steptoe PC, Edwards RG. Birth after re-implantation of a human embryo. Lancet 1978;2:366.
2. Seibel MM. A new era in reproductive technology: in vitro fertilization, gamete intrafallopian transfer, and donated gametes and embryos. N Engl J Med 1988;318:828.
3. Perone N. Gamete intrafallopian transfer (GIFT): historic perspective. J In Vitro Fert Embryo Transf 1991;8:1.
4. Shettles LB. Ova harvest with in vivo fertilization. Am J Obstet Gynecol 1979;133:845.
5. Krietman O, Hodgen GD. Low tubal ovum transfer: an alternative to in vitro fertilization. Fertil Steril 1980;34:374.
6. Tesarik J, Pilka L, Dvorak M, et al. Oocyte recovery, in vitro insemination and transfer into the oviduct after its microsurgical repair at a single laparotomy. Fertil Steril 1983;39:472.
7. McLaughlin DS, Troike DE, Tegenkamp TR, et al. Tubal ovum transfer. A Catholic approved alternative to in-vitro fertilization. Lancet 1987;1:214.
8. Asch RH, Ellsworth IR, Balmaceda JD, Wong PC. Pregnancy after translaparoscopic gamete intrafallopian transfer. Lancet 1987;21:1034.
9. Yee B, Rosen G, Chacon R, Soubrq S, Stone S. Gamete intrafallopian transfer; the effect of the number of eggs used and the depth of gamete placement on pregnancy initiation. Fertil Steril 1989;52:639.
10. Haines CJ, Oshea RT. Unilateral gamete intrafallopian transfer: the preferred method? Fertil Steril 1989;51:518.
11. Balmaceda JP, Gasllaldi C, Renioli J, et al. Tubal embryo transfer as a treatment for infertility due to male factor. Fertil Steril 1988;50:476.
12. Yovich J, Blackledge D, Richardson P, Matson P, Turner S, Draper R. Pregnancy following pronuclear stage tubal transfer. Fertil Steril 1987;48:851.
13. Devroey P, Braeckmans P, Smitz J, Wasesberghe L, Wisanto A, Van Steirteghem A. Pregnancy after translaparoscopic zygote intrafallopian transfer in a patient with sperm antibodies. Lancet 1986;2:1329.
14. Medical Research International, Society for Assisted Reproductive Technology, The American Fertility Society. In vitro fertilization and embryo transfer (IVF-ET) in the United States: 1990 results from the IVF-ET registry. Fertil Steril 1992;57:15.
15. Platia M, Krudy A. Transvaginal fluoroscopic recanalization of a proximally occluded oviduct. Fertil Steril 1985;44:704.
16. Rosch J, Thurmond A, Uchida B, Sovak M. Selective transcervical catheterization: technique update. Radiology 1988;168:1.
17. Confino E, Friberg J, Gleicher N. Transcervical balloon tuboplasty. Fertil Steril 1986;46:963.
18. Jansen R, Anderson M. Catheterization of the fallopian tubes from the vagina. Lancet 1987;2:309.
19. Bustillo M, Schulman J. Review: transcervical ultrasound guided intrafallopian placement of gametes, zygotes and embryos. J In Vitro Fert Embryo Transf 1989;6:321.
20. Hughes E, Shekelton P, Lenonie M, Leeton J. Ultrasound guided fallopian tube catheterization per vaginum; a feasibility study with the use of laparoscopic control. Fertil Steril 1988;50:986.
21. Jansen R, Anderson J, Radonic I, Smit J, Sutherland P. Pregnancies after ultrasound guided fallopian insemination with cryostored donor sperm. Fertil Steril 1988;49:920.
22. Balmaceda JP, Alam V, Borini A. Fallopian tube catheterization. In: Grunfeld L, ed. Infertility and reproductive medicine clinics of North America. Vol. 2. Philadelphia: WB Saunders, October 1991;789.

10
Transcervical Fallopian Tube Catheterization for Diagnosis and Treatment of Female Infertility

Andrew M. Singer and David H. Porter

Fluoroscopically guided hysterosalpingography (HSG) is a routine method of investigation of cervical, uterine, tubal, and peritubal anatomy and pathology. It is a fairly straightforward procedure to perform, has an extremely low complication rate, and is well tolerated by the patient.[1-3] However, there is a significant frequency of transient obstruction to flow of contrast through the tube(s) during HSG, often caused by debris within the tube or spasm of the fallopian tube.[4,5] Glucagon, terbutaline, and other substances have been used without significant success in attempts to prevent spasm.[6,7]

Another cause of pseudoobstruction exists when one fallopian tube has significantly increased resistance to flow of contrast compared to the other, causing preferential filling and selective spilling from the tube with lower flow resistance. These apparent obstructions cannot be differentiated from the true fixed ones on a routine HSG.

A technique of selective fallopian tube catheterization was devised by Platia and Krudy at the NIH in 1985.[8] Extensive technical refinements have been developed and large-scale clinical research has been conducted on the procedure.[5,9-11] Its advantage over conventional HSG is that a small 5-French catheter can be inserted directly into the ostium of the fallopian tube and a selective injection performed. This not only demonstrates tubal anatomy, but pseudoobstructions due to spasm or debris are usually overcome by the higher-pressure direct injection. If evidence of true obstruction exists, recanalization can be attempted by coaxially advancing a fine, floppy, 0.015-inch angiographic guidewire through a 3-French catheter through the region of obstruction. The procedure is safe, effective, and well tolerated by the patient.[10] It requires general anesthesia and is performed on an outpatient basis.

Technique

Fallopian tube catheterization is performed between the seventh and tenth days after onset of menses. Oral antibiotics are administered for 5 days, starting 2 days before the procedure. Oral doxycycline, 100 mg twice a day, is used unless contraindicated. Patients are examined in the angiography suite of the radiology department. The fluoroscopic C-arm in the angiography suite can tilt from side to side as well as from head to foot in the cranial-caudal plane, providing multiangular visualization of tubal and uterine anatomy without necessitating patient movement. The patient is placed in the lithotomy position. A 3l-inch, gradually inclined wooden buttocks support is placed for elevation and to aid in speculum insertion. The patient is prepped and draped in standard fashion. Povidone-iodine cleansing of the perineum and speculum insertion are completed. The cervical os is swabbed with povidone-iodine solution. Intravenous medications for sedation and comfort include midazolam and fentanyl. The vacuum cup is positioned on the cervix and negative pressure applied, forming a tight seal and thereby preventing reflux of contrast from the uterus into the vagina. A nonselective HSG is then performed using water-soluble contrast (Conray 60). Nonionic contrast is used if the patient has a strong history of allergy to iodine.

Under fluoroscopic guidance, a 9-French introducer sheath is inserted just beyond the tip of the Sovak Hysterocath (Cook Inc., Spencer, Indiana) to the approximate junction of the cervical canal and the endometrial cavity. A 0.035-inch (0.89-mm), J-tipped, soft guidewire is passed into the uterus through this sheath. The 9-French catheter is then advanced into the lower uterus. A 5-French curved catheter is then inserted coaxially over this guidewire. The catheter is never advanced without a guidewire beyond its end, since its tip is firm and can perforate the wall of the uterus or tube if not protected by the soft guidewire. Using angiographic techniques, the guidewire and catheter are manipulated and directed toward the proximal tubal ostium. The 5-French catheter is advanced slightly into the tubal ostium. It is sometimes necessary to exchange the J guidewire for a straight one. Contrast is then injected under fluoroscopic observation. If there is excessive reflux into the endometrial cavity from the tip of the 5-French catheter, a 0.015-inch (0.38-mm), platinum-tipped, floppy guidewire is inserted coaxially into the proximal tube and through the 5-French catheter. The catheter is advanced slightly over this wire to achieve better obturation of the tubal ostium. If the obstruction is not reversed by flushing the tube with hand-injecting contrast, gentle probing with the platinum-tipped guidewire is employed. If this is unsuccessful, a 3-French catheter is advanced coaxially to the level of the obstruction. Contrast is injected for better delineation of the distal tubal anatomy (Figs. 10.1, 10.2). Alternatively, a Bard (Bard Reproductive Systems, Billerica, MA) cervical cannula (shaft outside diameter 4 mm, length 25 cm) can be inserted into the uterus and held in plance by a balloon inflated within the uterus and immobilized by a second balloon inflated just below the cervical os (Fig. 10.3). A selective injection catheter (shaft 6-French, length 38 cm) is inserted to the obstructed tubal ostium and if the obstruction is not reversed by flushing the tube with hand-injected contrast, a Teflon-coated steerable guidewire (size 0.018 inch, length 80 cm) can be used to push out or pass through the obstruction (Fig. 10.4).

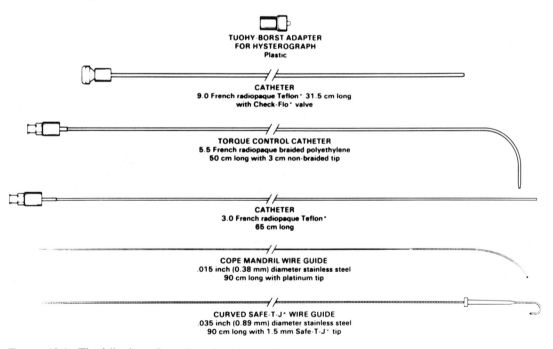

FIGURE 10.1. The fallopian tube catheterization set (Cook OB/GYN, 1100 West Morgan Street, P.O. Box 271, Spencer, Indiana, 47460, 1-800-541-5591).

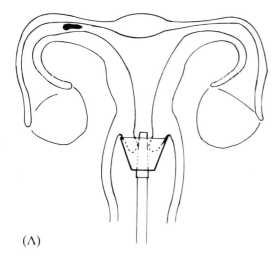

(A)

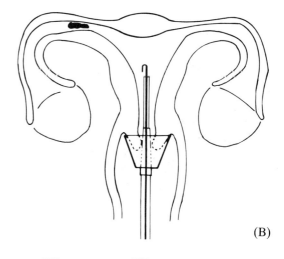

(B)

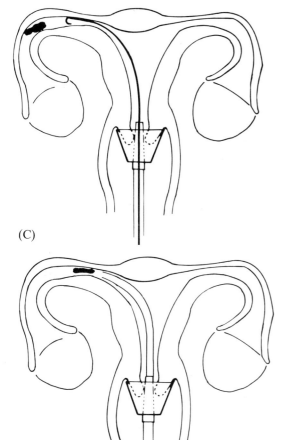

(C)

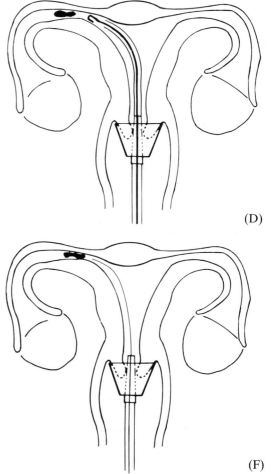

(D)

(E)

(F)

FIGURE 10.2. Fallopian tube catheterization procedure. (A) Vacuum hysterograph cup is inserted into the vagina and its tip directed into the cervical os. (B) A catheter is inserted, with 0.035-inch guidewire advanced just beyond the end of the catheter. (C) The guidewire is advanced to the region of the proximal tubal ostium. (D) A 5-French catheter is inserted over the guidewire and advanced into the proximal tube obstruction. (E) The guidewire is removed and selective ostial salpingogram is performed, demonstrating obstruction. (F) A platinum-tipped guidewire pushes out or passes through the obstruction. (G) A 3-French catheter is advanced over the 0.015-inch, platinum-tipped guidewire to the level of the obstruction. (H) The guidewire opens the obstructed tube by pushing the obstructing plug out of the isthmic portion.

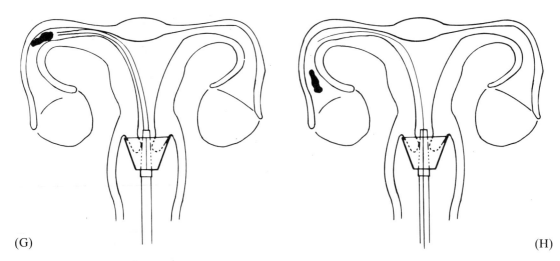

(G)   (H)

FIGURE 10.2. *Continued*

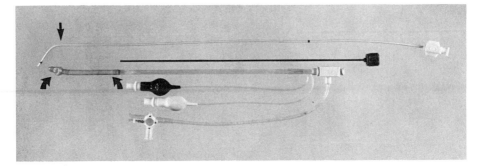

FIGURE 10.3. Fallopian tube catheterization set. Bottom: Bard cervical cannula with curved arrows pointing to location of balloons. Top: The straight arrow points to the selective injection catheter (Bard Reproductive Systems, 5 Federal Street, Billerica, MA 01822, Tel. 1-800-826-BARD). Courtesy of Machelle M. Seibel, M.D.

Another catheter we have found useful is a "directable" one designed by Confino et al.[12] for gamete intrafallopian transfer (GIFT) procedures (Fig. 10.5). This is a 7.5-French catheter whose shape can be changed within the uterus by tip deflection. This has been helpful in two types of patients: patients in whom the Sovak Hysterocath vacuum device (Fig. 10.6) did not seat well on the cervical os or did not provide an airtight seal due to anatomic factors, and those in whom the uterine shape or fibroids prevented introduction of the usual catheter or guidewire into the cornua of the uterus for selective tubal catheterization.

Discussion

This technique works well with mobile or soft obstructions that are often caused by mucus or debris within the fallopian tube. In one study, when 18 tubes resected for proximal tubal obstruction (documented by HSG and laparoscopy) were examined histologically, 11 were not obstructed.[4] Six had amorphous material forming casts, which were referred to as "plugs." Obstructions that are fixed or "hard," usually caused by extensive scarring from prior infections or surgery, may be opened by this guidewire and catheter technique, but often require surgical intervention. A selec-

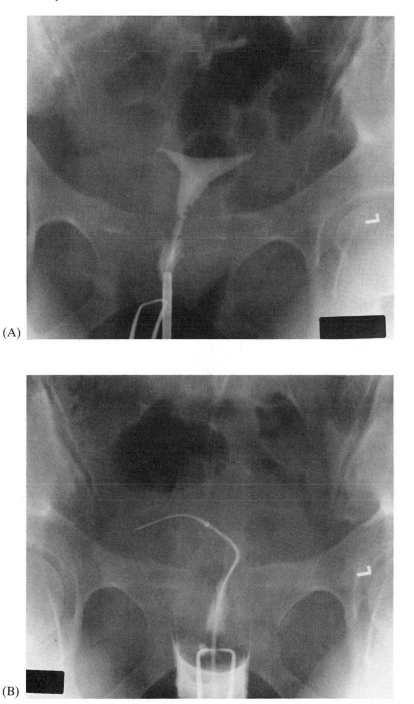

FIGURE 10.4. Fallopian tube catheterization procedure. (A) A baseline hysterosalpingogram is performed demonstrating obstruction. (B) A 0.018-inch Teflon-coated guidewire is advanced through the 6-French selective injection catheter pushing out or passing through the obstruction.

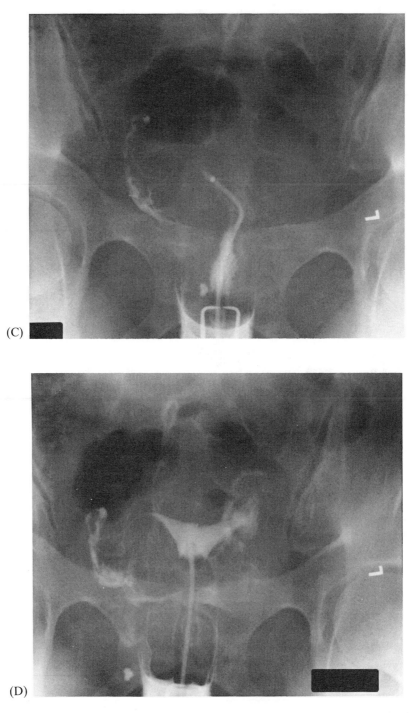

Figure 10.4. *Continued* (C) The guidewire is re- moved and selective ostial salpingogram is per- formed, demonstrating patency. (D) After repeating the procedure on the opposite tube, hysterosalpingo- gram demonstrates bilateral patency. (Courtesy of Machelle M. Seibel, M.D.)

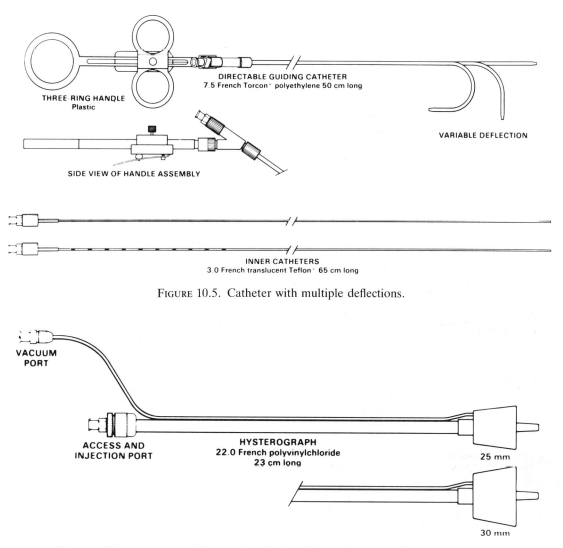

FIGURE 10.5. Catheter with multiple deflections.

FIGURE 10.6. A hysterosalpingography device with a vacuum cup (Cook Hysterocath).

tive injection proximal to this area will give excellent definition of tubal anatomy for planning microsurgical repair. The largest reported series achieved at least one patent tube in 86 of 100 consecutive patients using this technique.[10] The complication rate was very low (5%). There were five perforations by guidewire or catheter of the proximal fallopian tube early in their experience, but at surgery these could not be identified. The success rate in a smaller study group was 90%.[13] In these 22 patients, 38 obstructed tubes were catheterized. Nine tubes (24%) were opened by forceful selective hand

injection alone. In 25 tubes (66%), gentle probing with a guidewire was effective in achieving recanalization. There were four obstructed tubes (10%) in which recanalization was not possible.

Similar results were achieved in 157 patients, 96 of whom had obstructed tubes.[14] Seventy-nine (82%) of patients with obstructed tubes had one or both tubes successfully recanalized.

In our experience, 75% of obstructed tubes that were selectively catheterized were recanalized after selective injection alone or with guidewire probing.

The use of angioplasty balloons was suggested to dilate areas of narrowing.[15] At least one proximally occluded tube was opened in 71 of 77 patient (92%) studied using the balloon method.[16]

Radiation dosimetry calculations for this procedure estimate the fluoroscopic dose to be equivalent to that of a barium enema. This is based on an average exposure time of 8.5 minutes, with careful beam collimation. Total room time for the procedure averages about 1 hour.

Summary

This procedure is safe, effective, and well tolerated by the patient. It is useful for improved diagnosis of fallopian tube pathology, evaluation of previously ligated tubes prior to reanastomosis, and treatment of fallopian tube obstruction. It also has potential use with other infertility procedures such as intratubal placement of ova and sperm.

Questions and Answers

Question. I have a question for Dr. Singer. When attempting transuterine tuboplasty, I have often found that the tubes are open even after a prior laparoscopy or prior HSG has demonstrated obstruction. What percentage of tubes that have previously been shown to have bilateral obstruction either on HSG or on laparoscopy are actually open?

A.S. We found about 20%, and the question is why. I don't think we have a good answer. Part of it might be related to spasm, because most people performing HSG don't use sedation. We do use intravenous sedation during our procedure, which may have something to do with it. I don't know if we are injecting slightly more forcefully perhaps than was done originally. You may also be getting some reflux when you inject dye at laparoscopy. When we perform transuterine tuboplasty we can see fluoroscopically that we are getting reflux and we may be able to wedge the catheter in a little more firmly and know that we are not getting reflux. If we also see that we are not getting

spill, I think that is pretty good evidence that there is true obstruction.

Question. Do you use any premedication such as diazepam or naproxen prior to HSG to prevent tubal spasm?

A.S. I have never done a study with manometry to take a look, but we use the balloon catheters. We put them into the uterus and pull back, then inject, and perhaps we are able to inject at a higher pressure than when you are using the little nipple-ended catheters and tenacula. Maybe that is part of it.

Comment. I'd argue that initially you probably should perform very low-pressure injection because I am sure that the uterine distension causes uterine muscle to contract. Failing that, then approach at a higher pressure.

Dr. Dubuisson (Comment). We are very interested in transcervical catheterization of the tubes. Another indication for transcervical catheterization is ectopic pregnancy.[17] In our group in Paris Dr. Risquez published an article on the use of transcervical catheters for ectopic pregnancy. First we localize the ectopic pregnancy by ultrasonography or radiography. After identifying the ectopic site, we inject methotrexate by transcervical catheter. This is another indication for this very interesting technique.

References

1. Winfield AC, Wentz AC. Diagnostic imaging of infertility. Baltimore: Williams & Wilkins, 1987.
2. Whalen E. The Society of Uroradiology 1989 scientific session, September 23–24. AJR 1990; 154:11–15.
3. Wolf DM, Spatato RF. The current state of hysterosalpingography. Radiographics 1988; 8:1041–1058.
4. Sulak PJ, Letterie GS, Coddington CC, Hayslip CC, Woodward JE, Klein TA. Histology of proximal tubal occlusion. Fertil Steril 1987; 48:437–440.
5. Thurmond AS, Ropsch J, Patton P, Burry KA, Novy M. Fluoroscopic transcervical fallopian tube catheterization for diagnosis and treatment of female infertility caused by tubal obstruction. Radiographics 1988;8:621–640.
6. Thurmond AS, Novy M, Rosch J. Terbutaline in diagnosis of interstitial fallopian tube obstruction. Invest Radiol 1988;23:209–210.

7. Winfield AC, Pittaway D, Maxson W, Daniell J, Wentz AC. Apparent cornual occlusion in hysterosalpingography: Reversal by glucagon. Am Journal Radiol 1982;139:525–527.
8. Platia MP, Krudy AG. Transvaginal fluoroscopic recanalization of a proximally occluded oviduct. Fertil Steril 1985;44(5): 704–706.
9. Thurmond AS, Novy M, Uchida BT, Rosch J. Fallopian tube obstruction: Selective salpingography and recanalization. Radiology 1987; 163:511–514.
10. Thurmond AS, Rosch J. Nonsurgical fallopian tube recanalization for treatment of infertility. Radiology 1990;174:371–374.
11. Thurmond AS, Uchida BT, Rosch J. Device for hysterosalpingography and fallopian tube catheterization. Radiology 1990;174:571–572.
12. Confino E, Friberg J, Gleicher N. A new stirrable catheter for gamete intrafallopian transfer (GIFT). Fertil Steril 1986;46: 1147–1149.
13. Thurmond AS, Rosch J. Fallopian tubes: Improved technique for catheterization. Radiology 1990;174:572–573.
14. Lang EK, Dunaway HE, Roniger WE. Selective osteal salpingography and transvaginal catheter dilation in the diagnosis and treatment of fallopian tube obstruction. Am Journal Radiol 1990;154:735–740.
15. Confino E, Friberg J, Gleicher N. Preliminary experience with transcervical balloon tuboplasty. Am J Obstet Gynecol 1988;159: 370–375.
16. Confino E, Tur-Kaspa I, DeCherney A, et al. Transcervical balloon tuboplasty. A multicenter study. JAMA 1990;264:2079–2028.
17. Risquez F, Mathieson J, Zorn JR. Tubal cannulation via the cervix: a passing fancy—or here to stay? [editorial] J In Vitro Fert Embryo Transf 1990 Dec;7(6):301–3.

11
The Natural Cycle for In Vitro Fertilization

Machelle M. Seibel

Although the first in vitro fertilization (IVF) success occurred using natural cycles, the majority of IVF centers around the world favor the use of ovulation-inducing medications prior to oocyte retrieval. The concept of using ovulation-inducing medications for IVF evolved for a number of reasons. When the procedure was being developed, a laparotomy was required to retrieve oocytes. Laparoscopy replaced laparotomy as the method of choice for oocyte retrieval unless extensive adhesions made laparoscopy unsuitable. In addition, embryo culture techniques were less good, ultrasound had poorer resolution, and the detection of ovulation was less precise. For all of these reasons, the initial results using the natural cycle were poor and a tendency to use medication evolved. An increasingly large number of ovulation-inducing drugs are now being used individually or in combination for IVF. The primary goal of all medicated cycles is to increase the number of available oocytes for fertilization and transfer.

There are also potential disadvantages of using ovulation-inducing agents for IVF. These include the possibility of significant ovarian enlargement, pain, and ovarian hyperstimulation. The ovary develops a "swiss cheese" appearance reflecting multiple follicular development (Fig. 11.1). As a result, the oocyte retrieval requires a longer period of time to perform due to the need for multiple follicle punctures. This is both uncomfortable for the patient and increases the risk of ovarian bleeding.

Multiple births are also a risk following stimulated cycles of IVF. The issue of multiple births is compounded by the fact that the multiple embryos that commonly result may be cryopreserved and lead to subsequent ethical concerns. This potential problem has become more likely with the use of gonadotropin-releasing hormone (GnRH) agonists, which routinely yield large numbers of oocytes per retrieval.

The GnRH agonists do have advantages. Oocyte retrievals are less likely to be canceled, because GnRH agonists reduce the likelihood of a premature LH surge, and increased numbers of oocytes and increased numbers of embryos are typically obtained. However, GnRH agonists do not appear to increase the term pregnancy rate over other forms of treatment. Some disadvantages of GnRH agonists are the added cost of the agonist itself and of the increased gonadotropins that are typically required, as well as the addition of another injection to a patient already receiving an injectable medication.

By comparison, the natural cycle has certain advantages. It requires no medication, no multiple injections, and from the patient's perspective it is more natural and less technological. Only a single injection of human chorionic gonadotropin (HCG) is necessary in order to properly time the oocyte retrieval. The major advantage is simplicity. The natural cycle requires less monitoring than stimulated cycles and the oocyte retrieval is very rapid. The cost for a natural cycle is also reduced due to less need for monitoring and medication. There is virtually no problem of multiple birth, although in our experience both monozygotic and dizygotic twins are possible.

Monitoring with estradiol, luteinizing hormone (LH), and pelvic ultrasound can be

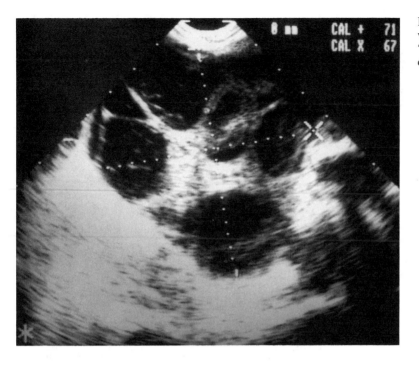

FIGURE 11.1. Ultrasound view of ovary depicting "swiss cheese" appearance of ovarian hyperstimulation.

initiated early in the cycle, although the first ultrasound can be delayed until cycle day 9 if there is no history of a hydrosalpinx, an ovarian cyst or a recent stimulated cycle. The estradiol level should be monitored until it reaches between 180 and 250 pg/ml and the dominant follicle diameter achieves at least 18 mm. Ovulation is triggered with 2,500 to 5,000 IU of HCG, and oocyte retrieval is performed 34 hours following HCG injection (Fig. 11.2). In those instances where there is a presumed LH surge, HCG can be given later in the day, with the retrieval that afternoon or the following morning if there is an absolute certainty about the time of LH surge onset. It is possible in those instances where an LH surge occurs to do the retrieval without administering HCG. In general, those patients who demonstrate an LH surge have a lower rate of conception than those who receive HCG after reaching the above criteria.

We provide luteal phase support, although its need has not been absolutely proven. Because there is only a single follicle present in natural cycles, removing granulosa cells may significantly lower progesterone production, and therefore the potential to alter the luteal

phase in this set of conditions is potentially greater than it is with multiple follicle puncture. Luteal phase support is provided with 1,500 IU of HCG at 3-day intervals, beginning with embryo transfer, for a total of three injections.

The experience gleaned from IVF patients choosing the natural cycle for ovulation monitoring has resulted in a better understanding of those individuals who do and do not achieve pregnancy. Age does not absolutely differentiate those individuals who will conceive, although patients aged 35 years and above are less likely to become pregnant, and those beyond age 38 have a poor prognosis. Cycle lengths are the same in conception and nonconception cycles. Estradiol levels are also similar on the day of HCG (Fig. 11.3). In contrast to stimulated cycles, FSH values on day 3 do not appear predictive of outcome. However, patients unsuccessful in achieving pregnancy with natural cycles appear to have higher FSH levels on cycle days 5 and 7 (Fig. 11.4). In contrast, among patients who do conceive, estradiol levels rise inversely with a diminution of FSH. In this group of patients, FSH levels on days 7 and 9 are quite low.

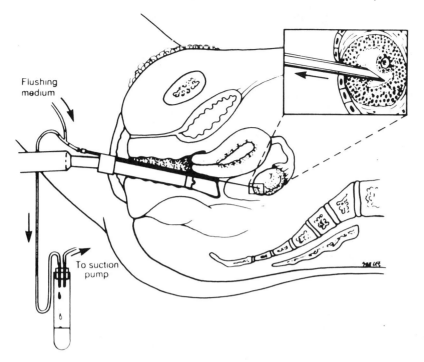

FIGURE 11.2. Schematic drawing of transvaginal ultrasound guided oocyte retrieval. Inset demonstrates needle within the follicle.

Among our patients, day 3 levels of LH are higher (above 19 mIU/ml) in patients for whom fertilization does not occur.

A third pattern of follicular phase estradiol and FSH values has been observed among patients who demonstrate an LH surge. Estradiol levels rise rapidly, and FSH values drop initially, then rise (Fig. 11.4). Finally, there are those individuals who do poorly due to poor follicle development. These patients

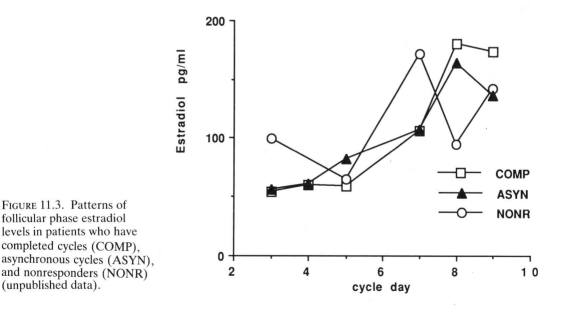

FIGURE 11.3. Patterns of follicular phase estradiol levels in patients who have completed cycles (COMP), asynchronous cycles (ASYN), and nonresponders (NONR) (unpublished data).

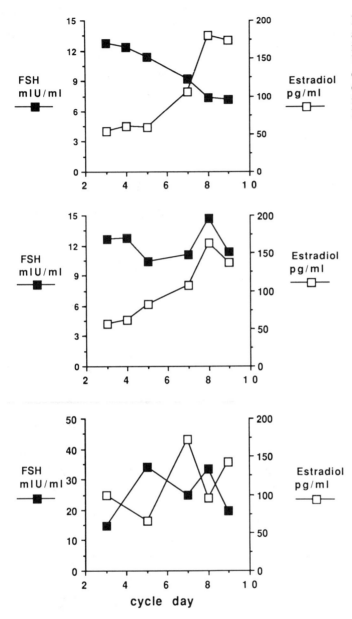

FIGURE 11.4. Patterns of estradiol (E_2) and follicle-stimulating hormone (FSH) in patients undergoing natural cycles. Upper panel is typical of completed cycles, middle panel is typical of asynchronous responders, and lower panel is typical of nonresponders (unpublished data).

demonstrate dysynchrony or a nonsychronized pattern of FSH and estradiol throughout the follicular phase. No pregnancies and occasionally failure to retrieve oocytes result among these patients.

In our experience of nearly 100 regular, natural cycles in which IVF was attempted, only approximately one-third proved to be endocrinologically normal and yielded an embryo for transfer. In an additional one-third of cycles, fertilization failed, and the remaining one-third failed to provide an oocyte. The most important independent variable was age. However, among those patients who did yield an embryo the overall pregnancy rate was 17% per transfer. For patients under age 34 the pregnancy rate was 32% per transfer. If further experience with the natural cycle allows us to select patients carefully, the results should rival those with stimulated cycles. However, it appears that medicated cycles will continue to be necessary for the majority of IVF patients, particularly those beyond 35 years of age.

Bibliography

1. Garcia J. Return to the natural cycle for in vitro fertilization (alleluia! Alleluia!). J In Vitro Fert Embryo Transf 1989;6:67.
2. Paulson RJ, Sauer MV, Lobo RA. In vitro fertilization in unstimulated cycles: A new application. Fertil Steril 1989;51:1059.
3. Foulot H, Ranoux C, Dubuisson JB, Rambaud D, Aubriot FX, Porirot C. In vitro fertilization without ovarian stimulation: A simplified protocol applied in 80 cycles. Fertil Steril 1989; 52:617.
4. Scott RT, Toner JP, Muasher SJ, Oehniger S, Robinson S, Rosenwaks Z. Follicle-stimulating hormone levels on cycle day 3 are predictive of in vitro fertilization outcome. Fertil Steril 1989; 51:651.

12
The Natural Cycle for In Vitro Fertilization: A French Experience

Herve Foulot

The use of the natural cycle for in vitro fertilization (IVF) began in our institution at the end of 1987. A simplified protocol was developed based upon an understanding of the physiology of the menstrual cycle. Three major points are of particular importance. The first point is the realization that the final stages of oocyte maturation are initiated by the luteinizing hormone (LH) surge and are achieved just prior to ovulation.[1,2] Second, spontaneous ovulation occurs between 35 and 42 hours after the onset of the LH surge. Therefore, if the endogenous LH surge is to be used for timing oocyte retrieval, it is necessary to detect its onset. The several LH determinations that are necessary to detect the LH surge are not compatible with laboratory scheduling in most IVF centers. Therefore, to avoid multiple daily measurements of LH we prefer to trigger ovulation with an injection of human chorionic gonadotropin (HCG) before the spontaneous LH surge occurs. Oocyte retrieval is timed for approximately 35 hours following HCG injection. The ideal time of HCG administration is just prior to or coincidental with the onset of the LH surge. HCG administration too early could lead to follicle atresia. To optimize timing of HCG injection, it is necessary to define complementary parameters for follicle maturation incorporating both estradiol (E_2) levels and follicular diameter.

The third point is the biological rhythm of the preovulatory LH surge demonstrated by Seibel et al.,[3] which occurs most often between 5 and 9 A.M. Therefore, a single serum LH determination performed daily at 9 A.M. allows the majority of the LH surge onsets to be detected.

Patient selection is obviously important. Not every candidate for IVF can benefit from unstimulated cycles. Only patients with ovulatory cycles can be included. The quality of the patient population can be indirectly appreciated by an evaluation of the luteal phase, but its proper assessment is cumbersome, requiring serum progesterone determinations and late luteal phase endometrial biopsies in more than one cycle. We therefore rely on an analysis of two recent consecutive basal body temperature charts. If at least one shows a biphasic profile with the luteal phase length greater than 12 days, the patient is offered IVF without stimulation. Two consecutive IVF attempts are currently performed, regardless of the results of the first one. Compared to stimulated cycles, natural cycles can be expected to produce better-quality oocytes because of the natural selection of the dominant follicle. The endometrium is also more receptive because of the lack of hyperestrogenicity induced by ovarian stimulation. Nevertheless, the synchronization between embryo stage and endometrial maturation is not adequate, since the embryo is transferred too early into the uterus. We therefore believe that in women with patent tubes the results may be improved using retrograde tubal transfer of early embryos.

On the ninth day of the cycle,[4] serum E_2 and LH are measured at 9 A.M. and pelvic ultrasound performed. A vaginal probe allows more accurate monitoring of follicular growth. These tests are repeated the next day or 2 days later, depending on the first results. When a preovulatory follicle diameter is observed about 18 mm and the LH surge has not occurred, ovulation is induced using 5,000 IU of HCG. If

TABLE 12.1. Results of 140 consecutive unstimulated IVF cycles.

Number of cycles	140
Cancelled cycles	13 (9.2%)
Spontaneous ovulations	7 (5%)
Recovered oocytes	111 + 4
Potentially fertilizable oocytes	108 + 2
Embryos	96 + 2
Clinical pregnancies	28 (20%/cycle)
Pregnancy deliveries	23 (16.4%/cycle)

there is an onset of the LH surge, the oocyte retrieval is timed for the next afternoon if LH $< 40 \, mIU/ml$, and for the next morning if LH $> 40 \, mIU/ml$.

Most of the first 80 oocyte retrievals we attempted were performed via the transurethral route. The prefilled bladder has the advantage of stabilizing the ovary, which makes follicular puncture easier. Because of its simplicity, follicular puncture is now performed via the transvaginal route. However, in some cases the ovary is extremely mobile, which occasionally results in follicular rupture during the procedure. The results of 140 consecutive IVF unstimulated cycles performed on 118 patients are shown in Table 12.1. The mean age of the patients was 33 years. The indications for IVF were tubal factor in 76%, unexplained infertility in 16%, endometriosis 8%, and cervical factor 0.4%. Couples with male factor infertility were excluded.

Thirteen cycles were canceled, with inadequate E_2 rise or premature LH surge being the main reasons. In seven cases pelvic ultrasound performed immediately prior to oocyte collection revealed follicle disappearance. One hundred ten preovulatory oocytes were recovered, of which 101 were fertilized (92%)

and 98 cleaved (89%) Two preovulatory oocytes were recovered in two patients, and 28 clinical pregnancies were obtained (20%). Table 12.2 shows the monitoring of a 33-year-old patient with tubal infertility who achieved an ongoing pregnancy. We have compared the LH surge group with the no surge–HCG group. Both groups attained similar plasma E_2 levels and follicular diameter on the day of HCG and on the LH surge day. The cleavage rate is significantly higher in the no surge–HCG group than in the LH surge group (Table 12.3), probably because of the short interval between the onset of the LH surge and the recovery of the oocyte. Significantly more patients became pregnant in the no surge–HCG group than in the LH surge group (pregnancy rates of 22.7 and 7.7%, respectively, $p < 0.05$) (Table 12.4).

These results excluded cases with male infertility because we wished to evaluate first the effectiveness of unstimulated cycles. When IVF is considered for male infertility, it may be necessary for women to undergo ovarian stimulation, since the fertilization rate is greatly reduced compared to other infertility etiologies. An open randomized study to compare the fertilization rate of oocytes obtained during stimulated and unstimulated IVF cycles

TABLE 12.3. Comparison of HCG group with LH surge group.

	HCG	LH surge
N	88	39
Fertilizable oocytes	74 + 2	34
Embryos	71 + 2	25
Cleavage rate	96%[a]	73.5%[a]

[a] $p < 0.05$.

TABLE 12.2. Monitoring a typical successful cycle.

Cycle day	E_2 (pg/ml)	LH (mIU/ml)	Follicle diameter (mm)	HCG 3,000 IU 11:00 P.M.	Oocyte retrieval 9:30 A.M.	Embryo transfer 4-cell
9	45	6				
10	90	6	17			
11	160	7	18			
12 A.M.	200	8	20			
12 P.M.	280	11		x		
14					x	
16						x

TABLE 12.4. Comparison of IVF outcome between LH surge group and HCG group.

	Pregnancies	Deliveries	Ectopic pregnancies	Spontaneous abortion
No LH surge	24 + 1 (DIPI)*	19 + 1 (22.7%[a])	4	1
LH surge	3	3 (7.7%[a])	0	0

[a] $p < 0.05$.
* DIPI = Direct intrapeutoneal insemination

for male factor is necessary. Compared to stimulated cycles, natural cycles can be expected to produce better-quality oocytes because of natural selection of the dominant follicle and a better endometrial receptivity due to the lack of hyperestrogenicity induced by ovarian stimulation. Nevertheless, the synchronization between embryo stage and endometrial maturation may not be adequate, since the embryo may be transferred too early into the uterus. We therefore believe that in women with patent tubes the results may be improved using retrograde tubal transfer of early embryos.

When medically assisted procreation is considered, it appears reasonable to begin by using the simplest, least expensive, and least dangerous techniques. Unstimulated cycles have these advantages in normally ovulating candidates for IVF.

Questions and Answers

Question. Among the patients you decide are good candidates for natural cycle IVF, is part of your selection process a serial ultrasound examination?

H.F. No. We use only basal body temperature charts.

Question. How about you, Dr. Seibel?

M.S. No. We simply go on the history of a normal cycle. When we first started using natural cycles, we were not using HCG to trigger ovulation. This made the procedure very complicated, because the patient would ovulate and invariably we would have problems getting access to the operation room. We were also often unable to measure LH

frequently enough to detect the onset of the LH surge in order to schedule the oocyte retrieval.

When LH is monitored throughout ovulation, at least three patterns are seen. The first is a typical pattern that rises to a peak and then returns to baseline. Another pattern rises less high and has a sawtoothed sustained plateau. The third pattern has a shoulder that rises slowly. It is helpful to know that most LH surges occur in the morning, so that if one sees a morning LH rise it is likely to be the LH surge. However, more than a single morning LH is often necessary to identify the LH surge onset in all patients.

Many of our initial natural-cycle patients were biologically older and had not done well with stimulated cycles. Therefore, it should not have been surprising that they did not do well with natural cycles either.

We calculated the FSH:LH ratio, and if it was below 1 on day 9 the patients usually did not make it to retrieval, even if serum E_2 and ultrasound appeared to be normal that same day.

Question. Do you monitor progesterone levels?

H.F. No, we don't monitor progesterone levels during the luteal phase.

Question. What was the average age of the patients in your study?

H.F. The average age was 33 years. We observed that in patients above 38 the results were very poor, and we now tend to eliminate these patients. We think that in patients over 38 the number of abnormal cycles with abnormal ovulation is greater than in patients less than 38. I think that if one wants to obtain good results with unstimulated cycles, it is important to treat patients under 38.

S.S. That is true with stimulated cycles also.

H.F. That is true.

M.S. Some of our patients had a picture of polycystic ovary syndrome that really wasn't picked up by biochemical parameters. On the day 3 baseline ultrasound they had an average of eight small follicles less than 8 mm in diameter, as opposed to 2.5 small follicles in the patients who ended up having a normal cycle. Of particular interest was the fact that in some patients the day 3 ultrasound did not show very many small follicles. However, a multitude of small follicles showed up on day 5 as if they had been there for a long time, finally appearing once they got the stimulus from FSH. There were many more small follicles in the patients who had asynchronus development.

H.F. We don't perform a baseline scan at day 3. Sometimes on day 9 we observe a lot of small follicles in patients who ovulated between day 16 and 18. Afterward there is a natural selection: the small follicles disappear and only the dominant follicle reaches a preovulatory diameter of, for example, 20 mm.

We do only one ultrasound on day 9 to draw a conclusion of synchrony of follicular development.

Question. What was the earliest day you saw a spontaneous LH surge that ended up in pregnancy?

H.F. I think day 9.

References

1. Testart J, Frydman R, Feinstein MC, Thebault A, Roger M, Scholler R. Interpretation of plasma luteinizing hormone assay for the collection of mature oocytes from women: Definition of a luteinizing hormone surge-initiating rise. Fertil Steril 1981;36:50
2. Seibel MM, Smith DM, Levesque L, Borten M, Taymor ML. The temporal relationship between the luteinizing hormone surge and human oocyte maturation. Am J Obstet Gynecol 142;569:1982.
3. Seibel MM, Shine W, Smith DM, Taymor ML. Biological rhythm of the luteinizing hormone surge in women. Fertil Steril 1982;37:709.
4. Foulot H, Ranoux C, Dubuisson JB, Rambaud D, Aubriot FX, Poirot C. In vitro fertilization without ovarian stimulation: A simplified protocol applied in 80 cycles. Fertil Steril 1989; 52:617.

13
Expression of Proto-Oncogenes in Mammalian Gametes and Embryos

A.A. Kiessling

The seminal discovery that the ability of retroviruses to transform normal cells into malignant cells is due to the incorporation of cellular genes into the viral genome[1] led to a new era of thinking about cancer. It became clear that malignant transformation was not the consequence of acquiring new genes, but the result of alterations in existing cellular genes. These findings heralded new ways of investigating malignant cells and, perhaps even more important, provided support for the concept that the similarities between malignant cells and embryonic cells are due to expressions of the same gene programs. Traits in common, such as growth patterns and protein expression, had long been noted by embryologists and oncologists, but investigational tools to examine these similarities in malignant and embryonic cells were unavailable. The knowledge that the transforming genes of retroviruses had their origins in the normal genetic repertoire of cells changed this by immediately creating a new scientific subspecialty: the isolation and characterization of the transforming genes, now known as oncogenes. This burgeoning field of research has led to the discovery of genes important to all aspects of cell function. Moreover, the sensitive molecular biological techniques developed as a result of these efforts have opened the way for similar explorations in the early embryo.

This chapter contains a general overview of oncogenes and proto-oncogenes. Also included is an introductory description of the molecular biological techniques used to explore expression of these interesting genes in gametes and embryos. The proto-oncogenes and growth factors known at this time to be expressed in mammalian gametes and embryos, principally mouse, are described individually.

Oncogenes and Proto-Oncogenes

Oncogenes are altered versions of normal cellular genes called proto-oncogenes.[1] An overview of the molecular biology of both will help clarify their possible roles as regulators of cell functions. To qualify as an oncogene, a gene must be shown to share base sequence homology with a retroviral oncogene, to transform cells in culture, or to be present in some neoplasia as a gene that is rearranged or amplified. Oncogenes can be grouped according to their type of genetic alteration and their possible cell function. The alterations in the normal cellular proto-oncogenes that give rise to oncogenes generally involve one or more of three mechanisms:

1. A change in the regulation of gene expression; this usually does not involve a mutation in the proto-oncogene itself.
2. A point mutation in the proto-oncogene; this leads to an amino acid substitution in the protein product, which results in a protein with altered function or response to cellular controls.
3. Gene sequence rearrangements; these usually result in protein products with

increased activity within the cell, either by virtue of being expressed at higher concentrations, or as the result of the synthesis of recombinant fusion proteins with altered cell functions or response to cellular controls.

Approximately 70 oncogenes (and their proto-oncogene counterparts) have been identified. They comprise a highly conserved class of genes found within vertebrates and invertebrates alike that profoundly influence cell behavior. With a few exceptions, they encode proteins in five functional groups: (1) growth factors; (2) plasma membrane proteins with tyrosine kinase activity, including several growth factor receptors; (3) plasma membrane guanine nucleotide binding proteins, including some known hormone receptors; (4) cytoplasmic proteins with serine-threonine kinase activity, known to function in signal transduction, as discussed below; and (5) nuclear proteins, including known regulators of messenger RNA (mRNA) transcription. It is important to note that these functional groups of proteins are key elements in the response of cells to external stimuli.

Proto-oncogenes immediately gained the interest of developmental biologists as a class of potentially important genes in the regulation of morphogenesis.[2-7] However, exploration of these possibilities had to await some refinements in molecular biology that allowed the investigation of these genes in small amounts of developing tissues. The three most important refinements are (1) nucleic acid hybridization in situ with RNA probes; (2) the introduction of synthetic gene sequences and constructs into developing gametes and embryos, and analysis of the results; and (3) detection of gene expression in single embryos by a combination of reverse transcription of RNAs to complementary DNAs (cDNAs) and amplification of cDNAs of interest by the polymerase chain reaction (PCR). A description and discussion of each of these techniques, in addition to more standard techniques of analyzing gene expression, will provide a useful reference for the findings presented later in this chapter.

Methods of Studying Gene Expression During Development

Northern Analysis

This method is standard for the analysis of messenger mRNA species within a cell. It requires isolation of RNA free of DNA, electrophoresis in a semisolid medium such as agarose gels for size separation, and transfer of the banded RNAs to a solid membrane filter such as nylon or nitrocellulose. The presence and size of specific mRNA gene products of interest are then determined by hybridization of the filter with radiolabeled DNA or RNA sequences (probes) homologous to the gene of interest. This method is semiquantitative for the amount of mRNA expressed per total RNA extracted and has become a routine technique for studies of gene expression. It requires on the order of thousands of copies of RNA for detection. Although this approach has led to the successful identification of several oncogenes in germ cells and postimplantation embryos, one disadvantage is that cells must be presorted to identify cell-type-specific gene expression.

Dot-Blot Analysis

A modification of the above method involves placing serial dilutions of RNA samples on filters as "dots." The filters are then hybridized with gene probes as described above. This approach has been used to investigate small amounts of RNAs in a semiquantitative way. It has the advantage of possibly increasing the concentration of RNAs and thus the sensitivity of detecting a specific transcript, but the disadvantage of not revealing any information about transcript sizes.

Hybridization In Situ

Gene expression is ultimately determined by the appearance of protein products. To this end, sensitive histologic methods of antibody detection of specific proteins in cells have been developed. A potential problem with these methods, however, is the risk that the site of protein detection may be the site of action rather than the cell of origin. To circumvent this problem, sensitive histologic methods of detecting mRNAs in cells have been developed. Early techniques used cDNA sequences as probes that were labeled with radioisotopes or bound to ligands that could be detected, such as biotin. These methods have been successful in a number of embryo experiments (e.g., cell lineage studies in chimeric mice) but have a major drawback in that there is a significant amount of nonspecific binding of DNA to proteins in many types of cells. This creates unpredictable background binding of the DNA probes, which limits the sensitivity of detection to those cells with large numbers of unique sequences.

Since RNA transcripts of interest may be expressed at relatively low abundance for brief periods of time, their detection requires sensitive techniques with low, measurable levels of background. For these reasons, plasmid vectors have been developed that contain transcriptional start sites which allow the synthesis of RNA strands complementary to both the plus and minus strands of the gene of interest. The gene sequences are inserted into the "ribo-vector" between transcriptional start sites (Fig. 13.1). RNA polymerases then synthesize single-stranded RNA molecules in each orientation, thus creating "sense" and "antisense" RNAs. The antisense RNA strands hybridize with the specific mRNA of interest in the cells, whereas the sense strands do not, but instead bind to nonspecific RNA-binding proteins that are present. Thus the sense control provides an essential assessment of nonspecific background binding. This approach has revealed proto-oncogene expression in oocytes and embryos, as discussed below.

Introduction of Synthetic Gene Constructs

Gene constructs are commonly introduced into gametes and developing embryos in two ways. The first is microinjection, the basis for the production of transgenic mice. Constructs containing oncogenes have been commonly used in these studies and have provided valuable information about the consequences of oncogene expression, but have not provided information about the normal role of proto-oncogenes during development. For this reason, experiments involving "oncomice" will not be considered further here.

Other work, however, involves microinjection of various types of constructs into oocytes and embryos for the purposes of probing gene function and gene expression. Gene function can be examined by measuring the effects of blocking gene expression as well as inducing gene expression. The first experimental approach uses synthetically prepared oligomers (approximately 20 bases long) of DNA whose sequence is complementary (antisense) to the

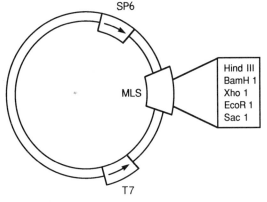

FIGURE 13.1. Schematic of a ribo-vector containing transcriptional start sites for SP6 and T17 RNA polymerases.

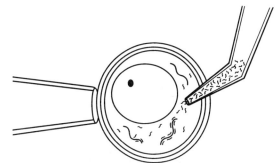

FIGURE 13.2. Microinjection of antisense oligonucleotides into the cytoplasm of a germinal vesicle stage oocyte.

mRNA of interest (Fig. 13.2). Such oligo-deoxyribonucleotides hybridize to the message and, with the help of a specific nuclease that degrades such RNA–DNA hybrids, render the cell depleted of message and hence the protein product. This is a powerful approach to blocking those functions that depend upon expression of the gene under study. A problem interpreting the results of such studies is the potential toxicity of the microinjected constructs to the oocyte or embryo, resulting in nonspecific aberrant oocyte behavior. It is possible to control for this problem by microinjecting random, nonsense oligomers of the same percent base composition and purity as the specific antisense oligomers. If not toxic, such control oligomers should have little or no effect on oocyte function. As discussed below, such an approach has been used to successfully probe the function of the proto-oncogene c-mos in oocytes.[8,9]

The effects of inducing gene expression can be measured by designing a synthetic construct in which the gene of interest is linked to a transcriptional promoter known to be active in the developing embryo. Examples of such promoters that have been used in mammalian oocytes and embryos are the promoters for thymidine kinase gene and the SV40 virus genes.[10,11] The introduction of such constructs leads to an overexpression of the gene, the consequences of which can be determined during subsequent development. This approach is analogous to the production of transgenic mice discussed above. Since its use

in probing gene function during defined stages of embryo development is just beginning, none of the studies described here result from these types of experiments, but it is anticipated that this approach will be useful in the future.

Studies of gene expression include ascertaining if a specific gene is normally active during development, and describing the nature of the regulatory elements necessary for its expression at that developmental stage. To determine if a specific gene is normally active during development, it is possible to take advantage of the specificity of the interaction between transcriptional regulators and their recognition sequences in the regulatory elements that control mRNA synthesis. Synthetic constructs can be engineered that involve the putative regulatory region of the gene of interest linked to a "reporter gene" that encodes a protein that is easily detected and for which there is no background activity in the cell of interest (Fig. 13.3). Examples of commonly used reporter genes are the bacterial genes CAT, which encodes chloramphenicol acetyl transferase, and lacZ, which encodes ß-galactosidase. Another sensitive reporter gene used more recently is the one encoding the firefly enzyme luciferase. If the reporter gene product is expressed, this suggests that the cells must be expressing the transcription factors specific for the gene of interest and, therefore, that the gene itself is normally expressed.

Alternatively, if the regulatory regions are not known, this approach can be used to map

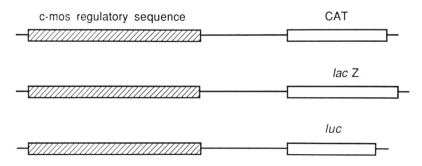

FIGURE 13.3. Example of synthetic gene constructs of the c-mos regulatory sequence linked to reporter genes. CAT encodes chloramphenicol acetyl transferase, lacZ encodes ß-galactosidase, and luc encodes luciferase.

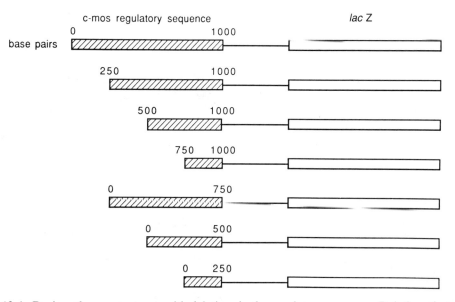

FIGURE 13.4. Design of gene constructs with deletions in the regulatory sequence. Deletions that result in a loss of activity help define the key sequences necessary for expression of the *lacZ* reporter gene.

them. For example, a construct can be made that contains the putative regulatory region of interest linked to a reporter gene. The precise location and nucleotide sequence of regulatory elements can be determined by construction of a series of deletion mutants in the suspected regulatory region (Fig. 13.4). Microinjection of each of the deletion mutants in parallel experiments will reveal the mutations that result in markedly decreased expression of the reporter gene. The regions sensitive to mutation likely comprise the regulatory region, a possibility that can be examined directly by introducing new constructs containing only the putative regulatory sequences and examining embryos for expression of the gene.

An alternative to microinjection of synthetic gene constructs takes advantage of the possibility of infecting early embryos with a retrovirus that contains the gene of interest. Retroviral vectors have been developed specifically for this purpose. Such vectors are retroviruses that are defective for replication because much of the genetic information for packaging their RNA genomes into infectious virus particles has been deleted and replaced by the synthetic gene constructs of interest. Such engineered virus vectors can be propagated in specially transformed cell lines designed to express the information necessary for virus packaging. Thus, the engineered viruses can undergo one round of infection in normal cells, but produce no infectious progeny. Therefore, embryonic cells infected at a specific stage of development (e.g., early blastocysts) will incorporate the viral genome into their own genes, but will not produce infectious progeny virus. Thus, the only cells that contain viral genes are those originally infected. By monitoring the expression of a reporter gene in cells throughout development, it is theoretically possible to track the cell lineages that arise from the originally infected stem cells. This approach has been applied successfully to studies of cell lineages[12] and may prove useful for understanding specific roles for proto-oncogenes in development, although such studies are just beginning.

Reverse Transcription and the Polymerase Chain Reaction

An alternative and theoretically more sensitive approach to studies of gene expression in embryos is the detection of mRNAs in single cells. Techniques to accomplish this have recently been developed as the combination of two molecular biology methods: reverse transcription of RNAs into cDNA copies, and amplification of single DNA copies to detectable levels by the PCR. See Chapter 24 for a complete description of this technique. This combined approach has already revealed the expression of three proto-oncogenes in pre-implantation mouse embryos, as discussed below.

Gene Expression in Early Development

To understand fully the controls on embryonic development, it is necessary to chronicle key switches in gene expression. Toward this end, it is useful to consider early development from the standpoint of changes in the genes being expressed. Three programs of gene expression are unique to conception and early cleavage:

1. The program expressed in mature gametes that directs fertilization;

2. The cleavage program that begins in the zygote or two-cell embryo and directs the early cleavages that occur without cell commitment;

3. The program of initial cell commitment at the late morula/early blastocyst stage that gives rise to trophoblast and inner cell mass (ICM) cells.

Discovering the factors that govern the transitions and expression of each of these three programs is an exciting chapter in developmental biology that is beginning to be written. The characteristics of proto-oncogenes, that is, highly conserved, powerful cell regulators of known DNA sequence, have made them attractive candidates for initial exploration. The work has begun by investigations of proto-oncogene expression in mammalian gametes.

Proto-Oncogenes Expressed During Gametogenesis

Spermatogenesis

The production of mature sperm includes premeiotic stages (spermatogenesis) and postmeiotic cell remodeling (spermiogenesis). Spermatogenesis encompasses all the stages of mitosis leading to type B spermatogonia and the subsequent two meiotic cleavages that give rise to round spermatids. Spermiogenesis is the morphologic remodeling of the haploid round spermatid into a flagellated, motile, fertile spermatozoon.[13] Methods for isolating purified populations of these cell types at distinct stages of development have been devised, and their RNA contents have been studied by Northern analysis and hybridization in situ. Most of the work has been done in mice. Three distinct patterns of proto-oncogene expression during spermatogenesis and spermiogenesis have been reported: (1) those proto-oncogenes expressed throughout spermatogenesis and spermiogenesis; (2) those expressed in cells late in spermatogenesis, at the transition to spermiogenesis; and (3) those expressed in postmeiotic cells undergoing spermiogenesis (Fig. 13.5).

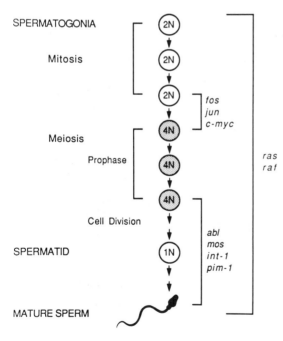

FIGURE 13.5. Summary schematic of proto-oncogenes expressed during spermiogenesis and spermatogenesis in the mouse.

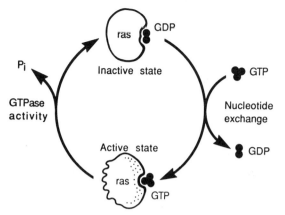

FIGURE 13.6. Activation pathway of *ras*, a guanine nucleotide-binding protein.

Proto-Oncogenes Expressed Throughout Sperm Maturation

Two proto-oncogenes, *ras* and *raf*, are expressed throughout spermatogenesis and spermiogenesis.[14–16] *Ras*, the first human oncogene discovered,[1] encodes a 21-kilodalton guanine nucleotide-binding protein. The three known members of the *ras* family are *ras*H (discovered as the oncogene in the Harvey rat sarcoma virus), *ras*N (discovered as the transforming gene in neuroblastomas), and *ras*K (the transforming gene of Kirsten leukemia virus). *Ras* is the only proto-oncogene for which the x-ray crystallographic structure is known. When bound to guanosine diphosphate (GDP) it is in an inactive state; when bound to guanosine triphosphate (GTP) it is activated. *Ras* possesses a GTPase activity that hydrolyzes GTP to GDP, thus down-regulating its own activity. The bound GDP must be displaced by incoming GTP for reactivation (Fig. 13.6).

GTP binding is an early event in several of the intracellular reaction chains known as signal transduction pathways. These pathways are the molecular events that link the cell's surface to internal responses such as synthesis of specific cell products for exportation or cell division. As most cell responses involve changes in gene expression, most signal transduction pathways link the cell's surface plasma membrane to the nucleus. The chain of bio-

chemical reactions that comprise the pathways regularly includes changes in the phosphorylation state of protein components, which leads to alterations in their enzyme activities. Many of these changes are mediated by small, soluble molecules such as cyclic adenosine monophosphate (cAMP) and inositol 1,4,5-triphosphate (IP3). These diffusible compounds are commonly called second messengers.

As a member of the G-protein family, *ras* is a candidate for regulation by a number of protein hormones. For example, one known function of gonadotropins is to activate a G protein, which in turn activates adenylate cyclase, which leads to increases in cAMP levels and consequent activation of cAMP-dependent protein kinase. Alternatively, G protein activation can lead to hydrolysis of the phospholipid, phosphatidylinositol 4,5-bisphosphate (PIP$_2$), by phospholipase C. This hydrolysis leads to the production of 1,2 diacylglycerol (DAG) and IP$_3$. DAG activates protein kinase C, and IP$_3$ stimulates the release of calcium stores. Although *ras* expression in yeast affects both of these G protein pathways, in mammalian cells there is no evidence that *ras* influences the cAMP-dependent pathways. Thus, *ras* appears to be a specialized G protein for which neither the effector that stimulates *ras* activity nor the target for its activity are known. It is known that the phospholipid pathway is influenced by *ras* expression in somatic mammalian cells, and the effect of this stimulation is cell division. Whether or not this same pathway is involved in male germ cells is not known. *Ras* has been reported to induce meiosis in *Xenopus* oocytes, which may be a clue to its function in male germ cells. It is certain that studies of the function of *ras* in maturing germ cells will provide important insights into its function in other mammalian cells as well.

Raf encodes a protein kinase that phosphorylates the amino acids serine and threonine. It was discovered as the oncogene in two retroviruses: a mouse sarcoma virus and an avian carcinoma virus.[1] Three members of the *raf* proto-oncogene family have been identified to date: c-*raf*-1, A-*raf*, and B-*raf*. The best-characterized are c-*raf*-1 and A-*raf*, which

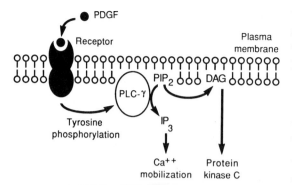

FIGURE 13.7. Example of *raf* activation by cell surface receptors of growth factors such as platelet-derived growth factor (PDGF).

encode proteins of 73 and 69 kilodaltons, respectively. *Raf* proteins contain protein kinase catalytic domains in their carboxyterminal halves and regulatory sequences in their aminoterminal halves. Phosphorylation of amino acid residues in the regulatory regions activates the protein kinase domain. Thus, as exemplified in Figure 13.7, binding of growth factors such as platelet-derived growth factor (PDGF), and epidermal growth factor (EGF) to their respective receptors on the cell surface results in phosphorylation of tyrosine in the *raf* protein, which converts it from an inactive to an active state. Treatment of cells with phorbol ester mitogens also results in increased *raf* activity. As expected, since phorbol esters act by stimulation of protein kinase C, which phosphorylates serine and threonine, *raf* contains phosphoserine when activated in response to phorbol ester treatment. Thus, the response of at least two plasma membrane sentinels to environmental stimuli is to activate *raf*, each by phosphorylating a different animo acid. As none of the targets for *raf* protein activity are known, it can only be speculated that the specific amino acid phosphorylated influences the target for *raf* phosphorylation of serine or threonine. Its position as a soluble, cytoplasmic protein suggests a central role for *raf* in the signal transduction pathways invoked by growth hormones and phorbol esters and leading to cell division. More recent evidence suggesting that *raf* activation can substitute for *ras* activation in cell division[1] further supports the role for *raf* as a central figure in mitosis signal transduction. The need for rapid cell cleavages without DNA replication suggests a possible role for *raf* in germ cell maturation.

Oncogenes Expressed at the Transition to Meiotic Prophase

Three nuclear oncogenes, *fos*, *jun*, and *myc*, are specifically expressed in type B spermatogonia, the final stage of sperm maturation prior to entry into meiosis.[15] *Fos* and *jun* are members of the diverse family of proteins that control gene expression known as transcription factors.[1] As discussed above, these proteins regulate gene expression by initiating or terminating mRNA synthesis. Although the process is not fully understood, it is known that transcription factors have a domain that binds to a specific DNA sequence and another domain that interacts with mRNA synthesis machinery. *Fos* was first identified as the oncogene of a murine osteosarcoma virus and *jun* as the oncogene of an avian sarcoma virus. Their proto-oncogene protein products form a heterodimer that binds to a symmetrical palindrome in DNA (Fig. 13.8). This palindrome is a member of a family of binding sequences whose consensus is TGA(C/G)TCA. Genes containing these sequences interact with a family of transcription factors known as AP-1. This family of transcription factors was first defined as responsible for gene expression after mammalian cells were exposed to phorbol esters.

As shown in Figure 13.8, the protein dimer is held together by hydrogen bonding between two leucine-rich regions of the proteins, the so-called leucine zipper. Since dimerization is essential for function, regulation of the expression of either *fos* or *jun* will affect the activity of this transcription factor. Three members of the *jun* family have been identified, c-*jun*, *jun*-B, and *jun*-D, encoding proteins of 47 and 40 kilodaltons respectively. Two members of the *fos* family have been identified, c-*fos* and *fos*-B, encoding proteins of 62 and 45 kilodaltons, respectively. These transcription factors appear to be essential for changes in cell status, presumably by acting to

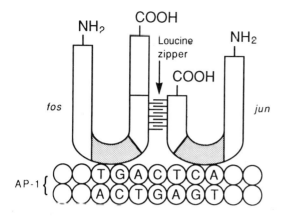

FIGURE 13.8. The heterodimer, *fos* and *jun*, forming the leucine zipper and binding to an AP-1 transcription regulating site in DNA.

turn on the expression of the gene program responsible for either differentiation or mitosis. Their role in male germ cells is unknown.

Myc was identified as the oncogene in an avian myelocytomatosis virus. There are three members of the *myc* proto-oncogene family, c-*myc*, L-*myc*, and N-*myc*, which encode proteins ranging from 60 to 66 kilodaltons. Although *myc* was one of the first oncogenes discovered,[1] little is known about its function. It binds nonspecifically to DNA and contains a lysine-rich leucine zipper region, suggesting its possible role as a transcription factor. In tumors it is frequently present in amplified DNA sequences and is overexpressed many-fold relative to normal cells. Its role in germ cells is unknown.

Oncogenes Expressed in Haploid Male Germ Cells

Transcripts of four proto-oncogenes have been detected in postmeiotic germ cells (Fig. 13.5). One (*int*-1) encodes an extracellular protein, and three (*abl, pim*-1, and *mos*) encode protein kinases.

Int-1 was first identified as the oncogene associated with mouse breast carcinomas induced by the retrovirus murine mammary tumor virus (MMTV).[17] This was an early example of oncogenicity by overexpression of a normal proto-oncogene. *Int*-1 overexpression was found to be necessary for tumor formation and was due to the integration of the MMTV

provirus adjacent to *int*-1. The powerful transcriptional promoter function of the retrovirus promoter is responsible for overexpression of *int*-1. Once identified, the sequence of *int*-1 was found to be that of a gene in *Drosophila* termed *wingless*. Mutations in *wingless* lead to malformations in the larval thorax that give rise to wingless offspring. It has been found more recently to be associated with the developing mouse embryo, discussed below. The sequence of the protein encoded by *int*-1 suggests that it is a secreted protein, a possibility corroborated by its characteristics in mammary tumors and developing *Drosophila* embryos. The mechanism by which it induces tumor formation and influences morphogenesis is unknown, but available evidence suggests that it is an extracellular matrix protein with growth-stimulating activity. Its role in male germ cells[18,19] is unknown.

Abl was first identified as the transforming gene in a murine leukemia virus and is the human oncogene activated by the Philadelphia chromosome translocation in chronic myelogenous leukemia.[1] It encodes a kinase of approximately 145 kilodaltons that phosphorylates tyrosine. It is not associated with the plasma membrane and appears to be a soluble, cytoplasmic enzyme, although more recent evidence indicates a significant amount is also found in the nucleus. Although it is clear that elevation of *abl* activity leads to cell proliferation, the target for *abl* has not been identified. It is expressed as a smaller transcript (4.7 kilobases) in mouse male germ cells (principally in postmeiotic cell types) than in somatic cells[20]; its role in male germ cells is unknown.

Pim-1 encodes a 36 kilodalton protein kinase that phosphorylates serine and/or threonine. It was originally isolated as the oncogene activated in mouse T-cell leukemias by adjacent integration of a murine leukemia provirus. Its oncogenic activity is due to overexpression of the normal gene product for which the target is unknown. It is expressed as a 2.4-kilobases transcript in postmeiotic stages of spermatogenesis[15]; its function is unknown.

Mos, like *pim*-1, encodes a relatively small protein kinase (43 kilodaltons) that phosphorylates serine and/or threonine and may be lacking a regulatory domain. *Mos* was originally identified as the oncogene in a murine sarcoma virus. A noteworthy characteristic of *mos* is that its normal expression is largely restricted to male and female germ cells.[21–24] *Mos* transcripts in male germ cells, most abundant in postmeiotic early spermatids, are somewhat larger (1.7 kilobases) than those in female germ cells (1.4 kilobases) because they are transcribed from different promoter regions. Its function in male germ cells is unknown, but the increasing body of evidence for its function in oocytes, discussed below, may provide some clues.

Summary

The identification of RNA transcripts of these nine proto-oncogenes (Table 13.1) has opened new avenues for investigation of male germ cell-specific processes. Protein products of some of the oncogenes[15] have also been localized to the developmental stages in which the transcripts are found. This suggests that the appearance of the transcripts coincides with protein function, although it is certainly possible that some products may function at later developmental stages. Understanding the role of proto-oncogenes in male germ cell maturation will provide important insights into the normal function of these powerful cell regulators that may lead to new approaches to the correction of male factor infertility.

TABLE 13.1 Proto-oncogenes expressed in male germ cells.

Gene	Principal cell type	Product
ras	Pre- and postmeiotic	G-binding protein
raf	Pre- and postmeiotic	Serine/threonine protein kinase
fos	B spermatogonia	Transcription factor
jun	B spermatogonia and PL spermatocytes	Transcription factor
myc	B spermatogonia and PL spermatocytes	Nuclear protein
int-1	Round spermatids	Extracellular protein
abl	Round and elongating spermatids	Tyrosine protein kinase
pim-1	Round spermatids	Serine/threonine protein kinase
mos	Round spermatids	Serine/threonine protein kinase

Oogenesis

In contrast to male germ cells, which can be obtained as purified populations of cells at discrete stages of development, oocytes arise from a more limited cellular pool whose maturation in most mammals begins in the fetal ovary. Thus, studies of gene expression in developing oocytes have long been hindered by the lack of sufficient cells for routine study by Northern analyses. More recent reports have utilized in situ hybridization of ovarian sections with riboprobes in an effort to localize specific oncogene transcripts in oocytes at various stages of maturation. This approach has identified two oncogenes expressed as maternal transcripts, *mos* and *kit*. Messenger RNAs of two other oncogenes, *sis* and *TGFα*, have been detected in mouse oocytes by the technique of reverse transcription/polymerase chain reaction (reviewed in Chapter 23).

As discussed above, *mos* was originally identified as the oncogene (v-*mos*) in a murine sarcoma virus. It encodes a relatively small (43-kilodaltons) protein kinase that phosphorylates serine and/or threonine, although its target protein(s) have not been identified. From the beginning, one of its most outstanding features was its apparent lack of expression of c-*mos* in normal cells. The discovery that it was expressed specifically in gonadal tissues led to renewed interest in its expression and function.

Mos is accumulated as a maternal transcript during oocyte maturation and reaches relatively high concentration in grown mouse oocytes (Fig. 13.9), with levels approximately equal to that of actin.[22–25] It is not polyadenylated in germinal vesicle stage oocytes and becomes polyadenylated in ovulated eggs.[25] This suggests, but does not prove, that it is not translated until after meiosis resumes. Studies to detect *mos* protein in oocytes are inconclusive with respect to the precise stage at which protein translation begins.

Studies to determine the function of c-*mos* in oocytes have relied on blocking translation of *mos* protein by microinjection of antisense oligodeoxyribonucleotides, as described above. These experiments have revealed that c-*mos* is essential for maintaining metaphase II

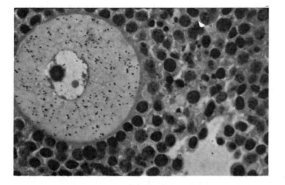

FIGURE 13.9. Photomicrograph of a cross-section of a germinal vesicle stage mouse oocyte following in situ hybridization with ^{35}S-labeled c-*mos* antisense RNA probes. Dark grains covering the oocyte cytoplasm show the location of c-*mos* mRNA. (Courtesy of D. Wolgemuth.)

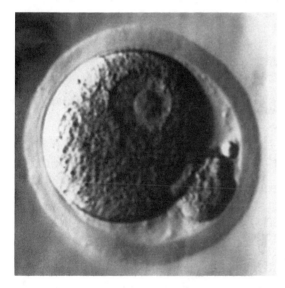

FIGURE 13.10. Antisense *mos*-injected egg: the nucleus with the morphology of a germinal vesicle reformed 2–3 hours following polar body extrusion.

arrest in gonadotropin-stimulated oocytes.[8] If *mos* translation is blocked, the oocytes undergo germinal vesicle breakdown and extrude a polar body, but within a few hours a nucleus is reformed (Fig. 13.10). Biochemical studies have revealed that histone H1 kinase activity is markedly depressed in the antisense c-*mos*-injected oocytes.[25] Histone H1 kinase is the functional activity of "maturation-promoting factor" (MPF), an "activity" in cytoplasm described several years ago[26] that initiates the resumption of meiosis in germinal vesicle stage oocytes. It is now known that MPF activity is due to a complex between cyclin, a protein that appears and disappears with each cell cycle, and p34^{cdc2}, a protein originally described in yeast as being necessary for cell division.[27,28] The finding that histone H1 kinase activity depends upon functional c-*mos* mRNA suggests a role for c-*mos* in the pathway that leads to cell division, an area of intense research interest at this time.

Studies to determine oocyte controls on c-*mos* expression have thus far focused on defining the regulatory sequence active in oocytes. These experiments have been accomplished by microinjection of a series of constructs (see Fig. 13.4) containing the reporter gene, *CAT*, described above, linked to deletion mutants of the upstream promoter region of c-*mos*. The theory behind this approach is that the CAT enzyme would be expressed only in those oocytes microinjected with constructs containing oocyte-active regulatory sequences. Those constructs in which oocyte-specific sequences have been deleted would not support the expression of CAT. The work has produced the interesting finding that all the upstream, nontranscribed regions of the c-*mos* gene can be deleted without altering CAT expression. Within the transcribed region, there is a 20-basepair sequence element to the 5′ side of the site of the start of translation that is necessary for CAT expression.[29] Thus, it appears that the oocyte-specific regulatory region for c-*mos* expression lies within the region of the gene that is transcribed into mRNA. This is consistent with similar findings in other oocyte systems.

Kit is a proto-oncogene which encodes a transmembrane tyrosine kinase receptor that has been identified as the W locus for sterility in mice.[1] It is structurally similar to *fms* and PDGF receptor. *Kit* mRNA is expressed in growing mouse oocytes, as detected by in situ hybridization, and disappears in two-cell embryos.[30] The protein is localized to the surface of oocytes from primordial to fully grown follicles, and declines in maturing oocytes.[31] *Kit* may therefore be involved in meiotic arrest.

Preimplantation Embryos

Investigation of proto-oncogene expression in preimplantation mammalian embryos is just beginning. A pioneering study of gene expression in isolated preimplantation mouse embryos by the method of reverse transcription/polymerase chain reaction (RT/PCR, see Chapter 23) identified expression of two proto-oncogenes, *sis* and TGFα.[32] The same study detected the growth factor TGFb in blastocysts but not in ova.

Sis was originally described as the oncogene in the retrovirus, simian sarcoma virus. Once isolated and sequenced, it was found to be PDGF.[1,33] *Sis* was thus the first proto-oncogene with a known physiologic role. Active PDGF preparations consist of a disulfide-linked dimer of two related proteins, PDGF chains A and B, with molecular weights of 31 and 28–35 kilodaltons, respectively. *Sis* encodes only PDGF-B, which is sufficient to cause transformation if expressed at elevated levels in those cells which normally express PDGF receptor. Overexpression of PDGF-A can also lead to transformation in some cells.[1]

PDGF stimulates cell division by binding to its receptor, which is a protein kinase that phosphorylates tryosine (see Fig. 13.7). Not all the substrates for the PDGF receptor are known, but in addition to *raf*, described above, another possibility is phospholipase C, which becomes activated and sets in motion the phosphatidyl-inositol signal transduction pathway. Cells that express PDGF and its receptor, stimulate their own division in an autocrine fashion. An interesting example of PDGF function in mammalian organogenesis is its probable role in lens development in the mouse. Intermittent exposure of lens tissue to PDGF in culture leads to normal development, whereas the continual presence of PDGF significantly inhibits normal lens development.[34]

TGFα is an extensively studied member of the EGF family that is expressed by a variety of tumors and dividing cells. TGFα binds to EGF receptor. As with PDGF, cells expressing TGFα and receptor stimulate their own division. In addition, in keeping with characteristics of EGFs, TGFα binding can also stimulate cell differentiation instead of mitosis.[35]

The study of gene expression in isolated preimplantation mouse ova and embryos by the recently developed molecular biology technique of RT/PCR revealed that PDGF-A and TGFα are present in ovulated ova, undetectable in two cells, and reappear at the morula–blastocyst transition.[32] This is consistent with the possibility that these growth factors are important during oocyte maturation or fertilization, not involved with the early cleavages, and are re-expressed during the initial differentiation stages of mouse embryos. This notion can be evaluated when information about the appearance of growth factor receptors is known. The growth factor receptors have not as yet been detected in the embryos. The increase in EGF receptors in the uterus at the time of implantation suggests that an alternate, or additional, possibility is that the blastocyst growth factors may signal decidualization of the uterus. These possibilities await the results of ongoing studies in a number of laboratories.

Postimplantation Development

An early study of proto-oncogene expression in embryonic tissues employed hybridization of specific DNA probes to RNA dot blots. The earliest day investigated was day 7 of mouse embryo development, which is approximately 48 hours after implantation and at the time of initiation of organogenesis. These studies revealed that *abl* and *ras* are expressed in embryonic and extraembryonic tissues throughout postimplantation development.[36] The characteristics and possible functions of these proto-oncogenes were discussed above. In addition, it was noteworthy that *fos* and *fms* were expressed at particularly high levels in extraembryonic membranes. The expression of *fms* in trophoblast cells was recently confirmed by two other laboratories.[37,38]

Fms was originally identified as the transforming gene of feline sarcoma virus.[1] The proto-oncogene encodes the monocyte/

TABLE 13.2 Proto-oncogenes expressed in eggs and embryos.

Gene	Principal cell type	Product
mos	Oocyte, ova	Serine/threonine protein kinase
kit	Oocyte, ova	Tyrosine kinase
sis	Ova, morula, blastocyst	PDGF
TGF_α	Ova, morula, blastocyst	Member of epidermal growth factor family
abl	Postimplantation conceptus	Transcription factor
ras	Postimplantation conceptus	G-binding protein
fms	Extraembryonic membranes	Colony-stimulating factor receptor
fos	Extraembryonic membranes	Transcription factor
int-1	Developing nervous system	Extracellular protein

macrophage cell surface receptor for colony-stimulating factor-1 (CSF-1). It is a relatively large (165–170 kilodaltons) membrane glycoprotein protein kinase that phosphorylates tyrosine. Its expression is necessary for monocyte-macrophage interaction with CSF-1 to bring about differentiation and maintenance of the macrophage phenotype.

CSF is itself an oncogene, as shown by transformation of monocytes following adjacent integration of a murine leukemia virus leading to overproduction of CSF.[1] CSF is expressed throughout the endometrium of the pregnant (not the virgin) mouse, in particularly high concentration in the periembryonic decidual cells. Thus, CSF-*fms* is the first proto-oncogene ligand–receptor pair to be identified during mammalian implantation.[37,38] One possible interpretation of the findings is that the uterine CSF is signaling the establishment of the uterine-specific population of macrophages present in the endometrium throughout pregnancy. Another possibility is that the maternal CSF is influencing the formation of syncytio- and cytotrophoblast cell populations during trophoblastic expansion in the decidua. The nature and function of the CSF-*fms* maternal–fetal interaction promises to provide an exciting chapter in early embryonic development.

A number of studies of later developmental stages have revealed developmentally restricted patterns of proto-oncogene expression during organogenesis. The types of expression range from elevations over normal adult tissue levels (e.g., the *myc* family) to specific expression of genes not found in adult tissues. *Int*-1 is an example of such expression. It is expressed in the developing nervous system of 8- to 13-day mouse embryos.[1,39] Northern analyses revealed *int*-1 mRNA in the diencephalon, mesencephalon, metencephalon, myelencephalon (but not the telencephalon), and spinal cord of 12- and 14-day mouse embryos. By day 16, *int*-1 expression was markedly reduced in the spinal cord.[39]

Summary

The eight proto-oncogenes detected as mammalian maternal and embryonic transcripts to date are listed in Table 13.2. These genes undoubtedly represent only the beginning of this exciting field of investigation that will lead to an understanding not only of proto-oncogene functions, but of the controls on gene expression during embryogenesis. The maturing oocyte may require unique maternal proteins for interaction with the ovarian environment and preparation for the enormous tasks of fertilization and early cleavage. The early cell cycles of embryogenesis may well be under maternal or blastomere controls. The initial cell divisions may not require outside stimulus, and thus the gene program being expressed would be the minimal set required for cell division. As cell differentiation begins, a different gene program may be turned on, thus giving rise to the appropriate receptors/ligands for the developing embryo cells to interact with neighbors and environment. Proto-oncogenes encode proteins involved in all of these activities and comprise the core set of genes with which to begin to explore the gene programs operational in these early developmental stages. The recent advances in molecular biology that create the opportunity to explore gene expression in individual embryos set the stage for an exciting era of developmental biology.

References

1. Cooper GM. Oncogenes. Boston: Jones and Bartlett, 1990.
2. Muller R, Slamon DJ, Trenblay JM, Cline MJ, Verma I. Differential expression of cellular oncogenes during pre- and postnatal development of the mouse. Nature (Lond.) 1982;299: 640–644.
3. Muller R. Differential expression of cellular oncogenes during murine development and in teratocarcinoma cell lines. Cold Spring Harbor Conference on Cell Proliferation 1983;10:451–468.
4. Muller R. Proto-oncogenes and differentiation. Trends Biochem Sci 1986;11:129–132.
5. Adamson ED. Oncogenes in development. Development 1987;99:449–474.
6. Kiessling AA, Cooper GM. The expression of oncogenes in mammalian embryogenesis. In: Rosenblum IY, Heyner S, eds. Regulation of Growth and Development. Boca Raton, FL: CRC Press, 1990.
7. Marcola M, Stiles CD. Growth factor superfamilies and mammalian embryogenesis. Development 1988;102:451–460.
8. O'Keefe S, Wolfes H, Kiessling AA, Cooper GM. Microinjection of antisense c-mos oligonucleotides prevents metaphase II arrest in the maturing mouse egg. Proc Natl Acad Sci USA 1989;86:7038–7042.
9. O'Keefe S, Kiessling AA, Cooper GM. The c-mos gene product is required for cyclin B accumulation during meiosis of mouse eggs. Proc Natl Acad Sci USA 1991;88:7869–7872.
10. Robl JM, Heideman JK, First NL. Strain differences in early mouse embryo development in vitro: Role of the nucleus. J Exp Zool 1988;247:251–256.
11. DePamphilis ML, Herman SA, Martinez-Salas E, Chalifour LE. Microinjecting DNA into mouse ova to study DNA replication and gene expression and to produce transgenic animals. BioTechniques 1988;6:662–680.
12. Rubenstein JLR, Nicolas JF, Jacob F. Introduction of genes into preimplantation mouse embryos by use of a defective recombinant retrovirus. Proc Natl Acad Sci USA 1986;83: 366–368.
13. Bellve AR, O'Brien DA. Isolation of mammalian spermatogenic cells and characterization of chromosomal proteins. In: The Spermatozoon; Maturation, Motility, Surface Properties, and Comparative Aspects. Ed by Urban & Schwarzenberg, Baltimore, nd. D.W. Fawcett and J.M. Bedford, 1979.
14. Leon JL, Guerrero I, Pellicer A. Differential expression of the ras gene family in mice. Mol Cell Biol 1987;7:1535–1540.
15. Wolfes HR, Kogawa K, Millette CF, Cooper GM. Specific expression of nuclear proto-oncogenes before entry into meiotic prophase of spermatogenesis. Science 1989;245:740–743.
16. Sorrentino V, McKinney MD, Giorgi M, Geremia R, Fleissner E. Expression of cellular proto-oncogenes in the mouse male germ line: A distinctive 2.4 kilobase pim-1 transcript is expressed in haploid postmeiotic cells. Proc Natl Acad Sci USA 1988;85:2191–2195.
17. Nusse R, Varmus HE. Many tumors induced by the mouse mammary tumor virus contain a provirus integrated in the same region of the host genome. Cell 1982;31:99–109.
18. Shackleford GM, Varmus HE. Expression of the proto-oncogene int-1 is restricted to post-meiotic male germ cells and the neural tube of mid-gestational embryos. Cell 1987;50:89–95.
19. Wilkinson DG, Bailes JA, McMahon, AP. Expression of the proto-oncogene int-1 is restricted to specific neural cells in the developing mouse embryo. Cell 1987;50:79–85.
20. Ponzetto C, Wolgemuth D. Haploid expression of a unique c-abl transcript in the mouse male germ line. Mol Cell Biol 1985;5:1791–1794.
21. Propst F, Rosenberg MP, Iyer I, Kaul K, Vande Woude GF. C-mos proto-oncogene RNA transcripts in mouse tissues: Structural features, developmental regulation, and localization in specific cell types. Mol Cell Biol 1987;7:1629–1637.
22. Goldman DS, Kiessling AA, Millette CF, Cooper GM. Expression of c-mos RNA in germ cells of male and female mice. Proc Natl Acad Sci USA 1987;84:4509–4513.
23. Mutter GL, Wolgemuth DJ. Distinct developmental patterns of c-mos proto-oncogene expression in female and male mouse germ cells. Proc Natl Acad Sci USA 1987;84:5301–5305.
24. Mutter GL, Grills GS, Wolgemuth DJ. Evidence for the involvement of the proto-oncogene c-mos in mammalian meiotic maturation and possibly very early embryogenesis. EMBO J 1988;7:683–689.
25. Goldman D, Kiessling AA, Cooper GM. Post-transcriptional processing suggests that c-mos functions as a maternal message in mouse eggs. Oncogene 1988;3:159–163.
26. Masui Y, Markert CL. Cytoplasmic control of nuclear behavior during meiotic maturation of frog oocytes. J Exp Zool 1971;177:129–145.
27. Murray AW, Kirschner MW. What controls the cell cycle. Sci Am 1991;3:56–63.
28. Lewin B, Driving the cell cycle: m phase kinase, its partners, and substrates. Cell 1990;61:743–752.
29. Pal SK, Zinkel SS, Kiessling AA. C-mos expression in mouse oocytes is controlled by initiator-related sequences immediately down-

stream of the transcription initiation site. Mol Cell Biol 1991;11:5190–5196.

30. Manova K, Nocka K, Besmmer P, Bachvarova RF. Gonadal expression of c-*kit* encoded at the W locus of the mouse. Development 1990; 110:1057–1069.

31. Horie K, Takakura K, Taii S, Narimoto K, Noda Y, Nishikawa S, Nakayama H, Fujita J, Mori T. The expression of c-*kit* protein during oogenesis and early embryonic development. Biol Reprod 1991;45:547–552.

32. Rappolee DA, Brenner CA, Schultz R, Mark D, Werb Z. Developmental expression of PDGF, TGFa, and TGFb genes in preimplantation mouse embryos. Science 1988,241:1823 1825.

33. Doolittle RF, Hunkapiller MW, Hood LE, Devare SG, Robbins KC, Aaronson SA, Antoniades H. Simian sarcoma virus *onc* gene, v-*sis*, is derived from the gene (or genes) encoding a platelet-derived growth factor. Science 1983;221:275–277.

34. Brewitt B, Clark JI. Growth and transparency in the lens, an epithelial tissue, stimulated by pulses of PDGF. Science 1988;242:777–779.

35. Sporn MB, Robert AB. Peptide growth factors are multifunctional. Nature 1988;332:217–219.

36. Muller R, Verma IM, Adamson ED. Expression of c-onc genes: c-fos transcripts accumulate to high levels during development of mouse placenta, yolk sac and amnion. EMBO J 1983;2:679–684.

37. Arceci RJ, Shanahan F, Stanley ER, Pollard JW. Temporal expression and location of colony-stimulating factor 1 (CSF-1) and its receptor in the female reproductive tract are consistent with CSF-1-regulated placental development. Proc Natl Acad Sci USA 1989; 86:8818–8822.

38. Regenstreif LJ, Rossant J. Expression of the c-fms proto-oncogene and of the cytokine, CSF-1, during mouse embryogenesis. Devl Biol 1989;133:284–294.

39. Shackleford GM, Varmus HE. Expression of the proto-oncogene int-1 is restricted to post-meiotic male germ cells and the neural tube of mid-gestational embryos. Cell 1987;50:89–95.

14
In Vitro Coculture of Mammalian Embryos

R.A. Godke, E.G. Blakewood, and J.K. Thibodeaux

The need for culturing early-stage mammalian embryos has increased markedly in recent years. This is in part because in vitro fertilization (IVF) procedures for farm animals were developed in the late 1980s,[1,2] thus making many laboratory-derived embryos available for research and commercial use in the livestock industry. This access to controlled animal embryo production enables researchers to use a vast number of early-stage zygotes for various embryo-engineering procedures such as developing embryo bisection methodology,[3] establishing of DNA insertion techniques for large animal embryos,[4] and refining embryo nuclear transfer techniques in domestic livestock.[5-7]

Experimental evidence now indicates that embryo transfer success markedly improves as the embryos of large animal species reach the morula and blastocyst developmental stages prior to recipient transfer. If simple, effective in vitro culture systems could be developed, pregnancy rates from nuclear transfer embryos and cryopreserved IVF-derived embryos would likely be improved. Also, the chances of successful pregnancy would likely increase with embryo micromanipulation and gene insertion experiments if embryos were cultured to morulae and blastocysts before transfer to surrogate females. Furthermore, embryo culture prior to transfer may also increase pregnancy rates of marginal-quality embryos harvested from donors prior to the blastocyst stage of development. Embryo culture methodology may also have potential application for use with questionable-quality embryos resulting from human IVF procedures. Although many attempts have been made to develop optimal embryo culture systems for mammals, much work is still needed to obtain optimal success rates.

Background

Mammalian embryo culture has been an active area of biological research for over half a century. Although a multitude of research papers have been published in the scientific literature, little is understood about the biochemical components necessary to maintain normal development of mammalian embryos in an in vitro environment.[8] Years of research have established, however, that effective in vitro culture systems require proper temperature, pH, buffering capacity, nutrients, and the presence of still undefined biologic components[9] for embryonic development to proceed.

Some of the earliest efforts in maintaining embryo development outside the female's reproductive tract were conducted using rabbit embryos. In a 1912 study Brachet[10] observed the development of primitive groove and rudimentary placental structures when culturing rabbit blastocysts within small plasma clots in glass dishes. However, it was not until some years later that Lewis and Gregory[11] reported using blood plasma as the medium for the development of 1-cell rabbit embryos to the 8-cell stage during 48 hours of in vitro culture.

Efforts to develop culture media have subsequently centered around the addition of diluted blood plasma or serum and other biological fluids to enhance embryo growth and increase buffering capacity of the in vitro culture system. Carrel[12] first noted that extracts from chick embryos increased the growth of mammalian cells maintained in vitro in 1913. Subsequently, Pincus[13] used hanging-drop cultures containing various mixtures of rabbit plasma, chick plasma, rabbit embryo, and chick embryo extracts, and observed early embryo cleavage in vitro, with the development of 2- and 4-cell rabbit embryos to the morula stage. Waddington and Waterman[14] showed that when chick embryo extracts and chicken plasma were incorporated into the culture medium for later-stage rabbit embryos, embryonic cell differentiation reached the primative streak developmental stage in vitro. One of the first successful cultures of mouse embryos incubated in a physiologic saline required supplementation with eggwhite and yolk of the domestic chicken egg.[15] However, when an attempt was made to culture bovine embryos in either eggwhite- or yolk-supplemented physiologic saline, it was reported not to be successful for embryo development.[16]

Chang[17] demonstrated that heat-inactivated serum could be used successfully to supplement the culture medium for 2-cell rabbit embryos in 1949. This success with rabbit embryos stimulated attempts to develop culture systems for farm animals using heat-inactivated bovine serum as a supplement to the culture medium. Brock and Rowson[18] were the first to attempt culturing cattle embryos in untreated bovine serum, and some years later Hafez et al.[19] reported their preliminary efforts in culturing 1-cell bovine embryos in serum-supplemented physiologic saline. Both laboratories failed to achieve acceptable in vitro development rates using bovine serum in the culture medium. In retrospect, this was likely due to use of fresh rather than heat-inactivated serum in the culture medium. Six years later success with in vitro embryo culture was reported when Onuma and Foote[20] used heat-treated bovine and rabbit sera in the medium while culturing 1-cell bovine embryos, and obtained a 45% cleavage rate from 184 fertilized ova incubated in vitro.

In 1975 Gordon[21] was one of the first to use phosphate-buffered saline supplemented with heat-treated bovine serum for short-term culture of bovine embryos, reporting that 60% of the embryos developed in vitro. The following year, Wright et al.[22] used a bicarbonate-buffered medium (Ham's F-10) with 10% heat-treated fetal bovine serum in a 5% CO_2 atmosphere to culture later-stage embryos and reported good success developing ovine embryos with this culture medium. These early studies and others[23,24] using phosphate-buffered saline, Ham's F-10 medium, and heat-treated fetal bovine serum formed the basis of the culture medium recipes for prehatched farm animal embroys in commercial embryo transplant units over the last 10 years.

In Vitro Block to Normal Development

One common finding in the early attempts at culturing early-stage mammalian embryos was the apparent in vitro developmental block that occurred at various morphological stages in the animal species evaluated. The "block" was first described for mouse embryos and subsequently documented for embryos of other laboratory and farm animal species (Table 14.1). Early studies indicated that the 1-cell mouse embryos could easily develop to the 2-cell stage in vitro; however, these 2-cell embryos failed to undergo further cleavage and characteristically degenerated in the culture medium.[25,26] This occurred in spite of the fact that corresponding

TABLE 14.1. In vitro development block stage for common mammalian species.

Mammal	Development stage (cells)
Mouse[25,26]	2
Hamster[27]	2–4
Rat[8,28]	4–8
Rabbit[29]	Morula
Cat[30]	Morula
Cow[31]	8–16
Sheep[32]	8–16
Goat[33]	8–16
Swine[34]	4–8
Horse[a]	?
Human[35]	No observed block

[a] Data not available, since little success has been reported for culturing precapsulated equine embryos.

embryos collected from mice at the 2-cell stage were capable of normal development to the blastocyst stage while remaining in vitro. In a classic paper, Whittingham and Biggers[36] transferred in vitro-cultured, developmentally blocked, 2-cell mouse embryos to oviducts placed in an organ culture system and were able to rescue them from the induced in vitro developmental block. Furthermore, blastocysts did develop from these previously blocked embryos, and pregnancies resulted after their transfer to recipient mice.

In early experiments involving bovine embryos, development of early-stage embryos (1–4 cells) proceeded to the 8- to 16-cell stage in vitro before they ceased in development.[31] It was noted, however, that corresponding bovine embryos collected from donors at the 8- to 16-cell stages would readily develop to the morula and blastocyst stages in vitro using a simple culture medium. Eyestone and First[37] showed that bovine embryos blocked at the 8- to 12-cell stage in vitro usually could not be rescued, even if they were returned to an in vivo environment. These culture observations with embryos of laboratory and farm animals suggest an inadequacy in the in vitro culture systems at this developmental stage, thus resulting in the characteristic in vitro block to development.

It was proposed[37] that the embryonic cells are live during the initial-stage block; however, they are not capable of dividing after being arrested in development. Although in vitro developmental blocks have not been shown to occur at different developmental stages in laboratory and farm animal species, they have not been reported for the human zygote.[35]

Early observations suggested that the timing of the developmental block in mouse embryos during in vitro culture is coincidental with an important biochemical transition occurring in the embryo. Initially, it was suggested that the murine embryonic genome is activated at the 2- cell stage and that protein synthesis is apparently no longer dependent on preexisting maternal messenger RNA (mRNA).[38] Correspondingly, evidence indicates that the transition from maternal to embryonic mRNA dependence in bovine embryos occurs at the same time as the 8- to 16-cell bovine developmental block. In a recent study, Frei et al.[39] cultured both fertilized oocytes and embryos of cattle with radiolabeled methionine and noted that a progressive decrease in protein synthesis occurred from the oocyte to the 8-cell stage. This was in contrast to an increase in protein synthesis from the 8-cell to the blastocyst stage. This decrease and subsequent increase in protein synthesis in bovine embryos suggests the transition from the translation of maternal mRNA accumulated during oogenesis and the translation of newly transcribed mRNA from the activated embryonic genome. Recently, King et al.[40] reported that bovine embryos began to synthesize ribosomal RNA (rRNA) at the time of maternal zygote transition, starting at the 8-cell stage, to further substantiate this hypothesis.

Jung[41] evaluated the effect of in vitro culture on protein synthesis by rabbit embryos and found that an in vitro environment resulted in accelerated protein degradation compared with corresponding blastocysts developing in vivo. It is interesting that this trend toward rapid protein degradation in vitro was partially reversed by supplementing the in vitro culture medium with uterine secretions of the female rabbit. This finding suggests that uterine secretory product(s) are important to maintain protein synthesis in developing rabbit embryos. From these results and those of others it should be emphasized that uterus—embryo interactions should not be overlooked when developing an effective in vitro culture system for early-stage mammalian embryos.

Attempts at Defining Culture Conditions

During early embryo culture experiments, Whitten[42] suggested the use of bicarbonate-buffered Krebs medium for mouse embryos in place of the standard physiologic saline to stabilize the pH of the culture environment. In this early study, no development of 8-cell mouse embryos was noted in Krebs medium alone; however, supplementation of the medium with 1% eggwhite resulted in development of these embryos to blastocysts. More important, Whitten[42] showed that crystalline bovine serum albumin (BSA) could be substituted for eggwhite in the culture system to produce similar embryo development in vitro. As research continued to identify a more definable culture medium, it was discovered that fertilized oocytes from some inbred strains of mice could develop from the pronuclear stage to the blastocyst stage in a defined medium, without the addition of BSA.[43] This is the primary reason why the developmental characteristics of embryos from each mouse strain should be evaluated before embryos are included in in vitro culture studies.

Following Whitten's discovery that various strains of mouse embryos could undergo development to the blastocyst stage in a defined medium, efforts were made to culture embryos of domestic species in different defined media. Restall and Wales[44] were among the first to report success culturing embryos using a defined medium based on components of sheep oviductal fluid. Some years later, Tervit et al.[45] cultured bovine and ovine embryos using synthetic oviductal fluid (SOF), reporting in vitro development from the 1-cell stage to the 16-cell stage and readily obtaining blastocyst-stage embryos when 8-cell embryos were incubated in this synthetic medium. In a subsequent study,[46] Brinster's modified ova culture medium (BMOC-3) was compared with SOF for in vitro culturing of 8- to 16-cell bovine embryos, resulting in development of 26 and 57% of the embryos to the morula stage, respectively. In contrast, Bowen et al.[47] compared SOF with Ham's F-10 medium and obtained 48 and 80% morulae, respectively, when 2- to 8-cell bovine embryos were cultured in vitro for 48 hours. Over the years, studies using SOF and other partially defined media have continued to produce variable results with farm animal embryos.

A more complete understanding of embryonic growth factors might be possible if embryos could be cultured in media with completely defined components. Although BSA is considered a component of virtually all defined culture media, individual batches of commercially supplied BSA are poorly

defined and are often found to have different growth-promoting effects on mammalian embryo development in vitro.[48,49] Unfortunately, attempts at in vitro culturing of mammalian embryos from the single-cell to the blastocyst stage in a completely defined medium have been consistently successful only with specific strains of mouse embryos.[43] Supplementation of culture medium with complex, undefined biologic fluids (e.g., fetal serum) apparently is still required to advance the embryos through the in vitro developmental block stage of domestic mammalian species.[24] The exception in this case may be the early-stage human embryo, which apparently does not require serum supplementation during early embryo culture,[50] nor does the embryo exhibit the characteristic in vitro block in culture.[35]

Intermediate Host Culture Systems

In Vivo Oviduct Culture

In an effort to overcome apparent inadequacies when in vitro culture is conducted in medium alone, alternative in vivo embryo culture methods were developed and evaluated. One of the early successful methods for enhancing early-stage mammalian embryo development was to use in vivo culture in the oviducts of an intermediate host animal (e.g., rabbit). In a classic study, Averill et al.[51] transferred early-stage 2- to 12-cell ovine embryos to the ligated oviducts of pseudopregnant rabbits for 4 or 5 days, resulting in development of morula and blastocyst-stage embryos for transfer to recipient ewes. This method was used by Hunter et al.[52] to transport sheep embryos collected in Cambridge, England to South Africa for subsequent transfer to recipient ewes. The storage intervals for embryos in rabbit oviducts ranged from 101 to 128 hours in this study, and 4 lambs were born after the transfer of 16 transported embryos.

In a more extensive study in England,[53] 456 early-stage ovine embryos (2–12 cells) were transferred to the ligated oviducts of pseudopregnant female rabbits. After in vitro culture, 87% were recovered from the intermediate host, with 93% of these developing to later-stage embryos while in the oviducts. Up to 69% survival rates were recorded when embryos were subsequently transferred to synchronized recipient ewes in this study. The same year, Lawson et al.[54] also transferred 48 1- to 8-cell bovine embryos to the ligated oviducts of pseudopregnant rabbits, and of the embryos recovered 2 to 4 days later, 83% advanced to later stages, with 15 embryos transferred and 73% live calves born. This finding substantiated the initial studies of successful development of bovine and caprine embryos in the oviducts of rabbits.[55-57] Boland[58] has written an excellent review and an evaluation of the feasibility of using rabbit oviducts for viability screening of bovine embryos prior to transfer.

Culture of agarose-embedded embryos in the ligated oviducts of sheep has become an important in vivo method when IVF and/ or micromanipulated farm animal embryos require culturing prior to recipient transfer. This in vivo culture procedure was developed by Willadsen[59] to facilitate the in vitro development of micromanipulated ovine reconstituted embryos. Blastomeres of 2-cell embryos were embedded in agarose and transferred to the ligated oviducts of ewes for 3 to 4.5 days. Of the 40 (65%) reconstructed embryos surgically recovered, 88% developed in the intermediate hosts to late morulae and early blastocysts. This same approach, using the ligated oviducts of sheep, was also successful for micromanipulated embryos of cattle, swine, and horses.[60] Although the rabbit oviduct was initially used for in vivo culture of farm animal embryos, the sheep oviduct culture system has become the method of choice in recent years for culturing IVF-derived[1,61] and nuclear transfer-derived zygotes.[62-64] As the expertise level increased with this method, embryo recovery rates have been reported to be in the range of 93 to 97%.[64]

In spite of the superior effectiveness of this in vivo culture technique over media culture systems, it has not been accepted readily for general use by most commercial animal embryo transplant units. The primary disadvantages of using ligated sheep oviducts for intermediate embryo culture are the time and amount of effort required, and the difficulty involved in performing multiple surgical procedures on the sheep intermediate host. In addition, a flock of ewes must be maintained as host animals, and this often proves to be costly for the transplant units.

In an effort to reduce the cost of in vivo embryo culture, Ebert and Papaioannou[65] evaluated mouse oviducts for culturing porcine embryos. In the initial study, 4- to 6-cell porcine embryos were transferred to the oviducts of immature mice, and 77% reached the blastocyst stage, compared with only 10% in the in vitro-cultured control group. Correspondingly, when early blastocysts were cultured in mouse oviducts for 2 days, the embryos recovered had twice as many cells than control embryos cultured in medium alone. Efforts are now underway in this and other laboratories to use the mouse as an intermediate host for culturing early-stage bovine and equine embryos. Although this in vivo method shows promise, placing the embryos in the oviducts of either mature or immature mice requires a great deal of time, skill, and patience.

Organ Culture

Biggers et al.[66] and Gwatkin and Biggers[67] were among the first to demonstrate successful in vitro embryonic development of murine embryos from the 1-cell stage through to the blastocyst stage using fresh explanted mouse oviducts. In the initial study,[66] oviducts from 8- to 9-week-old superovulated mice containing embryos were incubated in defined culture medium at 37°C on stainless steel grids in petri dishes. Of the 106 mouse embryos recovered after 4 days of organ culture, 13% had developed to morulae and 65% to blastocysts.

This organ culture system was subsequently tested on early-stage hamster embryos, which are notoriously difficult to culture in vitro.[27,68] Although 1-cell hamster embryos are known to readily cleave to the 2-cell stage, the in vitro developmental block has been shown to be near "absolute."[27] In a later study, Bavister and Minami[69] reported limited results in overcoming the hamster 2-cell block, with 11% of 830 1-cell embryos cleaving using mouse explanted oviduct cultures. Culture results improved when human chorionic gonadotropin (HCG) or pregnant mare serum gonadotropin (PMSG) was added to the mouse oviduct culture system while culturing 2-cell hamster embryos.[70]

Explanted mouse oviducts support in vitro development of early-stage embryos of various laboratory animals[71] and, as recently reported, farm animal species. In a recent example, Krisher et al.[72] cultured 1-cell porcine embryos in explanted oviducts of mated mice, and after 6 days of in vitro incubation 78% developed to the blastocyst stage, compared with only 36% developing to blastocysts in the control medium alone. It was proposed that the mouse oviducts needed systemic priming with endogenous estrogens prior to in vitro incubation to enhance embryotropic factors in the oviductal fluids during organ culture.

Attempts have been made to use the mouse oviduct culture system on early-stage bovine embryos at our laboratory, but at this stage only limited success has resulted. The mouse oviduct appears to have potential application for embryo culture with more than one species, but a high level of expertise and patience is necessary for consistent results with this procedure.

Embryo Coculture Systems

Trophoblastic Vesicle Coculture

Although early-stage mammalian embryos have proved difficult to culture in defined medium alone, later-stage embryos of the same species often readily develop in culture after their hatching from the zona pellucida. In the mid-1980s, Camous et al.[73] used this in vitro observation of hatched embryos to aid them in developing a coculture system for farm animal embryos. Heyman et al.[74] microsurgically sectioned trophoblastic cell layers of the day 12 to day 14 elongating conceptus (cattle and sheep) and noted that these pieces formed

spherical vesicles after several days of in vitro incubation at 37°C. These vesicles (termed trophoblastic vesicles) were thought to secrete cell-active luteotropic and embryo growth factors, and it was recommended that they be used for in vitro embryo culture procedures.

Camous et al.[73] overcame the 8- to 16-cell block to bovine embryo development in vitro by coculturing the embryos with trophoblastic vesicles prepared from trophoblastic layers of day 13 or day 14 elongating blastocysts of cattle. In this study, 46% of the 1- to 8-cell embryos developed to the morula stage when cultured with trophoblastic vesicles for 3 to 4 days, compared with less than 20% of the embryos cultured in the control Menezo B2 medium alone. Similar studies were conducted in which 1- to 8-cell bovine embryos were cocultured with trophoblastic vesicles prepared from day 14 bovine elongated blastocysts.[75] Again, 46% reached the morula stage, compared with only 18% of those cultured in medium. In a second experiment, 55 1-cell embryos were cocultured with trophoblastic vesicles, and 44% cleaved beyond the 8-cell stage, compared with only 13% of the 1-cell embryos cultured in medium alone. Correspondingly, when 1-cell sheep embryos were cocultured with trophoblastic vesicles from day 12 ovine blastocysts, 75% reached the morula stage, compared with only 35% cultured in the control medium.

These findings suggest that the day 12 to day 14 developing conceptus in sheep and cattle is capable of producing embryotropic factors that have the ability to enhance development of embryos from the 1-cell stage to the morula stage in vitro. It was suggested that trophoblastic vesicles may provide important metabolic component(s) (such as lipids), normally present in the uterine tract, that are required for embryo cleavage in utero.[73,76] Also, it was proposed that these embryotropic factors are secreted directly into the culture medium, and that there is no need for direct contact between developing embryo and the trophoblastic cells during the coculture interval. The latter was verified when 1- to 2-cell bovine embryos developed to the 16-cell stage by simply culturing them in conditioned

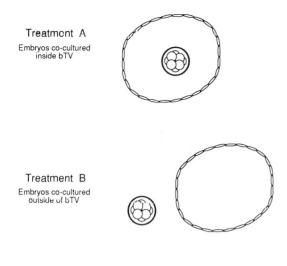

Treatment A
Embryos co-cultured inside bTV

Treatment B
Embryos co-cultured outside of bTV

Treatment C
Embryos cultured in medium alone

FIGURE 14.1. Controlled experiment in which bovine early morulae were randomly assigned either to a medium control group or to one of two bovine trophoblastic vesicle (bTV) treatment groups for a 96-hour culture interval. Embryos in treatment A were microinjected into the lumen of the bTV immediately prior to the onset of culture.[80]

increase in embryo transfer pregnancy rates was reported with the transfer of bovine trophoblastic vesicles along with the transfer of frozen-thawed embryos (blastocyst stage) in cattle.[77] In this case, the trophoblastic tissue apparently has the potential to exert both embryotropic and luteotropic stimuli to enhance the chance of a transplant pregnancy. It also was shown that the prehatched bovine embryo has the capability of producing arachidonic acid metabolites, and one or more of these metabolites (e.g., prostaglandin-E_2) may have luteotropic properties in the pregnant as well as the cyclic cow.[78,79]

In an attempt to improve the efficiency of the trophoblastic vesicle coculture system for farm animals, Pool et al.[80] used microsurgery to place early-stage bovine embryos (morulae) individually into bovine trophoblastic vesicles and evaluated subsequent embryo development in vitro (Fig. 14.1). Unexpectedly, embryos placed in the lumen of the trophoblastic vesicles had a lower percentage developing to quality grade 1 and 2 embryos (36%) compared with corresponding embryos cocultured outside of the trophoblastic vesicles (69%) during 60 hours of incubation (Table 14.2). This pattern of development was also evident after 96 hours of culture. This response subsequently was verified with bovine half-embryos (demi-embryos) cocultured either adjacent to or inside bovine trophoblastic vesicles in our laboratory. Why embryos are retarded in their development when placed inside the trophoblastic vesicle during culture is presently not clear. Possibly, the level of embryotropic

medium, as were corresponding embryos cocultured with bovine trophoblastic vesicles.[75]

In addition to having embryotropic activity in farm animals, these same trophoblastic tissues also have luteotropic capabilities in the cyclic cow and sheep.[74] Correspondingly, an

TABLE 14.2. Embryo viability assessments and quality grades during in vitro culture of bovine embryos.

Treatment[a]	0 hours — Number of embryos (grade 1)	60 hours — Viable embryos (%)	60 hours — Grade 1 & 2 embryos (%)	96 hours — Viable embryos (%)	96 hours — Grade 1 & 2 embryos (%)
bTV (inside)	36	64[b]	36[b]	58[b]	36[b,c]
bTV (outside)	36	81[b]	69[c]	72[b]	50[b]
Control	36	67[b]	22[b]	44[b]	17[c]
Total	108				

[a] Treatment A: embryos placed inside a bTV and cocultured; treatment B: embryos cocultured with a bTV; treatment C: embryos cultured in medium alone. Viable embryos: quality grades 1, 2, and 3.
[b,c] Means with different superscripts in the same column are significantly different ($p < 0.05$).[80]

factors produced by the trophoblastic cells becomes too concentrated inside the vesicle during incubation, and/or the metabolic by-products of the confined embryo accumulate to a toxic level in the lumen of the vesicle during coculture. Thus, placement of the bovine embryos inside trophoblastic vesicles was not effective as a simple coculture method, as was anticipated.

The timing of embryo harvest for trophoblastic vesicles production is important for the success of the coculture system. In one study, day 14 elongated ovine blastocysts were used to prepare trophoblastic vesicles.[81] When 1-cell sheep embryos were cocultured for either 24 or 72 hours, the cleavage rate was slightly less than when similar 1-cell embryos were cultured with medium alone. This lack of response was different from the positive response noted by French scientists when ovine embryos were cocultured with trophoblastic vesicles prepared from day 12 ovine blastocysts.[75] Similar findings of little or no embryotropic effect from trophoblastic vesicle coculture were noted when day 15 goat elongated blastocysts were used to prepare trophoblastic vesicles for the culture of early-stage caprine embryos.[82] In this case, the trophoblastic vesicles were apparently too morphologically advanced to stimulate the development of blastocysts from 2- to 8-cell goat embryos. Attempts have been made to produce trophoblastic vesicles from the equine conceptus at 10 days or more of age; however, the vesicles that formed showed limited abillity to grow and develop in vitro.[83,84] Based on the results with trophoblastic cocultures reported thus far, it appears that trophoblastic vesicles should be prepared after day 10 and before day 15 of development in the cow, sheep, and goat for maximum embryotropic activity during in vitro embryo coculture.

To use trophoblastic vesicles for in vitro culture effectively in animal embryo transplant units, these vesicles must be stored and ready for use when the need arises. A preliminary study conducted in this laboratory[85] found the bovine and caprine trophoblastic vesicles could be frozen and stored in liquid nitrogen

($-196°C$) for months for subsequent use in embryo coculture. After thawing, 30 to 70% of the vesicles gave evidence of becoming functional, having embryotropic properties. Although both fresh and frozen-thawed vesicles can appear viable for weeks in culture, their embryotropic properties are most evident during the first week after preparation or the first few days after thawing.

Uterine Cell Coculture

In a classic cell culture study, Cole and Paul[25] reported using irradiated HeLa cells to coculture 2-cell murine embryos through the hatching blastocyst stage. They noted marked improvement in developmental rates in vitro compared with that of embryos cultured in medium alone.

Many different coculture systems have been developed to enhance embryonic growth and development in vitro. Initial sources of cells for coculture were of reproductive origin, used in hopes of mimicking the in vivo environment of the uterus or the oviduct in vitro. In the early 1980s coculture systems incorporated monolayers of fibroblast and fibroblast-like cells derived from different animal sources. Today, most fibroblast monolayers for embryo coculture are prepared after three to five subpassages of cells after their initial outgrowth from uterine endometrial explants[86-88] (Fig. 14.2). In one of the earliest studies on cocultured cattle embryos,[86] morulae were placed with these helper cells and a higher percentage of hatched blastocysts resulted with the use of either uterine or testicular fibroblast monolayers (40 and 41%), compared with morulae cultured in medium alone (4%).

Subsequently it was shown that early-stage porcine embryos (4-cell to morula) had a higher developmental rate when cocultured on subpassed cells derived from porcine endometrial tissue than in medium alone.[89] In addition, the bovine uterine fibroblast coculture system was capable of enhancing in vitro development of porcine embryos.[87,90] Furthermore, porcine embryos cocultured on a bovine fibroblast monolayer resulted in a greater number that hatched and subsequently

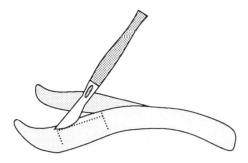

1. Cut uterus using sterile technique

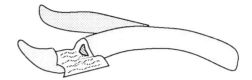

2. Expose endometrial tissue

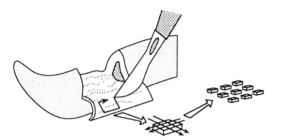

3. Cut out endometrial explants

4. Place sections in appropriate culture medium

FIGURE 14.2. Procedure for harvesting endometrial tissue from the uterus. The endometrial cells are incubated and subpassaged to produce fibroblasts for embryo coculture.

attached to the substratum during coculture. It was proposed that the fibroblasts of the monolayer released embryo growth factor(s) into the culture medium that enhanced embryo development, or possibly that the fibroblasts could be removing toxic substances from the medium, thus resulting in enhanced in vitro development.[86] It was further suggested that cell contact between embryos and the fibroblast monolayer was necessary to enhance embryonic development in a fibroblast monolayer culture system.[89]

Several years later, a similar monolayer system was evaluated using bovine half-embryos in a controlled study.[88] Improved viability of demi-embryos was evident on uterine fibroblast monolayers after 72 hours of coculture, compared with corresponding demi-embryos cultured with Ham's F-10 medium alone. Furthermore, a beneficial effect of the fibroblast monolayer on these micro-manipulated demi-embryos resulted during their in vitro cellular repair process. With renewed interest in fibroblast cocultures, Wiemer et al.[91-96] developed a fetal uterine cell monolayer culture system that incorporated uterine fibroblasts derived from near-term (≈270 days) bovine fetuses. This fetal cell coculture system has been shown to enhance in vitro development of mouse,[97] bovine,[91,92,96] equine,[93-95] and human [98-101] embryos over that of culturing in medium alone.

A majority of the reported studies on culturing embryos on uterine cell monolayer systems have used primarily fibroblasts originating from reproductive tissue (Table 14.3). In more recent studies, endometrial cells (e.g., epithelial or epithelial-like cells) for embryo culture have been isolated from the uterine lining of the cow,[102,103] goat,[104,105] and rhesus monkey.[106-108] Prichard et al.[105] cocultured 2- to 4-cell goat embryos on caprine oviductal

TABLE 14.3. Embryo culture studies using uterine monolayer cocultures.

Embryo type	Type of culture cells	Benefit of coculture[a]
Cow (morula)	Cow uterine fibroblasts	Yes[86]
Cow (morula/blastocyst)	Cow endometrial fibroblasts	Yes[88]
Cow (morula)	Fetal bovine uterine fibroblasts	Yes[91,92,96]
Cow (morula)	Fetal bovine uterine fibroblasts	Yes[110]
Cow (morula)	Cow uterine endometrium	Yes[102]
Cow (morula)	Goat uterine epithelium	Yes[104]
Cow (morula)	Rhesus uterine epithelium	Yes[107]
Pig (4-cell to morula)	Pig endometrium	Yes[89]
Pig (day 6 or 7)	Cow uterine fibroblasts	Yes[90]
Pig (blastocyst)	Cow uterine fibroblasts	Yes[87]
Pig (morula)	Cow uterine fibroblasts	No[87]
Sheep (1-cell)	Sheep fetal fibroblasts	Yes >3 days[120]
	Sheep fetal fibroblasts	No >6 days[120]
Sheep (1-cell)	Sheep uterine	No[81]
Goat (2- to 4-cell)	Goat uterine epithelium	Yes[105]
Goat (2- to 4-cell)	Fetal bovine uterine fibroblasts	Yes[82]
Horse (morula)	Fetal bovine uterine fibroblasts	Yes[93–95]
Rhesus (morula)	Rhesus uterine epithelium	Yes[107–109]
Human (pronuclear)	Fetal bovine uterine fibroblasts	Yes[98–100]

[a] Improvement in development compared with that of the culture in medium alone. Expanded from ref. 131.

and uterine epithelial monolayers. Adequate hatching rates were noted on uterine cell monolayers (63%); however, oviductal cell coculture had a greater number of embryos hatching (87%) than did the uterine cell monolayers. Unexpectedly, when the caprine embryos were sequentially transferred from the oviductal cell culture to the uterine cell culture in a third treatment group (changed in hope of sequentially mimicking the in vivo environment during the culture period), the hatching rate (73%) was not increased over that of the oviductal cell culture alone. Although caprine uterine cell monolayers were considered only adequate for goat embryos in this study, it was reported that caprine uterine epithelial monolayers could enhance postthaw development of bovine embryos when the embryos were cocultured prior to freezing.[104] Unfortunately, caprine oviductal cells were not used for bovine embryo coculture for in vitro comparison in the latter study.

The recent development of a nonsurgical embryo recovery technique in rhesus monkeys allows access to early-stage embryos for subsequent culture research.[106] Goodeaux et al.[107,108] reported increased development and hatching rates of rhesus monkey embryos

cocultured on rhesus uterine epithelial cells compared with those cultured in medium alone (63 versus 25%). Furthermore, this coculture procedure followed by nonsurgical embryo transfer resulted in the birth of a live offspring.[106,107] In addition, rhesus uterine epithelial monolayers were shown to be capable of supporting development of morula-stage cattle embryos.[107]

In an effort to maximize embryotropic capabilities within a single culture system, a controlled study was conducted by Pool et al.[110] to evaluate the use of both the endometrial fibroblast monolayer and trophoblastic vesicles in one culture system for developing bovine embryos in vitro. Quality grade 1 morulae were randomly and individually placed into single wells of culture and incubated in control medium with a bovine trophoblastic vesicle (bTV), with a fetal bovine endometrial fibroblast monolayer, or with a combination of a bTV and a fetal fibroblast monolayer cocultured with a morula (Fig. 14.3).

From previous coculture experience with various types of helper cells, it was anticipated that the coculture system with a combination of two different types of helper cells would be the most successful for culturing later-stage

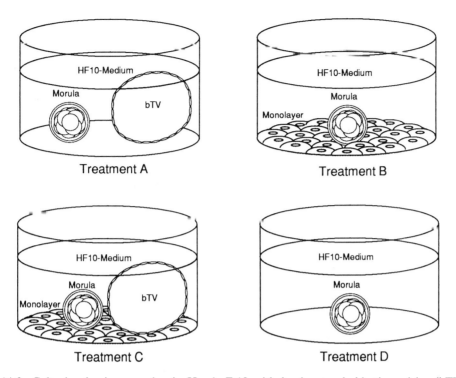

FIGURE 14.3. Culturing bovine morulae in Ham's F-10 with bovine trophoblastic vesicles (bTV), fetal bovine endometrial fibroblast cells, or a combination of these cell types during a 72-hour incubation period.[110]

bovine embryos. However, the number of viable embryos at 72 hours in both the control and the combination treatments was significantly less than those cocultured with either a bTV alone or with a fetal fibroblast monolayer (Table 14.4). The reason for the poor showing when the two different helper cell types were used in a combination treatment remains unclear. The results from this and other studies further indicate that we do not completely understand the functional dynamics of cell populations maintained in an in vitro environment.

In recent years the trend has been toward increasing the use of uterine epithelial cells for coculture of preimplantation embryos of farm animals. It now appears that the source of cells and the day of the cycle that cells are harvested influence the functional capability of the uterine cell coculture systems. Recently, Thibodeaux et al.[111,112] reported that changes in basic cell function in vitro were associated with a chang-

ing hormonal profile occurring across different days of the bovine estrous cycle. Both uterine and oviductal epithelial cells had the lowest percentage of cell attachment during primary culture when isolated from animals between days 8 and 10 and between days 14 and 16 of the estrous cycle. In contrast, the highest percentage of cell attachment was noted for cells isolated between days 4 and 6 (Fig. 14.4).

When flow cytometry was used to evaluate the mitotic index of isolated cells,[111,112] the lowest percentage of cell proliferation was inversely related to the highest percentage of cell attachment. Fundamental changes in uterine and oviductal epithelial cells in the culture system apparently coincided with the physiologic state of the cells isolated from each animal at the time of harvest. In addition, uterine or oviductal epithelial cells exhibited a cell crisis phase during in vitro incubation associated with cell death that occurred in cell populations from 20% of females evaluated. It

TABLE 14.4. Embryo viability assessments and quality grades during in vitro culture of bovine embryos.

| | 0 hours | 48 hours | | 72 hours | |
| | Number of embryos (grade 1) (%) | Viable embryos (%) | Grade 1 & 2 embryos (%) | Viable embryos (%) | Grade 1 & 2 embryos (%) |
Treatment					
bTV	28	71	90	75[a]	54[a*]
Monolayer	28	71	85	68[a]	61[a]
bTV + monolayer	28	75	76	36[b]	29[b]
Control medium	28	75	86	43[b]	31[b]
Total	112				

[a,b] Different superscripts in the same column are significantly different ($p < 0.05$ or $*p < 0.06$).[110]

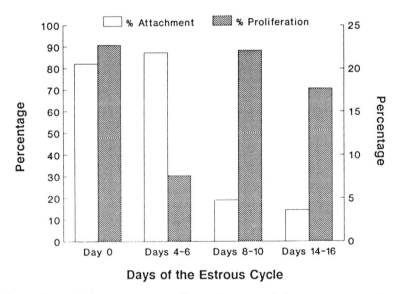

FIGURE 14.4. Comparison of the percentage cell attachment and the percentage cell proliferation of combined populations of uterine and oviductal epithelial cells (bovine) during in vitro culture.[112]

is becoming more evident that circulating hormone levels of cell donor animals ultimately affect the viability and the functional capacity of epithelial cells in the coculture system.[113] Certainly the type of culture medium[114,115] and the incubation temperature[115] may also affect the viability and functional capacity of epithelial cells during incubation and subsequent embryo coculture.

Oviduct Cell Coculture

Although positive results have been reported with the use of uterine cells as a coculture system, oviductal cells recently were shown to

be more effective in enhancing the development of early-stage embryos in vitro. It was proposed that oviduct epithelial cells would provide an in vitro environment similar to embryonic development in vivo.[8] It has also been shown that oviductal cells of various species are capable of stimulating embryonic development in other species. Earlier studies demonstrated the capabilities of the rabbit oviduct to enhance or maintain embryonic development in mouse, sheep, cow, pig, goat, and horse embryos.[8,58]

Over 25 years ago Biggers et al.[66] noted that 2-cell mouse embryos would develop through the in vitro block stage when cultured in

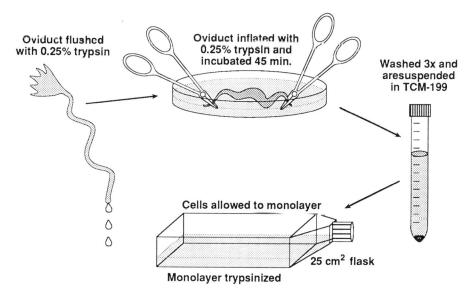

FIGURE 14.5. An effective method of harvesting fresh oviductal cells from the excised oviducts of farm animals.[105,168] It is recommended that fresh trypsin be purchased and used for optimal oviductal cell recovery with this procedure.

explanted mouse oviducts maintained in culture medium. Whittingham[116] later suggested that only the ampullar region of the murine oviduct was capable of maintaining embryo development in vitro. This stimulus to embryo development appears to be dependent on hormonal priming of the oviduct prior to placing the cells into culture.

Oviductal cells used for coculture are generally obtained by scraping the luminal surface of excised oviducts[81,117–119] or by collecting cells during embryo recoveries.[120] An effective method of flushing the excised oviducts of farm animals to harvest epithelial cells has recently been reported[105,112,113,168] (Fig. 14.5). Unlike earlier studies using explanted oviducts for culture, with this approach epithelial and epithelial-like cells from the interior lumen of the oviduct are harvested to prepare growing cell populations for in vitro embryo coculture.

In 1986 Rexroad and Powell[117,118] were among the first to report the use of oviductal epithelial cell monolayers for short-term culture of early-stage ovine embryos. Others have reported additional results, verifying that oviductal cell cultures are capable of

supporting development of early-stage ovine embryos when compared with control medium alone.[119,122,123]

Gandolfi and Moor[120] compared the developmental potential of pronuclear-stage ovine embryos cocultured on ovine oviductal epithelial and uterine fibroblast monolayers. In this study, both monolayer systems were capable of supporting embryo development to the blastocyst stage. After 6 days of incubation, however, 42% of the embryos developed into expanded blastocysts using oviductal cell monolayer coculture, compared with only 5% on uterine fibroblast monolayers. Furthermore, the transfer of embryos cocultured on oviduct cell monolayers resulted in higher pregnancy rates than those cultured on fibroblast monolayers.

Oviductal epithelial cell monolayers have also been successful for in vitro coculture bovine embryos.[102,124–128] Higher developmental rates of 5- to 8-cell embryos cultured for 4 to 5 days in an oviductal cell coculture system were reported than for Ham's F-10 medium alone.[124] Eyestone and First[126] further evaluated the effects of oviductal cell coculture on embryonic growth by comparing it with

TABLE 14.5. Embryo culture studies using oviductal monolayer cocultures.

Embryo type	Type of culture cells	Benefit of coculture[a]
Cow (5- to 8-cell)	Cow oviduct epithelium	Yes[124]
Cow (morula)	Cow oviduct epithelium	Yes[102]
Cow (morula)	Cow oviduct epithelium	Yes[137]
Cow (1- to 2-cell)	Cow oviduct epithelium	Yes[129]
Cow (IVF embryos)	Cow oviduct epithelium	Yes[113,125,130–133,135]
Pig (2- to 16-cell)	Pig oviduct epithelium	Yes[138]
Sheep (1- to 8-cell)	Sheep oviduct epithelium	Yes[81,117]
Sheep (1-cell)	Sheep oviduct epithelium	Yes >3 days[120]
Sheep (1-cell)	Sheep oviduct epithelium	Yes >6 days[120]
Sheep (1-cell)	Sheep oviduct cells	Yes[117]
Goat (2- to 8-cell)	Goat oviduct epithelium	Yes[105,121]
Rabbit (1-cell)	Rabbit oviduct epithelium	Yes[136]

[a] Improvements in development compared with culturing in medium alone. Expanded from ref. 131.

oviductal cell-conditioned medium. A higher rate of development was also obtained when 1- to 8-cell bovine embryos were cocultured on oviduct cell monolayers than when cultured in medium alone. Correspondingly, when oviductal cell coculture was compared with conditioned medium, in vitro developmental rates were similar. Recently, Ellington et al.[128] compared in vitro developmental rates of bovine embryos cocultured on oviductal monolayers in a simple medium (CZB) with in vivo developmental rates within the reproductive tract of the cow. Zygotes obtained 40 to 48 hours postestrus were cocultured in vitro for 5 days, and the developmental rates and number of nuclei per embryo did not differ from embryos developed in vivo. This and other studies[127,129] indicate that the developmental capacity of oviductal cell coculture systems can enhance development of bovine embryos with a simple serumfree medium.

Oviductal cell coculture systems provide adequate developmental rates for early-stage mammalian embryos (Table 14.5). These systems have been used in development of IVF-derived embryos of cattle[113,130–133] and IVF-derived chimeric embryos.[134] In each case, oviduct cell monolayers were more effective for culturing embryos than medium alone. In 1990 Japanese researchers evaluated the ability of six different culture systems to promote blastocyst development in IVF-derived bovine embryos.[135] These included culture medium alone, cumulus cells, oviductal epithelial cells, trophoblastic vesicles, amniotic sac cells, and in vivo culture in rabbit oviducts. The results showed no differences in blastocyst development among oviductal cells, trophoblastic vesicles, and amniotic sac cells, with developmental rates of 39 to 51%. These systems were also more effective for stimulating blastocyst development than cumulus cell coculture, culture in rabbit oviducts, or culture in medium alone.

Carney et al.[136] recently reexamined the use of rabbit oviductal cells for coculture of rabbit embryos. In the rabbit, the developmental rates generally are slower for in vitro-cultured than for in vivo-cultured embryos. However, the oviductal cell coculture system in this study resulted in developmental rates comparable with in vivo rates.

The ultimate endpoint of coculture systems is to provide optimum pregnancy rates. Ellington et al.[129] cocultured 1- to 2-cell cow embryos on oviductal epithelial cells in a simple medium or in the oviducts of an intermediate host rabbit. Embryos were cocultured to the morula or blastocyst stage and nonsurgically transferred to recipient animals. Pregnancy rates for oviductal cell coculture were 57% compared with 58% for embryos cultured in rabbit oviducts. It was concluded that oviductal epithelial cell coculture systems provided acceptable pregnancy rates, even when a simple medium was used with the embryos.

Recently a bilayered coculture system of bovine oviductal cells and bovine granulosa cells was developed to culture morula-stage bovine embryos.[137] Costar transwell culture plates with a collagen-treated, microporous membrane (0.4-μm pore size) were used to separate the two cell populations during in vitro culture. After 72 hours of culture, a greater percentage of hatched embryos resulted when they were cocultured in a bilayered system with oviductal and granulosa cells (75%) than when embryos were cultured in either oviductal cells (60%) or granulosa cells (50%) alone. This suggests a positive embryotropic interaction when bovine oviductal cells and granulosa cells are maintained in the same coculture system. This appears not to be the case when trophoblastic vesicles are maintained with a fetal bovine endometrial fibroblast monolayer during culture of bovine morulae.[110]

White et al.[138] reported enhanced development of 2- to 16-cell embryos cocultured on fetal porcine oviductal cell monolayers. In this study, in vitro development was evaluated during culture with medium alone, porcine oviductal cells, porcine endometrial fibroblasts, or a bilayer of porcine endometrial fibroblasts and oviductal cells. Higher percentages of hatched blastocyst were noted with coculture of porcine oviductal cells and a bilayer of oviductal and fibroblast cells (54 and 61%, respectively). It was concluded that oviductal cell coculture provided necessary factors to overcome the 4-cell in vitro block in the pig.

Oviductal secretory proteins have been isolated in the mouse,[139] rabbit,[140] sheep,[141] cow,[142] baboon,[143] and human.[144] Furthermore, oviductal cell monolayers capable of supporting development of ovine zygotes to the blastocyst stage in vitro have been found to secrete proteins similar to those detected in ovine oviductal fluid.[120] A present hypothesis suggests that oviductal epithelial cell feeder layers enhance the development of preimplantation embryos by one or more mechanisms. First, it is likely that oviductal cells secrete specific growth factors (e.g., proteins, peptides) that are required by early-stage embryos to maintain a normal rate of development.[120] Another possibility is that these cell feeder layers also have the ability to remove toxic components that are detrimental to the embryo from the surrounding medium during coculture.[8] Bavister[8] proposed that in addition to secreting embryotropic components and/or removing embryotoxic substances from the medium, the oviductal cells may lower oxygen tension in the culture medium to enhance embryo development. It was further suggested that like the oviductal epithelial cell monolayer, the uterine fibroblast feeder layer is also capable of reducing the oxygen tension and removing embryotoxic components from the culture medium, thus improving embryo development over that in culture medium alone. Although the uterine fibroblast monolayers have the ability to lower oxygen tension, they may lack the ability to produce embryotropic factors in vitro.[8]

Ouhibi et al.[145] evaluated protein secretions by subpassaged oviductal monolayers of mice, using radiolabeled methionine incorporation, and noted that monolayers maintained high protein secretion rates for 96 hours in culture. The protein secretion patterns in this study, and the monolayer viability and cell attachment patterns recently noted,[111,112] suggest that after subpassage these cells provide a more uniform in vitro cell population and reduced monolayer variability for subsequent use in embryo coculture systems. Recent findings also indicate that the culture medium used for in vitro culture of monolayers influences the growth and, to some degree, the proliferation rates of monolayers.[114,115] Growth curves for bovine oviductal and uterine epithelial cells indicate that CMRL-1066 medium provides a more suitable environment for cell growth than more popular media. In addition, flow cytometry has proved to be a reliable measurement of epithelial cell proliferation rates.[115] A comparison of growth rates and proliferation rates of oviductal epithelial cells incubated in different culture media is provided in Table 14.6. Identifying the factors that alter or directly influence cell monolayers of embryo coculture systems would provide the key to establishing the most efficient coculture systems for mammalian embryos.

The results thus far suggest that oviductal cell monolayers are the most effective coculture

TABLE 14.6. Proliferation rates for bovine oviductal epithelial cells during an 8-day growth incubation period comparing different culture media.

Item	Days in culture				
	Day 1	Day 2	Day 4	Day 6	Day 8
Tissue culture medium-199					
No. cells ($\times 10^5$)	2.1	3.1	5.6	9.5	12.4
Proliferating[a] (%)	44	31	25	23	22
CMRL-1066 medium					
No. cells ($\times 10^5$)	2.0	3.7	19.2	42.9	46.0
Proliferating (%)	40	37	24	17	15
Minimum essential medium					
No. cells ($\times 10^5$)	3.5	5.7	21.3	21.7	21.2
Proliferating (%)	34	41	30	17	17
Menezo B2 medium					
No. cells ($\times 10^5$)	3.5	4.3	8.2	14.9	25.3
Proliferating (%)	36	30	31	20	17
Ham's F-12 medium					
No. cells ($\times 10^5$)	2.2	2.6	7.9	13.1	14.5
Proliferating (%)	35	35	28	22	21

[a] Percent proliferation = number of cells in proliferative state of the cell cycle (G2, S, and M phases)/number of cells evaluated.[114]

system for early-stage farm animal embryos, and fibroblast monolayers are adequate for development of later-stage embryos (morula to blastocyst).[131] Correspondingly, Gandolfi and Moor[120] showed that pronuclear-stage sheep embryos cultured to later stages on fibroblast monolayers generally have lower pregnancy rates. Due to the limited number of studies conducted with uterine epithelial cells, it is unclear whether the development of early-stage embryos is dependent on the source of cells (uterus versus oviduct) or the specific cell type (epithelial versus fibroblast) needed for optimum coculture.

Granulosa Cell Coculture

Evidence is now accumulating to show that bovine granulosa/cumulus cells are important for the in vitro maturation of bovine oocytes obtained from abattoir ovaries. They also appear to play a role in subsequent development of IVF-derived embryos to the morula and blastocyst stages in vitro.[146] Faundez et al.[147] reported that in vitro fertilization rates were higher for bovine oocytes exposed to granulosa cells than for similar oocytes that were exposed to IVF procedures without the aid of granulosa cells. In this study the highest

were achieved when cumulus-intact bovine oocytes were incubated on granulosa cell monolayers prior to and during the in vitro fertilization procedure.

Recent findings suggest that coculture with granulosa cells continues to be beneficial after IVF with farm animals. Goto et al.[148] reported that bovine transplant pregnancies could be obtained after coculture of IVF-derived embryos with bovine cumulus cells for 6 or 7 days in vitro. In another study using granulosa cell coculture, Goto et al.[149] reported that 25% of in vitro-matured, in vitro-fertilized bovine oocytes reached the 8-cell stage after 3 to 4 days of incubation, with 21% reaching the morula and blastocyst stages after IVF. More recently Berg and Brem[150] noted a significantly higher rate of development to morulae and blastocysts (32%) with granulosa cell coculture compared with coculture on a monolayer of bovine oviductal epithelial cells (17%). These findings with granulosa cells are similar to those with in vitro-matured, in vitro-fertilized bovine oocytes cocultured with bovine cumulus cells in our laboratory.[151–156] Recently Zhang et al.[152] reported that 54% of the in vitro-fertilized bovine oocytes cleaved and 41% reached the morula stage of development in vitro with a simple bovine cumulus cell culture fertilization rates were achieved when cumulus-intact bovine oocytes were incubated on granulosa cell monolayers prior to and during the in vitro fertilization procedure.

Nakao and Nakatsuki[158] compared bovine trophoblastic vesicle and cumulus cell coculture systems using IVF-derived bovine embryos. In vitro development to the morula stage was similar when embryos were cocultured with either trophoblastic vesicles (17%) or cumulus cells (19%), or cocultured with both cell types (16%). Results suggested no additional embryotropic effect when both cell types were combined in a single culture unit. Rodriguez et al.[137] used day 6 bovine embryos to compare granulosa cells and oviductal cells in a bilayer transwell coculture system. After 72 hours in culture, significantly more embryos hatched in vitro with oviductal cells (24%), with granulosa cells (20%), and with oviductal cells in combination with granulosa cells (30%) when compared with embryos cultured in the control medium alone (4%). These results showed no clear advantage of a bilayer cell culture system over either cell type used individually for coculture.

The results thus far indicate that the use of granulosa cells in an embryo culture system gives similar results to the use of other helper cell coculture systems. The major advantage is that the granulosa cells are available for harvesting from the follicle at the time of oocyte collection. This makes the procedure simple to implement at little or no cost, compared with obtaining trophoblastic, uterine, and oviductal tissues for preparation of the other in vitro culturing systems. Baird et al.[159] reported good developmental success culturing mouse embryos with granulosa cells from hamsters, showing that this embryotropic response exists across animal species. In addition, the bovine and porcine cumulus cell coculture systems have been reported to be effective in developing porcine IVF-derived embryos.[153] Possibly in the future, embryo laboratories will be able to purchase frozen granulosa/cumulus cells from laboratory species and use them to prepare cocultures for farm animal embryos and possibly human embryos.

Chick Embryo Coculture

The avian egg represents a complete in situ environment for the development of the embryo from the blastoderm to the live chick at hatching. The albumen and yolk supply virtually all the nutrient requirements of the embryo during the early stages of development. Based on early observations describing the fertile chicken egg as a nearly perfect biologic unit, it was decided to evaluate the chick embryo amnion as a culture system for in vitro development of early-stage mammalian embryos.[160]

Chick embryo extract (CEE) was among the first agents used to stimulate the growth of mammalian cells in culture. Carrel[12] prepared CEE by grinding tissues of 6- to 20-day-old chicks in Ringer's solution, added the extracts to in vitro cultures of canine connective tissue, and noted a 3- to 30-fold increase in the rate of tissue growth. In a later study, Willmer and Jacobs[161] prepared CEE from 7-day-old chick embryos and found that this extract had the ability to stimulate the development of avian cells that had ceased to grow during in vitro culture. This rate of cell proliferation was found to be proportional to the concentration of CEE added to the culture medium.

New and Stine[162] first reported the use of CEE in mammalian embryo culture in 1964. Postimplantation-stage mouse and rat embryos (days 7 to 10) were placed in plasma clots that contained 15 drops of fowl plasma and 5 drops of CEE prepared from day 13 chick embryos. After 36 hours of culture, 50% of the mouse embryos at the one- to seven-somite stages developed blood circulation, and some developed tail and posterior limb buds. This finding further suggested that the developing fertile chicken egg produces unidentified growth-promoting factors that could be valuable in supplementation of mammalian embryo culture systems.

The use of the amniotic cavity of developing chick embryos to culture mammalian embryos was first reported by Blakewood et al.[160] In this procedure pronuclear mouse embryos were embedded in agarose, injected into the amniotic cavity of the 96-hour chick embryo,

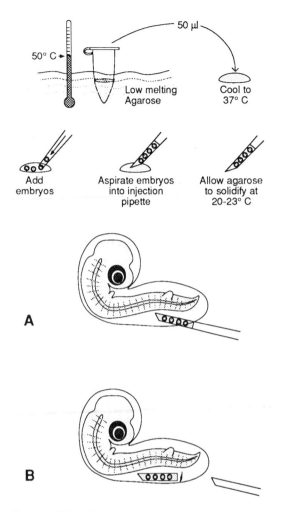

FIGURE 14.6. Procedure for agarose-embedding of mammalian embryos and placement of these embryos in the chick embryo amniotic cavity. Penetration of the 96-hour chick amnion with a beveled injection pipette (A) and removal of the pipette after injection of agarose-embedded mammalian embryos (B).[163,164] Reprinted, by permission, from Blakewood et al., 1989.[164]

TABLE 14.7. In vitro development of 2- to 8-cell caprine embryos in four culture systems during a 72-hour interval.

Treatment	Total	Expanded blastocyst (%)	Hatched blastocyst (%)
Control	20	0[a]	0[a]
Monolayer	20	50[b]	45[b]
Chick embryo	20	70[b]	55[b]
Trophoblastic vesicles	20	0[a]	0[a]
Total	80		

[a,b] Different superscripts in the same column are significantly different ($p < 0.01$).[82]

and incubated at 37°C[163] (Fig. 14.6). In the initial experiment,[160,164] pronuclear mouse embryos from two different lines were placed in the amniotic cavity of chick embryos for 72 to 96 hours of incubation. Following incubation, significantly more 1-cell mouse embryos developed into hatching blastocysts compared with those from the control culture medium alone, both within strains of mice and overall for treatments. Initial success using the chick embryo coculture system with precompaction-stage bovine morulae and 2- to 8-cell caprine embryos was also reported.[163,164] Significantly more expanded (80%) and hatching blastocysts (35%) resulted with precompaction-stage bovine morulae following culture in the chick embryo amnion compared with expanded (15%) and hatching blastocysts (0%) following culture in Ham's F-10 control medium.[165] Similar results to those obtained with bovine morulae were obtained when 2- to 8-cell goat embryos were cultured in the amniotic cavity of chick embryos.[166]

In a subsequent study with bovine embryos, Blakewood et al.[104] showed that culturing early-morula stage embryos either with a uterine cell monolayer or in the chick embryo culture prior to freezing resulted in significantly greater post-thaw embryo development than when embryos were cultured in the Ham's F-12 control medium. This approach of culturing prior to freezing was suggested as a way to improve post-thaw embryo survival in cattle and other mammalian species.

Blakewood et al.[82] further verified the ability of the chick embryo coculture system to enhance development of 2- to 8-cell goat embryos through the in vitro block stage of development. In the first experiment, both the fetal bovine uterine fibroblast monolayer and chick embryo coculture for 72 hours produced significantly more expanded and hatched blastocysts than the Ham's F-10 control medium alone (Table 14.7). The results were even more dramatic in the second experiment, where the 2- to 8-cell caprine embryos were placed in the amniotic cavity of the chick embryo for 96 hours compared with 72 hours in the first experiment. In this case, no early-stage goat embryos developed to the expanded or the hatched blastocyst stages with the fetal uterine monolayer or with the control medium; however, 86% of the embryos cocultured in the chick embryo amnion reached the expanded blastocyst stage and 82% developed to the hatched blastocyst stage in vitro. After culture, four recipient goat females received surgically transplanted chick embryo coculture morulae, two maintained pregnancies to term, and six live transplant offspring (50% of all embryos transferred) were born.[167] These findings further indicate that the developing chick embryo has potent embryotropic properties, and that these properties are evident with embryos across mammalian species.

Recently an attempt was made to culture fish embryos (*Oryzias latipes*) for 3 days in the unfertilized chicken egg yolk.[169] After 72 hours of incubation, the fish embryos developed with the best success rate under the vitelline membrane of the chicken ovum, developed moderately well in whole yolk suspension, but did not live more than 24 hours in culture medium alone. Although the embryotropic properties of avian amniotic fluids and yolk material remain largely undefined, the current need for a practical in vitro culture system may make chick embryo coculture an economical and viable alternative to coculture systems presently in use.

Cells Other Than Those of Reproductive Origin

Cole and Paul[25] first reported that a high percentage of mouse blastocysts hatched from the zona pellucida when cultured with a feeder layer of irradiated HeLa cells. Some years later, Glass et al.[170] evaluated several different types of helper cells (liver, L, JLS-V11, and teratocarcinoma cells) for culturing mouse embryos through to hatching stage and noted no differences in culture efficiency among these cell types.

More recently, Overskei and Cincotta[171] reported developmental success (83%) when 2-cell mouse embryos were cocultured in vitro on a monolayer of hamster hepatocytes. Correspondingly, excellent results were reported in this laboratory[172] when a commercially available cell line (Buffalo rat liver cells) was used to coculture 2-cell mouse embryos in vitro. It is interesting to note that the Buffalo rat liver cells produced better results during in vitro culture than did similar embryos incubated on mouse oviductal cells. In preliminary studies in this laboratory, these cells cocultured with early-stage and IVF-derived bovine embryos provided excellent results during in vitro culture.

An effort was made to coculture precompaction-stage mouse embryos in vitro using either bovine fetal spleen (BFS) cell monolayers or chicken embryo fibroblast (CEF) monolayers.[173] Although the latter offered no marked advantage over control medium, overall more of the murine embryos did hatch during coculture when the BFS cells were incorporated into the culture system. A similar study was conducted using BFS and CEF monolayers to coculture bovine morulae in vitro.[174] The BFS and CEF systems produced more hatched embryos (75 and 83%, respectively) than the control culture medium (45%). In addition, these two coculture systems were compared with a bovine cumulus cell coculture system using IVF-derived bovine embryos in the same laboratory.[175] The best success with development and hatching in vitro occurred with bovine cumulus cells rather than BFS cells or CEF monolayers.

Ouhibi et al.[145] evaluated the development of 1-cell mouse embryos cocultured on reproductive tract cells (oviductal epithelium) or established cell lines derived from cells other than those of reproductive origin (kidney cells). The oviductal cell coculture treatments consisted of mouse oviduct organ cultures, mouse oviductal cells, and bovine oviductal monolayers consisting of both polarized and unpolarized cells. Also, polarized and unpolarized oviductal cell monolayers and kidney cell monolayers (Vero and MDBK) were compared with control medium alone and the in vivo environment. The highest percentage of morulae and blastocysts were obtained from embryos placed in mouse oviductal organ cultures (77%). The percentage of morulae and blastocysts resulting from mouse oviductal, bovine unpolarized, and bovine polarized monolayers were 67, 48, and 14%, respectively. In addition, Vero unpolarized and polarized monolayers yielded lower developmental rates (8 and 4%) than MDBK unpolarized and polarized monolayers (74 and 21%). Overall, maintenance of cell polarization resulted in lower developmental rates during monolayer coculture. From this study it appears that the established Vero cell line was not suitable for development of mouse embryos.

These studies indicate that various cell lines and cell monolayers developed from tissues other than those of adult and fetal reproductive origins are capable of supporting development of early-stage embryos for up to 72 hours during in vitro culture. Certainly, being able to purchase a pathogen-free cell line with embryotropic capabilities and then thawing the cells for embryo culture would make coculture an acceptable procedure for commercial embryo transplant units.

Coculture of Human Embryos

The effectiveness of coculturing human IVF-derived zygotes on uterine cell monolayers has now been confirmed in several laboratories. Wiemer et al.[98] first reported coculturing human IVF-derived zygotes on fetal bovine uterine fibroblasts for intervals ranging from 26 to 32 hours prior to autotransfer. Significantly more embryos (resulting from 288 zygotes) were classified as having good morphology when incubated on bovine fibroblast monolayers (52%) than when incubated in medium alone (30%). Furthermore, the implantation rate was higher for the cocultured embryos than for embryos similarly cultured in medium alone. Similar findings were reported for cocultured human zygotes in another study from the same IVF group.[99]

Bongso et al.[176] reported improved in vitro development of IVF-derived human zygotes

following coculture with human ampullary cells. After culture, the formation of a blastocoelic cavity was noted in 78% of 23 human embryos in coculture, compared with only 33% of 18 embryos cultured in medium alone. Menezo et al.[177] used Vero kidney cells for the coculture of poor-quality human embryos that were judged to be unsuitable for freezing and not transferred. When these embryos were placed on a monolayer coculture for 5 days, 61% of 41 embryos reached the blastocyst stage, compared with only 3% of 31 cultured in medium alone. The potential of human oviductal and endometrial cells for culturing IVF-derived zygotes was recently reviewed by Bongso et al.[178] Certainly this option for culturing human embryos prior to their transfer cannot be overlooked in the years to come.

The primary element of concern to the medical community, however, would be the potential for transmission of pathologic agents from human coculture cells to the embryos during in vitro incubation. Studies with embryos from farm animals to date indicate that an intact zona pellucida during collection and transfer procedures protects the recipient female against extrazonal disease transmission.[179–181]

Amniotic Fluids in Embryo Culture

Human amniotic fluids have been used as an alternative to balanced salt solutions for in vitro fertilization and culture of human embryos. In an initial study, Gianaroli et al.[182] collected amniotic fluids from women during weeks 16 to 21 of gestation to culture murine embryos. The fluids were harvested by amniocentesis, and the supernatant after centrifugation was used for embryo culture. When 2-cell mouse embryos were cultured in this amniotic fluid, 91% developed to the blastocyst stage, compared with 85% cultured in Whittingham's T6 medium supplemented with fetal bovine serum. When amniotic fluids from different stages of gestation (20–21 weeks) were used to culture 2-cell mouse embryos, no differences in embryo growth rates were noted with fluids from different stages of pregnancy. These fluids were also used for fertilization, culture, and transfer of human embryos, resulting in four pregnancies from nine patients (44%). This compared with only two pregnancies in 12 patients (17%) when T6 medium supplemented with maternal serum was used during the procedure.

In a study using fresh and frozen-thawed amniotic fluids of human origin, Fugger et al.[183] noted no differences in the development of early-stage murine embryos when amniotic fluids were frozen prior to culture. Human amniotic fluids from weeks 14 to 23 of pregnancy were used for the in vitro culture of 2-cell murine embryos. When nonfrozen amniotic fluids were used, 96% blastocyst development occurred, compared with 97% in frozen-thawed amniotic fluids. The results from both amniotic fluid cultures were greater than the 78% blastocyst development in the control medium (Ham's F-10 with 10% human serum).

Embryotropic activity has been verified in human amniotic fluids by evaluating early-stage murine embryos cultured with amniotic fluids obtained from women during early pregnancy.[184] Amniotic fluids from later stages of pregnancy were also evaluated during the culture of 2-cell mouse embryos. Amniotic fluid from women at 35 to 39 weeks of pregnancy resulted in significantly less development to the hatching blastocyst stage than fluid from women at 15 to 16 weeks of gestation.

Oettle and Wiswedel[185] cultured 1,000 mouse embryos for 72 hours in human amniotic fluid extracted during the week 16 of pregnancy or in Earle's medium and noted significantly more expanded blastocysts compared with embryos cultured in control medium. In another study, 92% of the IVF-derived murine embryos cultured in human amniotic fluids underwent cleavage, compared with 86% in Ham's F-10 medium.[186]

Javed and Wright[187] were the first to use bovine amniotic fluids for the in vitro culture of mammalian embryos in 1990. Two-cell murine embryos were successfully cultured to the hatched blastocyst stage in frozen-thawed bovine amniotic fluids obtained at 70 days or less of gestation. The rates of development to the hatched blastocyst stage were less than those of 2-cell mouse embryos cultured in Whitten's medium (17 versus 60%). However, when the fluids were not frozen prior to culture, amniotic fluids from less than 70 days of gestation resulted in developmental rates equal to those obtained with culture in Whitten's medium (67 versus 64%).

The reported success with in vitro embryo development in amniotic fluids from several mammalian species suggests that these fluids may offer an alternative to serum-supplemented culture media. In addition, it was recently found in this laboratory that chick embryo amniotic fluids have embryotropic capabilities similar to those noted with human amniotic fluid. Thus, it should not be overlooked that fluids of embryonic or fetal origin could be suitable for the culture of animal or possibly human embryos.

Conclusion

Repeatable techniques for producing in vitro-fertilized farm animal embryos have made the early-stage zygote more accessible for experimentation and developmental study.[1,148,156] These studies have illustrated the need for culture systems that have the ability to promote normal in vitro development of early-stage farm animal embryos. Although the first live in vitro-fertilized calf was not produced until 1981,[188] the level of interest in developing early-stage embryos in vitro has continued, and this will likely rank as one of the major research areas of reproductive physiologists and embryologists in the 1990s.

The potential availability of a large number of in vitro-fertilized oocytes has stimulated increased efforts to develop gene transfer and embryonic cloning techniques for larger, economically important animals.[4,6,63,64] Unlike the human zygote, early-stage embryos of both laboratory and farm animals have consistently exhibited an in vitro developmental block that has hindered research progress with embryo culture experiments for decades. For farm animals, the ability to produce larger numbers of early-stage embryos in the laboratory would offer little benefit without developing an in vitro culture system that would allow the embryos to progress through the in vitro block stage. Correspondingly, early-stage embryos of these animals (e.g., cattle) are not considered to be good candidates for recipient transfer, since acceptable pregnancy rates are not usually achieved until embryos reach the morula and blastocyst stages of development.[189,190] If early-stage, IVF-derived embryos could be cultured in vitro to later morphologic stages, ultimately to improve embryo transfer success rates, marked gains could be made with a wide range of new reproductive technologies in the commercial livestock industry.

Recent published reports indicate that significant progress has been made in the in vitro culture of large animal embryos during the last 10 years. This progress has been due primarily to the development of new media recipes and the incorporation of helper cells into embryo culture procedures. These improvements in culture methodology have led to reproductive technology innovations never before considered in the livestock industry. A potential example of this technology would be bisecting the embryo (morulae and blastocysts), producing an offspring from a half-embryo, and storing the remaining half-embryo in liquid nitrogen to be used to produce a genetically identical twin at a later date.[3,60,191] Another example would be the administration of gonadotropin during pregnancy (e.g., in the cow) to stimulate follicular development[192] and the use of vaginal ultrasound-guided follicular puncture[193] to harvest supplemental oocytes from these gestating females for IVF. This approach would allow the pregnant female to produce her own natural offspring each year, in addition to allowing her to produce extra transplant offspring from IVF, embryo coculture, and recipient transfer procedures.

Prior to the 1980s the production of offspring from IVF and embryo micromanipulation techniques in most mammals was considerably restricted by the absence of suitable culture systems (with the exception of some strains of mice)[9,194] capable of effectively supporting in vitro development of early-stage embryos to transferable-quality morulae and blastocysts. The limitations imposed by inadequate culture

media for farm animal embryos were markedly reduced with procedures for the temporary culture of early-stage embryos in the oviducts of rabbits[58] and sheep.[59,60] This in vivo culture approach, however, is labor-intensive, time-consuming, and has not been well accepted by commercial embryo transplant units.

With recent advances made in embryo culture systems for farm animals, it appears that in vitro incubation problems may have been partially alleviated with the development of helper cell coculture systems, which permit embryonic growth and development through the in vitro block stage to morulae and blastocysts while in culture. In addition, coculture systems using trophoblastic vesicles have shown to enhance embryo development to the morula stage in vitro.[73,75] It now appears that uterine and oviductal epithelial and epithelial-like cells have an advantage over corresponding fibroblasts (those originating from these same tissue types) for culturing farm animal embryos. Recent studies suggest that oviductal cells (although more difficult to maintain in culture than fibroblasts) have become the first choice for embryo coculture by those producing laboratory-derived embryos for experimental studies. Others are now using the new chick embryo amnion culture system[163] and the cumulus cell coculture system[156,195] for embryo culture, and are reporting similar results to those using oviductal cell cocultures for IVF-derived farm animal embryos. Presently, efforts are being put forth to develop a completely defined medium for embryo culture.[129] However, progress has been slower than expected. Most research efforts at present are directed toward multicell bilayered or three-dimensional coculture systems, and efforts in this area will likely continue in years to come.

In humans developing embryos (≤8 cells) are usually transferred to the uterus of donor or recipient 2 days or more before their normal entry from the oviduct.[177] Premature entry of embryos into the uterus generally is not conducive to optimum embryo development in most animal species, and thus probably would not be advantageous to the human embryo. An added problem with human IVF is that the uterine environment of the donor female will probably not be normal at the time of embryo replacement. This is most often the result of daily doses of gonadotropic agents administered to stimulate follicular development, which often produce excess circulating steroid hormones and uterine hypertrophy during the treatment cycle. This is not a problem with animal embryo transplant procedures, since embryos are transferred to healthy, cyclic recipient animals or frozen and then subsequently transferred to recipients or to the donor at a later date, when she has resumed regular cyclicity. It is proposed that lengthening the usual culture interval with a helper cell coculture (e.g., oviductal or cumulus cells) for human IVF embryos may help overcome part of this problem and may increase the chance for pregnancy after embryo replacement.

In recent years researchers have begun to develop methods to coculture human IVF-derived zygotes.[98–101,176–178,196–198] Since the human embryo apparently does not have the an in vitro block such as occurs in laboratory and farm animals, the need to develop embryo culture technology has not been as great as with other mammalian species. Also, human embryos are transplanted into the uterus of the donor or surrogate female at the 2- to 8-cell stage rather than at the morula or blastocyst stage, as in animals, thus reducing interest in the culture of human embryos. However, since pregnancy rates from human embryo transfer have been considerably less than with research animals,[199] there may be a need to use embryo culture to develop the human embryo to more advanced morphologic stages in vitro prior to transfer to increase the chance of pregnancy.[99,200]

Possibly the most meaningful use of culture systems for human embryos in the future will be to nurture or rescue poor-quality or questionable-quality embryos in vitro prior to replacement in donors or transfer to surrogate females, thus increasing the overall pregnancy rate for oocytes harvested per donor collection. Coculture systems also should not be overlooked for use in enhancing post-thaw embryo survival. In addition, developing efficient coculture methods for humans would aid in evaluating embryo viability and conducting genetic analysis procedures prior to embryo replacement.

References

1. Lu KH, Gordon I, Gallagher M, McGovern H. Pregnancy established in cattle by transfer of embryos derived from in vitro. Vet Rec 1987;121:259–260.
2. First NL, Parrish JJ. In vitro fertilization of ruminants. J Reprod Fertil (Suppl) 1987; 34:151–165.
3. Godke RA, Rorie RW. Methods and applications of embryo bisection for cattle. Proc Eighth Amer Embryo Transf Conf, Reno, NV, 1988;66–84.
4. Hammer RE, Pursel VG, Rexroad CE Jr, Wall RJ, Bolt KJ, Ebert KM, Palmiter RD, Brinster RL. Production of transgenic rabbits, sheep and pigs by microinjection. Nature 1985;315:680–683.
5. Willadsen SM. Nuclear transplantation in sheep embryos. Nature 1986;320:63–65.
6. Robl JM, Prather R, Barnes F, Eyestone W, Northy D, Gilligan B, First NL. Nuclear transplantation in bovine embryos. J Anim Sci 1987;64:642–647.
7. Prather RS, Barnes FL, Sims MM, Robl JM, Eyestone WH, First NL. Nuclear transplantation in the bovine embryo: Assessment of donor nuclei and recipient oocytes. Biol Reprod 1990;37:859–866.
8. Bavister BD. Role of oviductal secretions in embryonic growth in vitro and in vivo. Theriogenology 1988;29:143–154.
9. Kane MT: Culture media and culture of early embryos. Theriogenology 1987;27:49–57.
10. Brachet A. Development in vitro de blastodermes et de jeunes embryons de mammiferes. CR Hebd Seanc Acad Sci 1912; 55:1191–1193.
11. Lewis WH, Gregory PW. Cinematographs of living developing rabbit eggs. Science 1929; 69:226–229.
12. Carrel A. Artificial activation of the growth in vitro of connective tissue. J Exp Med 1913; 17:14–19.
13. Pincus G. Observation of the living eggs of the rabbit. Proc Royal Soc Ser B 1930;107: 132–167.
14. Waddington CH, Waterman AJ. The development in vitro of young rabbit embryos. J Anat 1933;67:356–370.
15. Hammond J Jr. Recovery and culture of tubal mouse ova. Nature 1949;163:28–29.
16. Dowling DF. Problems of the transplantation of fertilized ova. J Agric Sci 1949;39:374–396.

78. Hwang DH, Pool SH, Rorie RW, Boudreau M, Godke RA. Transitional changes in arachidonic acid metabolism by bovine embryos at different developmental stage. Prostaglandins 1988;35:387–402.

79. Thibodeaux JK, Myers MW, Roussel JD, Godke RA. Intrauterine infusion of PGE_2 and subsequent luteal function in cattle. Prostaglandins 1992;49:531–541.

80. Pool SH, Rorie RW, Pendleton RJ, Menino AR, Godke RA. Culture of early-stage bovine embryos inside day-13 and day-14 precultured trophoblastic vesicles. Ann NY Acad Sci 1988;541:407–418.

81. Rexroad CE Jr, Powell AM. Co-culture of ovine eggs with oviductal cells and trophoblastic vesicles. Theriogenology 1988; 29:387–397.

82. Blakewood EG, Pool SH, Prichard JF, Godke RA. Culturing two- to eight-cell caprine embryos using domestic chicken eggs. Mol Reprod Develop 1990;27:288–294.

83. Ball BA, Altschul M, Hillman RB. Culture and transfer of equine trophoblastic vesicles. Proc Second Internatl Symp Equine Embryo Transf 1989;12(abstr).

84. Hehnke KE, Thompson DL Jr, Barry BE, White KL, Wood TC. Formation and characterization of vesicles from day-10 horse conceptuses. Theriogenology 1990;34:709–719.

85. Rorie RW, Pendleton RJ, Pool SH, White KL, Godke RA. Cryopreservation of bovine trophoblastic vesicles. Theriogenology 1987; 27:272(abstr).

86. Kuzan FB, Wright RW Jr. Observations on the development of bovine morulae on various cellular and noncellular substrata. J Anim Sci 1982;54:811–816.

87. Kuzan FB, Wright RW. Blastocyst expansion, hatching, and attachment of porcine embryos co-cultured with bovine fibroblasts in vitro. Anim Reprod Sci 1982;5:57–63.

88. Voelkel SA, Amborski GF, Hill KG, Godke RA. Use of uterine-cell monolayer culture system for micromanipulated bovine embryos. Theriogenology 1985;24:271–281.

89. Allen RL, Wright RW. In vitro development of porcine embryos in coculture with endometrial cell monolayers or culture supernatants. J Anim Sci 1984;59:1657–1661.

90. Kuzan FB, Wright RW Jr. Attachment of porcine blastocyst to fibroblast monolayers in vitro. Theriogenology 1981;16:651–658.

91. Wiemer KE, Denniston RS, Amborski GF, White KL, Godke RA. A fetal fibroblast monolayer system of in vitro culture of bovine embryos. J Anim Sci (Suppl 1) 1987;65: 122(abstr).

92. Wiemer KE, Amborski GF, Denniston RS, White KL, Godke RA. Use of a hormone-treated fetal uterine fibroblast monolayer system for in vitro culture of bovine embryos. Theriogenology 1987;27:294(abstr).

93. Wiemer KE, Casey PL, DeVore D, Godke RA. The culture of equine embryos using a new fetal uterine monolayer culture system. Theriogenology 1988;29:327(abstr).

94. Wiemer KE, Casey PL, Godke RA. Short term storage of equine embryos on a fetal bovine uterine monolayer followed by transfer to recipients. Proc Eleventh Internatl Congr Anim Reprod Artif Insem 1988;2:198.

95. Wiemer KE, Casey PL, Mitchell PS, Godke RA. Pregnancies following 24-hour co-culture of equine embryos on foetal bovine uterine monolayer cells. Equine Vet J (Suppl) 1989; 8:117–122.

96. Wiemer KE, Amborski GA, Denniston RS, Blakewood EG, Godke RA. Development of a fetal bovine uterine-cell monolayer culture system for bovine embryos. Theriogenology 1993;39 (in press).

97. Wiemer KE, Cohen J, Godke RA. Unpublished data, 1988.

98. Wiemer KE, Cohen J, Amborski GF, Wiker S, Wright G, Munyakazi L, Godke RA. In vitro development and implantation of human embryos following culture on fetal bovine uterine fibroblast cells. Human Reprod 1989; 4:595–600.

99. Wiemer KE, Cohen J, Wiker SR, Malter HE, Wright G, Godke RA. Coculture of human zygotes on fetal bovine uterine fibroblast: Embryonic morphology and implantation. Fertil Steril 1989;52:503–508.

100. Cohen J, Wiemer K, Wiker S, Malter H, Kort H, Massey J, Godke R. Co-culture of human zygotes on fetal bovine uterine fibroblasts. Proc Fifth World Congr In Vitro Fertil and Altern Assist Reprod, Jerusalem, Israel, 1989;41(abstr).

101. Cohen J, Wiemer K, Godke R. Helper cells from the bovine reproductive tract for culture of human zygotes. Proc Second In Vitro Fertil. and Embryo Transf Post-Graduate Course, UCLA, Santa Barbara, CA, 1989:1–2.

102. Rodriguez HF, Wiemer KW, Denniston RS, Godke RA. A bilayered fetal-cell co-culture system for culturing bovine embryos. Theriogenology 1990;33:309(abstr).

103. Thibodeaux JK, Roussel JD, Menezo Y, Godke RA, Goodeaux LL. A method for in vitro cell culture of superficial bovine uterine endometrial epithelium. J Tissue Culture Meth 1991;13:247–252.

104. Blakewood EG, Wiemer KE, Godke RA. Post-thaw viability of bovine embryos cultured in domestic chicken eggs or on epithelial

monolayers prior to freezing in liquid nitrogen (LN$_2$). Theriogenology 1989;31:177(abstr).

105. Prichard JF, Thibodeaux JK, Pool SH, Blakewood EG, Menezo Y, Godke RA. In-vitro co-culture of early stage caprine embryos with oviduct and uterine epithelial cells. Human Reprod. 1992;7:533–557.

106. Goodeaux LL, Anzalone CA, Thibodeaux JK, Menezo Y, Roussel JD, Voelkel SA. Successful nonsurgical collection of Macaca mulatta embryos. Theriogenology 1990;34:1159–1167.

107. Goodeaux LL, Thibodeaux JK, Voelkel SA, Anzalone CA, Roussel JD, Cohen JC, Menezo Y. Collection, co-culture and transfer of rhesus pre-implantation embryos. Assist Reprod Technol Androl 1990;1:370–379.

108. Goodeaux LL, Voelkel SA, Anzalone CA, Menezo Y, Graves KH. The effect of rhesus uterine epithelial cell monolayers in in vitro growth of rhesus embryos. Theriogenology 1989;31:197(abstr).

109. Goodeaux LL, Anzalone CA, Voelkel SA, Menezo Y, Thibodeaux JK, Roussel JD. The effect of CMRL-1066 and Menezo B2 media on co-culture of rhesus embryos. Theriogenology 1990;33:235(abstr).

110. Pool SH, Wiemer KE, Rorie RW, Godke RA. The use of trophoblastic vesicles and fetal uteirne fibroblast cells for the culture of precompaction-stage bovine embryos. Proc Eleventh Internatl Congr Anim Reprod Artif Insem 1988;4:479.

111. Thibodeaux JK, Goodeaux LL, Roussel JD, Amborski GF, Moreau JD, Godke RA. Stage of the bovine estrous cycle and in vitro characteristics of uterine and oviductal epithelial cells. J Dairy Sci (Suppl 1) 1991;74:295(abstr).

112. Thibodeaux JK, Goodeaux LL, Roussel JD, Menezo Y, Amborski GF, Moreau JD, Godke RA. Effects of stage of the bovine estrous cycle on in vitro characteristics of uterine and oviductal epithelial cells. Human Reprod 1991;6:751–760.

113. Thibodeaux JK, Menezo Y, Roussel JD, Hansel W, Goodeaux LL, Thompson DL Jr, Godke RA. Coculture of in vitro fertilized bovine embryos with oviductal epithelial cells originating from different stages of the estrous cycle. J Dairy Sci 1992;75:1448–1455.

114. Thibodeaux JK. In Vitro Culture of Bovine Uterine and Oviduct Epithelial Cells. PhD Dissertation, Louisiana State University, Baton Rouge, LA, 1991.

115. Thibodeaux JK, Myers MW, Goodeaux LL, Menezo Y, Roussel JD, Broussard JR, Godke RA. Evaluating on in vitro culture system of bovine uterine and oviduct epithelial cells for subsequent embryo co-culture. Reprod Fertil Dev 1992;4:573–583.

116. Whittingham DG. Development of zygotes in cultured mouse oviducts. I. The effect of varying oviductal conditions. J Exp Zool 1968;169:391–398.

117. Rexroad CE Jr, Powell AM. Co-culture of sheep ova and cells from sheep oviduct vesicles. Theriogenology 1986;25:187(abstr).

118. Rexroad CE Jr, Powell AM. Co-culture of sheep ova and cells from sheep oviduct. Theriogenology 1986;37:859–866.

119. Rexroad CE Jr, Powell AM. Co-culture of ovine eggs with oviductal cells in medium 199. J Anim Sci 1988;66:947–953.

120. Gandolfi F, Moor RM. Stimulation of early embryonic development in the sheep by co-culture with oviduct epithelial cells. J Reprod Fertil 1987;81:23–28.

121. Prichard JF, Pool SH, Blakewood EG, Menezo Y, Godke RA. Culture of early-stage caprine embryos using goat oviductal cell monolayers. Theriogenology 1991;35:259(abstr).

122. Bunch TD, Foote WC, Call JW, Wright RW Jr, Selgrath JP, Foote WD. Long term culture of two to eight-cell ovine embryos in various co-culture systems. Encyclia 1987;64:66–72.

123. Maciulis A, Bunch TD, Foote WC, Call JW. The influence of oviductal and embryo cell co-cultures on the development of one to two-cell ovine embryos. Encyclia 1987;64:73–78.

124. Eyestone WH, Vignier J, First NL. Co-culture of early bovine embryos with oviductal epithelium. Theriogenology 1987;27:228(abstr).

125. Eyestone WH, First NL. Co-culture of bovine embryos with oviductal tissue. Proc Eleventh Internl Congr Anim Reprod Artif Insem 1988;4:471(abstr).

126. Eyestone WH, First NL. Co-culture of early cattle embryos to the blastocyst stage with oviductal tissue or in conditioned medium. J Reprod Fertil 1989;85:715–720.

127. Ellington JE, Farrell PB, Carney EW, Simkin ME, Foote RH. In vitro development potential of bovine zygotes in oviduct epithelial cell co-culture systems. Theriogenology 1990;33:223(abstr).

128. Ellington JE, Farrell PB, Foote RH. Comparison of six-day bovine embryo development in uterine tube (oviduct) epithelial cell co-culture versus in vivo development in the cow. Theriogenology 1990;34:837–844.

129. Ellington JE, Farrell PB, Simkin ME, Foote RH, Goldman EE, McGrath AB. Development and survival after transfer of cow embryos cultured from 1- to 2-cells to morulae or blastocyst in rabbit oviducts or in a simple medium with bovine oviduct epithelial cells. J Reprod Fertil 1990;89:293–299.

17. Chang MC. Effects of heterologous sera on fertilized rabbit ova. J Gen Physiol 1949; 32:291–300.

18. Brock H, Rowson LEA. The production of viable bovine ova. J Agric Sci 1952;42: 479–488.

19. Hafez ESE, Sugie T, Gordon I. Superovulation and related phenomena in the beef cow. I. Superovulatory response following PMS and HCG injections. J Reprod Fertil 1963; 5:359–379.

20. Onuma H, Foote RH. In vitro development of ova from prepuberal cattle. J Dairly Sci 1969;52:1085–1087.

21. Gordon I. Cattle twinning by the egg transfer approach. In: Rowson LEA, ed. Egg Transfer in Cattle. Luxembourg: Commission of European Communities, 1976:305–319.

22. Wright RW Jr, Anderson GB, Cupps PT, Drost M, Bradford GE. In vitro culture of embryos from adult and prepubeal ewes. J Anim Sci 1976;42:912–917.

23. Renard JP, du Mesnil du Buisson F, Winterberger-Torres S, Menezo Y. In vitro culture of cow embryos from day 6 and day 7. In: Rowson LEA, ed. Egg Transfer in Cattle. Luxembourg: Commission of European Communities, 1976:154–159.

24. Wright RW Jr, Bondioli KR. Aspects of in vitro fertilization and embryo culture in domestic animals. J Anim Sci 1981;53: 702–729.

25. Cole RJ, Paul J. Properties of cultured pre-implantation mouse and rabbit embryos and cell strains developed from them. In: Wolstenhoume GEW, O'Conner M, eds. Preimplantation Stages of Pregnancy. Boston: Little, Brown & Co, 1965:82–155.

26. Whitten WK. Nutrient requirements for the culture of preimplantation embryos in vitro. Adv Biol Sci 1971;6:129.

27. Whittingham DG, Bavister BD. Development of hamster eggs fertilized in vitro or in vivo. J Reprod Fertil 1974;38:489–492.

28. Markert CH. Genetic manipulation of mammalian embryos: Current techniques and their potential usefulness in livestock improvement. Proc Tenth Internatl Congr Anim Reprod Artif Insem 1984;2:13–19.

29. Kane MT, Foote RH. Culture of two- and four-cell rabbit embryos to expanding blastocyst stage in synthetic media. Proc Soc Exp Biol Med 1970;133:921–925.

30. Johnson LA, Donoghue AM, O'Brien SJ, Wildt DE. Culture medium and protein supplementation influence in vitro fertilization and embryo development in the domestic cat. J Exp Zool 1991;257:350–359.

31. Thibault C. La culture in vitro de l'oeuf de vache. Ann Biol Anim Biochem Biophys 1966;15:159–164.

32. Wintenberger S, Dauzier L, Thibault C. Le development in vitro de l'oeuf de la brebis et de celui de la chevre. CR Seanc Soc Biol 1953;147:1971.

33. Betteridge KJ. Embryo Transfer in Farm Animals. Agricultural Monograph No. 16, Ottawa, Canada 1977;39.

34. Davis DL, Day BN. Cleavage and blastocyst formation by pig eggs in vitro. J Anim Sci 1978;46:1043–1053.

35. Edwards RG, Purty JM, Steptoe DC, Walters DE. The growth of human preimplantation embryos in vitro. Am J Obstet Gynecol 1981; 141:408.

36. Whittingham DG, Biggers JD. Fallopian tube and early cleavage in the mouse. Nature 1967; 213:942–943.

37. Eyestone WH, First NL. A study of the 8- to 16-cell developmental block in bovine embryos cultured in vitro. Theriogenology 1986;23: 152(abstr).

38. Flach G, Johnson MH, Braude PR, Taylor RAS, Bolton VN. The transition from maternal to embryonic control in the 2-cell mouse embryo. EMBO J 1982;1:681–686.

39. Frei RE, Schultz GA, Church RB. Qualitative and quantitative changes in protein synthesis occur at the 8-16-cell stage of embryogenesis in the cow. J Reprod Fertil 1989;86:637–641.

40. King WA, Chartrain I, Kopeony V, Betteridge KJ, Bergeron H. Nucleolus organizer regions and nucleoli in mammalian embryos. J Reprod Fertil (Suppl) 1989;38:63–71.

41. Jung T. Protein synthesis and degradation in non-cultured and in vitro cultured rabbit blastocyst. J Reprod Fertil 1989;86:507–512.

42. Whitten WK. Culture of tubal ova. Nature 1956;177:96.

43. Whitten WK, Biggers JD. Complete development in vitro of the preimplantation stages of the mouse in a simple chemically defined medium. J Reprod Fertil 1968;17:399–401.

44. Restall BJ, Wales RG. The fallopian tube of the sheep. III. The chemical composition of the fluid from the fallopian tube. Aust J Biol Sci 1966;19:687–698.

45. Tervit HR, Whittingham DG, Rowson LEA. Successful culture in vitro of sheep and cattle ova. J Reprod Fertil 1972;30:495–497.

46. Shea BF, Hines DJ, Lightfoot DE, Ollis GW, Olsa SM. In: Rowson LEA, ed. Egg Transfer in Cattle. Luxembourg: Commission of European Communities, 1976:145–152.

47. Bowen RA, Hasler JF, Seidel GE Jr. In vitro development of bovine embryos in chemically defined media. Proc Eighth Ann Res Conf, Colorado State University, Fort Collins, CO, 1975:171(abstr).

48. Kane MT. Variability in different lots of commercial bovine serum albumin affects cell

multiplication and hatching of rabbit blastocyst in culture. J Reprod Fertil 1983;69:555–558.

49. Roric RW, Ghedt DW, Miller GF, Lester TD. Development of in vitro produced bovine embryos in synthetic oviductal fluid (SOF) medium supplemented with different lots of fraction V bovine serum albumin (BSA). J Anim Sci (Suppl 1) 1991;69:47(abstr).

50. Menezo Y, Testart J, Perrone D. Serum is not necessary for human in vitro fertilization, early embryo culture, and transfer. Fertil Steril 1984;42:750–755.

51. Averill RLW, Adams CE, Rowson LEA. Transfer of mammalian ova between species. Nature 1955;176:167–168.

52. Hunter GI, Bishop GP, Adams JCE, Rowson LEA. Successful long-distance aerial transport of fertilized sheep ova. J Reprod Fertil 1962; 3:33–40.

53. Lawson RAS, Rowson LEA, Adams CE. The development of sheep eggs in the rabbit oviduct and their viability after re-transfer to ewes. J Reprod Fertil 1972;28:105–116.

54. Lawson RAS, Rowson LEA, Adams CE. The development of cow eggs in the rabbit oviduct and their viability after re-transfer to heifers. J Reprod Fertil 1972;28:313–315.

55. Sreenan J, Scanlon PF, Gordon I. Culture of fertilized cattle eggs. J Agric Sci 1968;70: 183–185.

56. Sreenan J, Scanlon PF. Continued cleavage of fertilized bovine ova in the rabbit. Nature 1968;217:867.

57. Agrawal KP, Mongha IV, Bhattacharyya NK. Survival of goat embryos in rabbit oviducts. Vet Rec 1983;112:200.

58. Boland MP. Use of the oviduct as a screening tool for the viability of mammalian eggs. Theriogenology 1984;21:126–137.

59. Willadsen SM. A method for culture of micromanipulated sheep embryos and its use to produce monozygotic twins. Nature 1979; 227:298–300.

60. Willadsen SM. Micromanipulation of embryos of the large domestic species. In: Adams CE, ed. Mammalian Egg Transfer. Boca Raton, FL: CRC Press, 1982:185–210.

61. Gordon I, Lu KH. Production of embryos in vitro and its impact on livestock production. Theriogenology 1990;33:77–87.

62. Westhusin ME, Slapak JR, Fuller DT, Kraemer DC. Culture of agar-embedded one and two cell bovine embryos and embryos produced by nuclear transfer in the sheep and rabbit oviduct. Theriogenology 1989;31: 371.

63. Marek DE, Pryor JH, Whitesell TH, Looney CR. Nuclear transplantation in the bovine: Effect of donor embryo age on subsequent embryo production. Theriogenology 1990; 33:283(abstr).

64. Bondioli KR, Westhusin ME, Looney CR. Production of identical bovine offspring by nuclear transfer. Theriogenology 1990;33: 165–174.

65. Ebert KM, Papaioannou VE. In vivo culture of embryos in the immature mouse oviduct. Theriogenology 1989;31:299–308.

66. Biggers JD, Gwatkin RBL, Brinster RL. Development of mouse embryos in organ cultures of fallopian tubes on a chemically defined medium. Nature 1962;194:747–749.

67. Gwatkin RBL, Biggers JD. Histology of mouse fallopian tubes maintained in organ cultures on a chemically defined medium. Int J Fertil 1963;8:453–457.

68. Bavister BD. Studies on the developmental block in cultured hamster embryos. In: Bavister BD, ed. The Mammalian Embryo: Regulation of Growth and Differentiation In Vitro. New York: Plenum Press, 1987:61–78.

69. Bavister BD, Minami N. Use of cultured mouse oviducts to bypass in vitro development block in cleavage stage hamster embryos. Biol Reprod (Suppl 1) 1986;34:119(abstr).

70. Minami N, Bavister BD, Iritani I. Development of hamster two-cell embryos in the isolated mouse oviduct in organ culture system. Gamete Res 1988;19:235–240.

71. Rumsey RE. Fetal mouse oviducts in tissue and organ cultures. Fertil Steril 1969;20: 149–162.

72. Krisher RL, Petters RM, Johnson BH, Bavister BD, Archibong AE. Development of porcine embryos from the one-cell stage of blastocyst in mouse oviducts maintained as organ culture. J Exp Zool 1989;249:235–239.

73. Camous S, Heyman Y, Meziou W, Menezo Y. Cleavage beyond the block stage and survival after transfer of early bovine embryos cultured with trophoblastic vesicles. J Reprod Fertil 1984;72:479–485.

74. Heyman Y, Camous S, Fevre J, Meziou W, Martal J. Maintenance of the corpus luteum after uterine transfer of trophoblastic vesicles to cyclic cows and sheep. J Reprod Fertil 1984;70:533–540.

75. Heyman Y, Menezo Y, Chesne P, Camus S, Garnier V. In vitro cleavage of bovine and ovine early embryos: Improved development using co-culture with trophoblastic vesicles. Theriogenology 1987;27:59–68.

76. Heyman Y, Menezo Y. Interaction of trophoblastic vesicles with bovine embryos developing in vitro. In: Bavister BD, ed. The Mammalian Preimplantation Embryo. New York: Plenum Press, 1987:175–191.

77. Heyman Y, Chesne P, Chupin D, Menezo Y. Improvement of survival rate of frozen cattle blastocysts after transfer with trophoblastic vesicles. Theriogenology 1987;27:477–484.

130. Fukui Y. Effects of sera and steroid hormones on development of bovine oocytes matured and fertilized in vitro and co-cultured with bovine oviduct epithelial cells. J Anim Sci 1989;67:1318–1323.

131. Rexroad CE Jr. Co-culture of domestic animal embryos. Theriogenology 1989;31:105–114.

132. Kitiyanant Y, Thonabulsombat C, Tocharaus C, Sanituongse B, Pavasuthipaisit K. Co-culture of bovine embryos from oocytes matured and fertilized in vitro to the blastocyst stage with oviductal tissue. J Sci Soc Thailand 1989;15:251–260.

133. Rorie RW, Xu KP, Betteridge KJ. Effects of culture on the post-thaw viability of cryopreserved in vitro fertilized bovine embryos. Theriogenology 1990;33:331(abstr).

134. Kinis A, Vergos E, Gordon I, Gordon A, Gallagher M. Studies in the production of chimeric cattle embryos by aggregation of blastomeres from embryos derived from oocytes matured and fertilized in vitro. Theriogenology 1990;33:268(abstr).

135. Aoyagi Y, Fukui Y, Iwazumi Y, Urakawa M, Ono H. Effects of culture systems on development of in vitro fertilized bovine ova into blastocysts. Theriogenology 1990;34:749–759.

136. Carney EW, Tobback C, Foote RH. Co-culture of rabbit one-cell embryos with rabbit oviductal epithelial cells. In Vitro Cell Dev Biol 1990;26:629–635.

137. Rodriguez HF, Denniston RS, Godke RA. Co-culture of bovine embryos using a bilayer of bovine oviductal and granulosa cells. Theriogenology 1991;35:264(abstr).

138. White KL, Hehnke K, Rickords LF, Southern LL, Thompson DL, Woods TC. Early embryonic development in vitro by coculture with oviductal epithelial cells in pigs. Biol Reprod 1989;41:425–430.

139. Kapur RP, Johnson LV. Selective sequestration of an oviductal fluid glycoprotein in the perivitelline space of mouse oocytes and embryo. J Exp Zool 1986;238:249–260.

140. Oliphant G, Reynolds AB, Smith PF, Ross PR, Marta JS. Immunocytochemical localization and determination of hormone-induced synthesis of sulfated oviductal glycoproteins. Biol Reprod 1984;31:165–174.

141. Sutton R, Nancarrow CD, Wallace ALC, Rigby NW. Identification of an estrous associated glyco-protein in oviductal fluid of the sheep. J Reprod Fertil 1984;72:415–422.

142. Roberts GP, Parker JM, Symonds HW. Protein from the luminal fluid of the oviduct. J Reprod Fertil 1975;45:301–313.

143. Fazleabas AT, Verhage HG. The detection of oviduct-specific protein in the baboon (Papio anubis). Biol Reprod 1986;35:455–462.

144. Edwards RC. The female reproductive tract. In: Conception in the Human Female. London: Academic Press, 1980;416–524.

145. Ouhibi N, Hamidi J, Guillaud J, Menezo Y. Co-culture of 1-cell mouse embryos on different cell supports. Human Reprod 1990; 5:737–743.

146. Critser ES, First NL. Use of a fluorescent stain for visualization of nuclear material in living oocytes and early embryos. Stain Technol 1986;61:1–5.

147. Faundez R, Spohr I, Boryczko Z. Effect of follicle cells on maturation and in vitro fertilization of cattle oocytes. Proc Eleventh Internatl Congr Anim Reprod Artif Insem 1988;5:325(abstr).

148. Goto K, Kajihara Y, Kosaka S, Koba M, Nakanishi Y, Ogawa K. Pregnancies after co-culture of cumulus cells with bovine embryos derived from in vitro fertilization of in vitro matured follicular oocytes. J Reprod Fertil 1988;83:753–758.

149. Goto K, Kajihara Y, Kosaka S, Koba M, Nakanishi Y, Ogawa K. Pregnancies after in vitro fertilization of cow follicular oocytes, incubation in vitro and their transfer to the cow uterus. Theriogenology 1988;29:251(abstr).

150. Berg U, Brem G. Developmental rates of in vitro produced IVM-IVF bovine oocytes in different cell culture systems. Theriogenology 1990;33:195(abstr).

151. Zhang L, Denniston RS, Godke RA. A method for in vitro fertilization in vitro matured bovine oocytes. Proc So African Soc Anim Sci 1990;20.

152. Zhang L, Blakewood EG, Denniston RS, Godke RA. The effect of insulin on maturation and development of in vitro-fertilized bovine oocytes. Theirogenology 1991;35: 30(abstr).

153. Zhang L, Denniston RS, Godke RA. The effect of insulin on the development of in vitro-fertilized porcine oocytes. J Anim Sci (Suppl 1) 1991;69:49(abstr).

154. Zhang L, Denniston RS, Bunch TD, Godke RA. Cow vs heifers for the production of in vitro-matured, in vitro-fertilized (IVF) embryos. J Anim Sci (Suppl 1) 1991;69: 49(abstr).

155. Zhang L, Flood MR, Bunch TD, Hansel W, Godke RA. Evaluating bovine oviduct cells used in combination with bovine cumulus cells to coculture IVF-derived bovine embryos in vitro. Proc Twelfth Internatl Congr Anim Reprod 1992;3:1375–1377.

156. Zhang L, Denniston RS, Godke RA. A simple method for in vitro maturation, in vitro fertilization and co-culture of bovine oocytes. J Tissue Culture Meth 1992;14:107–111.

157. Younis AI, Brackett BG. In vitro development of bovine oocytes into morulae and blastocysts. Theriogenology 1990;33.355(abstr).

158. Nakao H, Nakatsuji N. Effects of co-culture, medium components and gas phase on in vitro culture of in vitro matured and in vitro fertilized bovine embryos. Theriogenology 1990;33:591–600.

159. Baird JWC, Johnson CA, Williams SR, Godke RA, Jenkins CL, Schmidt G. Increased blastocyst formation in the mouse following culture of hamster cumulus cell monolayers. Proc Am Fertil Soc 1990;S9(abstr).

160. Blakewood EG, Jaynes JM, Godke RA. Culture of pronuclear mammalian embryos using domestic chicken eggs. Theriogenology 1988;29:226(abstr).

161. Willmer EN, Jacoby F. Studies on the growth of tissues in vitro. J Exp Biol 1936;13:237–248.

162. New CAT, Stein KF. Cultivation of post-implantation mouse and rat embryos on plasma clots. J Embryo Exp Morphol 1964; 12:101–111.

163. Blakewood EG, Godke RA. A method using the chick embryo amnion for mammalian embryo culture. J Tissue Culture Meth 1989; 12:73–76.

164. Blakewood EG, Jaynes JM, Johnson WA, Godke RA. Using the amniotic cavity of the developing chick embryo for the in vitro culture of early stage mammalian embryos. Poultry Sci 1989;68:1695–1702.

165. Blakewood EG, Pool SH, Wiemer KE, Godke RA. Culturing early stage bovine morulae using domestic chicken eggs. Theriogenology 1989;31:176(abstr).

166. Blakewood EG, Pool SH, Prichard JF, Godke RA. Culturing two- to eight-cell caprine embryos using domestic chicken eggs. Theriogenology 1989;31:175(abstr).

167. Blakewood EG, Prichard JF, Pool SH, Godke RA. Live births following transfer of caprine embryos cultured for 72 hours in domestic chicken eggs. Theriogenology 1990;33: 197(abstr).

168. Ouhibi N, Menezo Y, Benet G, Nicollet B. Culture of epithelial cells derived from the oviduct of different species. Human Reprod 1989;4:229–235.

169. Robertson JL, Schrick JJ, Minhas BS. The growth of fish embryos in chicken eggs. Theriogenology 1991;35:262(abstr).

170. Glass RH, Spindle AI, Pederson RA. Mouse embryo attachment to substratum and interaction of trophoblast with cultured cells. J Exp Zool 1979;208:327–335.

171. Overskei TL, Cincotta AH. A new approach to embryo co-culture. Theriogenology 1987; 27:266(abstr).

172. Hu Y, Voelkel SA, Godke RA. One-cell murine embryos cultured on rat liver cell monolayers and mouse oviduct cells. Proc First CAASS Conf, Cornell University, Ithaca, NY, 1989;83(abstr).

173. Kim HN, Hu YX, Roussel JD, Godke RA. Culturing murine embryos on bovine fetal spleen cell fibroblast and chick embryo fibroblast monolayers. Theriogenology 1989; 21:211(abstr).

174. Kim HN, Roussel JD, Amborski GF, Hu YX, Godke RA. Monolayers of bovine fetal spleen cells and chick embryo fibroblasts for co-culture of bovine embryos. Theriogenology 1989;31:212(abstr).

175. Kim HN, Zhang L. Roussel JD, Godke RA. Development of in vitro fertilized (IVF)-bovine oocytes using fetal spleen cell and chick embryo fibroblast monolayers. Biol Reprod 1991;44 (Suppl 1):73(abstr).

176. Bongso A, Soon-Chye N, Sathananthan H, Lian NP, Rayff M, Ratnam S. Improved quality of human embryos when co-cultured with human ampullary cells. Human Reprod 1989;4:706–713.

177. Menezo YJ, Guerin JF, Czyba JC. Improvement of human early development in vitro by co-culture on monolayers of vero cells. Biol Reprod 1990;42:301–306.

178. Bongso A, Ng SC, Ratnam SS, Sathananthan AH. Human oviductal/endometrial cell lines: Co-culture and assisted reproduction. Assist Reprod Technol Androl 1990;1:39–53.

179. Archbald LF, Godke RA. What are the risks for transmission of disease with embryo transplantation? Proc Conf Artif Insem Embryo Transf in Beef Cattle, Denver, CO, 1984:41–46.

180. Voelkel SA, Stuckey KW, Looney CR, Enright FM, Humes PE, Godke RA. An attempt to isolate Brucella abortus from uterine flushing of superovulated donor cows. Theriogenology 1983;19:355–366.

181. Singh EL. Disease transmission: Embryo-pathogen interactions in cattle. Proc Tenth Internatl Congr Anim Reprod Artif Insem, Champaign, IL, 1984;5:17–24.

182. Gianaroli L, Seracchioli R, Ferraretti AP, Trounson A, Flamigni C, Bovicelli L. The successful use of human amniotic fluid for mouse embryo culture and human in vitro fertilization, embryo culture and transfer, Fertil Steril 1986;46:907–913.

183. Fugger MB, Dormann A, Schulman JD. The effect of human amniotic fluid on in vitro development of mouse embryos. Biol Reprod (Suppl 1) 1987;36:177(abstr).

184. Ball GD, Arneson BW, Aaker DV, Benda AR. Human amniotic fluid as a culture

medium for 2-cell murine embryos. Biol Reprod (Suppl 1) 1988;38:71(abstr).

185. Oettle EE, Wiswedel K. Mouse embryos cultured in amniotic fluid. So Afr Med J 1990; 76:63–64.

186. Coetzee JC, Sevenster CBVO, Le R, Fourie F, Van Der Merwe JV, Helbeg LA. In vitro culture of mouse embryos in human amniotic fluid. So Afr Med J 1990;76:62–63.

187. Javed MH, Wright RW Jr. Bovine amniotic and allantoic fluids for the culture of murine embryos. Theriogenology 1990;33:257(abstr).

188. Brackett BG, Bosquet D, Boice ML, Donawick WJ, Evans JF, Dressel MA. Normal development following in vitro fertilization in the cow. Biol Reprod 1982;27:147–158.

189. Lindner GM, Wright RW Jr. Bovine embryo morphology and evaluation. Theriogenology 1983;20:407–416.

190. Hasler JF, McCauley AD, Lathrop WF, Foote RH. Effect of donor-embryo-recipient interactions on pregnancy rate in a large-scale bovine embryo transfer program. Theriogenology 1987;27:139–168.

191. Rorie RW, Pendleton RJ, Pool SH, Youngs CR, Godke RA. The viability of bovine "half" embryos produced before or after liquid nitrogen freezing. In: Feichtinger W, Kemeter P, eds. Future Aspects of Human In Vitro Fertilization. New York: Springer Verlag, 1987:26–35.

192. Ryan DP, Blakewood EG, Swanson WF, Rodriguez H, Godke RA. The use of follicle stimulating hormone (FSH) to stimulate follicle development for in vitro fertilization during the first trimester of pregnancy in cattle. Theriogenology 1990;33:315(abstr).

193. Kruip TAM, Pieterse MC, van Beneden TH, Vos P. Wurth YA, Taverne MAM. Increased success rate of IVM and IVF in the bovine after sonographic guided transvaginal collections of the oocytes. Theriogenology 1990; 33:269(abstr).

194. Whittingham DG. Culture of mouse ova. J Reprod Fertil (Suppl) 1977;14:7–21.

195. Goto K, Koba M, Takuma Y, Nakanishi Y, Ogawa K. Co-culture of bovine embryos with cumulus cells. AJAS 1989;2:595–598.

196. Purdy JM. Methods for fertilization and embryo culture in vitro. In: Edwards RG, Purdy JM, eds. Human Conception In Vitro. London: Academic Press, 1982:135.

197. Lindenberg S, Hyttel P, Sjogren A, Greve T. A comparative study of the attachment of human, bovine and mouse blastocysts to uterine epithelial monolayer. Human Reprod 1989;4:446–456.

198. Menezo Y, Plachot M, Heyman Y, Ducret L, Nicollet B, Beurlet J, Mandelbaum J, Junca AM. Culture of human trophoblastic tissue: A potential tool for improvement of early embryo culture and transfer. In: Fiechtinger W, Kemeter P, eds. Future Aspects in Human In Vitro Fertilization. New York: Springer-Verlag, 1987:77–81.

199. Menezo Y, Humeau AF, Ducret C, Nicollet B. Increased viscosity in embryo transfer medium does not improve the pregnancy rates in IVF and ET. Fertil Steril 1989;52:680–682.

200. Cohen J, DeVane GW, Elsner CW, Kort HI, Massey JB, Norbury SE. Cryopreserved zygotes and embryos and endocrinologic factors in the replacement cycle. Fertil Steril 1988;50:61–66.

15
The Intraovarian Insulinlike Growth Factor System: Basic and Clinical Implications

Eli Y. Adashi

The rationale for thinking of growth factors, insulinlike growth factors among others, in the context of ovarian physiology has to do with the recognition that the process of follicular development is exponential rather than linear. When the follicle finally takes off somewhere in the midfollicular phase it really grows in an exponential fashion. It increases its cell endowment in a manner not paralleled in its previous course of development, while producing a variety of steroid hormones, of which estrogens are just one example. This is a dramatic series of events in which somatic ovarian cells undergo marked differentiation and proliferation.

Although gonadotropins and gonadal steroids are the traditional regulators of ovarian function, it is hard to envision that by themselves they can account for this explosive agenda. Therefore many investigators have suggested that in addition to the traditional endocrine regulators of the ovary, there may be other intraovarian regulators that fine tune in situ the action of the traditional hormones. The general feeling is that some of these hormones may amplify the action of gonadotropins and gonadal steroids, providing us with a way of accounting for some still enigmatic processes in follicular development, including atresia and follicular selection, phenomena not fully accountable by traditional physiologic concepts.

Insulinlike growth factors (IGFs) are among the many growth factors and other intraovarian regulators that are under study. They are a family of homologous, low-molecular-weight, single-chain polypeptide growth factors that are named for their remarkable structural and functional similarity to insulin. Although there are types I and II IGF, this discussion is limited to IGF I. IGF I is a 70-amino acid, single-chain, linear polypeptide with three disulfide bonds. Its traditional role is to promote linear skeletal growth at the time of puberty. Without it dwarfism inevitably results.

Since the so-called somatomedin hypothesis was formulated, we have learned that IGF I is produced not just in the liver and is engaged not only in promoting linear skeletal growth, but may subserve a variety of functions in a variety of extrahepatic organs. It appears to adapt itself to the needs of the tissues where it is located. Since the ovary is such tissue, it is a good example to illustrate the peripheral IGF system.

Ovarian IGF I is both mitogenic and steroidogenic. Produced within the ovary itself, IGF I probably is a major amplifier of follicle-stimulating hormone (FSH) action. FSH action is suboptimal and compromised when there is no intraovarian IGF I production.

Two other roles assigned to IGF I are speculative. There is reason to believe that IGF I may engage in some intraovarian coordination between the various compartments, such as the granulosa and the thecal cells. It may also partake in the still-enigmatic process of follicular selection.

To show that the IGFs play a role in the ovary, we first have to show that they are produced there. No discussion of this question would be complete without mentioning the evidence for intraovarian IGF I production. The relative level of IGF I gene expression was surveyed in a variety of adult rat tissues. It is most active in the liver, which is responsible for the systemic generation of the protein. However, the second and third highest levels of IGF I gene expression are in the ovary and uterus, respectively. Thus, the ovary is capable of IGF I gene expression and, presumably, production of the corresponding protein.

Within the ovary, IGF I has been localized to the granulosa cell, with little seen at the level of the thecal interstitial cells. This is further illustrated by in situ hybridization studies in which the signal has been primarily localized to the membrana granulosa and the area around the follicle and the cumulus. Immunofluorescence studies also detected the protein in the granulosa cell layer, with little seen outside the follicle in the thecal interstitial cell compartment. Thus the ovary, and the granulosa cells in particular, are significant locations of IGF I gene expression. Ovarian IGF I production is constitutive and is subject to up-regulation by estrogens and, to some extent, by growth hormone as well.

The granulosa cells appear to contain most of the IGF I receptors. However, some receptors also exist on thecal interstitial cells. Thus the receptor, unlike the ligand, is more "promiscuous" and finds itself not only in the granulosa cells but probably also in the thecal interstitial cells. This is confirmed at the molecular level, where a signal emanating from both the granulosa and the thecal interstitial cells is evident.

Thus IGF I of granulosa cell origin has the possibility of binding to receptors not only on its cell of origin, the granulosa cell, but also on the adjacent thecal interstitial cells. The granulosa cell-derived IGF I molecules could find their way to the extracellular fluid, where they could recognize receptors on the very cell from which they emanated, or they could find their way to the immediately adjacent thecal interstitial cells, where they could interact with similar receptors. In the latter situation IGF I would be involved with the production of androgen rather than estrogen. This could allow the granulosa cells some degree of control over their own destiny, in that IGF I of granulosa cell origin might regulate androgen substrate provision to the granulosa cell, presumably suiting the aromatizing capabilities of the granulosa cell and of the follicle as a whole. This type of mechanism could increase the efficiency of follicular development by way of increased coordination.

Many actions have been ascribed to IGF I. However, it invariably requires gonadotropins to exert its effect. Thus IGF I is viewed as an amplifier or a synergizer with gonadotropins. It has been shown to amplify virtually every action of FSH, such as promoting progesterone or estrogen production and inducing luteinizing hormone (LH) receptors.

Increasing attention is being given to the proteins that bind circulating IGFs. IGFs do not differ from sex steroids, thyroid hormones, or cortisol, all of which have their corresponding binding proteins. Like all these hormone-binding proteins, the IGF-binding proteins probably play a role in regulating the fraction of IGF that is available to the cells. It is important to understand how much and what kind of binding proteins one is dealing with because they must affect the availability of IGFs to cell surface receptors. The more binding proteins, the less IGF I is bioavailable to exert its hormonal action. IGF I action can be regulated not only at the level of production but by changing the ambient concentrations of the binding proteins.

Little is known about the action of IGF-binding proteins in the ovary. We do know that several species of IGF-binding proteins in the ovary act as antigonadotropins. The addition of these proteins inhibits or substantially attenuates the action of both FSH and LH. This suggests and FSH and LH acting in vivo use endogenously generated IGFs to amplify their effects. Removing these IGFs by binding them to proteins will compromise gonadotropin action.

These and related findings have convinced us of the importance of endogenous IGFs in gonadotropin action. It appears that every time we give FSH or LH to a patient we are to some extent relying on the endogenous generation of IGFs to obtain optimum action. If for some reason that system is compromised, gonadotropin action will not be what we expect. Is it possible that low responses or other unexpected results have to do with intrinsic, as yet unrecognized, abnormalities in the intra-ovarian IGF I system? Only time will tell, but the possibilities clearly exist.

Clinical Implications

Some of the most esoteric work that has been done in vitro in this area has stimulated clinical investigation that suggests a number of avenues for application. This discussion is limited to the potential role of growth hormone in reproductive physiology and pathophysiology. Growth hormone is an adult hormone in search of a function. All we know is that it plays a major role in promoting prepubertal growth. It is not really clear what role, if any, it plays in adult life. The circulating levels of growth hormone progressively decrease with time, implicating it, at least in part, in the process of aging.

It occurred to us that if growth hormone is capable of regulating intraovarian IGF I generation in the adult female, it might play a role both in normal physiology and, most importantly, in pathophysiology. Although it is not really concentrated or focused, information suggests that although growth hormone may not be obligatory for reproductive function, it is at least permissive and is required for optimum gonadotropin hormonal action.

One large body of information that can be culled from the literature suggests that growth hormone deficiency is associated with delayed puberty which can be reversed by systemic replacement therapy. Every pediatric endocrinologist knows that small children, dwarfs with growth hormone deficiency, not only fail to grow but also enter puberty very slowly and in a much delayed fashion. Administering growth hormone to promote growth results in acceleration of the tempo of puberty in a manner that brings these patients back on schedule. One can conclude that growth hormone possesses some permissive puberty-promoting property, the exact nature of which or the exact target of which is not understood.

Given what we now know about the intra-ovarian IGF I system, it has been speculated that the ability of growth hormone to accelerate prepubertal maturation may be due at least in part to the generation of intraovarian IGF I and the consequent local amplification of gonadotropic action. In other words, intra-ovarian IGF I, under the influence of growth hormone, sensitizes the ovary to the action of gonadotropins, thereby accelerating puberty. In the adult growth hormone may be capable of decreasing gonadotropin requirements, so that women with growth hormone deficiency would require more gonadotropins for ovulation induction and vice versa.

To some extent this idea has been tested. The first evidence in the literature can be found in the work of Homburg and associates from the laboratory of Dr. Howard Jacobs in London, the title of which speaks for itself: "Growth hormone facilitates ovulation induction by gonadotropins." The data suggest that in patients undergoing in vitro fertilization (IVF) who were being treated with human menopausal gonadotropins (HMG), the addition of recombinant human growth hormone reduced the overall number of ampules per cycle required to achieve comparable levels of estradiol and comparable recruitment of preovulatory follicles at the time of human chorionic gonadotropin (HCG) administration. This limited preliminary information suggests that growth hormone has the ability to decrease overall gonadotropin requirements. If nothing else, it suggests that growth hormone is involved in some fashion in the reproductive process in the female.

These early studies raise more questions than they answer. Is the growth hormone action described by Jacobs and associates pharmacologic, or are we talking about growth hormone replacement therapy? Could some women who have a subtle, unrecognized deficiency benefit from replacement therapy? Some entities in reproductive endocrinology could well come under this heading.

Obesity is associated with growth hormone deficiency. Many of our patients in whom we induce ovulation are overweight. Estrogen deficiency decreases growth hormone release. A variety of circumstances in our specialty are associated with estrogen deficiency. An example is gonadotropin-releasing hormone

(GnRH) agonist-induced hypoestrogenism. It is well known that such patients require higher amounts of HMG to bring about comparable levels of follicular development. Is this because of a deficiency of gonadotropins or growth hormone or both?

Preliminary evidence and published reports demonstrate that the polycystic ovary syndrome (PCO) is associated with growth hormone deficiency. Is it possible that patients with PCO would benefit from growth hormone replacement therapy before ovulation induction is actually undertaken? All of these are truly unanswered questions, but ones that are finally perhaps available for study now that we have some understanding of the intraovarian IGF system.

In addition, are we going to see results from growth hormone therapy that are more substantive than a mere reduction in gonadotropin requirements? We are not really impressed by the fact that growth hormone decreases HMG requirements. That is merely substituting one drug for another. Are we actually going to see in selected patients improvement in terms of reproductive outcome? Will we see more eggs, more fertilization, more pregnancies? These unanswered questions clearly deserve pursuit.

Current information supports the existence of a complete, hormonally responsive, intraovarian IGF I system replete with ligands such as IGF I, its receptors, and its binding proteins. A major role of this system is presumed to be the amplification of gonadotropin hormonal action. In addition, we have tried to make a case for the possibility that the intraovarian IGF I system can be harnessed by gonadotropins, thereby disclosing the partial and, for that matter, self-serving IGF I dependence.

Even though the IGF I system is probably the best-studied intraovarian regulator so far, and even though all kinds of indirect evidence would suggest that it is relevant to in vivo ovarian function, we have no compelling evidence that would prove that these so-called intraovarian regulators are indispensable for ovarian function. Short of actual selective abolition of IGF I expression at the level of the ovary that would allow us to ask what consequences this might have on reproductive function, we cannot obtain the indispensable evidence that we so badly need. It is possible that when transgenic technology becomes refined enough to allow selective ablation of a principle in a tissue at will, we can answer this question in an elegant and convincing fashion. At this time, however, all that we have is a relatively large body of information that strongly suggests, but still does not absolutely prove, that the IGFs are an important component of intraovarian function.

Bibliography

1. Hammond JM. Peptide regulators in the ovarian follicle. Aust J Biol Sci 1981;34:491–504.
2. Hammond JM, Baranao JLS, Skaleris D, Knight AB, Romanus JA, Rechler MM. Production of insulinlike growth factors by ovarian granulosa cells. Endocrinology 1985;117:2553–2555.
3. Hsu C-J, Hammond JM. Gonadotropins and estradiol stimulate immunoreactive insulinlike growth factor I production by porcine granulosa cells in vitro. Endocrinology 1987;120:198–207.
4. Davoren JB, Hsueh AJW. Growth hormone increases ovarian levels of immunoreactive somatomedin-C/insulinlike growth factor I in vivo. Endocrinology 1986;118:888–890.
5. Hernandez ER, Roberts CT, LeRoith D, Adashi EY. Rat ovarian insulinlike growth factor (IGF I) gene expression is granulosa cell-selective: 5'-untranslated mRNA variant representation and hormonal regulation. Endocrinology 1989;125:572–574.
6. Murphy LJ, Bell GI, Friesen HB. Tissue distribution of insulinlike growth factor I and II messenger ribonucleic acid in the adult rat. Endocrinology 1987;120:1279–1282.
7. Voutilainen R, Miller WL. Coordinate tropic hormone regulation of mRNAs for insulinlike growth factor II and the cholesterol side-chain-cleavage enzyme, P450ssc, in human steroidogenic tissues. Proc Natl Acad Sci USA 1987;84:1590–1594.
8. Veldhuis JD, Furlanetto RW, Juchter D, Garmey J, Veldhuis P. Trophic actions of human somatomedin-C/insulinlike growth factor I on ovarian cells: In vitro studies with swine granulosa cells. Endocrinology 1985;116:1235–1242.
9. Davoren JB, Kasson BG, Li CH, Hsueh AJW. Specific insulinlike growth factor (IGF) I- and II-binding sites on rat granulosa cells: Relation to IGF action. Endocrinology 1986;119:2155–2162.

10. Adashi EY, Resnick CE, Hernandez ER, Svoboda ME, Van Wyk JJ. Characterization and regulation of a specific cell membrane receptor for Somatomedin C/Insulinlike Growth Factor I in cultured rat granulosa cells. Endocrinology 122:194–201.

11. Adashi EY, Rensnick CE, Svoboda ME, Van Wyk JJ. Follicle-stimulating hormone enhances somatomedin-C binding to cultured rat granulosa cells: Evidence for cAMP-dependence. J Biol Chem 1986;261:3923–3926.

12. Adashi EY, Rensnick CE, Rosenfeld RG. Insulin-like growth factor-I (IGF-I) and IGF-I hormonal action in cultured rat granulosa cells: Mediation via type I but not type II IGF receptors. Endocrinology 1990;126:216–222.

13. Adashi EY, Resnick CE, D'Ercole AG, Svoboda ME, Van Wyk JJ. Insulinlike growth factors as intraovarian regulators of granulosa cell growth and function. Endocr Rev 1985;6:400–420.

14. Adashi EY, Resnick CE, Svoboda ME, Van Wyk JJ, Hascall VC, Yanagishita M. Independent and synergistic actions of somatomedin-C in the stimulation of proteoglycan biosynthesis by cultured rat granulosa cells. Endocrinology 1986;118:456–459.

15. Binoux M, Hossenlopp P, Hardouin S, Seurin D, Lassarre C, Gourmelen M. Somatomedin (insulin-like growth factors)-binding proteins: Molecular forms and regulation. Hormone Res 1986;24:141–151.

16. Baxter RC. The insulinlike growth factors and their binding proteins. Comp Biochem Physiol 1988;91B:229–235.

17. Mottola C, MacDonald RG, Brackett JL, Mole JE, Anderson JK, Czeck MP. Purification and amino-terminal sequence of an insulinlike growth factor-binding protein secreted by rat liver BRL-3A cells. J Biol Chem 1986;261:11180–11188.

18. Brown AL, Chiariotti L, Orlowski CC, Mehlman T, Burgess WH, Ackerman EJ, Bruni CB, Rechler MM. Nucleotide sequence and expression of a cDNclone encoding a fetal rat binding protein for insulinlike growth factors. J Biol Chem 1989;264:5148–5154.

19. Margot JB, Binkert C, Mary J-L, Landwehr J, Heinrich G, Schwander J. A low molecular weight insulinlike growth factor binding protein from rat: cDNA cloning and tissue distribution of its messenger RNA. Mol Endocrinol 1989;3:1053–1066.

20. Ruoslahti E, Pierschbacher MD. New perspectives in cell adhesion: RGD and integrins. Science 1987;238:491–497.

21. De Vroede MA, Tseng LY-H, Katsoyannis PG, Nissley SP, Rechler MM. Modulation of insulinlike growth factor I binding to human fibroblast monolayer cultures by insulinlike growth factor carrier proteins released to the incubation media. J Clin Invest 1986;77:602–613.

22. Elgin RG, Busby WJ Jr., Clemmons DR. An insulinlike growth factor (IGF) binding protein enhances the biologic response to IGF-I. Proc Natl Acad Sci USA 1987;84:3254–3258.

23. Drop SLS, Valiquette G, Guyda HJ, Corvol MT, Posner BI. Partial purification and characterization of a binding protein for insulinlike activity (ILAs) in human amniotic fluid: A possible inhibitor of insulinlike activity. Acta Endocr (Copenh) 1979;90:505–518.

24. Ritvos O, Tanta P, Jalkanen J, Suikkari AM, Voutilainen R, Bohn H, Rutanen EM. Insulinlike growth factor (IGF) binding protein from human decidua inhibits the binding and biological action of IGF-I in cultured choriocarcinoma cells. Endocrinology 1988;122:2150–2157.

25. Seppala M, Wahlstrom T, Koskimies AI, et al. Human preovulatory follicular fluid, luteinized cells of hyperstimulated preovulatory follicles, and corpus luteum contain placental protein 12. J Clin Endocrinol Metab 1984;58:505–510.

26. Seppala M, Than G. Insulinlike growth factor binding protein PP12 in ovarian cyst fluid. Arch Gynecol Obstet 1987;241:33–35.

27. Suikkari AM, Jalkanen J, Koistinen R, Butzow R, Ritvos O, Ranta T, Seppala M. Human granulosa cells synthesize low molecular weight insulinlike growth factor binding protein. Endocrinology 1989;124:1088–1090.

28. Davoren JB, Hsueh AJW. Growth hormone increases ovarian levels of immunoreactive somatomedin C/insulinlike growth factor I in vivo. Endocrinology 1986;118:888–890.

29. Ui M, Shimonaka M, Shimasaki S, Ling N. An insulinlike growth factor-binding protein in ovarian follicular fluid blocks follicle-stimulating steroid production by ovarian granulosa cells. Endocrinology 1989;125:912–916.

30. Adashi EY, Resnick CE, Hernandez ER, Hurwitz A, Rosenfeld RG. Follicle-stimulating hormone inhibits the constitutive release of insulinlike growth factor binding proteins by cultured rat ovarian granulosa cells. Endocrinology 1990;126:1305–1307.

31. Homburg R, Eshel A, Abdalla HI, Jacobs HS. Growth hormone facilitates ovulation induction by gonadotropins. Clin Endocrinol 1988;29:113–117.

16
Medical Treatment of Ectopic Pregnancy

Donald P. Goldstein

Ectopic pregnancy is the commonest cause of maternal death in the United States. Because hemorrhage may be both acute and severe, surgical correction of an ectopic gestation is often indicated (Fig. 16.1). However, due to diagnostic improvements such as laparoscopy, ultrasound, and more sensitive β-human chorionic gonadotropin (β-hCG) assays, the diagnosis of ectopic pregnancy is being made much earlier. As a result, medical treatment of ectopic pregnancy is currently under active investigation by a number of clinicians. Although a number of nonsurgical systemic treatments such as RU 486 (mifepristone), actinomycin D, or local injections of potassium chloride or prostaglandins under laparoscopic or ultrasound guidance have been used (Table 16.1), this chapter will focus on methotrexate as a treatment for ectopic pregnancy. This type of treatment can be administered either systemically or locally. A summary of systemic treatment with methotrexate for tubal pregnancy is shown in Table 16.2.

Methotrexate (MTX) is an antifolate compound that inhibits the action of dihydrofolate reductase, thus preventing the conversion of dihydrofolic acid to tetrahydrofolic acid. Since its introduction in 1956, MTX has been the principal drug used in the treatment of gestational trophoblastic disease. In 1956 Hreshchyshyn treated patients with abdominal pregnancy for retained placenta, but this proved excessively toxic for use with benign disease.

Workers in Japan first reported the use of MTX for treatment of a persistent cornual gestation, with good results. MTX was subsequently used in the management of a cervical pregnancy. In 1986 a number of investigators reported the use of MTX with citrovorin factor (CF) rescue for ectopic pregnancies. Intramuscular MTX was alternated with CF, with excellent results in selected patients. That same year intravenous infusion of MTX followed by intramuscular or oral CF rescue was described as an alternative and effective regimen. Since that time publications have detailed the successful use of transvaginal and translaparoscopic injection of the conceptus with MTX and also the use of oral MTX.

It is quite clear that by using quantitative hCG determinations, ultrasound examination, and, in some instances, dilation and curettage (D&C), one can select suitable candidates for medical management (Fig. 16.2). In general, these are patients who have a positive β-hCG titer that is not doubling appropriately and who have no evidence of an intrauterine pregnancy by D&C or ultrasound examination. In some instances, it is necessary to perform a diagnostic laparoscopy to determine whether or not the ectopic pregnancy is about to rupture or bleed (Fig. 16.3). This is certainly true with larger gestations visible on ultrasound, in which the risk of impending rupture or hemoperitoneum secondary to tubal bleeding would be present. In smaller, asymptomatic gestations it may be possible to circumvent laparoscopy and proceed with medical therapy.

Patient Demographics

Between July 1984 and February 1990, we managed 74 patients with ectopic pregnancies medically. Their age range was 15 to 41 years.

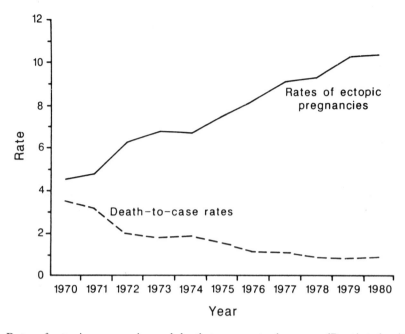

FIGURE 16.1. Rates of ectopic pregnancies and death-to-case rates by years. (Reprinted, with permission, from Ectopic Pregnancies–United States, 1970–1980. JAMA 1984;251:2327. Copyright by the American Medical Association, 1984.

TABLE 16.1. Local injection in unruptured tubal pregnancy.

Drug	Author	No. of cases	Success rate No.	Success rate %	Tubal patency No.	Tubal patency %	Side effect
Local injection (vaginal ultrasonography)							
Methotrexate	Feichtinger et al.[26,27]	9	8	89	—	—	0
	Robertson et al.[28]	9	4	44	—	—	0
	Leeton et al.[29]	2	2	100	—	—	0
	Robertson et al.[30]	2	1	50	—	—	0
Potassium chloride	Timor Tritsch et al.[21]	1	1	100	—	—	0
PGE_2	Ribic-Paucelj et al.[31]	2	0	0	—	—	0
	Feichtinger et al.[27]	1	0	0	—	—	1
Local injection (laparoscopy)							
Local PGF_{2a} and systemic PGE_2	Lindblom et al.[34]	23	22	96	—	—	0
	Egarter et al.[36,37]	71	57	81	22/24	92	3
	Vejtorp et al.[38]	11	10	91	6/7	85	0
	Lang et al.[39]	9	8	89	—	—	6
Hyperosmolar glucose	Lang et al.[39]	9	9	100	3/3	100	0
Methotrexate	Pansky et al.[11]	27	24	88	19/21	90	0

Reprinted, with permission, from ref. 40.

Gravidity ranged from one to six pregnancies. Eleven patients had had one previous ectopic pregnancy, four had had two, and two had three. The mean pretreatment β-hCG was 823 mIU/ml (range 45–5,400 mIU/ml).

Indications

The 74 patients were divided into three groups on the basis of the clinical status of the ectopic pregnancy: proved, persistent, or presumed.

TABLE 16.2. Results of systemic treatment with methotrexate for tubal pregnancy.

Author	No. of cases treated	Failure rate		Dose of methotrexate	Route of administration	CV factor	Tubal patency	
		No.	%				No.	%
Miyazaki et al.[41]	9	1	12	60–300 mg	IM	No	5/6	83
Ory et al.[10]	6	1	17	1 mg/kg × 4 days	IV	Yes	—	—
Goldstein et al.[42]	13	1	8	1 mg/kg × 4 days	IM	Yes	4/4	100
				200 mg/m²	IV			
Rodi et al.[15]	7	0	0	1 mg/kg × 4 days	IM	Yes	4/5	80
Sauer et al.[16]	21	1	5	1 mg/kg × 4 days	IM	Yes	15/20	75
Hans et al.[43]	1	0	0	50 mg × 5 days	IM	Yes	—	—
Ichinoe et al.[44]	22	1	4.5	0.4 mg/kg × 5 days	IM	No	10/19	53
Stovall et al.[19]	36	2	5.5	1 mg/kg × 1–4 days	IM	Yes	—	—
Chotiner et al.[3]	1	0	0	25 mg/kg × 3 days	IM	Yes	—	—
Brandes et al.[1]	1	0	0	1 mg/kg × 3 days	IM	Yes	1/1	100
Cowan et al.[4]	1	0	0	1 mg/kg × 3 days	IM	Yes	—	—
Total	118	7	6				39/55	71

CV, citrovorum; MTX, methotrexate; IM, intramuscular; IV, intravenous.
Reprinted with permission from ref. 40.

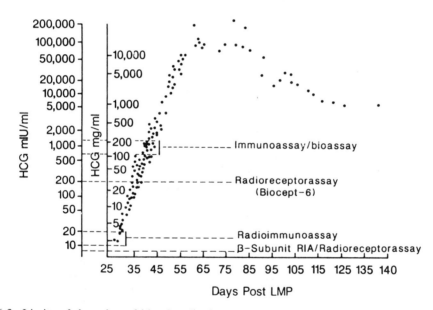

FIGURE 16.2. Limits of detection of blood and urine pregnancy tests. Reprinted, with permission, from Batzer FR. Hormonal detection of early pregnancy. Fertil Steril 1980;34:1.

The 39 women whose ectopic pregnancies were diagnosed by laparoscopy were placed in the proved group and represented 53% of the total patient population. Eighteen patients were in the persistent category because they had already undergone removal of an ectopic pregnancy at laparoscopy or laparotomy, and had evidence of a plateau or reelevation of their hCG titer. Seventeen were presumed to have ectopic pregnancy on the basis of an elevated hCG level and no evidence of intrauterine pregnancy on D&C or extrauterine pregnancy on laparoscopy. In all of these patients the hCG titer plateaued or rose. The only other possible diagnosis would have been trophoblastic disease, and since this condition

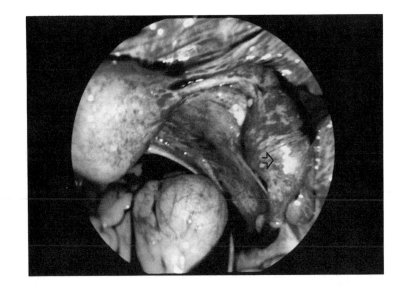

FIGURE 16.3. Laparoscopic view of ampullary ectopic pregnancy. Arrow within ectopic. Photo courtesy of Machelle Seibel, M.D.

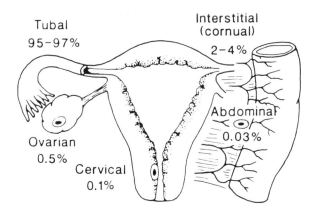

FIGURE 16.4. Distribution and incidence of ectopic implantation sites. Reprinted, with permission, from Mattingly RF. Ectopic pregnancy. In: TeLinde, ed. Operative Gynecology. 5th ed. Philadelphia: Lippincott, 1977:369.

would be managed medically in reproductively active women it was decided to place them in a separate category, despite the fact that the location of their pregnancy was undetermined.

Location

The locations of the 39 proved ectopic pregnancies were 4 cornual, 18 isthmus, 14 ampulla, and 3 cervical (Fig. 16.4). In the 18 women with persistent ectopic pregnancies, the pregnancy was isthmic in 14 and ampullary in 4.

Contraindications

The contraindications to medical treatment of ectopic pregnancy are summarized in Table 16.3. Generally, in patients with serum hCG levels of 5,000 mIU/ml and a tubal pregnancy

TABLE 16.3. Contraindications to medical treatment of ectopic pregnancy

1. Laparoscopic evidence of impending rupture or hemoperitoneum secondary to bleeding from the tube
2. Serum HCG > 5,000 mIU/ml
3. Diameter of tubal pregnancy >3 cm
4. Evidence of hematologic, renal, or hepatic abnormalities that would be affected by the use of high-dose MTX therapy
5. Fetal heart motion present on ultrasound

diameter of 3 cm, fetal heart motion is seen on ultrasound. These pregnancies are best treated surgically or perhaps with direct injection of MTX into the conceptus.

Treatment Regimens

Two MTX regimens were used in this series. The initial seven patients were treated with alternating intramuscular doses of MTX and CF. The average dose of MTX per course of therapy was 246 mg. Mean hospitalization was 9.2 days (range 8–12 days). When it was realized tthat these patients were more stable than we previously considered them to be, we switched to the use of intermediate-dose (300 mg/m^2) MTX infusion, and the subsequent 67 patients were treated with a total of 74 courses. In seven patients (approximately 10%) the initial dose was repeated because of poor

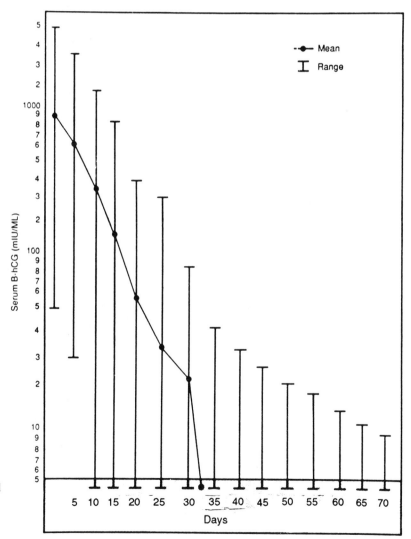

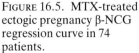

FIGURE 16.5. MTX-treated ectogic pregnancy β-NCG regression curve in 74 patients.

TABLE 16.4. Side effects after systemic methotrexate therapy.

Author	No. of cases treated	Cases with side effects		Dermatitis	Stomatitis	Gastritis	LFT	BMS	Pleuritis
		No.	%						
Miyazaki et al.[41]	9	3	33	—	3	—	3	—	—
Ory et al.[11]	6	3	50	—	2	1	2	—	—
Goldstein et al.[42]	13	0	0	—	—	—	—	—	—
Rodi et al.[15]	7	2	28	—	2	—	2	—	—
Sauer et al.[16]	21	5	23	1	2	1	1	—	1
Hans et al.[43]	1	0	0	—	—	—	—	—	—
Ichinoe et al.[44]	22	5	22.5	—	—	—	4	1	—
Stovall et al.[19]	36	3	8.3	—	1	—	2	—	—
Chotiner et al.[3]	1	1	100	—	—	1	—	1	—
Brandes et al.[1]	1	0	0	—	—	—	—	—	—
Cowan et al.[4]	1	0	0	—	—	—	—	—	—
Total	118	22	18.6	1	10	3	14	2	1

LFT, liver function tests; BMS, bone marrow suppression.
Reprinted, with permission, from ref. 40.

response. The average dose of each course was 356 mg based on the patient's height and weight. The mean hospitalization was 2.3 days (range 1–4 days). Originally we administered CF intramuscularly; now we administer it orally, and the mean hospitalization time is approximately 18 hours.

The protocol used for the majority of patients in this study was an infusion of intermediate-dose MTX: $100 \, mg/m^2$ administered as an intravenous bolus, followed by a 12-hour infusion of $200 \, mg/m^2$. Twenty-four hours after the initiation of the MTX infusion, the patient began taking CF 15 mg every 12 hours for four doses. Serum hCG titers were monitored twice weekly (Fig. 16.5).

Toxicity

Only one patient experienced a drop in her platelet count to under $100,000/mm^3$. She had idiopathic thrombocytopenic purpura and was treated with a borderline platelet count or $80,000/mm^3$. She experienced a transient drop in her platelet count to about $20,000/mm^3$ which resolved spontaneously. Eight (11%) of patients experienced a transient elevation of serum glutamic oxalacetic transaminase (SGOT) to over 50 IU, but no serious hepatic consequences or jaundice was noted. In all cases the SGOT level returned to normal

within 10 days. Epithelial toxicity was the most common side effect (26%); it consisted of stomatitis and conjunctivitis that lasted 4 or 5 days and did not require hospitalization or any particular therapy. We no longer are required to perform any hematologic or hepatic studies because we have found that in treating over 250 patients with trophoblastic disease with this regimen, no significant hematologic or hepatic toxicity has occurred. A summary of the side effects after systemic MTX therapy is shown in Table 16.4.

Results

Six (15%) of the 39 patients with proved ectopic pregnancies had to undergo subsequent surgical intervention because of bleeding or rupture. Two (11%) of the 18 patients with persistent disease also had subsequent surgery, and all responded to therapy. The mean solution time in the mean β-hCG level was 33 days (range 6–8 days). Intercurrent surgery, which constituted the treatment failures, was performed in 8 (11%) of the 74 patients.

It is important to remember that patients should be monitored both endocrinologically and clinically, because even while they are experiencing apparently good regression in β-hCG titer, rupture can occur. In analyzing the treatment failures, we did not find

TABLE 16.5. Patients who failed medical treatment of ectopic pregnancy.

Intercurrent surgery	Pretreatment HCG (mlU/ml)	Remarks
L salpingooophorectomy	632	Hemoperitoneum without rupture (early intervention)
L salpingooophorectomy	3,330	Pain during therapy
L salpingectomy	5,300	No response
R salpingostomy	4,300	No response
R salpingectomy	5,800	Hemoperitoneum, 2nd-degree rupture (good response)
L salpingectomy	4,321	Hemoperitoneum, 2nd-degree rupture (good response)
R salpingectomy	876	Hemoperitoneum, 2nd-degree reupture (good response)
R salpingectomy	1,825	Hemoperitoneum without rupture (good response)

L, left; R, right.

TABLE 16.6. Expectant management of tubal pregnancy.

Author	No. of cases	Laparoscopy for diagnosis	Success rate		Patency		Pregnancy rate	
			No.	%	No.	%	No.	%
Ohel et al.[45]	1	Yes	1	100	1/1	100	—	—
Carp et al.[46]	14	12 only	11	79	5/5	100	4/5	80
Derricks et al.[47]	12	No	11	89	—	—	—	—
Garcia et al.[48]	13	No	12	92	7/10	70	5/12	42
Fernandez et al.[49]	14	Yes	10	71	6/6	100	3/6	50
Sauer et al.[14]	5	Yes	5	100	4/5	80	—	—
Total	61		50	82	23/27	85	12/23	52

Reprinted, with permission, from ref. 40.

any dominant factor that would predict rupture or hemoperitoneum. In some cases hemoperitoneum required surgical intervention, even though it appeared that the response to hormonal therapy was good. Only two patients had no apparent hCG response to treatment (Table 16.5).

Recommended Protocol

Once a diagnosis of ectopic pregnancy is made, the patient is considered to be a candidate for study (Table 16.6). She should be admitted to the hospital for appropriate laboratory studies, including a complete blood cell count, platelet count, SGOT, blood urea nitrogen, and creatinine. As mentioned, not all patients require diagnostic laparoscopy, but some may be admitted for medical treatment based on negative findings on D&C and ultrasound. Once it is ascertained that there is no evidence of any hematologic, hepatic, or renal abnormalities, treatment with MTX followed by calcium leucovorin factor may be instituted. The patient should be monitored twice weekly until the hCG titer is negative. Once that occurs, no follow-up is indicated. Patients should be treated if the β-hCG titer does not fall 1 log in 18 days, plateaus, or reelevates.

Hysterosalpingogram should be performed 3 months after a normal titer to ascertain if gross damage to the tube has occurred. In 10 of 43 women who underwent subsequent hysterosalpingography, diverticula of the tube or interstitial area were found. Eighteen patients underwent subsequent laparoscopy, in five of whom tubal adhesions were present, presumably from the previous ectopic pregnancy. So far, 45 patients treated with this protocol have subsequently conceived. Of these, 27 delivered at term, 8 had spontaneous miscarriages, and 10 had repeat ectopic pregnancies.

In summary, medical treatment of ectopic pregnancy with intermediate-dose MTX infusion followed by CF rescue appears to offer an alternative to surgical intervention in selected cases. This treatment is particularly well suited for patients with persistent ectopic pregnancies when surgery has failed to remove all trophoblastic tissue, for women with rising hCG levels, and for those with presumed ectopic pregnancies who have rising HCG levels and in whom the site of the pregnancy cannot be determined.

Suggested Reading

1. Brandes MC, Youngs DD, Goldstein DP, Parmlay TH. Treatment of cornual pregnancy with methotrexate; case report. Am J Obstet Gynecol 1986;155:655–657.
2. Carson SA, Stovall T, Umstot E, Anderson R, Ling F, Buster JE. Rising human chorionic somatomammmotropin predicts ectopic pregnancy rupture following methotrexate chemotherapy. Fertil Steril 1989;51:593–597.
3. Chotiner MC. Nonsurgical management of ectopic pregnancy associated with severe hyperstimulation syndrome. Obstet Gynecol 1985; 66:740–743.
4. Cowan BD, McGehee RP, Bates GW. Treatment of persistent ectopic pregnancy with methotrexate and leukovorum rescue; a case report. Obstet Gynecol 1986;67(Suppl):50(S)–52(S).
5. Farabow WS, Fulton JW, Fletcher V Jr, Velat CA, White JT. Cervical pregnancy treated with methotrexate. NC Med J 1983;44:91.
6. Firth LA, Pierre AW, Wilson PD. Choriocarcinoma presenting at a ruptured ectopic pregnancy. Aust NZ Obstet Gynecol 1985; 25:22–25.
7. Hreshchyshyn MM, Naples JD Jr, Randall CL. Amethopterin in abdominal pregnancy. Am J Obstet Gynecol 1965;93:286.
8. Martin DC. Nonsurgical treatment of ectopic pregnancy [letter]. Fertil Steril 1987;48:344–346.
9. Ory SJ. Nonsurgical treatment of ectopic pregnancy. Fertil Steril 1986;46:767–769.
10. Ory SJ, Villanueva AL, Sand PK, Tamura RK. Conservative treatment of ectopic pregnancy with methotrexate. Am J Obstet Gynecol 1986; 154:1299–1306.
11. Pansky M, Bukovsky L, Golan A, et al. Local methotrexate injection: A nonsurgical treatment of ectopic pregnancy. Am J Obstet Gynecol 1989;161:393.
12. Patsner B, Kenigsberg D. Successful management of ectopic pregnancy with oral methotrexate therapy. Fertil Steril 1988; 50:982–983.
13. Peterson HB. Extratubal ectopic pregnancies, diagnosis and treatment. J Report Med 1986; 31:108–115.
14. Rahman MS, Al-Suleiman SA, Rahman J, et al. Advanced abdominal pregnancy: Observation in 10 cases. Obstet Gynecol 1982;59:366.
15. Rodi LA, Sauer MV, Gorrill MJ, et al. The medical treatment of unruptured ectopic pregnancy with methotrexate and citrovorum rescue: Preliminary experience. Fertil Steril 1986;46:811–813.
16. Sauer MV, Gorrill MJ, Rodi LA, et al. Nonsurgical management of unruptured ectopic pregnancy: An extended clinical trial. Fertil Steril 1987;48:752–755.
17. Shapiro BS. The nonsurgical management of ectopic pregnancy. Clin Obstet Gynecol 1987; 30:230–235.
18. Silva PD. A laparoscopic approach can be applied to most cases of ectopic pregnancy. Obstet Gynecol 1988;12:944.
19. Stovall TG, Ling FW, Buster JE. Outpatient chemotherapy of unruptured ectopic pregnancy. Fertil Steril 1989;51:435–438.
20. Tanaka L, Hayashi H, Kutsuzawa T, Fujimoto S, Jehinoe K. Treatment of interstitial ectopic pregnancy with methotrexate: Report of a successful case. Fertil Steril 1982:37:851–852.
21. Timor-Tritsch L, Baxi L, Plesner DB. Transvaginal salpingocentesis: A new technique for treatment of ectopic pregnancy. Am J Obstet Gynecol 1989;160:459–461.
22. Vermesh M. Conservative management of ectopic gestation. Fertil Steril 1989;51:59.
23. Kojima E, Abe Y, Morita M, Ito M, Hirakawa S, Manose K. The treatment of unruptured tubal pregnancy with intratubal methotrexate injection under laparoscopic control. Obstet Gynecol 1990;75:723–725.
24. Tulandi IT, Hemmings R, Khalifa F. Rupture of ectopic pregnancy in women with low and declining serum β-human chorionic gonadotropin concentrations. Fertil Steril 1991;56:786–787.
25. Diamond MP, Lavy G, DeCherney AH. Diagnosis and management of ectopic pregnancy. In: Seibel MM, ed. Infertility: A Comprehensive Text. Norwalk, CT: Appleton & Lange, 1990: 447.

26. Feichtinger W, Kemeter P. Conservative treatment of ectopic pregnancy by transvaginal aspiration under sonographic control, and injection of methotrexate. Lancet 1987;1:381–382.

27. Feichtinger W, Kemeter P. Treatment of unruptured ectopic pregnancy by needling of sac and injection of methotrexate or PGE$_2$ under transvaginal sonography control. Arch Gynecol Obstet 1989;246:85–89.

28. Robertson DE, Smith W, Craft I. Reduction of ectopic pregnancy by ultrasound methods. Lancet 1987;2:1524.

29. Leeton J, Davison G. Nonsurgical management of unruptured tubal pregnancy with intra-amniotic methotrexate: Preliminary report of two cases. Fertil Steril 1988;501:67–69.

30. Robertson DE, Moye MAH, Hansen JN, et al. Reduction of ectopic pregnancy by injection under ultrasound control. Lancet 1987;2:974–975.

31. Ribic Paucelj M, Novak-Antolic Z, Urhovec I. Treatment of ectopic pregnancy with prostaglandin E$_2$. Clin Exp Obstet Gynecol 1989;16:106–109.

32. Zakut H, Sadan O, Katz A, Dreval D, Bernstein D. Management of tubal pregnancy with methotrexate. Br J Obstet Gynecol 1989;96:725–728.

33. Hahlin M, Bokstrom H, Lindblom B. Ectopic pregnancy: in vitro effects of prostaglandins on the oviduct and corpus luteum. Fertil Steril 1987;47:935–940.

34. Lindblom B, Hahlin M, Källfetlt B, Hamberger L. Local prostaglandin F$_{2a}$ injection for termination of ectopic pregnancy. Lancet 1987; 1:776–777.

35. Lindblom BO, Emk L, Hahlin M, Kallfelt B, Lundorff P, Thornburn J. Nonsurgical treatment of ectopic pregnancy. Lancet 1988;1:1403.

36. Egarter CH, Husslein P. Treatment of tubal pregnancy by prostaglandins. Lancet 1988;1:104–105.

37. Egarter C, Fitz R, Spona J, et al. Behandlung der eileiterschwangers-chaft mit prolaglandinen: ene multizenterstudie. Geburtshilfe Frauenheilkd 1989;49:808–812.

38. Vejtorp M, Vejerslev LO, Ruge S. Local prostaglandin treatment of ectopic pregnancy. Hum Reprod 1989;4:464–467.

39. Lang P, Weiss PAM, Mayer HO. Local application of hyperosmolar glucose solution in tubal pregnancy. Lancet 1989;2:922–923.

40. Pansky M, Golan A, Bukovsky I, Caspi E. Nonsurgical management of tubal pregnancy. Necessity in view of the changing clinical appearance. Am J Obstet Gynecol 1991;164:888–895.

17
GnRH Agonists in the Treatment of Fibroids

Ralph Philosophe

Uterine leiomyomas (fibroids) are the most common solid pelvic tumor in women. They are found clinically in approximately 25% of women, and pathological serial sectioning shows that their prevalence is even higher.[1] Fibroids represent the most common indication for hysterectomy for benign disease in the United States.[2,3]

Fibroids may be intramural, submucosal, or subserosal, or they may develop in other müllerian tissues such as the round ligaments, broad ligaments, cervix, and vagina.[4] Their size and location may significantly affect their symptomatology. Menorrhagia, possibly leading to iron deficiency anemia, occurs in approximately 30% of patients and is more commonly seen in association with submucous fibroids. Large fibroids may cause pressure on adjacent structures such as nerves, ureters, bladder, and bowel, causing pelvic pain and pressure, and urinary or bowel difficulties. Distortion of the uterine cavity may cause reproductive difficulties such as cornual obstruction, premature labor, and increased fetal loss. Fibroids are more common in nulliparous than multiparous women and in black than white women. The peak incidence occurs during the reproductive years, and regression generally occurs after the menopause. For this reason, the creation of a pseudomenopause with gonadotropin-releasing hormone agonists (GnRHa) has come under investigation in the medical management of fibroids.

Etiology

The factors involved in the initial neoplastic transformation giving rise to these tumors are unknown. They are, however, clearly stimulated by ovarian sex steroids. Growth is evident in pregnancy, and shrinkage occurs after the menopause or in hormonally suppressed women. At the cellular level, a higher number of estrogen and progestin receptors have been found in fibroid tissue than in normal myometria,[5,6] accounting for an enhanced responsiveness of fibroid tissue to circulating estrogens. Furthermore, the conversion of estradiol to estrone, a much weaker estrogen, is significantly lower in fibroids than in normal tissue,[7] resulting in an elevated intramyomal estradiol concentration.[8] This would enable fibroids to be less dependent on the circulating estradiol level and may explain their variable response to medical therapy among patients with equal estrogen suppression.[9] The elevated local intramyomal estradiol level is further substantiated clinically by the finding of endometrial hyperplasia at the margins of the submucous fibroids.[10]

Management

Surgical Management

By far the mainstay of treatment for fibroids is surgery. Myomectomy is the surgical procedure of choice for symptomatic women trying to retain their reproductive potential. Nevertheless, intraoperative hemorrhage, postoperative adhesion formation, weak uterine scars, postoperative fever, and damage to adjacent normal tissue are commonly associated. Furthermore, the reoperative rate following myomectomy is 15 to 30%.[11] Although fibroids can be treated safely and effectively by myomectomy, large fibroids may require treatment by hysterectomy. However, hysterectomy has inherent risks that include anesthetic complications, hemorrhage, infection, adhesion formation, and inadvertent injury to other organs. The death-to-case ratio from hysterectomy is 1 to 2 per 1,000 operations, and as many as 25 to 50% will sustain some type of complication.[12] In addition, psychologic and emotional sequelae including sexual dysfunction, low self-esteem, and alterations in the perception of femininity may occur. The rate of depression within 3 years following hysterectomy in nearly five times greater than in unoperated control patients.[13] As will be discussed in more detail later, GnRHa may be administered preoperatively to decrease fibroid size, allowing some patients to become candidates for laparoscopic and/ or hysteroscopic myomectomy, or vaginal hysterectomy, which carry lower morbidity than abdominal myomectomy and abdominal hysterectomy, respectively. Furthermore, the prognosis is expected to improve following agonist preoperative therapy, as the success of myomectomy appears to be inversely related to tumor volume at the time of surgery.[14]

Medical Management

Medical management is emerging as a significant alternative to surgery for fibroids in a select group of patients. As most of the fibroids will become asymptomatic in the menopause, controlling the associated symptoms during the years before the menopause with medical therapy may make certain hysterectomies unnecessary. Because uterine leiomyoma is the most common indication for hysterectomy, medical management is expected to have a significant role in reducing the rate of hysterectomy. Furthermore, because reduction in size may be achieved preoperatively, vaginal hysterectomy may become feasible, thereby reducing operative morbidity.[15]

Agents Used

Medical management in the form of ovarian suppression may be achieved by a number of agents, including progestins,[16] androgens (danazol),[17] antiestrogens (gestrinone),[18] oral contraceptive pills,[19] or GnRH agonists or antagonists. GnRHa are among the best alternatives, as they are devoid of intrinsic steroid effects, have a wide safety margin, and appear to be highly efficacious at tumor reduction and symptom alleviation. The value of the other forms of medical therapy in the reduction of leiomyoma size is limited. They may, however, be of clinical value in maintaining volume reduction brought about by GnRHa. For example, progesterone, although not very effective in reducing fibroid size, seems quite adequate at maintaining the shrunken state of a fibroid previously reduced by GnRHa. This finding is quite useful, since discontinuation of GnRHa is often followed by a rapid regrowth of the fibroid to pretreatment size (Fig. 17.1). Characteristically, GnRHa produce symptoms of hypoestrogenism, which include hot flashes, vaginal dryness, mood changes, decreased libido, and headaches. Although side effects are common, tolerability is good and discontinuation of treatment because of side effects is unusual.

RU 486 in preliminary work has been shown to decrease fibroid size by about 50% after 3 months of therapy and may be effective for preoperative adjunctive therapy. Further studies are needed to establish its safety and efficacy, as a transient elevation of androgens in blood was noted during initial therapy.[20] GnRH antagonists have also been studied and have the advantage of a very rapid onset of action without an initial "flare" or stimulatory release of gonadotropins, as seen with GnRHa. However, at present, their low potency, short half-life, and histamine-related side effects have limited their use.

Mechanism of Action of GnRHa

The effects of GnRHa on fibroid smooth muscle cells are complex. The major mode of action is to create a hypoestrogenic state, thereby decreasing the occupancy of estrogenic receptors, whose volume is increased in fibroid smooth muscle cells. Continuous administration of GnRHa results in down-regulation of its

FIGURE 17.1. Uterine volume changes during 6 months of therapy with Nafarelin, 200 μg b.i.d. and at follow-up. Reprinted, with permission, from ref. 42.

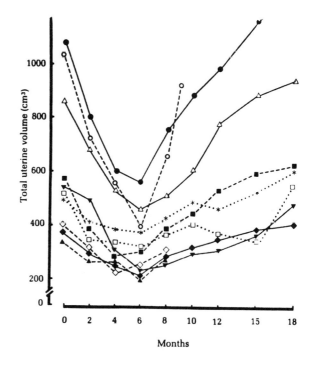

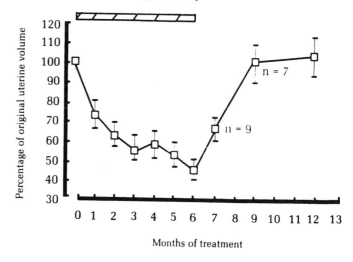

own receptors in the pituitary gland, with resultant suppression of both pulsatility and basal gonadotropin release. Following the first subcutaneous administration, maximal gonadotropin release is obtained within 4 hours. With daily administration, the response is abolished within 1 week, and pituitary desensitization follows. GnRHa also appear to substantially decrease estrogen receptors in fibroid tissue while increasing progesterone receptors.[21] The combined effects of lower estradiol levels and lower receptor concentration cause a markedly shrunken cytoplasmic volume, as assessed by electron microscopy. These cells, however, can rapidly regenerate with the return of normal estrogen concentration and receptors.

Estrogen may exert its effects by influencing epidermal growth factor (EGF) receptor volume in the smooth muscle cell. EGF is a peptide hormone that controls, in part, the rate and extent of cell proliferation. It binds to all cell types within the human uterus. Treatment with GnRHa decreases binding of EGF to leiomyoma smooth muscle cells but not to myometrial cells when compared with untreated women.[22] This would be expected to result in a more selective reduction of fibroid mass compared with myometria. However, the effect induced by GnRHa on fibroids cannot be explained solely by the degree of hypoestrogenic state achieved nor its resultant influence on EGF, because variable effects are noted despite adequate estrogen suppression (<20 pmol/L). Furthermore, maintaining patients on a GnRHa regimen which preserves basal estrogen levels sufficient to prevent analog side effects does not result in regrowth of the fibroids. A direct effect of GnRHa on the fibroids is suggested and supported by the finding of GnRH receptors in fibroid smooth muscle cells.[23] Treatment with GnRHa has been found to decrease secretion of insulinlike growth factors (IGF I and IGF II) by explant cultures of myometria and fibroids when compared with tissue obtained from placebo-treated controls.[24] Both IGF I and IGF II have been implicated in the initiation or promotion of fibroid growth. Therefore, the effect of the analogs may be mediated directly by GnRH receptors, which in turn act on intracellular growth factors, thereby reducing size. This may explain in part why regrowth does not occur even when basal estrogen levels are maintained during GnRHa therapy.

Another mechanism by which fibroid size may be reduced is by the reduction in uterine arterial blood flow. Estrogens have been shown to produce vasodilation and increased blood flow in uterine vasculature in rat models.[25] Conversely, if estrogen levels are reduced, as by GnRHa therapy, vasoconstriction and decreased blood flow occur. This is demonstrated by ultrasound doppler measurements of uterine blood flow in which the resistance of uterine artery vessels was found to increase significantly following 4 months of treatment with GnRHa.[26] A significant reduction in prominent vessels adjacent to the uterus or indicidual fibroids in patients treated with GnRHa compared with placebo has also been observed using magnetic resonance imaging.[27] The histology from uteri of women pretreated with GnRHa shows intense hyalinization around blood vessels.[28] Ultrasound doppler studies of uterine arteries do not show any significant change prior to the third week of treatment. The response is a gradual one, though after 4 months there is no further reduction in doppler wave forms. The blunted arterial blood supply, therefore, is believed to represent another method by which fibroid size is reduced. It also explains the reduced blood loss that occurs during myomectomy in women pretreated with GnRHa. Postoperative morbidity may also be reduced because of the lowered risks of infection, adhesion formation, and the need for blood transfusions secondary to reduced blood loss.

Route of Administration

GnRHa demonstrate increased binding affinity for GnRH receptors and a reduced susceptibility to proteolytic degradation compared to the native hormone.[29] The majority of studies have used nasal sprays or subcutaneous injections of GnRHa. If administered orally, the native GnRH molecule and its analog have less than 1% bioavailability content compared to intravenous (IV) injection. The nasal route has the advantage of rapid absorption and avoids the hepatic first-pass effect. Absorption, however, may depend upon the physiologic conditions of the nasal mucosal membranes. The efficacy of the intranasal delivery route has been found to be lower than[30,31] or similar to[9,32] subcutaneous injections of analog. A long-acting depot formulation has been developed. The analog is incorporated into biodegradable microspheres composed of a polymer of polyacetic and polyglycolic acid. As with the daily subcutaneous injections, a brief stimulation or "flare" period is seen with the depot injection in the first days of treatment. Recurrence of the "flare" phenomenon does not occur with subsequent doses. The efficacy of the depot formulation appears to be similar to that of daily subcutaneous injections. The availability of a long-acting depot formulation

TABLE 17.1 Advantages of preoperative GnRH agonist treatment for leiomyomas.

1. Reduced size	Pfannensteil vs. midline abdominal incision
	Vaginal hysterectomy vs. abdominal hysterectomy
	Laparoscopic/hysteroscopic resection more feasible
	Less damage to adjacent myometrium
	Improved fertility outcome
	Reduced operating time
2. Reduced blood flow to fibroids	Less intraoperative blood loss
	Reduced postoperative fever
	Reduced transfusions and inherent risks
3. Reduced menstrual blood loss	Corrects or improves anemia
	Optimizes surgery

allowing once-a-month administration has made this form of therapy much more convenient for the patients.[33,34]

Effectiveness

GnRHa are highly efficacious at reducing fibroid size. Most studies show approximately a 50% reduction following 6 months of therapy (Table 17.1). Larger fibroids demonstrate a greater decrease in size and are more likely to shrink than smaller tumors.[32] The greatest reduction in size occurs during the first month of therapy, after which the rate tapers off until by the sixth month of treatment, very little continued reduction is evident.[42] Approximately 10% of patients may be refractory to this treatment and show no reduction. Continued growth of fibroids during agonist therapy must also be recognized as a sign of possible sarcomatous development.[44] Regardless of the response by the fibroids, the analogs also induce endometrial atrophy and reduce uterine volume. This contributes significantly to the resolution of heavy uterine bleeding and/or symptoms due to compression on the adjacent organs. Unfortunately, when GnRHa are discontinued, the fibroids almost invariably return to their pretreatment size,[41,45] and approximately one-third of patients have recurrence of symptoms. It follows that long-term treatment with GnRHa is required, and concern has emerged over the safety of chronic estrogen depression.

Associated Risks

GnRHa induce a postmenopausal state in an accelerated time frame. The effects of menopause on lipids and bones may also occur more precipitously than following natural menopause. It is known that the natural menopause is associated with a rise in serum low-density lipoprotein (LDL) cholesterol and total cholesterol, while high-density lipoprotein (HDL) cholesterol remains essentially unchanged.[46] Premenopausal women rendered acutely estrogen-deficient by surgical castration have lower HDL cholesterol in addition to elevated LDL cholesterol, and demonstrate a sevenfold increase in the rate of myocardial infarction.[47] The rapid onset of menopause induced by GnRHa is analogous to undergoing bilateral salpingo-oophorectomy, and similar adverse effects on lipid metabolism may also occur. Theoretically, the long-term effects of these changes in the lipid profile on cardiovascular disease are expected to be similar.

Bone loss associated with GnRHa use also appears to occur more precipitously than in natural menopause. Small but significant losses of 6 to 8.2% in trabecular bone of the lumbar vertebrae were noted after only 6 months of GnRHa therapy.[48,49] The effects of GnRHa on bone turnover and the subsequent risk of osteoporosis are nevertheless controversial, as numerous variables affecting alterations in bone turnover exist. These variables include the sensitivity of tests for detecting bone loss, the extent of the hypoestrogenic state induced by analogs, insufficient calcium intake, exercise, and lifestyle. Methods that assess only the wrist are limited because the appendicular skeletal bone mass is measured, whereas the clinically important spinal bone may differ significantly from the former. Furthermore, cortical bone, which comprises 95% of distal wrist bones, turns over much less rapidly than trabecular bone. It is thought that the latter is more reflective of acute changes in the balance of bone mineral content. Bone turnover is increased during GnRHa therapy.[50] However, the net loss of body calcium may be reversed by supplemental calcium intake.[51] Several authors have found no bone loss,[52-54] while others suggest a decrease in bone density[55-58] following 6 months of GnRHa therapy. This loss appears to reverse itself by 3 to 6 months posttreatment, although some authors have observed patients without complete reversibility.[55,56b] This finding is worrisome, and the potential combined long-term risks of heart disease and osteoporosis may outweigh the benefits from long-term medical therapy with GnRHa versus surgery. These concerns have precluded the use of GnRHa as single-agent medical therapy for longer than 6 months.

Clinical Applications

Because of safety issues with long-term use of GnRHa, its clinical use when administered as a sole agent is limited to less than 6 months. Short-term treatment ($\leq$ 6 months) is expected to offer benefit to two groups of women: (1) perimenopausal women with symptomatic fibroids and (2) premenopausal patients requiring conservative surgery for symptomatic fibroids.

For perimenopausal patients, GnRHa may alleviate symptoms related to fibroid growth until spontaneous ovarian failure occurs. Surgery may thus be avoided in these patients. Premenopausal women with symptomatic

fibroids may benefit from an adjunct, preoperative short course of GnRHa treatment. Therapy for 1 or 2 months allows anemic patients to normalize their hemoglobin, diminishes intraoperative blood loss, minimizes damage to adjacent normal uterine tissue during myomectomy, and makes laparoscopic or hysteroscopic resection of fibroids more feasible (Table 17.2).[36,59-62]

Advances in Long-Term Therapy

The rapid regrowth of fibroids that almost invariably occurs following the cessation of GnRHa treatment has prompted the search for adjunctive medical therapy. This includes the addition of a progestin with the rationale that it can antagonize the estrogen-stimulated uterine growth.[63] GnRHa may therefore be used to reduce fibroid volume to an acceptable size, and progesterone may then be used to maintain the effect induced by GnRHa without the disadvantages of chemical castration. The reduction in estrogen receptors and the increase in progesterone receptors in fibroid tissue by GnRHa[21] creates favorable conditions for adjunctive progesterone therapy.

Preliminary work in 18 patients who received 6 sequential months of GnRHa therapy followed by 6 months of medroxyprogesterone

TABLE 17.2 Effects of GnRH agonists on leiomyomata uteri.

Authors	No. of patients	GnRH agonist	Dose	Duration	Month	Reduction %
Maheux et al. (1985)[35]	10	Buserelin	500 μg SC	Daily	6	LV-55
West et al. (1987)[33] SC	13	Goserelin	3.6 mg	Monthly	6	UV-55
Kessel et al. (1988)[36]	14	Histerelin/ Triptorelin	20–50 μg SC	Daily	6	UV-40
Collins RL (1988)[37]	21	Imbzl-D-His-Pro-Net-GnRH	4 μg/kg SC	Daily	6	UV-50
Andreyko et al. (1988)[38]	10	Nafarelin	400 μg IN	b.i.d.	6	LV-46 UV-57
Van Leusden H.A.I.N. (1988)[39]	28	Triptorelin	4 μg IM	Monthly	6	UV-77
Benagiano et al. (1988)[40]	20	Buserelin	1,500 μg IN	Daily	6	LV-62
Matta et al. (1989)[41]	10	Buserelin	300 μg IN	t.i.d.	6	LV-57 UV-44
Vollenhoven et al. (1990)[32]	17	Buserelin	200 μg SC	Daily	6	LV-54
	19	Buserelin	1,200 μg IN	Daily	6	LV-51
Williams et al. (1990)[42]	13	Nafarelin	200 μg IN	b.i.d.	6	UV-45
Friedman et al. (1991)[43]	60	Leuprolide	3.75 mg IM	Monthly	6	UV-45
Zawin et al. (1990)[27]	17	Leuprolide	3.75 mg IM	Monthly	6	LV-68
			1 mg SC	Daily	6	UV-56

LV, Leiomyoma volume; UV, uterine volume; SC, subcutaneously; IN, intranasally; EM, Intramuscularly.

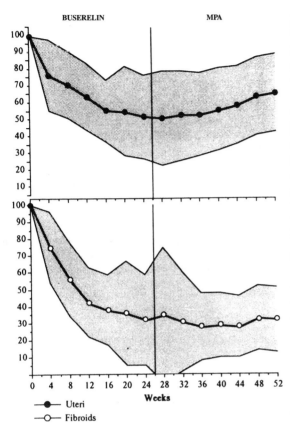

BUSERELIN   MPA

—●— Uteri
—○— Fibroids

FIGURE 17.2. Variation in the volume of the uterus (o) and of fibroid masses (●) in 18 women during 26 weeks of Buserelin therapy, followed by 26 weeks of treatment with MPA. Shaded areas represent one standard deviation. Reprinted, with permission, from ref. 45.

acetate (MPA) (200 mg/day for the first month, 100 mg/day for the second month, 50 mg/day for the third and fourth months, and 25 mg/day for the fifth and sixth months) showed an initial regression in fibroid size of 52%, followed by no significant regrowth of fibroid during the ensuing 6 months (Fig. 17.2). Symptoms such as hot flashes, sweating, depression, vaginal dryness, and decreased libido while on analog therapy improved when GnRHa was replaced with MPA. Vaginal spotting, however, increased to involve approximately 50% of patients. No women discontinued therapy with GnRHa or MPA due to side effects. MPA also prevented recurrence of those symptoms reported prior to initiating any therapy. Nine

patients have completed 18 months of observation (6 months GnRHa followed by 12 months MPA), and the fibroids have remained at approximately half of the pretreatment volume.[64]

The lipid changes induced by 6 months of GnRHa in 40 patients showed a significant increase in total cholesterol, a significant decrease in HDL cholesterol, and no significant change in LDL cholesterol. Treatment with MPA in 20 patients was associated with a significant decrease in HDL cholesterol but with no significant change in LDL cholesterol.[64] The long-term consequences of these unfavorable lipid changes remain to be elucidated.

Progesterone may also be administered simultaneously with GnRHa (as opposed to sequential therapy). In a study involving 16 women with symptomatic fibroids, 7 women received daily GnRHa therapy and placebo pills for 6 months, while 9 women received daily GnRHa and oral MPA 20 mg/day for 6 month.[65] Although women treated with GnRHa and MPA experienced significantly fewer hypoestrogenic side effects, they failed to demonstrate significant reduction (14%) in mean uterine volume compared with the GnRHa/placebo group (53%), despite achieving equally profound estrogen suppression. Two interesting conclusions were drawn from this study. First, MPA or its metabolite may somehow interfere with GnRHa action on fibroids. Second, estrogen suppression does not appear to be the only factor involved in tumor shrinkage, as had been previously noted. This observation, along with the finding of GnRHa receptors in leiomyoma cells, reinforces a direct action of GnRHa on fibroids and suggests that severe hypoestrogenemia may not be necessary to achieve sufficient tumor regression. In another study, the mean fibroid volume and estradiol (E_2) levels were assessed in four groups of patients receiving different doses of GnRHa to achieve different basal E_2 levels. The reduction of uterine volume was statistically the same among the four groups, although the basal E_2 levels were different.[66] Therefore, maintaining a slightly higher basal E_2 level (20–50 pg/ml) does not adversely affect tumor shrinkage but may have an impact on reducing reported side effects.

An alternative approach to titrating the GnRHa dose to maintain a desired E_2 level would be to profoundly suppress E_2 levels with GnRHa and to add back low doses of estrogen to maintain a desired basal level (20–50 pg/ml). The long-term effects on uterine and fibroid size and the resolution of disturbing symptoms following prolonged therapy remain unanswered. A small preliminary study was done on five perimenopausal women treated with GnRHa for 3 months, followed by 24 months of daily GnRHa and cyclic hormone replacement therapy consisting 0.625 mg/day of conjugated estrogen (days 1–25) and 10 mg/day of MPA (days 16–25) each month. The study found a decrease in uterine volume of approximately 50%, which persisted during the ensuing 24 months of combination therapy.[53] Bone loss by single photon absorption photometry did not change significantly in the five patients over the 27-month treatment period. Hot flashes were reported in all women during the 3-month period of GnRHa therapy only, and were eliminated in all women within 1 month following addition of cyclic estrogen-progestin replacement.

The data presently available are insufficient for clinical recommendations, but a monthly depot of GnRHa combined with low-dose estrogen and progesterone replacement therapy may prevent lipid and bone changes that occur in the menopause.[67] Larger and longer studies are still needed to ascertain the length of the suppressive effect on fibroid growth and the potential deleterious lipid effects associated with prolonged GnRHa use with or without the addition of estrogen and MPA.

References

1. Cramer SF, Patel A. The frequency of uterine leiomyomas. Am J Clin Pathol 1990;94:435–438.
2. Lee NC, Dicker RC, Rubin GL, Ory HW. Confirmation of the preoperative diagnoses for hysterectomy. Am J Obstet Gynecol 1984; 150:283–287.
3. Easterday CL, Grimes DA, Riggs JA. Hysterectomy in the United States. Obstet Gynecol 1983;62:201–212.
4. Robins SL, Cotran RS. Leiomyomata (fibromyoma). In: The Pathogenic Basis of Disease. Philadelphia: W.B. Saunders Co., 1979:1271.
5. Tamaya T, Fujimoto J, Okada H. Comparison of cellular levels of steroid receptors in uterine leiomyoma and myometrium. Acta Obstet Gynecol Scand 1985;64:307.
6. Sadan O, Vanidelekinge B, Van Gelderen CJ, Savage N, Becker PJ, Van Der Walt LA, Robinson M. Estrogen and progesterone receptor concentrations in leiomyomas and normal myometrium. Ann Clin Biochem 1987;24:263.
7. Pollow K, Sinnecker G, Boquoi E, Pollow B. In vitro conversion of estradiol 17ß into estrone in normal human myometrium and leiomyoma. J Clin Chem Clin Biochem 1978;16:493–502.
8. Otubu JA, Buttram VC, Besch NF, Besch PK. Unconjugated steroids in leiomyomas and tumor-bearing myometrium. Am J Obstet Gynecol 1982;143:130.
9. Maheux R, Lemay A, Merat P. Use of intranasal leuteinizing hormone-releasing hormone agonist in uterine leiomyomas. Fertil Steril 1987;47:229–233.
10. Deligdish L, Loewenthal M. Endometrial changes associated with myomata of the uterus. J Clin Pathol 1970;23:676–680.
11. Berkeley AS, DeCherney AH, Polan ML. Abdominal myomectomy and subsequent fertility. Surg Gynecol Obstet 1983;156:319–322.
12. Dicker RC, Greenspan JR, Strauss LT, Cowart MR, Scully MJ, Peterson HB, DeStefano HB, Rubin AL, Ory HW. Complications of abdominal and vaginal hysterectomy among women of reproductive age in the United States. The collaborative review of sterilization. Am J Obstet Gynecol 1982;144:841–848.
13. Richards DH. Depression after hysterectomy. Lancet 1973;2:430–433.
14. Buttram VC, Reiter RC. Uterine leiomyomata: Etiology, symptomatology and management. Fertil Steril 1981;36:433–445.
15. Stovall TG, Ling FW, Henry LC, Woodruff MR. A randomized trial evaluating leuprolide acetate before hysterectomy as treatment for leiomyomas. Am J Obstet Gynecol 1991; 164:1420–1425.
16. Goldzieher JW, Macqueo M, Ricaud L, Aguilar JA, Canales E. Induction of degenerative changes in uterine myomas by high dosage progestin therapy. Am J Obstet Gynecol 1966;96:1078–1087.

17. DeCherney AH, Maheux R, Polan ML. A medical treatment for myomata uteri. Fertil Steril 1983;39:429–430.

18. Coutinho EM, Boulanger GA, Goncalves MT. Regression of uterine leiomyomata after treatment with gestrinone, an antiestrogen, anti-progesterone. Am J Obstet Gynecol 1986; 155:761–767.

19. Ross RK, Pike MC, Vessey MP, Bull D, Yeates D, Casagrande JT. Risk factors for uterine fibroids: Reduced risk associated with oral contraceptives. Br Med J 1986;293:359–362.

20. Murphy AA, Kettel LM, Morales A, Yen SSC. Response of uterine fibroids to the antiprogesterone RU 486. A pilot study. Abstract 071, AFS, Orlando, Florida 1991.

21. Baird DT, Bramley TA, Hawkins TA, Lumsden MA, West CP. Effect of treatment with GnRH analogue zoladex on binding of estradiol, progesterone and epidermal growth factor to uterine fibromyomata.

22. Lumsden MA, West CP, Bramley T, Rumgay L, Baird DT. The binding of epidermal growth factor to the human uterus and leiomyomata in women rendered hypoestrogenic by continuous administration of LH RH agonist. Br J Obstet Gynec 1988;95:1299–1304.

23. Wiznitzer A, Marbach M, Hazum E, et al. Gonadotropin-releasing hormone specific binding sites in uterine leiomyomata. Biochem Biophys Res Comm 1988;152:1326.

24. Rein MS, Friedman AJ, Pandian MR, Heffner LJ. The secretion of insulin-like growth factors I and II by explant cultures of fibroids and myometrium from women treated with a gonadotropin-releasing hormone agonist. Obstet Gynecol 1990;76:388–394.

25. Resnik R, Killam AP, Battaglia FC, Makowski EL, Meschia G. The stimulation of uterine blood flow by various estrogens. Endocrinology 1974;94:1192–1196.

26. Matta WHM, Stabile I, Shaw RW, Campbell S. Doppler assessment of uterine blood flow changes in patients with fibroids receiving the gonadotropin-releasing hormone agonist buserelin. Fertil Steril 1988;49:1083–1085.

27. Zawin M, McCarthy S, Scoutt L, Lange R, Lavy G, Vulte J, Comite F. Monitoring therapy with a gonadotropin-releasing hormone analog: Utility of MR imaging. Radiology 1990;175: 503–506.

28. Benagiano G, Morini A, Abbondante A, et al. Sequential GnRH analogue (buserelin)—medroxyprogesterone acetate MPA treatment of uterine leiomyomata. In: Vickery BH, Lunenfeld B, eds. GnRH Analogues in Cancer and Human Reproduction. Lancaster: MTP Press.

29. Loumaye E, Naor Z, Catt KJ. Binding affinity and biological activity of gonadotropin-releasing hormone agonists in isolated pituitary cells. Endocrinology 1982;111:730–736.

30. Fraser HM. LHRH analogues: Their clinical physiology and delivery systems. In: Healy DL, ed., Balliere's Clinical Obstetrics and Gynecology—International Practice and Research. Anti-Hormones in Clinical Gynecology. Vol 2. London: Balliere Tindall, 1988:639.

31. Friendman AJ, Barbieri RL, Benacerraf BR, Schiff I. Treatment of leiomyomata with intranasal or subcutaneous leuprolide, a gonadotropin-releasing hormone agonist. Fertil Steril 1987;48:560–564.

32. Vollenhoven BJ, Shekleton P, McDonald J, Healy DL. Clinical predictors for buserelin acetate treatment of uterine fibroids: A prospective study of 40 women. Fertil Steril 1990;54:1032–1038.

33. West CP, Lumsden MA, Lawson S, Williamson J, Baird DT. Shrinkage of uterine fibroids during therapy with goserelin (Zoladex): A leuteinizing hormone-releasing hormone agonist administered as a monthly subcutaneous depot. Fertil Steril 1987;48:45–51.

34. Van der Spuy ZM, Fieggan AG, Wood MJA, Pienaar CA. The short-term use of luteinizing hormone-releasing hormone analogues in uterine fibroids. Horm Res 989;32(Suppl 1): 137–140.

35. Maheux R, Guilloteau C, Lemay A, Bastide A, Fazekas ATA. Luteinizing hormone-releasing hormone agonist and uterine leiomyoma; a pilot study. Am J Obstet Gyn 1985;152:1034–1038.

36. Kessel B, Liu J, Mortola J, Berga S, Yen SSC. Treatment of uterine fibroids with agonist analogs of gonadotropin-releasing hormone. Fertil Steril 1988;49:538–541.

37. Collins RL. Treatment of symptomatic leiomyomata uteri with a long acting gonadotropin-releasing hormone agonist: Long-term follow-up. Gynecol Endocrinol (Suppl 1) 1988;2: 89.

38. Andreyko JL, Blumenfeld Z, Marshall LA, Monroe SE, Hricak H, Jaffe RB. Use of an agonist analog of gonadotropin-releasing hormone (nafarelin) to treat leiomyomas: Assessment by magnetic resonance imaging. Am J Obstet Gynecol 1988;158:903–910.

39. Van Leusden HAIM. Triptorelin to prevent hysterectomy in patients with leiomyomas. Lancet 1988;2:508–519.

40. Benagiano G, Primiero F, Morini A, Isidori C, Addi G, Tunner G. Multimodal pharmacological approach to the treatment of leiomyomata uteri. Gynecol Endocrinol (Suppl 2) 1988; 2:50.

41. Matta WHM, Shaw RW, Nye M. Long-term follow-up of patients with uterine fibroids after treatment with the LHRH agonist buserelin. Br J Obstet Gynecol 1989;96:200–206.

42. Williams IA, Shaw RW. Effect of Nafarelin on uterine fibroids measured by ultrasound and magnetic resonance imaging. Eur J Obstet Gynecol Reprod Biol 1990;34:111–117.

43. Friedman AJ, Hoffman DI, Comite F, Browneller RW, Miller JD. Treatment of leiomyomata uteri with leuprolide acetate depot: A double-blind, placebo-controlled, multicenter study. Obstet Gynecol 1991;77: 720–725.

44. Meyer WR, Mayer AR, Diamond WP, et al. Unsuspected leiomyosarcoma: Treatment with a gonadotropin releasing hormone analogue. Obstet Gynecol 1990;75:529.

45. Benagiano A, Morini A, Aleandri V, Piccinno F, Primiero FM, Abbondante A, Elkind-Hirsch K. Sequential GnRH superagonist and medroxyprogesterone acetate treatment of uterine leiomyomata. Int J Obstet Gynecol 1990;33: 333–343.

46. Lipid Research Clinics Program. The Lipid Research Clinics Coronary Primary Prevention trial results. Reduction in the incidence of coronary heart disease. JAMA 1984;251:351.

47. Rosenberg L, Hennekens CH, Rosner B, Belanger C, Rothman KJ, Speizer FE. Early menopause and the risk of myocardial infarction. Am J Obstet Gynecol 1981;139:47–51.

48. Matta WH, Shaw RW, Hesp R, Katz D. Hypogonadism induced by luteinizing hormone releasing hormone analogues: Effects on bone density in premenopausal women. Br Med J 1987;294:1523.

49. Dodin S, Lemay A, Maheux R, Dumont M, Turcot-Lemay L. Bone mass in endometriosis patients treated with GnRH agonist implant or danazol. Obstet Gynecol 1991;77:410.

50. Van Leusden HAIM, Dogterom AA. Rapid reduction of uterine leiomyomas with montly injections of Δ-trp-GnRH. Gynecol Endocrinol 1988;2:45-51.

51. Comite F, Jensen P. Bone density changes associated with GnRH analogues. International Symposium on GnRH Analogues in Cancer and Human Reproduction. Geneva, Switzerland, Feb 1988.

52. Comite F, Jensen P, Lewis A, et al. GnRH analog therapy in endometriosis: Impact on bone mass. Society for Gynecologic Investigation Atlanta, IGA, March No. 112, 1987.

53. Tummon IA, Ali A, Pepping ME, Radwanska E, Binor Z, Dmowski WP. Bone mineral density in women with endometriosis before and during ovarian suppression with gonadotropin-releasing hormone agonists or danazol. Fertil Steril 1988;49:792–796.

54. Bianchi G, Costantini S, Anserini P, Rovetta G, Monteforte P, Menada MV, Faga L, DeCecco L. Effects of gonadotropin-releasing hormone agonist on uterine fibroids and bone density. Maturitas 1989;11:179–185.

55. Dawood MY, Lewis V, Ramos J. Cortical and trabecular bone mineral content in women with endometriosis: Effect of gonadotropin-releasing hormone agonist and danazol. Fertil Steril 1989;52:21–26.

56. Devogelaer JP, Huaux JP, Donnez J, et al. Differential effects of the GnRH agonist buserelin on the axial and the appendicular skeleton at different scanning sites. Preferential loss of trabecular bone. In: Christiansen C, Johansen JS, Riis BJ, eds. Osteoporosis 1987. Proceedings of the International Symposium on Osteoporosis. Viborg: Norhaven Bogtrykkeri, p. 588.

56b. Devogelaer JP, De Deuxchaisnes CN, Donnez J, Thomas K. LHRH analogues and bone loss (letter). Lancet 1987;1:1498.

57. Johansen JS, Riis BJ, Hassager C, Moer M, Jacobson J, Christiansen C. The effect of gonadotropin-releasing hormone agonist analog (nafarelin) on bone metabolism. J Clin Endocrinol Metab 1988;67:701–706.

58. Matta WHM, Shaw RW, Hesp R, Evans R. Reversible trabecular bone density loss following induced hypoestrogenism with the GnRH analogue buserelin in premenopausal women. Clin Endocrinol 1988;29:45–51.

59. Lumsden MA, West CP, Baird DT. Goserelin therapy before surgery for uterine fibroids (letter). Lancet 1987;1:36–37.

60. Friedman AJ, Rein MS, Harrison-Atlas D, Garfield JM, Doubilet PM. A randomized, placebo controlled, double-blind study evaluating leuprolide acetate depot treatment before myomectomy. Fertil Steril 1989;52:728–733.

61. Healy DL, Lawson SR, Abbott M, Baird DT, Fraser HM. Toward removing uterine fibroids without surgery: Subcutaneous infusion of a luteinizing hormone-releasing hormone agonist commencing in the luteal phase. J Clin Endocrinol Metab 1986;63:619–625.

62. Dubuisson JB, Mandlebrot L, Lecuru F, Aubriot FX, Foulot H, Mouly M. Myomectomy by laparoscopy: A preliminary report of 43 cases. Fertil Steril 1991;56:827–830.

63. Hsueh AJW, Peck EJ, Clark JH. Progesterone antagonism of the estrogen receptor and estrogen induced uterine growth. Nature 1975;254: 337–339.

64. Benagiano G, Morini A, Aleandri V, Piccinno F, Angelini R, Goldzieher JW. Sequential buserelin-medroxyprogesterone acetate treatment of leimyomata uteri. In: Brosens I, Jacobs HS, Runnebaum B, eds. LHRH Analogues in Gynecology. New Jersey: The Parthenon Publishing Group, 1990.

65. Friedman AJ, Barbieri RL, Doubilet PM, Fine C, Schiff I. A randomized, double-blind trial of gonadotropin-releasing hormone agonist (leuprolide) with or without medroxyprogesterone acetate in the treatment of leiomyomata uteri. Fertil Steril 1988;49:404–409.

66. Maheux R. The use of LHRH analogues in the treatment of leiomyoma uteri. In: Brosens I, Jacobs HS, Runnebaum B, eds. LHRH Analogues in Gynecology. New Jersey: The Parthenon Publishing Group, 1990.

67. Friedman AJ. Treatment of leiomyomata uteri with short-term leuprolide followed by leuprolide plus estrogen-progestin hormone replacement therapy for 2 years: A pilot study. Fertil Steril 1989;51:526–528.

18
GnRH Agonists in the Treatment of Endometriosis

Ricardo Serta

Endometriosis is present in approximately 5 to 7% of reproductive age women and is believed to cause infertility in 20 to 40% of those affected. There is some evidence supporting a hormone-dependent mechanism for endometriosis, as it is rarely found prior to or beyond reproductive age. Furthermore, it regresses following bilateral oophorectomy. Although definitive treatment can best be accomplished by surgery, the potential need for repetitive operative procedures and the inability to remove all endometrial implants at the time of surgery have resulted in the introduction of several types of medical treatment, including progestogens, estrogen-progestogen combinations, and danazol. In recent years gonadotropin-releasing hormone agonists (GnRHa) have experienced enormous popularity for the medical treatment of endometriosis. The substitution of native GnRH amino acids at position 6 and 10 by D-amino acids and ethylamides, respectively (Table 18.1),[1] led to the development of several synthetic GnRHa. These substitutions greatly increased the half-life and potency of the native compound and allowed widespread clinical application.

Administration of GnRHa

The objective of administering GnRHa to endometriosis patients is to induce a prolonged hypoestrogenic period without endometrial shedding and menstrual bleeding. The impact on endometriotic implants is believed to reduce local tissue reaction and adhesion formation.[2]

GnRHa are available in a number of formulations and may be administered via intra-vaginal, rectal, intranasal, percutaneous, and depot routes (Table 18.2). Oral administration is ineffective because these peptides are rapidly destroyed by digestive enzymes. The biological efficacy of GnRHa is related to their absorption, affinity to the gonadotropin receptor, bioavailability, and metabolic clearance. Because of their prolonged half-life and potency, GnRHa are effective even when administered subcutaneously once daily. Multiple daily intranasal insufflations are widely employed in long-term treatment, but absorption through the nasal mucosa is poor and variable. Therefore, a dose of 200 to 1,000 µg repeated two or three times daily is usually required to reduce steroid levels to the menopause range. A more profound and constant decrease in serum estrogen levels can be achieved with subcutaneous administration than with intranasal spray.

Slow-release formulations such as biodegradable microcapsules, microspheres, or small subcutaneous implants have also been developed for the continuous delivery of GnRHa.[3] Pituitary gonadal function is more completely inhibited with delayed-release formulations than with aqueous solutions. The suppression is more constant, probably due to the absence of absorption problems, as in the intranasal route, and to the absence of compliance problems associated with multiple daily injections, as required with the subcutaneous or intramuscular routes. When used to suppress endometriosis, GnRHa are usually administered for 6 to 9 months. An initial rise in estradiol (E_2) levels is generally observed if therapy is initiated in the early follicular phase. Initiating therapy in the early or midluteal

TABLE 18.1 GnRHa currently in clinical use.

Name	Structure
	1 2 3 4 5 6 7 8 9 10
GnRH	ProGlu-His-Trp-Ser-Tyr-Gly-Leu-Arg-Pro-Gly-NH$_2$
Leuprolide	-D.Leu- -Pro.NEt
Buserelin	-D.Ser(tBu) Pro.NEt
Nafarelin	-D.Nal-
Zoladex	-D.Ser(tBu) AzaGly
Lutrelin	-D.Trp -Me-Leu- -Pro.NEt

TABLE 18.2 Formulation and route of administration of GnRHa.

Name	Route of administraton	Formulation	Dose
Leuprolide	SC injections	Aqueous solution	1×500–$1000\,\mu g$/day
	IN spray		$2 \times 800\,\mu g$/day
	IM injection		3.75 mg/4 weeks
Buserelin	SC injections	Aqueous solution	$1 \times 200\,\mu g$/day
	IN spray		$3 \times 400\,\mu g$/day
	Implants injection		6.6 mg/5 weeks
Nafarelin	IN spray	Aqueous solution	$2 \times 200\,\mu g$/day
			$2 \times 400\,\mu g$/day
Goserelin	Cylindrical implants	SC injection of implant	1×3.6 mg/4 weeks

phase avoids this initial stimulation and reduces the risk of luteinization or ovulation during the first month of treatment.

Hormonal Pattern

As seen in Figure 18.1, estrogen values can reach menopausal levels following 2 or 3 months of GnRHa therapy. Following a slight initial rise, the mean serum luteinizing hormone (LH) concentration maintains early midfollicular phase levels throughout therapy. The mean follicle-stimulating hormone (FSH) levels remain in the low range of the early follicular phase. Serum concentrations of progesterone, Δ^4-3 ketosteroids, 17-α hydroxyprogesterone, androstenedione, and testosterone decrease during therapy, but no significant changes in 17-hydroxypregnenolone or dehydroepiandrosterone (DHEA) are detected. Serum levels of aldosterone and cortisol can initially rise due to the stimulatory effects of estrogens on transcortin and aldosterone-binding globulin but return to normal levels within the first weeks of therapy. There

is also a slight decrease in 5-α-reduced androgens, dihydrotestosterone (DHT), and androstenediol during GnRHa therapy.[4]

Side Effects

The administration of GnRHa is associated with a variety of undesirable symptoms, primarily due to hypoestrogenism. Almost all therapies achieve menopausal estrogen levels within 3 months, at which time virtually all patients experience amenorrhea and hot flashes. These hot flashes can be reduced by the addition of 20 to 30 mg daily of medroxyprogesterone acetate (MPA). Vaginal dryness, emotional lability, sweating, dyspareunia, and insomnia are usually present but to a lesser extent (Fig. 18.2). Some patients report vaginal bleeding within the first month of therapy, and approximately 60% of the remaining cases occur within the next 2 months. Side effects are usually well tolerated, with cessation of therapy required in only a small percentage of cases.

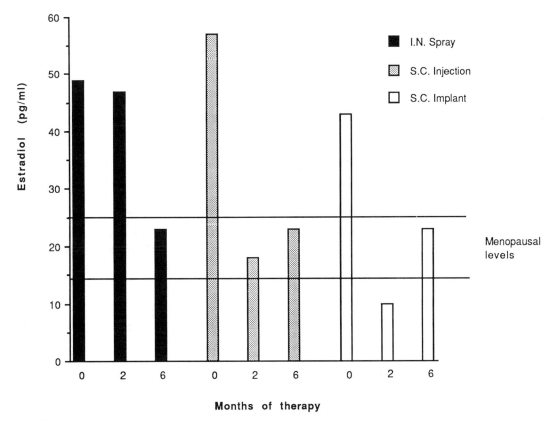

FIGURE 18.1. Estrogen levels in endometriosis patients treated with three different routes of administration of GnRHa.

Metabolic Effects

GnRHa have been shown to alter lipoprotein metabolism when administered long-term.[5] Low-density lipoproteins (LDL) are thought to lead to atherosclerotic plaque formation. High-density lipoproteins (HDL), particularly the subfraction HDL-2, are known to confer protection against plaque formation.[6-8] Most of the GnRHa have been shown to increase total plasma cholesterol, but no significant changes have been reported in the LDL subfraction. There is some controversy about the effects of GnRHa on the HDL subfraction, with some reports showing an increase and others a decrease in plasma levels. The total effect of GnRHa on lipid metabolism makes them a relatively safe drug in this respect. This is particularly welcome in view of the signi-

ficant adverse effects of other agents, such as danazol, on HDL cholesterol (Fig. 18.3).

The loss of bone mass during therapy due to hypoestrogenemia has been a topic of concern associated with GnRHa.[9-12] GnRHa have been shown to reduce vertebral bone density in several sites, including the proximal femur, an important site of osteoporotic fracture. The decrease in bone mass is significant even with calcium replacement. Urinary calcium excretion increases to menopause levels, with approximately 5% reduction in trabecular bone density following 6 months of GnRHa therapy.

Johansen et al.[13] reported a 2 to 5% decrease in bone mineral content of the radius after 6 months of GnRHa therapy. The use of a depot formulation of leuprolide acetate[14]

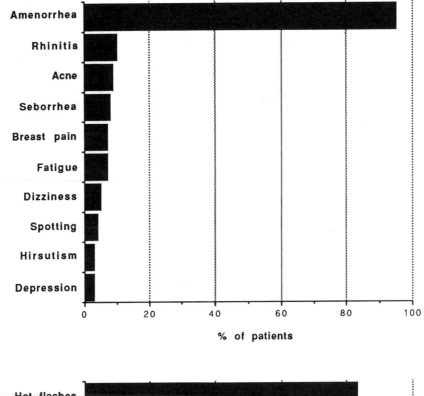

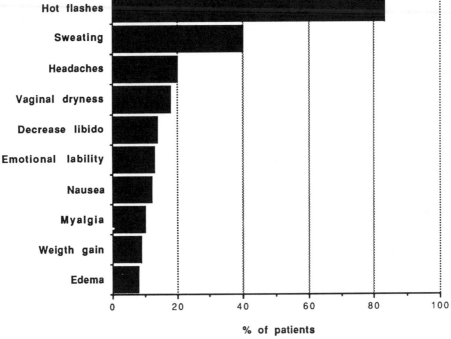

FIGURE 18.2. Common side effects of GnRHa therapy for endometriosis.

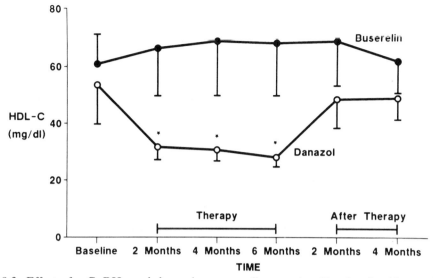

FIGURE 18.3. Effect of a GnRHa and danazol on serum lipoproteins. Reprinted, with permission, from ref. 33.

resulted in a decrease in spinal trabecular bone mineral density of 3.4%, but 90% of the patients had a partial to complete recovery of their bone mineral density when the GnRHa was discontinued. Surrey et al.,[15] associating a progestogen with the GnRHa Histrelin, observed a mean 5.6% decrease in bone density of the lumbar spine. This decrease was completely reversed 24 weeks after completion of therapy. In one study employing a depot formulation of leuprolide,[16] a reduced mineral content of trabecular, but not cortical, bone mass was observed after treatment. Although there are some reports of regaining of trabecular bone density 6 months after resumption of ovarian activity, this point remains controversial, and further studies are necessary to evaluate the effect of various GnRHa on bone mass when used in a long-term fashion.

Systemic Effects

No clinically relevant changes in blood, renal, and hepatic function were observed with GnRHa administration. Slight increases in arterial blood flow resistance can be observed, and in one study a significant decrease in white blood cell count and neutrophils was documented.[17]

Relief of Symptoms

The most prevalent indications for the use of GnRHa in the treatment of endometriosis are relief of pain and infertility. Almost all reports of GnRHa administration for endometriosis report a high percentage of improved symptoms and resolution of lesions following treatment. In general the extent of improvement is related to the stage of the disease. In one report,[18] GnRHa resulted in decrease of pelvic pain (73 to 19%), pelvic tenderness (63 to 18%), and dyspareunia (45 to 2%). Women who responded to therapy and were observed for 13.7 months demonstrated a decrease in premenstrual pain (26 to 17%), pelvic pain (15 to 6%), and dyspareunia (12 to 4%). Donnez et al.[19] reported a decrease of 72% and 82% in ovarian endometrial cysts size following treatment with buserelin spray and buserelin implant, respectively. Treated cases of mild endometriosis demonstrated reduced American Fertility Society (AFS) classification[20] (Fig. 18.4) scores from 18.2 to 16.8 and from 18.5 to 14 following therapy with buserelin spray and buserelin implant, respectively. Steingold[21] reported an overall decrease in mean AFS scores from 9 to 4 after subcutaneous administration of Histrelin. In one

THE AMERICAN FERTILITY SOCIETY
REVISED CLASSIFICATION OF ENDOMETRIOSIS

Patient's Name _____ Date _____

Stage I (Minimal) · 1-5
Stage II (Mild) · 6-15
Stage III (Moderate) · 16-40
Stage IV (Severe) · >40
Total _____

Laparoscopy _____ Laparotomy _____ Photography _____
Recommended Treatment _____

Prognosis _____

	ENDOMETRIOSIS	<1cm	1-3cm	>3cm
PERITONEUM	Superficial	1	2	4
	Deep	2	4	6
OVARY	R Superficial	1	2	4
	Deep	4	16	20
	L Superficial	1	2	4
	Deep	4	16	20

	POSTERIOR CULDESAC OBLITERATION	Partial	Complete
		4	40

	ADHESIONS	<1/3 Enclosure	1/3-2/3 Enclosure	>2/3 Enclosure
OVARY	R Filmy	1	2	4
	Dense	4	8	16
	L Filmy	1	2	4
	Dense	4	8	16
TUBE	R Filmy	1	2	4
	Dense	4*	8*	16
	L Filmy	1	2	4
	Dense	4*	8*	16

*If the fimbriated end of the fallopian tube is completely enclosed, change the point assignment to 16.

Additional Endometriosis: _____ Associated Pathology: _____

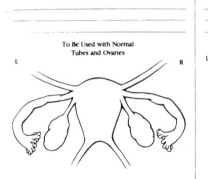

To Be Used with Normal
Tubes and Ovaries

To Be Used with Abnormal
Tubes and/or Ovaries

For additional supply write to: The American Fertility Society, 2131 Magnolia Avenue.
Suite 201, Birmingham, Alabama 35256

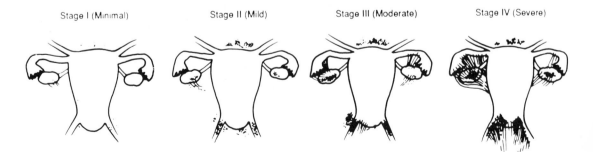

Stage I (Minimal) Stage II (Mild) Stage III (Moderate) Stage IV (Severe)

FIGURE 18.4. Revised AFS classification of endometriosis. Reprinted with permission. Copyright by the American Fertility Society.

study[22] scores for the subjective symptoms of pelvic pain, dyspareunia, and dysmenorrhea were combined, and by the end of therapy 94% of patients reported improvement, 58% had complete relief, and 6% related no changes in symptoms after therapy.

Recurrence of Symptoms

Several studies have shown by laparoscopy that virtually all patients have an improvement in the extent of the disease, but most do not show complete eradication of the lesions. Kennedy et al.[22] using Nafarelin (400 μg daily) found 36% of the patients studied were free of disease, 50% had a partial regression, and in 14% the disease was unchanged at a second-look laparoscopy performed approximately 175 days after therapy. A recurrence rate of 40 to 60% suggests that GnRHa induces a remission rather than a cure of endometriosis. The suppression of ovarian activity immediately following cessation of therapy can induce an underestimation of the number of implants at a second-look laparoscopy.[23,24] For this reason it is recommended to allow normalization of menses before evaluating the recurrence of implants and symptoms. When endometriomas are diagnosed, only a low percentage show significant improvement in their disease stage, despite the fact that the size

of endometriomas, determined ultrasonographically, may decrease more than 50%.[17]

Reversibility of Drug Effect

Resumption of menses occurs in 98% of cases within 3 months after the medication is discontinued. Schriock[25] observed a mean of 47 ± 8 days from discontinuation of treatment until the first ovulatory menses. Hormone levels tend to return to baseline levels approximately 4 weeks after cessation of therapy.

Conception Rates

The prompt reversibility of the drug effect may be beneficial to infertile patients who could conceive immediately after suppression of their endometriosis. Franssen[23] reported that one-third of the subgroup of patients with long-standing infertility conceived during the 6-months posttreatment follow-up. In this study, of seven pregnancies, four had AFS scores for endometriotic implants only ranging from 1 to 5 and 3 had scores ranging from 6 to 9, at the beginning of treatment. Tummon[26] observed a cumulative pregnancy rate of 70% after 12 months of therapy in patients with a mean AFS score of 24 ± 7. Buhler et al.[18] documented a conception rate of 60% within 12 months after the cessation of therapy.

TABLE 18.3 Conception rates in endometriosis patients treated with GnRHa.

Author	Drug (route)	No. patients	No. conceived	Pregnancy rates (%)	Follow-up period (mo.)
Buhler[18]	Buserelin (IN)	43	26	60	12
Lemay[30]	Buserelin (IN)	4	2	50	5
Fraser[24]	Buserelin (SC)	5	2	40	4
Henzl[29]	Nafarelin (IN)	56	17	30	12
Henzl[29]	Nafarelin (IN)	48	25	52	12
Tummon[26]	Leuprolide (IN)	10	7	70	12
Zorn[28]	Decapeptil (IM)	16	7	43	12
Franssen[23]	Buserelin (IN)	22	7	31.8	6

They observed that 31% conceived in the first month, 75% conceived within 6 months, and 25% conceived within 8 to 12 months after cessation of therapy. However, this study does not specify the stage of endometriosis at the beginning of treatment in patients achieving pregnancy. Dmowski[17] reported that conception occurred in 60% of patients treated with intranasal buserelin and in 25% of patients treated with subcutaneous buserelin. The AFS scores for endometriosis at the beginning of the treatment were 28 ± 7 and 27 ± 7 for the buserelin intranasal and subcutaneous groups, respectively. Fraser et al.[27] using buserelin implant injections observed a pregnancy rate of 40% within 4 months of returning to cyclical ovarian function. In this study only two patients achieved pregnancy. At the beginning of the treatment one was staged as minimal and the other as severe endometriosis, according to the AFS classification. Zorn et al.[28] using microcapsules of D-Trp^6-LH-RH obtained a 43% pregnancy rate after completing agonist therapy. In this study 22 patients were infertile, 16 of them due only to endometriosis. The stages of endometriosis were I, II, III, and IV in 2, 1, 10, and 9 infertile patients, respectively. Table 18.3 sumarizes conception rates in endometriosis patients treated with GnRHa.

Summary

GnRHa have proven to be effective therapy for patients with symptomatic endometriosis. Reports employing a variety of GnRHa preparations and routes of administration have shown a significant improvement in pelvic pain, dyspareunia, and dysmenorrhea after therapy. Between 30 and 60% of patients infertile due to endometriosis achieve pregnancy within 12 months following therapy, depending upon their stage of the disease. However, the hypoestrogenic status caused by long-term therapy has resulted in a high incidence of vasomotor symptoms, alterations of the lipoprotein profile, and loss of bone mineral density. Maintaining estrogen at a level that could induce regression of the lesions without producing these adverse effects would optimize GnRHa therapy. The maintenance of specific estrogen levels to alleviate the adverse effects caused by hypoestrogenism, while eliminating the extent and symptoms of endometriosis, is the ultimate goal of endometriosis therapy.

Progestational agents have been shown to ameliorate vasomotor symptoms and retard both urinary calcium excretion and radiological evidence of loss of bone mineral density in menopausal women. Surrey[15] showed that association of a GnRHa and norethindrone could produce a significant reduction in both painful symptoms and visible implants with minimization of vasomotor symptoms in comparision to GnRHa alone.

Mild systemic effects, lipoprotein metabolism changes, and hormonal alterations may occur with GnRHa therapy. However, the only potentially serious side effect of ovarian suppression by GnRHa consists of transient negative effects on bone metabolism. Despite these side effects, GnRHa therapy is relatively safe and effective when compared to the alternative modalities currently being used to treat endometriosis.

References

1. Seibel MM. Infertility A Comprehensive Text. Norwalk: Appleton & Lange, 1990:122.
2. Shaw RW. Rationale in use of LHRH analogues in endometriosis. Horm Res 1989; 32(Suppl 1):110.
3. Furr BJA. Pharmacology of the luteinizing hormone-releasing hormone (LHRH) analogue, Zoladex. Horm Res 1989;32(Suppl 1):86.
4. Dupont A, Dupont P, Belanger A, et al. Hormonal and biochemical changes during treatment of endometriosis with luteinizing hormone-releasing hormone (LHRH) agonist (D-Trp^6,des-Gly-NH$_2$^{10}) LHRH ethylamide. Fertil Steril 1990;54:227.
5. Dlugi AM, Rufo S, D'Amico JF, Seibel MM: A comparision of buserelin versus danazol on plasma lipids. Fertil Steril 1988;49:913.
6. Miller NE. Associations of high-density lipoprotein subclasses and apolipoproteins with ischemic heart disease and coronary atherosclerosis. Am Heart J 1987;113:589.
7. Crook D, Gardner R, Worthington M, et al. Zoladex versus Danazol in the treatment of pelvic endometriosis: Effects on plasma lipid risk factors. Horm Res 1989;32(Suppl 1):157.

8. Gordon T, Castelli WP, Hjortland MC, et al. High density lipoproteins as a protective factor against coronary heart disease. Am J Med 1977;62:707.
9. Devogelaer J-P, Nagant de Deuxchaisnes C, Donnez J, et al. LHRH analogues and bone loss. Lancet 1987;1:1498.
10. Matta WH, Shaw RW, Hesp R, et al. Reversible trabecular bone density loss following induced hypo-oestrogenism with the GnRH analogue buserelin in premenopausal women. Clin Endocrinol 1988;29:45.
11. Cann CE, Henzl M, Burry K, et al. Reversible bone loss is induced by GnRH agonists. Endocrine Society 68th Annual Meeting. Program and Abstracts, 1986, p. 24.
12. Stevenson JC, Lees B, Gardner R, et al. A comparison of the skeletal effects of Goserelin and Danazol in premenopausal women with endometriosis. Horm Res 1989;32(Suppl 1): 161.
13. Johansen JS, Riis BJ, Hassager C, et al. The effect of a gonadotropin-releasing hormone agonist (Nafarelin) on bone metabolism. J Clin Endocrinol Metab 1988;67:701.
14. Dlugi AM, Miller JD, Knittle J, et al. Lupron depot (Leuprolide acetate for depot suspension) in the treatment of endometriosis: A randomized, placebo-controlled, double-blind study. Fertil Steril 1990;53:419.
15. Surrey ES, Gambone JC, Lu JKH, et al. The effects of combining norethindrone with a gonadotropin-releasing hormone agonist in the treatment of symptomatic endometriosis. Fertil Steril 1990;53:620.
16. Barnes RB, Mercer LJ, Montner S. Characteristics of bone loss during treatment with a depot gonadotropin-releasing hormone agonist (GnRH-a). Abstract Presented at the 44th Annual Meeting of The American Fertility Society, Atlanta, GA, October 10–13, 1988; p. 23.
17. Dmowski WP, Radwanska E, Binor Z, et al. Ovarian suppression induced with Buserelin or danazol in the management of endometriosis: A randomized, comparative study. Fertil Steril 1989;51:395.
18. Buhler K, Schindler AE. Long-term follow-up of patients treated for endometriosis with LHRH analogue buserelin. In: Brosens I, Jacobs HS, Runnenbaun B, eds LHRH Analogues in Gynecology. Park Ridge, New Jersey: The Parthenon Publishing Group, 1990:159.
19. Donnez J, Nisolle M, Clerckx F, et al. The ovarian endometrial cyst: The combined (hormonal and surgical) therapy. In: Brosens I, Jacobs HS, Runnenbaun B, eds LHRH Analogues in Gynecology. Park Ridge, New Jersey: The Parthenon Publishing Group, 1990:165.
20. American Fertility Society: Revised American Fertility Society Classification of Endometriosis. Fertil Steril 1985;43:351.
21. Steingold KA, Cedars M, Lu JKH, et al. Treatment of endometriosis with a long-acting gonadotropin-releasing hormone agonist. Obstet Gynecol 1987;69:403.
22. Kennedy SH, Williams IA, Brodribb J, et al. A comparison of nafarelin acetate and danazol in the treatment of endometriosis. Fertil Steril 1990;53:998.
23. Franssen AMHW, Kauer FM, Chadha DR, et al. Endometriosis: Treatment with gonadotropin-releasing hormone agonist Buserelin. Fertil Steril 1989;51:401.
24. Evers JLH. The second look laparoscopy for evaluation of the result of medical treatment of endometriosis should not be performed during ovarian suppression. Fertil Steril 1987;47:502.
25. Schriock E, Monroe SE, Henzl M, et al. Treatment of endometriosis with a potent agonist of gonadotropin-releasing hormone (nafarelin). Fertil Steril 1985;44:583.
26. Tummon IS, Pepping ME, Binor Z, et al. A randomized prospective comparision of endocrine changes induced with intranasal Leuprolide or danazol for endometriosis. Fertil Steril 1989;51:390.
27. Fraser HM, Sandow J, Cowen GM, et al. Long term suppression of ovarian function by a luteinizing-hormone releasing hormone agonist implant in patients with endometriosis. Fertil Steril 1990;53:61.
28. Zorn JR, Mathieson J, Risquez F, et al. Treatment of endometriosis with a delayed release preparation of the agonist D-Trp[6]-luteinizing hormone-releasing hormone: Long term follow-up in a series of 50 patients. Fertil Steril 1990; 53:401.
29. Henzl MR, Corson SL, Moghissi K, et al. Administration of nasal nafarelin as compared with oral danazol for endometriosis. N Engl J Med 1988;318:485.
30. Lemay A, Maheux R, Faure N, et al. Reversible hypogonadism induced by a luteinizing hormone-releasing hormone (LH-RH) agonist (buserelin) as a new therapeutic approach for endometriosis. Fertil Steril 1984;41:863.

19
GnRH Agonists in the Treatment of Hyperandrogenism

Eli Y. Adashi

Although hirsutism is a common clinical entity, treatment options are limited and management continues to be challenging. This discussion will address the potential utility of gonadotropin-releasing hormone agonists (GnRHa) in hyperandrogenic disorders. This form of treatment is an exciting advance because the use of GnRHa for the treatment of hirsutism is not duration-limited, in that the inevitable hypoestrogenism can be managed by concurrent estrogen replacement therapy. This is in contrast to using GnRHa to treat estrogen-dependent conditions such as endometriosis or uterine fibroids.

Pathophysiology of Hirsutism

Hirsutism due to ovarian or adrenal hyperandrogenism is a result of a chain of events that culminates in the clinical manifestation of hirsutism and virilization. It begins with the excess production of androgens at glandular sources by the ovaries or the adrenals, followed by the delivery of the circulating androgen, in this case testosterone, to the periphery by the circulating sex hormone-binding globulin (Fig. 19.1). There it undergoes further processing, for example, by the enzyme 5-α-reductase, which converts it to a more biologically potent androgen such as dihydrotestosterone. Dihydrotestosterone in turn interacts with the androgen receptor at the level of the hair follicle, where it exerts its well-known effects, in this case the promotion of follicle hair growth. It goes without saying that the various strategies that have been designed to address hirsutism have attempted to interrupt this

chain of events at one point or another, preferably at several, in an effort to minimize the hyperandrogenic effect.

Historically, the first agent that was successfully applied in the treatment of hirsutism was the combination of oral contraceptives followed in short sequence by spironolactone, which became increasingly popular in the 1980s. I would like to suggest, although this is relatively recent and by no means widely acceptable, that we at least consider the use of GnRHa in ovarian hyperandrogenism, particularly the moderate and severe varieties.

Combination Oral Contraceptives

These agents for the most part have a salutary effect in hirsutism by diminishing ovarian androgen production (Fig. 19.2). They do so by at least partially suppressing the circulating levels of pituitary gonadotropins, thereby depriving the ovary of gonadotropic support, which is essential for the promotion of thecal interstitial cell androgen biosynthesis.

In addition, the estrogenic component, through direct effects on the liver, stimulates the circulating levels of sex hormone-binding globulin, increasing the ability of serum to bind or trap testosterone and decreasing the bioavailable form of testosterone for consumption by hair follicles. Thus, combination oral contraceptives as a rule have a double mechanism of action whereby they have a positive effect on the hyperandogenic state. In a relatively short application, a combination oral contraceptive preparation (no longer on the market) that contained mestranol $100\,\mu g$ produced progressive time-dependent

**ANDROGEN HORMONAL ACTION
OPERATIONAL CHARACTERISTICS**

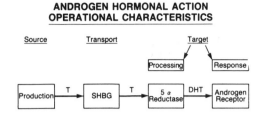

FIGURE 19.1. T, Testosterone; SHBG, sex hormone-binding globulin; DHT, dihydrotestosterone.

**COMBINATION ORAL CONTRACEPTIVES
SITES OF ACTION**

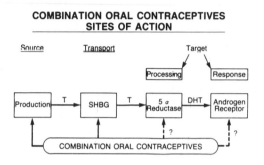

FIGURE 19.2. T, Testosterone; SHBG, sex hormone-binding globulin; DHT, dihydrotestosterone.

increments in the circulating levels of testosterone while concurrently producing progressive increments in the circulating levels of sex hormone-binding globulin. These two effects have, for the most part, been credited for the salutary results of the agents in the treatment of ovarian hyperandrogenism.

Combination oral contraceptives are not without their shortcomings, however. For the most part, they are not selective for the reproductive axis, and they have a variety of familiar systemic side effects. Sex steroid receptors exist in a variety of tissues; there is no reason to believe that they will limit themselves to the reproductive tract.

In addition, combination oral contraceptives are only moderately effective in modifying androgen economy or excessive hair growth, for two major reasons. First, these compounds usually suppress gonadotropin release only enough to suppress ovulation, and do not reduce gonadotropin levels as low as a GnRHa would. Second, combination oral contraceptives generally are prescribed to be taken cyclically, which means that in 1 of every

4 weeks treatment is inevitably suboptimal. Some of the gains that may have been made could potentially be lost.

Spironolactone

Spironolactone now constitutes an option and an additional modality that has been used fairly widely over the last several years (Fig. 19.3). It is an aldosterone antagonist that is used primarily as a potassium-sparing diuretic in the management of hypertension. Spironolactone interacts at the periphery, both by inhibiting the enzyme 5-μ-reductase and by competing with the androgen receptor for binding with circulating androgens. Thus, spironolactone acts in a manner distinct from that of combination oral contraceptives and provides a different way of addressing treatment in hyperandrogenism. It stands to reason, although information is limited, that if one were to coadminister combination oral contraceptives and spironolactone, one could reach a very high degree of potency, because all of the different steps involved in androgen hormonal action would be perturbed.

The efficacy of spironolactone is now well established. It has been clearly shown that taking it orally for about 12 months results in time-dependent decrements in circulating levels of total as well as free testosterone, with no effect on the circulating levels of sex hormone-binding globulin. Clinically the decrease in testosterone is manifested in a decrease in hair shaft diameter, an acceptable although imperfect measure of improvement in

**SPIRONOLACTONE
SITES OF ACTION**

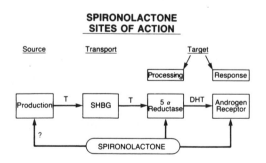

FIGURE 19.3. T, Testosterone; SHBG, sex hormone-binding globulin; DHT, dihydrotestosterone.

hirsutism. Placebo-treated women notice no difference in hair shaft diameter.

Like combination oral contraceptives, spironolactone is not without its shortcomings. For the most part, it is not selective for the reproductive axis because it was designed only to perturb electrolyte economy. In addition, like combination oral contraceptives, it is only moderately effective in modifying androgen economy or excessive hair growth, and is mostly suited for a mild, or at most moderate, degree of hyperandrogenism. Neither one is selective for the reproductive axis, and neither is as potent as we would like it to be.

GnRH Agonists

It was hoped that GnRHa might have application in the treatment of ovarian hyperandrogenism, particularly the moderate and severe varieties (Fig. 19.4). These agents are highly specific for the reproductive axis, having no actions outside the reproductive tract, and they are known to be extremely potent in terms of their ability to deactivate the reproductive tract for the duration of treatment (Fig. 19.5).

Of course some practical issues arise with long-term application of GnRHa. The ability of these agents to put the reproductive axis to rest at will has been used to advantage in a variety of circumstances, for example, endometriosis and uterine fibroids. Suppression of circulating levels of estrogens would have a salutary effect on both of these conditions, which depend on estrogens for their very genesis and maintenance. These are estrogen-

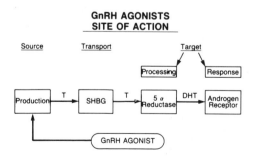

FIGURE 19.4. T, Testosterone; SHBG, sex hormone-binding globulin; DHT, dihydrotestosterone.

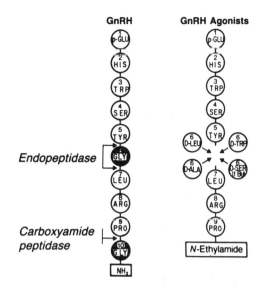

FIGURE 19.5. GnRHa: structural formulas.

dependent conditions that would benefit from a short course of treatment with GnRHa because a long-term treatment inevitably leads to hypoestrogenism, which has a variety of problems associated with it, the most important being the development of osteoporosis. Thus, at least in obstetrics and gynecology, we are unable to use these drugs for extended periods of time, the limit generally being around 6 months.

Ovarian hyperandrogenism is rather distinct in that it is not an estrogen-dependent condition but an estrogen-independent one. There is no reason why these women could not concurrently have replacement with estrogens and progestins to offset the otherwise inevitable hypoestrogenic side effects. Thus, for hirsutism, we can apply GnRHa in an open-ended fashion, over the long term, together with concurrent estrogen and progesterone replacement therapy, maintaining both endogenous estrogens and androgens in a very low state but correcting the estrogen deficiency. This is perhaps one of the few disorders in which GnRHa find a long-term application in obstetrics and gynecology. We propose that GnRHa are at least a possibility to be considered in moderate to severe ovarian hyperandrogenism.

Previous Work

Let me share with you our own experience in this connection, and touch on a variety of clinical conditions in which this paradigm ˙ay be applicable. First, however, it is important ι cite the work that made it possible or that to some degree showed us the way. I am referring specifically to the work of Chang and associates, which dates back to 1983.

A group of women with polycystic ovary disease (PCO) and normally cycling controls were treated for 4 weeks parenterally with a GnRHa on a daily basis with regular monitoring of circulating levels of androstenedione and testosterone (Fig. 19.6). The circulating levels of both hormones in the women with PCO displayed time-dependent decrements around four weeks. Substantial decrements in the release of immunoreactive gonadotropins were also documented. These findings suggested that residual circulating androgens in all

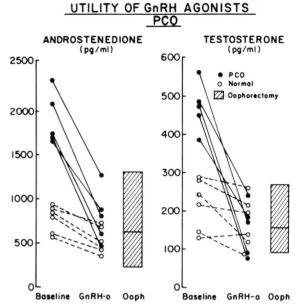

FIGURE 19.7. Polycystic ovarian syndrome: effect of a GnRHa on the circulating levels of androgens. (From ref. 3).

likelihood derived exclusively from the adrenal glands, and the ovarian contribution of androgens was all but eliminated, thereby selectively turning off ovarian androgen production (Fig. 19.7). This suggested the possibility that one could use these agents long-term in women with ovarian hyperandrogenism, provided one addressed the hypoestrogenic complications that would inevitably arise.

Clinical Experience

The first example is that of an individual who suffered from severe hyperinsulinemic hyperandrogenism. There is a close association between these two entities, in that hyperinsulinemia often leads to and is closely associated with excessive androgen production. The woman was 22 years old. In addition to extreme hirsutism, she had severe insulin resistance that required the administration of 2,000U crystalline zinc insulin per day. In itself this was able to maintain her only in a fragile state of euglycemia, punctuated by admissions to the hospital for ketoacidosis. By the time we saw

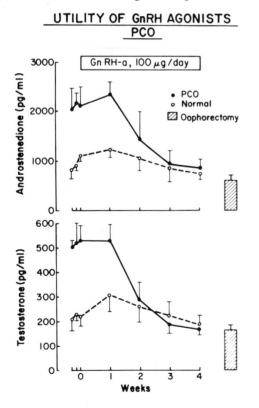

FIGURE 19.6. Polycystic ovarian syndrome: effect of a GnRHa on the circulating levels of androgens. (From ref. 3).

her she had already had two laparotomies. During the first, one ovary was removed. During the second, the residual ovary was wedged. In both cases the concern was that this patient might harbor an ovarian androgen-producing tumor. This was a legitimate concern, given the degree of virilization that she experienced.

As we now know in retrospect, given experience with a large number of such patients, few if any of these women actually have an ovarian androgen-producing tumor, despite the intensity of their hyperandrogenic state. Rather, they have a functional disorder, namely, hyperplasia and hypertrophy of the ovarian androgen-producing cells, presumably driven by a combination of insulin and gonadotropins.

In addition to hirsutism, the patient had a hyperpigmented hyperkeratotic lesion that is commonly referred to as acanthosis nigricans. This feature is commonly but not exclusively seen in patients with hyperinsulinemia, as it also occasionally occurs in certain oncologic conditions.

This patient suffered from a systemic deficiency or diminution in the number of insulin receptors that affected her entire body. This is a congenital condition that recently was traced at the molecular level. The insulin receptor molecule suffers from a single amino acid mutation that is responsible for the systemic constellation of symptoms of which hirsutism is probably the least distressing.

When we first saw the woman, her circulating levels of testosterone were about 800 ng/dl. This is about 10 to 12 times the normal mean for normally cycling women and clearly well into the normal male range. Combination oral contraceptives or spironolactone were not likely to be helpful for this patient, as both had been tried and to no avail. At about this time the GnRHa were being introduced. Lupron was the first that was commercially available. We decided to try it, knowing that it had been used successfully in suppressing testicular androgen production in patients with metastatic prostatic cancer. In the initial experiment with this patient, we treated her with Lupron 1 mg/day subcutaneously for 6

weeks, during which we observed progressive decrements in the circulating levels of total testosterone. After 6 weeks, however, we were not able to return the circulating levels of testosterone to normal. This puzzled us because we knew that, at least in normally cycling women, a 6-week course of a GnRHa at that dosage is more than sufficient to deactivate the ovaries and to bring the androgen and estrogen levels into the postmenopausal range.

When treatment was discontinued, circulating levels of testosterone rebounded (Fig. 19.8). That is something one would now expect, but at the time it was a new phenomenon, reaffirming once again that if we were to provide continuous sustained relief to this patient, we would have to administer the agonist on a continuing basis.

We wondered at one point whether the residual circulating levels of testosterone reflected the insulin levels that were perhaps driving the ovaries or our inability to suppress the circulating levels of gonadotropins. That question was easily testable by measuring both the immunoreactive levels and the biologically active levels of luteinizing hormone (LH) before and 6 weeks into therapy. The biologically active concentrations of LH were virtually nondetectable while circulating levels of testosterone were still readily measurable. We went through a series of additional trials trying to determine why we were unable to suppress testosterone in this patient, only

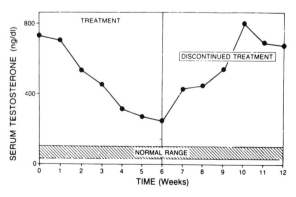

FIGURE 19.8. Utility of Lupron in the management of severe hyperinsulinemic hyperandrogenism.

to realize later that these steroidogenically superactive ovaries simply needed a longer period of suppression before they could actually cease their activity. All that was necessary was a longer course of therapy, which we ultimately carried out. In retrospect, it probably should have been self-evident. In fact, we could drive the circulating levels of testosterone of this patient well into the subnormal range and close to the castrate range during the course of therapy.

At this point we were prepared to carry out a longer-term study to demonstrate that the now suppressed circulating levels of testosterone could translate into clinical improvement for this patient. Unfortunately, the woman was diagnosed with an early form of breast cancer that required bilateral mastectomy and chemotherapy. She is still taking the agonist for reasons that are obvious but have nothing to do with hyperandrogenism. This patient is now 4 or 5 years beyond her mastectomy and is doing well; we have every reason to believe that she is or will be cured. We did do long-term studies with a series of patients not quite as severely affected as this one.

Hyperthecosis

I would like to briefly discuss hyperthecosis, another condition for which all we had to offer until recently was a surgical approach. Hyperthecosis may be treated by wedge resection if the woman is relatively young and anticipating a family. Bilateral oophorectomy is offered in a woman in her late thirties or early forties whose family is completed. We had little to offer an individual who was still young, perhaps not married, and who wished to have symptomatic therapy for hirsutism prior to embarking on a more definite form of therapy at a later date. In this respect GnRHa are ideal.

One woman was treated with a parenterally administered GnRHa for 6 months. She experienced a prompt and sustained suppression of circulating levels of both androstenedione and testosterone. By the time suppression was virtually complete, the levels approximated

those in oophorectomized control women, suggesting once again that the ovarian contribution was all but eliminated and that the only residual androgens presumably were derived from the adrenals. This woman chose to conceive. Pergonal was superimposed on Lupron, resulting in successful conception. If she had stopped taking the agonist and been given a conventional form of ovulation induction such as clomiphene citrate, she may or may not have responded, since many of these patients are known to be resistant to such therapy.

Even the use of GnRHa does not provide a total androgenic blockade. These patients still have ambient levels of testosterone and androstenedione that probably will continue to support hair growth, albeit at a lower rate. Thus, if one is ever to achieve complete suppression of hair growth and a marked, dramatic improvement of hirsutism, one will have to consider a total androgenic blockade. This would include either elimination of the residual adrenal contribution or blockade of the action of those residual androgens by an antiandrogen. This is commonly done in patients with prostatic cancer, whose life is at stake, and where no chances are taken of leaving any androgens to exert their effect peripherally.

Over the last several years we have collected several patients with moderate to severe hyperandrogenism. Some had hyperthecosis, some PCO, some idiopathic hirsutism. They were rather heterogeneous in degree or severity of hyperandrogenism, but all of them suffered from clinical hyperandrogenism with testosterone levels in excess of 150 ng/dl. None of the patients had adrenal pathology as determined by adrenocorticotropic hormone (ACTH) stimulation test. These patients underwent a 6-week course of treatment with a GnRHa, discontinued treatment, and recovered thereafter.

The mean circulating level of testosterone at the outset was about 300 ng/dl, approximately 6 times the normal mean, albeit a far cry from the patient in whom the levels were clearly in the normal male range. Unfortunately, we were unable to return the circulating levels of testosterone to normal, and the recovery phase promptly reaffirmed the need for continuous application of the drug.

We continued to follow this group of patients for at least 6 months, and several of them for many years, allowing us to observe progressive improvement in circulating levels of androgens that can be accomplished with longer therapy. We have noted, for example, that the circulating levels of testosterone decreased further when treatment was extended for as long as 24 weeks or 6 months. A further decrease in the circulating levels of androstenedione was also apparent, although it was not statistically significant. No effect was observed on the circulating levels of dehydroepiandrosterone (DHEAS) and adrenal androgen, attesting once again to the selectivity of GnRHa for the reproductive axis that spares the adrenal glands.

Clinically these patients were scored at the beginning and end of therapy using two systems that are acceptable but admittedly imperfect. One of these is the Ferriman Galwey score, an arbitrary system that assigns four points to nine different body areas, depending on the severity of the condition. The poorest score is 36 points. These patients began with a pretreatment score of 24 and ended up 6 months later with a score of 12.

Another scoring system is to measure the hair shaft diameter under the microscope with a micrometer. Thus, it is possible objectively to quantify improvement of hirsutism. These patients experienced marked reduction in overall hair shaft diameter. Our findings are in keeping with those reported when an intranasally administered analog, nafarelin, was used for a similar period of time. The hirsutism score decreased and hair shaft diameter clearly diminished as well. Thus the long-term application of GnRHa does provide clinical improvement, although it does not provide complete androgenic blockade. Presumably turning off the ovaries and reducing the circulating levels of androgens over the long term will have comparable clinical consequences evident either in the hirsutism score or in hair shaft diameter, as well as in the patient's subjective assessment of hirsutism.

Hormone Replacement Therapy

Prolonged administration of GnRHa requires concurrent estrogen and progesterone replacement therapy. However, several issues have to be addressed before replacement therapy can be provided effectively and safely. First, one would want to see what effect the replacement regimen would have on the efficacy of the agonist in relation to androgen economy. Second, one would have to determine what estrogen and progestins do to protect women from bone density loss that would otherwise occur when they took the agonist alone. Finally, one would have to know what the addition of estrogen replacement therapy might do to the cardiovascular risk of these women, in whom it is already somewhat increased due to hyperandrogenism. Some of these questions are clearly unanswered.

We do not have any data on the ability of estrogen replacement to protect women from loss of bone mass. Hyperandrogenic women have somewhat increased regular bone density to begin with, however, suggesting that at least initially they would be protected from the adverse effects of the agonist.

Although there is no definite evidence to support it, we think these women may be at increased cardiovascular risk because their hormonal profile is closer to that of men. Presumably this is a result of the high levels of testosterone that lead to a less favorable lipoprotein pattern. If that is the case, suppressing androgens in hyperandrogenic women may have benefits that go far beyond the cosmetic goals of therapy. In fact, if we are in a position to return the circulating hormonal pattern of such women to normal over time, we could significantly improve their cardiovascular risk, something that we did not originally envision when we began this line of investigation.

This benefit from normal circulating levels of androgens could be augmented by adding estrogens, which would feminize the lipoprotein profile and other risk variables, thereby further reducing the cardiovascular risks to which these women may be subject. Thus, I suggest that giving GnRHa with estrogen replacement therapy to hyperandrogenic women over the long term may have benefits that have nothing to do with reducing hirsutism and may be most important with respect to decreasing cardiovascular risk.

The application of GnRHa in hirsutism has received relatively little attention. In our opinion, this is the preferred therapy for moderate or severe forms of the disorder. I hope that some day these women might benefit from total androgenic blockade. We believe this is indispensable if we are ever to achieve what amounts to a cure of hirsutism, as opposed to the mediocre, rather frustrating, and disappointing results we now tend to achieve.

Questions and Answers

P. What protocol are you using for a replacement therapy?

E.A. At this time we give 0.625 mg Premarin on days 1 through 25, and Provera 10 mg on days 13 to 25. There is no particular reason why we settled on that regimen, but it happens to be the one most commonly employed in the United States. Any other protocol would probably be applicable.

P. Would you use a patch or would you be worried about a first-pass effect?

E.A. In principle, I have no problem with the patch. Questions still exist as to whether it provides women with a comparable protective effect with respect to bone density and cardiovascular risks. The patch is obviously a recent development, but I have every reason to believe, and I hope we are all right in assuming, that it will prove effective in both categories.

P. Did you measure estradiol (E_2) levels in these patients?

E.A. We did. Initially they are stimulated, as you might expect, but once we get into the suppressing phase they are in the menopausal range, less than 20 pg/ml. In that respect, these women are no different from normally cycling women.

P. Would you consider giving them intermittent Provera to find out if they withdraw, to be a biologic index of estrogenicety? They have estrone, they have estriol, both non-E_2-type estrogens. I would assume they are obese. It

seems to me you would not have to give many of them estrogen replacement therapy, even if their testosterone levels were decreased. Some of our patients had endometriosis, and because they had so much pain we gave them a GnRHa. One woman took it for 3 months. Then we tried to induce ovulation, and at laparoscopy she had empty follicles.

E.A. We have not made the distinction with respect to body weight, but I agree that not every individual with ovarian failure necessarily is estrogen insufficient. Yes, there are occasions when body weight compensates enough to make estrogen replacement redundant. We have not had morbidly or extremely obese patients that I can think of. We have not made a conscious effort to separate them by weight.

P. Have you used depot leuprolide?

E.A. Once depot leuprolide became available, many patients took it. Some of them have been taking it for years. They refuse to stop treatment once they start, for a variety of reasons, not necessarily hirsutism. There are facets to the response to the agent that we do not comprehend, which have to do with the sense of well-being that these patients report. These are women who may have had a touch of depression, or may have experienced something along the lines of a premenstrual stress syndrome, and who are extremely happy to continue therapy. I do not know what it is that prompts them to continue, but many of them are, in fact, taking the depot form at this point.

P. How much GnRHa do you administer? We had severe side effects with the 7.5 mg dose and when I called the company they said that was not the recommended dose; they only recommend 3.75 mg.

E.A. A daily subcutaneous dose of 20 μg/kg for hirsutism is recommended by Ritmaster from Halifax, which translates in an average 50-kg woman to 1 mg a day, which means the full dose. There are no comparable studies for the depot form, but extrapolating from the subcutaneous GnRHa dose we use 7.5 mg for this indication. That does not necessarily mean that that would be the dose for endometriosis, but for hirsutism we presume that we want to use the full dose.

Bibliography

1. Andreyko JL, Marshall LA, Dumesic DA, Jaffe RB. Therapeutic uses of gonadotropin-releasing hormone analogs. Obstet Gynecol Surv 1987; 42:1.
2. Friedman AJ, Barbieri RL. Leuprolide acetate: Applications in gynecology. Curr Probl Obstet Gynecol Fertil 1988;11:205.
3. Chang RJ, Laufer LR, Meldrum DR, DeFazio J, Lu JKH, Wylie WV, Rivier JE, Judd HL. Steroid secretion in polycystic ovarian disease after ovarian suppression by a long-acting gonadotropin-releasing hormone agonist. J Clin Endocrinol Metab 1983;56:897.
4. Calogero AE, Macchi M, Montanini V, Mongioi A, Mauferi G, Vicari E, Coniglione F, Sipione C, D'Agata R. Dynamics of plasma gonadotropin and sex steroid release in polycystic ovarian disease after pituitary-ovarian inhibition with an analog of gonadotropin-releasing hormone. J Clin Endocrinol Metab 1987;64:980.
5. Andreyko JL, Monroe SE, Jaffee RB. Treatment of hirsutism with a gonadotropin-releasing hormone agonist (nafarelin). J Clin Endocrinol Metab 1986;63:854.
6. Faure N, Lemay A. Ovarian suppression in polycystic ovarian disease during six-month administration of luteinizing-hormone releasing hormone (LH-RH) agonist. Clin Endocrinol (Oxf) 1987;27:703.
7. Faure N, Lemay A. Acute pituitary-ovarian response during chronic luteinizing hormone-releasing hormone agonist administration in polycystic ovarian syndrome. Clin Endocrinol (Oxf) 1988;29:403.
8. Steingold K, DeZiegler D, Cedars M, Meldrum DR, Lu JKH, Judd HL, Chang RJ. Clinical and hormonal effects of chronic gonadotropin-releasing hormone agonist treatment in polycystic ovarian disease. J Clin Endocrinol Metab 1987;65:773.
9. Couzinet B, Le Strat N, Brailly S, Schaison G. Comparative effects of cyproterone acetate or a long-acting gonadotropin-releasing hormone agonist in polycystic ovarian disease. J Clin Endocrinol Metab 1986;63:103.
10. Schaison G, Couzinet B. Comparative effects of cyproterone acetate or a long-acting LHRH agonist in polycystic ovarian disease. Horm Res 1987;28:169.
11. Rittmaster RS. Differential suppression of testosterone and estradiol in hirsute women with the superactive gonadotropin-releasing hormone agonist leuprolide. J Clin Endocrinol Metab 1988;67:651.
12. Ceders MI, Steingold KA, de Ziegler D, Lapolt PS, Chang RJ, Judd HL. Long-term administration of gonadotropin-releasing hormone agonist and dexamethasone: assessment of the adrenal role in ovarian dysfunction. Fertil Steril 1992;57:495.
13. Kennedy L, Traub AI, Atkinson AB, Sheridan B. Short-term administration of gonadotropin-releasing hormone analog to a patient with a testosterone-secreting ovarian tumor. J Clin Endocrinol Metab 1987;64:1320.
14. Parr JH, Abraham RR, Seed M, Short F, Wynn V. The treatment of a hyperandrogenic and virilizing state in an elderly female with a synthetic LHRH agonist. J Endocrinol Invest 1988;11:433.
15. Adashi EY. Potential utility of gonadotropin-releasing hormone agonists in the management of ovarian hyperandrogenism. Fertil Steril 1990;53:765.

20
The Neuroendocrine Basis of Infertility

Andrew Herzog

This chapter describes neuroanatomic substrates and physiologic mechanisms by which the brain, in particular mental processes, may contribute to infertility and its treatment. I propose a three-part hypothesis: (1) mental processes promote the development of some reproductive endocrine disorders that cause infertility; (2) reproductive endocrine disorders alter mental processes; and (3) an understanding of the reciprocal relationships between mental processes and hormonal secretions may be important in the diagnosis and treatment of infertility. This hypothesis is based on the pivotal role that the limbic system of the brain plays in both mental processes and ovarian regulation. By mental processes, that is, the workings of the mind, we generally assume that we are dealing with brain function.

Mental processes are generally attributable to the brain (Fig. 20.1), in particular to the cerebrum, and specifically to the cerebral cortex. The cerebral cortex appears to be a rather homogeneous covering of the brain that, in order to be accommodated by the relatively small skull, has to be folded in rather irregular patterns. On closer examination of the cortex, however, we find that it is not entirely homogeneous, and as one moves from one part of the brain to another, the organization of different cell types in each region of the brain is different. In fact, approximately 50 different regions have been identified (Fig. 20.2), each one having a specific type of cellular architecture, chemistry, pharmacology, physiology, connectivity, and function.[2]

One can look over the convexity of the cerebral hemisphere and see most of the cytoarchitectonic regions. One can then go to the medial surface and again follow the different cytoarchitectonic regions until one reaches the edge of the cortex. The edge of the cortex is where the limbic system is found. "Edge" in Latin is *limbus*, and the limbus of the cerebral cortex is made up of the cingulate gyrus, the hippocampal gyrus, the amygdala, and the septum.

The limbic system, that is, the various architectonic regions of the limbic system, has to do with behavior related to the primitive drives of feeding, drinking, sex, sleep, and aggression. In 1937 it was suggested that the limbic system is the mechanism of emotion.[3] This suggestion was based on a great deal of animal experimental evidence showing that when these regions in the brain were stimulated, the animal produced a rage reaction, fought, or appeared afraid. These areas of the brain have been stimulated to produce reward and also punishment. Ablation of them produces a loss of emotional response in animals.

How does this whole system work? To provide a simplistic view of how the brain perceives, I suggest the example of how we see a chair. The retina of the eye sees a chair in terms of dots of light, dots of darkness, and contrasts. This information is sent by way of the thalamus to the occipital cortex where the dots are put together into lines. The information is then transmitted to the inferior part of the temporal lobe where the lines are put together into the image of a chair. Indeed, specific neurons in the inferior temporal gyrus are visual object-specific. They will fire if you see a chair regardless of whether it is an ordinary brown chair on the floor or a 10-foot pink chair with purple stripes upside down on a

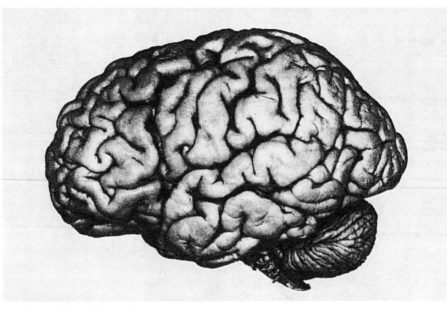

FIGURE 20.1. The brain: a view of the convexity of the left cerebral hemisphere.

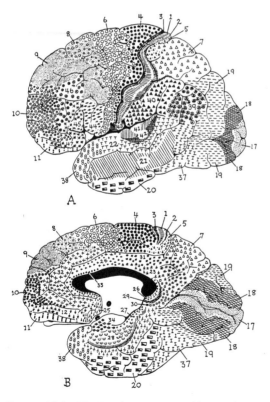

FIGURE 20.2. The Brodmann cytoarchitectonic map of the cerebral cortex.

billboard. We still recognize it as a chair, and the same neuron in the inferior temporal gyrus will discharge.

The brain does more than identify lines and make them into chairs. It wants to relate what it perceives with past experiences of "chair" and also with emotional and motivational context. This is the job of the limbic system. Take, for instance, a bentwood rocking chair. I might have seen a similar chair at 10 years of age when I celebrated my birthday, and seeing it now makes me feel happy. Then I may remember that last week I saw a lady light a match, burn her dress, and suffer third-degree burns while she sat in the same type of chair. In this case, the chair could make me feel afraid. The recollection of previous experiences in relation to our present perception and the attachment of our present perception to motivational and emotional context is the job of the limbic system.

The limbic system plays an important role in emotion. If the anterior temporal lobes, especially the amygdala, are bilaterally removed from a monkey, the animal develops behavioral changes known as the Kluver-Bucy syndrome.[4] One feature is psychic blindness.

FIGURE 20.3. The brain: a cross section at the level of the anterior temporal lobes and hypothalamus.

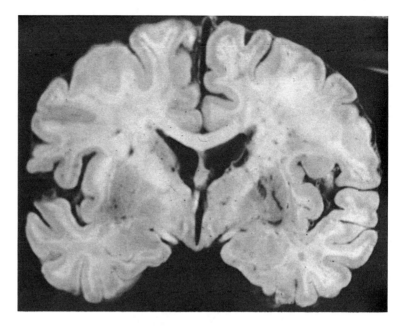

If you put the animal in a room with objects it likes and objects it fears, the animal will navigate without problems; however, it will show no fear and no pleasure in relation to these objects.

In contrast, we can have more than normal discharges, that is, more than normal function in limbic structures such as the amygdala. The most notable example is temporal lobe epilepsy. People with this disorder are filled with emotion. They have vivid memories and show familiarity with everything. Everything that they see carries an inordinate amount of emotional and motivational significance.[5] Everything is important, thereby making these individuals tangential and circumferential in their communication because there is no one focus of their attention. This suggests that the limbic system plays a major role in the representation of emotion in the brain.

The limbic system also plays a major role in regulating ovarian function. This regulation is carried out using two mechanisms: neuroendocrine and neural.

Figure 20.3, a cross section of the brain, shows the cerebral cortex ending dorsomedially in the cingulate gyrus on top and ventromedially in the amygdala. It also shows the third ventricle, the hypothalamus, and the optic tract. The ovary secretes estradiol and progesterone under the control of pituitary luteinizing hormone (LH) (Fig. 20.4). Pituitary LH is in turn regulated by gonadotropin-releasing hormone (GnRH), which is secreted by hypothalamic neurosecretory cells (hns) into the pituitary portal circulation (pps), by which it reaches the pituitary gland.

The hypothalamus, however, despite the illustrations in most endocrinology textbooks, does not function in a vacuum. It has extensive reciprocal connections with other parts of the brain, most notably the limbic system. The amygdala can be divided into morphologically distinct divisions, corticomedial and basolateral, with each one exerting the opposite influence on individual hypothalamic cells, thereby being able to modulate neurosecretion by hypothalamic cells.[6] The amygdala does not only modulate endocrine secretion, as has been evidenced by a number of stimulation and ablation studies showing concordant changes of gonadotropin secretion. It also has the densest array of gonadal steroid receptors of any part of the brain except the hypothalamus.[7]

Estrogen acts on nerve cells in a strongly stimulating fashion.[8] It produces increased discharges in cells with estrogen receptors, and

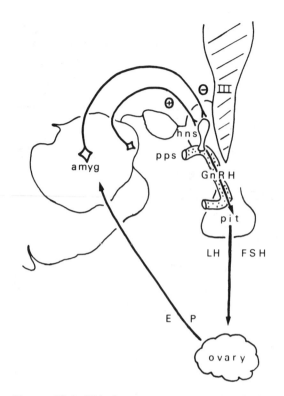

FIGURE 20.4. This figure represents a cross section of the anterior lobe and diencephalon. It depicts direct projections from the two anatomically distinct functional divisions of the amygdala (amyg) to the same ventromedial hypothalamic neurons. The different influences of these projections on hypothalamic neurosecretory cells (hns) modulate pulsatile gonadotropin-releasing hormone (GnRH) secretion. Releasing hormones enter the pituitary portal system (pps) and regulate the pattern of luteinizing hormone (LH) and follicle-stimulating hormone (FSH) secretion by the pituitary (pit). These gonadotropins induce ovulation and stimulate estradiol (E) and progesterone (P) production. Gonadal steroids, in turn, bind to specific amygdaloid hormone receptors and influence neural activity, including epileptiform discharges.

it can even produce seizures. Progesterone, in contrast, lowers nerve cell discharge rates. It can produce sedation or sleep, and is an antiseizure hormone.[9] Thus the limbic structures not only modulate hormonal secretion but are also sensitive to hormonal feedback.

The amygdala can also regulate the ovary and be influenced by the ovary through the autonomic nervous system, consisting of vagal

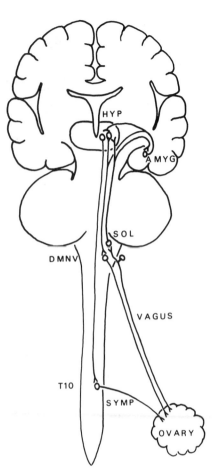

FIGURE 20.5. This illustration depicts the neural pathways that may mediate limbic influences on gonadal structure and function. The amygdala (AMYG) has direct fiber projections to the dorsomedial and lateral regions of the hypothalamus (HYP). These regions are connected directly to the preganglionic sympathetic neurons in the intermediolateral cell column of the thoracolumbar spinal cord, from which originate sympathetic nerve fibers to the gonads. The amygdala also has direct and indirect projections to the dorsal motor nucleus of the vagus (DMNV), from which originate vagal fibers to the gonads. Afferent vagal fibers from the gonads project to the solitary nucleus in the medulla (SOL). The solitary nucleus has direct projections to the amygdala as well as to the hypothalamus.

parasympathetic and thoracic sympathetic fibers to the ovary (Fig. 20.5). The amygdaloid cells are directly connected with the dorsal motor nucleus of the vagus, which innervates the ovary. In other words, there is only one neuron between the amygdala and the ovary. Similarly, any changes that occur in the ovary are only one neuron away from the neurons of the solitary nucleus, which project directly to the amygdala. A similar story exists for the sympathetic pathway, where there are two interposed levels of neurons. Destruction of either the vagal or the sympathetic innervation of the ovary leads to changes in ovarian structure and lack of compensatory hypertrophy after ovarian injury.[10] It leads to changes in the responsivity of LH and follicle-stimulating hormone (FSH) and to altered menstrual cycles.[10] Furthermore, one can stimulate different portions of the limbic system in the amygdala and the hippocampus and produce predictable up- or down-regulation of ovarian secretion of estradiol and progesterone.[11] This occurs in animals whose pituitary gland has been removed, thereby making the neuroendocrine mechanism of regulation impossible and suggesting that a direct neural innervation may be acting.

Thus the limbic system may represent a mechanism of behavior, specifically emotion. It regulates the autonomic nervous system, which regulates internal organs such as the ovaries. It also modulates hormonal secretion. Each of these actions in turn can feed back to change the limbic system. For example, emotion may change autonomic activity and endocrine secretion as well. We know this is true because when we are angry, breathing becomes deeper and faster, the heart starts to pound and beat faster, epinephrine and norepinephrine are secreted, and glucagon is secreted to produce more glucose in the bloodstream. In women prone to panic attacks, a close relationship exists between the level of estradiol in the serum and a tendency to produce the panic attacks. When estradiol is elevated relative to progesterone, the result is panic attacks with concomitant palpitations and heart racing. The limbic system coordinates the response of the body to emotional change through autonomic and hormonal regulation of internal organs.

The limbic system is also the site of origin of most epilepsy.[12] Specifically, medial temporal structures such as the amygdala are the site of

origin, or at least involvement, for epilepsy in most adults. The work we have done on temporal lobe epilepsy can demonstrate how altered limbic activity can affect ovarian function.

First, reproductive dysfunction is overrepresented in men and women with temporal lobe epilepsy (TLE). Fourteen percent to 20% of women with TLE have amenorrhea.[13–15] More than 50% have some menstrual dysfunction such as too long or too short a cycle, intermenstrual bleeding, or heavy bleeding. Their fertility rate is reduced by one-third.[16] Among men with epilepsy, 49 to 71% have been reported to have diminished potency or hyposexuality.[17] Sperm count, morphology, and motility are abnormal in the great majority.[18]

We studied a group of 50 women with clinically and electrically documented TLE and found that reproductive endocrine disorders, including those that contribute to infertility, were overrepresented.[13] The overall occurrence of reproductive endocrine disorders was 38%, compared to our estimate of 8% in the general population. Polycystic ovarian syndrome was perhaps the most notable, occurring in one out of five women in this group, compared to the 4 or 5% in the general population. Hypogonadotropic hypogonadism was also strongly overrepresented, as were premature menopause and hyperprolactinemia. These disorders could not be attributed to the use of antiseizure medication, and the conclusion was that the only specific factor that distinguished them from healthy control women was TLE. Another fact that suggests an important role for the brain in the development of reproductive endocrine disorders is the finding that the two most prevalent reproductive endocrine disorders were associated with the opposite sides of the brain involved with epilepsy. Specifically, polycystic ovarian syndrome was associated with TLE emanating from the left hemisphere in 10 women and from the right in only 1. Hypogonadotropic hypogonadism was overwhelmingly associated with right-sided temporal lobe discharges. In a larger review of our cases from the last few years,[19] we found the following among 30 women with

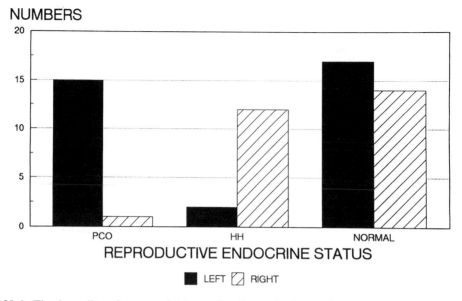

FIGURE 20.6. The laterality of temporal lobe epileptiform discharges in women with polycystic ovary syndrome (PCO), hypogonadotropic hypogonadism (HH), and normal reproductive endocrine function.

reproductive dysfunction and 30 women who had normal reproductive function (Fig. 20.6). Sixteen women who had temporal lobe spikes or sharp waves had polycystic ovary syndrome; 15 of the 16 had a left-sided lateralization of their temporal lobe epileptic discharges. Only one had right-sided lateralization. Among hypogonadotropic hypogonadal women we found the reverse. Two had left-sided epileptiform discharges in the temporal lobe and 12 had right-sided discharges.

I emphasize that these were temporal lobe discharges, because with the other lobes of the brain the findings are different. Among women who had TLE but no reproductive dysfunction, that is, normal menstrual cycles between 26 and 32 days, we found very little difference between left- and right-sided origin of temporal lobe discharges (left 57%, right 43%).

How does TLE relate to ovarian function? The first level at which these limbic discharges can affect hormonal regulation is the hypothalamus. The ventromedial hypothalamus produces GnRH. This secretion is pulsatile. We asked whether the pulsatile secretion of GnRH was altered among men and women with TLE. We are nearing the completion of our study on the women whom we studied

specifically between days 2 and 7 of the menstrual cycle. We completed our evaluation of the men.[20] We also studied healthy controls. Specifically, we drew blood samples to measure LH levels every 15 minutes from 8 A.M. to 4 P.M. while the subjects were sitting or lying comfortably in a room with electroencephalographic leads on their heads.

Of our eight control men, five had 4 pulses, one had 2, one had 3, and one had 6, which turns out to be a statistically normal distribution (Fig. 20.7). Among the 13 men with epilepsy, none had 4 pulses in 8 hours. Rather, the distribution was bimodal with peaks at 2 and 6 pulses in 8 hours. We tried to correlate the two peaks with duration of epilepsy, types of seizures, types of medications, and so on. The only retrospective correlation that we found is as follows. Among the men who had 6 and 7 pulses in 8 hours, all had either right temporal lobe epileptiform discharges or left-sided bursts of slowing in the temporal lobe. The men who had 2 pulses in 8 hours all had left temporal lobe epileptiform discharges or right temporal slowing. The data suggest that the pattern of GmRH pulse secretion by the hypothalamus varies in relation to the laterality of limbic discharges in the brain and also to

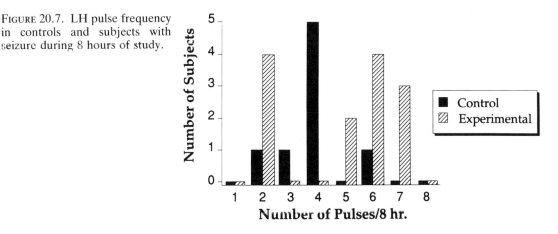

FIGURE 20.7. LH pulse frequency in controls and subjects with seizure during 8 hours of study.

the specific type of discharges, spikes versus slowing.

If limbic seizure discharges can alter the pattern and amount of GnRH pulse secretion, we may be able to explain the over-representation of reproductive endocrine disorders in women with epilepsy. We know from work in monkeys[21] that a decrease in GnRH pulse frequency results in a pattern of pituitary secretion in which LH levels are decreased and FSH levels remain normal. This is the pattern one sees in patients with hypogonadotropic hypogonadism. We know that if GnRH pulse amplitude is increased in monkeys, LH secretion is increased and FSH secretion is decreased, which is the pattern in polycystic ovarian syndrome. A proposed mechanism of the interactive nature of limbic seizure discharges and reproductive endocrine abnormalities is shown in Fig. 20.8. In addition, monoamine levels in the spinal fluid of men and women with epilepsy are normal, elevated, or decreased.[13] They show a much greater variability than in healthy controls. Since dopamine inhibits prolactin and LH secretion, it would follow that depletion of dopamine levels in the brain may be associated with elevated prolactin and LH levels such as one sees in polycystic ovarian syndrome. Elevated dopamine content in the brain would decrease LH secretion and perhaps contribute to the development of hypogonadotropic hypogonadism. The depletion of brain dopamine by epilepsy is now well demon-

strated in animals,[22] and it is also seen in the spinal fluid of humans with epilepsy.[23] Elevated dopamine levels occur only in human epilepsy and have not been demonstrated in animals.[23]

To complete the development of this reciprocal interaction between limbic system and ovarian function, there is not much in common between hypogonadotropic hypogonadism and polycystic ovary syndrome other than the fact that they produce anovulatory cycles with inadequate luteal phases and diminished progesterone levels.[13] We know that high estradiol/progesterone ratios in the serum increase limbic seizure discharges, thereby completing a vicious cycle in which limbic seizure discharges produce ovarian dysfunction and ovarian dysfunction exacerbates the limbic dysfunction (Fig. 20.8).

Questions and Answers

Participant. Did you look at the frequency of menstrual dysfunction in grand mal seizures?

A.H. The frequency of menstrual disorders is increased in grand mal seizures.[24] Grand mal seizures, however, are a peculiar control for this study because they involve the amygdala. Using depth electrodes, that is, putting an electrode into the human brain and recording from various regions, Sperling[25] showed that when medial temporal lobe limbic structures

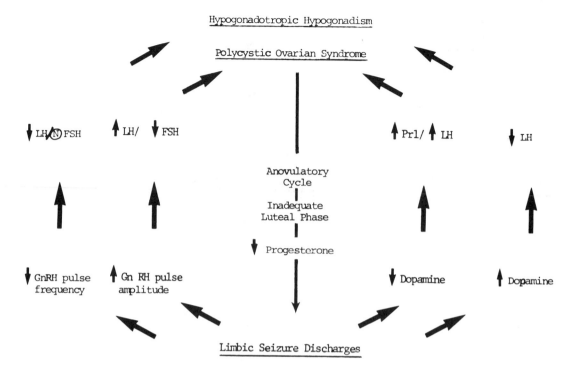

FIGURE 20.8. This illustration depicts possible mechanisms by which limbic seizure discharges may promote reproductive endocrine disorders and how abnormal reproductive hormone levels may influence epilepsy. It is based on the hypothesis proposed by Herzog et al.[1,13,17] that suggests that involvement of limbic structures with epileptiform discharges may disrupt normal limbic modulatory influences on hypothalamic gonadotropin-releasing hormone (GnRH) secretion. Altered frequency or amplitude of GnRH secretion may lead to patterns of pituitary luteinizing hormone (LH) and follicle-stimulating hormone (FSH) secretion that are found in hypogonadotropic hypogonadism and polycystic ovary syndrome. Limbic seizures alter brain dopamine levels. Hypothalamic dopamine exerts an inhibitory effect on pituitary LH and prolactin (Prl) secretion. Abnormal brain dopamine levels may alter pituitary gonadotropin and prolactin secretion and promote the development of reproductive endocrine disorders. Reproductive endocrine disorders that are associated with seizures of temporal lobe origin are characterized by anovulatory cycles and diminished progesterone secretion. An elevated serum estrogenprogesterone ratio may promote the development of seizure discharges in the brain.

are extensively involved, pituitary hormonal secretion is altered. If seizure discharges do not spread to involved medial temporal lobe limbic structures, these endocrine changes do not occur.

Participant. Could you comment briefly on the studies that showed increased sedation from progesterone?

A.H. Progesterone has been known for over 45 years to be a sedative, hypnotic, and anesthetic as well as antiseizure medication.[9,26] Selye in the 1940s was able to anesthetize rodents using high doses of progesterone.[26] Studies are still carried out that show this. The side effects of natural progesterone use in excessive amounts are sedation, depression, apathy, and lethargy. It is a good sleeping medication or hypnotic. We showed that progesterone significantly decreases seizure frequency in women with temporal lobe seizure disorder who have an inadequate luteal phase.[27] Natural progesterone can be used in lozenge form conveniently and is easily measured in the serum by routine endocrine laboratory testing.

Participant. When I was reviewing the literature on infertility, I found studies that supposedly showed that mental illness caused infertility, and only a few that said that stress was a result rather than a cause of infertility. Fortunately, more studies have come out and organizations like Resolve have been careful to try to dispel that myth. Could you address the extent to which infertility may cause depression or depression may lead to certain kinds of infertility problems?

A.H. I have worked mostly in the area of epilepsy and hormones, but I have received increasing numbers of referrals to evaluate individuals with emotional disorders. The complaint was that the emotional disorder, and here I will restrict myself to women, fluctuated in a cyclic fashion. We now have over 150 cases and have published one series on brain dysfunction in women with perimenopausal depression. We see exacerbations of agitated depression also in relation to menses or the entire second half of the menstrual cycle, postpartum and in the years approaching menopause. Many studies have concluded that hormones are not critical, and to say that they are critical is not a popular view these days.

How does one resolve the issue that the majority of women go through menstruation, delivery, and menopause without being emotionally disabled, and yet a significant minority become devastated at a particular point in their cycle, or in relation to delivery of a baby, or in the years approaching menopause? Most women during these times of their life go through the same hormonal changes. I grant that studies have suggested that levels may differ in some of these women, and I suspect that in some, they may. If the hormonal changes are the same in most women in these phases of life, however, it is not just the hormones that are the basis of disabling emotional syndromes. There must be something special about the brains of these women. We evaluated the possibility that something special makes certain people unusually sensitive to hormonal influence. Our findings in a perimenopausal depression study[28] were that a special brain substrate shows unusual sensitivity to hormones and to other chemicals as well. We know, for example, that the effect of any medication or chemical in the body is based not only on the dosage and regimen but also

on what it is acting on. I have patients who take 40 mg of Valium, and they come trotting into the office. I have had others for whom I prescribe 2 mg and they call up the next day saying, "You idiot, are you trying to kill me?" It is not just the medication or chemical that determines the effect but also what it is acting on.

It is interesting that our group of women with perimenopausal depression had a much higher frequency of postpartum psychosis and menstrual depression than our controls. They also had a significantly higher frequency of left-handedness, neurologic findings, and electroencephalographic (EEG) disturbances with or without clinical seizure concomitants, and a significantly higher frequency of personal or family history of depression. Each of these is a marker for anomalous brains, and I believe that it is the presence of this anomalous brain that confers unusual responsivity to hormones and chemicals. A number of years ago Geschwind suggested that idiosyncratic reaction to medications is more common among men and women who are left-handed, or have a family history of left-handedness or its concomitants, such as other than brown hair and eyes, and early gray hair.

References

1. Herzog AG. A hypothesis to integrate partial seizures of temporal lobe origin and reproductive endocrine disorders. Epilepsy Res 1989; 3:151–159.
2. Brodmann K. Vergleichende lokalisationlehre der grosshirnrinde in ihren prinzipien dargestellt auf grund des zellenbaues. Leipzig: J.A. Barth, 1909:1–324.
3. Papez JW. A proposed mechanism of emotion. Arch Neurol Psychiatry 1937;38:725–743.
4. Kluver H, Bucy PC. An analysis of certain effects of bilateral temporal lobectomy in the rhesus monkey. J Psychol 1938;5:33–54.
5. Bear D, Fedio P. Quantitative analysis of interictal behavior in temporal lobe epilepsy. Arch Neurol 1977;34:454–467.
6. Kaada B. Stimulation and regional ablation of the amygdaloid complex with reference to functional representation. In: Eleftheriou BE, ed. The Neurobiology of the Amygdala. New York: Plenum Press, 1972:205–281.

7. Pfaff DW, Keiner M. Estradiol-concentrating cells in the rat amygdala as part of a limbic-hypothalamic hormone-sensitive system. In: Eleftheriou BE, ed. The Neurobiology of the Amygdala. New York: Plenum Press, 1973: 775–792.

8. Longo LPS, Saldana LEG. Hormones and their influence in epilepsy. Acta Neurol Latinoam 1969;12:29–47.

9. Herzog AG. Progesterone in seizure therapy. Neurology 1987;37:1433.

10. Burden HW, Lawrence IE. The effect of denervation on compensatory ovarian hypertrophy. Neuroendocrinology 1977;23:368–378.

11. Kawakami M, Kubo K, Vemura T, Nagase H, Hayashi R. Involvement of ovarian innervation in steroid secretion. Endocrinology 1981; 109:136–145.

12. Falconer MA, Serafetinides EA, Corsellis JAN. Etiology and pathogenesis of temporal lobe epilepsy. Arch Neurol 1964;10:233–248.

13. Herzog AG, Seibel MM, Schomer DL, Vaitukaitis JL, Geschwind N. Reproductive endocrine disorders in women with partial seizures of temporal lobe origin. Arch Neurol 1986;43:341–346.

14. Jensen I, Vaernet K. Temporal lobe epilepsy: Follow-up investigation of 74 temporal lobe resected patients. Acta Neurochir 1977;37: 173–200.

15. Trampuz V, Dimitrijevic M, Kryanovski J. UIga epilepsije u patogenezi disfunkeije ovarija. Neuropsihijatrija 1975;23:179–183.

16. Dansky LV, Andermann E, Andermann F. Marriage and fertility in epileptic patients. Epilepsia 1980;21:261–271.

17. Herzog AG, Seibel MM, Schomer DL, Vaitukaitis JL, Geschwind N. Reproductive endocrine disorders in men with partial seizures of temporal lobe origin. Arch Neurol 1986; 43:347–350.

18. Christiansen P, Deigaard J, Lund M. Potens, fertilitet of konshormonudskilleiss hos yngre manglige epilepsilidende. Ugeskr Laeger 1975; 137:2402–2405.

19. Herzog AG. Lateralized asymmetry of the cerebral control of endocrine secretion in women with epilepsy. Neurology 1991;41:366.

20. Herzog AH, Drislane FW, Schomer DL, et al. Abnormal pulsatile secretion of luteinizing hormone in men with epilepsy: Relationship to laterality and nature of paroxysmal discharges. Neurology 1990;40:1557–1561.

21. Knobil E. The neuroendocrine control of the menstrual cycle. Rec Prog Horm Res 1980; 36:53–80.

22. Sato M, Nakashima T. Kindling: Secondary epileptogenesis, sleep and catecholamines. Can J Neurol Sci 1975;2:439–446.

23. Papeschi R, Molina-Negro P, Sourkes TL, et al. The concentration of homovanillic and 5-hydroroxyindoleacetic acid in ventricular and lumbar CSF. Neurology 1972;22:1151–1159.

24. Bilo L, Meo R, Nappi C, et al. Reproductive endocrine disorders in women with primary generalized epilepsy. Epilepsia 1988;29:612–619.

25. Sperling MR, Pritchard PB, Engle J Jr, Daniel C, Sagel J. Prolactin in partial epilepsy: An indicator of limbic seizures. Ann Neurol 1986; 20:716–722.

26. Selye H. The antagonism between anesthetic steroid hormone and pentamethylenatetrazol (Metrazol). J Lab Clin Med 1941;27:1051–1053.

27. Herzog AG. Intermittent progesterone therapy and frequency of complex partial seizures in women with menstrual disorders. Neurology 1986;36:1607–1610.

28. Herzog AG. Perimenopausal depression: Possible role of anomalous brain substrate. Brain Dysfunct 1989;2:146–154.

21
Oocyte Donation

Zev Rosenwaks

In the past, infertility due to absent or abnormal gametes in females was considered to be irreversible. Whereas male gametes were accessible, available on demand in large numbers, and able to be cryopreserved and stored, the same was not true for the female. The report of a pregnancy following donor embryo transfer in 1983 was the first description of pregnancy in patients with absent or abnormal oocytes. The original technique described by Buster involved intracervical artificial insemination of a normal female volunteer with the infertile couple's husband's spermatozoa, uterine lavage during the perinidatory period, and subsequent intrauterine embryo transfer to a synchronized recipient. Concerns regarding infectious diseases, technical difficulties, and the possibility of pregnancy in the donor have limited the application of this technique. More recently, in vitro fertilization (IVF) has been utilized for human oocyte donation. In this circumstance, ovarian stimulation of the donor is used prior to oocyte retrieval to increase the number of oocytes recovered at harvest. Insemination is performed in vitro with the recipient's husband's spermatozoa; after fertilization and embryo culture, the embryo(s) is transferred transcervically into the endometrial cavity. Additionally, there are now reports of comparable pregnancy rates following gamete intrafallopian transfer (GIFT) using donor oocytes.

Although oocyte donation (OD) is medically analogous to sperm donation, the relative inaccessibility of female gametes, their availability in low numbers, and the requirement of embryo-endometrial synchronization make the procedures technically very different. Successful OD requires an established IVF and/or GIFT program, appropriately screened and selected donors, complete evaluation and preparation of recipients, synchronization of embryo and endometrial development, and systematic short- and long-term follow-up after embryo transfer.

Indications for Oocyte Donation

There are a wide variety of pathologic disorders that can only be treated by OD. Simply stated, patients with ovarian failure of any cause, anatomically inaccessible ovaries, poor-quality oocytes at the time of IVF, or certain genetic disorders may be candidates for OD. Other therapeutic options must be excluded prior to resorting to OD. Potential patients can generally be divided into those with and those without ovarian function.

Women with endogenous ovarian function who are candidates for OD may be divided in turn into those with and those without normal gametes. The one indication for OD in patients who ovulate normally and have presumably normal gametes is ovarian inaccessibility preventing oocyte retrieval. Although modern techniques make the ovaries of most women accessible, rare patients may still require OD.

Patients who still have endogenous ovarian function may also be candidates for OD if they have failed IVF or GIFT secondary to persistently poor oocyte quality or have known genetic disorders. An increasing percentage of women presenting for OD are carriers for a

TABLE 21.1. Diagnosis of patients entering an oocyte donation program.

Diagnosis		n
Ovarian failure		
Autoimmune		4
Radiation therapy		6
Chemotherapy		8
Surgical castration		14
Gonadal dysgenesis		26
Idiopathic		59
	Total	117
Nonovarian failure		
Failed IVF		26
Inaccessible ovaries		7
Genetic disorder (carrier state)		8
	Total	41

variety of genetic disorders, especially X-linked disorders.

Patients with ovarian failure comprise the largest group of women presenting for OD. While the specific etiology may be identified in some cases, the majority of these women have idiopathic ovarian failure. Known causes of ovarian failure include chemotherapy or pelvic irradiation for the treatment of malignancies, surgical castration, autoimmune disorders, and gonadal dysgenesis. The various diagnoses of women entering our OD program are presented in Table 21.1.

Preparatory Cycles

With OD, events leading to egg harvest (ovarian hyperstimulation) are dissociated from the events (endometrial development) of the natural cycle in the recipient.

In the natural cycle, oocyte development, subsequent embryo development, and endometrial receptivity are coordinated as naturally synchronous events, allowing the embryo to arrive in the endometrial cavity and implant, presumably at the optimum time. With OD the oocytes are harested after ovarian stimulation outside the endometrium. Therefore, it is important to have a means of reproducibly creating an endometrial environment with defined limits of receptivity so that appropriate synchronization between donor (embryo) and recipient may be achieved. Since

there are no definitive markers of endometrial receptivity, circulating steroid levels and endometrial histology on specific days of the menstrual cycle are presumed to equate with development of normal endometrial receptivity.

Patients with Ovarian Function

In patients with natural ovarian function, normal endometrial receptivity may be presumed following documentation of normal midluteal progesterone levels and an in-phase endometrial biopsy in the late luteal phase.

Patients with Ovarian Failure

Patients with ovarian failure require the administration of endogenous estrogen and progesterone to produce endometrial growth and differentiation. The goal of this replacement therapy is to reproducibly create a sufficient level of circulating steroids, properly sequenced endometrial development, and consequently normal endometrial receptivity. To document the appropriateness of hormonal replacement therapy, the patients undergo two preparatory cycles in which they receive hormonal replacement therapy, have serial determinations of serum estrogen and progesterone concentrations, and undergo endometrial biopsies to ensure adequate endometrial development.

Estrogen replacement therapy can be delivered orally, transdermally, or transvaginally in polysiloxane-impregnated rings. Limited availability of the estradiol-containing rings and poor patient compliance secondary to discomfort and vaginal infections have limited their application. Most programs now use either transdermal or oral estrogen replacement. There are a number of different hormonal replacement regimens. Our regimen, using oral micronized estradiol and the associated serum estradiol and estrone levels, is demonstrated in Figures 21.1 and 21.2. While circulating estradiol levels are physiologic, the estrone concentrations are clearly supraphysiologic.

Transdermal estradiol administration using skin patches is described in Figure 21.1.

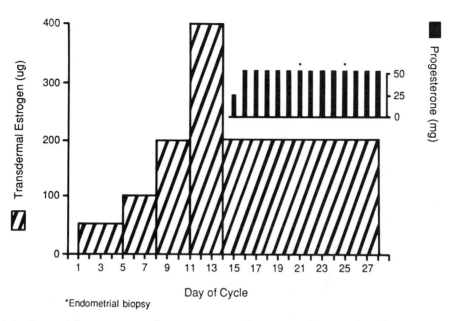

FIGURE 21.1. Protocol for estrogen and progesterone replacement using transdermal estrogen patches and intramuscular progesterone.

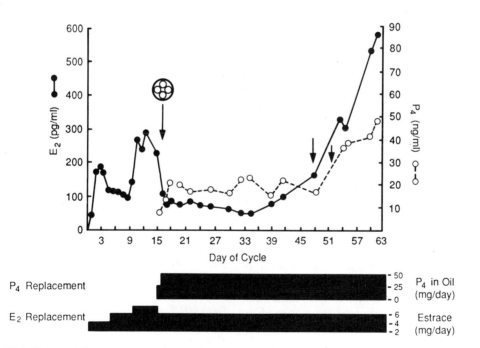

FIGURE 21.2. Protocol for estrogen and progesterone replacement using oral estrogen and intramuscular progesterone.

Estradiol levels are considered adequate if late follicular values exceed 200 pg/ml and midluteal concentrations exceed 100 pg/ml.

Progesterone replacement has been provided with oral, transvaginal, and intramuscular preparations. The most reliable circulatory levels have been obtained with intramuscular replacement. Additionally, intramuscular replacement has produced the most consistent secretory changes at the time of endometrial biopsy. The protocols for progesterone replacement and associated serum levels are shown in Figure 21.2. Midluteal progesterone levels of 20 ng/ml or higher are considered adequate.

Endometrial biopsies for histological dating are performed on days 20–21 in the first preparatory cycle and on days 25–26 in the second. The inflammatory reaction that follows the first biopsy can induce pseudodecidualization, and therefore the second biopsy must be performed in a second cycle. The biopsies taken on days 20–21 consistently have some degree of glandular–stromal dysynchrony. Most patients will have either sub- or supranuclear vacuoles indicative of days 17–18 glandular development, but will also have significant stromal edema consistent with days 21–22 stromal maturity. The adequacy of endometrial development should be judged by the stromal component. The late luteal biopsy generally demonstrates exhausted secretory glands and pseudodecidualization consistent with days 25–26. Studies in naturally cycling women have demonstrated that there are changes in the surface glycocalyx of the endometrial surface epithelium during the perinidatory period which are felt to be specific for implantation. Extensive studies evaluating these changes in the day 20 biopsies of the ovarian failure patient's preparatory cycles reveal the same changes. This supports the contention that hormonal replacement can reproduce biochemical changes consistent with the natural cycle.

Oocyte Donors

Sources

The most difficult part of establishing and maintaining a good OD program is maintaining an adequate supply of donor oocytes. Sources may be divided into two—anonymous and nonanonymous. Anonymous donors include IVF patients who choose not to cryopreserve their excess oocytes, women willing to undergo ovarian stimulation and oocyte retrieval at the time of tubal sterilization procedures, and volunteers willing to undergo ovarian stimulation and oocyte retrieval electively. The advent of cryopreservation has drastically reduced the number of oocytes available from IVF patients.

As OD has gained increasing public attention, more women undergoing tubal sterilization procedures are interested in donating oocytes, and this group is now the primary source of anonymously donated oocytes. Some centers are permitting women who do not have an indication for any type of operative procedure to donate oocytes. Nonanonymous donors may be relatives, friends, or paid donors. The legal and ethical issues surrounding nonanonymous donation from paid donors are complex, and many centers are not currently accepting this type of donor.

Screening

Appropriate screening of donors requires a complete history and physical examination, detailed review of genetic and infectious disease histories, a psychologic evaluation, and extensive counseling regarding the risk of the procedure (Table 21.2).

The complete history and physical examination should pay particular attention to potential contraindications to ovarian hyperstimulation. A detailed menstrual and pregnancy history is important because potential donors who have

TABLE 21.2. Screening of potential oocyte donors.

Genetic history
HIV
VDRL
Hepatitis screen
Rh type
Psychological evaluation
Counseling regarding risks of donation
Reproductive history
CBC
SMA-20
Sickledex or hemoglobin electrophoresis

histories of infertility, recurrent miscarriages, or very irregular cycles may be suboptimal candidates. Women under the age of 35 are preferred; however, in certain cases where the recipient is aware of the donor's age and has undergone the appropriate genetic counseling regarding the risk of chromosomal anomaly and the need for amniocentesis, older donors may be acceptable.

All donors, including family members of the recipient, are required to undergo a psychologic evaluation to make certain that they understand the implications of gamete donation and the risks they may be assuming, and to ensure that they are not being coerced to donate. If the donor is undergoing tubal sterilization, the evaluation should also provide documentation that her decision to undergo sterilization has not been altered by her desire to donate oocytes.

Laboratory screening includes a complete blood count (CBC) and a metabolic profile to determine the general metabolic state of the donor. The blood type including Rh factor is also determined, since Rh$^-$ negative recipients should be informed if they are transferred oocytes from an Rh$^-$ positive donor. The low incidence of isoimmunization (0.2%) with adequate appropriate prenatal care does not contraindicate the use of Rh$^-$ positive oocytes in Rh$^-$ negative women. Infectious screening includes hepatitis, Venereal Disease Research Laboratory (VDRL), and human immunodeficiency virus (HIV) testing. When appropriate, donors are also screened for sickle trait, Tay Sachs, or other inheried disorders.

A complete genetic history is obtained. Formats identical to those used for sperm donation are comprehensive and may be used. What constitutes exclusion criteria must be decided on an individual basis. For example, potential donors with family histories of diabetes or serious psychiatric diseases are generally excluded. Less significant medical problems such as myopia, which may be familial, are presented to the recipient and decisions made on an individual basis.

Finally, informed consent must be obtained. The patient must be extensively counseled as to the risks of undergoing gonadotropin stimulation and retrieval—up to and including death. All donors are told that we are uncertain of any long-term psychologic complications of OD; however, they are informed that sperm donation has not produced long-term problems among donors.

Ovarian Stimulation and Oocyte Retrieval

Gonadotropin stimulation begins on day 3 of the donor's menstrual cycle in a manner identical to that used for patients attempting to conceive through routine IVF. Decisions regarding the specific stimulation protocol should be based on contemporary criteria used within the particular IVF program. Monitoring and decisions regarding the timing of human chorionic gonadotropin (HCG) administration and oocyte retrieval should be identical to the standard IVF criteria. During office visits donors are kept separate from routine IVF patients and the recipient to protect their anonymity.

Oocyte retrieval is performed routinely and may be done either laparoscopically or by ultrasound guidance. In patients not undergoing tubal sterilization, ultrasound-directed retrievals may be indicated, since these procedures usually do not require general anesthesia.

Follow-up is handled routinely with an office visit approximately 4 weeks after the procedure. All patients are told to use barrier contraception until their next menses to avoid the risk of pregnancy. (This includes the patients who underwent tubal ligation, since the possibility of ovulation prior to retrieval cannot be absolutely excluded.)

Synchronization of the Donor and Recipient

Appropriate synchronization of embryonic and endometrial development is necessary if the implantation is to occur. With natural in vivo conception, the hormonal events in the follicle surrounding oocyte maturation and ovulation also direct endometrial development, thus providing intrinsic synchronization. There is no natural mechanism assuring synchronous development in OD patients. Therefore, control of this critical relationship becomes the responsibility of the physician.

The principle of synchronization is to transfer embryos to the recipient at a time when the embryonic and endometrial development will allow subsequent implantation. Prior animal work has demonstrated some biologic tolerance to developmental dysynchrony between embryo and endometrium. Sheep tolerate up to 2 days of dysynchrony. Cattle and primates may tolerate up to 3 days of dysynchrony, although with reduced reproductive efficiency.

In reviewing the literature regarding synchronization, it is critical to appreciate the importance of the number of days of progesterone exposure and not the total cycle length. With in vivo conception, the length of the follicular phase may be highly variable while still allowing conception; however, the secretory changes following ovulation still progress in concert with ovulation, fertilization, and embryo development. Loss of synchronization of these events may occur naturally, as in some cases of corpus luteum deficiency, and may lead to infertility.

For the purpose of this discussion, the first day of progesterone exposure will be considered day 15. This is a logical choice, since during natural cycles the luteinizing hormone (LH) surge usually peaks on cycle day 14 with ovulation approximately 24 hours later. Significant progesterone production begins in the periovulatory period, making cycle day 15 the first day with significant circulating progesterone levels. Finally, this discussion addresses the window of transfer as well as the window of receptivity of the human endometrium. However, these terms must be taken with the knowledge that there is currently no precise means of determining when the embryo will implant following transfer without producing some risk to a possible pregnancy.

The Window of Transfer

Embryo transfers have been performed on cycle days 16–24, but pregnancies have been reported only from transfers done on cycle

TABLE 21.3. Pregnancy rates by cycle day of transfer.

Cycle day	Total transfers	Total		Pregnancies		Miscarriages	
		n	%	n	%	n	%
16	5	0	(0)	0	(0)	0	(0)
17	31	10	(32)	8	(25)	2	(20)
18	14	6	(42)	5	(35)	1	(17)
19	13	6	(46)	4	(30)	2	(30)
20	5	1	(20)	0	(0)	1	(100)
21	2	0	(0)	0	(0)	0	(0)
24	2	0	(0)	0	(0)	0	(0)
Total	72	23	(31)	17	(23)	6	(26)

days 16–19. The Monash group performed transfers on cycle days 16–18, whereas we typically have transferred embryos on days 17–19. Usually the embryos are transferred at approximately the same developmental stage (2–15 blastomeres, most commonly 4 blastomeres) so that differences in pregnancy rates for the given cycle days reflect changes in endometrial receptivity. Since the embryos are usually transferred 2 days following retrieval, day 17 transfers are synchronous, day 16 and day 18 transfers are dysynchronous by 1 day, and day 19 transfers are dysynchronous by 2 days. However, this applies to in vitro fertilized oocytes and ensuing in vitro developed embryos. It is possible that embryo development in vivo may occur at a different rate. The pregnancy results by day of transfer are demonstrated in Table 21.3. There are no differences in the pregnancy rates of patients transferred on days 17–19. Notably, there were no pregnancies from cycle day 16 transfers. These data indicate that with 48-hour embryos, the human system can tolerate up to 2 days of dysynchrony.

Synchronizing Natural Cycle Patients

Patients requiring OD who are still having spontaneous menstrual cycles may be difficult to synchronize. The patients should monitor their urine for the presence of LH and have their surge confirmed by a serum LH determination. The day of the LH surge is arbitrarily designated as day 14 and the day of spontaneous ovulation as day 15. When available, ultrasound monitoring is also useful in confirming the time of ovulation. If oocytes are donated on the recipient's cycle days 15, 16, or 17, then the embryos will be tranferred 48 hours later on cycle days 17, 18, or 19. Since the donation of excess oocytes from IVF patients is now quite uncommon, most patients receive oocytes from scheduled donors, and the embryos are cryopreserved for future transfer.

Synchronizing Ovarian Failure Patients

We previously demonstrated that there is substantial flexibility in the quantity and duration of estrogen exposure needed to allow subsequent normal secretory transformation with progesterone therapy. This fact allows great flexibility in synchronizing patients who are receiving hormonal replacement to induce endometrial receptivity.

Most women undergoing gonadotropin stimulation will be ready for HCG administration on cycle day 9 (±1 day) and undergo retrieval 34–36 hours later. This is substantially shorter than the "follicular phase" (estrogen administration only) commonly used in the hormonal replacement regimens. Therefore, the recipient must begin her replacement regimen prior to the anticipated menses of the donor. Variability in the onset of the menses of the donor and the subsequent duration of her gonadotropin stimulation may result in errors of 3 or more days in the estimate of when the oocytes will be retrieved. This problem is overcome by beginning the recipient on her replacement regimen 5 days prior to the anticipated menses of the donor. If the donor's menses is earlier or later than expected or takes shorter or longer than usual to stimulate, the duration of the follicular phase is adjusted accordingly. Progesterone administration is withheld until the day prior to or the day of oocyte retrieval. Since the first day of progesterone administration is always considered cycle day 15, this results in oocyte retrieval on the recipient's cycle day 15 or 16 and embryo transfer on cycle day 17 or 18.

Cryopreservation

There are now a number of reports detailing the use of cryopreservation in OD programs. This eliminates the need for donor–recipient synchronization. Precise control of the thawing process allows the recipients to choose the time of transfer. Embryo–endometrial synchronization is still required and is obtained by thawing the embryos on the recipient's cycle day 16 and transferring them on cycle day 17. However, when 8 to 16 cell embryos are thawed, transfer may be required on the recipient's day 18 or 19. To date, limited experience with cyropreservation and OD precludes the assessment of its impact on success rates. However, if no adverse impact is identified, this technique will be extremely useful in simplifying the scheduling of OD transfer.

Follow-Up After Transfer

Patients are allowed to return to their normal activities the day after transfer. They remain on the estrogen and progesterone replacement in the same dosage used in the luteal phase of their preparatory cycles. All patients have serum samples taken three times weekly to confirm adequate absorption by assessment of serum estrogen and progesterone concentrations. There are no special precautions beyond emphasizing that the medication schedule should be maintained unless instructed otherwise.

Since these patients have no endogenous estrogen and progesterone production except from the placenta, an increase in serum estrogen and progesterone concentrations in the face of a constant hormonal replacement schedule indicates the onset of placental steroid production. Once a significant increase has been detected, the medications are reduced by half and rechecked the following week. If they continue to rise, then all medications are discontinued and again serum values are checked throughout the following week. Maintenance of estrogen and progesterone levels indicates adequate placental steroid production. An example of an individual patient's replacement therapy and serum estrogen

TABLE 21.4. Success rates with oocyte donation from the literature.

Group	Method	N	Pregnancies		Viable pregnancies	
			n	%	n	%
Rosenwaks	IVF	58	22	(38)	17	(29)
Lutjen	IVF	31	6	(19)	4	(13)
Navot	IVF	8	2	(25)	2	(25)
Levran	IVF	27	10	(37)	4	(15)
Feichtinger	IVF	4	1	(25)	1	(25)
Devroey	IVF	31	3	(10)	2	(6)
Salat-Baroux	IVF	18	5	(28)	3	(17)
Yovich	Prost	3	1	(33)	1	(33)
Asch	GIFT	8	6	(25)	5	(63)
Abdalla	ZIFT	1	1	(100)	1	(100)

and progesterone levels is shown in Figure 21.2. Generally, for most patients estrogen and progesterone are discontinued by week 10 of pregnancy, day 1 being the first day of the replaced transfer cycle.

Once placental steroid production is established, the patients are returned to the care of their personal obstetricians and generally have unremarkable pregnancies. We request an early ultrasound to confirm an intrauterine pregnancy. Initial concerns that the lack of ovarian relaxin production would make vaginal delivery ill-advised have been discontinued. The route of delivery should be determined by contemporary obstetrical indications.

Success Rates with Oocyte Donation

Success rates with OD should be defined per attempt and also per attempt within the window of transfer. Embryo transfers performed outside of the established window of transfer are not representative of potential ongoing success rates. Patient counseling should reflect the success rates within the window of transfer, since future transfers will be done within this predefined time period.

Our results are presented to Table 21.3 as a function of the cycle day of transfer. Our viable pregnancy rates within the window of transfer (days 17–19) are 29%. A summary of results compiled from various groups is presented in Table 21.4.

The Physiologic Model Provided by Oocyte Donation

The ability to control the circulating hormonal milieu, the endometrial environment, and the timing and number of embryos replaced, combined with the ability to measure placental hormonal production in the absence of ovarian function, provides unique insight into the physiology of reproduction.

Placental Steroidogenesis

The OD model provides an opportunity to study the onset of placental steroid production isolated from any corpus luteum function. In a review of eight patients with ovarian failure who conceived through OD, an increase in estrogen and progesterone was seen during the sixth and seventh gestation weeks (fourth and fifth weeks after transfer), respectively. Furthermore, extrapolation of the rise in both estrogen and progesterone serum levels to baseline replacement levels as determined during the third and fourth gestation weeks demonstrated the probable onset of production in the fifth gestational week (3 weeks after transfer).

This information is helpful in counseling patients regarding the probable duration of hormonal replacement therapy. It also has relevance to patients with luteal phase dysfunction requiring progesterone supplementation; they should not require treatment beyond the ninth gestational week.

Embryo Quality and Pregnancy Rates

Morphologic criteria used for assessing the quality of embryos transferred to IVF patients correlate well with the pregnancy rates. However, these women have supraphysiologic estrogen levels and estrogen/progesterone ratios that may impact on endometrial development by altering the receptivity of the endometrium. The OD model offers the opportunity to evaluate the impact of embryo quality when embryos are transferred into defined endometria.

TABLE 21.5. Pregnancy rates based on morphologic grading of the embryos transferred.

Embryo quality	Total transfers	Total		Pregnancies ongoing		Miscarriages	
		n	%	n	%	n	%
1	17	14	(82)	12	(70)	2	(14)
2	20	6	(30)	4	(20)	2	(33)
3	1	0	(0)	0	(0)	0	(0)
4	15	1	(7)	0	(0)	1	(100)
5	3	0	(0)	0	(0)	0	(0)

TABLE 21.6. Pregnancy rates following the transfer of fresh and cryopreserved embryos

Embryo status	Total transfers	Total		Pregnancies ongoing		Miscarriage	
		n	%	n	%	n	%
Fresh	46	19	(41)	15	(33)	4	(27)
Cryopreserved	12	3	(25)	2	(17)	1	(33)

The pregnancy rate for grade 1 embryos exceeds 80%, while the transfer of grade 2 embryos resulted in pregnancies in 33% of cases. Transfer of poor-quality grades 3–5 embryos resulted in only one pregnancy, which subsequently miscarried (Table 21.5). This information demonstrates that embryo quality, as determined by morphologic criteria, is highly predictive of the ability of that embryo to implant into relatively normal endometria. The ability to transfer embryos of "good" quality into defined endometrial environments allows the assessment of embryo versus endometrium in determining reproductive efficiency in the human.

The Impact of Cryopreservation on Pregnancy Rates

Cryopreservation has become an integral part of many IVF programs, since it provides patients with the option of limiting the number of fresh embryos transferred during the IVF cycle, thus decreasing the chances for multiple pregnancies.

The OD model is an ideal way to assess the efficiency of cryopreservation, since most oocytes are obtained from fertile, non-IVF donors and the oocytes are all given to the recipient. The indication for cryopreservation is usually dysynchrony between the donor and the recipient. Since the endometria of the recipients are well defined and reflect a physiologic, controlled menstrual cycle, this is an ideal model to answer this question.

Our experience with the transfer of cryopreserved embryos to OD patients is listed in Table 21.6. There were no differences in success rates between fresh and cryopreserved transfers with these preliminary data. Salat-Baroux had 3 pregnancies in 18 patients, which is a pregnancy rate of 19%. This was not statistically different from the remainder of their program, but it is lower than the pregnancy rates in most OD programs. More data will be required to answer these questions adequately.

Summary

OD has become an established method of treating patients who cannot conceive because of absent, inaccessible, or poor-quality oocytes, as well as patients who are carriers of genetic disorders. Exogenous estrogen and progesterone replacement can induce endometrial receptivity with a well-defined temporal window of transfer, and the transfer of high-quality oocytes results in excellent pregnancy rates.

References

1. Steptoe PC, Edwards RG. Birth after the reimplantation of a human embryo. Lancet 1978;2:336.
2. Lutjen P, Trounson A, Leeton J, et al. The establishment and maintenance of pregnancy using in vitro fertilization and embryo donation in a patient with primary ovarian failure. Nature 1984;307:174.
3. Navot D, Laufer N, Kopolovic J, et al. Artificially induced endometrial cycles and establishment of pregnancies in the absence of ovaries. N Engl J Med 1986;314:806.
4. Buster JE, Bustillo M, Thorneycroft IH, et al. Nonsurgical transfer of in vivo fertilized donated ova to five infertile women: Report of two pregnancies. Lancet 1983;2:223.
5. Bustillo M, Buster JE, Cohen SW, et al. Nonsurgical ovum transfer as a treatment in infertile women: Preliminary experience. JAMA 1984;25:1171.
6. Bustillo M, Buster JE, Cohen SW, et al. Delivery of a healthy infant following nonsurgical ovum transfer. JAMA 1984;251:889.
7. Rosenwaks Z. Donor eggs: Their application in modern reproductive technologies. Fertil Steril 1987;47:895.
8. Heape W. Preliminary note on the transplantation and growth of mammalian ova within a uterine foster mother. Proc R Soc Lond 1890; 48:457.
9. Wilett EL, Black WG, Casida LE, Stone WH, Buckner PJ. Successful transplantation of a fertilized bovine ovum. Science 1951;113:247.
10. Seidel GEJ Jr. Supervulation and embryo transfer in cattle. Science 1981;211:351.
11. Newcomb R, Rowson LE. Conception rate after uterine transfer of cow eggs in relation to synchronization of oestrus and age of eggs. J Reprod Fertil 1975;43:539.
12. Beatty RA. Transplantation of mouse eggs. Nature 1951;168:2995.
13. Rowson LEA, Moor RM. Embryo transfer in the sheep: The significance of synchronizing oestrus in the donor and recipient animal. J Reprod Fertil 1966;11:201.
14. Rowson LEA, Lawson RAS, Moor RM, Baker AA. Egg transfer in the cow: Synchronization requirements. J Reprod Fertil 1972;28:427.
15. Hodgen GD. Surrogate embryo transfer combined with estrogen-progesterone therapy in monkeys, implantation, gestation and delivery without ovaries. JAMA 1983;250:2167.
16. Friedman C, Barrows H, Kim MH. Hypergonadotropic hypogonadism. Am J Obstet Gynecol 1983;145:360.
17. Tulandi T, Kinch RAH. Premature ovarian failure. Obstet Gynecol Surv 1981;36:521.
18. Turkington RW, Lebovitz HE. Extra-adrenal endocrine deficiencies in Addison's disease. Am J Med 1967;43:499.
19. Irvine W, Chan MMW. Immunological aspects of premature ovarian failure associated with idiopathic Addison's disease. Lancet 1968; 1:883.
20. DeMoraes-Ruehsen M, Blizzared RM, Garcia-Bunuel R, Jones GS. Autoimmunity and ovarian failure. Am J Obstet Gynecol 1972; 112:693.
21. Caldwell BV, Luborsky-Moore JL, Kase N. A functional LH agonist and LH receptor antagonist in serum from a patient with premature ovarian failure syndrome. Presented at the meeting of the Endocrine Society, Miami, June 15, 1978.
22. Navot D, Rosenwaks Z, Margalioth EJ. Prognostic assessment of female fecundity. Lancet 1987;2:645.
23. Van Stierteghem AC, Van den Abbeel E, Braeckmans P, et al. Pregnancy with a frozen-thawed embryo in a woman with primary ovarian failure. N Engl J Med 1987;317: 113.
24. Trounson A, Leeton J, Besanda M, Wood C, Conti A. Pregnancy established in an infertile patient after transfer of a donated embryo fertilised in vitro. Br Med J 1983;286:835.
25. Lutjen PJ, Findlay JR, Trouson AO, Leeton JF, Chan LK. Effects on plasma gonadotropins of cyclic steroid replacement in women with premature ovarian failure. J Clin Endocrinol Metab 1986;62:419.
26. Jones HW Jr. Ethical considerations of the new reproductive technologies. Fertil Steril (Suppl 1) 1986;46.
27. Muasher SJ, Garcia JE, Rosenwaks Z. The combination of follicle stimulating hormone and human menopausal gonadotropins for the induction of multiple follicular maturation for in vitro fertilization. Fertil Steril 1985;44:62.
28. Rosenwaks Z, Muasher SJ. Recruitment of fertilizable eggs. In: Jones HW Jr, Jones GS, Hodgen GD, Rosenwaks Z, eds. In Vitro Fertilization—Norfolk. Baltimore: Williams & Wilkins, 1986:30.
29. Veek LL, Maloney M. Insemination and fertilization. In: Jones HW Jr, Jones GS, Hodgen GD, Rosenwaks Z, ' eds. In Vitro Fertilization—Norfolk. Baltimore: Williams & Wilkins, 1986:168.
30. Seed RG, Seed RW. Artificial embryonation—human embryo transplant. Arch Androl 1980; 5:90.

31. Bustillo M, Buster JE. Nonsurgical ovum transfer: The Harbor, UCLA experience. In: Feichtinger W, Kemeter P, eds. Future Aspects in Human In Vitro Fertilization. Berlin: Springer-Verlag, 1987:122.

32. Jones HW Jr, Acosta AA, Andrews MC, et al. Three years of in vitro fertilization at Norfolk. Fertil Steril 1984;42:826.

33. Formigli L, Formigli G, Rocciio C. Donation of fertilized uterine ova to infertile women. Fertil Steril 1987;47:162.

34. Asch RH, Balmaceda JP, Ord T, et al. Oocyte donation and gamete intrafallopian transfer in premature ovarian failure. Fertil Steril 1988; 49:263.

35. Robertson JA. Ethical and legal issues in preimplantation genetic screening. Fertil Steril 1992;57:1.

36. Ryan KJ. Placental synthesis of steroid hormones. In: Tulchinsky D, Ryan KJ, eds. Maternal–Fetal Endocrinology. Philadelphia: Saunders, 1980:3.

37. Seibel MM. A new era in reproductive technology: In vitro fertilization gamete intrafallopian transfer, and donated gametes and embryos. N Engl J Med 1988;318:828.

38. Schenker JG, Frenkel DA. Medico-legal aspects of in vitro fertilization and embryo transfer practice. Obstet Gynecol Surv 1987; 42:405.

39. German Medical Association: Statement. Dtsch Arzteibl 1985;22:91.

40. Committee of Enquiry into Human Fertilization and Embryology: Report. London: Her Majesty's Stationery Office, 1984.

41. Committee to Consider the Social, Ethical, and Legal Issues Arising from In Vitro Fertilisation: Reports. Melbourne, Australia, 1983, 1984.

42. Salat-Baroux J, Cornet D, Alvarez S, et al. Hormonal secretions in singleton pregnancies arising from the implantation of fresh or frozen embryos after oocyte donation in women with ovarian failure. Fertil Steril 1992;57,150.

22
New Animal Embryo Engineering Technology

Robert A. Godke

Animal reproduction is entering the era of embryo engineering, having as its ultimate goal the production of increased numbers of genetically superior offspring. Not since the commercial development of artificial insemination methods for cattle in the 1950s has any new technical research development caused such an interest in the livestock industry. Along with artificial insemination procedures, embryo transplantation and embryo freezing techniques have precipitated the beginning of a new age in animal reproduction technology. Although the greatest genetic impact on domesticated animal populations still originates from the male through artificial insemination, embryo transfer technology now offers new opportunities to expand superior maternal genetics in planned breeding programs.[1-5] Recent developments in molecular biology and genetic engineering are now giving new dimensions to research and development for future application to seedstock farm animals.

Historical Perspective

The first part of this developing technology actually occurred near the end of the nineteenth century, when the first live birth of mammalian offspring (rabbits) from embryo transfer was reported in the scientific literature in 1881.[6] In the original paper, Walter Heape, then a student at Cambridge University, surgically transferred two embryos (4-cell stage) from an Angora doe rabbit to the fallopian tube of a Belgian hare female that had been mated 3 hours previously by a Belgian hare male. On May 29, 1880, the Belgian hare gave birth to six live offspring. Four were from the Belgian × Belgian mating and two were albino, long-haired Angora transplant offspring, originating from the embryos of the Angora donor doe.

Unfortunately, the account of embryo transplantation in rabbits in the 1890s lay dormant in the research archives of the Royal Society of London for a number of years. Subsequently, other researchers became keenly interested in mastering this technique in other laboratory animals in hope of studying various aspects of mammalian developmental biology. During the progressing decades of the twentieth century (starting in the 1930s), embryo transplantation success was reported in laboratory mice, rats, hamsters, and guinea pigs, in addition to further embryo transfers in the domestic rabbit. As interest in this technique developed, other researchers conducted successful transfers with more exotic species such as the snowshoe hare, wild rabbit, mink, ferret, quokka, and wallaby. More recently, successful transplants have been reported with the gerbil, dog, cat, bighorn sheep, zebra, Przewalski's horse, bongo antelope, Indian gaur, water buffalo, eland, suni antelope, llama, and baboon. In 1978 the first in vitro fertilized human embryo baby was born in England as a result of autotransplantation by Drs. Steptoe and Edwards.[7] However, the first human embryo transplant baby (donor to a surrogate) was not born until February 1984 at the UCLA Medical Center in California. It has been very difficult to produce live offspring of subhuman primates using transfer techniques. It was only in 1989 that the first rhesus monkey transplant offspring was produced using nonsurgical collection and transfer techniques.[8,9]

Prior to the 1930s little effort was made to adapt embryo transplant procedures to domestic farm animals. The first established report of an offspring born after homologous embryo transfer in the domestic sheep or embryo reimplantation in the domestic goat was in Texas in 1934.[10] Subsequently, Warrick and Berry[11] in 1949 verified live offspring born after homologous embryo transfer and autotransfer in both the sheep and the goat. Although successful methods for producing viable swine embryo transplant offspring were first reported in the early 1960s in Europe and the United States,[12–14] the Russian scientist Kvasnickii has been given credit for producing the first successful embryo transplant offspring in swine in 1951.[15] The same year, researchers at the University of Wisconsin were the first to report a live offspring from surgical embryo transplantation in cattle.[16] This calf caused a great deal of excitement among researchers and cattle producers alike.

Success with equine embryo transplantation prior to the 1970s has not been verified in the scientific literature. Although there were some claims of equine embryo transfer some years earlier, they apparently were not well documented. In 1972 reproductive physiologists in Cambridge, England, used surgical collection and transfer techniques to produce the first donkey × mare hybrid offspring (mule) and the first stallion × donkey hybrid offspring (hinny) using donkey recipient females.[17] That same year a nonsurgical method was used for recovering embryos from domestic mares in Japan.[18] Using the same basic nonsurgical uterine flushing method, 18 fertilized ova were subsequently collected from 29 mares.[19] When 15 of the embryos were transplanted to recipient mares, six pregnancies producing embryo transplant offspring resulted. The first nonsurgical transfer of an embryo in the United States resulting in a live foal was reported in 1978 at Texas A&M University.[20]

Development of Nonsurgical Embryo Transfer Methodology

The development of nonsurgical collection and transfer techniques for applied use in cattle

embryo transplantation is now considered one of the major milestones in the commercial cattle embryo industry in North America. Historically, Mutter et al.[21] at the University of Kentucky are given credit for being the first to nonsurgically transfer a bovine embryo that produced a viable offspring in 1964. A single 16-cell embryo was collected from a cow's reproductive tract at slaughter and transferred by a small-bore cannula to a recipient female, resulting in a live embryo transplant calf. Prior to 1970, Sugie[22] of Japan was accredited with producing the only documented live embryo transplant calf that had been collected and transferred nonsurgically. Using specially designed equipment, Sugie reported in 1965 collecting and transferring 32 bovine embryos to recipient females, which resulted in the birth of one Holstein transplant offspring. During the late 1960s and early 1970s many other attempts were made to develop a practical and efficient procedure for nonsurgical embryo transplantation in cattle, but with little success.

In July 1976 a practical procedure for nonsurgically collecting bovine embryos using a flexible rubber catheter (transcervical) was independently reported by three different research groups.[23–25] Single embryo recoveries from nonstimulated donor females can similarly be executed using this procedure.[26] In addition to nonsurgical bovine recovery procedures, a nonsurgical embryo transplanting procedure for cattle using a bovine semen insemination apparatus was reported from Europe the same year.[27] With this procedure, a small synthetic rubber catheter (16–24 French) is inserted through the cervix of the donor cow and a phosphate-buffered saline medium is flushed through the uterus to harvest the embryos 6 to 8 days after mating (Fig. 22.1). This collection procedure is relatively simple and can be completed in 30 minutes or less without harm to the cow. After collection, the embryos are transplanted into recipient cattle using a nonsurgical transfer procedure that has been refined so that it now is similar to the standard artificial insemination (AI) procedure used by many cattle producers. Embryos (with holding medium) are individually placed in 0.25- or 0.50-ml semen straws and inserted directly into

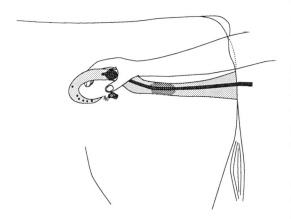

FIGURE 22.1. The standard method for nonsurgically collecting embryos from donor cattle. The method for collecting embryos is similar for horses; however, a surgical approach is used for embryo collection in sheep, goats, and swine.

the uterus of recipient cattle with the standard Cassou AI device. Similar to the procedure for AI, this nonsurgical method takes 10 minutes; however, with the nonsurgical embryo transfer a 7- to 8-day embryo is placed into the uterus of the female instead of semen at the time of estrus.

With the development of embryo transfer technology in the mid-1970s, cattle reproduction entered a new age of technical advancement. Prior to 1973 no more than 20 embryo transplant pregnancies had been produced by researchers, yet by 1976 there were 20 newly established units in North America. In 1976 the basic techniques for nonsurgical collection and transfer of bovine embryos became available to veterinarians and technicians in the cattle industry. The development of nonsurgical methods then made transplanting embryos a realistic possibility for cattle producers.

It has been estimated that up to 10,000 pregnancies resulted from cattle embryo transfer in 1978.[28] By the end of 1980 the number was estimated to have reached 20,000 annually.[29] The number and size of commercial transplant units increased, resulting in 35,000 or more pregnancies from cattle embryo transfer in 1982. To reduce the cost of producing transplant pregnancies, mobile transplant teams expanded this technology to fit on-the-farm situations, which stimulated nationwide usage of the procedure. It was estimated that 55,000 or more bovine pregnancies were achieved by the end of 1984. When the final tabulations for 1986 were in, this figure reached 100,000 embryo transplant pregnancies in North America alone. Current projections indicate that the number of transplant offspring will increase markedly in the years to come.

After the development of the basic nonsurgical techniques, embryo recovery percentages and posttransfer pregnancy rates were initially lower for these procedures than with the standard surgical approach to transplantation. However, refinement of techniques and technician experience have greatly improved success rates and have made transplanting embryos a meaningful part of cattle reproductive management, especially for the seedstock producers.

Today, with nonsurgical collection procedures, one would expect to harvest 75 to 95% of the resulting ova from an adequately stimulated, hormone-treated donor cattle. Usually 60 to 85% of the ova collected from inseminated beef or dairy donors will be fertilized. Often single ovum collection rates from unstimulated donors are greater than from superovulated cattle. With an experienced technician, one could expect a 50 to 75% pregnancy rate for viable embryos transferred nonsurgically to good-quality recipient animals. For neophytes lacking transfer experience, the results are often lower, even disastrous in some cases. There is little doubt that the development of nonsurgical collection and transfer technology was the largest single contributing factor to the rapid growth of the commercial embryo transplant business in North America today.

Nonsurgical collection and transfer procedures are also applicable to the horse but have not been developed for practical use in sheep, goats, and swine, likely due to the anatomic structure of these animals. Nonsurgical transfer procedures in the mare, however, are usually less successful than transferring equine embryos by the standard surgical method.

Embryos and Disease Transmission

In recent years the question has arisen, Does embryo transplantation spread animal diseases? Although there presently is not a wealth of information on the subject in the scientific literature, studies have been underway in this area in at least four research laboratories in North America. For an overall review of the potential for embryo disease transmission see recent reviews on this subject.[30-32] Findings thus far indicate that the zona pellucida of the early-stage farm animal embryo is a primary defense barrier against the invasion of pathogenic microorganisms. As long as the zona pellucida remains intact, the embryos of larger mammals are generally considered not to harbor transient pathogens under the zona pellucida at the time of transfer. Washing the intact embryos through a series of 10 washes with holding medium and a trypsin solution has been successful in removing pathogenic microorganisms on the surface of the zona pellucida in studies reported with the bovine embryo.

One bacterial disease of major concern to cattle owners in the United States is brucellosis. If proper embryo handling techniques are used, *Brucella abortus* should not be transmitted from seropositive donor females to transplant offspring or respective recipient animals using nonsurgical embryo transfer procedures.[33,34] These findings should offer encouragement to cattle producers considering embryo transfer as a means of saving valuable germ plasm seedstock that have become infected with the brucella organism.

Bovine viral diseases (e.g., blue tongue, foot and mouth, bovine viral diarrhea, bovine leukemia) are in the process of being evaluated under laboratory conditions for the potential of transmission with embryo transfer.[32] Results reported thus far suggest that none of the diseases investigated are transmitted when infected seropositive donor cattle are superovulated and the recovered embryos are properly transferred to seronegative recipient females. To ensure safe worldwide embryo import and export markets in the years to come, it is imperative that animal embryos not transport disease organisms from donors to recipients.

Freezing Farm Animal Embryos

In 1972 David Whittingham in England amazed the world when he produced the first mammalian offspring (mice) from embryos that had been frozen at −196°C in liquid nitrogen (LN_2).[35] The next year, Ian Wilmut reported the first calf born in the world from a frozen embryo at the Animal Physiology Research Unit in Cambridge, England.[36] This offspring, a healthy male, had been frozen as an embryo for 6 days in LN_2 before being thawed and transferred to a crossbred recipient cow. After this event, researchers all over the world began working diligently to develop an applied procedure for the livestock industry.

In 1978 the first frozen-thawed embryo transplant calf was born in the United States at Carnation Genetics, California. During 1980–1981 it was estimated that over 100 frozen embryo calves were born on ranches in the United States. A fivefold increase in the number was estimated for 1982, and in 1983 layman publications began carrying advertisements of both small and large commercial companies offering this service to the cattle industry. One estimate suggested that 21,000 frozen-thawed embryo transplant calves were born in North America in 1984. Although scientists still consider this technology to be in the developmental stages, it would appear that the future for freezing farm animal embryos is indeed promising.

The first frozen-thawed transplant lambs were produced in England during the mid-1970s,[37] and in 1982 the first reported frozen embryo lambs were born in the United States in Louisiana.[38] Today several commercial transplant units in the United States have incorporated this technology into their services for sheep producers. Live offspring were first produced from frozen-thawed goat embryos in Australia in 1976[39] and in the United States in 1986.[40] In 1982 the first frozen-thawed embryo foal was born to a recipient mare in

Japan,[41] and in 1983 Colorado State University reported the birth of the first frozen embryo transplant foal in North America.[42] Despite 15 years of effort by a multitude of researchers, the first live offspring from frozen-thawed swine embryos were not produced until August 1984, at Trans World Genetics in California (Genetic Engineering News, September, 1984). It was not until recently that Japanese scientists documented live births in the scientific literature from frozen-thawed porcine embryos.[43] At this stage, however, a repeatable freezing procedure for porcine embryos has not been verified by other laboratories and subsequently reported in the scientific literature. The high lipid content of individual blastomeres had been proposed as the major contributing factor to the poor success.

What are the success rates from frozen embryos? In cattle, for example, the pregnancy rates after nonsurgical transfer of frozen-thawed day 7 to day 8 embryos usually range between 30 and 55%. Some of the more experienced professionals have reported pregnancy rates approaching 70%. However, this success rate often requires a surgical paralumbar approach for embryo placement into the uterine horn of recipients. The transfer pregnancy rates decline dramatically when embryos earlier than the morula stage are frozen for subsequent transfer. Scientists generally are optimistic that success rates for transferred frozen-thawed bovine embryos will improve with continued basic research in cryobiology. Frozen-thawed embryo transfers in sheep, goats, and horses have been completed primarily in research studies, with some commercially transferred. However, pregnancy rates under field conditions have generally been less than the average rates after fresh embryo transfer in these species, especially with equine embryos. Recently it has been reported that freezing is more detrimental to the inner cell mass than to the trophoblast cells of equine blastocysts.[44] This is likely the reason why equine blastocysts may appear viable on visual assessment after thawing, but pregnancies often do not result from the transfer of these embryos to recipient mares.

Recent advances have refined various aspects of this freezing technology. A table-top freezing unit was developed in Louisiana that freezes embryos without the use of LN_2.[45,46] This unit uses a standard 110-volt electrical power source, and small thermoelectric cells in the cooling chamber to reduce the temperature of the embryos at a controlled rate (Fig. 22.2). Testing and evaluation of this new freezing method shows similar results to that of the standard LN_2 vapor freezing units now on the commercial market. Different embryo cryoprotective agents, such as glycerol and sucrose, are now being used in place of dimethylsulfoxide (DMSO) for freezing and thawing of farm animal embryos. Vital stains for embryos, such as fluorescein diacetate (FDA), are now being used to assess the viability of embryos before and after freezing.[47,48] These stains assist in detecting the highest-quality embryos for transfer to recipients. Various staining techniques have improved pregnancy rates when selecting frozen-thawed embryos for transplantation.

New culture systems (co-cultures) have been developed for holding embryos before and after freezing. Embryos are placed in culture medium (e.g., Ham's F-10) in wells of culture plates on a layer of cells (monolayer) and allowed to develop in vitro while being maintained in a temperature-controlled incubator. These monolayer cultures (fibroblasts or epithelial cells) are derived from endometrial cells collected at the abattoir from uterine tissues of fetal or adult females. Using a standard monolayer culture system, bovine embryos develop for 1 to 4 days in vitro with excellent viability.[49] Recent studies have shown that epithelial cells collected from the uterine lumen or the oviduct may be better for culturing embryos than fibroblasts from uterine origin.[50–53] In vitro culturing allows for careful post-thaw evaluation of questionable-quality embryos before selection is made for transfer.

A method of freezing embryos in semen straws has both the cryoprotectant and the rehydrating agent stored in the same unit when the embryo is frozen.[54–58] With this procedure (termed the one-step method), embryos can be removed from LN_2 storage, warmed, and

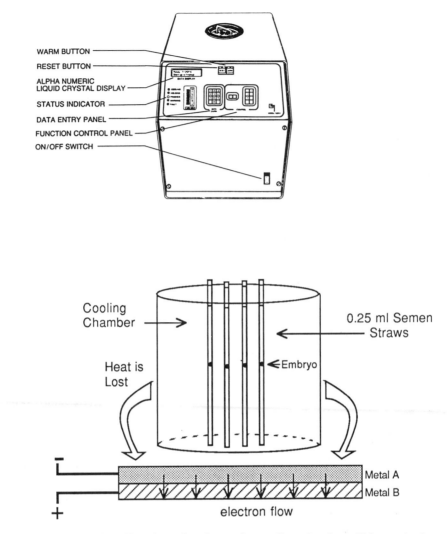

FIGURE 22.2. Thermoelectric cell embryo freezing unit. When voltage is applied (110 volts), electrons flow from metal A and metal B. When energy is lost by the metal, it becomes cooler, removing heat from the cooling chamber. This results in a controlled method for freezing embryos prior to storage in liquid nitrogen.[45]

placed directly into the uterus of the recipient cow with a Cassou AI device, similar to the methods used by producers to artificially inseminate their cattle with frozen-thawed semen.

Individual cattle embryos in a small amount of a cryoprotectant–buffer medium [e.g., glycerol and Dulbecco's phosphate-buffered saline (PBS)] are placed in 0.25-ml plastic semen straws, and the remainder of each straw is filled with a specific concentration sucrose–buffer solution. The cryoprotectant–buffer medium containing the embryo is separated from the sucrose–buffer solution by a small air bubble (Fig. 22.3). The embryo is maintained in position within the straw by a second air bubble. After freezing, the straws are stored in a LN$_2$ tank ($-196°C$) until suitable recipient females are available for transfer. Straws containing the embryos are then either thawed in warm water (e.g., 37°C) for 1 minute or allowed to thaw at room temperature in air. Each straw is then shaken briskly to move the thawed embryo from the cryoprotectant–

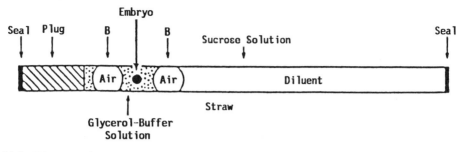

FIGURE 22.3. Diagram of a one-step, 0.25-ml straw containing the glycerol–buffer medium, an embryo, and the sucrose solution. Note the two air bubbles (B) used to separate the two solutions until the straw is briskly shaken to move the embryo into the sucrose solution prior to transfer.[56]

buffer medium into the diluted sucrose–buffer solution within the straw. The sucrose–buffer solution aids in rehydrating the embryo after thawing, and the warmth of the uterus brings the thawed embryo up to body temperature in the recipient female.

It has been estimated that well over 2,000 transplant calves resulting from this procedure have been born in the United States. Several modifications of this embryo handling method are now under evaluation. This one-step procedure eliminates the need for micropipettes, sterile dishes, a stereomicroscope, and handling of individual embryos before their transfer. There are no intermediate steps of opening the packaged unit and handling the embryos, as has been the case in the past. The thawing and transfer procedure is relatively simple, taking only a few minutes to complete. This packaging method will likely be the key to development of cattle frozen embryo banks in the future.

The Use of Embryo-Freezing Technology

The potential applications of freezing farm animal embryos have only recently been realized by the livestock industry. For example, transferring frozen-thawed embryos at the time of choice would dictate the season of the year when offspring would be born. Storing frozen embryos would allow producers to market out-standing females at production sales, or even to market the entire herd at peak prices. Freezing embryos would allow for disease testing while embryos were kept in quarantine, and would save valuable germ plasm by permitting storage of embryos from quarantined herds destined for slaughter (e.g., for brucellosis). Embryo freezing is beneficial when valuable donor females produce more embryos per collection than the number of recipients available on the day of transfer. Without freezing, these embryos are often discarded or in desperation placed in recipient animals that have virtually no chance for a successful pregnancy.

With the advent of national and international marketing of animal embryos, freezing and storing of embryos in LN_2 appears to be the method of choice. Thousands of embryos ($<200\,\mu m$ in diameter) can be placed in one small semen storage tank and shipped to seedstock owners worldwide. This could be accomplished for a mere fraction of the cost that it would take to transport live animals to similar destinations. Also, transplant offspring born from native surrogate females should gain acquired immunity from maternal transfer that imported adult animals would likely not possess.

With the new, one-step packaging method, the producer could purchase frozen embryos of choice from an embryo bank and, as the breeding season approaches, transplant them directly into the recipient cattle 7 or 8 days after estrus. This could be done in place of inseminating these females with frozen-thawed semen. A progressive rancher could establish a top-quality replacement herd in a reasonable length of time using this new embryo technology. Commercial embryo banks are now in existence for bovine embryos in both the United States and Europe.

Long-Term Storage of Frozen Gametes and Embryos

How long might farm animal embryos remain viable stored in LN_2? This question has yet to be fully answered. It has been reported that processed bull semen frozen in LN_2 for 30 years or more produced live viable calves when placed in the reproductive tract of suitable females. A healthy Holstein male calf was born from frozen bull semen in Wisconsin that was collected and processed at American Breeders Service on November 19, 1953 (Advanced Animal Breeder, August, 1984). The first calf produced in this country from frozen-thawed bull semen was born on May 29, 1953, in Janesville, Wisconsin. All indications are that if properly prepared and frozen, bovine sperm cells will remain viable as long as they are maintained in LN_2 at $-196°C$.

Studies in England were conducted to evaluate the viability of mouse embryos frozen in LN_2 for 5 to 10 years. Long-term storage of mouse embryos did not significantly reduce their viability when thawed and transferred to recipient mice.[59] Reports from commercial cattle transplant units indicate that bovine embryos frozen for 12 years in LN_2 have produced viable transplant calves. At this time there is no reason to believe that good-quality embryos, frozen under proper conditions, will be any less viable in long-term storage than frozen semen. Since the first frozen-thawed embryo transplant calf was only produced in 1973, it will be a matter of time before this question is answered fully. Most of the farm animal research in cryopreservation is focused on freezing both in vivo and in vitro matured oocytes. This approach would offer genetic opportunities never before realized in planned animal breeding programs. If the technology can be developed in the near future, frozen oocyte banks will surpass frozen embryo banks in popularity. The opportunity to freeze oocytes should not be overlooked in human-assisted fertility programs.

Natural Twinning in Farm Animals

The birth of dizygotic twins often occurs in sheep and goats and only very rarely in horses (1:500 to 1:1,000). Swine are litter-bearing animals, and both monozygotic and dizygotic twin offspring occur in dairy and beef cattle. The incidence of twin births generally tends to be slightly higher for dairy (1–7%) than for beef cattle (0.5–5%). It has been estimated that only 1 to 10% of all twin calves born are the result of an embryo's dividing into two similar parts during an early stage of gestation (monozygotic twins). It is likely that the occurrence of monozygotic twins in cattle is a random event rather than a hereditary trait. However, since dizygotic twins are the result of multiple ovulations, genetic involvement of the dam is likely associated with the production of such twin births. The total number of twins born in dairy herds can be affected by nutrition and season of the year.[60] The occurrence of a natural set of triplets (trizygotic) in domestic cattle is estimated to be 1:65,000 to 1:100,000 births.

In theory, the production of twins from single-ovulating farm animals (e.g., cattle) could be a method of improving reproductive efficiency. This approach has some merit and has been evaluated extensively in several countries (Ireland, Japan) that have a very small land area for agriculture. Seidel[2] indicated that approximately 70% of the nutrient intake of a mature beef female is used for body maintenance, and the remaining 30% is used for growth and maintenance of her fetus during pregnancy. Consequently, cattle carrying twin fetuses would tend to be more efficient in feed utilization per offspring produced, and make better use of available grazing acreage.

Micromanipulation of Embryos to Produce Multiple Offspring

The fertilized ovum of farm animals divides into two approximately equal-size blastomeres within hours after the sperm cell has entered the ovum. The 2-cell embryo then divides, producing duplicate cells in a systematic pattern, into 4 cells, 8 cells, and so on until it reaches the 64-cell or the 128-cell stage of development as morphologically undifferentiated embryonic cells. Shortly thereafter, a small blastocoele cavity forms in the center of this spherical mass of differentiating cells. The embryos of farm animals reach the blastocyst stage of development a little later than the embryos of laboratory animals, at 7 to 9 days after fertilization. As the blastocyst develops, two characteristic cell types become evident: the inner cell mass, which subsequently forms the fetus, and the trophectoderm layers, which contribute to the development of the fetal placenta. Unlike laboratory animals and humans, the earliest that any of the farm animals begin implantation is 12 days postfertilization for swine, extending to more than 35 days post-fertilization for horses.

Blastomere Separation

Early studies in mammalian embryo micromanipulation involved evaluation of the developmental potential of single blastomeres isolated from early-stage embryos of the rabbit,[61–63] rat,[64] and mouse.[65] These studies provided evidence that individual blastomeres of early-stage laboratory animal embryos (<8 cells) were totipotent, and that the potential existed for the production of multiple offspring from a single embryo.

Embryo micromanipulation to produce multiple transplant offspring is a newly developed technique in farm animals, which involves opening the zona pellucida around the blastomeres with a finely drawn glass needle and surgically dissecting the cell mass of the embryo into individual cells or embryo segments. Since each blastomere at the early stage of development is capable, in itself, of developing into individual animal offspring (totipotent),

this approach has been employed to produce identical twin, triplet, and quadruplet offspring from a single embryo in farm animals. In 1979 Steen Willadsen of Cambridge, England, was credited with a major breakthrough in farm animals when he produced the first live sets of identical twin offspring (lambs) from micromanipulation of early-stage sheep embryos using blastomere separation techniques.[66] Two years later he reported the birth of identical twins and a set of triplet calves from micromanipulation of early-stage bovine embryos.[67] Keen interest was generated from the birth of these embryo-engineered offspring, since researchers had been attempting this feat in farm animals for over 25 years without notable success.

A major barrier to the production of multiple offspring from early-stage embryos was the inability of precompaction-stage embryos to survive in vivo without an intact or near-intact zona pellucida. Evidence to this effect has been shown in the rabbit,[68] mouse,[69,70] pig,[71] and sheep.[72] The obstacle was later overcome by the development of an agar embedding technique for micromanipulated mammalian embryos.[66,73]

To produce identical offspring using microsurgery on sheep and cattle embryos, Willadsen used the nonpregnant sheep as an intermediate host for the micromanipulated embryos. Early-stage embryos were collected surgically from the donor and micromanipulated (blastomere separation), and then the agar-embedded blastomeres were transferred into the ligated oviducts of intermediate host sheep until they advanced to the late morula or blastocyst stage. At this time, the developing embryos were removed from the intermediate host and surgically or nonsurgically transferred to the respective host species recipients. This novel method of producing identical offspring in sheep, cattle, and the horse[73–76] is now considered a classic work. Using this procedure, five surgeries are needed on at least four different animals to obtain one set of genetically identical twin lambs from two recipient females. Unfortunately, this method for multiple offspring production from a single embryo requires a great deal of skill, time, and labor, and therefore was not readily accepted by the commercial livestock industry.

Embryo Splitting

In 1982 three research groups, one in France and two in the United States (Colorado and Louisiana), produced genetically identical twin calves by splitting single later-stage bovine embryos without the use of animal surgery or an intermediate host to serve as an incubator animal.[77-79] Subsequently, more in-depth studies with bovine morulae and blastocysts in Europe and the United States confirmed that bisecting embryos and transplanting resulting half-embryos (demi-embryos) produced respectable transplant pregnancy rates in recipient females.[80-88] This simplified approach includes nonsurgical transfer of micromanipulated embryos to recipient females with the use of a standard artificial insemination catheter. The development of this technique has recently made the production of genetically identical offspring by micromanipulation a reality to cattle producers the world over. Embryo collection, micromanipulation, and transfer to recipient females can be completed in a matter of an hour with this methodology.

The basic embryo-splitting procedure used in most physiology research laboratories is performed with two microinstruments made from soft glass microliter pipettes. The first microinstrument consists of a suction pipette with a fire-polished tip. This pipette has an inside diameter slightly smaller than that of the embryo and is used to hold the embryo stationary during the manipulation process. The second microinstrument is a finely drawn glass surgical needle used to bisect the embryo. The right and left arms of a commercial micromanipulator unit (e.g., Leitz) are used to mechanically reduce the coarse motions of the hands to very fine and exacting movements. The microinstruments are firmly attached to the arms of the micromanipulator unit, thus enabling the operator to perform minute dissection of the embryos as they are viewed under a stereomicroscope ($60-100\times$). The day 6 to day 8 bovine embryo (diameter 120–200 μm) used for embryo dissection is generally not visible to the naked eye.

Individual embryos are held in position for microsurgery under Dulbecco's PBS holding medium by a 1-ml syringe (creating slight negative pressure) attached by plastic tubing to the suction pipette. The fine glass surgical needle is then used to mechanically remove the acellular zona pellucida. This is done by making a rent, or cut, around 60% of the circumference (216°) of the zona pellucida. Once the embryo proper has been removed from the zona pellucida, the surgical needle is used to bisect the embryonic cell mass (on a vertical plane) into halves[80] (Fig. 22.4). Each of the resulting half-embryos can be reinserted either into the original zona pellucida or into another zona pellucida removed from an unfertilized ovum (e.g., cattle, swine). The half-embryos, either one or both of them, are then individually drawn into 0.25-ml french semen straws for nonsurgical transfer to recipient females. Subsequently, Mertes and Bondioli[88] suggested that using the glass surgical needle to bisect bovine embryos outside the zona pellucida[80] might have an advantage over bisecting the embryo with an ophthalmic blade or scalpel blade, as prescribed in the basic procedure developed by Colorado State University.[84]

Since the birth of genetically identical twin calves from later-stage embryos in 1982, 2,500 or more split-embryo transplant offspring have been born to recipient cows in North America. Today embryo splitting is being offered as a service to livestock producers by several commercial embryo transplant units in the United States and Canada. Usually a set charge ranging from $25 to $150 is placed on each embryo that is microsurgically divided into halves for transfer.

The results to date indicate that usually 45 to 65% of the half-embryos transferred to good-quality recipients result in pregnancies. Correspondingly, results from transferring whole embryos range from 50 to 75%. However, when these results are evaluated from the standpoint of the number of transplant offspring produced per number of embryos collected, 100 good-quality whole embryos

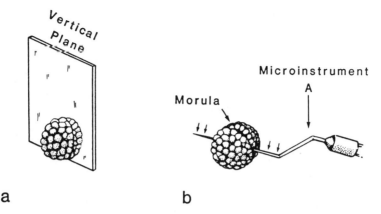

FIGURE 22.4. An early-stage bovine embryo (a morula) is bisected on a vertical plane. A flexible, fine glass needle (microinstrument) attached to the arm of a commercial micromanipulator unit is used to divide the embryo into halves while in holding medium.[80]

may result in 70 transplant offspring born, whereas 100 similar-quality embryos divided into halves would yield 200 half-embryos, which then may result in 110 split-embryo calves born, or a 110% pregnancy rate from 100 embryos. One should keep in mind that 100 recipient females would be needed for the 100 whole embryos, but 200 would be needed to transfer the half-embryos, if single births were desired.

Several years after the birth of identical twin calves from this new procedure, the first genetically identical twin lambs from bisected ovine embryos (morula and blastocyst stages) were reported in 1984 by Willadsen and Godke in England[89] and Gatica et al. in Ireland,[90] and more recently in Louisiana.[91] Split-embryo goat transplant twins were born in Japan,[92] and in 1986 in the United States.[93] In June 1984 the first set of identical twin foals resulted from a single equine split embryo (blastocyst stage) in Colorado,[94,95] and the first swine split-embryo transplant litter was born in Louisiana in August 1984.[96,97] More recently, live identical twin offspring have been produced after the dissection of domestic rabbit embryos.[98]

Producing embryo-engineered twin calves from early- or later-stage embryos will result in genetically identical offspring of the same sex. For cattlemen this would remove the concern for freemartinism, if both half-embryos were transferred to the same recipient female. In the initial studies with cattle, both micromanipulated half-embryos were transplanted into the same recipient. However, more recently a single half-embryo was placed in each recipient female without significantly reducing transplant pregnancy rates. In this case, the twin set would be produced by two different surrogate mothers. It is interesting to note that pregnancy rates have been similar when either a single half-embryo or two half-embryos have been nonsurgically transplanted into suitable recipient females. Apparently a viable bovine demi-embryo is capable of producing enough luteotropic factor to override the endogenous maternal luteolytic factor to maintain pregnancy in these recipient animals.

We have noted at our embryo laboratory that genetically identical split-embryo calves do not always have identical coat color patterns. This also was brought to our attention by concerned cattle owners who noted phenotypically different color patterns in sets of split-embryo twins born from bisected bovine embryos. Recently Seidel[99] confirmed these observations and suggested that coat color patterns form individually as the transplanted fetus develops in the uterus of the recipient female (an epigenetic effect).

As the fetus develops during the second trimester, millions of hair follicles are formed under the epidermal surface. Then melanoblast cells migrate away from the neural crest and invade the hair follicles as the cells ventrally migrate. These melanoblast cells change into melanocytes once they invade the hair follicles. The melanocytes are capable of producing melanin granules that are added to the hair as it grows, giving its characteristic color shades. In most cases there appear to be no specific genetic instructions as to which hair follicles are to be invaded by the melanoblast cells during migration. The only genetic instructions are related to the general rather than the specific migration pattern, giving a greater chance variation in coat color pattern, even with genetically identical twins. Therefore, the coat color patterns of identical twins (e.g., Simmental beef breed) would be very similar, but likely not identical. Even though their coat color patterns may not be phenotypically identical, split-embryo twin calves are considered to be genetically identical.

Embryo splitting of farm animals may have a far-reaching impact on the seedstock industry in the years to come. The possibility exists that one-half of a micromanipulated embryo could be transferred to a recipient and the remaining half could be frozen for use at a later date. If the offspring derived from the first half-embryo was of the quality the owner desired, the remaining half-embryo could then be thawed and transferred to another recipient to produce the remaining twin offspring, or possibly marketed as a sexed embryo with known genetic and phenotypic characteristics. The possibility also exists that the first half-embryo transplant female could serve as the recipient for the remaining frozen half-embryo of the pair. The half-embryo female could carry its identical twin sister to term, serving as its mother as well as its sister. This feat is not out of the realm of possibility, since fresh and frozen-thawed twins have already been produced from two portions of a sheep embryo, one half used as a fresh transfer and the other as a frozen-thawed transfer.[73,100]

Cattle have produced live offspring after embryo transfer of frozen-thawed half-embryos.[101] This technology may offer numerous opportunities to expand procedures for progeny testing of full sibs, evaluating undesirable recessive traits, studying maternal uterine influence on offspring, and performance testing sires. Frozen-thawed bovine demi-embryos have now produced viable transplant offspring at commercial cattle transplant units in North America. Commercial bull studs have become interested in this technology for potential use in their young sire evaluation programs. In addition, with the increase in the number of superior quality dairy goats in North America during the last 15 years, embryo engineering and transplant technology should not be overlooked as a tool in the reproductive management of caprine seedstock.[102]

In a subsequent study, later-stage embryos (late morulae) from a beef donor female were split into half-embryos, then carefully dissected in quarters by microsurgery. In February 1984 the first live quarter-embryo calves were produced from separate surrogate mothers.[103,104] All four quarter-embryos were transferred nonsurgically, and two live, genetically identical, twin heifer calves were born. Some success also occurred ($\leq 25\%$) with in vitro production of bovine blastocysts from bisecting developing blastocysts derived from half-embryos.[105,106] Unfortunately, embryo loss was too great from this approach to make this procedure practical at the present time. In this laboratory it has been noted that each time the bovine embryo is bisected, the resulting demi-blastocysts that develop in vitro have approximately one-half the cell number and size as the intact control blastocysts maintained under the same culture conditions. A quarter-embryo blastocyst would be one-half the size of a half-embryo blastocyst during the same culture interval. As the developing blastocyst becomes smaller in mass (cell number at the time of blastulation), the overall potential for producing viable conceptus after transfer is subsequently reduced. This same observation was made some years ago with the developing mouse blastocyst.[107] Further studies are needed to improve the efficiency of this procedure for farm animal embryos.

In an effort to improve the efficiency of the embryo splitting procedure, Rorie et al.[108] in this laboratory developed a simplified, less costly technique for bisecting farm animal embryos. With this simplified procedure, a double-edged razor blade is used in place of the glass microinstruments and the commercial embryo micromanipulation unit for making half-embryos from later-stage embryos. The Louisiana State University (LSU) razor blade technique can be performed on either morulae or blastocysts (e.g., days 6–8 bovine embryos) with an intact zona pellucida or with embryos with the zona removed with a pronase solution prior to bisection.[109] Results indicate embryos bisected with the hand-held razor blade are as viable as similar-quality embryos bisected with the standard glass needle method. Using this new procedure for bisection has made embryo splitting more practical for in-field use and thus less costly for livestock producers already participating in an embryo transplant program.

Another study reported that when later-stage bovine morulae and blastocysts were bisected into half-embryos, they did not have to be replaced into an empty zona pellucida before being transferred to recipient cattle.[32] Results to date indicate that zona-free and zona-encased demi-embryos produce similar transplant pregnancy rates in beef cattle recipients. It is interesting to note that occasionally when a later-stage bovine half-embryo is nonsurgically transferred either with a large rent in the zona pellucida or without a zona pellucida, it divides, also producing a set of genetically identical twins. During the last 2 years this embryo splitting in utero has happened with bovine and ovine embryos in our laboratory. In these known cases, three transplant offspring developed from a single pair of twin demi-embryos (one half-embryo transferred to each of two recipient females). If half-embryos (from later-stage morulae) were transplanted without a zona pellucida, and this frequently resulted in twin offspring from each demi-embryo in utero, the existing embryo splitting procedure would be more efficient for on-the-farm use by livestock producers.

Embryo Sexing

From both the research and the applied viewpoints, the possibilities of developing new procedures using microsurgery and micromanipulative techniques with farm animal embryos appear to be endless. In addition, other new laboratory procedures and techniques, supplemental to basic micromanipulation, will likely be developed to aid embryo engineering research and enhance the commercial embryo transfer industry in the coming years. One possibility is to be able to sex embryos before their transfer to recipient females.[29] During the last 14 years most attempts at sexing bovine embryos have been with chromosome analyses (e.g., karyotyping) on cells extracted from the embryo proper.[110–113] These procedures are time-consuming, tedious, and require a well-trained technician to give meaningful results. Although several research laboratories have had respectable results with karyotyping and then transferring sexed bovine embryos, most commercial transplant units that have used this approach indicate that the extra handling involved with this sexing procedure lowers transplant pregnancy rates.

With increased interest in embryo freezing technology and micromanipulation, attempts are intensifying to make embryo sexing a simple and efficient procedure for use in commercial embryo transplant stations. Researchers have been carefully evaluating H-Y antibodies for sex determination of mammalian embryos.[114–117] In a review of the subject, Ohno[118] indicated that a histocompatibility antigen (H-Y antigen) was present in or on the surface of male cells of those mammals evaluated, but that it was not found to be associated with corresponding female cells. With this in mind, researchers then developed specific antibodies to the male H-Y antigen (primarily of the IgM subclass) in the hope of devising a method of identifying male and female embryos immediately after donor collection.

Most approaches evaluated have used a fluorescent-labeled H-Y antibody so the sexing procedure can be completed while viewing the embryos under a laboratory microscope. Progress in this area, however, has been slower than expected. Success in sexing embryos with the H-Y antibody technique has been reported in mice, sheep, swine, cattle, and recently horses.[119] An earlier report[117] suggested that fluorescent H-Y antibody techniques would be a useful tool in bovine embryo sex determination in the future. Today there are continued claims of embryo-sexing antibodies and/or embryo-sexing kits for cattle being evaluated under field transplant conditions; however, these have yet to reach the commercial market for use by the livestock industry. Most of the research efforts with farm animal embryos today revolve around developing a Y-specific DNA probe to detect male embryos.[120] With a specific probe, the embryo could be bisected, sex determination made on one demi-embryo, and the remaining demi-embryo transferred to the recipient. Developing an efficient embryo-sexing procedure for farm animals is a priority for embryo engineering research.

Genetic Engineering—Its Potential for Farm Animals

Genetic engineering has recently been re-defined for animals as those technologies that induce direct changes in genetic materials (genes) or genetic frequencies (genotype), or that change life history characteristics of individuals or the genetic material (gametes) produced by that individual.[3] In recent years the definition has had to be redefined to include aspects of the new technology that were never before thought possible by the scientific community.

Chimeric Embryos

Efforts have been made with farm animal models to incorporate the cells (blastomeres) of two different embryos together in vitro to form one embryo with more than two parents. An offspring produced in this way is called a chimera. In 1982 Steen Willadsen verified his earlier studies[100,121] and that of Tucker et al.[122] showing that chimeric offspring could be produced by aggregating blastomeres from two or more sheep embryos (e.g., from two or more breeds) into one embryo. The offspring

produced following the surgical transfer of these embryos are called intraspecies chimeras. Subsequently in the United States later-stage chimeric sheep embryos (two breed types) were microsurgically constructed by either blastomere aggregation[123] or inner cell mass microinjection techniques[124,125] to produce viable ovine chimeric transplant offspring.

In 1981 Willadsen produced the first chimeric bovine offspring using multiple blastomeres from embryos of two cattle breeds in England. Attempts have also been made to produce *Bos taurus/Bos indicus* chimeric calves using an inner mass cell-injection technique.[126] Although seven transplant calves were born in this study, none were overtly chimeric. One calf, however, did have tissues that gave some evidence of being chimeric. More recently Brem et al.,[127] Rorie et al.,[128] and Pool et al.[129] have reported the birth of viable overt chimeric offspring produced by aggregation of later-stage bovine embryos of domestic cattle breed types (Fig. 22.5). Preliminary observations on the early stages of life of the intraspecies chimeric farm animals suggest they may have some growth or production advantage over individuals of either of the two parent breeds. These observations need to be verified. This area of research appears to offer a multitude of opportunities to study and evaluate animal development and growth patterns.

It should not be overlooked that the idea of producing chimeric or tetraparental embryos was developed some years earlier for laboratory animals.[130] Early techniques for chimeric embryo production in mice included both blastomere aggregation[131,132] and micro-injection of inner cell mass cells of one genotype into the inner cell mass of a blastocyst of a second genotype.[133,134] The in vitro development of microsurgically derived intraspecies allophenic (chimeric) embryos has allowed researchers a unique opportunity to study early-stage embryo development in the mouse.[135,136] Intraspecies chimeric offspring have also been produced in the laboratory rat[64,137] and the rabbit.[138–140] More recently, a new simplified procedure has been developed for producing viable transplant offspring from chimeric rabbit

Aggregation Chimera

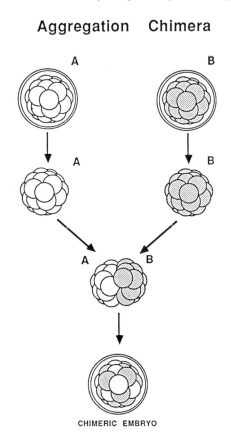

FIGURE 22.5. Using embryo micromanipulation and blastomere aggregation of individual morulae from two different donor animals to make a chimeric embryo.

embryos (morulae),[141,142] and a novel approach has been reported to produce intraspecies chimeric mouse embryos by injecting the inner cell mass into a large trophoblastic vesicle derived from microsurgically engineered blastocyst formed by the aggregation of multiple compact morula-stage embryos.[143]

Research confirms that embryos of animals from two different species (sheep and goat) can be aggregated into one embryo to produce an interspecies chimera. The first viable sheep-goat chimera (male) was reported by Fehilly et al.[144] from England in 1984. West German researchers subsequently duplicated this feat with sheep-goat embryos and produced live transplant offspring.[145] Attempts have been made at producing horse-donkey reconstruct-

ed embryos, but no live offspring have been reported[146] New simplified methods have been tried for producing sheep-goat chimeras by introducing sheep-goat hybrid inner cell mass into an ovine embryo (blastocyst).[147,148] In a recent report, Rorie et al.[149] described a simplified procedure for micromanipulation and reconstruction of blastocysts to facilitate reciprocal inner cell mass transfers and chimeric embryo production using a microscalpel, a culture dish, and a glass microinjection pipette. With this microsurgical procedure sheep-goat chimeric offspring were produced, and healthy lambs were born with a goat placenta to a goat recipient female at this station in 1989. This method is easy to learn and only takes several minutes to construct an allophenic embryo.

Inner Cell Mass Transfers Between Embryos

A new technique developed for farm animals in Cambridge, England, is the transfer of the cells that form the embryo (inner cell mass cells), using micromanipulation techniques, to another embryo of that species or to another species. If successfully completed, the embryo that has received the inner cell mass cells (by microsurgery and/or microinjection) will develop normally when transferred to a recipient. The beauty of this method is that the placental membranes will develop from the trophectoderm of the second embryo and the fetus will develop from the inner cell mass of the first embryo (Fig. 22.6). This would allow the genetically engineered embryo to be placed in a recipient female of the second embryo's breed type (or species) to ensure an optimum environment for placental membrane attachment. However, the developing fetus would originate from the first embryo.

For example, the sheep and goat (two different animal species) could be used as embryo donor females. When a sheep embryo is transferred to a female goat or a goat embryo is transferred to a female sheep, the embryo does not develop to term. If the inner cell mass of

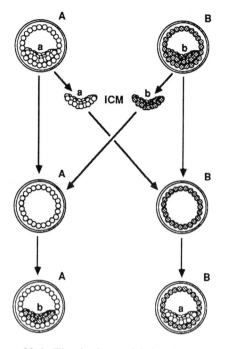

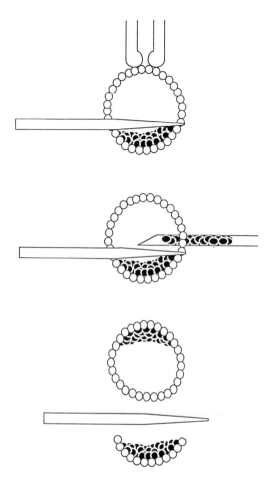

FIGURE 22.6. The basic model for the construction of reciprocal inner mass cell (ICM) transfers
from two different blastocysts. The first embryo is
derived from the ICM cells (b) and the corresponding placental tissue is derived from the trophoblast
cell (A). In the reciprocal, the second embryo is
derived from ICM cells (a) and the corresponding
placental tissue is derived from the trophoblast
cells (B).

FIGURE 22.7. A new method used for inner cell mass
transfer procedure between blastocysts. The foreign
ICM is placed in the blastocoelic cavity of the host
blastocyst, and the host ICM is then microsurgically
removed.[149]

the sheep embryo was microsurgically removed
and placed in the goat embryo, the composite
embryo could then be transferred to a goat
recipient. The chance for an offspring to be
produced from this composite embryo would
be greatly enhanced, since the placental membranes that developed from this embryo would
be derived from the original goat embryo. In
this procedure the goat inner cell mass could
then be placed in the remaining trophectoderm
cells of the sheep embryo, and this composite
embryo could be transferred to a female sheep
recipient. The end result would be an interspecies transfer of two embryos, with the goat
giving birth to a lamb and the ewe giving
birth to a goat. This laboratory produced
viable lambs from a goat recipient using this
new inner mass cell transfer procedure (Fig.
22.7).[149] The recipient goat accepted, nursed,

and raised the transplant lambs as if they were
her own natural offspring.

This new technique could be put to use in
saving some of our endangered species, where
more abundant recipient species could carry
the embryos of endangered species to term.
Examples might include rare Indian gaur cattle
embryos placed in domestic cattle or embryos
of the rare Przewalski's horse placed in domestic quarter horse mare recipients. Requests are
being put forth by zoological societies the
world over to help them develop ways to use
the inner cell mass transfer procedures to
engineer embryos of exotic mammals.

Fertilization Using Sperm Cell Microinjection

Several research groups in the United States and abroad have been attempting to develop techniques to produce offspring from micro-injection of sperm cells into unfertilized ova.[150–153] The idea of mechanically fertilizing ova with individual sperm cells has intrigued scientists for decades. The original idea was to microinject sperm cells into sperm-activated ova. Using this first approach, the ovum would be activated by a single sperm cell during either the in vivo or the in vitro fertilization process, after which the activated ovum would be subjected to a microinjection procedure to introduce a second sperm cell. The genetic material from the first male's sperm cell (male pronucleus) would be removed from the ovum with a fine microsuction needle, allowing the genetic material from the female and the sperm cell of the second male to join at syngamy to form a mechanically fertilized 1-cell embryo.

Using basic sperm microinjection techniques in more recent studies, full-term conceptus development and live offspring have been reported in laboratory mice,[154] and live off-spring were produced by the microinjection of sperm cells into the ooplasm of rabbit ova.[155,156] Using improved methodologies, such as hypertonic medium (0.5 M sucrose) to increase the perivitelline space and electrofield induction, the success rate of oocyte activation in the rabbit has markedly improved.[157–159]

The possibility now exists that sperm cell microinjection techniques can be developed for unfertilized ova of cattle.[160] Success has been reported for in vitro fertilization (IVF) and normal cleavage of in vitro-matured cattle oocytes after sperm cell microinjection of in vitro-capacitated bovine sperm cells.[161] More recently, sperm cell microinjection of bovine oocytes has resulted in live transplant offspring in Japan. With recent improvement of in vitro oocyte maturation and sperm cell maturation methods, IVF rates of bovine oocytes without the use of microinjection would now be expected to be above 85%.[162] Identifying appropriate in vitro embryo culture

systems for IVF-derived embryos seems to be one of the major drawbacks to efficient IVF procedures in farm animals at the present time.

By using a partial zona-renting technique (partial zona dissection) to facilitate sperm passage and fresh ejaculated human sperm cells for IVF, pregnancies and live births have recently resulted from human oocytes.[163–165] Pregnancies also have resulted from the injection of multiple, acrosome-reacted sperm cells into the perivitelline space of human ova.[166] Using a subzonal insemination procedure (SUZI) and the transfer of multiple sperm cells, six IVF babies were recently reported in Rome.[167] In an effort to improve zona-renting technology, a laser microbeam from a dye-tuned, compact nitrogen laser was used to make a small opening in the zona pellucida of bovine and murine oocytes and embryos.[168] Although the method was successful at a wave-length of 440 nm, the acridine orange stain used to activate the laser beam for microsurgery at the zona surface was found to be detrimental to subsequent in vitro development of the laser-exposed embryos. Further studies in this area are needed to evaluate the feasibility of this approach.

The possibility exists that freeze-dried sperm cells could be used to fertilize farm animal oocytes with sperm cell microinjection techniques in the future. It is interesting to note that at least two calves have been born after oocyte fertilization with previously dried bovine sperm cells.[169–170] Certainly the potential for using this technology with freeze-dried sperm cells or with DNA extracted from preserved sperm cells from extinct animals to produce new embryos merits reevaluation by the scientific community.

In the new oocyte activation approach now under consideration, two sperm cells would be injected into an ovum and the female genetic material (female pronucleus) would then be removed with a microsuction needle, leaving the genetic material of the two sperm cells to form a developing embryo (androgenesis). The two sperm cells could be from one male or from two different males (Fig. 22.8). With this theoretical approach, it is expected that two-thirds of the offspring would be males and one-

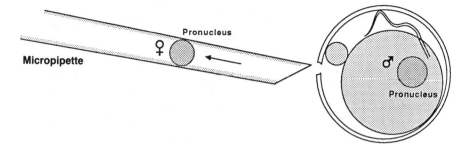

Removal of Female Pronucleus from a Sperm-Activated Ovum

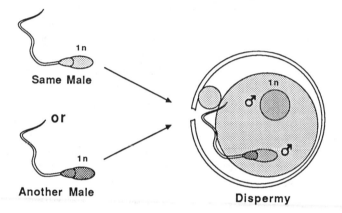

Sperm Injection or In Vitro Fertilization

FIGURE 22.8. A model for producing animal embryos from two sperm cells from one male or two different males without input from the female genome.

third females. The possibilities of producing an offspring from two males or from two sperm cells from the same male (and no female genome) could revolutionize the bull stud industry. A classic study using the mouse gamete model suggested that this approach may not be feasible for mammals any time in the future.[171]

Embryonic Cloning (Nuclear Transplantation)

Embryonic cloning (nuclear transplantation) in mammals as we know it today involves the fusion of a single blastomere from an early-

stage embryo with the vitelline membrane of an enucleated, unfertilized ovum (Fig. 22.9). After the blastomere containing a 2n zygotic nucleus is transferred to the ooplasm of an enucleated ovum, the blastomere nucleus re-initiates embryonic development at the appropriate stage to produce a reconstructed embryo that develops in a normal manner. This nuclear reprogramming seems to occur up to the time of early embryonic cell differentiation in ovine and bovine embryos. Willadsen[172] suggested that nuclear-reprogrammed embryos would, therefore, produce offspring similar to those transplant offspring derived from individually separating blastomeres at the 2-, 4-, and 8-cell stages of development. Successful nuclear

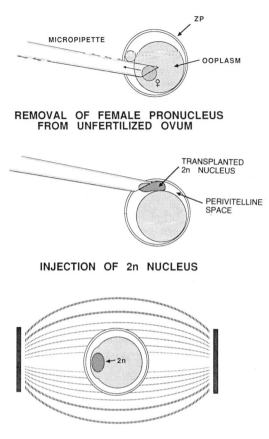

REMOVAL OF FEMALE PRONUCLEUS
FROM UNFERTILIZED OVUM

INJECTION OF 2n NUCLEUS

ELECTROFUSION

FIGURE 22.9. Method used for nuclear transfer to produce embryonic clones using farm animal embryos.

transfers have been recently reported for laboratory mice[173-175] and rabbits.[176] The first embryonic cloned lambs were reported by Willadsen in 1986,[177] and he produced the first embryonic cloned bovine offspring while conducting experiments in Texas later that year. Further success at producing nuclear transplant calves has been reported by Prather et al.[178] and Bondioli et al.[179] at the Granada Genetics research unit in Texas.

Nuclear transplantation offers the opportunity for livestock owners to produce multiples of genetically identical offspring from a single, genetically superior embryo. A single 16-cell embryo could theoretically produce 16 offspring using nuclear transfer. Recently, researchers at Granada Genetics research unit

have been able to recycle the nuclear material from nuclear transfer embryos to produce live offspring from the third-generation recycled embryos. This offers potential for embryo engineering to produce vast numbers of offspring from a valuable donor female.[179,180]

With the basic procedure described by Willadsen[172,177] for farm animals, a blastomere of a 4-, 8-, or 16-cell embryo, and in some cases a 32-cell embryo, is placed adjacent to the cytoplasmic membrane of an enucleated ovum using a simple direct microinjection technique. In sheep and cattle, the cytoplasm of the blastomere (along with the 2n nucleus) is combined with the ooplasm of the enucleated ovum by fusing adjacent plasma membranes with electrically induced fusion. As the reconstructed embryos begin to develop, they are placed either in an intermediate host (e.g., rabbit or sheep oviduct) or in an embryo coculture system to develop to morulae or blastocysts before transfer to recipient females. In cattle this transfer is made as a single embryo using a nonsurgical approach between days 6 and 8 of the recipient estrous cycle.

The production of multiple offspring from individual embryos has the potential not only for amplifying superior genetics in livestock but also for providing valuable animals for research. It has been suggested that the genetic uniformity of these monozygotic animals could permit the number of animals per experiment needed for research to be reduced while maintaining the same level of statistical validity.[181]

Gene Insertion into Embryos

This area of research surfaced in 1981 and has subsequently become one of the leading developmental areas for commercial genetic engineering companies in North America. The basic approach to gene injection or insertion involves taking genetic material (genes) and, with microinjection techniques, placing this material (usually synthesized or from another species) near or into the pronuclei of recently sperm-penetrated ova in the process of in vitro fertilization.[182] These DNA-injected embryos are then transplanted into recipient animals. If the DNA material becomes incorporated into the 2n nucleus, the resulting transplant offspring then will have the potential of genetically altered capability at some time during their own life. A classic study in 1981 reported that a DNA sequence controlling the production of hemoglobin in the rabbit was injected into the male pronuclei of recently sperm-activated mouse ova.[183] When the transplant mice were born they were able to produce rabbit hemoglobin in addition to mouse hemoglobin for their red blood cells. Even more important to the future of this transgenic technique was that some of the natural born offspring of these genetically engineered mice were able to produce rabbit hemoglobin, implying that this was a heritable characteristic for these mice.[183] Subsequently, Wagner et al.[184] suggested that genes could be introduced into sperm-activated ova of farm animals to produce transgenic embryo transplant offspring.

New genetic engineering companies have been working to isolate and identify specific genes and then duplicate them in the molecular biology laboratory. Scientists are now looking into ways of inserting these man-made genes into activated ova and embryos of farm animals. For example, some researchers are evaluating the possibility of incorporating the growth hormone (GH) gene into swine, sheep, and cattle ova. If the genetic material introduced into the activated ova becomes incorporated in the nuclear DNA, the possibility exists that the GH gene could be activated to stimulate rapid growth as these offspring develop en route to maturity. Successful incorporation and expression of the GH gene has already been reported for embryo transplant mice.[185]

Daily injections of GH have resulted in 10% or greater increase in milk production in dairy cows.[186,187] If the GH gene could be incorporated into the nuclear material of dairy cattle embryos, milk production might be increased, if gene expression occurred during lactation. This could eliminate the need for daily exogenous administration of GH for the lactating dairy cow. Research is needed to explore this possibility.

The first extensive attempt at producing transgenic farm animals was with ovine and porcine sperm-activated oocytes. The most notable success resulted when transgenic pigs expressed an exogenous GH gene at the USDA Research Laboratory in Beltsville.[188] These animals had increased circulatory levels of GH, but they did not increase in body stature over the control animals. As the animals matured, they had increased physical/structural problems that have been attributed to the supplementary increase in GH production from the foreign gene. Some limited success with gene insertion was also reported by these authors for rabbits and sheep, but the incorporation efficiency was extremely low.[188] Researchers in New Zealand, Australia, the United Kingdom, and the United States have continued with serious efforts to produce transgenic farm animals during the last 7 years. However, progress has been much slower than expected.

Other genes with the potential to be used in farm animal genetic engineering research are now being identified and evaluated. Davis et al.[189] described the ovine Booroola gene that affects ovulation rate in sheep. When this gene is present and expressed in Australian merino ewes, ovulation and multiple lambing rates increase in the flock. In a subsequent report, another gene(s), now referred to as the Spearow gene, was identified that is involved in increasing ovulation rates up to sixfold in mice.[190] Possibly, the Booroola gene could be incorporated into ovine embryos of single-ovulating sheep breeds in the hope of increasing ovulation rates of ewes in subsequent generations. The Spearow or similar genes should not be overlooked for their potential to increase the ovulation rate and the number of offspring produced in single and litter-bearing animals. Several research groups have gene-injected embryo transplant pregnancies now underway in swine and cattle in North America.

For the livestock producer, gene insertion techniques now offer a unique approach to animal breeding strategies with the introduction of selected gene sequences into either genomic or embryonic DNA prior to embryo transfer. In the future, genetically engineered animal herds may produce biomedically important compounds for use by humans. These life-giving compounds (e.g., selected peptides, proteins) could then be harvested from the body tissue, serum, or milk produced by these transgenic animals. Human clotting factor IX and α_1-antitrypsin have been produced and identified in the milk secretions of transgenic mice and sheep,[191] and just recently in pigs. This new technology certainly offers a great deal of potential for future research.

This area of research is but one example of many advances now being made in animal reproductive technology. There appears to be a very short lag-time between discovery and implementation in this area of animal agriculture. In the months and years to come, we will probably see farm animals that express incorporated genes, true embryonic clones produced from a multitude of animals, and diseased or genetically defective animals treated with gene therapy. Animal reproductive technology is truly entering a new era.

References

1. Bradford GE, Kennedy BW. Genetic aspects of embryo transfer. Theriogenology 1980; 13:13–26.
2. Seidel GE Jr. Superovulation and embryo transfer in cattle. Science 1981;211:351–358.
3. Rutledge JJ, Seidel GE Jr. Genetic engineering and animal production. J Anim Sci(Suppl 2) 1983;57:265–272.
4. Dickerson GE, Willham RL. Quantitative genetic engineering of more efficient animal production. J Anim Sci 1983;57:248–264.
5. Humes PE, Godke RA. Genetic impact of embryo transfer in beef cattle. Proc Conf Artif Insem Embryo Transf Beef Cattle, NAAB, Denver, CO 1985:38–44.
6. Heape W. Preliminary note on the transportation and growth of mammalian ova within a uterine foster mother. Proc Royal Soc B 1891; 48:457–458.
7. Steptoe PC, Edwards RG. Birth after the reimplantation of a human embryo. Lancet 1978;2:366.
8. Goodeaux LL, Anzalene MK, Webre MK, Graves KH, Voelkel SA. Nonsurgical technique for flushing the Macaca mulatta uterus. J Med Primatol 1990;19:59–67.
9. Goodeaux LL, Anzalone CA, Thibodeaux JK, Menezo Y, Roussel JD, Voelkel SA. The birth of a live Macaca mulatta from a nonsurgically collected and transferred embryo. Lab Primate Newsletter 1990;29:12–13.
10. Warwick BL, Berry RO, Horlacher WR. Results of mating rams to Angora female goats. Proc 27th Ann Mtg Amer Soc Anim Prod 1934:225–227.
11. Warwick BL, Berry RO. Inter-generic and intra-specific embryo transfers. J Hered 1949; 40:297–303.
12. Hancock JL, Hovell GJR. Egg transfer in the sow. J Reprod Fertil 1962;4:195–201.
13. Vincent CK, Robison OW, Ulberg LC. A technique for reciprocal embryo transfer in swine. J Anim Sci 1964;23:1084–1088.
14. Smidt D, Steinback J, Scheven B. Modified method for the in vivo recovery of fertilized ova in swine. J Reprod Fertil 1965;10:153–156.
15. Kvasnickii AV. Interbreed transplantation of ova. Sovetsk Zooteh 1951;1:36–42. Animal Breeding Abstracts 1951;19:224.
16. Willet EL, Black WG, Casida LE, Stone WH, Buckner PJ. Successful transplant of a fertilized bovine ovum. Science 1951;113:247.
17. Allen WR, Rowson LEA. Transfer of ova between horses and donkeys. Proc Eighth Internatl Congr Anim Reprod Artif Insem, Munich 1972;1:483–488.
18. Oguri N, Tsutsumi Y. Non-surgical recovery of equine eggs, and an attempt at nonsurgical egg transfer in horses. J Reprod Fertil 1972;31: 187–195.
19. Oguri N, Tsutsumi Y. Non-surgical egg transfer in mares. J Reprod Fertil 1974;41:313–320.
20. Vogelsang SG, Sorensen AM Jr, Kraemer DC. Fertility of donor mares following nonsurgical collection of embryos. J Anim Sci (Suppl 1) 1978;47:397.
21. Mutter LR, Graden AP, Olds D. Successful non-surgical bovine transfer. AI Digest 1964; 12:3.
22. Sugie T. Successful transfer of a fertilized bovine egg by nonsurgical techniques. J Reprod Fertil 1965;10:197–201.
23. Drost M, Brand A, Aarts MH. Device for non-surgical recovery of bovine embryos. Theriogenology 1976;6:503–507.
24. Elsden RP, Hasler JF, Seidel GE Jr. Nonsurgical recovery of bovine eggs. Theriogenology 1976;6:523–532.
25. Rowe RF, Del Campo MR, Eilts CL, French LR, Winch WP, Ginther OJ. A single cannula for nonsurgical collection of ova from cattle. Theriogenology 1976;6:471–483.
26. Baker BA, Guillory BM, Abdulla GJ, Godke RA. A technique for nonsurgical collection of single ovulated bovine embryos. Proc Louisiana Acad Sci 1979;42:76.

27. Brand A, Drost M, Aarts MH, Gunnink JW. Device for nonsurgical transfer of bovine embryos and its effect on uterine contamination. Theriogenology 1976;6:509–514.

28. Seidel GE Jr, Seidel SM. Bovine embryo transfer: Costs and success rates. Adv Anim Breeder 1978;26:6–10.

29. Seidel GE Jr. Management of reproduction of cattle in the 1990's. Proc 1979 Carl B and Florence E King Visiting Scholar Lectures. University of Arkansas, Fayetteville, AK, Special Report No. 77:51–59.

30. Eaglesome MD, Hare WCD, Singh EL. Embryo transfer: A discussion on its potential for infectious diseases control based on a review of studies on infection of gametes and early embryos by various agents. Can Vet J 1980;21:106–112.

31. Archbald LF, Godke RA. What are the risks for transmission of disease with embryo transfer? Proc Conf Artif Insem Embryo Transf Beef Cattle, NAAB, Denver, CO 1984:41–46.

32. Singh EL. Disease transmission: Embryo-pathogen interactions in cattle. Proc Tenth Internatl Congr Anim Reprod Artif Insem, June 10–14, University of Illinois, Urbana, IL 1985;4:17–24.

33. Stringfellow DA, Howell VL, Schnurrenberger PR. Investigations into the potential for embryo transfer from Brucella abortus infected cows without transmission of infection. Theriogenology 1982;18:733–743.

34. Voelkel SA, Stuckey KW, Looney CR, Enright FM, Humes PE, Godke RA. An attempt to isolate *Brucella abortus* from uterine flushings of brucellosis-reactor donor cattle. Theriogenology 1983;19:355–366.

35. Whittingham DG, Leibo SP, Mazur P. Survival of mouse embryos frozen to −196°C and −269°C. Science 1972;178:411–414.

36. Wilmut I, Rowson LEA. Experiments on the low temperature preservation of cow embryos. Vet Rec 1973;92:686–690.

37. Willadsen SM, Polge C, Rowson LEA, Moor RM. Preservation of sheep embryos in liquid nitrogen. Cryobiology 1974;11:560.

38. Sims DR, Voelkel SA, Looney CR, Humes PE, Godke RA. Transplant lambs born from frozen embryos. Louisiana Agric 1982;25(4):4–5.

39. Bilton RJ, Moore NM. In vitro culture, storage and transfer of goat embryos. Australian J Biol Sci 1976;29:125–129.

40. Pendleton RJ, Youngs CR, Rorie RW, Pool SH, Memon MA, Godke RA. Offspring from frozen goat embryos born in Louisiana. Dairy Goat J 1987;67:182,189.

41. Ogrui N, Tsutsumi Y, Hachinohe Y. Nonsurgical transfer of equine embryos. In: Hafez ESE, Semm K, eds. In vitro Fertilization and Embryo Transfer. Lancaster: MPT Press, 1982:287–295.

42. Takeda T, Elsden RP, Squires EL. In vitro and in vivo development of frozen-thawed equine embryos. Proc Tenth Internatl Congr Anim Reprod Artif Insem, June 10–14, University of Illinois, Urbana, IL 1984;2:246.

43. Hayashi S, Kobayashi K, Mizuno J, Saitoh K, Hirano S. Birth of piglets from frozen embryos. Vet Rec 1989;125:43–44.

44. Barry BE, Thompson DL Jr, White KL, Wood TC, Rabb MH, Colborn DR. Viability of inner cell mass versus trophectodermal cells from frozen-thawed horse embryos. Theriogenology 1989;31:171.

45. Voelkel SA, Viker SD, Lambeth VA, Godke RA. A new approach to freezing bovine embryos without the use of liquid cooling agents. Theriogenology 1984;21:272.

46. Viker SD, Voelkel SA, Rorie R, Lambeth VA, Godke RA. A new method for freezing embryos using microprocessor-controlled thermoelectric cells. Proc Third World Conf In Vitro Fertil Embryo Transf, May 14–17, Helsinki, Finland 1984:128.

47. Looney CR, Jackson DA, Voelkel SA, Godke RA. The use of fluorescein diacetate (FDA) to assess viability of bovine embryos in vitro. Proc Second World Congr Embryo Transf Mammals, September 20–22, Annecy, France 1982:56.

48. Looney CR, Voelkel SA, Jackson DA, Godke RA. In vitro culture of bovine embryos with fluorescein diacetate indicator. J Anim Sci (Suppl 1) 1982;55:62.

49. Voelkel SA, Amborski GF, Hill KG, Godke RA. Use of a uterine-cell monolayer culture system for micromanipulated bovine embryos. Theriogenology 1984;21:271–281.

50. Rexroad CE, Powell AM. Co-culture of ovine eggs with oviductal cells and trophoblastic vesicles. Theriogenology 1988;29:387–397.

51. Gandolfi F, Brevinin TAL, Moor RM. Effect of oviduct environment on embryonic development. J Reprod Fertil (Suppl) 1989;38:107–115.

52. Prichard JF, Pool SH, Blakewood EG, Godke RA. Culture of early-stage caprine embryos using oviductal and uterine cell monolayers. Theriogenology 1990;33:300.

53. Rodriguez HF, Wiemer KW, Denniston RS, Godke RA. A bilayered fetal-cell co-culture system for culturing bovine embryos. Theriogenology 1990;33:309.

54. Leibo SP. A one-step method for direct nonsurgical transfer of frozen-thawed bovine embryos. Proc Second World Congr Embryo Transf Mammals, September 20–22, Annecy, France, 1982:97.

55. Leibo SP. Field trial of one-step frozen bovine embryos transferred non-surgically. Theriogenology 1983;19:139.

56. Leibo SP. A one-step method for direct non-surgical transfer of frozen-thawed bovine embryos. Theriogenology 1984;21:767–790.

57. Leibo SP, West AW, Perry B. A one-step method for direct nonsurgical transfer of frozen-thawed bovine embryos. I. Basic studies. Cryobiology 1982;19:673.

58. Leibo SP, West AW, Perry B. A one-step method for direct nonsurgical transfer of frozen-thawed bovine embryos. II. Basic studies. Cryobiology 1982;19:674.

59. Glenister PH, Lyon MF, Wittingham DG. The effect of radiation on frozen mouse embryos. Proc European Cryobiol Soc Mtg, London 1982:1.

60. Ryan DP, Godke RA, Boland MP. Frequency of twins from Friesian cows in a warm dry climate. Theriogenology 1988;29:300.

61. Seidel F. The development potential of an isolated blastomere in the 2-cell stage mammalian egg. Naturwissenschaften 1952; 39:355–356.

62. Daniel JC, Takahashi K. Selective laser destruction of rabbit blastomeres and continued cleavage of survivors in vitro. Exp Cell Res 1965;39:475.

63. Pincus G, ed. The Eggs of Mammals. New York: Macmillan, 1936:76.

64. Nicholas JS, Hall BV. Experiments on development in rats. II. The development of isolated blastomeres and fused eggs. J Exp Zool 1942;90:441–549.

65. Tarkowski AK. Experiments on the development of isolated blastomeres of mouse eggs. Nature 1959;184:1286–1287.

66. Willadsen SM. A method for culture of micromanipulated sheep embryos and its use to produce monozygotic twins. Nature 1979; 277:298–300.

67. Willadsen SM, Polge C. Attempts to produce monozygotic quadruplets in cattle by blastomere separation. Vet Rec 1981;108:211–213.

68. Moore NW, Adams CE, Rowson LEA. Developmental potential of single blastomeres of the rabbit egg. J Reprod Fertil 1968;17:527–531.

69. Bronson RA, McLaren A. Transfer to the mouse oviduct of eggs with and without the zona pellucida. J Reprod Fertil 1970;22:129–137.

70. Modlinski JA. The role of the zona pellucida in the development of mouse eggs in vivo. J Embryol Exp Morphol 1970;23:539.

71. Moore NW, Polge C, Rowson LEA. The survival of single blastomeres of pig eggs transferred to recipient gilts. Australian J Biol Sci 1969;22:979–982.

72. Trounson AO, Moore NW. The survival and development of sheep eggs following complete or partial removal of the zona pellucida. J Reprod Fertil 1974;41:97.

73. Willadsen SM. Micromanipulation of embryos of the large domestic species. In: Adams CE, ed. Mammalian Egg Transfer. Boca Raton, FL: CRC Press, 1982:185–210.

74. Willadsen SM, Pashen RL, Allen WR. Micromanipulation of horse embryos. Proc Ann Conf Soc Study Fertil 1980:28.

75. Willadsen SM, Lehn-Jensen H, Fehilly CB, Newcomb R. The production of monozygotic twins of preselected parentage by micromanipulation of nonsurgically collected cow embryos. Theriogenology 1981;15:23–29.

76. Willadsen SM, Fehilly CB. The development potential and regulatory capacity of blastomeres from two-, four- and eight-cell sheep embryos. In: Bier HM, Lindner HR, eds. Fertilization of the Human Egg In Vitro. New York: Springer-Verlag, 1983:353–357.

77. Ozil J-P, Heyman Y, Renard J-P. Production of monozygotic twins by micromanipulation and cervical transfer in the cow. Vet Rec 1982;110:126–127.

78. Lambeth VA, Looney CR, Voelkel SA, Hill KG, Jackson DA, Godke RA. Micromanipulation of bovine morulae to produce identical twin offspring. Proc Second World Congr Embryo Transf Mammals, September 20–22, Annecy, France, 1982:55.

79. Williams TJ, Elsden RP, Seidel GE Jr. Identical twin bovine pregnancies derived from bisected embryos. Theriogenology 1982;17:114.

80. Lambeth VA, Looney CR, Voelkel SA, Jackson DA, Hill KG, Godke RA. Microsurgery on bovine embryos at the morula stage to produce monozygotic twin calves. Theriogenology 1983;20:85–95.

81. Ozil J-P. Production of identical twins by bisection of blastocysts in the cow. J Reprod Fertil 1983;69:463–468.

82. Voelkel SA, Humes PE, Godke RA. Pregnancy rates resulting from nonsurgical transfer of micromanipulated bovine embryos. Proc Tenth World Congr Anim Reprod Artif Insem, June 10–14, University of Illinois, Urbana, IL 1984;2:251.

83. Voelkel SA, Viker SD, Humes PE, Godke RA. Micromanipulation and nonsurgical transfer of bovine embryos. J Anim Sci (Suppl 1) 1984;59:393.

84. Williams TJ, Elsden RP, Seidel GE Jr. Pregnancy rates with bisected bovine embryos. Theriogenology 1984;22:521–531.

85. Brem G, Kruff B, Szilvassy B, Tenhumberg H. Identical Simmental twins' through micro-surgery of embryos. Theriogenology 1984; 21:225.

86. Baker RD, Eberhard BE, Leffel RE, Rohde RF, Henschen TJ. Pregnancy rates following surgical transfer of bovine demi-embryos. Proc Tenth Internatl Congr Anim Reprod Artif Insem, June 10–14, University of Illinois, Urbana, IL 1984;2:220.

87. Baker RD, Shea BF. Commercial splitting of bovine embryos. Theriogenology 1985; 23:3–12.

88. Mertes PC, Bondioli KR. Effect of split-ting technique on pregnancy rate from half embryos. Theriogenology 1985;23:209.

89. Willadsen SM, Godke RA. A simple pro-cedure for the production of identical sheep twins. Vet Rec 1984;114:240–243.

90. Gatica R, Boland MP, Crosby TF, Gordon I. Micromanipulation of sheep morulae to produce monozygotic twins. Theriogenology 1984;21:555–560.

91. McFarland CW, Rorie RW, McNeill DR, Voelkel SA, Hembry FG, Godke RA. Micro-surgery on sheep embryos to produce genetic-ally identical twin lambs. Louisiana Agric 1985;28(3):3.

92. Tsunoda Y, Wakasu M, Yasui T, Sugie T. Micromanipulation and freezing of goat embryos. Proc Tenth Internatl Congr Anim Reprod Artif Insem, June 10–14, University of Illinois, Urbana, IL 1984;2:249.

93. Pendleton RJ, Youngs CR, Rorie RW, Memon MA, Godke RA. The birth of split-embryo goat offspring in Louisiana. Dairy Goat J 1987;67:58–59.

94. Slade NP, Williams TJ, Squires EL, Seidel GE Jr. Production of identical twin pregnancies by microsurgical bisection of equine embryos. Proc Tenth World Congr Anim Reprod Artif Insem, June 10–14, University of Illinois, Urbana, IL 1984;2:241.

95. CSU Equine Sciences Newsletter 1984;3(1): 1–2.

96. Rorie RW, Voelkel SA, McFarland CW, Southern LL, Godke RA. Micromanipulation of day-6 porcine embryos to produce split-embryo piglets. Theriogenology 1985;23:225.

97. Rorie RW, Pendleton RJ, Youngs CR, Southern LL, Memon MA, Hembry FG, Godke RA. The use of microsurgery to pro-duce split-embryo transplant offspring from sheep, goat and swine. Proc Eleventh Internatl Congr Anim Reprod Artif Insem, June 26–30, Dublin, Ireland 1988;2:188.

98. Yang X, Foote RH. Production of identical twin rabbits by micromanipulation of embryos. Biol Reprod 1987;37:1007–1014.

99. Seidel GE Jr. Are identical twins produced from micromanipulation always identical? Proc Conf Artif Insem Embryo Transf Beef Cattle, NAAB, Denver, CO 1985:50–53.

100. Willadsen SM. The viability of early cleavage stages containing half the normal number of blastomeres in the sheep. J Reprod Fertil 1980;59:357–362.

101. Lehn-Jensen H, Willadsen SM. Deep-freezing of cow "half" and "quarter" embryos. Therio-genology 1983;19:49–54.

102. Godke RA, Overskei TL, Voelkel SA. The potential for micromanipulation and embryo transfer in breeding goats. Proc Dairy Goat Conf, California State Polytechnic University, Pomona, CA 1984;10:3–12.

103. Voelkel SA, Viker SD, Johnson CA, Hill KG, Humes PE, Godke RA. First calves produced from quartered embryo. Louisiana Agric 1984;27(3):5.

104. Voelkel SA, Viker SD, Johnson CA, Hill KG, Humes PE, Godke RA. Multiple embryo transplant offspring produced from quartering a bovine embryo at the morulae stage. Vet Rec 1985;117:528–530.

105. Voelkel SA, Rorie RW, McFarland CW, Godke RA. An attempt to produce quarter embryos from non-surgically recovered bovine blastocysts. Theriogenology 1986;25:207.

106. Voelkel SA, Godke RA. Unpublished data, 1986.

107. Tarkowski AK, Wroblewolsa J. Development of blastomeres of mouse eggs isolated at the 4- and 8-cell stage. J Embryol Exp Morphol 1967;36:155–180.

108. Rorie RW, McFarland CW, Overskei TL, Voelkel SA, Godke RA. A new method of splitting embryos without the use of a commercial micromanipulator unit. Therio-genology 1985;23:224.

109. McFarland CW, Rorie RW, Voelkel SA, Godke RA. The use of pronase to success-fully remove the zona pellucida from bovine embryos. Theriogenology 1985;23:208.

110. Hare WCD, Betteridge KJ. Relationship of embryo sexing to other methods of prenatal sex determination in farm animals: A review. Theriogenology 1978;9:27–43.

111. Moustafa LA, Hahn J, Roselius R. Versuche zur Geschlechtsbestimmung an Tag 6 und 7 alten Runderembryonen. Tierarztl Wschr 1978; 91:236–238.

112. Singh EL, Hare WCD. The feasibility of sexing bovine morula stage embryos prior to embryo transfer. Theriogenology 1980;14: 421–427.

113. Winterberger-Torres S, Popescu PC. Transfer of cow blastocysts after sexing. Theriogenology 1980;14:309–318.

114. White KL, Lindner GM, Anderson GB, BonDurant RH. Survival after transfer of "sexed" mouse embryos exposed to H-Y antisera. Theriogenology 1982;18:655–662.

115. White KL, Lindner GM, Anderson GB, BonDurant RH. Cytolytic and fluorescent detection of H-Y antigen on preimplantation mouse embryos. Theriogenology 1983;19: 701–705.

116. Zavos PM. Preconception sex determination via intravaginal administration of H-Y antisera in rabbits. Theriogenology 1983;20:235–240.

117. Wachtel SS. H-Y antigen in the study of sex determination and control of sex ratio. Theriogenology 1984;21:18 28.

118. Ohno S, Nagi Y, Ciccarese S, Iwata H. Testis-organizing H-Y antigen and the primary sex-determining mechanism of mammals. Rec Progr Horm Res 1979;35:449–476.

119. White K. Embryo and gamete selection. In: Moo-Young M, Babiuk L, Phillip J, eds. Animal Biotechnology, Comprehensive Biotechnology. Oxford: Pergamon Press, 1989:179–202.

120. Bondioli K, Ellis S, Pryor J, Williams M, Harpold M. The use of male-specific chromosomal DNA fragments to determine the sex of bovine preimplantation embryos. Theriogenology 1989;31:95–104.

121. Willadsen SM. The development capacity of blastomeres from 4- and 8-cell sheep embryos. J Embryol Exp Morphol 1981;65:165–172.

122. Tucker EM, Moor RM, Rowson LEA. Tetraparental sheep chimeras induced by blastomere transplantation. Changes in blood type with age. J Immunol 1974;26:613–621.

123. Voelkel SA, Godke RA. Unpublished data, 1984.

124. Butler JE, Anderson GB, BonDurant RH, Pashen RL. Production of ovine chimeras. Theriogenology 1985;23:183.

125. Butler JE, Anderson GB, BonDurant RH, Pashen RL, Penedo MCT. Production of ovine chimeras by inner cell mass transplantation. J Anim Sci 1987;65:317–324.

126. Summers PM, Shelton JN, Bell K. Synthesis of primary Bos taurus-Bos indicus chimaeric calves. Anim Reprod Sci 1983;6:91–102.

127. Brem G, Tenhumberg H, Kruff B, Kräußlich H. Production of cattle chimerae through embryo microsurgery. Theriogenology 1985; 23:182.

128. Rorie RW, Pool SH, Pendleton RJ, White KL, Godke RA. The use of micromanipulation and cellular aggregation to produce chimeric bovine embryos. Proc Congr Peruano Genetica, December 8–13, 1986, Lima, Peru 1987:45.

129. Pool SH, Rorie RW, White KL, Godke RA. Growth rates of calves resulting from aggregated embryos. Theriogenology 1988;29:288.

130. Rossant J, Croy BA, Chapman VM, Siracusa L, Clark DA. Interspecific chimeras in mammals: A new experimental system. J Anim Sci 1982;55:1241–1248.

131. Tarkowski AK. Mouse chimaeras developed from fused eggs. Nature 1961;190:857–860.

132. Mintz B. Formation of genetically mosaic mouse embryos. Am Zool 1962;2:432.

133. Gardner R. Mouse chimeras obtained by the injection of cells into the blastocyst. Nature 1968;220:596–597.

134. Gardner RL. Production of chimeras by injecting cells or tissue into the blastocyst. In: Daniel J, ed. Methods in Mammalian Reproduction. New York: Academic Press, 1978:137–166.

135. Gardner RL. Microsurgical approaches to the study of early mammalian development. In: Moghassi K, ed. Birth Defects and Fetal Development: Endocrine and Metabolic Factors. Springfield, IL: CC Thomas, 1971: 212–233.

136. Gardner RL, Papaioannou V, Barton S. Origin of the ectoplacental cone and secondary giant cells in mouse blastocysts reconstituted from isolated trophoblast and inner cell mass. J Embryol Exp Morphol 1973;30:561–572.

137. Mayer JF, Fritz HJ. The culture of preimplantation rat embryos and the production of allophenic rats. J Reprod Fertil 1974;39:1.

138. Gardner RL, Munro AJ. Successful construction of chimaeric rabbit. Nature 1974;250:146.

139. Moustafa LH. Chimeric rabbits from embryonic cell transplantation. Proc Soc Exp Biol Med 1974;147:885–888.

140. Babinet C, Bordenave GR. Chimaeric rabbits from immunosurgically-prepared inner-cell-mass transplantation. J Embryol Exp Morphol 1980;60:429–440.

141. Yang X, Foote RH. Production of chimeric rabbits from morulae by a simple procedure. Gamete Res 1988;21:345–351.

142. Yang X, Foote RH. Term development of chimeric rabbit from combined day 2 and day 3 morulae. Theriogenology 1989;31:275.

143. Loskutoff N, Kraemer D. Intraspecies blastocyst reconstruction in mice using giant trophodermal vesicles produced by multiple embryo aggregation. Biol Reprod 1991;43:1037–1044.

144. Fehilly CB, Willadsen SM, Tucker EM. Interspecific chimaerism between sheep and goat. Nature 1984;307:634–636.

145. Meinecke-Tillmann S, Meinecke B. Experimental chimaeras—removal of reproductive barrier between sheep and goat. Nature 1984; 307:637–638.

146. Pashen RL, Willadsen SM, Anderson GB. Attempts to produce horse-donkey chimeras by blastocyst aggregation. J Reprod Fertil (Suppl) 1987:659–694.

147. Polzin VJ, Anderson DL, Anderson GB, BonDurant RH, Butler JE, Pashen RL, Penedo MCT, Rowe JD. Production of sheep-goat chimeras by inner cell mass transplantation. J Anim Sci 1987;65:325–330.

148. Roth TL, Anderson GB, BonDurant RH, Pashens RL. Survival of sheep × goat hybrid inner cell masses after injection into ovine embryo. Biol Reprod 1989;41:675–682.

149. Rorie RW, Pool SH, Prichard JF, Betteridge K, Godke RA. Production of chimeric blastocysts comprising sheep ICM and goat trophoblast for intergeneric transfer. J Anim Sci (Suppl 1) 1989;67:401–402.

150. Uehara T, Yanagimachi R. Microsurgical injection of spermatozoa into hamster eggs with subsequent transformation of sperm nuclei into male pronuclei. Biol Reprod 1976; 15:467.

151. Thadani VM. A study of heterospecific sperm-egg interactions in the rat, mouse and deer mouse using in vitro fertilization and sperm injection. J Exp Zool 1980;212:435–453.

152. Markert CL. Fertilization of mammalian eggs by sperm injection. J Exp Zool 1983;228: 195–201.

153. Shaikh AA, Minhas BS, Bowen MJ, Westhusin JE, Kraemer DC. Pronucleus formation following microinjection of spermatozoa into baboon ova. Proc Soc Study Reprod, 1984; No. 294.

154. Mann, J. Full term development of mouse eggs fertilized by a spermatozoon microinjected under the zona pellucida. Biol Reprod 1988; 38:1077–1083.

155. Hosoi Y, Miyake M, Utsumi K, Iritani A. Development of oocytes after microinjection of spermatozoon. Proc Eleventh Internatl Congr Anim Reprod Artif Insem, June 26–30, Dublin, Ireland 1988:231.

156. Iritani A. Current status of biotechnical studies in mammalian reproduction. Fertil Steril 1988; 50:543–551.

157. Yang X, Chen J, Foote RH. Blastocyst development from rabbit ova fertilized by injected sperm. J Reprod Fertil (Abstr Ser) 1988;1:13.

158. Yang X, Chen J, Chen Y, Foote RH. Improved developmental potential of rabbit oocytes fertilized by sperm microinjection into the perivitelline space enlarged by hypertonic medium. J Exp Zool 1990;255:114–119.

159. Yang X, Jiang S, Kovacs A. Electro-field induced oocyte activation in rabbits. Proc 25th Mtg Soc Study Reprod 1990:70.

160. Iritani A, Kasai M, Niwa K, Song HB. Fertilization in vitro of cattle follicular oocytes

with injected spermatozoa capacitated in a chemically defined medium. J Reprod Fertil 1984;70:487–492.

161. Younis AI, Keefer CL, Brackett BG. Fertilization of bovine oocytes by sperm microinjection. Theriogenology 1989;31:276.

162. Zhang L, Blakewood EG, Denniston RS, Godke RA. The effect of insulin on maturation and development of in vitro-fertilized bovine oocytes. Theriogenology 1991;35:30.

163. Malter H, Cohen J. Partial zona dissection of the human oocyte: A nontraumatic method using micromanipulation to assist zona pellucida penetration. Fertil Steril 1989;51:139–148.

164. Malter HE, Cohen J. Blastocyst formation and hatching in vitro following zona drilling of mouse and human embryos. Gamete Res 1989;24:67–80.

165. Cohen J, Malter H, Wright G, Kort H, Massey J, Mitchell D. Partial zona dissection of human oocytes when failure of zona pellucida penetration is anticipated. Human Reprod 1989;4:435–442.

166. Ng S, Bongso A, Sathananthan H, Ratnam S. Micromanipulation: Its relevance to human in vitro fertilization. Fertil Steril 1990;53: 203–219.

167. Antinori S, Fischel S, Versaci C, Chairiell F, Lisi F. Evaluating 6 pregnancies established by subzonal insemination, "SUZI". Proc Eighth World Congr Human Reprod, June 26–July 1, Helsinki, Finland, 1990;No. 262.

168. Godke RA, Beetem DD, Burleigh DW. A method for zona pellucida drilling using a compact nitrogen laser. Proc Eighth World Congr Human Reprod, June 26-July 1, Helsinki, Finland, 1990; No. 258.

169. Meryman HT. Drying of living mammalian cells. Ann NY Acad Sci 1960;85:729.

170. Graham EF, Larson EV, Crabo BG. Freezing and freeze-drying bovine spermatozoa. Proc Fifth Tech Conf Artif Insem Reprod 1974.

171. Surani M, Barton S, Norris M. Experimental reconstruction of mouse eggs and embryos: An analysis of mammalian development. Biol Reprod 1987;36:1–16.

172. Willadsen S. Cloning of sheep and cow embryos. Genome 1989;31:956–962.

173. McGrath J, Solter D. Nuclear and cytoplasmic transfer in mammalian embryos. In: Gwatkin R, ed. Developmental Biology: A Comprehensive Synthesis. Manipulation of Mammalian Development. New York: Plenum Press 1986;4:37–55.

174. Tsunoda Y, Yasui T, Nakamura K, Uchida T, Sugie T. Effect of culturing the zona pellucida on the pronuclear transplantation in the mouse. J Exp Zool 1986;240:119–125.

175. Hogan B, Constantini F, Lacy E. Manipulating the Mouse Embryo: A Laboratory Mannual.

New York: Cold Spring Harbor Laboratory, 1986.

176. Stice S, Robl J. Nuclear reprogramming in nuclear transplant rabbit embryos. Biol Reprod 1988;39:657–664.
177. Willadsen S. Nuclear transplantation in sheep embryos. Nature 1986;320:63–65.
178. Prather R, Barnes F, Sims M, Robl J, Eyestone W, First N. Nuclear transplantation in the bovine embryo: Assessment of donor nuclei and recipient oocyte. Biol Reprod 1987;37:859–866.
179. Bondioli K, Westhusin M, Looney C. Production of identical bovine offspring by nuclear transfer. Theriogenology 1990;33:165–174.
180. Smith L, Wilmut I. Factors affecting the viability of nuclear transplanted embryos. Theriogenology 1990;33:153–164.
181. Robl J, Stice S. Prospects for the commercial cloning of animals by nuclear transplantation. Theriogenology 1989;31:75–84.
182. Gordon JW, Scangos GA, Plotkin DJ, Barbosa JA, Ruddle FH. Genetic transformation of mouse embryos by microinjection of purified DNA. Proc Natl Acad Sci 1980;77:7380–7384.
183. Wagner TE, Hoppe PC, Jollick JD, Scholl DR, Hodinka RL, Gault JB. Microinjection of a rabbit beta-globin gene into zygotes and its subsequent expression in adult mice and their offspring. Proc Natl Acad Sci 1981;78:6376–6380.
184. Wagner TE, Murray FA, Minhas B, Kraemer DC. The possibility of transgenic livestock. Theriogenology 1984;21:29–44.
185. Palmiter RD, Norstedt G, Gelinas RE, Hammer RE, Brinster RL. Metallothioncin-human GH fusion genes stimulate growth of mice. Science 1983;222:809–814.
186. Bines JA, Hart IC, Morant SV. Endocrine control of energy metabolism in the cow: The effect on milk yield and levels of some blood constituents with injection of growth hormone and growth hormone fragments. Br J Nutr 1980;43:179–186.
187. Peel CJ, Bauman DE, Gorewit RG, Sniffen CL. Effect of exogenous growth hormone on lactation performance in high yielding dairy cows. J Nutr 1981;111:1662–1671.
188. Hammer RF, Pursel VG, Rexroad CE, Wall RJ, Bolt DJ, Ebert KM, Palmiter RD, Brinster RL. Production of transgenic rabbits, sheep and pigs by microinjection. Nature 1985;315:680–683.
189. Davis GH, Montegomery GW, Allision AJ, Kelly RW, Bray AR. Segregation of a major gene influencing fecundity in progeny of Booroola sheep. New Zealand J Agric Res 1982;25:525–529.
190. Spearow JL. Mechanism of action of genes controlling reproduction. Proc 1983 Edinburgh Workshop on Prolific Sheep. The Genetics of Fecundity 1983:11–16.
191. Wilmut I, Archibald A, Harris S, McClenaghan M, Simons J, Whitelow C, Clark A. Methods of gene transfer and their potential use to modify milk composition. Theriogenology 1990;33:113–123.

23
The Role of the Embryo in Prenatal Diagnosis

A.A. Kiessling

The risk to offspring of inherited debilitating disease has created a need for prenatal genetic analyses. The standard of care in this regard has historically been karyotyping fetal cells recovered from amniotic fluids during the second trimester of pregnancy. The stress to parents of several months of pregnancy with an unknown outcome provided the impetus for development of a procedure to evaluate the fetus earlier in gestation. Sampling the chorionic villus during the first trimester became possible as a result of improvements in the techniques for ultrasonic guidance of biopsy needles. Karyotypic analysis, or, more recently, mapping the DNA of the sampled cells, has successfully provided information about fetal genetics during the first trimester. Although chorionic villus biopsy has proven a valuable tool in genetic counseling of parents, it is not without risk to the developing embryo and may provide somewhat ambiguous results if the embryo is female. Thus, a more ideal approach would be genetic assessment of a developing embryo before a pregnancy is established.

Recent advances in the molecular biologic analyses of single cells have opened the door to this possibility. Genetic assessment of single cells of the embryo before placement in the womb for establishment of pregnancy is now possible. The theory is simple: one blastomere is sampled for genetic or gene expression analysis and the remaining blastomeres are sufficient for normal development of the conceptus following transfer to the uterus. The precise methods for these types of analyses are described below.

In addition to genetic analysis, it is also becoming possible to noninvasively analyze some aspects of the physiology of individual embryos by sampling culture conditions for uptake or secretion of metabolic products. Although these methods are early in their development, some techniques of microanalysis will be described below.

Molecular Biologic Analysis of Genes and Gene Expression

The current possibilities for analysis of early cleaving embryos stem from developments in two areas: micromanipulation of single cells and the polymerase chain reaction.

Micromanipulation of Embryos

During the past decade, major advancements have been made in the techniques and equipment available for micromanipulation of gametes and embryos. Inverted compound microscopes are fitted with fine caliper pipet holders that are capable of incremental movements in microns in x, y, or z coordinates. Pipet pullers can be programmed to melt and pull glass pipets of standard bore to yield capillary tubes of reproducible dimensions in microns for holding and/or insertion into the egg. Microforges have been developed to melt the ends of such tubes to yield safe, non-damaging "holders" for embryos and eggs. Heated microscope stages and controlled gas atmospheres support embryo manipulations under conditions that lessen the opportunity for retarding or damaging embryonic cells. These technical advancements make it possible

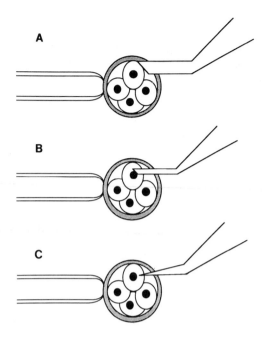

FIGURE 23.1. Micromanipulation of embryos. Whole blastomeres (A) or nuclei (B) can be removed for analysis without damaging the remaining cells of the embryo. In addition, small amounts of cytoplasm can be withdrawn for analysis, or substances can be microinjected for treatment (C).

to conduct microsurgery (embryo biopsy) on early cleaving, zona-enclosed embryos (Fig. 23.1). Several types of embryo biopsy are possible: (1) removal of an entire cell; (2) removal of a nucleus from a cell; and (3) cytoplasm sampling for analysis of gene expression.

Whole Cell Biopsy

This approach was first applied to bovine blastocysts (see Chapter 22 for a review). One or a few trophoblast cells are removed for cell culture and chromosome analysis in order to determine the sex of the embryo before transfer to recipients. The desirability of female offspring for most dairy cattle producers provided the impetus for development of this technique. The length of time required for cell culture and karyotyping means it is necessary to cryopreserve the biopsied embryo prior to transfer. The combined logistics and expense for embryo biopsy, culture, and

cryopreservation have made this approach untenable for most commercial applications.

The development of the DNA amplification technique known as the polymerase chain reaction (PCR) allows genetic analysis of the DNA in single cells. This is a powerful new molecular biology technique that promises to allow analysis not only of DNA sequences, but also gene expression in single cells. A description of this method is included below.

Nuclear Biopsy

Removal of a single nucleus has been employed as an experimental technique for studies of nucleus/cytoplasm interaction.[1,2] Although not applicable to human embryos, the technique has become so advanced that calves have developed from the individual nuclei of bovine morulae transferred into unrelated oocytes. The basic approach is to remove all genetic information from recipient oocytes, and then insert a nucleus recovered from one blastomere of an 8- to 32- cell morula. The "nuclear transfer embryo" undergoes aparently normal cleavage and development to off-spring. As this methodology is being developed commercially, details of success rates are proprietary information. However, the technology presents the possibility of maintaining an unending supply of cloned individuals. Each nucleus from an 8- to 32-cell morula can give rise to a new 8- to 32-cell morula which can be transferred to a recipient cow for gestation, cryopreserved intact, or cryopreserved following the removal of a few nuclei to give rise to new individuals. Now only does this technology provide the opportunity to immortalize individual genomes, but will also answer a number of basic questions about cytoplasmic versus genetic control of development and gene expression.[3]

Cytoplasm Sampling

Egg cytoplasm has been shown to have profound effects on embryonic development.[4,5] It is possible that analysis of cytoplasm for content of mRNAs or proteins may provide valuable information about the developmental potential of the egg before fertilization, or the zygote following fertilization. Techniques for relaxing cytoplasmic structural proteins to allow withdrawal of small aliquots of cytoplasm have been reported[6] and provide the opportunity for extracellular analysis of picoliter quantities of cytoplasm without deleterious effects on developmental potential. Although reports of this experimental approach have not yet appeared, it is anticipated that these methods will become routine in the next decade. Proteins will have to be detected by sensitive measurements of enzyme activity or immune reactivity. mRNAs can be detected and quantified by reverse transcription into complementary (c) DNAs, and amplification of the resulting DNA of interest by the polymerase chain reaction.

DNA Amplification by the Polymerase Chain Reaction

Studies of thermophilic organisms that replicate their DNA at temperatures exceeding 80°C opened the way for the development of a technique that will revolutionize biological studies. For years, the need to generate sufficient copies of specific gene or mRNA sequences for study has been satisfied by a previous molecular biological advancement, that of gene cloning and amplification in vectors that infect bacteria. The new technique described below allows specific amplification and identification of DNA sequences in an afternoon.

The theory is simple and is based on the specificity of enzymes that replicate DNA. All DNA polymerases initiate DNA replication by adding individual nucleotides to the 3′ carbon of the ribose moiety at the end of a polymer already hydrogen-bonded to the DNA strand. This initiating polymer (the primer) can be either RNA or DNA, can be as short as 15 nucleotides and still be highly sequence specific, but must have a free 3′-OH group to interact with the incoming triphosphate moiety of the next base in the sequence. Once polymerization is initiated, the enzyme adds specific nucleotides at an astonishing speed, dozens of nucleotides per second[7] for most DNA polymerases. The newly replicated strand thus replaces the previous double strand, resulting in semi-conservative replication. Once the enzyme comes to the end of the single strand being replicated, it must pause until a new primed, single-strand is available. Much research has been directed at understanding the mechanism for the generation of single stranded, primed regions of DNA for replication. In vitro model systems generate such regions by simply melting the two strands apart and, in the presence of excess concentrations of primers, allowing reassociation to take place at lower temperatures. The melting temperatures are extreme, however, greater than 85°C in most instances in physiologic solutions. These temperatures irreversibly heat inactivate mammalian DNA polymerases, and thus most studies of DNA replication have been limited to one round of synthesis of new strands homologous to primed single-stranded regions.

Studies of *Thermus aquaticus*, however, revealed DNA polymerases that were not denatured at temperatures exceeding 85°C and thus paved the way for not only understanding how thermophilic organisms replicate their DNA, but also the development of an elegant molecular biology technique for continuous melting, reannealing and polymerization of specific, oligo-primed DNA stretches. Kary Mullis, the developer of the methodology, maintains the power of this observation came to him one afternoon while on a Sunday drive with a girl friend who, after listening to his idea, stated "it would never work."

The procedure is generally known as the Polymerase Chain Reaction (PCR). Primers of deoxyribonucleotides of sequences specific for the gene in question can be synthesized relatively inexpensively. Should the exact sequence of the gene under study not be known, but related sequences known, it is possible to synthesize primers with more than one base at a given position. Such "degenerate" primers are synthesized by adding mixtures of bases at the desired step of polymerization, instead of a single bases. Reannealing with such primers allows the simultaneous hybridization of related, but slightly different, primer sequences.

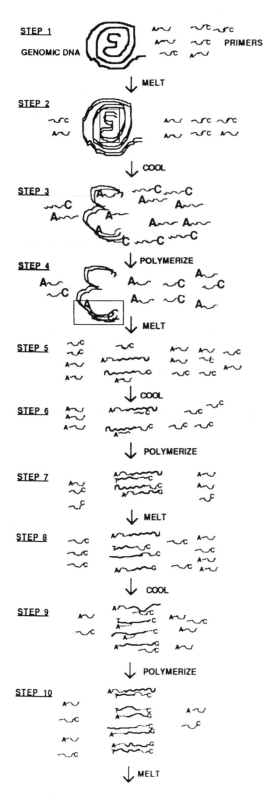

To initiate the chain reaction, the DNA under investigation is heated to separate the strands, allowed to reanneal with the oligos which are present in excess, followed by enzyme-catalyzed polymerization. Once strand synthesis is completed, the heating, reannealing, and polymerization process is repeated. Thus, each round, which requires only three or four minutes, will double the amount of DNA product formed, effectively a chain reaction. Twenty such cycles will result in 2^{20}-fold (approximately 10^7) amplification, and require about one hour.

Amplified DNA products can be detected and identified in several ways. The simplest way is to electrophorese the product through a polyacrylamide gel, and detect it by staining with eithidium bromide which binds to double stranded DNAs and results in a fluorescent complex which can be recorded on film with the aid of an ultraviolet light box. This is a common laboratory procedure. The threshold sensitivity of detection is approximately 10^{11} copies of a 100 base pair product. Thus, a single round of amplification will allow visualization of single copy genes from 10^4 cells (Fig. 23.3). Assay conditions yielding this result must include at least 10^{12}–10^{13} primer molecules (10- to 100-fold excess over new product), and at least one unit (approximately 10^{10} molecules) of enzyme.

In practice, there are limitations to the reaction, such as inhibitory substances (e.g., heparin) in the target DNA, and competing reactions brought about by the aberrant interaction of the high concentration of oligo primers with each other (the so called "primer-

FIGURE 23.2. Schematic of steps involved in the amplification of a specific gene sequence in cellular DNA by the method of polymerase chain reaction (PCR). In the presence of oligodeoxyribonucleotide primers complimentary in base sequence to the target gene, genomic DNA is heated to melt apart the double strands, and then cooled to allow the primers to anneal. The presence of a heat-stable DNA polymerase and deoxyribonucleotide triphosphate bases will support synthesis of the remaining strand attached to the primers. Repeated heating, annealing, and polymerization cycles bring about amplification of the target squence.

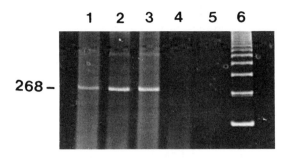

FIGURE 23.3. Electropherogram of amplified sequences of the single copy human gene, β-globin, in formaldehyde-fixed white blood cells. lanes 1–3, 10^4, 5×10^4, 10^5 cells, respectively; lanes 4 and 5, assay reaction blanks with no cells; lane 6 is molecular weight DNA ladder of 123 base pair repeats. The band amplified is a 268 base pair sequence of human β-globin amplified approximately 10^7-fold and visualized by staining with ethidium bromide.

dimer") or with the target DNA. Competing products formed during the first few rounds of amplification are the most inhibitory since they may quickly reach the concentration of the genomic DNA sequences in question. For these reasons, an ideal circumstance would be to initiate the reaction under the most stringent and specific conditions that would allow the amplification process to begin, i.e. temperatures just below annealing temperatures, and primer and enzyme excesses of only 100- to 1000-fold. In practice, this would mean starting and stopping the reaction process several times, which leads to the notion of a two stage PCR process in which the second stage amplifies an inner portion of the original sequence. This would allow not only an additional 10^7-fold amplification, but also the added specificity of the DNA sequence in question containing the inner primer sequence. In this instance, product would be identified by size in acrylamide gel electrophoresis, as described above.

Three other approaches are routinely used to identify the amplified DNA product. One is to treat the product with a specific restriction enzyme that cleaves the product into two known sizes which are then identified on a polyacrylamide gel. Another is to detect amplified DNA product by hybridization with

a third oligonucleotide homologous to an inner region of the amplified DNA. The homologous oligonucleotide is labelled either with radioactivity, or with a ligand, such as digoxigenin or biotin, that can be detected by ligand-specific antibody that is linked to an enzyme for which a color specific reaction can be used for detection. The hybridization can be carried out with product DNAs on a nitrocellulose filter, such as a dot-blot or a Southern blot, and hybridized product detected by exposing X-ray film if the probe is radioactive, or incubating with enzyme substrate, if enzyme-linked antibody is used to detect probe. The sensitivities of these two approaches are comparable. Alternatively, the hybridization can be carried out in solution, one half of the product subjected to restriction nuclease digestion, and then the cut and uncut products compared for size by electrophoresis, as described above. This latter approach is particularly useful in those instances when non-specific products are known to be synthesized during the PCR reaction.

Application of this methodology to genetic analysis of human embryos has already been reported[8-10] and will soon become a routine procedure in centers of assisted reproductive technology. Current approaches have focused on detection of Y-chromosome specific sequences in order to identify fetuses carrying known sex-chromosome-linked genetic disorders.

Another application of this technology to pre-implantation embryos will be to ensure that embryos arising from donor eggs and/or sperm are free of dangerous pathogens, such as hepatitis virus and human immunodeficiency virus. Such methodology may supplement or possibly eventually replace the current quarantine period required for donor sperm samples in order to allow repeat antibody testing of the donor.

Microanalysis of Embryo Metabolism

A need to be able to study and analyze single eggs and embryos has long been recognized. It is important to establish baseline parameters for intracellular constituents such as amino acid pools, nucleotide pools, ionic composition, energy substrates, etc., in order to more fully understand the metabolic requirements of the developing embryo. In addition, it may be possible to predict developmental potential of individual embryos by assessing critical processes at defined stages of pre and post-fertilization development. Toward this end, techniques of micro-fluorometry have been applied to individual eggs and embryos with useful information resulting, but most of these approaches result in destruction of the cells.[11,12]

More recently, using nanoliter microdrops under oil as culture conditions, it has been possible to assess the uptake of glucose and glutamine by individual embryos.[13,14] Such studies have provided the basis for normal metabolism, which may prove to be useful parameters for assessment in the future. The current equipment requirements for these assays prevent their common use, but selected culture conditions can be evaluated and the information applied for more general use. For example, the glucose uptake studies confirmed the toxicity of HEPES buffer to calcium ion channels in mouse embryos.[14]

Microscopy of Single Oocytes and Embryos During Culture

Although of unknown utility to normally developing embryos, this approach will be useful to diagnose malfunctions of fertilization and early cleavage in those couples for whom there is evidence of conceptions that repeatedly fail to develop normally. An example of such a situation is the report of a couple with multiple conceptuses that resulted in hydatiform moles.[15] In this case the zygotes were found to exhibit defects in cell division that lead to disparate chromosome segregtion. Advances in videomicroscopy and time-lapse, computer controlled videorecorders open the possibility of continuous examination of oocytes and/or embryos during culture under ultra low light exposure.

In summary, advances in molecular biology and computer enhancements in detection of low levels of light have opened the way for studies of individual preimplantation embryos. Methods are rapidly being developed that are not detrimental to the embryo. The 1990s will see a rapid increase in the application of these technologies to human reproduction and genetic diseases.

References

1. Tarkowski AK. Experiments on the transplantation of ova in mice. Acta Theriol. 1959; 2:251–267.
2. Mann JR. DDK egg-foreign sperm incompatibility in mice is not between the pronuclei. J Reprod Fertil 1986;76:779–781.
3. Collas P, Robl JM. Relationship between nuclear remodeling and development in nuclear transplant rabbit embryos. Biol Reprod 1991; 45:455–465.
4. Muggleton-Harris A, Whittingham DG, Wilson L. Cytoplasmic control of preimplantation development in vitro in the mouse. Nature, 1982;299:460–62.
5. Pratt HPM, Muggleton-Harris AL. Cycling cytoplasmic factors that promote mitosis in the cultured two cell mouse embryo. Development 1988;104:115–20.
6. Fissore R, O'Keefe S, Kiessling AA. The purine-induced block to mouse embryo cleavage is reversed by compounds that elevate cyclic-adenosine monophosphate. Biol Reprod 1992;47:1105–1112.
7. Innis MA, Myambo KB, Gelfand DH, Brow MAD. DNA sequencing with Thermus aquaticus DNa polymerase and direct sequencing of polymerase chain reaction-amplified DNA. Proc Natl Acad Sci USA 1988;85: 9436–9440.
8. Handyside, AH, Kontogianni EH, Hardy K, Winston RML. Pregnancies from biopsied human preimplantation embryos sexed by Y-specific DNA amplification. Nature 1991; 344:768–770.
9. Handyside AH, Pattinson JK, Penketh RJA, Delhanty JDA, Winston RML, Tuddenham EGD. Biopsy of human preimplantation embryos and sexing by DNA amplification. Lancet 1989; Feb. 18, 347–349.
10. Verlinsky Y, Pergament E, Strom C. The preimplantation genetic diagnosis of genetic diseases. J In Vitro Fertil Embryo Transf 1990;7:1–5.
11. Leese HJ, Biggers JD, Mroz EA, Lechene CP. Nucleotides in a single mammalian ovum or

preimplantation embryo. Anal Biochem 1984; 140:443–448.

12. Baltz JM, Biggers JD, Lechene C. Two cell stage mouse embryos appear to lack mechanisms for alleviating intracellular acid loads. J Biol Chem 1991;266(10):6052–6057.

13. Butler JE, Biggers JD. Noninvasive measurement of glucose uptake by two populations of murine embryos. Biol Reprod 1988;39: 779–786.

14. Gardner DK, Clarke RN, Lechene CP. Development of a non-invasive ultramicrofluorometric method for measuring net uptake of glutamine by single preimplantaton mouse embryos. Gamete Res 1989;24:427–438.

15. Edwards R, Crow J, Dale S, MacNamee M, Hartshorne G, Brinsden P. Preimplantation diagnosis and recurrent hydatiform mole. Lancet 1990; April 28, 1030–1031.

24
Historical Perspective of the Infertile Experience

Barbara Eck Menning

A historical perspective of the infertile couple's experience might be subtitled "We've Come a Long Way, Baby." The past 20 years have been a period of tremendous growth and change in the area of infertility, both in diagnosis and treatment, and in the patient's approach to the health care system. Technology has had an enormous affect on infertile couples. More importantly, however, these couples have had a dramatic impact on the industry, perhaps the strongest of any consumer advocacy group.

How did I come to work in this field? I certainly didn't set out to be an infertility counselor or nurse specialist. It is one of the ironies of my life that as a young nurse graduate I chose to specialize in the area of maternal child health. In that role, first as a bedside nurse and later as an instructor, I saw many labors and deliveries, and I helped many women put their first baby to breast. I never saw a birth that didn't move me profoundly. I always assumed that one day this would happen for me too, but it was not to be.

I spent the first 4 years of my marriage enduring every test and many of the attempted treatments of infertility. The one pregnancy I did achieve was lost to an early miscarriage. Even though I was a nurse, I found I did not know much about this complex area of infertility, and I knew even less about negotiating the health care system. I had four different doctors in four years and only the last doctor was a specialist. By then, there was nothing left to work with. After two ovarian surgeries and a hyperstimulation, my ovarian function had ceased. In those days, that was the ball game. I was only 31 years of age.

I did not know a single infertile person and

such was the power of my feelings that I really believed that I was going crazy. I was fortunate to find a woman therapist who helped me over several years to identify my feelings of anger, guilt, and grief and to work them through. There were two problems with individual therapy. First, I had to teach this person all about infertility and why it hurt so badly, and second, I was not relieved of my sense of isolation, my sense of being all alone.

With time I pursued a family by adoption, bringing three multiracial children into my home in only 5 years. Those children are now aged 20, 18, and 17. Life is very interesting at my home.

I thought about what I had been through, and I believed that there were many people like me out there if only I could find them. I knew if I could find them, that I could help them.

In the early 1970s infertility was not discussed openly, and I have to believe that such has been the case from the beginning of time. Couples with this problem assumed it was a female disorder and did not talk about it. They were often filled with guilt and shame, the so-called stigma of infertility, that finds its roots in the earliest of religious and social teachings. All the major religions have contributed to pressure on young men and women to marry and bear children. Since Adam and Eve the command has been go forth, be fruitful, and multiply.

In recent times, however, with growing awareness of world overpopulation, such pressure has become more subtle, with most faiths pressuring now for only the 2.11 children allowed to us by Zero Population Growth.

Some, most notably Roman Catholicism, Orthodox Judaism, and the Mormon faith, still encourage couples to bear all the children that God will provide.

Infertility, which was called "barrenness" in the Bible, was considered a fall from grace, a punishment from God. There were those who viewed infertility in the same light 20 years ago, who blamed themselves, and who were told by others, "It must be something you did." This is blaming the victim, and much of my work has been aimed at correcting this attitude.

A large area of influence on infertility is psychoanalytic psychology, which views parenthood as the only normal outcome of development into adulthood. Freud had a negative view of female psychology in general. His so-called penis envy theory concluded that the only way women could compensate for having been born without a penis was through childbearing, ideally, of male children. More recent reiterations are seen in the works of Helena Deutsch, Erik Erikson, and others.

It is shocking how totally these concepts have permeated the fields of mental health, medicine, nursing, and education. We still hear it said that a couple does not truly grow up if they do not procreate, and that a women is not complete if she has never borne children. Most damning is the idea that infertility is motivated; a woman could conceive if she really wanted to.

In addition, a host of punitive terms label women's dysfunctions. Endometriosis is known as the career woman's disease. There is the incompetent cervix. There is habitual abortion. Women have blighted ova, and that most outrageous condition of all, hostile cervical mucus.

Infertile couples have been prey to many myths and superstitions over the years. To the woman who worked, the answer was, quit your job. To the woman languishing at home, it was get a job. The tense and the frantic were told to relax or take a second honeymoon and, of course, adopt and you will get pregnant. All of these myths imply that the problem is all in our heads. All of these suggestions blame the victim.

Debunking the Myth

Infertility as a Medical Specialty

Infertility came into its own as a specialty in the early 1970s for several important and connected reasons. First, the supply of adoptable, healthy infants slowed to a trickle. Contrary to some beliefs, this was the result not of the increased availability of safe and legal abortion, but rather of the proliferation of birth control and social acceptance of single motherhood. Today 90 to 95% of all single mothers and women pregnant out of wedlock keep their babies. Therefore, as couples became less able to turn to adoption as an easy alternative, they were willing to try more experimental options, often begging physicians to do more for them.

Second, research in the area of fertility control was burgeoning in the 1970s, and many serendipitous discoveries benefited infertility. A good example is the drug clomiphene, which was first tested as a possible birth control agent, being an antiestrogen. When tried on laboratory rats, however, it proved to have quite the opposite effect of stimulating ovulation. Finally, the decade was characterized by a new sexual candor and a consumer movement that led more people to seek treatment for infertility than ever before.

The Consumer Movement

I believe that the consumer movement in health care was a direct benefit of the feminist movement. No longer was the physician seen as God. Women and, eventually, men came to demand equality and a partners-in-care approach to medicine. They demanded to be informed, to be able to read their charts, to be able to seek second opinions, and to be treated with respect. We started to see the patient bill of rights in hospitals and clinics; the model was written by George Annas for the American Civil Liberties Union.

Hospital economics contributed much to the power of the consumer movement. For example, we experienced a population decline in the 1970s and the 1980s, and hospitals were forced for the first time to market to the public. They either succeeded in meeting the public's demands or they failed. One of these demands was for more homelike and humane birthing rooms, less anesthesia, unrestricted visiting for spouses and partners, and rooming-in. Hospitals complied. The patient advocate was a regular staff position in most hospitals.

The Beginning of Resolve

In 1973, 2 years after I adopted my first child and shortly before I adopted my second, I was asked to participate in the annual Conference of the Open Door Society, a Massachusetts-based adoptive parent's group. They asked me to choose a topic, and I told them that I wanted to speak on infertility. They reacted in horror and told me that no one would come. I said I would take my chances. I was convinced that people attending an adoption conference needed to talk about their infertility too, and that many had unresolved feelings. We had the conference, and I had my panel with a standing-room-only crowd.

So many feelings and so many questions were left over at the end of this panel that we decided to circulate a sign-up list for those wishing to have further contact. All the people that signed the list were women. They became the first support group, meeting on a weekly basis for the better part of a year. At the same time, I volunteered to be a telephone counselor for the Open Door Society, fielding the medical questions and questions about infertility. It was not long before I was even taking some of these calls at my home. The idea of infertility advocacy began, although we were nameless and not really a formed organization.

We chose the name Resolve as a word (not an acronym) that explained what we were trying to do—resolve infertility. We wrote a small newsletter and some simple fact sheets to help educate our callers, because they wanted to be educated. I led several support groups each year. As our numbers grew, we charged a small membership fee for the newsletter and for attendance at groups. In the first 3 years

Resolve was a kitchen table organization run strictly by volunteers. A small nucleus of us formed the board of directors and we incorporated in 1974. One of our reasons for incorporating was to attract some of the grants and donations that were available. Unfortunately, those in charge of distributing such funds did not beat a path to our door.

Finally, in 1976 we were able to move out of the kitchen and into a one-room office. That same year I published my book *Infertility: A Guide for the Childless Couple*, which was revised completely in 1988. It provided exposure of our mission and brought Resolve to a national level. We heard from people all around the country who wanted to duplicate our services. We began to think about chapter affiliations and how we might go about being more than just a local organization.

The first nine years were years of great struggle. We never had enough money. We never had enough office space, staff, or time, but we were dedicated to offering education, referral, and support to infertile couples. No one else seemed to care.

I looked everywhere for additional funding. I wrote grant proposal after grant proposal. One time I took what I thought was a very well-thought-out proposal to a group that was heavily funding family planning services in the Boston area. After an excellent presentation, I was told by the director of this organization that on a scale of 1 to 10 we were a 1.

We also had trouble having access to the media in those days. People simply did not want to hear about just infertility. We were only invited on television or radio talk shows when something scandalous was going on, such as when children of donor insemination were searching for their donor fathers. If anything smacked a little bit of the risqué we might be invited to come on the air. We could never discuss infertility in its own right. I cannot fully impress on you how hard it was to campaign for a cause whose time had not yet come. There were many times I was demoralized and close to quitting. The one thing that kept me going was the response of the infertile couples whose needs we were meeting, because there was nothing else for them. In retrospect, I wouldn't change those years for anything.

By 1982, when I stepped down as director of Resolve, we had over 40 chapters around the country and over 10,000 members. Today Resolve boasts 50 chapters and 20,000 members and is still going strong. The reason is that the need still exists.

We help the some 10 million infertile Americans with education, referral, and support. We also offer educational programs to associated professionals in the area of medicine, nursing, mental health, and adoption. Our advocacy has one advantage over that offered by institutions: we are free from bias, we are free from motives. We do not profit from the referrals that we make or the programs that we offer. We do not endorse products. Our support group leaders are not even permitted to be on the staff of any institution offering infertility or adoption services. We have no conflict of interest.

The Effects of Infertile Couples

Infertile couples have had an impact on the medical field of infertility. The first is in vitro fertilization (IVF).

IVF

In 1972 Dr. Pierre Soupart, a biologist at Vanderbilt University in Nashville, was the first American to fertilize a human egg in vitro. This received wide press coverage. In 1974 Dr. Soupart applied to the National Institutes of Health (NIH) for a 3-year study to determine the safety of human IVF. The next year NIH decided that it would fund this proposal only after review by an ethical advisory board, which was created by federal law to study this issue. That same federal law banned further work in human IVF until the conclusion and the findings of the board were known. Nothing was able to go forward in America. It took 2 years to appoint the members to this board and another 6 months to convene the first hearing. In addition, they broadened their scope beyond Dr. Soupart's request to consider all

scientific, legal, ethical, social, and religious issues involved in the procedure. Ironically, just 2 months after the hearings began, baby Louise was born in England.

The 15-member board was composed of physicians, medical ethicists, lawyers, civic leaders, and a psychiatrist. They worked from May 1978 to May 1979 holding hearings in each of the eight regions of the country in preparing their report. Resolve was represented at each of these hearings by infertile couples, many of whom presented personal cases that could only be helped by this technology. In spite of a favorable ruling by the board in May 1979, Secretary Joseph Califano of the Department of Health, Education, and Welfare took no action on the recommendation. He did not agree with the findings. Dr. Soupart died in 1981 without ever receiving his grant or seeing IVF go forward in this country.

With the lack of federal support and federal funding, the private sector was called on to pioneer the first efforts in this country, and indeed it did. Infertile couples demanded access to the technique. Today we have over 200 IVF clinics in this country. The births that result are no longer front-page news items. Several thousand children have been born with this procedure.

Insurance

Another area in which infertile couples have had a dramatic impact is insurance. One of the greatest injustices they had to face was discrimination when submitting their tests and treatments for coverage. Usually insurance covered disease or illness, but the fact that infertility is not a disease or an illness provided the loophole for denying reimbursement. Infertility insurance was targeted early on by Resolve as one of its advocacy projects. Members of the Bay State chapter organized, lobbied, and brought before the legislature a bill to mandate all private insurers to cover infertility tests and treatments to the same extent that benefits are provided for other pregnancy-related procedures. This bill was passed into law in January 1988 and was signed by the governor.

Contrary to the fears of insurers, the mandate has not proved to be expensive. Blue Cross/Blue Shield estimates that premiums rose in 1989 only by $0.59 per family per month. By comparison, the inclusion of chiropractic services in the same year boosted rates $7.55 per family per month. Resolve is now spearheading a state-by-state campaign to win insurance coverage. So far nine states have passed such laws and more are in the works.

Federal employees who are not covered by these laws should be aware that Patricia Schroeder, congresswoman from Colorado, is sponsoring the Federal Employee Family Building Act. If enacted, this piece of legislation would cover infertility tests and treatments, and more important, it would also cover the usual costs of adoption. This would set an important precedent in this country for future employee benefits that infertile couples may ask for.

Additional Progress

Several other changes in the field have taken place in the last 20 years and deserve mention. For example, more and more couples are coming to us, not just women. Thus, they are diagnosed and treated as couples. When men are reluctant, the doctors and nurses tell the wives that their husbands must come in for tests. They must be regarded as a couple. This is not the way it was in the early 1970s.

Counseling and support groups are aimed at couples, and partners are encouraged to work together. In this way they air their feelings with each other and listen to what other couples are going through. This is far more constructive than working only with women's groups.

Another change that has taken place over the years is that couples are much more informed consumers. We put a large burden on them to educate themselves and to enter into their own advocacy. They want to be educated. They want to make proper decisions for themselves, because after all, they have to live with the consequences.

Institutions and private physicians are providing much more in the way of written literature. These couples are often anxious,

and they do not hear or remember well what caregivers may tell them. Therefore, it is essential to have written materials that explain the terminology and the course of the workup, such as what might be the next test to be performed, and what might be some suggestions for treatment.

Infertility is no longer the poor relation of family planning. In fact, it is now a multibillion-dollar industry. Public awareness of infertility as an issue, as a real and possible event, has increased greatly. The media are giving the subject more responsible coverage rather than treating it with sensationalism.

Physicians are more specialized in infertility treatment and thus more qualified than ever before. In the early 1970s it was not uncommon for doctors with family practice, obstetrics, and gynecology backgrounds to be doing a smattering of infertility therapy, even carrying patients as far as ovulation stimulation and tubal surgery, and not making referrals. We are increasingly aware that this truly is a specialty that requires considerable training and we are referring to doctors who have subspecialty certification. In many cases the local doctor can begin the workup, but there are logical points of referral, as there are some problems for which a specialist and only a specialist is appropriate.

The alternatives to combined genetic children are increasingly complex. Donor insemination has been available for many years and continues to be a popular choice for couples with problems of male infertility. In addition to the already difficult decision to pursue this option, however, couples are extremely concerned about the possibility of semen contaminated with sexually transmitted diseases. This has changed the protocols for donor selection and semen storage. More programs use frozen rather than fresh semen. Egg donation is also a possibility; this, of course, is the female equivalent of donor insemination with a somewhat more invasive means of collection.

Surrogate motherhood is proliferating. I was uncomfortable with this option when it surfaced in the late 1970s and early 1980s, and I continue to be uncomfortable with it. Try as I might, I cannot look at surrogate motherhood as anything other than renting a womb for 9 months: literally purchasing a baby and paying usually a poor person to carry that baby. I know that a lot of people disagree, but my deepest feeling is that this will be ruled illegal in this country within the next few years.

Traditional adoption still exists, but the local, healthy infant that looks like the parents is becoming unusual, and the wait for any child may be up to 5 years. More open adoptions are taking place, with couples encouraged to advertise in newspapers or magazines to solicit a birth mother who might want to give her baby up. Contact between the adoptive couple and the birth mother is encouraged. Even visitation of the birth mother with her baby can be written into the contract, which obviously raises all kinds of questions for the future. Legal risk adoptions are frequent, where the child who is not totally legally free for adoption is nevertheless placed with an adoptive family. There is a trial time before the family will know for sure whether or not that child is free for them to adopt. International adoptions are increasing, including children from all different countries and ethnic and racial backgrounds. Finally, we are seeing an increase in special-needs adoptions. All of these raise concerns and issues for the adoptive parents as well as the adopted children.

Conclusion

New technology offers new hope, but it also raises moral, ethical, and legal dilemmas, and it certainly puts the infertile couple more at risk than ever before for physical, emotional, and financial burdens. As we push ahead for better technology, we must not forget the lives of the people who will be affected by it. We must work together toward alleviating their financial burden through helping them obtain infertility insurance. We must support their emotional burden through thoughtful counseling, careful selection into programs, and continuing support mechanisms.

For the future, I have hopes and I have some concerns. I look forward to the day when our cure rate in infertility will be not merely 50% but more like 80 to 90%. Technology might be defined as the application of science to solve problems. Science inevitably moves much more rapidly than ethical and legal safeguards. Just because a technology is possible does not necessarily mean it is appropriate. Even though I speak as an advocate for infertile couples, I would be the first to say that they are vulnerable and exploitable because some of them would literally have a baby at any cost. Sometimes they have to be protected from themselves. I do not agree with the philosophy of a baby at any cost.

As we move ahead, and we must, we should be willing to subject our science to the review of enlightened and reasonable minds. We must be willing to say no, or at least not yet, when science exceeds the realm of current acceptable practice. This will slow our progress, but ultimately history and society will be the judge of the appropriateness of our technologies, and determine whether humanity has been helped or harmed.

Questions and Answers

Participant. I understand that Massachusetts has a bill pending to limit infertility insurance. Do you know anything about that?

Barbara Menning. I am not surprised, because even from the beginning Blue Cross/Blue Shield and others tried to limit what was covered. They tried to exempt IVF, for example, because they feared it would be very expensive, and an experimental procedure besides. If such a bill is pending, the Bay State chapter of Resolve is extremely organized, and they will be aware of it and be ready to attend any hearings and to discuss the issue. All diagnostic work, tests, and attempted treatments must be covered. The insurers must not start making exclusions, because that is how they nibble away at the law.

Q. What other states have this insurance?

Machelle Seibel. Nine states so far have this insurance and at least 15 or 20 have bills that are pending. I receive a regular report from Washington describing the various states and what they are trying to pass. Surprisingly, a number of these bills fail to pass. Also, the coverage in other states usually do not provide the same comprehensive coverage as Massachusetts. For instance, in certain states only IVF or assisted technologies might be covered, whereas in others basic infertility workup and treatment are covered but not the advanced technologies. Some states have a ceiling on the number of cycles allowed or the total money available. In Massachusetts it has been a very interesting experience as a clinical person trying to help patients get coverage. For example, a couple may live in Massachusetts, but their insurance company is in Connecticut. Or they work in Massachusetts, but they live in New Hampshire. In these cases an insurance company may try to avoid responsibility for payment. Reversal of a tubal ligation is often not covered because the resulting sterility is considered to have been inflicted on the woman by herself. If a woman had a tubal ligation reversed and paid for it herself, and the reversal failed, she would be a candidate for IVF, but it would not be covered. There is still a long way to go.

Q. Could you cite some examples of the costs of some of the medical procedures?

Machelle Seibel. Depending on where you go and the type of cycle, IVF costs between $6,000 and $8,000 per cycle. That means the beginning of the cycle to the pregnancy test, more or less. Tubal surgery probably would cost about $8,000 to $12,000. This includes the hospital stay, anesthesia, operating room, and the physician. The total cost is great.

Barbarn Menning. What about the cost of a general workup from the first test to the more invasive test?

Machelle Seibel. The basic workup exclusive of a laparoscopy is probably somewhere around $1,500 to maybe $2,000.

Barbara Menning. Especially for those in a middle-income or low-income bracket, it is highly discriminatory. People who are not covered by insurance are stopped before they begin.

Suggested Reading

Menning, BE. *Infertility: A Guide for the Childless Couple*. 2nd ed. New York Prentice-Hall Press, 1988.

25
Psychological Issues in Infertility: An Historical Overview

Judith Bernstein

The mental health profession has taken an interesting odyssey through infertility during the last 50 years. The twists and turns of that journey reveal as much about the state of the psychiatric arts as they do about infertility. The following is a historical and evolutionary overview of some of the salient psychological issues in infertility.

The Diagnosis of Psychogenic Infertility: The Era of Scapegoating

In the 1940s and 1950s, both the medical and the psychiatric literature contained numerous case reports of men and women who sought psychiatric care for major depression, obsessive-compulsive behavior, and neurosis who were incidentally found to have infertility as well. As a result of these few cases, a theory of the psychogenicity of infertility evolved. Because reproductive endocrinology was in its infancy, and barely 50% of patients carried a diagnosis, psychiatrists incorrectly concluded that the other 50% of diagnoses were psychogenic. They reasoned that hostility or ambivalence toward an appropriate gender identification or anger toward the marital partner was preventing conception in the female.[1-28] It was postulated that men with infertility exhibited extreme animosity and aggressiveness toward their wives, thereby preventing conception.[29-39] According to Rutherford et al.,[40] the composite profile of the psychogenically infertile male includes

above-average educational background, a domineering mother who is sexually unsatisfied herself, the childhood threat to withdraw love for "naughty" (i.e., sexual) behavior, lack of sexual aggression before marriage, and conflict within marriage between sexual desire and fear of offending the love object.

It is easy to understand how such thinking evolved. As early as 1945, Helena Deutsch, writing in *The Psychology of Women*, identified five types of women who she believed caused their own infertility: (1) the infantile, dependent woman who somatizes for attention; (2) the woman who expends her motherliness on her husband and knows that he would not welcome the competition of a child; (3) the woman whose motherliness is "consumed in a fire of erotic love . . . or devotion to an ideology"; (4) the masculine, aggressive woman who refuses to accept her properly passive, masochistic role (as defined for women in Freudian dogma); and (5) the emotionally disturbed woman who fears additional burdens.[3] By 1957 when the classic article by Bos and Cleghorn was written,[1] these five types had become the standard for the examination of emotional issues in female infertility.

Although it is easy today for us to be amused at the notion that more than 50% of infertility is caused by psychic conflicts as described by these early Freudians, the consequences of applying these constructs are far from amusing. A generation of infertile couples were in effect scapegoated. They were blamed for their own infertility and sent wandering to discover their unconscious conflicts—all for lack of the more precise science now available to pinpoint organic causes.[41,42]

The Emergence of an Insight: Infertile Couples Are Normal, but Infertility Is a Major Life Stressor

In the 1960s and 1970s, psychologists, social workers, nurses, and infertility specialists joined psychiatry in the quest to understand the relationship between emotional distress and infertility. With the advent of this new mental health team, major breakthroughs were achieved. Standard quantitative tests (MMPI, Rorschach, Neuroticism Scale, and the TAT) were applied to infertile couples, who were found to be no different from the fertile population in psychometric response. Distress related to infertility was not sufficient to manifest psychiatric symptomatology.[43–68] Medical treatment of psychiatric symptoms among infertility patients experiencing depression and anxiety improved their sense of well-being, but did not change their infertility status.[47] Instead of cutting off the foot to fit the shoe, researchers began to describe accurately and quantitatively the emotional experience of infertility.[69,78]

Denber, Noyes and Chapnick, Mai and Eisner were the main leaders of this movement to debunk psychogenic theories. They were effective in shifting the focus of investigation from a small number of psychiatric patients with infertility to the large, little-studied population of normal couples with infertility who experienced distress as a consequence of their condition. As a result of this redirection, some common themes began to be elucidated about the emotional issues related to infertility.

Despite the rapidly mounting evidence that couples with infertility had normal psychological profiles, psychiatry was slow to let go of the Psychogenic Morbidity Model. It was not until Berg and Wilson's critical article in Fertility and Sterility in 1990[79] that emotional dysfunction was officially recognized as psychological strain resulting from infertility.

Development of Constructs for Understanding the Emotional Impact of Infertility: The Crisis Model

Barbara Eck Menning, founder of Resolve, the self-help group for couples with infertility, was instrumental in developing a cognitive construct for understanding how couples are affected emotionally by infertility, how they process the diagnosis, and how they move forward to resolution of psychological distress caused by infertility.[80,81] By 1980 the crisis model initially described by Kubler-Ross had been refined and applied to infertility. Infertility became recognized as a disruption in the normal equilibrium which taxes existing resources, threatens life goals, and may awaken unresolved psychic problems.

As part of this conceptualization, crisis theory was modified to take into account the emotional roller coaster of infertility. Unlike other life crises, infertility is not strictly time-related, but seems to consist of multiple crisis events before either resolution or emotional acceptance is final. As in any crisis, the end product could be either maladaptive change or increased maturity and strength. The couple may experience several emotions and behaviors at different times and in different order from each other: surprise, denial, anger, isolation, guilt, grief, and finally, resolution or acceptance. For the first time, physicians treating infertility were asked to consider patients' emotional needs simultaneously with their medical needs. The concept of an appropriate mental health professional joining forces with the medical team began to solidify.

Elaboration and Refinement of Menning's Model

Several other researchers have been instrumental in expanding the description of the emotional state of infertile couples. Kraft[88] elucidated the intrapsychic conflicts that infertility arouses, while Griffin[89] described gender differences and the effect on the marital relationship. Davis and Dearman[90] isolated six coping strategies commonly used by infertile women: increasing space, regaining control, being the best, looking for hidden meaning, giving in to feelings, and sharing the burden. The aspects of loss of control and the negative effects on self-image and generational identity have also been elaborated and refined.[90,93]

Eight stages of passage through infertility treatment have been identified: diagnosis, assimilation, hope, intensifying treatment, spiralling down, letting go, quitting, and shifting focus.[94] This passage is not without cost. Mahlstedt[95] depicted eight major losses implicit in infertility: loss of a relationship, loss of health, loss of status or prestige, loss of self-esteem, loss of self-confidence, loss of security, loss of a fantasy, and loss of something or someone of great symbolic value.

These observations are more complex when one considers the many types of ambiguity involved in infertility diagnosis and treatment, along with their sociocultural and intrapersonal meanings and consequences.[96] Seibel and Taymor[97] described in detail the interrelationship between the neuroendocrine hormones and stress effects. Others working along those same lines have been evaluating the mediating effects of anxiety, as measured by state-trait testing, on stress-related production of the target hormones prolactin, cortisol, and testosterone.[98,99]

Gender differences also play an important role. Men are generally less directly involved, less obsessive and depressed, but more hostile and angry in their reaction to infertility.[99] They are more likely to describe themselves as being primarily concerned about the threat to the marriage relationship.[101,102] This may reflect the effect of stress on the couple's sexual relationship as attention shifts from making love to making babies.

Sociocultural patterns among infertile couples have also been described.[103] In our society, parenting confers adult status.[104] Generativity (the stage of adulthood described in Erikson's developmental model) tends to be defined narrowly, especially for women, as procreativity rather than creativity. Childlessness can isolate both men and women from their families of origin and their peers.[41,42,103]

Cultural differences have been identified that shape the social perception of infertility, and change its meaning and impact.[105] There are conflicting data about the effects of infertility on sexual relationship and marriage; some studies show no deficit, others show improvement, and still others show diminution of marital satisfaction and sexual enjoyment.[106–111] New tools are currently being developed for measuring emotional effects of infertility, among them a questionnaire from the Psychological Special Interest Section of the American Fertility Society, and the IFQ (Infertility Questionnaire) designed by Bernstein, Potts, and Mattox.[67] An NIH-funded study has been undertaken by the group responsible for the IVF Registry data collection that plans to follow infertility patients for a decade in order to describe both physical and emotional consequences. As information becomes available, appropriate intervention may prevent some of the psychological distress that infertility creates.

Psychological Intervention

Support groups for couples with infertility have proven their value.[112,113] These may be sponsored by a self-help group like Resolve, an infertility practice, or a counseling office. Support groups with a therapeutic approach should be led by mental health professionals, while groups with an educational focus or networking goals may be led by infertility nurses or lay members. Groups may be mixed but often have a specific focus based on gender, diagnosis, or type of treatment.

Supportive counseling may take place in the infertility office or on a referral basis. A growing number of infertility experts make a cogent argument for initial psychological evaluation, support services, crisis intervention, and sexual counseling as required.[91,114–117] As many as 20% of couples may seek out some type of psychological support, and many more will have wished they had.[118] Short-term individual therapy and psychotherapy may be indicated for those for whom infertility awakens old issues. Women who have experienced abuse, and anyone who has been traumatized or has not met usual developmental goals in childhood, will be more vulnerable to the losses infertility brings and may benefit from longer, more intense intervention. Behavioral therapies are being suggested, both individually and in groups, for stress reduction.[96,119,120] Biofeedback training has been utilized, and a successful mind–body program has recently been described.[121] Couples therapy is indicated for those having a difficult time making joint decisions about treatment options, as well as those who have deep-seated conflicts that express themselves through issues related to infertility.[114,115] Group therapy has also been shown to be effective.[122]

A supportive nursing role has been developed to assist couples in getting through the maze of infertility diagnosis and treatment. Education puts control back in patients' hands, and individualized attention helps rebuild self-esteem. Sometimes validation of the difficulty of the experience and the normalcy of the grieving process is all a patient needs to feel better and cope more positively. Permission to feel grief without shame is immensely important. All of these techniques are well within the capabilities of the specialty nurse and consistent with standard nursing philosophy.[112-114]

Evaluation of the Effects of High-Tech Therapies

Much effort has been focused on establishing norms for couples who undergo IVF or other high-tech treatment. Couples typically enter their first IVF cycle hopeful, although often with unrealistic expectations.[123] It is not surprising that Hazeltine and colleagues[54] described elevated levels of anxiety and depression post-IVF, and Garner[124] found 64% of patients to have elevated scores on the Beck Depression Inventory after a failed cycle. An experience of extreme grief and devastation with the first failure is also commonly reported.[125] Others have clarified that couples

who utilize IVF, like infertility patients in general, are normal people experiencing a major life challenge.[126-129] A majority of one study sample found infertility to be the most upsetting experience in their lives, and a large number of respondents to Mahlstedt's questionnaire about the effects of IVF rated infertility as equally distressing as the death of a loved one.[130]

Bombadieri has investigated the special situation of couples who find it impossible to stop therapy, characterized stages of the decision-making process, and developed interventions to enable couples to let go.[131] This process is probably related to patients' motivations for parenthood. Those perceiving greater social pressure to become parents or who view parenting as a prerequisite for personal fulfillment exhibit higher levels of depression.[125] Some of the newer techniques such as surrogacy and gamete donation probably increase the potential for stress.[132] This type of information can often be made available at an initial education and assessment interview with a counselor. Should couples experience difficulty as they move through the assisted reproduction process, they will then have someone to reach out to who is not a stranger.[133,134]

Issues related to surrogacy are just beginning to be investigated.[135] Little is known about the psychological dynamics of any of the parties, and even less about the emotional consequences. Certainly the surrogacy cases that have gotten our attention through the courts imply the potential for suffering inherent in these procedures.

Long-Term Emotional Consequences of Gamete Donation

Donor insemination of sperm and the new therapy of oocyte donation may permanently alter the configuration of family relations, change self-esteem, affect gender identity, modify power relations in the marital context, and have major implications for the emotional health of offspring.[131] Although a growing body of information is evolving about this subject, little is known. Most reports have been subjective, confused by multiple variables, and not controlled. Much remains to be done to describe actual effects of this therapy and the secrecy that surrounds it. Interventions have been developed (e.g., educational efforts, support groups, offspring self-help organizations) but have yet to be objectively tested.[136,137]

Pregnancy After Infertility

Investigation is just beginning to elaborate the potential effects of previous infertility on adaptation to pregnancy and parenting. One article speculates that infertility may make couples more vulnerable to depression and anxiety, and that they may take a much longer time to adjust to pregnancy.[138] Other problems may include control during labor, and possibly overprotectiveness of the child in early infancy. Differences in maternal identity, but not in early mothering, have been described in a small pilot study comparing previously infertile women and never-infertile women.[139] Moreover, the effects of previous infertility may linger; Bernstein et al. found women to remain mildly depressed compared to matched, never-infertile controls 1 year after delivery of a healthy child.[100]

A study currently in progress by Bernstein, Lewis, and Seibel involves both psychometric testing and structured, in-depth interviews in each trimester of pregnancy, matching former IVF patients with those receiving basic therapies and with never-infertile controls. Emerging themes include extensive denial of the pregnancy, increased anxiety, delayed bonding with the fetus, continuance of the self-image as an infertile person, and preoccupation with the next pregnancy while still experiencing the first pregnancy.

State of the Art

Work is proceeding rapidly, and many academic centers now encourage participation of mental health professionals on the infertility team. A special section within the American Fertility Society has been a major resource for dissemination of data, networking, and collegial support. Several multicenter grant applications have grown out of these efforts, and the level of research continues to become more sophisticated. A strong research base will allow us to avoid the pitfalls and misdirections that come from relying on anecdotal experience.

The field of infertility treatment is moving extremely rapidly, and it is imperative that those who study psychological effects and develop supportive interventions move with equal speed. Infertility patients are faced with a confusing array of options, as well as uncharted ethical and legal implications that are very stressful. All of us—physicians, nurses, and mental health professionals—must join our efforts to forge a comprehensive team, so that we can keep pace with technology, anticipate new directions, and help couples make the decisions that enable science to best meet their needs, physical and emotional. This is the mission for the nineties!

References

1. Bos C, Cleghorn RA. Psychogenic sterility. Fertil Steril 1958;9:84–96.
2. Brody H. Psychologic factors associated with infertility in women. Unpublished doctoral dissertation, New York University, 1955.
3. Deutsch HC. The Psychology of Women. Vol. 2. New York: Grune & Stratton, 1945.
4. DeWatteville H. Psychologic factors with treatment of sterility. Fertil Steril 1957;8:12.
5. Fisher C. Psychogenic aspects of sterility. Fertil Steril 1953;4:466–470.
6. Ford E, Forman I, Wilson JR, et al. A psychodynamic approach to the study of infertility. Fertil Steril 1953;4:456.
7. Greenhill JP. Emotional factors in female infertility. Obstet Gynecol 1956;7:602.
8. Hampson JL. Objective personality studies of infertile couples. Unpublished study, University of Washington School of Medicine, Seattle, 1963.
9. Igarashi M, Tohma K, Ozawa M, Hosaka H, Matsumoto S. Pathogenesis of psychogenic

amenorrhea and anovulation. Int J Infertil 1965;10:311.

10. Kroger WW. Evaluation of personality factors in the treatment of infertility. Fertil Steril 1952;3:542.

11. Kroger WW. Psychosomatic Obstetrics, Gynecology and Endocrinology. Springfield, IL: Charles C. Thomas, 1962.

12. MacLeod AW. Some psychogenic aspects of infertility. Fertil Steril 1964;15:125.

13. Karahasanoglu A, Barglow P, Growe G. Psychological aspects of infertility. J Reprod Med 1972;9:241–247.

14. Nesbitt RE, Hollendor M, Fisher S, Osofsky HJ. Psychologic correlates of the polycystic ovary syndrome and organic infertility. Fertil Steril 1968;19:778–786.

15. Norris AS. Psychological aspects of infertility. J Iowa Med Soc 1965;55:122–124.

16. Pohlman E. Childlessness, intentional and unintentional, psychological and social aspects. J Nerv Ment Dis 1970;15:2–12.

17. Rothman O, Kaplan AH, Nettles E. Psychosomatic infertility. Am J Obstet Gynecol 1962;8:373.

18. Rubenstein BB. An emotional factor in infertility: A psychosomatic approach. Fertil Steril 1951:80–86.

19. Sandler B. Infertility of emotional origin. J Obstet Gynecol Br Commonwealth 1961; 68:809.

20. Sandler B. Conception after adoption: A comparison of conception rates. Fertil Steril 1965;16:313–322.

21. Sandler B. Emotional stress and infertility. J Psychosom Res 1968;12:51–59.

22. Seward GH, et al. The question of psychophysiologic infertility: Some negative answers. Psychosom Med 1965;27:533–545.

23. Abse DW. Psychiatric aspects of human male infertility. Fertil Steril 1966;17:133–139.

24. Andrews RG. Adoption and the resolution of infertility. Fertil Steril 1970;21:73–76.

25. Arronet GH, Bergquist CA, Parekh MC. The influence of adoption on subsequent pregnancy in infertile marriage. Int J Fertil 1974;19: 159–162.

26. Banks AL. Counseling in infertility problems. In: Klemer RH, ed. Counseling in Marital and Sexual Problems. Baltimore: Williams and Wilkins Co., 1965:239–252.

27. Wenz FV. Fertility and suicidal behavior (Abstract). Psychol Rep 1976;39:600.

28. Cooper H. Psychogenic infertility and adoption. So Afr Med J 1971;45:719–722.

29. Bullock JL. Iatrogenic impotence in an infertility clinic: Illustrative case. Am J Obstet Gynecol 1974;120:476–478.

30. Calef The hostility of parents to children: Some notes on infertility, child abuse, and

abortion. Int J Psychoanal Psychother, 1972; 1:76–79.

31. Heiman M. Psychoanalytic evaluation of the problem of "one-child sterility." Fertil Steril 1955;6:405.

32. Kaplan E, Blockman L. The husband's role in psychiatric illness associated with childbearing. Psychiat Ann 1969;43:396–409.

33. Klemmer RH, Rutherford RN, Banks AL, Coburn WA. Marriage counseling with the infertile couple. Fertil Steril 1966;17:104–109.

34. Laitmon M. Psychodynamic factors associated with functional infertility in married couples: A comparative study of psychological factors in a group of fertile married couples and a group of infertile married couples without a medical basis for their condition. Unpublished doctoral dissertation, New York University 1963.

35. Palti Z. Psychogenic male infertility. Psychosom Med 1969;31:326–330.

36. Rubenstein BB. An emotional factor in infertility. Clinics in Obstetrics and Gynecology 1965;8:100.

37. Rutherford RN. Emotional aspects of infertility. Clinical Obstetrics and Gynecology 1965;8:100–114.

38. Ginsberg GC, Frosch WA, Shapiro TL. The new impotence. Arch Gen Psychiat 1972; 26:218.

39. Goldberg C. More on the infertile couple (Letter to the Editor) J Psychosoc Nursing 1984;22:43.

40. Rutherford RN, Klemer RH, Banks AL, Coburn WA. Psychogenic infertility from the male viewpoint. Pacif Med Surg 1966;7: 434–439.

41. Benedek T. Parenthood, Its Psychology and Psychopathology. New York: Little, Brown, 1970.

42. Benedek T, Ham GC, Robbins RP, et al. Some emotional factors in infertility. Psychosom Med 1953;14:484.

43. Berger DM. The role of the psychiatrist in the reproductive biology clinic. Fertil Steril 1977; 20:89–90.

44. Berger DM. Psychological assessment of the infertile couple. Can Fam Physician 1974; 20:89–90.

45. Debrovner CH. Sexual problems associated with infertility. Med Aspects Hum Sexual 1976;10:161–162.

46. Debrovner CH, Shubin-Stein R. Sexual problems in the infertile couple. Med Aspects Hum Sexual 1975;9:140–152.

47. Denber HCB, Rolan M. Effect of tybamate on psychosomatic symptoms in a group of infertility patients. Fertil Steril 1969;20: 373–379.

48. Donovan JC. Psychiatric evaluation of the infertile couple. In: Gold JJ, ed. Gynecologic Endocrinology. 2nd ed. Hagerstown, MD: Harper & Row, 1975.

49. Dubin L, Amelar RD. Sexual causes of male infertility. Fertil Steril 1972;23:579–582.

50. Eisner BG. Some psychological differences between fertile and infertile women. J Clin Psychol 1963;19:391.

51. Elstein M. Effects of infertility on psychosexual function. Br Med J 1975;3:296–299.

52. Fagan PJ, Schmidt CW, et al. Sexual functioning and psychologic evaluation of in vitro couples. Fertil Steril 1986;46:668–672.

53. Freeman EW, Boxer AS, Rickels K, Tureck R, Mastroianni L. Behavioral and emotional factors: Comparisons of anovulatory infertile women with fertile and other infertile women. Fertil Steril 1985;43:48–53.

54. Hazeltine FP, Mazure CM, et al. Psychologic testing of couples in the in vitro program suggested dysphoria among the males and high anxiety component in the couples. Fertil Steril 1984;41:575–578.

55. Link PW, Darling C. Couples undergoing treatment for infertility: Dimensions of life satisfaction. J Sex Marital Ther 1986; 12:46–59.

56. Mai FMM. Psychiatric and interpersonal factors in infertility. Aust NZ J Psychiat 1969; 3:31–36.

57. Mai FMM. Conception after adoption: An open question. Psychosom Med 1971; 33:509–514.

58. Mai FMM. Interesting sexual cases: Psychogenic infertility. Med Aspects Hum Sexual 1971;5:26–28.

59. Mai FMM. Fertility and psychiatric morbidity. Aust NZ J Psychiat 1972;6:165.

60. Mai FMM, Munday RN, Rump EE. Psychiatric interview comparisons between infertile and fertile couples. Psychosom Med 1972; 34:431–440.

61. Mai FMM, Munday RN, Rump EE. Psychosomatic and behavioral mechanisms in psychogenic infertility. Int J Psychiat 1972; 120:199–204.

62. Mai FMM, Rump EE. Are infertile men and women neurotic? Aust J Psychol 1972; 24:83–86.

63. Noyes RW, Chapnick EM. Literature on psychology and infertility. Fertil Steril 1964; 15:543–558.

64. Paulson JD, Haarmann BS, Salerno RL, Asmar P. An investigation of the relationship between emotional maladjustment and infertility. Fertil Steril 1988;49:258–263.

65. Piatt JJ, Fisher I, Silver MJ. Infertile couples personality traits and self-ideal concept discrepancies. Fertil Steril 1973;24:972–976.

66. Shirai GH, Bloch SK, Heinrich JF. Sexual behavior in male infertility. Tohoku J Exp Med 1968;95:313–316.

67. Bernstein J, Potts N, Mattox J. Assessment of psychological dysfunction associated with infertility. JOGN Nurs 1985;6:63s.

68. Daniluk C. Infertility: Intrapersonal and interpersonal impact. Fertil Steril 1988; 49:982–990.

69. Downey J, Yingling S, et al. Mood disorders, psychiatric symptoms, and distress in women presenting for infertility evaluation. Fertil Steril 1989;52:425–429.

70. McGuire LS. Psychologic management of infertile women. Postgrad Med 1975; 57:173–176.

71. Murphy MJ. Fertility, birth timing, and marital breakdown: A reinterpretation of the evidence. J Biosoc Sci 1984;16:487–500.

72. Roland M. Management of the Infertile Couple. Springfield, IL: Charles C. Thomas, 1968.

73. Rosenfield DL, Mitchell E. Treating the emotional aspects of infertility—Counseling services in an infertility clinic. Am J Obstet Gynecol 1979;135:177–180.

74. Walker HE. Psychiatric aspects of infertility. Urol Clin No Am 1978;5:481–488.

75. Walker HE. Sexual problems and infertility. Psychosomatics 1978;19:477–484.

76. Wiehe VR. Psychologic reaction to infertility: Implications for nursing for resolving feelings of disappointment and inadequacy. JOGN Nurs 1976;18:20.

77. Williams LS, Power PW. The emotional impact of infertility in single women: Some implications for counseling. J Am Med Womens Assoc 1977;32:327–333.

78. wilson EA. Sequence of emotional response induced by infertility. J Kentucky Med Assoc 1979;77:229–233.

79. Berg BJ, Wilson JF. Psychiatric morbidity in the infertile population: A reconceptualization. Fertil Steril 1990;53:654–661.

80. Menning BE. Infertility: Facts and feelings. Nurs Dig 1976;3–7.

81. Menning BE. Counseling infertile couples. Obstet Gynecol 1979;22:1–8.

82. Menning BE. The emotional needs of infertile couples. Fertil Steril 1980;34:313–319.

83. Menning BE. Donor insemination: The psychological issues. Contemp OB Gyn 1981; 18:155–172.

84. Newton CR, Hearn MT, Yupze AA. Psychological assessment and follow-up after IVF: Assessing the impact of failure. Fertil Steril 1990;54:879–886.

85. Rutledge AL. Psychomarital evaluation and treatment of the infertile couple. Clin Obstet Gynecol 1979;22:255–267.

86. Bernstein J, Mattox J. An overview of infertility. JOGN Nurs 1982;11:309.

87. Walker HE. Sexual and psychological problems and infertility. In: Crockett ATK, Urry RL eds. Male Infertility: Workup, Treatment and Research. Grune and Stratton New York 1977.

88. Kraft AD, Palombo J, Mitchell P, Dean C, Meyers S, Schmidt AW. The psychological dimensions of infertility. Am J Orthopsychiat 1980;50:618–628.

89. Griffin ME. Resolving infertility: An emotional crisis. AORN J 1983;38:597–601.

90. Davis DC, Dearman DN. Coping strategies of infertile women. JOGN Nurs 1991;20:221–228.

91. Frank DI. Counseling the infertile couple. J Psychosoc Nurs 1984;225:17–23.

92. Mazor M. Barren couples. Psychol Today 1979;12:101–112.

93. McCormick TM. Out of control: One aspect of infertility. JOGN Nurs 1980;9:205–206.

94. Blenner JL. Passage through infertility: A stage theory. Image 1990;22:153k–158.

95. Mahlstedt PP. The psychological components of infertility. Fertil Steril 1985;43:335–346.

96 Sandelowski M. The color gray: Ambiguity and infertility. Image 1987;19:70–74.

97. Seibel M, Taymor M. Emotional aspects of infertility. Fertil Steril 1982;37:137–145.

98. Demyttenaere K, Nojs P, Evers-Kiebooms G, Kroninckx PR. The effect of a specific emotional stressor on prolactin, cortisol, and testosterone concentrations in women varies with their trait anxiety. Fertil Steril 1989;52:942–948.

99. Rose R. Androgen responses to stress. Psychosom Med 1969;31:405–417.

100. Bernstein J, Mattox JH, Kellner R. Psychological status of previously infertile couples after a successful pregnancy. JOGN Nurs 1988;17:404.

101. Nachtigall RD, Becker G. The differential experience of men and women undergoing an infertility evaluation. Paper presented at the meeting of the Pacific Coast Infertility Society, Las Vegas, NV, 1985.

102. Wright J, Duschesne C, et al. Psychosocial distress and infertility: Men and women respond differently. Fertil Steril 1991;55:100–108.

103. Benedek T. Parenthood as a developmental phase. J Am Psychoanal Assoc 1959;7:389.

104. Veevers JE. The social meanings of parenthood. Psychiatry 1973;36:291–310.

105. Agunloye K. Infertility—A sociocultural definition. Nigerian Nurse 1978;10(3):27–28.

106. Barnes J. Psychosexual problems and infertility. Ir J Med 1979;148:6–10.

107. Bell J. Psychological problems among patients attending an infertility clinic. J Psychosom Res 1981;25:1–3.

108. Keye WR. Psychosexual responses to infertility. Clin Obst Gynecol 1984;27:760–766.

109 Hirsch AM, Hirsch SM. The effect of infertility on marriage and self concept. JOGN Nurs 1989;18:13–20.

110. Kaufman SA. Impact of infertility on the marital and sexual relationship. Fertil Steril 1969;20:380–383.

111. Shrednick A. The impact of infertility on the marital relationship. Paper presented at the meeting of the Pacific Coast Fertility Society, Las Vegas, NV, 1985.

112. Christianson C. Support groups for infertile patients. JOGN Nurs 1986; 15:293–297.

113. Sanfilippo JS, Galbraith E, Yussman MA. In office infertility support group. Obstet Gynecol 1989;74:405–407.

114. Milne BJ. Couples' experiences with in vitro fertilization. JOGN Nurs 1988;17:347–352.

115. Sarrel PM, DeCherney AH. Psychotherapeutic intervention for treatment of couples with secondary infertility 1985; 43:897–900.

116. Taymor ML, Bresnick E. Infertility counseling. In: Taymor ML, ed. Infertility. New York: Grune & Stratton, 1978:94–98.

117. Bresnick E, Taymor ML. The role of counseling in infertility. Fertil Steril 1979;32:154–156.

118. Seibel MM, Bernstein J, Levin S, Seibel SG. Epidemiologic insights into the importance of emotional support in infertility treatment. American Fertility Society, Orlando, Florida, October 1991.

119. Moore AM, O'Moore RR, Harrison RF, Murphy G, Carruthers ME. Psychosomatic aspects in idiopatic infertility: Effects of treatment with autogenic training. J Psychosom Res 1983;27(2):145–151

120. Hellhammer H, Hubert W, Freishem CW, Nieschlag E. Male infertility: Relationships among gonadotropins, sex steroids, seminal parameters, and personality attitudes. Psychosom Med 1985;47:58–66.

121. Domar A, Seibel MM, Benson H. The mind/body program for infertility: A new behavioral treatment approach for women with infertility. Fertil Steril 1990;53:246–249.

122. Abarbanel AR, Bach G. Group psychotherapy for the infertile couple. Int J Fertil 1959;4:151.

123. Kopotzke EJ, Berg BJ, Wilson JF, Owens D. Physical and emotional stress associated with components of the infertility investigation: Perspectives of professionals and patients. Fertil Steril 1991;55:1137.

124. Garner CH, Kelly M, Arnold ES. Psychological profile of IVF patients (Abstract). Fertil Steril 1984;44:57S.

125. Newton R, Hearn MT, Yupze AA. Motives for parenthood as a predictor of psychological vulnerability to failed in vitro fertilization. Paper presented at the 7th World Congress of In Vitro Fertilization, Paris, 1991.

126. Callan VJ, Kloske B, Kashima Y, Hennessey JF. Toward understanding women's decisions to continue or stop in vitro fertilization: The role of social, psychological and background factors. J In Vitro Fert 1988;5:363–369.

127. Morse C, Dennerstein L. Infertile couples entering an in vitro program: A preliminary survey. J Psychosom Obstet Gynecol 1985; 4:207–210.

128. Seibel M, Levin S. A new era in reproductive technologies: The emotional stages of in vitro fertilization. J In Vitro Fert 1987;4:135–140.

129. Leiblum SR, Kemmann E, Lane MK. The psychological concomitants of in vitro fertilization. J Psychosom Obstet Gynecol 1987; 6:165–169.

130. Mahlstedt PP, MacDuff S, Bernstein J. Emotional factors and the in vitro fertilization and embryo transfer process. J In Vitro Fert 1987;4:232–236.

131. Mahlstedt P, Greenfield DA. Assisted reproductive technology with donor gametes: The need for patient preparation. Fertil Steril 1989;52:908.

132. Bombadieri M. When to call it quits. In: Seibel MM, et al., eds. Technological Advances in Infertility and Their Psychosocial, Ethical and Legal consequences. New York: Springer-Verlag, 1991.

133. Greenfeld PA, Lavy G, Greenfeld D, Holm CT, DeCherney AH. Helping patients end treatment: The IVF follow-up clinic as a tool for continuing psychological assessment. In: Mashiach et al., eds. Advances in Assisted Reproductive Technologies. New York: Plenum Press, 1990.

134. Mikesell S, Falk R. The utilization of assessment of marital satisfaction and interpersonal perceptions with IVF couples to develop intervention strategies to reduce the psychological impact of the stress associated with infertility. Fertil Steril 1984;41:58s.

135. Reame NE. Maternal adaptation and psychologic responses to a surrogate pregnancy. Paper presented at the American Fertility Society Meeting, Atlanta, Georgia, 1988.

136. D'Andrea KG. The role of the nurse practitioner in artificial insemination. JOGN Nurs 1984;13:75–78.

137. Mahlstedt PP, Probasco KA. Sperm donors: Their attitudes toward providing medical and psychosocial information for recipient couples and donor offspring. Fertil Steril 1991;56:747.

138. Garner CH. Pregnancy after infertility. JOGN Nurs 1985;6:58s.

139. Dunnington RM, Glazer G. Maternal identity and early mothering behavior in previously infertile and newly infertile women. JOGN Nurs 1991;20:309.

26
Psychological Evaluation of the Infertile Couple

Susan Levin

A couple beginning their infertility workup is generally optimistic and hopeful that their problem will be diagnosed and solved quickly, and that they will soon have a baby. Paradoxically, at the same time they can also be frightened and anxious about what is wrong with them and deeply concerned about whether or not they will be able to have a child. Each couple has a different style of managing fears and anxieties. Each has a personal history that predates their infertility problem and may directly affect how they react to all of the medical tests and to the final results of their treatments.

Psychologic evaluation or assessment can offer emotional support for these patients as well as provide the medical team with a thorough understanding of their needs. A complete evaluation should include a full history revealing the psychodynamics of each individual and couple. This information places the couple and their infertility within the context of their lives rather than isolated in the doctor's office. An effort should be made to integrate the evaluation into the total infertility workup. This can be accomplished by an early introduction to the mental health professional. The patient then experiences the evaluation as routine, thus avoiding the stigma usually attached to such a referral.

It is essential that the clinician understand that many of the tests involved with infertility are intrusive, painful, embarrassing, and cause great disruptions in people's lives. This knowledge will assist in the understanding of the impact of the problem on the couple. For example, taking one's temperature in the morning may seem painless and easy. A

therapist might be puzzled by someone's inability to comply unless he or she knows that many women find this simple act extremely difficult because it is a persistent reminder that they are infertile and that their sexual relationship has deteriorated.

Another example is the hysterosalpingogram. Whereas some women find the procedure relatively painless, others can find it excruciating. This reaction could be related to the condition of the tubes, the woman's anxiety, or her pain tolerance. Sometimes they are difficult to sort out. The clinician who is knowledgeable about the medical part of the workup is better able to prepare, educate, and support these patients. However, it is important for the mental health provider to resist the temptation to give medical opinions about the treatment. If the patient needs a second opinion, she can be encouraged to arrange for that from the appropriate source.

It is important to remember that referral to a psychiatrist, a social worker, a psychologist, or a psychiatric nurse can be experienced as yet another intrusive test. Generally, individuals or couples who come for a psychiatric consultation are anxious but hopeful that they will be helped and eventually feel relief. When infertility is the problem, patients may seem more anxious, guarded, or even angry. They are sensitive about their bodies not working properly. Control and self-esteem issues are central.

The infertility workup has exposed the most intimate parts of their lives and their relationship. Patients can often be embarrassed and extremely vulnerable as they describe their situation. They may feel awkward when they mispronounce a medical procedure. They may be afraid to cry and express their feelings. They are concerned about being judged or diagnosed as "crazy". Now, not only are their bodies out of control, but perhaps their minds are too. They may fear being blamed for causing their problem: for example, that some deep secret or past event, or even ambivalence about having a child, will be discovered. Again they will lose control over what occurs in the interview.

The first task is to provide a comfortable environment where these patients can feel safe and begin to form a trusting relationship. This starts with simple and obvious items such as where the interview takes place; a box of tissues makes it clear that tears are not surprising and helps give their personal experiences a feeling of normalcy. Introducing yourself, handshakes if appropriate, explanation of the purpose of the interview and what you hope to gain from the session are important to the patient. Finding out if there has been a previous experience with a therapist and whether it was a negative experience can help explain expectations. All of this may help patients feel more in control.

Several areas should be examined to establish the psychologic status of the infertile couple or individual.

The Couple's Relationship

How is the couple currently functioning and how has infertility changed their relationship? Are they closer now, or are they more distant? How are they communicating? What is their style of coping with this crisis and other crises? How has infertility affected their sexual relationship? What level of intimacy have they been comfortable with past and present? What is the history of the relationship? How long have they known each other? How long have they been married? How much time in their relationship has been focused on having children? Have there been other crises, medical problems, or stresses that they have had to cope with? Were they aware of an infertility problem prior to marriage? How

important are children to each of them? Have they broken up during their relationship? Has either one been married before? Do they have any biologic children from previous relationships? Has the woman had any abortions from this relationship? Has she had other pregnancy losses?

The history allows you to assess the foundation of the couple's relationship with a better understanding of each partner's expectations and goals. There is potentially a big difference between a couple in their mid-thirties who have been married for 1 year with a diagnosis predating their relationship and a couple of the same age who have been trying to conceive for 8 of the 10 years that they have been married. Couples who have had a difficult relationship prior to infertility may have a lot of anger toward each other and may have difficulty with the issues around blame and guilt.

The Meaning and Dynamics of Infertility

Much of this is gathered from the history. Has the couple always known that they were going to have children and planned their lives around parenthood? Some couples have chosen their careers, their houses, and even their automobile based on that expectation. Others married knowing that they never wanted children and later changed their minds.

A recent death in a family may lead a couple to believe that a baby would replace the loss. A couple may start their infertility treatment and find that a parent is diagnosed with a terminal illness. Obviously, they are feeling increased emotional strain and pressure. They may not only be grieving the potential loss of their parent but also be responsible for the parent's care. It becomes quite difficult to juggle medical appointments for everyone and keep functioning at work and at home. The couple may want to produce the first grandchild before the parent dies and be devastated when this is not possible.

The following questions help unfold some of the unspoken. What is motivating the couple, and what underlying meaning does a biologic child hold for them? When the couple thinks about having a baby, which is more important, the pregnancy or the baby? Do they think about a child or someone to keep them company in their old age? If one of the partners already has a biologic baby, is the other one more motivated and perhaps even asserting more pressure and displaying more affect around infertility? Often one member of the couple is more invested in the infertility treatments and the biologic child. Understanding what is motivating both partners helps to understand their pain and perhaps answer questions that the medical team may have as they provide their care.

The Couple's Support System

Does the couple have established supports? Do they live near family? Do they have friends or are they more isolated? Who have they told about their infertility?

Is this the way they normally deal with a problem? Do they feel more isolated because of infertility? Do people at work know about their situation, and does work provide the necessary flexibility so that they can go for the many doctor's appointments? Do they feel their friends and family are empathic and supportive?

It is not unusual to find that couples who usually turn to friends and family for support have decided to keep this problem a secret. This of course leads potentially to social isolation, which can then exaggerate their feeling of being damaged, out of sync with their peers, and alone.

The Psychodynamics of the Individual

How is each member of the couple functioning? What is their affective response (i.e., depressed, anxious, sad, angry, etc.) and is it typical for them? What has been their recent and past experience with loss (both real and symbolic) and other traumatic events? How has their self-esteem been affected?

What other medical problems have they had? Many years ago a woman was referred after an interrupted IVF cycle. While waiting for her retrieval, she panicked, and went home before the procedure. This very erratic behavior made more sense when she was able to explain to her consultant that earlier in her life she had undergone surgery that required anesthesia. She had an extremely bad experience with the anesthesia and was frightened by the IVF procedure. After explaining her fears, she was able to tell the anesthesiologist and to have a retrieval.

Has the couple had a drug or alcohol problem? Does either one have a psychiatric history? A family history is also important. Female patients have had mothers with serious psychiatric illnesses that seemed to relate to childbirth and pregnancy. This often frightens these women when they feel "crazy" after taking different hormones. It is a reasonable concern and they are possibly at risk for a similar illness.

Goals, Expectations, and Plans

How long will the couple pursue the quest for the biologic child? Many people may not have thought about this, but it is important because it helps them conceptualize an end to the treatment, even if no child results. If they start to plan for closure, it helps them to regain some of the control that they have given to the medical staff. Some couples may think in terms of how many treatment cycles they will try, how many years they will wait, or what is the oldest they want to be. What level of technology will they pursue in their treatment? What other options have they considered? Are adoption, surrogacy, or donor programs possible for this couple?

Although the couple may change their mind about these goals or plans, it can be helpful to the medical team to have some idea about what is initially tolerable and expected. These questions also establish how realistic the couple is as they approach treatment.

Obviously this information is gathered over time, and one interview is not enough time.

The mental health clinician is not the only one who has access to the patient. With a team approach, everyone can plan, evaluate, and provide support for the patients.

Case Reports

The following vignettes illustrate the benefit of an evaluation. Each of these happened at different points during the patients' medical workup.

The As

Mrs. A called the clinical social worker after she had been referred by her infertility specialist. She had been trying to conceive for a little more than a year and had sought help only a few months earlier. She was feeling desperate and was in tears in her physician's office. Initially, she wanted to come alone to the first sessions, saying that she was too vulnerable and needed the time for herself. During these meetings she expressed a great deal of anger and sadness about her infertility, and in some ways her affect seemed out of proportion to where she was in her workup. She was ready to quit and adopt.

At the time of the evaluation the cause of her infertility was undiagnosed, and she was frustrated with all of the tests and negative results. Gradually, she was able to describe how torn she felt between her role as a high-powered professional woman and her desire to be a mother. Was her ambitiousness interfering with her ability to conceive and to be a good wife? She was able to reveal that she felt her marriage was at a difficult place and worried that her husband was having an affair. She said that he was never home and was always unavailable, and that the pleasure that they used to have with each other was greatly diminished. She feared that she and her infertility were driving him away.

Mr. A had not been able to complete his medical tests. It was possible that he had an infertility problem. Whenever they were supposed to have sexual relations, they would either have a fight or he would have to work late and be too tired. The couple's ability to communicate had deteriorated significantly.

Mrs. A's anxiety about her marriage was quickly connected to the fact that her own parents had a difficult marriage with many separations, that ultimately ended in divorce. She feared that the same would happen to her marriage, which was why she resisted asking her husband to join her at these sessions. She also feared that he would turn down her request. She described her husband as very fragile and mute when it came to discussing feelings. When she did ask him to come to a session, to her surprise, he eagerly accepted. Within a few meetings he was quite talkative and seemed easily able to allay her fears about an affair or divorce. He was clearly committed to their relationship and had strong positive feelings for his wife. However, he was very upset about the infertility and knew how desperately Mrs. A wanted a child. He feared that medical tests would reveal that it was his problem and that it would be hopeless. There was no medical basis for his fears. Eventually he was able to describe his negative feelings about hospitals, doctors, and medical procedures.

Several years before Mr. A had met his wife, his sister had died of cancer. He had been quite close to this sister and had spent a great deal of time at the hospital with her and had talked to her doctors frequently. She had undergone many tests and treatments, and in the end her case was hopeless. Whenever he went to the hospital for procedures he was reminded of his loss. Mr. A showed a great deal of affect during this interview and was able to connect the past with the present. He used these sessions to do delayed grief work. Afterward, he was able to complete his part of the workup and provide support to his wife. Their relationship improved. Mrs. A was less angry and more sympathetic with her husband's concerns and vice versa.

To understand and evaluate this couple, the past and the present were crucial. They had a good relationship prior to infertility, but it was deteriorating quickly. Each partner had experienced losses that infertility was bringing back to the surface. In this case, it was hard to separate evaluation from therapy, since the evaluation became therapeutic. This case also raised the question of when to see the couple and when to see the individual. Some might suggest always to see the couple on the first visit, since infertility is a couple's problem; however, not all patients agree. Sometimes one member wants time alone because, just like Mrs. A, he or she feels too vulnerable, confused, and perhaps angry. Often it is important to respond to the request to be alone with the therapist with the idea that eventually both should be seen at least a few times, even if by a different therapist.

The Bs

In this case the nurse practitioner was the evaluator. As the team nurse, she faced with Mrs. B a very angry and unhappy patient. Mrs. B came to have a uterine sounding and was impatient with the support staff and somewhat hostile to the nurse. She was quite confused about the purpose of the procedure and resistant to having it done. Explanations were almost useless and just seemed to make Mrs. B more disturbed.

The nurse invited Mrs. B into her consultation room so that they could talk about starting the procedure. It was soon discovered that Mrs. B had had several ectopic pregnancies and had undergone surgery. Coming in for a uterine sounding brought back the emotional pain that she experienced with these earlier losses. She had not had the oportunity to talk about these losses. During this tearful session she expressed the sadness and the anger that she had felt. Her anger was connected to feeling that the medical staff had not listened to her when she was complaining of pain. Thanks to the sensitive intervention of the nurse, Mrs. B was able to proceed with the uterine sounding and the rest of the medical workup.

The Cs

Mr. and Mrs. C had been trying to conceive for 4 of the 5 years they had been married. They had not had any conceptions and were about to try IVF. Mr. C's sperm count was low, with poor morphology and motility. A chronic illness required him to have repeated blood transfusions from which he contracted another chronic illness. The doctor kept insisting that the couple try donor sperm, but they never responded.

After their first failed IVF cycle, Mrs. C became upset and was referred to the mental health consultant. During the first session she was able to discuss the pressure she was feeling from the physician to use a donor. She and her husband didn't want a donor and felt that they were not being listened to, yet they worried that the team would not allow them to try another cycle unless they agreed to the recommendation.

Their reluctance to use the donor was based on Mr. C's experience with the blood transfusion, and they feared that they might contract something a lot worse. They had both decided that they would like to try one more cycle of IVF and, if unsuccessful, quit their infertility treatments and either adopt or remain child free. The pressure was very painful, as they wanted very much to do the "right" thing and please the doctor. Once this couple's goals and plans were clear, the doctor was able to stop offering what she thought was right for them. The evaluation allowed the patients to explain what they wanted.

Questionnaires

Each of these vignettes demonstrates different types of evaluations done in an interview format. Questionnaires can also be used to help fill in the psychologic picture (Appendix 1). However, they should be used together with a mental health professional, not instead of one. The professional provides a relationship that can be a safety net.

Questionnaires must be used carefully so that they are not experienced as cold and intrusive. They are best used with the personal consultation, and can be completed while patients are waiting for their appointment or after the consultation. Usually the questionnaire takes at most 10 minutes to complete, and it can provide information that the consultant may not have had time to ask about or highlight areas that need more in-depth evaluation.

Evaluations for Special Therapies

Mention should be made of the mental health evaluations done prior to high-tech procedures, including in vitro fertilization (IVF), gamete intrafallopian transfer (GIFT), zygote intrafallopian transfer (ZIFT), and donor egg. Many programs require that an evaluation be done before patients proceed with these treatments rather than making it optional. Although the evaluation is more like a consultation to the team, patients perceive it more like a screening. The requirement may only be one interview and therefore, the goals are different.

A required interview automatically creates certain problems. The mental health provider is immediately perceived as a gatekeeper. Patients often are resistant and angry about the meeting. They may fear that something about them will interfere with their being able to undergo the procedure. This anxiety may interfere with their being able to use the session for a consultation. They may feel that they have to hide who they are in order to appear presentable and pass the "test."

Great effort must be made to allay these fears when possible. If there is only one session, the following goals are realistic: (1) provide education about the emotional component of the procedure; (2) assess and share with the couple potential risks and vulnerabilities as they prepare for the procedure; (3) gather information to share with the team to assist the couple in coping; and (4) offer to be an impartial go-between for the couple and team if problems develop.

Usually one interview is required for IVF, GIFT, and ZIFT. The various donor programs often involve more contacts because of the complexity of the issues. In the donor egg programs where the donor is known, more interviews are required because more people than the infertile couple are involved. The number of interviews should be left to the judgment of the mental health professional. There should be a certain amount of flexibility.

It is clear that infertility deeply affects people psychologically and socially. The purpose of the psychologic evaluation is first to provide information that will help other medical professionals manage patients' care in a way that fits with their patients' needs. Second, and equally important, this information lets us know if other interventions are necessary. Some of these interventions are as follows:

1. Groups provide support and information as they help individuals and couples deal with their isolation.
2. Individual counseling appeals to some patients who find a group overwhelming and uncomfortable.
3. Intensive psychotherapy may be indicated for those with longstanding issues who have the motivation to work toward change.
4. Behavioral therapies aimed at reducing stress and anxiety have been quite successful.
5. A referral to a psychopharmacologist may be indicated in cases of severe depression, active psychosis, or severe anxiety. The professional chosen should be well aware of the issues of pregnancy and medication.
6. Psychiatric hospitalization may be indicated for patients who are severely depressed or suicidal.

In dealing with these last two interventions, a mental health professional should already be involved. With all of them, however, the goal is to provide this population with the opportunity for emotional growth and to enrich their lives in spite of their infertility.

Suggested Reading

1. Bernstein J, Potts N, Mattox J. Assessment of psychological dysfunction associated with infertility. JOGN Nurs 1985;6:635.
2. Bresnick E, Taymor ML. The role of counseling in infertility. Fertil Steril 1979;32:154–156.
3. Menning BE. Infertility: A Guide for the Childless Couple. New York: Prentice-Hall, 1977.
4. Benedek T. Parenthood: Its Psychology and Pathology. New York: Little, Brown, 1970.
5. Lidz RW. Conflicts between fertility and infertility. In: Notman MT, Nadelson C, eds. The Woman Patient. Vol. I. Sexual and Reproductive Aspects of Women's Health Care. New York: Plenum Press, 1978.
6. Mazor MD. The problem of infertility. In: Notman MT, Nadelson C. The Woman Patient. Vol. I. Sexual and Reproductive Aspects of Women's Health Care. New York: Plenum Press, 1978.
7. Friedman R, Gradstein B. Surviving Pregnancy Loss. Boston: Little, Brown, 1982.
8. Mazor M. Barren couples. Psychol Today 1979;12:101–112.
9. Manlstedt PP. Psychological components of infertility. Fertil Steril 1985;43:335–346.
10. Berg BJ, Wilson JF. Psychiatric morbidity in the infertile couple: A reconceptulization. Fertil Steril 1990;53:654–661.
11. Domar AD, Seibel MM, Benson H. The mind/body program for infertility: A new behavioral treatment approach for women with infertility. Fertil Steril 1990;53:246–249.
12. Paulson JD, Haarmann BS, Salerno RL, Asmar P. An investigation of the relationship between emotional maladjustment and infertility. Fertil Steril 1988;24:972–976.
13. Seibel M, Levin S. A new era in reproductive technologies: Emotional stages of in vitro fertilization. J In Vitro Fert 1987;4:135–140.
14. Taymor ML, Bresnick E. Infertility counseling. In: Taymor ML, ed. Infertility. New York: Grune & Stratton, 1978.
15. Seibel M, Taymor M, Emotional aspects of infertility. Fertil Steril 1982;37:137–145.
16. Glazer E. Group therapy and support groups. In: Seibel. MM, Kiessling AA, Bernstein J, Levin S, eds. Technology and Infertility:

Clinical, Psychosocial, Legal and Ethical Aspects. New York: Springer-Verlag, 1992.

17. Cooper S. Couples therapy. In: Seibel MM, Kiessling AA, Bernstein J, Levin S, eds. Technology and Infertility: Clinical, Psychosocial, Legal and Ethical Aspects. New York: Springer-Verlag, 1993.

18. Cooper S. Sexual dysfunction and treatment. In: Seibel MM, Kiessling AA, Bernstein J, Levin S, eds. Technology and Infertility: Clinical, Psychosocial, Legal and Ethical Aspects. New York: Springer-Verlag, 1993.

19. Wright J, Duschesne C, Sabourin S, et al. Psychosocial distress and infertility: Men and women respond differently. Fertil Steril 1991; 55:100–108.

APPENDIX 1. IFQ

Instructions: Please circle the number closest to the reaction that most accurately expresses your current feelings.

Answer:	Strongly Agree	Agree	Neutral	Disagree	Strongly Disagree
Circle:	5	4	3	2	1

1. I feel bad about my body because of our inability to have a child.
   5   4   3   2   1

2. Since our infertility I feel I can do anything as well as I used to.
   5   4   3   2   1

3. I feel I am as attractive as before our infertility.
   5   4   3   2   1

4. I feel less masculine/feminine because of our inability to have a child.
   5   4   3   2   1

5. Compared with others, I feel I am a worthwhile person.
   5   4   3   2   1

6. Lately, I feel I am sexually attractive to my partner.
   5   4   3   2   1

7. I feel I will be incomplete as a man/woman if we cannot have a child.
   5   4   3   2   1

8. Having an infertility problem makes me feel physically incompetent.
   5   4   3   2   1

9. I feel guilty about somehow causing our infertility.
   5   4   3   2   1

10. I wonder if our infertility problem is due to something I did in the past.
    5   4   3   2   1

11. My spouse makes me feel guilty about our problem.
    5   4   3   2   1

12. There are times when I blame my partner for our infertility.
    5   4   3   2   1

13. I feel I am being punished because of our infertility.
    5   4   3   2   1

14. Lately, I feel I am able to respond to my spouse sexually.
    5   4   3   2   1

15. I feel sex is a duty, not a pleasure.
    5   4   3   2   1

16. Since our infertility problem, I enjoy sexual relations with my spouse.
    5   4   3   2   1

17. We have sexual relations for the purpose of trying to conceive.
    5   4   3   2   1

18. Sometimes I feel like a "sex machine" programmed to have sex during the fertile period.
    5   4   3   2   1

19. Impaired fertility has helped our sexual relationship.
    5   4   3   2   1

20. Our inability to have a child has *increased* my desire for sexual relations.
    5   4   3   2   1

21. Our inability to have a child has *decreased* my desire for sexual relations.
    5   4   3   2   1

Questionnaire especially for infertility patients designed by Judith Bernstein.

Infertility Questionnaire: Scoring Sheet

A: Self-esteem (Q 1–8)	B: Blame/guilt (Q 9–13)	C: Sexuality (Q 14–21)
Q 1: 5=5 4=4 3=3 2=2 1=1 _____	Q 9: 5=5 4=4 3=3 2=2 1=1 _____	Q 14: 5=1 4=2 3=3 2=4 1=5 _____
Q 2: 5=1 4=2 3=3 2=4 1=5 _____	Q 10: 5=5 4=4 3=3 2=2 1=1 _____	Q 15: 5=5 4=4 3=3 2=2 1=1 _____
Q 3: 5=1 4=2 3=3 2=4 1=5 _____	Q 11: 5=5 4=4 3=3 2=2 1=1 _____	Q 16: 5=1 4=2 3=3 2=4 1=5 _____
Q 4: 5=5 4=4 3=3 2=2 1=1 _____	Q 12: 5=5 4=4 3=3 2=2 1=1 _____	Q 17: 5=5 4=4 3=3 2=2 1=1 _____
Q 5: 5=1 4=2 3=3 2=4 1=5 _____	Q 13: 5=5 4=4 3=3 2=2 1=1 _____	Q 18: 5=5 4=4 3=3 2=2 1=1 _____
Q 6: 5=1 4=2 3=3 2=4 1=5 _____		Q 19: 5=1 4=2 3=3 2=4 1=5
Q 7: 5=5 4=4 3=3 2=2 1=1		Q 20: 5=1 4=2 3=3 2=4 1=5 _____
Q 8: 5=5 4=4 3=3 2=2 1=1 _____		Q 21: 5=5 4=4 3=3 2=2 1=1 _____

Total: _____ A   Total: _____ B   Total: _____ C
Divide by 8 = _____ X̄   Divide by 5 = _____ X̄   Divide by 8 = _____ X̄

Total test score: Add subscale A, B, and C and divide by 21 = _____ X̄

        Mean score of 1–3 = no distress
        Mean score of 3.1–4 = mild to moderate distress
        Mean score of 4.1–5 = severe distress

27
Male Infertility: The Psychologic Issues

R. Tracy MacNab

If one looks at the popular media, the scientific journals, and some recent books, it is clear that we have rediscovered fatherhood. Fathers are important, and maybe more important than we thought, both in the family and in the lives of their children. Increasing scientific evidence indicates too that fathering has enormous effects on children in ways that we had not previously suspected, and also modifies tremendously the life of the men involved. We have only recently considered the psychologic aspects of infertility in men. This is partially because of our biases, partially because the psychological aspects of male infertility were not apparent much of the time, and partially because we did not have a scientific model for thinking about them. However, we now know that infertility is a traumatic interruption in the life of both women and men. It really should not come as any surprise that we can make that statement; we really should not even have to make it.

When I set out to do a study on infertility, the subject were very polite, smiled and wished me well, and ushered me out the door. I heard statistics from them about the number of men who would return for the second appointment. Fewer than 50% even came back to hear results from the first evaluation. Many men would be interviewed and not even call back to remain in touch with us.

The number of men who stayed involved and agreed to a full-fledged workup was very low. Of those, the number who were willing to fill out and return a questionnaire, and then have an interview was about 1 in 500. I mailed thousands of questionnaires and made hundreds of phone calls over a 2 year period, and

wound up with only 50 subjects, 30 of whom made it into the study. As I reached the interview phase, it became apparent that, for some of the men with whom I spoke and who had been experiencing infertility for a year or two, fatherhood did not seem important. These were not men who failed to notice that their wives were having psychologic difficulties about their infertility. They were not men who were reporting significant sexual dysfunction in their relationship. By and large most of them were able to say that, no matter what the cause of the infertility, no matter whose diagnosis it was, they themselves were doing pretty well. Their lives were not disrupted in any dramatic way. Their work went on. Their leisure activities went on. Their connection to their extended family and their circle of friends continued essentially as usual.

What they all said was something like this: "I am very concerned about my wife. I am worried about her problems with infertility and wondering how she's dealing with it. I am doing everything I can to be supportive of her, and I am trying hard to adjust my work schedule to be there for appointments, or sometimes to comfort her when she needs comforting. I am just plain worried about these tears she keeps crying all the time."

So I ran into this paradox, and I did not know how to explain it. These men had not changed either their career direction or their philosophical orientation. Then I met the men who had been struggling with infertility for at least 3 years or more. Their lives were changing, things were happening. They were in crisis, and they were having significant emotional reactions.

After I performed that study, I reviewed and examined the differences between male and female development, particularly the psychologic development of gender identity. When gender is assigned, many profound social mechanisms come into play. If you dress two babies in pink or blue, regardless of sex, and put them in a room full of toys, both men and women will select the doll or the stuffed animal for the one dressed in pink and the train and the truck for the one dressed in blue. Instantly, from the moment we know a child's sex, a magnet is turned on that draws all the stereotypes from the culture. We begin to transform the child into what he or she is going to do and be as an adult.

Girls are born in a state of merger or strong identification with their mothers, gradually over their lifetime moving away from the mother within the context of a relationship. This is a primary role model that requires no switch of genders. The girl moves out and away from her mother, but within the context of relatedness. Eventually, she chooses another love object and makes a family.

Boys have an additional step. A good deal of relatively recent literature deals with boys' identification with their mothers. We are, for instance, used to talking about penis envy. We do not talk too much about womb envy or breast envy, but we should. Who is the primary model for identification from early years? Who does most of the child care in this country? Women. Who are the first-, second-, third-, fourth-, and fifth-grade teachers? Mostly women. Boys who are looking for role models are going to have a hard time finding them in a culture where the collective amount of time that fathers spend with newborns is 39 seconds a day. A boy moves out of a tremendous identification with his mother, reaching out for a father model and experiences significant difficulty finding it. A lot of today's fiction describes a little boy letting go of his mother's hand and reaching for his father—and not finding him. So you have grieving on one side and loss on the other, and this happens over and over, when a boy is 18 months, 3 years, and 6 years old. Children are not prepared to take on massive grief reactions, but by the time they are 6, boys have essentially lost both parents.

Having made whatever attachment to whatever male figures are accessible, men go on through life, move on to the outside love object, and marry. When they are faced with infertility, they reach out again, toward fatherhood, toward that model they thought they would be, and again find that their hand is empty. That leaves them with the woman who is there (their wife), sometimes with other women, and sometimes back to mother.

There are two general male configurations in response to infertility. The first could be characterized as a sort of fifties man, the fellow who is much more comfortable with patriarchal privilege, who wants to go to work and have that be the place where he invests his time, while his wife is at home and waiting. For him the notion of his wife going into the marketplace is a big challenge, and there is a lot of struggle around that. There is still a struggle with mother and with early issues of disidentification with the mother and the lack of a father to hold on to.

Then there is the other configuration, the nineties man who has been to support groups and many conferences. He has taken over all the household chores; he does the laundry, he does windows, and he cleans the boiler. While the fifties man attempts to cope by withdrawing, this nineties man solves his problem by over-identifying. He is going to help his wife through this by being tremendously solicitous, supporting her through thick and thin. This man comes to every single appointment, he arranges his work schedule to be there, he takes notes, he asks the right questions, he is engaged. He is the new age man who represents the evolving consciousness in society.

Both of these men have said in their very different ways that their pride was hurt. The first man says, "I'm not going to do that. That's her business, not mine. I have a job to do. I can't cancel this or my boss will yell at me." The second man stuffs his feelings and is solicitous of his wife. But both men let the woman continue to bear the emotional burden of the infertility.

That dilemma is difficult for men because mama's boy is not a term of praise in our culture. To be caught in such a dilemma due to infertility is to not only be faced with the necessity for grieving, which is not an affect that we allow particularly in men, but also with a repeat of those early developmental moments, when both hands were empty.

These men are living with a tremendous amount of feeling. They have grief that has to be let out somewhere but has no real place to go. We know that what happens at that point. Those men do feel grief, and they do have feelings, but their grief and feelings become hidden, and laden with shame.

One can start off with mama's boy, and with the attachment to the mother and the failure of masculine gender identity as the original shame issue. As one moves into adult life infertility creates the problem all over again. Unfortunately for men, infertility itself does not have informal public forums. There is no place for men to resolve it. A man does not go to a group of friends and say, "I am shooting blanks." He does not talk about the miscarriage that happened, or sit down with the boys at work and talk about how his wife's monthly cycle came around again and they both are filled with grief. Instead, shame occurs.

Shame is an enemy of normal adult development, psychologic development in general. What does a man do with his shame if it has nowhere to go? When we work with families of parents who abuse their children we know where the shame goes. Physical, verbal, and sexual abuse puts the shame in the child. Where does a man who has no children put the shame? In his wife, and she takes it on. He says, "I am so terribly sorry you're upset," and she says, "I will cry the tears for you. I will assume the burden. I will even take the blame." A number of studies of couples in whom the male factor has been identified describe the wives continuing to go for medical treatment and continuing to seek new experts to explain the condition.

The woman is now carrying the shame. Why is she doing this seemingly crazy thing? It is because of what Erikson called a generative identity; the stage of life that follows the young adult struggle for selfhood and the resulting capacity for negotiating an intimate relationship. Notice what happened with the couple I described. They are managing shame in order to preserve intact the idea that one of them is going on to become a generative adult. In this case and in many, many others it is the husband who does that, even if he has the diagnosed infertility factor.

We are going to see this pattern frequently because the men do not come for treatment, because they are being supportive, or because they do not talk about their feelings. We must not be fooled into believing that infertility is not a major life stressor for them, because it is. We must not regard them with hostility, but identify what is adaptive and positive about their reaction. That is, two people are working together to preserve a sense of hopefulness about the future and a notion that something good about them is going to go on. They have been denied a child as a recipient of those projections, at least for now. They must create some way to do it so they create an image, and that is at least one of the partners will go on as though life were normal. This approach will last only for about 3 years because it is at best a temporary coping mechanism. After that it all falls apart.

When you are working with couples, and I cannot say it too strongly, it is essential to have both partners involved no matter who has the infertility problem, no matter how uninvolved the husband appears to be. At some point things will begin coming apart if they continue to go it alone.

At that time both partners are going to need a different kind of support than they required previously. This is particularly important for the men who do not appear to be grieving. For example, a couple moves to adoption or to donor insemination during those first 3 years, and it is not evident that the man is in any particular distress. His wife has gone through the grieving process and is ready to take the next step. He has not done that, however. How is he going to love the child that might result from these options when he has not given up the one he was hoping for? Somebody somehow has to leave the door open for him to grieve.

We need groups in which men can talk to men. How can we do that? We all know how difficult it is to involve them, and we need to be clever. Someone made the suggestion that we drive a '56 Chevy into the waiting room of the office, open the hood and let the men all stand around with their hands in their pockets, looking at the alternator and debating why it will not start. That could be a novel beginning for a men's infertility discussion group. Now, if you don't have room for a '56 Chevy in your waiting area, what I recommend you do is make use of some of the informal, subterranean resources in which there can be couples' groups.

The wives can still lead the men there, and then the men go off in one room, and the women go off in the other. This is the way that men cleverly, almost deviously, create a men's group within the context of a couples' group. Those men get to support one another in doing that necessary grieving. It is tremendously important, and it is very, very hard for us to achieve in any other way, because if you put up a sign saying, please attend the men's discussion group, you know how few are going to show up.

The study of infertile men that I mentioned earlier showed that the men who were in the most trouble and resolved things the least in their lives were from the group where the diagnosis was indeterminate, and the infertility had lasted more than 3 years. Those folks who tended to get locked into struggles with physicians and treatment teams were the ones who had never given up and had a chance to grieve. Because they never met that moment at which somebody said, "Quit," they were unable to initiate the grieving process. A lot of those people went on being irritated, frustrated, and hating the whole medical establishment for years and years. This created a corrosive effect in all of life, not just in their relationships with their doctors.

Summary

Infertility is a major life stres for men as well as for women. Husbands need to be involved in the fertility workup and treatment from the beginning. This includes not only the obvious medical testing, but also any discussions, referrals for counseling, or related care. The signs of distress in most men will not be apparent initially, but the door should be left open to frankly discuss feelings about any aspect of the workup, diagnosis and treatment. Follow-up is important, because difficulties may not be apparent until months or years later. This is particularly important if the couple considers adoption or donor insemination during the first several years of their infertility struggle. The wife may be more emotionally prepared to accept an adopted child into her life than her husband who may not have dealt with his feelings. If he has not grieved his own losses, he will be unprepared to welcome a genetically unrelated child into his life. A highly desireable setting for this kind of work is a focused men's group. These groups are difficult to arrange, and perhaps even more difficult to complete. However, most men study with an extended infertility experience uniformly long to have a place where men can talk about their feelings. Occasionally male groups do form spontaneously within the context of mixed-gender and couples groups.

In order to empathize with the emotional struggle experienced by infertile couples, we must learn to understand the role of gender in adaptation to infertility. The ultimate goal of infertile couples is to preserve generative hopes in the marriage. The better these hopes can be acknowledged, the better they can express the necessary grief at their failure.

Bibliography

1. Astrachan A. How Men Feel. New York: Anchor Press, 1988.
2. Blatt SJ, Schichman S. Two primary configurations of psychopathology. Psychoana Contemp Thought 1983;6:187–254.
3. Erikson EH. Identity: Youth and Crisis. New York: W.W. Norton, 1968.
4. Farrell MP, Rosenberg SD. Men at Midlife. Boston: Auburn House, 1981.
5. Gilligan C. In a Different Voice: Psychological Theory and Women's Development. Cambridge: Harvard University Press, 1982.
6. Herzog JM. On father hunger: The father's role in the modulation of aggressive drive and fantasy. In: Cath SH, Gurwitt AR, Ross JM, eds. Father and Child: Developmental and Clinical Perspectives. Boston: Little, Brown, 1982.
7. Horney K. The denial of the vagina. Int J Psychoanal 1933;14:57–70.

8. Jacobson E. Development of the wish for a child in boys. The Psychoanalytic Study of the Child. 1950;5:139–152.

9. Kohut H. The Restoration of the Self. New York: International Universities Press, 1977.

10. MacNab RT. Infertility and men: A study of change and adaptive choices in the lives of involuntarily childless men. Unpublished doctoral dissertation, 1984.

11. Mazor MD. Psychosexual problems of the infertile couple. Med Aspects Hum Sexual 1980;14(12):32–49.

12. Menning BE. Infertility: A Guide for the Childless Couple. Englewood Cliffs: Prentice-Hall, 1977.

13. Ogden TH. Projective Identification and Psychotherapeutic Technique. New York: Jason Aronson, 1982.

14. O'Leary J, Wright F. Shame and gender issues in pathological narcissism. Psychoanal Psychol 1986;3:327–339.

15. Osherson S. Finding Our Fathers: The Unfinished Business of Manhood. New York: The Free Press, 1986.

16. Pleck JH. Working Wives, Working Husbands. Beverly Hills: Sage Press, 1985.

17. Raphael R. The Men from the Boys: Rites of Passage in Male America. Lincoln: University of Nebraska Press, 1988.

18. Ross JM. In search of fathering: A review. In: Cath SH, Gurwitt AR, Ross JM, eds. Father and Child: Developmental and Clinical Perspectives. Boston: Little, Brown, 1982.

19. Seibel MM, Graves WL. The psychological implications of spontaneous abortions. J Reprod Med 1980;25:161–175.

20. Stolorow RD, Lachmann FM. Early loss of the father: A clinical case. In: Cath SH, Gurwitt AR, Ross JM, eds. Father and Child: Developmental and Clinical perspectives. Boston: Little, Brown, 1982.

21. Tyson P. A developmental line of gender identity, gender role, and choice of love object. J Am Psychoanal Assoc 1982;30:61–86.

22. Wright F, O'Leary J, Balkin J. Shame, guilt, narcissism, and depression: Correlates and sex differences. Psychoanal Psychol 1989; 6:217–230.

23. Wurmser L. Shame: The veiled companion of narcissism. In: Nathanson DL, ed. The Many Faces of Shame. New York: The Guildford Press, 1987.

24. Zilbach JJ. The family life cycle: A framework for understanding children in family therapy. In: Combrinck-Graham L, ed. Children in Family Contexts. New York: Guilford Press, 1988:46–66.

28
Paradise Lost: Sexual Function and Infertility

Susan Cooper

The crisis of infertility involves experiencing a series of losses. Some are primary and some are secondary, but all are significant. The loss of the biologic experience of pregnancy and childbirth, the inability to pass on one's genes to the next generation, and the loss of children in one's home are the fears as well as the realities with which infertile couples struggle. Some or all of these losses can be ameliorated by medical technology or by alternatives such as adoption or the use of donor gametes. Another profound loss involves the damage done to one's self-esteem and is not easily repaired. This injury affects one's deepest sense of self, including feelings about masculinity or femininity, and sexuality.

It is probably not surprising, therefore, that a couple's sexual relationship is often the area of their life that is most negatively affected by infertility. Lovemaking, once a warm, intimate, physically pleasurable experience, becomes a dreaded chore, a means to an end that can continue to result in failure. Even the thought of sexual intercourse signals the pavlovian response of tension and avoidance in many, perhaps most, infertile couples. To make matters worse, sex often becomes the battleground on which a couple's fears, anxieties, and depression are played out.

There are many reasons why a couple's sexual relationship is so adversely affected by infertility, but since sex is usually considered a private matter they are rarely talked about. In fact, one of the paradoxes of infertility is that although couples often have an extremely difficult time talking with close friends or even to each other about sex, they are expected to discuss this most private of acts freely with a physician who may be a virtual stranger.

Depression and Loss of Libido

For many infertile people, depression is the emotional state that permeates all others. Even when they have reason to be optimistic about achieving a pregnancy, this hope is usually coupled with depression that becomes worse as the months and years pass by without conceiving. One of the clinical manifestations of this is loss of libido, for when people are depressed they usually do not feel like being sexual.

Various psychologic and physiologic theories exist about the relationship among sex, stress, and depression, the mechanisms of which are only recently being investigated. One theory suggests that people engaged in a crisis have to expend all their emotional energy mastering that crisis, and that they have no energy left over for anything peripheral. A depressed libido is therefore an adaptive accommodation that conserves energy for life's essentials.

Another theory postulates that depression leads to major physiologic changes that affect the central nervous system at the neurotransmitter level by lowering the androgen supply. Still other theories postulate that depression causes and is caused by a decreased amount of catecholamines, mainly norepinephrine, in the brain, which in turn decreases the sexual response. At any rate, there seems to be a cause-and-effect relationship between the brain, environment, and reproductive system.

Sexual Identity

Infertility deals a severe blow to both men's and women's identities. Their sense of themselves as sexual people becomes distorted as their inability to procreate becomes manifest. Unfortunately, in this society the notions of masculinity, virility, fertility, and potency are equated. Men who are part of an infertile couple often feel emasculated, especially if a male factor is involved. Their identity as men and as sexual beings suffers a real setback. Sometimes men with no history of sexual inadequacy or dysfunction become impotent for periods of time after they learn about their infertility problem.

A woman whose identity is closely tied to being a mother, and this is most of us, feels the burden of infertility constantly. Her sense of herself as a sexually desirable person becomes distorted. She suffers feelings of inadequacy and may experience herself as unlovable, unfeminine, damaged, or defective. Her life may seem purposeless.

For both partners sex comes to mean failure—failure to conceive and therefore failure to be a real man or a real woman. These negative features become magnified as infertility continues and they often are generalized so that global self-esteem is affected. The ability to enjoy sex presupposes the ability to take pleasure in one's body and one's self, and to feel that one deserves pleasure in life. This in turn is dependent on having a positive self-image as a man or as a woman. When self-images are damaged by infertility, and depression saps libido, the convergence of these factors can lead to a couple's poor sexual relationship.

Structured Sex

Infertility takes the spontaneity out of sex. Attempting to conceive means having sex on the right days. Often it means every other day during the middle of the month, every day or every 36 hours, or whatever frequency the couple believes will be most conducive to conception. The man must be able to maintain an erection and reach orgasm. The woman only has to be a receptacle for his sperm, although some theories decree that female orgasm facilitates conception by helping the egg move down the tubes and sperm move upward. Other theories claim that orgasm makes no difference. Whatever the theory, though, trying hard to reach orgasm in most instances produces the effect that is the opposite of what was intended. For couples experiencing infertility, sex begins to resemble a clinical procedure rather than a loving passionate act between husband and wife.

Scrutinized Sex

Also contributing to a couple's sexual decline is the fact that infertility takes the privacy out of sexuality. Despite the sexual revolution, men and women rarely discuss this aspect of their lives. To some extent our sexual arousal, and hence our enjoyment, are dependent upon sex remaining behind closed doors. By its very nature, the infertility workup necessitates that sex lives are open to scrutiny. Physicians have to know when a couple has had intercourse, how often, and sometimes in what position. They ask detailed questions in an effort to ascertain whether infertility results from a sexual dysfunction or from a structural or physiologic problem.

All infertile couples are familiar with the daily chart on which the woman records her basal body temperature taken before getting out of bed each morning. The purpose of the chart is to predict ovulation. When a dip in temperature is followed by a rise, it means that ovulation is occurring. Couples are instructed to circle the days on which they had intercourse so the physician can determine whether their timing makes conception possible. Believe it or not, many couples report faking their circles so the doctor will not think they were not trying hard enough to get pregnant. Other couples report having been admonished by their physician for not having frequent enough sexual relations. It can be humiliating to have to describe one's sexual conduct.

Diagnostic tests such as the postcoital test (PCT) magnify feelings of invasion. Couples must have intercourse for the purpose of learning whether the sperm can live in the woman's cervical environment. The woman may be asked to appear in her doctor's office a few hours after she has had intercourse (although most often the test is performed the morning after). Couples often feel that their physician is literally in the bedroom with them watching their performance. In fact, the PCT test is graded and, depending on the results, couples can leave the doctor's office with their self-esteem either intact or in ruins.

A 1984 study of 50 women[1] indicated that a significant number of them experienced a decrease in their sexual enjoyment, including less foreplay and fewer orgasms, just prior to the postcoital test. A more recent study comparing overnight PCT test results with those done the same morning[2] showed that women who took the overnight test felt less pressure and therefore had a more enjoyable sexual experience. The study also indicated that for both groups there was a significant positive correlation between the quality of the sexual encounter and the results of the postcoital test, indicating that an enjoyable sex act is more likely to enhance the quality of the sperm–cervical mucus interaction.

Performance

The anxiety and tension that surround infertility often build up to such a degree that successful intercourse with ejaculation becomes impossible. Husbands feel anxious about having to perform. Wives feel anxious that their husbands will not be able to perform. Both feel pressure and tension related to sex, and as a result, negative habits develop. Since it is the woman who is most tuned into her cycle or to her temperature chart, it is usually she who plays quarterback in the baby-making venture. For many couples, at least those who have experienced long-term infertility, neither partner is especially interested in making love. Usually, however, they are intent on having sex during ovulation so as not to lose an opportunity to conceive that month. The purpose of sex thus becomes procreation, not recreation, and many couples develop quick

and unfortunately unsatisfying routines to achieve their desired purpose.

A common occurrence is as follows. Foreplay is minimal, sometimes even nonexistent. When the husband appears to have a secure erection, the wife signals him to penetrate her. The quicker he comes, the happier she is. In other cases women do try to become aroused or to let their husbands stimulate them, but often the pressure of the moment interferes with the ability to experience pleasure. These women also usually end up feeling dejected and signaling their mates to hurry and get it over with.

Another common occurrence is that the husband becomes impotent. The more they work at arousing him the worse it gets. He just cannot maintain an erection. Invariably both partners become frustrated and feel like failures.

A woman can feel resentful if she does not reach orgasm or become sexually aroused, particularly if she believes her mate is enjoying himself while she is not. She may be irritated with her partner if he takes too long to reach orgasm. A man can get annoyed if he feels his mate is merely lying there and not participating in the sex act, or if he senses she cannot wait to get it over with. Often he feels used. When men have trouble reaching orgasm, women become understandably frustrated.

Yet frustration only increases the tension, and when anger builds up, particularly if it is unexpressed, couples either withdraw from each other emotionally and sexually or they have an unproductive fight. Neither way contributes to the well-being of a relationship.

When these kinds of sexual patterns occur, a man tends to feel rejected, believing a baby is far more important to his wife than he is. The woman may begin to question whether her husband really wants a child, since he seems so uninterested in sex. In fact, for most couples it is the woman who first feels the losses associated with infertility. A man can lag months or even years behind in coming to terms with his grief about not having a child. So while the wife experiences the emptiness and loss of not having a baby, her husband experiences the loss of not having a wife.

Although she has not left him physically, he feels emotionally abandoned by her as she appears to be consumed with desire for a child and not for a husband.

Conflict

The fights that so often occur during infertility are a result of the enormous stress and constant pressure to produce a child. Many couples begin quarreling about trivial matters that never would have bothered them before their infertility. To the extent that the partners wish consciously or unconsciously to avoid intercourse because it is associated with failure, anger can serve a useful purpose: it can prevent the dreaded sex act.

It is probably not surprising that infertile couples often manage to have their worst fights around the middle of the menstrual cycle. When people are angry with each other, they do not feel like being sexual, and if a couple does not have sex during their fertile time, they probably will not feel they have failed when conception does not occur. Some couples might even sacrifice a month of trying for the relief they feel at not having failed.

On the other hand, many couples have an abhorrence of anger and will do anything to avoid overtly expressing it. They often withdraw from each other physically and emotionally. Their anger is acted out by their being unavailable, ill, or perhaps having to deal with an unexpected emergency. Still other couples manage to keep the peace midcycle and have their fights at other times. Thus they are able to avoid sex during their nonfertile days while not losing their chance to conceive in a given month.

Resolving the Problem

Because of all these factors, sex is rarely enjoyable for infertile couples and they should be reassured that such negative experiences are normal. Sex on demand for the purpose of procreating and sex for pleasure are two different phenomena. As mentioned earlier, infertility is about losses, some big, some little.

For most couples, however, the loss of the pleasure and intimacy they previously experienced from their sexual relationship is a big one, and in the midst of all the other losses they may not even know consciously that they are grieving it.

There are ways in which infertile couples can begin to pick up the pieces of their sexual relationship even before their infertility is resolved. Some things they can do and ways of being with each other can ease the pain as well as minimize their sexual problems, and in the long run enrich their relationship.

The following case report is probably a good illustration of a couple who had some sexual problems before their marriage, but infertility brought them to the surface and exacerbated them.

Case Report

Cathy and Bob are an attractive couple in their mid-thirties who have gone through 6 years of infertility treatment, including several failed IVF cycles. Cathy was exposed to diethylstilbestrol (DES) in utero, and prior to undergoing in vitro fertilization (IVF) she and Bob spent years with various specialists who misdiagnosed their problem and attempted various treatments, none of which worked.

The couple are both professionals in high-level jobs. Cathy is extremely outgoing and cheerful. Her husband is more laid-back but pleasant, warm, and loving. They recently decided to end treatment and adopt, a choice that was made with the aid of counseling.

After reaching this decision, they sought further counseling because sex was no longer pleasurable, and they missed the intimacy they used to have. During the initial interview, Cathy was quick to tell me they had had no sexual problems before their infertility. She had become depressed about her infertility early on, however, about a year after they began trying to become pregnant. Bob remained optimistic until about the fourth failed IVF attempt. Over the years sex had become so associated with failure that Cathy lost all her sexual desire and considered intercourse a duty that she had to perform. Bob easily sensed this and over time became adept at performing his function speedily, assuming that quickness would please her.

Both Cathy and Bob came from unhappy homes. Cathy's mother, who had several children, complained constantly, particularly about her husband. She threatened divorce all during Cathy's childhood and finally left her husband when Cathy was a young adult. Bob describes his mother as having a mean streak. She was the dominant force in the family and ruled either by giving orders or by becoming depressed. In fact, she was hospitalized at least a few times for depression during his childhood and adolescence. In neither family was conflict handled in a positive way. Disagreement usually turned into anger, which turned into verbal abuse and, on a few occasions in each of their families, into physical abuse. Thus anger frightened both of them, and each became determined in their outward dealings with one another to act kindly and avoid any issues that might create conflict.

Cathy in particular had fantasies about creating the kind of loving family she wished she had experienced as a child. The longer their infertility dragged on, the more depressed she became, yet her outward demeanor was always cheerful. She began to feel emotionally estranged from her husband, who she felt did not understand why she was in so much pain. Nor could Cathy understand how he could still be so hopeful. However, she remained, for practical purposes, a devoted wife determined to be caring and supportive to her husband.

In the first few months of counseling, it became clear that even though they had talked at length about their infertility treatment and later about adoption, they had never really spoken about their innermost feelings related to infertility or its effect on their marriage. Both Cathy and Bob described themselves as being physically very affectionate. Unfortunately, as infertility progressed, she stopped initiating any signs of affection, fearing that Bob would misread them as an expression of sexual desire. In turn, when he initiated affection, Cathy would either stiffen up or not respond, fearing that he was signaling the desire for sex. Gradually, the physical affection they had enjoyed became almost nonexistent. Bob felt rejected as a husband, lover, and friend. Cathy felt alone and misunderstood in her pain. Coitus occurred rarely—about three or four times during the year preceding our initial visit—and was quite unsatisfactory to both of them. Cathy stated matter-of-factly that Bob reached orgasm almost immediately upon entering her. Bob felt guilty about this, but for the past couple of years he had not been able to control when he ejaculated.

My first intervention after about two sessions was to instruct this couple not to have sex. I encouraged them to be physically affectionate as often as they wanted, but I clearly stated that physical touching was not to lead to sexual touching even if they

felt like it. As it turned out, they felt enormously relieved by this directive and were free to be affectionate, which in turn made them feel closer. As the pressure was off, they felt safer to talk about how infertility had affected their relationship. It became apparent that they had stopped sharing their feelings for fear it would lead to irreparable conflict. The directive made it safe for them to do so, knowing that all the hurts, angers, and misunderstandings must be aired before they could begin to heal.

I spent a good deal of time in the beginning of treatment educating them about infertility and reassuring them that their reactions to this crisis were normal. At the same time, we explored enough of their family histories to form an understanding of how individual dynamics contributed to their current problem, including how anger was expressed in their families. They developed a renewed appreciation for each other, were able to reaffirm their love and commitment, and reassured each other of their ability to tolerate angry feelings directed at themselves. About 2 or 3 months after beginning counseling, they were ready to deal with many of the deeper hurts and angers.

Several insights developed that enabled Bob and Cathy to become closer so that we could focus more on their sexual relationship. Although they did not consider themselves religious, both came from families that were. Cathy in particular remembered her mother remarking on a few occasions that the purpose of sex and of being female was to bear children. Since she could not do that, she felt like a failure and imagined that her lack of enjoyment of sex was an additional punishment for her shortcomings as a woman.

During one poignant session, Cathy began to talk about how defective she felt, as her cervix as well as other parts of her reproductive system were malformed due to being exposed to DES. An incident that had taken place several years ago was in many ways a metaphor for how she felt about her body. She had undergone a painful surgical procedure in which her cervix had been cauterized. That evening while showering she passed some dead, brownish tissue. As she watched it run down her legs and eventually disappear in the shower drain, she burst into tears, feeling like a freak, overcome with shame and disgust about her body. Even as she spoke she began to sob, remembering the incident and the pain. Bob, who had tears in his eyes, as did I, reached over and held her while she cried. When her tears subsided, he looked at her lovingly and said, "I never knew how awful it was for you," and he hadn't. Cathy finally felt that he understood.

During one session about 5 or 6 months into treatment, they both fully acknowledged that their sex life was never really very good. Although in the beginning Cathy usually had orgasms, and Bob was able to sustain intercourse for a reasonable length of time, it was never exciting. They had not consciously lied to me during our initial session when they told me that they had no sexual problems prior to infertility. Rather, they had been afraid to face the truth themselves. Slowly the details emerged, together with an important revelation. I learned that early on their relationship was characterized by a whirlwind, passionate courtship. They described it as love at first sight and were married about a year after they met. During one session Cathy offhandedly commented that their sexual relationship had gotten off to a bad start. When I inquired about that, they confessed to having made love after the first date. Cathy in particular felt enormously guilty. She had never behaved that way before. Bob, too, regretted how it had happened, although he did not feel guilty. Cathy was so worried that Bob would think she was a bad girl that she unconsciously resolved to act in the future like a good girl, which meant to her behaving passively and sticking to the basics. Bob, on the other hand, was so smitten with Cathy that he did not want her to think he was interested only in her body. Therefore he constantly held back from initiating anything but the standard movements for fear she would think he was enjoying himself too much.

I decided to interview each of them separately about their sexual history, feeling that I needed more information about each of them, and hypothesizing that there may have been some important information they did not yet feel comfortable revealing to each other. I probably should have done this earlier in my work with them, but I had not sensed that it was necessary. I learned, and later shared with them, that both Cathy and Bob had had at least one previous relationship in which sex was highly important and enjoyable. Yet with each other they had become inhibited and fearful. Because of the history of their relationship, which was compounded by infertility, negative unsatisfactory patterns had developed. Clearly, both had the capacity to experience pleasurable and uninhibited sex. They would just have to find their way out of the woods. By now they had established a foundation of trust, understanding, and mutuality so that we could begin to focus more on sex and begin standard behavioral interventions. At this point their sex life has seen some improvement, but it is not where they would like it to be. Cathy still rarely desires sex, although her feelings toward Bob have deepened. Bob has made some headway, but not enough, in improving his tendency to premature ejaculation. Actually my work with Bob has focused less on this problem and more on helping him not to feel so guilty by finding ways other than intercourse to satisfy Cathy. The work continues.

Specific Suggestions

Most infertile couples do not meet with a psychotherapist during the course of infertility treatment, but their sexual relationship may still be suffering. I hope that physicians who specialize in this area will feel comfortable talking to couples about the difficulties of maintaining a satisfying sexual relationship in the midst of treatment. The following are some suggestions for both physicians and psychotherapists, although clearly the former will not be able to explore them in as much depth as the latter.

Couples who have difficulty having sex close to ovulation can be counseled to view midcycle sex as work, a job that must be done in order to reach a desired goal. During that time, however, couples can be encouraged to reaffirm their love for one another and their commitment to working on expanding their family. Their feelings can be expressed tenderly and lovingly even though deep sexual passion may be missing. Husband and wife must understand the pressures each of them feels about performance, and be patient with, not critical of, one another.

Being angry with a man who is temporarily impotent only makes matters worse. If ejaculation is not achieved, the couple should take a few hours off or a day off, and try again. When it is achieved, they can congratulate themselves, even if it was not the sexual experience of the century. To feel sexual, most men and women, particularly women, have to feel close to their mate. They have to feel emotionally connected and understood, which means sharing their innermost feelings, worries, fears, and thoughts. Unfortunately, many women have difficulty doing this, as they fear rejection by their spouse. In addition, most men have been taught since they were little boys not to express their emotions. Yet people tend to feel less depressed and hence more sexual when they can say what they feel and know that they are loved and accepted regardless.

Couples must be helped to understand that feelings are not decisions. There is a time for both. Expressing anger about a physician does not necessarily mean that they want to switch. Nor does expressing dissatisfaction about a sexual encounter mean they want a divorce. The extent to which individuals feel like attractive, desirable people in part determines the extent to which they allow themselves to experience and to act on their sexual feelings.

Infertile couples have to remind themselves and each other that infertility should not determine one's self-worth or one's sexuality. Being a real man has about as much to do with the quality of his semen as it does with whether or not he eats quiche. Being a real woman is simply not related to whether she has endometriosis, or "hostile" mucus, or blocked tubes. These concepts, however, are easier said or believed than they are felt, and they must be reinforced over and over again.

What comes to mind is Alfred Adler's theory of organ inferiority in which he claims that people who have a physical defect have a tendency to generalize the defect to their body as a whole, which affects their global self-esteem as well. This is the case whether that defect is something major like blindness, deafness, or a missing limb, or something as innocuous as missing part of a finger. These individuals begin to feel completely defective, rather than just focusing on the one aspect that is in fact defective.

It is desirable that infertile couples continue the same kinds of behavior that used to make them feel sexual, whether it is dressing in a certain way, sharing a romantic dinner, or whatever. It is especially important to exercise, eat properly, get enough sleep, and, in general, keep one's body in good shape. The healthier one is, the better, and the more sexual he or she will feel. If medications related to infertility treatment are producing physically undesirable side effects, it is important to acknowledge this fact to oneself and to each other. The unaffected spouse can make a point of being especially supportive, and the one whose body must bear these traumas—usually the woman—can focus on the time when the medications will end, and she can feel like her old self.

When feelings are expressed openly and honest communication is established between a couple, a solid foundation is created for discussing the most intimate and difficult of subjects, including sex. In working with couples over the years, including those who are fertile and infertile, I have discovered that sex often has different meanings for men and women. Men tend to need sex to feel loved. It may be the primary way in which they feel needed and desired by their mate. To many it is essential to maintaining their relationship, and without it they may have difficulty feeling connected to their wives. If sex is infrequent or missing, they feel empty, rejected as a man. Women, on the other hand, tend to experience sex as a means by which they mutually reinforce the love that has already been expressed in other ways. It is the dessert that enhances the delicious meal, but is not necessary in order to feel comfortably full. This does not mean that women enjoy sex less than men, but it is not essential for their emotional survival in the relationship. Thus, while women may desire sex when they are feeling particularly close to their mate, men may desire it most when they are feeling more distant and want to be closer, perhaps after a fight.

The loss of an enjoyable sexual relationship during infertility may therefore affect husbands in a more profound and depressing way than it does their wives. If a woman feels unable to participate in sex, sometimes talking about her reluctance helps, particularly if she is able to communicate her love and commitment to her partner. A man, in turn, often feels better knowing that his partner's lack of interest in making love does not mean that she is rejecting him. Communicating the meaning about this particular loss is essential so that both partners can try to convey through additional words or actions what was previously conveyed through sex.

Loving couples need physical contact. It enables them to feel connected, and it enhances intimacy. Physical contact and sexual contact, however, are not the same. The first is essential, the second desirable. During the ordeal of infertility couples can make extra efforts to touch or hug each other, snuggle in bed, kiss each other goodnight or good morning, or give and receive nonsexual massages. If their emotions can bear it, reserving some time during the nonfertile part of the month, even once is enough, for recreational sex, can be extremely rewarding. Sex then is no longer viewed solely as a means to an end, but it is also a reminder that it once was, and can be again, a loving and pleasurable activity.

Often, however, even the thought of sex when it is not necessary seems intolerable. In fact, it is the idea of intercourse that is most distasteful, but couples do not have to have intercourse to give and receive sexual pleasure. It helps to remember the earliest period in their relationship when passion was probably at its peak, and even a goodnight kiss was highly arousing. They can experiment with sexual activities that they may have long forgotten about. Gentle caressing, massaging, necking, petting, mutual masturbation, and oral sex are all ways in which they can indulge in sexual pleasure without having to engage in intercourse. Couples too easily become conditioned to the negative sexual patterns they developed and forget the repertoire of behaviors they once enjoyed. Again, however, communication is essential. Husbands and wives must talk with each other about what they most enjoy and how they like to be touched, kissed, or stroked.

The bad news is that in some ways paradise is truly lost. Most infertile couples who once had good sexual relationships will probably not regain their prior sex life unless they decide to remain child free, and even then it will probably be a long time before sex is no longer associated with infertility. When couples, fertile and infertile, go on to have children by birth or adoption, the sexual freedom and spontaneity they once had fades into the past. Couples parenting after infertility can certainly derive great pleasure from their sexual relationship, particularly if they start working on it before children arrive, but it may always be a reminder of their infertility.

The good news is that paradise can be regained. Although infertility may interfere with the enjoyment of sex, it can also provide couples with an opportunity to become closer. The majority of infertile couples who have resolved their infertility have unsatisfactory sex lives, yet they are increasingly close in their marriages. Thus infertility deprives couples of one resource for intimacy, enjoyable sex, but supplies them with another, the enhanced communication that comes from facing a problem together.[3] Infertility, particularly if it is long-term, is probably one of the most difficult times in a couple's life. Nothing can erase the pain; they must go through it in order to come out of it. Yet struggles tend to make us stronger.

In conclusion, the Chinese have two definitions for the word *crisis*: danger and opportunity. Although infertility is not dangerous in the sense of being life-threatening, the emotional pain that accompanies it can threaten the marital and sexual relationship. Yet the opportunity for increased intimacy and growth is profound. If we avail ourselves of this opportunity, we can discover paradise: the silver lining behind the dark cloud of infertility.

Questions and Answers

Machelle M. Seibel. I was involved in sexual function studies related to pelvic malignancy some years ago. People who did well sexually after treatment, say colostomy, which can be very disfiguring, were those whose spouse was most accepting of the problem. Obviously, the more one's partner accepts one's problems, the better the relationship is and the less it is altered. The second important factor related to outcome was information. The more discussion there was about the problem before it became a fact, the less of a problem it became after the fact.

It would seem for infertility patients also that the best intervention time would be before something becomes a big problem. However, the receptivity for the problem often does not exist until it's about to explode. What does one do about that?

S.C. I think it explodes at different times for different couples, but I think that you are right, particularly with infertility. Its so frightening that the tendency is to deny, not to want to believe that this is happening. A number of couples told me that they avoided for years joining a support group because that meant that they really were infertile. I think couples have to find their own timetable for when they can best deal with these sorts of things. I think what physicians can do if they have an extra couple of minutes is say, "This has been going on for 3 years now. How are you two doing with it?"

Machelle M. Seibel. What happens when they come to me, the subspecialist, is that they experience a renewed belief that things are now definitely going to work out. They are starting all over, and they drop all their previous experiences. In many ways this delays dealing with the emotional aspects of their problem.

S.C. Denial is not necessarily a bad thing; it is also functional. It is when denial breaks down that couples are really willing and able to deal with their feelings.

Bibliography

1. de Vries K, et al. The influence of the post coital test on the sexual function of infertile women. Psychosom Obstet Gynaecol 1984;3.
2. Boivin J, Takefman J, Tulandi T, Brender W. The psychosexual influence of the same morning versus the over-night post coital test on physiological results. Department of Psychology, Concordia University, Montreal, Canada.
3. Greil AL, Porter KL, Leitko TA. So near and yet so far: Sex and intimacy among infertile couples. Association Paper for the Society for the Study of Social Problems, 1987.
4. Glazer E, Cooper S. Without Child: Experiencing and Resolving Infertility. Lexington Books, Lexington, MA, 1989.
5. Kaplan HS. The New Sex Therapy. New York: Brunner/Mazel, 1974.

29
Secondary Infertility

Dianne Clapp

I often think about the concept of family in our society. It seems that the standard image in the advertising world is that the perfect family consists of two kids, a mom, and a dad. I went to buy a toothbrush holder and there were four slots. I bought a set of placemats, and they came in fours. All the car ads show mom and dad getting into the car with two kids in the back. The couple who is experiencing secondary infertility is constantly being bombarded with that image.

People ask me if I have any children, never if I have a child. It is always assumed that I have more than one. If someone does have one, the response usually is "Oh, only the one." The message is loaded and it puts a lot of pressure on couples.

The assumptions that are made by society are interesting. One clearly is that if a couple has only one child, it is not because they are infertile, but because they have decided to have only one. In this era of population control such a decision is sometimes sanctioned, but the inference is that it is selfish: you only have one child because you are interested in your career, or because you really don't enjoy parenting that much. In addition, remarks so innocently made—"When are you going to have another child?"—can really cut to the bone. We just do not consider that the couple who has only one child may not do so because of choice.

One Diagnosis, Two Different Populations

Secondary infertility in the classic sense is defined as an inability to conceive or carry a pregnancy to term after 1 year of trying following a successful pregnancy. Some couples who experience secondary infertility previously experienced primary infertility. They struggled to achieve that first child, and now they are struggling to have a second child. All the horrors of the previous workup and the old tensions within themselves as a couple begin to surface. The pain of the old infertility, largely resolved if the pregnancy resulted in the birth of a child, begins to become acute again.

Another part of the population conceives very quickly and easily. They may have even used birth control to try to space their children perfectly. Now they can't conceive, and they are in total shock and disbelief that this is happening.

With the couples who have conceived easily and are now struggling with infertility, it is more difficult to involve husbands in therapy. They seem more content with the status quo. They feel that they have done it once, and it is going to be all right, they will be able to do it again. Also, this group feels a lot of acute guilt: pregnancy happened so easily before, but it is not happening now. We must have done something wrong, or I did something wrong. No one parents perfectly, and unfortunately, many couples tend to believe that they are being punished with infertility for past parenting inadequacies.

If they experienced infertility in the past, they frequently expect that the treatment that enabled them to conceive will work again. If it doesn't, they often respond with denial. They stubbornly hold on to an ineffective treatment and find it hard to go on to the next stage of therapy, even if new diagnoses are uncovered.

The couple who has previously experienced infertility may feel they have been granted one miracle, and they are uncomfortable asking for another. They tend to be silent about their need and their desperation. They feel guilty for wanting one more when some people don't even have one. This sense of lack of entitlement fosters more isolation for the couple.

Special Contradictions

Secondary infertility requires a thorough assessment, and many medical examinations lie ahead for the couple. It may be necessary to switch from the obstetrician/gynecologist who has managed their previous pregnancy to an infertility specialist. Many people feel half fertile and half infertile, and to go to an infertility specialist doesn't seem to quite fit them. They are reluctant to move away from their obstetrician and accept the diagnosis of infertility.

What does it feel like to be going through secondary infertility? I asked one of my clients how it really feels. She said, "It is sort of like when I used to be a really good tennis player. I won a lot of trophies that I have at home. Then suddenly I stopped being able to play tennis. I started taking classes, reading books, and watching videos, because for some reason I lost the knack. All my friends I used to play with on a women's team are doing just great, and I am not. The trophies haunt me because they show me what I could do so well in the past." The comparison between the former fertile self and the present infertile self is very painful.

Couples are also concerned that their child is getting older. Their plan to space their children is no longer in their control, because by now the first child is older than they had wanted him or her to be when they had their second. They are older too, and that causes a lot of distress. They begin to think how old they will be when the second child goes into high school or college.

Being out of synchrony with their friends and siblings is frequently an issue for women, particularly with those friends who shared the first childbirth or play group. Now they want to share the second child experience with them, and they feel left out of that sisterhood.

Although the emotional consequences of infertility are similar for primary and secondary infertility, the two groups cannot use the same coping mechanisms. Frequently a woman with primary infertility becomes enmeshed in her career. She decides that she is going to focus on that as a way to heal herself and build up an identity. But the woman who has a child is having a lot of her energy drained off by motherhood. She is probably not in a position to go back to graduate school or expand her job to a point at which she can really get a tremendous amount of fulfillment from it. She is often on hold with her own development as she is waiting for this second child to come along. Her creativity may be more narrowly channeled into biologic generativity.

These couples also can't just take off on vacation together. Those with primary infertility frequently find it helpful to avoid holidays so as not to be around all the nieces and nephews. They often go skiing or plan some other fabulous vacation to avoid Christmas at home with the family. In contrast, couples with secondary infertility feel responsible to be part of the child's world. The woman with secondary infertility feels obligated to give her child the family Christmas experience, no matter how difficult she finds the questions and comments she will receive. Other activities such as play groups, Parent–Teacher Association meetings, and kindergarten classes can also be excruciatingly painful for people going through secondary infertility. They cannot use the avoidance techniques that work for those with primary infertility.

I think these couples have been neglected. We don't have enough support groups for them, we don't have enough literature available to them, and we don't have enough support from the medical community for them. When people seek therapy for secondary infertility, the tendency is for the medical team to look at them as not being the interesting cases. They have conceived before, so they are not considered particularly challenging.

The couple is experiencing all the stages that Kubler-Ross, Barbara Menning, and others have talked about in terms of infertility: denial, shock, anger, sadness, and guilt all mixed together, and they don't feel comfortable sharing those feelings with society. Thus they become more and more isolated. I see it happening also within the couple, and I am concerned that the isolation has even more ramifications for their relationship. The husband may be impatient with his wife for not being happy with their present child. I think he misunderstands. The wife is obviously happy with their child, but she is also dealing with a lot of unhappiness because she feels out of control and unable to achieve what she ultimately wants. I spend a great deal of time exploring that issue with couples and trying to find out the motivation for a second pregnancy. I don't think we can do much in the way of intervention unless we know why the struggle is so intense.

Motivations for Pregnancy

One of the reasons couples have for wanting a second pregnancy so desperately is that they are anxious to redo something in the past. If the first pregnancy or delivery was not as they wanted it to be, they want to do it again. They want to go through it this time without drugs, or use the birthing room instead of the monitors.

A second component of this is that they may want to be parents in a different way. If the first few months or the first years were difficult, or if they think they made some mistakes but have learned something useful, they want to do better the second time.

I usually ask two questions: Which partner wants to have a second child the most? and What is hardest about this experience? Answers to both are important because sometimes husbands and wives don't realize what is difficult for the partner, and verbalizing and hearing the responses is helpful. It is important for the couple to know what the motivation

is behind all this. Maybe the husband didn't realize that pregnancy was so crucial for his wife. Maybe the wife didn't undertstand that her husband wanted to be a more active parent when the babies were young. We have to know what they are grieving besides a pregnancy and the child, and we have to address some symbolic losses as well.

Potential Effects for Existing Children

The experience of secondary infertility is different also because it does not occur in a vacuum: a third person experiences this infertility with the couple, and that is the child they already have. It is helpful to ask a couple immediately how they think their child at home is perceiving this time. Sometimes the child is too young to perceive much of anything, but if they are 2 years old or older they usually experience something. It is good to sensitize people about that. Couples frequently have seen that their children feel different. They feel different from their friends and their cousins. They feel different when people talk about what they did with their brothers and sisters. They feel different when they have friends over and there is only their room and not a brother's or sister's room. They feel angry and disappointed with the mother particularly. Instead of feeling "Gee, Mom, can't we have another child?" or "Can't you give me a baby brother or sister?" they may construe the situation as "Mom won't." They may also sense the unhappiness in their parents, and that gives us concern because the child can interpret the parents' pain as meaning that somehow they are not enough. Perhaps they did something wrong, and their parents are being driven to get a better child or maybe even a replacement. It is of major importance to make sure that a child is not feeling that.

Because infertility involves so many medical interventions, a young child may have fantasies that the mother is very sick because she is taking her temperature, having injections, having x-rays, and going to the doctor. It is not unusual for a child to feel frightened and have a fantasy that the mother is dying. It is very important that any woman who is going through active infertility treatment be reassuring to her child in whatever way necessary, to be clear that she is all right, not sick or dying.

Secondary infertility can have a profound effect on parenting when the parents are preoccupied and even obsessed with their struggle. For one thing, the existing child feels the mother distancing herself due to preoccupation. For another, parents miss out on the growth and development of their child because they are concentrating on what isn't happening. They are busy with their medical appointments, and like all infertile couples, they are on an emotional roller coaster. Eventually, it is exhausting for everyone.

Clearly, in all of this there is a tendency or a danger to overindulge the only child. Some parents do this because they just enjoy having an only child, but I am talking here about the overindulgence that comes from the guilt of having been preoccupied and not paying attention to the child: "I'm so depressed that my IVF attempt didn't work, I'll go out and buy him a new swing set." These couples also fantasize about the death or illness of their existing child and how they would cope or even survive. This can create terror in them, which can lead to overprotectiveness.

One of the peak times for people to go through conflict over overprotectiveness is when their children reach age 2 or 3 and are beginning to assert themselves by rejecting the parental image. They start with "No," and "I don't want to," and "I hate you," and "I'm going to do it myself." That can cut really deeply in any mother's heart, obviously, but when she is going through secondary infertility it is just devastating because if feels like a whisper of the future. The child is getting on the school bus and going off to school, and there is not much to celebrate for a mother going through secondary infertility. She thinks, "My God, he really is school age. He is growing away from me." The loss of the first child's busy stage is harder when there is fear that there will never be another to experience infancy with.

Moving On

Unlike couples with primary infertility, those with secondary infertility are not grieving a dream. They know what parenthood is like. They know what it feels like to give birth and to have a child. What they are grieving is the size of their family, the spacing of a sibling for their child, the closeness of their children, and the possible loss of the expected pleasure of a repeat pregnancy.

Being able to say enough is enough is very difficult when a couple has had a success before, but that is part of the resolution these couples have to face at some point. It means saying it to each other and possibly to a child as well. It also means opening up the option of alternatives.

Sometimes neither the option of adoption nor that of having only one child feels right. In my work with couples I begin to explore their pros and cons. This is not to move the couple to one decision or another, but to allow the grief work to begin and to let them feel that they can take some control over their future.

One step in unlocking the grieving process is to be specific. I usually spend at least one session with the couple talking about the option they find least desirable. They are always surprised that we focus that way, but I find that it is helpful to say, in the case of adoption, "Let's spend the next session talking about your worst fears about adoption." It is really helpful for them to hear these fears together and in a safe place.

I also ask them to write down the pros and cons of adoption and not share them with their partner until they come together to talk with me. That can be very enlightening for them. If they stay at home and talk about it, they can go off on tangents and not reach any conclusion. The next time we meet we do the same about having only one child. Again, I ask them their worst fears, and the pros and the cons. I try to give them books on both options, particularly the one they are least comfortable with. It is important for them to understand all possibilities before they make any kind of decision.

A special issue arises in considering adoption. I always ask people how they think their extended family will feel about an adopted child. They have to think about grandparents, aunts and uncles, cousins, and all, and assess whether an adopted child would be considered second best in the wider family circle because they already have a biologic child. Another question is how their biologic child would feel about an adopted child. Clearly, adopting is going to make their infertility much more visible, and they are opening themselves up to personal questions: Why did you adopt? Which one is your own?

Nursing and Counseling Support

Although many couples move through secondary infertility to resolution—either acceptance of the loss of the hoped-for biologic child or adoption—without requesting anything but purely medical help, many would benefit from supportive psychological intervention.

Nurses and physicians can give permission to show distress, even though the couple is considered lucky, in other circles, to have the family they do have. They can validate people's right to try to build families constituted according to their ideas of what feels right. They can help couples explore the meaning to them of a pregnancy and a larger family, and communicate with each other about differences in motivation or intensity of feeling. They can educate about potential effects of the workup on the existing family, and help the couple explore nonbiologic options. Referral to a therapist is always appropriate for assistance with decision making or exploration, either short-term or in depth, of intrapsychic issues that may make the experience of infertility more difficult. Secondary infertility may have aspects that are distinct from primary infertility, but it is no less intense or painful, no easier to resolve, and no less deserving of attention from the mental health community.

Suggested Reading

1. Collection: "Secondary Infertility" Resolve Fact Sheet, available from Resolve Inc., 5 Water Street, Arlington, MA.
2. Diamant A. One and only. Boston Globe Magazine, December 3, 1989:18–54.
3. Glazer E, Cooper S. Without Child: Experiencing and Resolving Infertility. Lexington, MA: DC Heath, 1988.
4. Harkness C. The Infertility Book: A comprehensive Medical and Emotional Guide. San Francisco: Volcano Press, 1987.
5. Hawke S, Know D. One Child by Choice. Englewood Cliffs, NJ: Prentice Hall, 1977.
6. Kappelman M. Raising the Only Child. New York: New American Library, 1977.

30
Coping with Pregnancy Loss: Ectopic Pregnancy, Recurrent Abortion, and Stillbirth

Rochelle Friedman

Too often women's illnesses, concerns, and issues have been overlooked, minimized, and not infrequently blamed on them. Unfortunately, the area of pregnancy loss falls in this category of social history. Until recently, women who had lost a pregnancy were told that it was all for the best, that they had not lost anything of significance. Most horrifying, the classic psychoanalytic literature, when it addressed the issue at all, maintained that pregnancy loss was a physical expression of the mother's negative or ambivalent feelings about her femininity or about being a mother.

Until recently physicians and patients each had their own perspective on pregnancy loss. Medical caregivers tended to see early losses as nature's failure, as demonstrated by descriptive phrases such as blighted ovum, nonviable fetus, ectopic pregnancy, and miscarriage. From their perspective, pregnancy loss was a medical problem that they had to deal with by emptying the uterus, or performing surgery to deal with an ectopic implantation.

The parents' perspective has tended to focus less on the medical aspects, which most experience as an ordeal to be lived through, and more on what they have lost. For them the loss of a pregnancy, even an extremely early one, is likely to be experienced as the loss of their future child. Failure to understand this leaves caregivers in a position in which they cannot but disappoint.

To understand the parents' experience of losing a pregnancy involuntarily, or giving one up voluntarily because of medical necessity, social circumstances, or personal circumstances, we have to understand what relationships are formed between the parents and their unborn child. What was not understood until recently is that attachment does not begin at birth. Pregnancy loss hurts terribly because the mother and perhaps also the father become attached to their future child very early in the pregnancy. They begin to fantasize about what the baby will be like, what sex it will be, what they will name it, and much more. The child becomes real to them before anything like a real baby is present.

In many areas of life, disappointment is profound when one's deepest wishes are thwarted, and so it is with pregnancy loss. Even when the embryo is minute or abnormal, the emotional importance of its loss may be tremendous. This is particularly true for couples who have put off childbearing, those with a history of infertility or repeated pregnancy loss, and those who soon will be too old to have a child.

One of the most important factors determining how a given couple will experience the loss of a pregnancy is the strength of their wish for a child. A 20-year-old, unmarried mother of two may find herself saddened by the loss of her third pregnancy, but not uncommonly, her grief will be tempered by relief. There is no relief for the couple in their late thirties or early forties, or for the couple who are thrilled about being pregnant only to learn that the fetus carries a major genetic or structural abnormality.

The desire for a child and the attachment to both the wished-for and the real baby are important in determining how the loss of a pregnancy will be experienced. Other determining factors are how long a couple has been trying to become pregnant; whether they have a history of infertility or pregnancy loss; whether they have other children; their personality structure, including how they cope with stressful events; whether they have had other losses and when in their lives they occurred; whether these losses were resolved; how supportive they are to each other; and how supportive their friends, family, and caregivers are.

As those who care for individuals who are in the process of losing a pregnancy, our first task is to get to know the people to whom we are ministering. Circumstances will dictate whether we can learn a lot or just the bare minimum. Asking questions such as, "Will you tell me what brings you in? Tell me a bit about what is going on? Tell me about the difficulty you have been having?" will elicit responses that convey valuable information. They should provide information about whether the couple understands what is happening, how accurate their understanding is, how upset they are, and whether they can respond positively to efforts to reach out to them.

In early interactions with patients, there are several ways in which caregivers can be helpful:

1. Try to clarify the situation.
2. Keep patients informed about what is going on, what tests and procedures are being planned, what they involve, and what information they will yield.
3. When options exist, these should be explained carefully: patients should be helped to think them through. Where possible, patients should be encouraged to have input into decision making.
4. We can provide support and a comforting presence; convey caring by tone of voice and by willingness to listen, explain, answer questions, and spend time.
5. It is helpful to express sympathy directly. Patients are touched by a caregiver's concern.
6. Try to have a spouse or other relative or friend present to offer support and help in decision making.
7. Try to understand what the patients' needs

are, what they are experiencing, and what might be helpful to them. Put yourself in their shoes. Few people in the middle of crisis have the presence of mind to know what they need. They are too panicky, confused, or frozen to think clearly.
8. We have to understand that grief is a process, and depending on where in the process our patients are, our role will differ.

Caregivers must be aware of what the patient's experience is: whether she is in the process of having a miscarriage, in pain from a ruptured ectopic pregnancy, in hospital to have ultrasound confirmation of intrauterine death, or awaiting a therapeutic abortion. It is important to focus on the situation at hand and to ask ourselves, "How can I help the person get through this acute crisis?"

When we are caring for someone who has already experienced a loss, our role depends on how recently the loss has occurred. Early on, we are dealing with people in crisis whose usual coping mechanisms are not functioning properly. Their grief is acute, and it affects their sleep, appetite, and ability to concentrate and take interest in things. They cry frequently and easily, they cannot make a decision, they may be irritable or feel fragile, and their judgment as well as their ability to function may be impaired. What they need at this point is support, reassurance, comfort, and help in taking care of practical matters. Farther along in the grief process their needs shift from requiring assistance in areas of basic functioning to needing help in coping with enduring emotional pain.

In dealing with these patients it is important not to encourage them to push feelings aside. When one does not grieve a loss, pain does not disappear, it just goes underground, emerging to cause difficulty later in life. Some caregivers worry that in asking patients about their emotional state they may be putting ideas into their heads. In fact, the opposite is true. When one's feelings are validated, they are much less likely to be exaggerated in order to be heard.

In order to provide sensitive emotional support to our patients, we need to understand the mourning process. Because parents experience the fetus as a child, pregnancy loss or stillbirth is perceived as a death. Individuals who have lost a loved one usually experience several stages of grief. Couples who have lost a pregnancy commonly go through a parallel grief process. The initial stage of grief is often a state of shock in which the person may have a difficult time believing that the loss has occurred. They may report feeling emotionally numb or dead. As the reality of what has happened sinks in, numbness fades and active mourning begins. During the mourning process it is usual to feel sad or preoccupied by one's loss and uninterested in the outside world. Common symptoms include wide fluctuations in mood; irritability, anger, and jealousy; blaming others for the loss; and wanting to avoid contact with anyone or anything that reminds one of the loss.

Although mourning is a slow and painful process that may continue for weeks or months, it must take place before healing can occur. Grieving is a personal process. How a person experiences and expresses grief is determined by how one normally handles feelings, how one deals with stress, whether there is a history of previous losses, one's religious beliefs, the presence or absence of other children, prognosis for future success in childbearing, and the extent of support from family and friends.

As the reality of what has happened sinks in, it is common to feel an intense, consuming sadness that may be experienced as a physical sensation—tightness in the chest, a knot in the pit of the stomach, or a feeling of being empty inside, which may be continuous or occur in waves. Feelings of isolation and detachment are common, and it is often difficult to take pleasure in people, places, or activities that were previously enjoyable. For most people the climb back is an emotional roller coaster, fluctuating between sadness and the depths of despair.

It is also common to feel irritable and easily upset, or to experience overly sensitive reactions to real or imagined slights, many of which would not ordinarily be of concern. Even when they are aware that their reactions are somewhat irrational, the parents feel unable to control them. Feelings of guilt often torment both parents. Most people find it difficult to cope with events that are beyond their control or that they do not understand. We are used to living in a world where things happen for a specific reason. However, the majority of couples are unable to learn very much about the cause of their pregnancy loss, either because the cause was not sought, or if sought, no definitive answer was found.

Given the lack of a scientific, or at least a satisfactory, answer, most couples are thrown back on their fantasies or become preoccupied with trying to discover what caused their pregnancy to fail. For some this leads to obsessive ruminations about what may have gone wrong or what they may have done wrong. Typically, women focus on having lifted something heavy, not resting enough, having had intercourse, or traveling. Some couples carry a burden of guilt, related to a past event, that leaves them particularly vulnerable to blaming themselves. This may have been a previous therapeutic abortion, premarital sex, or guilt about particular sexual practices. Sometimes one or both parents feel guilty about having had ambivalent feelings about the pregnancy at the outset.

Many couples find that their own tendency to search for a cause and to blame themselves is reinforced by much of society's mythology about pregnancy loss. Everyone has a theory about what might have gone wrong that they are eager to share with the bereaved couple, ostensibly provided as "helpful information." Often, however, such ideas come across as blame rather than help.

Couples may exhaust themselves searching for an explanation. Since they probably will never turn up one that satisfies them, their energies can be tied up in this pursuit for a significant period of time. One thing that can be done to short-circuit the process is to address the problem of how difficult it is not to know, perhaps engaging the larger issue of how we live with things in life that are beyond our control.

A common reaction to pregnancy loss that surprises and dismays most people is envy toward anyone more fortunate, which means anyone who is either pregnant or the parent of an infant. In their sadness and anger, a couple may wish others ill. Even while acknowledging the irrationality of their feelings, they may find it impossible not to feel envious of someone who has what they want.

Some women experience feelings of inadequacy in the aftermath of a pregnancy loss. This usually begins as concern about whether or not they are physically adequate, whether they are feminine enough, or whether or not their body works well enough to carry a pregnancy. They tend to see other women as competent and complete, and themselves as inadequate and damaged.

Another insidious consequence of losing a pregnancy is that as a result, life tends to seem fragile. Frightening thoughts, feelings of danger, and concern about terrible things happening are difficult to push away when the unthinkable has, in fact, happened. I look on this as a loss of innocence and consider it one of the more disturbing and far-reaching consequences of losing a pregnancy. Feeling that the world is a dangerous place and being aware of the limited amount of control we have over our own destiny are usually issues of midlife. In the population of parents who have lost pregnancies, these issues arise one or two decades earlier than they otherwise would.

When grief does not diminish as time passes, caregivers should be concerned. Persistent denial and symptoms of depression (sleep disturbance, loss of appetite, irritability, crying, and fatigue) are indications that grief is not resolving as it should. Unexplained pain, chronic headache or stomach discomfort, lack of sleep, and self-destructive thoughts or behavior are other red flags. When a pathologic grief reaction is suspected, patients should be referred to individual treatment or to a professionally led support group (leaderless support groups are useful, but not for this population).

While all forms of pregnancy loss share much in common, each type has specific features that we should be aware of.

Miscarriage

Because miscarriage occurs early in pregnancy, there is a tendency to minimize its importance. One of the most important things caregivers can do is to understand the emotional magnitude of early fetal loss. The reality that the ovum was blighted, or that miscarriage is nature's way of making sure that severely damaged embryos do not survive is one thing. The psychologic experience, however, is not one of losing a "blighted embryo," but of losing a desired child.

Although miscarriage is common, ending one in five pregnancies, it is almost always unanticipated. When miscarriage threatens, one leaves the happy world of pregnancy and enters the nightmarish world of uncertainty, fear, pain, and hospitals. It consumes one's life (women describe running to the bathroom to check for blood, and being hypervigilant about every pain and twinge).

Most women are unprepared for the physical experience of miscarriage and find it frightening. It is good practice for women who are threatening to miscarry to be seen by a physician or nurse. Those who are told to wait it out at home, that nothing can be done, are most likely to feel unattended to and to voice complaints about the care they received, often holding on to the belief that if they had been seen, something could have been done.

When the fetus dies but is not expelled, a missed abortion has occurred. Women who experience this tend to feel in limbo—not pregnant and not able to go on with life. Women who have had a missed abortion must make a choice to have labor induced or to wait until it begins spontaneously. In both cases, they tend to experience a resurgence of grief at the time of delivery, because the magical hope that a mistake has been made and the fetus is really alive must be abandoned.

When a woman who has miscarried has to be hospitalized, it is best for this to be on a regular surgical floor. The maternity floor is no place for those with any type of pregnancy loss.

Ectopic Pregnancy

The occurrence rate of ectopic pregnancy is 1 in 100 live births.

Ectopic pregnancy is a loss even more difficult for patients to comprehend than miscarriage. Most people have no idea what an ectopic pregnancy is until they have one. It is an early loss and therefore invisible. Moreover, it is overshadowed by the fact that it is a medical emergency requiring surgery. Characteristically, the woman has had twinges of pain for hours or days, and only enters the hospital when the pain is intolerable. The person we meet is in the throes of a medical crisis, in acute pain, and perhaps unaware that she is pregnant.

Ectopic pregnancy is an upsetting experience for several reasons. It is often not diagnosed until the tube ruptures, and rupture of an ectopic pregnancy is accompanied by severe pain. It is not uncommon to learn of the pregnancy simultaneously with learning that the pregnancy is lost. Ectopic pregnancy almost always requires surgery; it is potentially a life-threatening event.

Couples are likely to feel grief and sadness on many levels. First, there is the loss of the pregnancy. There is also the possibility that fertility has been impaired. Only 50% of women conceive after an ectopic pregnancy. Those who do conceive have a 7 to 12% risk that a future pregnancy will also be ectopic.

The emotional recovery entails coming to terms with what has happened, what one has lost, and what is still possible. It may be complicated by lack of understanding and support from family and friends, who tend to focus on the life-threatening aspects of the surgery and not appreciate the less dramatic aspects: that the pregnancy has been lost or that fertility has been compromised.

Guilt and blame tend to be significant. Patients blame themselves for having contracted sexually transmitted diseases, for past abortions, or for having chosen to use an intrauterine device (IUD). They blame their doctors for having inserted an IUD, for not treating pelvic inflammatory disease early enough or well enough, and for subjecting them to mutilating surgery.

Stillbirth

Because stillbirth occurs between the 20th week of gestation and birth, it is a public loss. As the pregnancy has been carried for a significant amount of time, anticipation is high and disappointment is profound.

When stillbirth is diagnosed prior to the onset of labor, the physical and emotional issues are similar to those encountered with a missed abortion: feelings of loss, horror at carrying a dead fetus, disbelief, the choice to have delivery induced or to wait for labor to begin spontaneously, and the resurgence of grief at the time of delivery. When death occurs during labor or delivery, anticipation is at a maximum. The mother is exhausted, and her coping ability is compromised by stress, fatigue, and pain.

Working with couples who have had stillbirths has taught us that it is important to acknowledge that a baby has died and that the loss is significant. Anything we can do to make the loss real will help. It is important to give the couple the choice about whether they want to see their baby, hold their baby, have pictures taken that they can keep, or have a lock of hair, handprints or footprints, or the baby's blanket to take home.

When the child has severe abnormalities, for example, when the skin is severely deteriorated, it is best to describe the damage in some detail to the parents and leave the decision of whether they want to see the child to them. It is important not to let the current practice of urging couples to see and hold their stillborn child become routine. We must consider the specific nature of each situation and the expressed wishes of each couple.

Arranging a religious ceremony or burial may be of comfort to some people. Others may find it an unwelcome burden and may prefer that the hospital take care of arrangements. Each couple should be helped to figure out what is best for them.

When one has a stillbirth, hospitalization is an inevitable part of the experience. The woman who enters the hospital with a known fetal death is too often treated as if she has the plague. No one knows what to say so they avoid her. She is upset, which engenders more avoidance, and since the fetus is known to be dead, the medical necessity for frequent contact does not exist. In the worst of cases, the bereaved woman is left alone for long periods of time. Her emotional pain is ignored and her physical pain is responded to only when it has to be or when more important things have been attended to.

With a stillbirth the time for lifesaving heroics is past. Yet there is much a caregiver can do. Being with the woman or the couple can help; warmth and understanding are healing. The staff must be informed about what has happened. They can help by stopping to talk, asking how the woman is doing, offering to sit with her if she wishes, commiserating, and giving her a chance to talk about her experiences. Ask when she realized the baby had died, what the pregnancy was like up to then, if she had any premonition, and so on.

As with miscarriage and ectopic pregnancy, hospitalization on a maternity floor should be avoided unless it is preferred by the parents. Whenever possible, the hospital stay should be as brief as possible.

The postpartum period is difficult, as it is a time of brutal emotional pain and of physical discomfort without the compensation of a baby. The woman must deal with postpartum physical concerns, episiotomy, lochia, and breast engorgement, often without preparation. Because she feels like a failure, the mother may feel she is not entitled to attention and so may have trouble resting, taking time out from work, or asking for help. Many women have difficulty recognizing that they need time to recover from this exhausting, emotionally draining ordeal.

Parents have to inform friends and extended family of the stillbirth. When there are other children, they have to inform them of the death, deal with their reactions, and comfort and reassure them.

Voluntary Losses

The grief women experience after a voluntary loss (therapeutic abortion necessitated by the presence of a fetal abnormality or elective abortion) is in many ways similar to that described by women who have had involuntary losses. What is different about the experience of voluntarily terminating a pregnancy is that making the choice to end a pregnancy, even an ill-fated one, carries with it an enormous psychologic burden. Even those who feel they have made the right choice may feel the weight of responsibility for ending a life: feelings of ambivalence and guilt are also commonly experienced.

Advances in prenatal diagnostic technology have made the in utero diagnosis of fetal malformations possible. With the ability to detect abnormalities before birth comes the necessity of making painful decisions. National Institutes of Health statistics report that 95% of women who learn through amniocentesis that the fetus is deformed choose to abort. It is important to understand that the decision to terminate a pregnancy rather than to deliver a grossly abnormal child is not a real choice at all, but one that is dictated by circumstances. It is an agonizing decision because often there is some element of uncertainty, and because what is being terminated is a wanted pregnancy. Women who have made this choice mourn their lost child, lose faith in their own bodies, and must deal with implications for the health of future offspring who may be similarly affected. They also must bear a burden in addition to the grief normally experienced with a fetal loss. They are burdened by guilt at destroying a life, at not wanting to live with a severely damaged child, at feeling that they have made a selfish decision, and perhaps at violating their own deeply held religious or ethical beliefs. Both the decision and the resolution of loss are further complicated when spouses do not agree on the decision, when one spouse is known to be a carrier of the genetic defect found in the fetus, the couple has an existing child with the defect, or the full extent of the defect cannot be determined prenatally.

Although elective abortion seems to be the only form of pregnancy loss that involves choice, for many women it does not feel like one they have chosen. Perhaps they would like to have had a child in their life if the situation was different or their life was different. These women grieve the child they would have wanted, but their grief is complicated by several factors, such as ambivalence about the choice they have made, guilt at ending the life of a future child, and worry about the effect of an abortion on their ability to carry future pregnancies. They experience shock at the feelings of loss that they did not anticipate. The pregnancy may have come at a time when the woman was also dealing with disappointment in a relationship or the loss of one. Finally, the decision to have an abortion is often made in secret, against one's better judgment, or in conflict with religious beliefs or moral values.

Caregivers must recognize that women who choose abortion can suffer the same grief as those who have involuntary losses. They also must put aside their own feelings about abortion if they are to offer healing compassion rather than the punishing experience these patients often unconsciously expect.

Summary

In summary, somewhere between one-third and one-fifth of women who conceive lose their babies through miscarriage, stillbirth, ectopic pregnancy, or infant death. Another 1.5 million pregnancies are terminated by abortion. Of the approximately 3.5 million infants born in 1983, about 200,000 had some birth defect, of which 75,000 were serious enough to cause premature death or require lifelong family or institutional care. This adds up to a significant number of poor outcomes. It also adds up to a significant number of patients who blame either themselves or their physicians for failing to deliver a perfect baby.

We unwittingly contribute to the displacement of blame when we fail to make patients aware that pregnancy is a process over which caregivers have limited control. Even the best medical care and the best self-care do not guarantee a good outcome. We have to help patients understand that there are many risks inherent both in development and in delivery, that we will do whatever we can to ensure a healthy infant, and that we expect that they will follow our guidelines so as to do the same. We must make them aware that we can offer good care but that we are not able to offer guarantees.

Questions and Answers

Question. Do you feel there is a true post-abortion syndrome?

Rochelle Friedman. Absolutely, but not for everyone. I think one sees this most often in women who have the highest level of ambivalence about the pregnancy. Often, as I said, they decide to have an abortion even though they would like to have had the baby because there are compelling reasons not to have it. These are people who grieve what they would like to have had. Their grief process is just as I described and lasts a long time, and often comes up over and over again with other life events. It may be a miscarriage, it may be a period of infertility, it may be the birth of a child that brings back feelings about the child they did not have.

Machelle M. Seibel. I would like to make a comment about two types of pregnancy loss that I think have been created by technology. One is selective abortion and its natural correlate, a twin gestation in which one of the fetuses is abnormal or dies naturally. In selective termination you are sacrificing, if you will, one or more fetuses to allow the others to survive. The second one is routine embryo transfer after IVF. I remember clearly one patient immediately after her embryo transfer who popped her head up and asked, "Do I have that maternal glow yet?" The perception that one is in fact pregnant for the moment creates the potential for that individual to perceive every embryo transfer that does not turn into a clinical pregnancy as a pregnancy loss. I do not know if there is any answer. I do think that consciousness has to be raised about the technologic creation of pregnancy loss.

Rochelle Friedman. Those are important points, and in fact, some women do have feelings about the embryos that do not take, about the ones that are not transplanted. We have to look at these issues in the future and understand more about them. Selective reduction is a nightmare psychologically because it feels like making a choice between children. As with many aspects of pregnancy loss, there is a wide discrepancy between the psychologic experience and the way in which it is handled medically.

Diane Clapp. Many women feel guilty about abortions they had a long time ago, and they have not grieved them because they simply felt relieved that they were no longer pregnant. Only in retrospect, as they are unsuccessfully trying to be come mothers, do they feel guilty, even though physicians and nurses have told them they did not cause their infertility by these abortions. Realizing now that they may never be a mother and that they might have a 20-year-old today causes the loss to take on a new meaning.

Question. These people are also angry at their bodies, and nature, and God, and fate. Why were they pregnant at the wrong time, and now cannot become pregnant or retain a pregnancy?

Rochelle Friedman. All of us think in cause-and-effect terms. It is our way of making sense of a world that does not seem to be rational. What these people are doing is saying that this is happening to me now because something happened to me then, or I chose to do something then. They are making their mental calculation and we are seeing the end product of it.

Question. Please comment on husbands in relationship to pregnancy loss, because I feel that they are really neglected in our working with couples, particularly in the hospital.

Rochelle Friedman. What often happens is that because the woman is carrying the pregnancy she forms an attachment to their future child earlier than the husband does. This makes perfect sense. The baby is in her body. She experiences all that is going on and she has a constant awareness that it is inside her, whereas her husband only experiences this secondarily. So when an early pregnancy, in particular, is lost, the two people tend to have a different attachment to the baby. This may be true even when the loss occurs at the time of delivery. The other factor that seems to make a difference is that men and women are socialized differently in terms of allowing themselves to experience their feelings and, particularly, to show them publicly. Women experience far fewer constraints in terms of crying, being sad, and being disappointed than men do. Therefore, the woman experiences her feelings directly and the man may put his aside. His social role is to hold the two of them together, and he is also conditioned not to fall apart. So he copes for both of them and his wife grieves for both of them, and that is how they go through the first stage. Although this is an adaptation to a stressful situation, often it does not work well, because on a psychologic level, what often happens is that over a period of time the wife becomes resentful that her husband is not feeling anything. She wonders if he really wanted the baby, if he really cares about her, and whether he has any feelings at all. He is trying to cope and keep the family together, and she is feeling emotionally abandoned. From his point of view, what seems to be happening is that his wife is grieving far longer than he thinks she should. He wonders why she is not back to normal and starts wondering if he really knows the woman he married. They end up at opposite ends of the universe in terms of dealing with their pain. What one can do to short-circuit all this misery is to explain that men and women often react differently and that one way is no better or worse than the other. This information seems to help to defuse things. Another fact that surprises people is that some men have delayed grief reactions. In the immediate period after loss it may be the woman whose feelings predominate. The man copes stoically, and maybe 3 or 4 months later he finds that he is depressed for no reason, or that he just cannot concentrate or that his work is falling apart. Now that his wife is feeling somewhat better, his feelings break through because it is safe to grieve.

Suggested Reading

1. Bibring GL. Some considerations of the psychological processes in pregnancy. In: Psychoanalytic Study of the Child. Vol. 14. New York: International University Press, 1959.
2. Blumberg B, et al. The psychological sequelae of abortion performed for a genetic indication. Am J Obstet Gynecol 1975;122:122.
3. Bowlby J. Attachment and Loss. New York: Basic Books, 1969.
4. Corney RT, Horton FT Jr. Pathological grief following spontaneous abortion. Am J Psych 1974;131:825–827.
5. Costello A, Gardner SL, et al. Perinatal grief and loss. J Perinatol 1988;8:361–370.
6. Davis D, Steward M, et al. Postponing pregnancy after perinatal death: Perspectives on doctor advice. J Am Acad Child Adol Psych 1989;28:481–487.
7. Donnai P, Charnes N, et al. Attitudes of patients after genetic termination of pregnancy. Br Med J 1981;282:621.
8. Friedman RR, Cohen KA. Emotional reactions to the miscarriage of a consciously desired pregnancy. In: Notman M, Nadelson C, eds. The Woman Patient. Vol. 3. New York: Plenum Press, 1982.
9. Friedman R, Gradstein B. Surviving Pregnancy Loss. Boston: Little, Brown, 1992 (in press).
10. Friedman T, Gath D. The psychiatric consequences of spontaneous abortion. Br J Psych 1989;155:810–813.
11. Furlong RM. Grief in the perinatal period. Obstet Gynecol 1983;61:497.
12. Glass RH, Golbus MS. Habitual abortion. Fertil Steril 1978;29:257–265.
13. Graham MA, et al. Factors affecting psychological adjustment to a fetal death. Am J Obstet Gynecol 1987;157:254–257.
14. Grimm ER. Psychological investigation of habitual abortion. Psychosom Med 1962;24:369–378.
15. Kaij L, Malmquist A, Nilsson A. Psychiatric aspects of spontaneous abortion. II. The importance of bereavement, attachment and neurosis in early life. J Psychosom Res 1969;13:53–59.
16. Kennell JH, Slyter H, Klaus MH. Mourning response of parents to the death of a newborn infant. N Engl J Med 1970;283:344–349.
17. Kirk EP. Psychological effects and management of perinatal loss. Am J Obstet Gynecol 1984;149:46–51.
18. Michel-Wolfromm H. The psychological factor in spontaneous abortion. J Psychosom Res 1968;12:67–71.
19. Seibel M, Graves WL. The psychological implications of spontaneous abortion. J Reprod Med 1980;25:161–165.
20. Simon NM, et al. Psychological factors related to spontaneous and therapeutic abortion. Am J Obstet Gynecol 1969;104:799–806.
21. Seitz PM, Warrick LH. Perinatal death: The grieving mother. Am J Nursing 1974;74:166–170.
22. Wolff JR. The emotional reaction to a stillbirth. Proceedings, Third International Congress of Psychosomatic Medicine in Obstetrics and Gynecology, London 1971:330–332.

31
Implementation of Ovum Donation Technology: Start-up Decisions, Challenges, and Problems

Judith Bernstein, Mara Brill, Susan Levin, Machelle Seibel, and Sharon Steinberg

The technology that makes pregnancy possible for women with little or no ovarian function is a recent and highly successful addition to the infertility specialists' therapeutic armamentarium. Ovum donation, perhaps more than any other advance in reproduction, creates unknown ethical, social, psychological, and legal circumstances for modern day family builders. In the narrowest sense, women who would previously have had to adopt in order to parent may now bear children who are genetically their husband's and gestationally their own.[1-5] In the largest sense, the female life cycle has been dramatically altered. Age boundaries for reproduction have been expanded beyond menopause, potentially allowing women of any age to become pregnant,[6] theoretically extending reproductive potential indefinitely. Daughters and mothers may donate eggs to each other, violating natural generational barriers.[7] Aunts may in fact be genetic mothers, and children raised in the same social circle may be biologically siblings with no knowledge of that relationship.[8] The effects of these new connections on egg donor offspring and their families are generally unknown.[9-14] This chapter will discuss the startup decisions, challenges, and problems involved in implementing an ovum donation program.

A Scientific Success Story

From a scientific point of view, ovum donation is a resounding success. The methodologies for exogenously preparing a uterine lining to receive an embryo among women with diminished or absent ovarian function are clearly established.[15] Pregnancy rates, even from early reports,[16-21] range between 30 and 50% which represents substantial improvement over conventional in vitro fertilization. Information learned about the relative contribution of egg, endometrial quality, and timing issues related to implantation will no doubt help improve success rates for many of the new reproductive technologies.

The Social Response to Scientific Advances in Reproduction

Although the technology necessary for ovum donation is relatively straightforward, the implementation, or social integration of that technology is not. Many people feel that "any sufficiently advanced technology is indistinguishable from magic".[22] Society at large is apprehensive about the unknown consequences of scientific tinkering with reproduction. As stated by C.P. Snow, "If the scientists have the future in their bones, then the traditional culture responds by wishing the future did not exist. It is the traditional culture, to an extent remarkably little diminished by the emergence of the scientific one, that manages the Western world."[23] Such social attitudes and concerns, fears, and vulnerabilities dictate the importance of developing egg donation programs with caution, scrupulous attention to detail, and clearly thought out responses to ethical and psychological issues.

This work was funded in part by the Faulkner Institute for Reproductive Medicine.

Establishing an Ovum Donation Program

The Key Building Blocks

The cornerstone of successful ovum donation is a successful IVF program: reliable hormone assays and ultrasounds; clinicians experienced with ovulation induction, oocyte retrieval, and embryo transfer techniques; and technicians and scientists expert in andrology and embryo culture. Institutional support is essential from the onset, as is the involvement of a mental health team and an ethics advisory group. Substantial nursing energies must also be available for startup problem solving, patient education and emotional support, donor screening and matching, and cycle coordination. Because ovum donation is considerably more labor intensive than IVF, appropriate nursing support should be anticipated. In our experience, each egg donation cycle requires approximately a fourfold increase in nursing time and effort over conventional IVF.

Key Areas for Early Decision-Making

A successful egg donation program rarely evolves without complex planning. Intensive analysis and coordination are required throughout the entire process. There are four necessary phases: (1) preprogram planning, (2) patient selection and evaluation, (3) procedure planning, and (4) follow-up.

Preprogram Planning

Institutional Coordination

The preprogram planning stage requires project personnel to work with hospital administrators to review a number of important issues (Table 31.1). We have divided these into seven areas.

(1) Protection of Patient Confidentiality

The goal of confidentiality is to permit the involved parties the opportunity to choose what

TABLE 31.1. Pre-program planning.

- Protect patient confidentiality (staff education).
- Establish admission procedures, costs, billing mechanisms; coordinate with other specialties.
- Develop appropriate recordkeeping forms.
- Consider legal issues related to informed consent and financial responsibility.
- Plan introduction of the program to the community.
- Involve a mental health team.
- Review ethical issues that affect proposed policies.

they tell families, friends, community, and offspring. Record keeping must be designed to protect confidentiality in the case of known donors, and anonymity in the case of both donors and recipients matched by the program. The name of the recipient should not appear in the donor's record, nor the donor's name in the recipient's record. Similarly, the name of the donor should not appear on records released for insurance purposes. A numerical coding system, with the master list held by the program director, best accomplishes this goal. If medications for the donor are to be billed to the egg recipient, care should be taken not to release the name. On the day of retrieval, if the operating room schedule is circulated widely, it may be advisable to register the donor under an assumed name. Because hospital staff who will interact with either donors or recipients are likely less familiar with oocyte donation and its related ethical, legal and emotional issues, an in-service should be provided by the assisted reproduction team.

(2) Admission Procedures, Costs, and Billing Mechanisms

Special procedures are required in most institutions to prevent medical records from generating billing records. This is necessary so the donor's records can be kept in her own name and made accessible to her at any time in the future, without initiating a corresponding bill for services. In most hospitals this will require a separate registration method and hand-billing to ensure that charges are posted to the appropriate account (the recipient). Appropriate billing mechanisms must also be worked out for services provided by other departments such as anaesthesia, radiology, pharmacy, and laboratory. Cycle charges vary greatly with the type of practice and region of the country. A detailed fee structure and written billing policies should be available to all patients who are inquiring about egg donation. Special insurance codes may be necessary in those instances where coverage is provided. Inquiry should be made to each carrier likely to be involved prior to program startup, since coverage can be either minimal, partial, or complete, and restrictions may apply to type of diagnosis and selection criteria. Some companies cover egg donation under reproductive benefits, and others under organ donation. State insurance commission regulations may also affect billing formats. While the final responsibility for insurance may rest with the patient, early acquisition of this type of information makes for a smoother running program. If donors are to be compensated monetarily for their inconvenience, special mechanisms may need to be developed. The purpose of the compensation, amount, method, and timing should be clearly delineated in advance. Finally, the party responsible for hospital bills in the event of complications for the donor must be identified prior to retrieval.

(3) Medical Records

An effort should be made to anticipate future needs for medical records. From a practical point of view, flow sheets provide useful organization for administrative issues, genetic screening, medical history, matching characteristics, physical examination, laboratory results, and cycle information. Hospital based records should be coded for anonymity, accessible to the donor for future use, and separated from account generation. Practice-based records should provide long-term access to donor health information, matching criteria, genetic screening, and consent forms. A decision should be made prior to program startup about future handling of requests for information from either donor or recipient. Provision should be made for requests based on medical necessity, and the possibility of future laws requiring disclosure of identifying information should be considered. All pro-

grams should think seriously about acquiring nonidentifying biographical information for later release to adult offspring.

(4) Consent Development

Consent forms for oocyte donation are complicated documents. In addition to providing information and legal protection, forms must delineate the rights and responsibilities of all involved parties including the medical team, the institution, the donor and spouse, the recipient and spouse, and offspring. Explanation of screening and preparation requirements, risks and benefits, the matching process, what to expect during ovulation induction, uterine preparation, retrieval, and transfer are necessary. Discussion of confidentiality and anonymity, compensation and financial responsibility, ownership of oocytes and embryos, responsibility for offspring, pregnancy, and any risks incidental to donation should be included. If cryopreservation is to be utilized, a separate consent should describe couple requests in the event of death, divorce, or other unanticipated catastrophes.

(5) Introduction of the Program to the Community

Plans should be made with the institutional public affairs department for announcement of the new program. This may simply be information provided so staff can answer questions as they arise, or may be a formal introduction —an open house or newspaper interview describing the egg donation program. All individuals who interact with the public should be aware of the American Fertility Society Guidelines for egg donation, and feel comfortable discussing the general ethical, psychological, and legal ramifications. They also need to be familiar with specific program policies and the discussions involved in developing them.

(6) Mental Health Team Planning

Ovum donation is more complex than in vitro fertilization because it involves a third party, the egg donor. Inclusion of mental health professionals is imperative in selecting donors stable enough to make a firm commitment. Equally important is the need to safeguard the potential donor by evaluating risks and benefits to that person as realistically and completely as possible. A psychologist or social worker or psychiatrist familiar with reproductive issues can assess the donor's mental health, and help examine possible outcomes of donation. Many programs use the Minnesota Multiphasic Personality Index (MMPI) to identify potential donors at risk for having emotional difficulties being a donor. Issues for discussion with a donor include motivation for donation, future childbearing desires, attitudes of family, friends, and significant other toward donation, perception of legal risks, possible complications, and what to tell existing children about the multiple doctor's visits, needle sticks, and medications required for donation. Scenarios to explore might be future infertility offspring seeking information, fantasies about the recipient, or contact with children. Scheduling problems for work should be reviewed as well as feelings about compensation.

If the donor is known to the recipient couple, the effect of donation on that ongoing relationship should be explored. For sisters there are special issues—sibling competition, guilt and manipulation, effect of the act of donating on the family of origin, what to tell the child about this special relationship, the potential for over-involvement on the part of the aunt-genetic mother, and/or a feeling of being threatened on the part of the rearing-gestational mother. Friends who donate also have special issues, such as what to tell children who will be raised in the same social circle about their genetic relationship.

The recipient couple benefit from a mental health evaluation during which they can frankly discuss risks and benefits, feelings about what to tell the child, and the potential for imbalance in parenting between a father who is genetically related to the child and a mother who is not. The interview might also provide the opportunity to discuss expectations, and explore options if the procedure is not successful.

The mental health contribution could take on many formats. Counseling could be either a requirement or a recommendation which could

include or exclude spouses. Either interviews, a panel of instruments, or both could be used to assess patients. However, it is important to remember that information included in a formal write-up becomes part of the patient's legal chart. In those circumstances in which a potential donor is rejected due to a question of emotional dysfunction, explaining the rejection to the potential donor creates a special challenge for the health professional.

(7) Ethical Decision-Making

Extensive ongoing consideration of the ethical concerns related to egg donation is essential for the program to function smoothly and successfully in an environment that safeguards the rights of all involved parties. Although some issues will need to be decided on a case by case basis, there should be broad agreement among the team members about general requirements. In the ideal setting, a team of IVF professionals, accustomed to discussing issues through to consensus, would have an ethics advisory board available to them for instruction on fundamental ethical principles. The team and the ethics board would jointly decide issues such as unacceptable donor attributes, or criteria for matching. Because information is lacking about the long-term emotional and social outcomes, and few laws are applicable to guide clinical action, this process is essential. Time spent in this type of program development is rewarded by time saved in crisis problem-solving once the procedures start. Issues for ethical decision-making may involve as yet unanswered questions specific to the donor, the recipient, or the offspring.

Donor Issues

What constitutes acceptable motivation? If compensation is to be provided for time, trouble, effort, and risk, how can it be distinguished clearly from an unacceptable compensation for body parts? Will patients be permitted to come to their own agreements with donors about financial matters, and if so, will the program choose to review those agreements or make stipulations about them? Is it necessary for contracts between donor and recipient to be drawn formally by a private attorney? How many times is it appropriate for a donor to donate? For how many individuals? How can a program avoid the problem of manipulation of donors or recipients, either by family pressures or for economic gain? To what extent should donor preferences about the recipient couple be taken into account? What defines an "acceptable" background for the donor—should candidates with family histories of depression or alcoholism be utilized? How will anonymous donor recruitment take place —from among IVF patients, from newspaper advertising, from among hospital employees? If IVF candidates are used, how will optimal egg quality be assured, and what might be the effect on an IVF patient who does not conceive herself, but fantasizes that the recipient has? If women are used who have no children, how might they feel if they develop infertility later on, knowing that someone else may have a child who is genetically theirs? If hospital employees are used, how will anonymity be assured?

Recipient Issues

How much information about the donor will be imparted? What voice does the recipient couple have in the matching process? Will two recipients be assigned to each donor, maximizing availability but reducing opportunity, or will all the eggs from that donor be provided to one individual and cryopreserved? If a single recipient is chosen, is there concern about the potential for stockpiling multiple excess embryos, most of which may never be used? Should recipients be permitted to locate their own donors through advertising, or should anonymous donors be provided exclusively by the program? If recipients bring their own donors, who are then intentionally switched with other couples' donors to create anonymity, are methods for confidentiality going to be adequate to prevent the individuals from finding out information couples would prefer to conceal?

Offspring Issues

What right does a child have to information about the manner of its conception or its genetic identity? If the donor is an aunt, will that information clarify or confuse the family relationship? If the donor is a family friend, what will be the effect on the child's identity? If the donation has been anonymous, what is the program's obligation to provide nonidentifying information, and what should be its response to a request, later on, for a search? How should a program counsel couples about the risks and benefits of keeping the child's genetic origins secret? Does a child have a right to a traditional family, and if so, should the program limit recipients on the basis of age or marital status? Will the program permit donation across generations (mother to daughter or the reverse), and should donations that fall into societal definitions of incest be prohibited? How many offspring are appropriate from any one donor, in the interest of preventing problems of consanguinity? What guarantees should be provided for the health of recipients, especially those who have survived treatment for cancer, in the interests of increasing the likelihood that parents will survive to see a child's majority? For many of these questions there are no answers. For this reason time, teamwork and ethical advice are essential in program development.

Patient Selection and Evaluation

Donor and recipient selection and matching should follow guidelines published by the American Fertility Society.[24] Four additional areas also require planning: education and emotional support, choice of stimulation protocol, geographical and temporal separation of anonymous donor and recipient during ovulation induction, and special arrangements for the days of retrieval and transfer (Table 31.2).

Education and Emotional Support

Ovum donation has enormous potential for confusion that can be reduced only through

TABLE 31.2. Patient selection and evaluation.

- Follow American Fertility Society Guidelines.
- Provide education and emotional support for donors, recipients and spouses.
- Make arrangements for confidentiality/anonymity during testing, retrieval and transfer.
- Plan for long-term follow-up.

education. Protocols are complicated and arrangements for confidentiality and anonymity are complex. Two couples may have to be coordinated around retrieval of one set of eggs. When sisters are involved, information may have to be transmitted to both sisters and their respective spouses, but other family members may also be calling to see how the pair are doing, in essence giving rise to a situation of multiple patients. Because donors are presumed fertile, they may have unrealistic expectations or knowledge deficits about infertility. Furthermore, a known donor's eggs may fail fertilization, leaving her worried that she herself is infertile. Recipients who have premature ovarian failure or have been treated for cancer may have been focusing on health concerns totally unrelated to infertility, and may lack essential knowledge of reproduction. Recipients who are former IVF patients may experience exhaustion of their emotional reserves, and exhibit anxiety, depression, or obsessive behaviors that inhibit information processing.

All of these factors combine to make educational materials essential. Each program should develop a detailed description packet for initial contact, an acceptance packet outlining all steps necessary for evaluation, and a cycle calendar packet that includes all information necessary for medication, testing, and preop requirements. In addition, one-on-one teaching after the first consultation, during the preparation phase, at the time of cycle start, and during daily callbacks for test results and medication instructions is often necessary. Support groups and seminars can also play a useful role, especially if they permit networking of recipient couples. Emotional support should be integrated into all phases of the egg donation experience. The six main goals are illustrated in Table 31.3.

Stimulation Protocols

Most programs use ovulation induction protocols that work well in their IVF programs. If stimulation is medically contraindicated or not desired by the donor, a natural cycle could be utilized. Otherwise, most programs administer a GnRH agonist/gonadotropin protocol in

TABLE 31.3. Goals of emotional support.

- *Assess*: emotional stability.
- *Clarify*: Individual/couple values.
- *Discuss*: secrecy vs. openness altruism vs. manipulation control issues potential losses.
- *Negotiate*: couple differences sibling issues concerns about parenting.
- *Define*: potential problem areas sources of future support, if needed.
- *Balance*: needs of donor and recipient couple.

TABLE 31.4. Endometrial preparation.

Estrogen	Progesterone
Estradiol valerate	Injectable
Conjugated estrogen	Micronized tablets
Micronized estradiol	Vaginal suppositories
Transdermal estradiol	Intravaginal rings
Estradiol impregnated intravaginal rings	Natural P only; given QD or QOD; the day P is started
Incremental increase and decrease mimics normal estradiol release pattern	becomes cycle day 15; usually begun day after donor receives hCG

order to obtain a maximum number of oocytes from each donor.

The goal of recipient preparation is steroid levels that mimic the normal cycle and produce an in-phase biopsy in a practice cycle. Many forms of estrogen and progesterone supplementation will achieve this goal (Table 31.4). Pregnant patients are generally maintained on therapy until 16 weeks of gestation.

Special Arrangements for Testing, Retrieval, and Transfer

For anonymous donation to work, donor and recipient have to be separated geographically or temporally. This may mean that donor bloods are drawn in one location and recipient bloods in another, for example, or that donor ultrasounds are done in the afternoon when no recipients are present. Otherwise, waiting room geography will allow patients to determine for themselves who is to get whose eggs. On the day of retrieval, when ejaculate must be collected from recipients' husbands, specimens will have to be scheduled for different times or different locations. If more than one recipient is involved, and GIFT is planned for one patient, ZIFT may have to be used for the other to prevent both being in the OR at the same time. To allow smooth coordination, key people in the operating room, recovery, registration, and anesthesia need to be informed. If the donation is between sisters, and the mother is planning to wait in the OR waiting area, the recipient's husband may be more comfortable receiving a call in his office about the time to report for a semen specimen, rather than being told in front of his mother-in-law. A very few experiences with donor cycles will point out some of the sensitive areas that require special planning.

Preparation of nursing staff will prevent many of the insensitive remarks that originate in natural curiosity and good intentions. Patients waiting for transfer do not appreciate confusion about why there is no retrieval record in their hospital chart. Basic information should be shared with nursing staff at the time of OR scheduling.

On the day of transfer, care should be taken not to schedule two couples receiving eggs from the same donor at the same time and place, allowing husbands to meet over the coffee pot. Because there is a window of implantation between days 17 to 19, two couples who have their donated eggs fertilized the day of retrieval could have their resulting embryos transferred on sequential days within that window. Attention paid to these issues during program development will short-circuit potential problems.

Follow-up

Ovum donation is part of the frontier of reproductive science, and long-term investigation will be required before the medical team can predict with certainty, either physical or emotional outcomes for any one patient's family or society.

Society is clearly apprehensive about new reproductive techniques, and confused about fundamental ways that technology might change human relationships. Responsible scientists and clinicians can help alleviate these concerns by careful preprogram planning, and well designed followup research studies involving large numbers of patients. Long-term

followup of ovum donation patients (both donors and recipients) and their families can provide answers to some of the questions now being debated by ethics committees, scientific bodies, religious organizations, legal groups, the press, and the public at large.

References

1. Junca AM, Cohen J, et al. Anonymous and non-anonymous oocyte donation preliminary results. Hum Reproduct 1988;3:121.
2. Kennard EA, et al. A program for matched, anonymous oocyte donation. Fertil Steril 1989; 51:655.
3. Ben-Nun I, et al. Egg donation in an in vitro fertilization program: an alternative approach to cycle synchronization and timing of embryo transfer. Fertil Steril 1989;52:683.
4. Asch RH, et al. Oocyte donation and gamete intrafallopian transfer in premature ovarian failure. Fertil Steril 1988;49:263.
5. Rosenwaks Z. Donor eggs: their application in modern reproductive technologies. Fertil Steril 1987;47:895.
6. Sauer MV, Paulson RJ, Lobo RA. A preliminary report on oocyte donation extending reproductive potential to women over 40. N Engl J Med 1990;323:1157.
7. Kapetanakis E, Pantos KJ. Continuation of a donor oocyte pregnancy in menopause without early pregnancy support. Fertil Steril 1990;54: 1171.
8. Leeton J, Harman J. The donation of oocytes to known recipients. Aust NZ J Obstet Gynaecol 1987;27:248.
9. Kirkland A, et al. An analysis of the psychological aspects of women who have delivered babies after ovum donation. Hum Reproduct 1991;6:224.
10. Mahlstedt P, Greenfield DA. Assisted reproductive technology with donor gametes: the need for patient preparation. Fertil Steril 1989; 52:908.
11. Leeton J, Harman J. Attitudes toward egg donation of thirty-four infertile women who donated during their in vitro fertilization treatment. J In Vitro Fert Embryo Transfer 1986;3: 374.
12. Leeton J, Caro C, et al. The search for donor eggs: a problem of supply and demand. Clin Reprod Fertil 1986;4:337.
13. Schiver LR, Collin RL, et al. Long-term followup of women evaluated as oocyte donors. Hum Reproduct 1991;6:165.
14. Schiver LR, Rothmann S, Collins RL. Oocyte donors and semen donors: personality and motivation. Hum Reproduct 1991;6:164.

15. Navot D, et al. Hormonal manipulation of endometrial maturation. J Clin Endocrinol Metab 1989;68:801.

16. Sauer MV, et al. Establishment of a non-anonymous donor oocyte program; preliminary experience at the University of Southern California. Fertil Steril 1989;52:433.

17. Sauer MV, et al. Oocyte and pre-embryo donation to women with ovarian failure: an extended clinical trial. Fertil Steril 1991;55:39.

18. Leeton J, Trounson A, Wood C. The use of donor eggs and embryos in the management of human infertility. Aust NZ J Obstet Gynaecol 1984;24:265.

19. Rosenwaks Z, Veeck LM, Hung-Ching L. Pregnancy following transfer of in vitro fertil-ized donated oocytes. Fertil Steril 1986;45:417.

20. Rotztejn D, et al. Results of tubal embryo transfer in premature ovarian failure. Fertil Steril 1990;54(2):348.

21. Serhal PF, Craft IL. Ovum donation—a simplified approach. Fertil Steril 1987;48:265.

22. Clarke AC. Profiles of the future. New York: Holt Reinhardt, 1984.

23. Snow CP. The two cultures with the scientific revaluation. Cambridge University Press, New York, 1959.

24. The ethics committee of the American Fertility Society. Donor eggs in in vitro fertilization. In Ethical Considerations of the New Reproductive Technologies. Fertil Steril (Suppl 2) 1990;53:485.

32
The Long-Term Psychologic and Social Effects of Gamete Donation

Judith Bernstein

Medical and mental health professionals involved in therapeutic donor insemination (TDI) have a multitude of happy stories—baby pictures, telephone calls from ecstatic parents, repeat performances. For many couples TDI is an excellent method of family building. Over the last few years, however, many of us have become increasingly concerned with our lack of substantive knowledge about possible long-term psychologic effects of gamete donation, and the consequent inadequacy of our informed consent process. Most practitioners are very good at detailing the physical risks of TDI, and can talk at great length about potential infection, the risk of congenital anomalies, and the controversy of using fresh vs. frozen sperm. We acknowledge with our patients the probable benefits of couples experiencing pregnancy together and avoiding the costs and stresses of adoption. What is less certain is the degree to which we carefully and knowledgeably prepare couples to make intelligent decisions about possible psychological risks associated with TDI. What do we really know about the potential emotional or social consequences of sperm or ovum donation for individuals who choose these therapies, for their marriages and extended family units, or for the lives and self-perceptions of their donor offspring?

We have 100 years of medical experience with gamete donation. The first human insemination in the United States occurred in 1874,[1] but the roots of this procedure can be found as far back in human history as a third century A.D. collection of Jewish law, the Talmud,[2] which discusses the legal position of women who achieve pregnancy without physical contact.

In the United States alone, an estimated 15,000 to 20,000 infants per year are born through TDI, roughly equal to the number of adoptions of newborns.[3] Despite the prevalence of gamete donation, the worldwide medical literature contains follow-up reports on fewer than 1,500 TDI pregnancies, and fewer than 800 offspring. More than 80% of these reports represent less than 5 years of follow-up. The evidence presented is largely narrative and subjective, and the few studies using quantitative instruments and objective data have not been well designed.

Anecdotal information about families originating from TDI is reassuring. The divorce rate following TDI is low,[4-6] and offspring intelligence, as measured by standard testing procedures, is at least as high as in the normal population.[7] The medical literature does not, however, provide us with a solid scientific basis for assessing and discussing issues that are of equally critical importance to our patients as they make the choice to accept donor gametes. Some of the more important questions include: (1) What processes encourage good mental health and effective use of coping skills as couples make the transition from the trauma of a diagnosis of male infertility to an intelligent choice of appropriate alternatives for family building? (2) Will secrecy or openness about a choice of TDI be the better alternative for a specific couple and for their child, and what will be the pitfalls and benefits of either choice? (3) What effect might a couple expect TDI to have on their marriage, and what could they do now to prepare for possible problems? (4) What motivates donors, and what description of donors' attitudes might be given to offspring if parents choose to be open about gamete donation? (5) What could be learned from experiences with donor insemination that might be applicable to the new field of ovum donation? (6) Would public education programs about gamete donation be beneficial in reducing potential social stigmas for offspring, and if so, what agency should initiate such a campaign?

Processing the Need for TDI

Several articles have discussed the impact of the need for TDI on the couple. The majority of 62 French couples interviewed by Cyzba[8] viewed the diagnosis of male infertility as a traumatic event, and described it in highly colored language as a wound, a knife in the belly, a castration. Wives tended to be very protective of husbands and worried about injury to the man's self-esteem.

David and Avidan[9] analyzed questionnaires returned by 44 French couples who had recently completed TDI therapy. Guilt feelings were expressed by 80% of the men about their failure to meet marital expectations by producing a biologic child. The majority of the wives reported guilt for not sharing that failure, and distress over the inequality thus introduced into the relationship. They were upset for their husbands, but angry over being denied a normal pregnancy, and the conflict between these feelings was uncomfortable. Frank clinical depression was reported by 32% of couples.

Berger, who has written extensively on the reaction to male infertility, reports that as much as 3 months after diagnosis, only 3 of 16 men in one study were free of major symptoms such as insomnia, depression, weight loss, and interruption of normal marital sexual life.[10]

He subsequently studied larger groups of Canadian couples who were receiving donor insemination therapy, and followed them for a longer period of time. Many couples were offered TDI immediately following diagnosis,

so that gamete donation was presented as a cure for male infertility. The discussion surrounding TDI did not include emotional reactions to infertility or potential emotional or social consequences of therapy. Other couples had been encouraged to take time to grieve the loss of fertility, consider alternatives, and communicate clearly with each other. Delays in treatment were positively associated with increased marital satisfaction and improved self-concept. If TDI was initiated within 6 months of diagnosis, couples were more likely to exhibit marital strain, anxiety, and depressive symptoms.[11,12] These findings have been confirmed by others.[13–15]

Secrecy Versus Openness

The first successful U.S. donor insemination occurred in Philadelphia in 1874 and was performed under anesthesia. The patient and her husband were not informed.[16] During the first half of the twentieth century, many physicians required couples to promise never to tell TDI children their manner of conception.[17] There were no laws to protect couples, offspring, or physicians, and concern about social stigma was understandable.

Although TDI is now commonplace in developed industrial countries, a pattern of secrecy is still the norm. In France, where extensive public education about gamete donation has occurred, approximately half of couples inform their children conceived by TDI. In New Zealand 60% of couples do not inform their children.[18] In the United States 95% of couples interviewed by several TDI clinics planned to withhold this information from their offspring.[20] What do we understand about this secret? What does it protect, whom does it protect, and why? What are the consequences of keeping it? The legal rights of rearing fathers are now protected, and it is unlikely that physicians can be sued for wrongful life. Is it still wise to withhold information about a child's genetic origin that might be an important part of his or her identity concept?

The issue of secrecy is complex. The main reason given by 92 English couples for not telling the child was fear of social rejection,[21] but several other reasons for concealment emerged that were designed to protect the rearing father, not the child. Donor insemination was perceived as humiliating by 42% of the men and 19% of the women, and there was a strong desire to prevent male infertility from becoming common knowledge. It was hoped that by concealing the origin of conception, the injury to self would be bandaged over and the father–child relationship might be less impaired. Women feared that every time the husband looked at the child he would be looking at his own infertility and would come to reject the child; they hoped that keeping the secret would help the rearing father forget the initial trauma.

The intense emotional need to keep TDI a secret was confirmed in a study of 830 French couples receiving TDI therapy.[22] Although 40% of this group would tell a child eventually about the manner of his conception, only 1 of 830 would be willing to tell the husband's father. This unwillingness has been interpreted psychodynamically as protection from a narcissistic injury to the most critical of all selves, the internalized father.[23] In addition, TDI is not really a medical act, although insemination has been medicalized to reduce social discomfort. The specimen used in therapeutic donor insemination has been produced by a sexual act, masturbation, and TDI is still perceived by the Roman Catholic Church as adulterous. Damage to masculine self-esteem from this donor–wife–husband sexual triangle is greatly feared, and the secret can be seen by the couple who experience shame as a vital defense of ego.

The need for secrecy extends so deeply that many TDI patients have even given false addresses to the physicians on whom they were depending for pregnancy.[8] Thirty-eight couples who were so satisfied with donor insemination that they were returning for a second pregnancy were asked why they prefered TDI over adoption.[24] The majority of men stated that TDI, unlike adoption, enabled them to conceal the painful memory of their sterility; wives were concerned with protecting their husbands from what might be seen as a defect in masculinity. A study of parental attitudes in Sweden after donor insemination

reports that 48% of couples returning for a second pregnancy had never discussed male infertility or TDI with each other after the initial diagnosis.[25] Thus denial and repression may even extend to the couple themselves.

Secrecy is an understandable human response, but often not a healthy one. Psychiatric literature abounds with examples of the destructive effects of secrets on family and individual functioning. Secrets that are shame-based can corrode families. Lies that begin with a baby book multiply and may provide a weakened foundation for family trust based on authentic communication. Case histories describe the termination of intimate marital communication with insemination therapy and the subsequent negative effects of unresolved guilt, anger, and blame on the new family unit.[26] Concern has been expressed that the secrecy surrounding TDI stops the grieving process prematurely, and denial of unpleasant feelings leads to serious depression.[11] Long-term denial is at best a primitive, inadequate solution to ego injury.

Secrecy can pose potential emotional risk for offspring, as well as TDI parents. Eloquent accounts of distress caused by discovery as an adult of TDI conception have been published by donor offspring groups. These intense narratives remind us of a powerful example in literature, an archetype for feelings that can be experienced by children who question whether they are truly their parent's child:

My father was a Corinthian and my mother was a Dorian. At home I rose to be a person of some preeminence until a strange thing happened. A curious thing. Although perhaps I took it more to heart than it deserved. One day at table a fellow who had been drinking deeply made bold to say I was not my father's son. For the time I suffered in silence as well I could. Next day I approached my parents and told them to tell me the truth. They were bitterly angry, and I was relieved. Yet somehow that smart remained, and a thing like that soon passes from hand to hand. . . . I must pursue the trail to the end, and I must unravel the mystery of my birth.[27]

Sophocles' description of Oedipus' state of mind and his parents' over-vigorous denial are very similar to case histories of troubled donor offspring.

If the secret is kept successfully, the adolescent will have to build an identity based on inaccurate genetic information. "Why don't I have my father's musical ability, or look like him?" the child may ask himself, or "Why am I so bad at sports, when everyone in the family is so athletic?" Case histories attest to donor insemination children feeling different and tending to act out rebelliously in response to overcompensation on the part of uneasy parents.[28] Confusion about genetic origin has been described as genealogical bewilderment. The task of adolescent identity-building and separation from the father image is difficult if the child does not truly know that which he is to separate from.[29]

TDI in many ways resembles a form of unacknowledged adoption. The American Academy of Pediatrics, in discussing adoption states, "Unresolved feelings of infertility, concern about biologic identity, and attempts to try harder on the part of the parents because of perceived biologic inadequacy are factors that may stress the parents and subsequently the child."[30] Although only 5% of TDI parents interviewed in a New Zealand study thought their children would ever wish to know about the genetic parent,[31] 75% of adopted children are known to seek information about birth parents, although the majority express no desire to meet them directly.[32] Thus TDI parents may be unrealistic in assuming that offspring have no need to know their genetic identity. Society may also decide at some time in the future, as is beginning to be the case with adoption, that offspring have not only a need but a right to know, and disclosure may occur despite the wishes of rearing parents. What would then happen emotionally to offspring who discovered later in life that a secret had been kept from them, and one parent is not biologically "theirs"?

Inadvertent disclosure of the secret is a serious concern. Only 1 of 92 Swedish couples stated that they planned to disclose TDI to their child if they were to become pregnant, but 15% had already told someone else—a friend or family member—who might be much less invested in keeping the secret 10 or 20 years down the road.[33] Numerous case histories have been compiled of TDI offspring who learned the truth of their conception inadvertently in adolescence or later, in circumstances that were destructive or explosive.[34–36] One national organization of TDI offspring hopes to help individuals assimilate the knowledge and reform identities. "It is an awesome responsibility," writes one woman, "to be the solution to someone else's problem."[34]

Comprehensive, scientific, long-term research simply has not yet been designed, and the literature provides us only with these anecdotal accounts of the pain caused to TDI offspring by secrecy. Since there are few published accounts of successful TDI, we are left with a significant potential for bias. Assumptions about a large group of individuals, most of whom never present for psychiatric treatment, should never be made on the basis of a handful of case histories describing the pain and distress of those for whom the TDI experience has been unremittingly negative. Clinical experience suggests that the majority of families are quite normal, and their children are well-adjusted and happy. The potential for problems must be investigated in the context of the ability of most couples to accept infertility, make an appropriate decision about TDI, and go on to build successful families.

Several recently published books advocate openness about gamete donation, and the secrecy surrounding artificial insemination continues to be the subject of magazine articles and talk shows. The argument against secrets has been stated clearly by many types of mental health professionals:

Those who do not have secrets are totally free to be. They are not burdened by any need to hide. They do not have to slink around in the shadows. They do not have to construct new lives to hide old ones. They need waste no effort covering tracks or maintaining disguises. Ultimately they find that the energy required for the self-discipline of honesty is far less than the energy required for secretiveness. . . . People dedicated to the truth . . . become free from fear.[37]

What do we really know, though, about the ability of children to understand and process complex information about conception? Might certain extended family values and beliefs lead to rejection of a child conceived by TDI, and could exclusion from the family cause more harm than secrets? Is society still likely to react negatively to a child who announces innocently to his friend's parents or his teacher that mommy and daddy got someone else to give sperm to help make him? If we encourage couples to be open and they feel unequal to the task, will they then fear that they are inadequate or doing something wrong, and that they are a poor role model to their children? If parents tell a child about TDI despite their discomfort, against their own instincts, judgment, and feelings, and their words and nonverbal behavior are not authentic, will that child have more serious problems with his or her identity and the development of a positive relationship with his or her parents? Should medical professionals make recommendations to patients about secrecy or openness, or should their role be restricted to raising questions, not answering them? The medical literature provides no guidance on these issues.

Marital and Family Functioning

Although several studies have indicated that the divorce rate is low for couples who have conceived through TDI,[38] gamete donation can create stress within marriages. Numerous case histories[34-42] document male sexual dysfunction based on revival of oedipal conflicts, with displacement of libido into work, and less marriage and life satisfaction. The powerful fantasies of many women about the donor can be disruptive to the marriage bond. Couples can also experience an upset in the balance of power, with the woman who has been able to achieve a pregnancy without her husband's participation becoming dominant in the relationship. She may act out anger against her spouse for having had to resort to TDI. The husband may be angry with the wife for her success in the face of his failure, and withdraw or take a more passive role. Delaisi de Parseval[43] has coined an overly clever but still valid term for men who rear a child conceived through sperm bank donation: "the fathers who come in from the cold." The donor has been kept on ice, but the rearing father has indeed been left out in the cold at that very important moment of his child's conception, and this may set a pattern for the marital relationship. He may continue to be excluded when parenting decisions have to be made or discipline is required.

As the child grows, parent–child relationships may be altered. Children conceived by TDI are often denied traditional family names (Jr. or III) and perhaps grow up with less of a sense of entitlement in the family, even when the secret is well kept.[41] Fathers whose sense of masculinity has been damaged by infertility report feeling particularly threatened by an adolescent male child who is busily developing a sexual identity;[41] it is hard under these circumstances to provide the requisite approval and guidance. Case histories abound of parent–child relations thought to have been damaged by TDI.[30,34,35,41-45]

Although stressors on the marital and family bond have certainly been identified as a result of TDI, the medical literature has been confined to case history and divorce data, both of which are problematic. The case histories, of course, represent a small subset of the TDI experience (parents who were in sufficient distress to seek out a mental health professional). It is impossible to generalize from such a potentially biased sample about quality of life issues for those who never seek counseling. In a single larger study, 92 couples were asked if they had experienced marital stress as a result of TDI.[24] All 92 stated that they had not, but these data are suspect on two grounds: (1) All of the couples questioned were requesting the questioner to provide them with a second child and might have been careful not to include negative material. (2) There was no anonymity for responses. Although low divorce rates are reassuring, divorce statistics alone can never be sufficient to describe marital satisfaction, since couples may stay together to protect the TDI secret despite severe marital division and discord. The medical literature certainly raises questions, but fails altogether to answer them.

Physical and Emotional Health of Donor Offspring

Two aspects of offspring physical health, IQ and congenital anomaly rate, have been examined in well-designed studies, although neither has been replicated. Japanese TDI children scored higher than the norm for intelligence.[7] Of 362 American children conceived through gamete donation, 2.9% had a major anomaly at birth, and 6.9% at later follow-up; both figures were within the normal range.[38] Birth weight and developmental milestones were normal, and a large number of children, 10.5%, were found to be gifted.

Investigation of the emotional health of donor offspring has been haphazard. The vast majority of those reported have been followed by anecdote alone—Christmas cards, grocery store encounters, telephone calls. On this basis, one physician asserts that only 3 children of 303 pregnancies produced by TDI in his practice came to his attention as discipline problems.[46] Hundreds of happy patients were described by another doctor, again through anecdotal follow-up.[47] A third anecdotal report states that only 4 of 50 families experienced any difficulty claiming the child as their own.[48] Respondees to a questionnaire corroborated this positive outcome; all 134 of these parents declared that their parental self-esteem was not diminished by donor insemination, and some couples believed that TDI had improved their ability to function in the parental role.[49] The study of congenital anomalies previously discussed also included a question about whether or not couples thought they might benefit from counseling; few thought counseling was needed.[38] This was taken by the investigators to mean that few families had significant problems.

These reports are reassuring, but problematic. The discrepancy between this information and the previously cited studies describing TDI as humiliating is obvious. Couples may have rejected the idea of counseling because they did not understand how it might be helpful to them, or out of concern about costs. If they are using denial as a coping mechanism, they would certainly not wish to expose well-protected feelings to a counselor. Furthermore, in any group of nondonor children, many would be expected to be identified as discipline problems, and many completely normal parents, especially first-time parents, report difficulty with bonding, yet TDI couples seemed to be dramatically healthier than the average. One might suspect that some of these couples are either intent on keeping their "story" together, or desirous of another pregnancy and reluctant to disclose problems to a physician they might need in the future. It is also possible that TDI parents are extremely motivated to be parents and have therefore been more successful at childrearing.

Donor Beliefs and Attitudes

Donors originally were recruited by physicians on an informal basis, usually from a circle of friends or medical students. Cryobanks draw from a larger group, often using college undergraduates or newspaper advertisements. It was always assumed that protection of anonymity was essential for recruitment, and that the main motivator was financial.[50] Neither of these commonly held assumptions has proved to be true.

An investigation of English sperm donors revealed that 60% would not mind meeting a child, and more than half would want to know the name of the donor if they had themselves been conceived by artificial insemination.[21] When a law was passed in Sweden requiring donor information to be registered with a central agency and provided to the child at majority, the number of donors decreased temporarily but soon returned to adequate levels.[2] Sperm bank donors in New Zealand have expressed willingness to donate even if identifying information were provided to the child.[19] An investigation of 85 donors with standard psychological instruments disclosed that their primary motivation was not financial reward, but altruism.[51] A majority of donors at two large sperm banks (Houston and Louisiana) would continue to provide specimens if anonymity could not be guaranteed, and 96% would wish to share nonidentfying information with recipient families.[52] In-depth psychosocial information would be willingly provided by 90% of donors. Attitudes of potential ovum donors are just now being explored.[53,54]

Public Education Programs

France has had the longest experience with a supervisory agency for TDI. Their Centre d'Etude et de Conservation du Sperme (CECOS) is responsible for collecting statistics and forming public policy. Under the aegis of CECOS, extensive public education programs have been undertaken, issues have been debated, and changes have occurred in public opinion, with the result that almost half of the couples who receive TDI no longer feel that this fact has to be kept secret from a child so conceived.[22] Unfortunately, no information is available in the medical literature about the extent or format of this educational campaign.

Implications for Ovum Donation

Much of what has been learned about the emotional issues involved in sperm donation can be applied to ovum donation. If oocytes are offered anonymously, couples will face the same issues of genetic discontinuity for the child and secrecy versus openness. They may also experience inequality in the marriage, with one partner feeling more related to the child than the other. The choice of this therapy may stress a marriage, and individuals may feel lingering sadness and experience depression over perceived inadequacy, and these factors may adversely affect child-rearing. If oocytes are donated by a family member, questions arise about what to tell the child, and complications in relations between donor and recipient may strain the family system or change it in unforeseen ways. Issues of manipulation or family pressure may be involved, as we have learned from the literature about psychiatric complications in kidney donation.[55–58]

Until recently, TDI was viewed narrowly as a purely medical procedure, a "cure" for infertility instead of one of many alternatives for family building. We now know that the emotional issues are of at least as much concern to patients as the mechanics of technique, and patients benefit greatly from preprocedure counseling that explores some of these issues.

Ovum recipients and their donors would also benefit from preprocedure preparation. A report on the first follow-up of small numbers of offspring born from ovum donation from sisters shows that donors express a strong, continuing sense of connection to the child.[59] Will this have an effect on the relationship between the sisters later on, with competition developing for the right to parent this child? Will infertile women who have donated ova anonymously but never conceived themselves experience depression later on in life, or regret the donation, and how might they be counseled to prepare themselves? If we are going to offer information, we must begin to gather it systematically; the medical literature does not provide it.

Implications for Medical, Nursing, and Mental Health Interventions

It is essential that medical professionals avoid two dangerous extremes: either pretending that there are no potential long-term problems for the TDI family, or being paralyzed by our knowledge deficit about what emotional or social consequences might result from this particular choice for resolving infertility.

Compelling reasons have been offered for immediate reform of the process of preparing couples for donor insemination.[60] Secrecy should not be routinely advocated. Couples should instead be given opportunities to discuss methods of coping with infertility and its impact on individual, marital, and parenting issues. Risks and benefits of secrecy versus openness should be elaborated, and the couple given tools to make a choice that is appropriate for their own situation.

What can we offer to couples considering donor conception to assist them to develop healthy strategies? We can outline for couples the issues related to donor gametes, the questions that may come up for them, and the concerns that may arise about genetic discontinuity. We can describe the current state of medical research in this area and present the findings with as little bias as possible. We can provide readings in the adoption literature that may have some bearing on TDI issues. Couples will need to make the difficult adaptation to the stigmas that still surround nonbiological parenthood, and the psychological literature about shame may also be helpful.

Based on what can be gleaned from the existing literature about gamete donation, medical professionals counseling patients about TDI should adopt the orientation that they are helping normal, healthy people make a life decision for which there is very little support and potentially considerable social stigma. The social work perspective of looking at the person in the situation is very useful; if these couples need assistance, it is generally not because of their pathology, but as a result of the stress inherent in the situation. A mental health consultation pre-TDI may be useful in preparing couples to examine the issues they will possibly face, and to identify coping mechanisms and support systems that they can utilize.

Information and opportunity to explore concerns can be provided in many different types of settings. Workshops, networking of patients, consumer organizations, literature lists, specialized individual and couple counseling, and support groups all offer a productive framework for pre-TDI preparation.

Workshops and short-term groups can be designed to relate to issues at different stages. There can be groups for couples who have just received a diagnosis of male infertility, and are exploring the idea of TDI. This is the place where people can feel free to voice their doubts, questions, anger, and grief. It can be normalizing to exchange feelings, wonder aloud if they are the only Roman Catholics in the whole state who would be doing such a thing, or make comments like, "Fresh or frozen? It sounds like do I buy fresh broccoli or go to the freezer to get the frozen stuff!" or "I'd rather have a daughter . . . a son should be a chip off the old block." Other groups may consist of couples who have made the decision to do TDI and are needing support while they go through the often lengthy process. A third group needing support consists of parents of TDI children who wish to work out decisions about what to tell the child, or concerns about inequality in power in the parenting relationship. For others who find that the choice of TDI has awakened deep-seated problems, individual therapy may be appropriate.

Summary

Available medical literature in the area of psychosocial issues related to gamete donation exposes an astonishing paucity of information about a commonly used therapy (TDI), and a virtual absence of information about sequelae of ovum donation, a newer procedure now being widely disseminated. Long-term, multi-center follow-up studies must be planned. Investigation should be prospective in design and controlled for variables such as age, education, geography, cultural differences, pre-existing psychiatric illness or dysfunctional family history, and length of marriage. The teams that design these studies would ideally be composed of reproductive endocrinologists and nurses who provide gamete donation, and mental health specialists who deal with the consequences of this therapy. With information from this type of study, we will be able to answer patients' questions accurately, raise issues for patients to consider, and provide emotional support for their choices.

Acknowledgment

Carol Frost Vercollone presented a series of case histories at the conference, drawn from her extensive experience specializing in TDI counseling and education. Her contribution during the conference and in the writing of this review was invaluable. Her positive outlook provided a continual reminder of the resilience of the human spirit in the face of difficult decisions and directions.

Bibliography

1. Reuben B. The psychological aspects of human artificial insemination. Arch Gen Psychiatry 1965;13:121.
2. Richardson JW. The role of a psychiatric consultant to an artificial insemination by donor program. Psychiatr Ann 1987;17:101.
3. Office of Technology Assessment. Artificial Insemination Practice in the U.S. Washington, DC: US Government Printing Office, 1988.
4. Rosenkvist H. Donor insemination: A prospective socio-psychiatric investigation of 48 couples. Dan Med Bull 1981;28:133.
5. Bendvold E, Skjaeraasen J, Moe N, Sjoberg D, Kravdal O. Marital break-up among couples raising families by artificial insemination by donor. Fertil Steril 1989;51:980.
6. Henahan J. Artificial insemination has few untoward effects. JAMA 1983;250:1256.
7. Iizuka R, Sawada Y, Nishina N, Ohi M. The physical and mental development of children born following artificial insemination. 1968; Int J Fertil 13:24.
8. Czyba JC, Chevret M. Psychological reactions of couples to artificial insemination with donor sperm. Int J Fertil 1979;24:240.
9. David A, Avidan D. Artificial insemination donor: Clinical and psychological aspects. Fertil Steril 1976;27:528.
10. Berger DM. Couples' reactions to male infertility and donor insemination. Am J Psychiatry 1980;137:1047.
11. Berger DM. Psychological aspects of donor insemination. J Psychiatry Med 1982;12:49.
12. Berger DM, Eisen A, Shuber J, Doody KF. Psychological patterns in donor insemination couples. Can J Psychiatry 1986;31:818.
13. Back KW, Snowden R. The anonymity of the gamete donor. J Psychosom Obstet Gynecol 1988;9:191.
14. Lovesett J. Artificial insemination: The attitude of patients in Norway. Fertil Steril 1981;42:415.
15. Manuel C, Cyzba JC. Aspects psychologique de l'insemination artificielle. Lyon: Symep, 1983.
16. Rubin B. Psychiatric aspects of human artificial insemination. Arch Gen Psychiatry 1965; 13:121.
17. Walker A, Gergson S, McLaughlin E. Attitudes toward donor insemination—a post-Warnock survey. Hum Reprod 1987;2:745.
18. Chevret M. Le vecu de l'insemination artificielle. These de Medecine, Lyon, 1977.
19. Daniels KR. Artificial insemination using donor semen and the issue of secrecy: The views of donors and recipient couples. Soc Sci Med 1988;27:377.
20. Reading AE, Sledmere CM, Cox DN. A survey of patient attitudes towards artificial insemination by donor. J Psychosom Res 1982;26:429.
21. Rowland R. The social and psychological consequences of secrecy in artificial insemination by donor programmes. Soc Sci Med 1985;21:391.
22. David D, Soule M, Mayaux MJ, Guilmard-Moscato ML, Czglik F, et al. Gynecol Obstet Biol Reprod 1988;17:5.
23. Novaes SB. Social integration of technical innovation: Sperm banking and AID in France and the United States. Soc Sci Inform 1985; 24:569.
24. Farris EJ, Garrison M. Emotional aspects of successful donor insemination. Obstet Gynecol 1954;3:19.
25. Milsom I, Bergman P. A study of parental attitudes after donor insemination (AID). Acta Obstet Gynecol Scand 1982;61:125.
26. Penochet JC, Moran P, Jarrige A. Psychiatric complications linked to AID. Ann Med Psychol 1979;137:635.
27. Sophocles. King Oedipus. Trans. Watling EF. London: Penguin, 1947.
28. Clamar A. Psychological implications of donor insemination. Am J Psychoanal 1980;40:173.
29. Sants HJ. Genealogical bewilderment in children with substitute parents. Br J Med Psychol 1964;37:133.
30. Sokoloff BZ. Alternative methods of reproduction: Effects on the child. Clin Pediatr 1986;26:11.
31. Daniels KR. The new birth technologies: A social work approach to researching psychosomatic factors. Soc Work Health Care 1986; 11:49.
32. Sorosky AD, et al. Adoption and the adolescent: An overview. Adolescent Psychiatry, Vol V. New York: Aronson, 1977.
33. Nijs P, Rouffa L. A.I.D. couples: Psychological and psychopathological evaluation. Andrologia 1975;7:188.
34. Baran A, Pannor R. Lethal Secrets. New York: Warner, 1989.
35. Snowden R, Snowden E. The Gift of a Child. Boston: Allen & Unwin, 1984.
36. Noble E. Having Your Baby by Donor Insemination. Boston: Houghton Mifflin, 1987.
37. Peck, S. The Road Less Traveled. New York: Simon & Schuster, 1978.
38. Amuzu B, Laxova R, Shapiro S. Pregnancy outcome, health of children, and family adjustment after donor insemination. Obstet Gynecol 1990;75:899.

39. Waltzer H. Psychological and legal aspects of artificial insemination (A.I.D.): An overview. Am J Psychother 1982;36:91.

40. Levie LH. An inquiry into the psychological effects on parents of artificial insemination with donor semen. Eugenics Rev 1967;59:97.

41. Gerstel G. A psychoanalytical view of donor insemination. Am J Psychother 1963;17:64.

42. Lamson HD, Pinard WJ, Meaker SE. Sociologic and psychologic aspects of insemination with donor semen. JAMA 1951;145:1062.

43. Delaisi de Parseval G, Hurstel F. Paternity a la francoise. In: Lamb ME, ed. The Father's Role: Cross-cultural perpectives. Hillsdale, NJ: Lawrence Erlbaum, 1987.

44. Bok S. Lying to children: The risks of paternalism. Hastings Center Rep 1978;8:10.

45. Snowden R, Mitchell GD. The Artificial Family. London: Allen & Unwin, 1985.

46. Haman JO. Therapeutic donor insemination: A review of 440 cases. Calif Med 1959;90:130.

47. Jackson MH. Artificial insemination (donor). Eugenics Rev 1957;48:203.

48. Clayton CE, Kovaks GT. AID offspring: Initial follow-up study of 50 couples. Med J Austr 1982;171:338.

49. Kremer J, Frijling BW, Nass JLM. Psychosocial aspects of parenthood by artificial insemination donor. Lancet 1984;1:628.

50. Kovacs GT, Clayton CE, McGowan PE. The attitudes of semen donors. Clin Reprod Fertil 1983;2:73.

51. Handelsman DJ, Dunn SM, Conway AJ, Boylan LM, Jansen RPS. Psychological and attitudinal profiles in donors for artificial insemination. Fertil Steril 1985;43:95.

52. Mahlstedt P, Probasco K. Sperm donors: Their attitudes toward providing medical and personal information for donor offspring. Presented at the American Fertility Society Annual Conference, Washington DC, 1990.

53. Templeton AA, Glasier A, Angell RR, Aitken RJ. What potential ovum donors think. Lancet 1984;1:1081.

54. Sauer MV, Rodi IA, Scrooc M, Bustillo M, Buster J. Survey of attitudes regarding the use of siblings for gamete donation. Fertil Steril 1988;49:721.

55. House RM, Thompson TL. Psychiatric aspects of organ transplantation. JAMA 1988;260:535.

56. Morris P, St. George B, Waring T, Nanra R. Psychosocial complications in living related kidney donors: An Australian experience. Transpl Proc 1987;19:2840.

57. Sharma VK, Enoch MD. Psychological sequelae of kidney donation: A 5–10 year follow up study. Acta Psychiatr Scand 1987;75:264.

58. Steele CI, Altholz JAS. Donor ambivalence: A key issue in families of children with end-stage renal disease. Soc Work Health Care 1988; 13:47.

59. Leeton J, Harman J. The donation of oocytes to known recipients. Aust NZ Obstet Gynecol 1987;27:248.

60. Mahlstedt PP, Greenfeld DA. Assisted reproductive technology with donor gametes: The need for patient preparation. Fertil Steril 1989;52:908.

33
Individual Psychotherapy for Infertile Patients

Susan R. Levin

Many individuals and couples resolve their infertility crisis with the help of couples' therapy or group support therapy, or without any intervention. Others experience tremendous personal growth in an individual psychotherapy. Selecting the appropriate patients for this treatment modality is challenging. Often these patients are self-selected. They want to come in alone for consultation and for various reasons find it difficult to convince their spouse to join them. A history revealing early abuse, trauma, or loss would be a strong indication for referral for individual psychotherapy.

A complete assessment is important to understand if the dysfunction observed and described was caused by the infertility or is prexisting. This also provides insight about the personal meaning the patient has given the wished-for pregnancy and baby. Infertility and the intrusive medical treatments can substitute for other previously maladaptive behaviors.

There are general themes and reactions that seem characteristic of infertility. Individuals often are in intense emotional pain. They describe feeling as though their lives are on hold, and they are stuck waiting for a pregnancy to occur, to have their own family, and finally to become parents. They feel out of control of their lives and their bodies and experience a deep sense of being damaged. A chronic state of grieving intensifies at the start of every menstrual period.

Affective responses tend to be intense—competition, jealously, envy, rage, guilt, and sadness. Often these feelings are repressed and the individual appears quite depressed or expresses anger at others, most often their doctor, spouse, or unempathic friends. Social isolation is a common result. It is important not to generalize, however. As with any other problem, each person has his or her own way of reacting or defending himself or herself, and has a personal internal view of this problem.

When patients come to a psychotherapist they usually express their frustration and sadness about their infertility quite easily. They also tenaciously hold the belief that having a biologic child would make their problems go away, which can create difficult resistance to deepening their therapeutic work. Infertility may camouflage other difficulties and vulnerabilities, creating a challenge the therapist must accept when doing individual treatment.

Narcissistic issues are primary with most infertile individuals, no matter what their diagnosis. Understanding this is important when therapists consider their approach or technique. Initially, an empathic and supportive listener will allow the patient to be more open and settle into beneficial treatment. The silent, distant therapist may be perceived as judgmental and depriving which can lead to humiliation, despair, or further regression. Some patients may just abandon treatment, adding to their feelings of failure.

As with any therapy, begin with what the patient wants to talk about. It is unlikely that they will want to focus on their own childhood. Since a good history is important, however, it can be elicited gradually in the context of the infertility issues.

Some flexibility in designing treatment is important and including patients in this process may help them feel more in control. However, the standard psychotherapy practice of working with patients once or twice a week for the 50-minute hour is usually appropriate. Occasionally, patients may want to come in every other week or more frequently than two times a week.

The most common treatment pattern for this patient population is weekly visits for several months, cessation for several months, followed by their return to continue work for a year or more. Understanding changes, interruptions, or other deviations from the treatment plan may help avoid acting out and potentially allow access to vital unconscious material.

It is not unusual therapy to focus on the patient's medical care. Hours may be devoted to identifying which treatments are comfortable or appropriate. This allows an opportunity to analyze resistances to continuing regimens when continuing is still considered reasonable, to help them recognize when it is time for a second medical opinion, to decide whether to change or not change physicians, to begin considering options other than a biologic child, and to identify when to stop medical treatment either temporarily or permanently. Gradually, intolerable feelings, wishes, and fantasies can be recognized, articulated, and then tolerated. This new self-understanding and self-acceptance can eventually help the infertile patient feel more in control of their feelings and their lives which directly affects and improves their self-esteem.

Understanding and working with transference can allow personal change and growth to occur. Since these patients are in crisis, it is also important to avoid further regression. Negative affect can be more intense in individual than in group treatment and can often be directed at the therapist. Being supportive doesn't mean avoiding these feelings or overgratifying these patients. Often they will ask personal questions about the therapist's fertility history, or try to stretch the hour beyond the established limit, or find the bill intolerable. Underneath this entitlement expressed by rage, intrusiveness, and envy are deeply felt shame, guilt, and sadness. Patients will imagine what they need to, and project these images onto the therapist. Some will need to see the therapist as "having it all"

and be horrified by the extremely envious and even murderous feelings they experience in response. Others will imagine the therapist "without" and be fearful of the therapist's envy. These situations can test the limits of any good therapy and therapist. Helping the patient to become aware of their feelings, fantasies, motivations, and wishes allows for acceptance, growth and the ability to make informed decisions about fertility and life.

The following two vignettes illustrate the importance of historical data and a good assessment. For each of these women, infertility became woven into their traumatic past, and the medical treatments began to replicate their own tendency toward self-punishment. Their wish for pregnancy/baby became their pathologic attempt to repair their premorbid damaged selves. Infertility became a part of maladaptive and repetitive behavior that already existed. Individual psychotherapy was the only intervention that could stop the cycle they were in.

Mrs. W (late thirties) is a lawyer and functions on the surface quite well. She referred herself for treatment after 3 years working with several infertility specialists. She was about to enroll in a gamete intrafallopian transfer (GIFT) program and was aware of feeling quite anxious and panicky, with accompanying physical symptoms. At first, she was not eager to talk about her personal history, and she was very clear that she didn't want her husband to come in. Initially and at different times throughout treatment she seemed depressed, frightened, and somewhat guarded.

It was clear that she was fragile. Control was very important, as pertaining to frequency of visits and what we talked about. When she cried, she was embarrassed, frightened at her loss of control, and relieved. She described desperately wanting a baby, but being worried that she wouldn't be able to do GIFT. She described the other treatments as intrusive, but she had felt comfortable with her doctors. Now she was going to have to change doctors, and having someone else examine her was frightening. She was quite anxious.

Over several weeks Mrs. W was able to talk about her history. She stated that her sisters and brothers had been physically abused by her mother's uncle and alluded to the fact that she had some vague memory of experiencing sexual abuse. These memories were resurfacing as she started her medical evaluation for GIFT and they frightened her. She feared that she was going to lose control. Things seemed to intensify around the GIFT because she saw it as the last treatment before she gave up the pursuit of a biologic child. Her husband had been resistant to continuing and would not consider adoption.

As the treatment unfolded, it became clear that Mrs. W felt damaged not just because of the infertility but because of her history. Although she seemed fragile psychologically, she appeared to be quite satisfied with her financially rewarding legal career. Her quality of life far surpassed that of her siblings and her parents.

Mrs. W suffered a great deal, with torment similar to that of survivors' guilt. Although she had experienced sexual abuse, she felt that her suffering didn't compare to what she had observed others in her family experience. She was plagued with thoughts that she should have done more to intervene on her siblings' behalf. Not being able to carry a pregnancy to term was further proof that she was a bad, incompetent, and undeserving person. It seemed that she had an idea that if she could have a pregnancy and a child she would have the opportunity to correct all the wrong that had been done, and if she didn't it was proof that her long-held beliefs about herself were true.

With this belief system came punishment. At times during therapy it became clear that the infertility treatments were her punishment and replaced earlier abuse. The infertility specialist was now her abuser. Later, while continuing in psychotherapy, the infertility treatments ended and Mrs. W became suicidal. She expected the therapist to feel helpless, much as Mrs. W must have felt as a child observing and experiencing her all-powerful parents neglect and abuse her and her siblings. In some ways her therapist *was* powerless, but the therapeutic relationship was quite powerful. This relationship, together with Mrs. W's intelligence and her strong wish to improve her internal life and ultimately survive, has helped her so far to weather extremely difficult times. These included several unsuccessful GIFT cycles, her therapist's pregnancy, stopping infertility treatments, and the death of a sibling. However, her suicidality was a serious concern for a long time.

The 3-year treatment is far from complete. Mrs. W is not involved in infertility treatments and remains ambivalently childless. She is far less isolated then she was when she began treatment. Although her suicidal thoughts are still there, she feels it is her work with the therapist that has kept her sane and alive.

Another case is that of Mrs. L, who came for counseling after a second miscarriage. She was insistent that she was in crisis and needed only brief and supportive therapy. Her focus was the loss of her pregnancy and the possible loss of future pregnancies. Approximately 9 months after our first meeting, Mrs. L felt better and decided to discontinue therapy. A year later, almost at the anniversary of her miscarriage, she returned feeling depressed with suicidal ideation. Mrs. L feared that she could never have a biologic child. Her primary goal was to be a mother. However, she was unable to complete a pregnancy, and she was also unable to complete her career ambitions.

This extremely bright, talented woman was unable to complete many of her life projects. Long-term therapy twice a week was suggested, and after a great deal of thought and discussion, Mrs. L agreed to try this approach. It soon became apparent that her struggle with infertility mirrored many of her life conflicts and provided a screen that fended off painful memories. Inability to resolve these conflicts prevented her from feeling successful.

Mrs. L had experienced trauma by loss at early and crucial times in her development. As she was entering her oedipal stage, her sister, 3 years older, died suddenly. Initially there was no access to memories or feelings about these events. She was too young to understand death's permanency and grieve her loss effectively.

During her adolescence another sister died. This time she understood death but was still unable to mourn. She acted out her grief with the first of several unwanted pregnancies followed by therapeutic abortions. This behavior was an unconscious effort to change the outcome of her original trauma, that is, to recreate her first sibling loss and provide punishment for her guilt due to her aggressive and competitive feelings resulting from normal sibling rivalry at the different stages of development. Throughout, there was a wish to have her mother there to help her during developmentally crucial times, but her mother was understandably overwhelmed with her own grief.

For Mrs. L infertility became part of this repetition. The miscarriages, the medical treatments, and every menstrual cycle continued to repeat the experience of her earlier losses. They proved her feelings could be damaging to her unborn babies and to herself. In psychotherapy she could finally experience the depth of her pain and her losses safely. I believe this intervention allowed her to leave her infertility treatments and eventually adopt.

These cases raise important issues in the psychotherapy of infertile women. They illustrate how patients' histories create personal meaning and interpretation of their infertility and medical treatments. For both of these women the stress of their medical treatment brought out earlier repressed childhood memories that were reexperienced with the psychotherapist present. The therapist provided support as well as interpretation of behavior and wishes, and attempted to stop self-destructive repetitive behavior. During this process both patients came to be aware that the coveted biologic baby was to be a cure for earlier childhood trauma. This situation allows the therapist to make use of transference as it develops.

Suggested Reading

1. Mann J. Time Limited Psychotherapy. Cambridge, MA: Harvard University Press, 1973.
2. Prarad H, ed. Crisis Intervention: Selected Readings. New York: Family Service Association of America, 1965.
3. Schoenberg B, Carr AC, Peretz D, Kutscher AH, eds. Loss and Grief: Psychological Management in Medical Practice. New York: Columbia University Press, 1970.
4. Winnicott DW. The Maturational Process and the Facilitating Environment. New York: International Universities Press, 1965.
5. Fenster S, Phillips SB, Rapoport ERG. The Therapist's Pregnancy: Intrusion in the Analytic Space. New Jersey: Analytic Press, 1986.
6. Bellak I, Faithorn P. Crises and Special Problems in Psychoanalysis and Psychotherapy. New York: Bunner/Mazel, 1981.
7. Applegarthe A. Some observations on work inhibitions in women. J Am Psychoanal Assoc (Suppl) 1976;24:251–268.
8. Chehrazl S. Female psychology: A review. 1984;141–162.
9. Freud S. Mourning and Melancholia. London: Hogarth Press, Standard Edition, Vol 14. 1957:275–300.
10. Galenson E, Roiphe H. Some suggested revisions concerning early female development. J Am Psychoanal Assoc (Suppl) 1976;24:29–55.
11. Grossman WI, Stewart WA. Penis envy: From childhood wish to developmental metaphor. J Am Psychoanal Assoc (Suppl) 1976;24:193–212.
12. Kestenberg JS. On the development of maternal feelings in early childhood. Psychoanalytic Study of the Child 1956;11:257–291.
13. Kleeman JA. Freud's view on early female sexuality in the light of direct child observation. J Am Psychoanal Assoc (Suppl) 1976;24:3–27.
14. Kohut H. A Note on Female Sexuality. The Search for the Self. New York: International Universities Press, 1978;2:783–792.
15. Nagera H. Female sexuality and the oedipus complex. New York: Jason Aronson, 1976.
16. Parens, et al. On the girl's entry into the oedipus complex. J Am Psychoanal Assoc (Suppl) 1976;24:79–107.
17. Pollock GH. Childhood sibling loss: A family tragedy. Annual of Psychoanalysis, International University Press 1986;14:5–33.
18. Robbins ET. Search for mother: The psychotherapy of two young women who lost their mothers during their oedipal years. Presented at the Annual Advanced Training Psychotherapy Symposium, Boston, 1987.
19. Russell P. Beyond the wish: Further thoughts on containment. Unpublished paper, 1979.
20. Stoller RJ. Primary femininity. J Am Psychoanal Assoc (Suppl) 1976;24:99–77.
21. Williams BL. Reproductive motivations and contemporary feminine development. 1985;167–193.
22. Zetzel E. An obsessional neurotic: Freud's rat man. Capacity for Emotional Growth. New York: International Universities Press, 1970;216–228.

34
Management of Patients with Preexisting Psychiatric Illness

Susan M. Fisher

How do we deal with infertility protocols for patients with preexisting mental illness? What are the psychodynamic issues of disappointment, loss, the limits of trying, failed grandiosity, or the meaning of a baby? What is the relationship between infertility protocols and medication for the chronically medicated, mentally ill patient who wants to become pregnant? These are very big problems. They are also problems that, strikingly, almost no one knows anything about.

It is impossible to talk about the dangers of psychotropic medication during a fertility workup separately from the dangers of those medications during pregnancy. If a woman is taking any psychotropic medications during a fertility workup and becomes pregnant, the medications have been constantly in her circulation. The majority of those agents are most dangerous in the earliest days of the pregnancy when organs are being laid down. If there is any possibility that the patient may become pregnant, it is mandatory to consider the dangers of the drugs for pregnancy. In other words, we cannot think of these women as nonpregnant once they have stopped birth control or are attempting a technique that could cause them to become pregnant.

In utero exposure to psychotropic medications can produce four kinds of problems for the infant: (1) morphologic anomalies; (2) subtle, long-term behavioral changes, known as behavioral teratogenicity, resulting from the effects of the drug on the developing brain; (3) intoxication when the maternal circulation no longer metabolizes the drug; and (4) passive addiction, which produces withdrawal symptoms in the newborn.

One would like to eliminate medications during a fertility workup and during pregnancy, but we can't. The risks are too great for seriously ill women: malnutrition, attempts at premature self-delivery, fetal abuse, refusal of care, precipitous delivery, and the serious disruption of functioning with its concomitant collapse of the social network.

Bipolar Disease

Lithium is the most effective agent in preventing episodes of bipolar disease. It is a wonderful drug—unless you are pregnant. Carbamazepine (Tegretol) and valproic acid are alternatives, but cannot be used. If a woman wants to become pregnant, she must stop taking all of these drugs before she tries. Carbamazepine produces fetal head growth retardation and other defects as well as developmental delay. Valproic acid produces neural tube defects, among others. Lithium ions diffuse across the placenta, so their concentrations in umbilical cord blood, neonatal serum, and maternal serum are the same; in amniotic fluid they are higher. Every study comes to the same conclusion: they cause a fivefold increase in congenital cardiovascular disease, and a 400-fold increase in other cardiac anomalies.

The mother also is at risk because she requires progressively greater doses of lithium to maintain a given serum level as pregnancy proceeds, because her plasma volume is greater and her glomerular filtration rate increased. At delivery, when the plasma volume drops and the glomerular filtration rate drops, the patient has an enormously greater concentration of lithium in her tissues, and the difference between the toxic versus therapeutic level of lithium is minimal.

Many women with manic-depressive disease are perfectly fine while they are taking lithium. They are happy, well-functioning people in the community. If they wish to become pregnant, however, they have to stop the lithium. Therefore, they must be followed closely for early signs of mood episodes. If a mood disorder recurs, they should be hospitalized with a structured environment and receive psychotherapy. If that is insufficient, electroconvulsive therapy (ECT) is the treatment of choice, as well as antipsychotic drugs. This is an instance in which ECT is a blessing. For some women with severe disease, none of this works. They must be treated with lithium because it is betterr then the other drugs.

Lithium should not be given during the period of organogenesis, days 18–55 after conception. Days 20–45, the period of cardiac differentiation, is the most vulnerable time. If a patient either inadvertently or of necessity has taken lithium during the period of organogenesis, the only alternative to abortion is fetal ultra sonography at 16 to 20 weeks to exclude cardiac abnormalities.

Depression

Ten percent of pregnant women are depressed. Many drugs are available for them, but only the tricyclic antidepressants have been widely studied. The fetus can metabolize and excrete these agents, but how well is unclear. No major teratogenic effects are documented, but subtle, infrequent effects, particularly behavioral ones, are related to the neurochemical changes in the nervous system. These have not been studied adequately.

Monoamine oxidase inhibitors (MAOI) are absolutely never to be used. They are teratogenic. Maprotiline is absolutely contraindicated because it causes seizures.

If a woman has been taking antidepressants, she should stop them before she attempts to conceive. Psychotherapy and other psychosocial intervention may be effective. If using

medication, is essential, it should be a tricyclic. If the patient is extremely depressed, ECT is safer than any drug.

The recommended antidepressants are nortryptiline and despiramine. They are the two most widely assessed for teratogenicity, and have the fewest side effects that are problematic in pregnancy. The therapeutic serum levels are relatively well known. These must be checked at least once a trimester in order to be reliable because of changes in maternal blood volume.

If a woman is taking antidepressants and learns that she is pregnant, she must taper the dosage. She should not stop suddenly because withdrawal risks exist for both mother and fetus.

Women taking antidepressants must be counseled about their options before they attempt pregnancy. They can discontinue the drug, continue it, or switch to another agent that will be safer in pregnancy.

Psychotic Illness

It is not known whether psychotic illness tends to get better or worse during pregnancy. There is also controversy about whether babies born to schizophrenic mothers are at greater risk of congenital anomalies even without drug exposure. Antipsychotic medications cross the placenta. Just as with antidepressant drugs, they can cause anticholinergic effects. Although numerous equivocal studies suggest that antipsychotic medications are safe during pregnancy, it cannot be conclude that they are.

Reversible physiologic and behavioral effects occur in neonates from exposure to antipsychotics, including a range of extrapyramidal dysfunctions such as tremors, posturing, increased muscle tone, extra-vigorous sucking, deep tendon reflex, a shrill cry, and episodic hyperactivity, as well as Jaundice, respiratory depression, and behavioral abnormality. These symptoms begin 1 to 3 days after birth. If the mother has taken a depot medication such as fluphenazine hydrochloride, the effects begin three to four weeks after birth. These symptoms remit gradually over several months.

It is a greater risk for the psychotic patient to be untreated. One of the first things to remember is that antipsychotic drugs can produce false positive results in some urinary pregnancy tests. Therefore it is important to make sure a woman actually is pregnant. If an antipsychotic medication is necessary, one of the higher-potency agents is advised because they tend not to produce orthostatic hypertension, sedation, gastrointestinal slowing, and tachycardia. The best studied of these are trifluoperazine hydrochloride (Stelazine) and haloperidol (Haldol). One should never use a depot neuroleptic for noncompliant patients.

A family history of extrapyramidal dysfunction in relation to using neuroleptics is essential. Benadryl (diphenhydramine) can ease extrapyramidal symptoms once the baby is born, but taken during pregnancy it is associated with oral cleft and must not be used. If possible, the woman should stop all medications during the period from 4 to 10 weeks after fertilization. If she does experience extrapyramidal symptoms with Haldol or Stelazine, her dose can be lowered or she can be switched to a lower-potency agent such as chlorpromazine (Thorazine).

Anxiety Disorders

Benzodiazepines (diazepam, chlordiazepoxide, lorazepam) are the only drugs that have been studied in anxiety disorders. Benzodiazepines cross the placenta and the fetus accumulates them, so cord plasma concentrations are higher than maternal plasma concentrations. The specific anomaly most frequently associated with diazepam exposure is oral clefts. Evidence also exists for physiologic effects on the newborn. They are hypothermic, they suck poorly, they are hypotonic, they are lethargic, and their reflexes are down. They also can experience withdrawal symptoms, such as hypertonia, hyperreflexia, restlessness, tremors, and worse, lasting up to several months.

For panic disorder, tricyclic antidepressants are the best treatment in the first place. Behavioral techniques, relaxation techniques, and psychotherapy are also effective. If a benzodiazapine is necessary, the ones most studied are diazepam, chlordiazepoxide, and lorazepam. Lorazepam has some theoretical advantage in that it does not tend to accumulate in fetal tissues. It must be tapered long before delivery. Diazepam should not be prescribed until after the 10th week of gestation when closure is complete, to avoid an oral cleft.

Acknowledgment

Particular gratitude goes to Dr. L.J. Miller for advice in preparation of this material.

Suggested Reading

1. Aarskog D. Association between maternal intake of diazepam and oral clefts. Lancet 1975;2:921.
2. Burr WA, Falek A, Strauss LT, et al. Fertility in psychiatric outpatients. Hosp Commun Psychiat 1979;30:527–531.
3. Calabrese JR, Gulledge AD. Psychotropics during pregnancy and lactation: A review. Psychosomatics 1985;26:413–426.
4. Coverdale JH, Aruffo JA. Family planning needs of female chronic psychiatric outpatients. Am J Psychiat 1989;146:1489–1491.
5. Coyle I, Wayner MJ, Singer G. Behavioral teratogenesis: A critical evaluation. Pharmacol Biochem Behav 1976;4:191–200.
6. Dal Pozzo EE, Marsh FH. Psychosis and pregnancy: Some new ethical and legal dilemmas for the physician. Am J Obstet Gynecol 1987;156:425–427.
7. Dubovsky SL. Generalized anxiety disorder: New concepts and psychopharmacologic therapies. J Clin Psychiatry 1990;51(Suppl):3–10.
8. Edlund MJ, Craig TJ. Antipsychotic drug use and birth defects: An epidemiologic reassessment.
9. Gelenberg AJ, Carroll JA, Baudhuin MG, et al. The meaning of serum lithium levels in maintenance
10. Gitlin MJ, Pasnau RO. Psychiatric syndromes linked to reproductive function in women: A review of current knowledge. Am J Psychiat 1989;146:1413–1422.
11. Gutheil TG. Psychodynamics in drug prescribing. Drug Therapy (Hosp) 1977;35–40.
12. Hartz SC, Heinonen OP, Shapiro S, et al. Antenatal exposure to meprobamate and chlordiazepoxide in

13. Jones KL, Lacro RV, Johnson KA, et al. Pattern of malformations in the children of women treated with carbamazepine during pregnancy. N Engl J Med 1989;320:1661–1666.

14. Kallen B, Tandberg A. Lithium and pregnancy: A cohort study on manic-depressive women. Acta Psychiat Scand 1983;68:134–139.

15. Kellogg CK. Benzodiazepines: Influence on the developing brain. Prog Brain Res 1988;73:207–228.

16. Kerns LL. Treatment of mental disorders in pregnancy: A review of psychotropic drug risks and benefits. J Nerv Ment Dis 1986;174:652–659.

17. Livezey GT, Marczynski TJ, Isaac L. Enduring effects of prenatal diazepam on the behavior, EEG, and brain receptors of the adult cat progeny. NeuroToxicology 1986;7:319–334.

18. Mackay AVP, Loose R, Glen AIM. Labour on lithium. Br Med J 878:1976

19. Mandelli M, Morselli PL, Nordio S, et al. Placental transfer of diazepam and its disposition in the newborn. Clin Pharmacol Therapeut 1975;17:564–572.

20. McNeil TF. A prospective study of postpartum psychoses in a high-risk group: 1. Clinical characteristics of the current postpartum episodes. Acta Psychiat Scand 1986;74:205–216.

21. Miller L.J. Clinical strategies for the use of psychotropic drugs during pregnancy. Psychiat Med 1991;9:275–298.

22. Mogul KM. Psychological considerations in the use of psychotropic drugs with women patients. Hosp Commun Psychiat 1985;36:1080–1085.

23. Morrell P, Sutherland GR, Buamah PK, et al. Lithium toxicity in a neonate. Arch Dis Child 1983;58:538–539.

24. Nora JJ, Nora AH, Toews WH. Lithium, Ebstein's anomaly, and other congenital heart defects. Lancet 1974;2:594–595.

25. Nurnberg HG. Treatment of mania in the last six months of pregnancy. Hosp Commun Psychiat 1980;31:122–126.

26. Parry BL. Reproductive factors affecting the course of affective illnes in women. Psychiat

27. Platt JE, Friedhoff AJ, Broman SH, et al. Effects of prenatal exposure to neuroleptic drugs on children's growth. Neuropsychopharmacology 1988;1:205–212.

28. Prien RF, Gelenberg AJ. Alternatives to lithium for preventive treatment of bipolar disorder. Am J Psychiat 1989;146:840–848.

29. Day D, Singh M. Anticonvulsants during pregnancy and lactation: Fetal and neonatal hazards. Ind Pediat 1988;25:185–191.

30. Rumeau-Rouquette C, Goujard J, Huel G. Possible teratogenic effect of phenothiazines in human

31. Sachs GS. Adjuncts and alternatives to lithium therapy for bipolar affective disorder. J Clin Psychiat 1989;50(Suppl):31–39.

32. Van Gent EMV, Nabarro G. Haloperidol as an alternative to lithium in pregnant women. Am J Psychiat 1987;144:1241.

33. Whitelaw AGL, Cummings AJ, McFadyen IR. Effect of maternal lorazepam on the neonate. Br Med J 1981;282:1106–1108.

34. Wilson N, Forfar JC, Godman MJ. Atrial flutter in the newborn resulting from maternal lithium ingestion. Arch Dis Child 1983;58:538–549.

35. Winter RM, Donnai D, Burn J, et al. Fetal valproate syndrome: Is there a recognisable phenotype? J Med Genet 1987;24:692–695.

36. Wisner KL, Perel JM. Psychopharmacologic agents and electroconvulsive therapy during pregnancy and the puerperium. In: Cohen RL, ed. Psychiatric Consultation in Childbirth Settings: Parent- and Child-Oriented Approaches. New York: Plenum Medical Book Company, 1988.

35
Application of Behavioral Medicine Techniques to the Treatment of Infertility

Alice D. Domar and Herbert Benson

Background Information

One of the early scientific understandings of how the mind and body interact was achieved by Walter Cannon at Harvard Medical School. By injecting cats with catecholamines from an extract of their adrenal glands he found a consistent arousal of the sympathetic nervous system: increased blood pressure, increased heart rate, increased metabolism, and 300 to 400% increase in muscle blood flow. He reasoned that this prepared the animals for running or for fighting—hence the name "fight-or-flight" response. It is also called the "emergency response."

All humans have this response. It is elicited by any circumstance that requires behavioral adjustment. It can be an acute adjustment, such as a near car accident or being late for an appointment. It can be chronic, such as an adjustment to illness or to the stress of infertility.

The fight-or-flight response has been implicated in causing or making worse a number of disorders. The symptoms of anxiety, such as nausea, vomiting, diarrhea, constipation, short-temperedness, insomnia, and inability to get along with others, are all part of this response. All forms of pain are made worse by the elicitation of the fight-or-flight response. This same response may interfere with the reproductive cycle. Certainly, anxiety and worry in men can impede sexual performance. Furthermore, the hypothalamic area is sensitive to stress, and thus a woman's ovulation can be affected by the same process.

What can be done to alter this stress-related response? If it is injurious, how should we treat

it? Drugs are frequently not appropriate. One could take tranquilizing drugs, but there are many side effects. There are no surgical procedures to counteract this response.

Since the fight-or-flight response is often a mind/body effect, it would seem logical to use the mind in an alternative fashion to bring about decreased stress. The relaxation response is the physiologic counterpart to the fight-or-flight response. It is not a technique, but a set of physiologic changes that occur when certain thought patterns occur.

The original studies that defined the relaxation response used transcendental meditation to elicit the response. These studies were performed in the same physiologic laboratories that Cannon had occupied in defining the fight-or-flight response half a century earlier.

During elicitation of the relaxation response, the amount of oxygen being consumed decreases from rest by 16 to 17%. This occurs simply by changing the mode of thinking, continues for as long as this mode of meditative thinking continues, and returns to normal with everyday thoughts. Parallel changes in carbon dioxide elimination also occur and in the overall metabolism of the body. The respiratory rate also decreases from 13 or 14 breaths per minute to 10 or 11 per minute. Heart rate and blood pressure also decrease.

The relaxation response is different from sleep. The changes in oxygen consumption associated with sleep occur over a period of hours. In contrast, changes in oxygen consumption during the relaxation response occur within 3 to 5 minutes and last as long as the mental instructions are maintained.

Just as there is more than one way to sweat or to increase one's heart rate, there are many techniques that elicit the relaxation response. Transcendental meditation is but one of many ways.

Regardless of the technique used, two basic steps elicit the relaxation response. The first step is the repetition of a word, sound, prayer, phrase, or muscular activity. The second is the passive disregard of other thoughts that come to mind and a return to the repetition. These instructions exist in virtually every human culture. The earliest example is from the *Upanishads* dating back to the seventh or eighth century B.C. There it was written that to achieve a union with God, one should pay attention to one's breathing. On each out-breath the practitioner is instructed to repeat silently to himself or herself an appropriate word or sound or prayer. Should other thoughts come to mind, they should be passively disregarded and there should be a return to the repetition. Another example comes from Judaism, dating back to the Second Temple in a practice called Merkabolism. Within Christianity, prayers evolved dating back to the time of Christ that were passed on by word of mouth through the monasteries and ultimately codified on Mt. Athos in Greece. The instructions were to say a prayer over and over. Secular techniques also elicit the relaxation response. In Concord, Massachusetts, Thoreau, Emerson, and Alcott achieved the same state by fixed gazing at sunlight as it shimmered off leaves.

The repetition of any word, sound, prayer, phrase, or muscular activity can evoke consistent changes. If one thinks a certain way, measurable, predictable, reproducible physiologic changes occur. We and others have found that the elicitation of the relaxation response is an appropriate therapy in disorders, such as infertility, that are contributed to or made worse by stress.

Application to Infertility

Two questions arise from the association of infertility and stress. First, do women with infertility have a different psychologic profile from fertile women? Second, what is the effect, if any, of psychologic and/or behavioral treatment interventions on the psychologic and reproductive status of infertile women?

There is a longstanding bias in the medical literature that infertile women are mentally ill. A medical textbook from 1797 cited barren women as more anxious, more depressed, and beset with psychologic problems. The psychiatric literature has also suggested that infertility results from psychologic causes.

The current difficulty in studying the interaction between psychopathology and infertility is distinguishing between the chicken and the egg. If one compares a group of infertile women with a group of fertile women, the former will have more psychologic symptoms than the latter. Although many psychiatrists have drawn the conclusion of psychogenic causes for infertility from this type of history, it is unclear that such is the case. It is equally likely that infertility has caused psychologic symptoms.

Two studies attempted to address this question by comparing women diagnosed as having idiopathic infertility with those known to have an organic cause such as blocked tubes or endometriosis. Brand examined three groups of women. Group 1 had functional infertility that was idiopathic. Group 2 consisted of women with organic infertility. Group 3 were women considered reproductively normal but whose husbands had very low sperm counts. Patients were assessed for basal pulse volume, heart rate, skin resistance, and muscle tension, which were called the physiologic measures. Four psychologic scales were also administered, including the Tennessee Self-Concept Scale, the IPAT Anxiety Scale, the Eysenck Personality Inventory, and a personal, home, social, and formal relation questionnaire.

No significant differences were identified on any of the physiologic measures among the three groups, or between the functional and organic groups on any of the subscores of the four questionnaires. The authors concluded that there could be no psychologic cause for the infertility, and that women with idiopathic infertility did not differ significantly from those with an organic etiology for their infertility.

A second study assessed 294 women, 49 of

whom were anovulatory, 141 fertile, and 104 with an infertility diagnosis other than anovulation, such as endometriosis or blocked tubes. These women completed the Hopkins System Check List, the Eysenck Personality Inventory, the Langer Screening Scale, the Mood Analog Scale, the entire Minnesota Multiphasic Personality Inventory, and the Sexual Function Inventory.

All subjects in this study scored in the normal range. There were no significant differences among the groups on any measures, with one exception. Women who did not ovulate did report lower self-esteem and more inhibited sexual attitudes than those in the other two groups. It is not known whether these minor differences resulted from or preceded infertility.

These two studies concluded that because they found no differences between patients with idiopathic and organic infertility, psychopathology does not cause infertility. The belief that psychologic conditions per se cause infertility appears not to be substantiated.

An extensive literature review indicates that infertility can have a devastating psychologic impact. Women commonly report that it is the worst experience of their lives. A modified Beck Depression Inventory was administered to 51 couples before and after an unsuccessful IVF attempt. Prior to IVF, 38% reported depressive symptoms. Following an unsuccessful cycle, the number increased to 64%. Two other studies found that women with infertility consistently have much higher anxiety scores than fertile controls. In general, although it appears that psychopathology does not cause infertility, it does appear that infertility contributes greatly to symptoms of depression and anxiety.

A group in South America evaluated 42 women with unexplained infertility using a battery of psychologic scales at the beginning and the end of the study. In addition, each patient completed a situational anxiety scale every other week. These were specific questions regarding infertility and pregnancy. A timed series analysis of that scale showed opposite and statistically significant trends indicating that spontaneous decreases in anxiety were related to pregnancy and increases in anxiety were related to nonpregnancy. The total qualitative analysis showed that all patients who became pregnant had significant decreases in measured anxiety prior to conceiving. Women who had increases in anxiety did not become pregnant.

These findings raise interesting questions concerning the interactions between anxiety per se and infertility. If anxiety somehow contributes to infertility, what might be the effect, if any, of psychologic and behavioral treatments on the reproductive status of women? If the data suggest that anxiety contributes to infertility, or if a decrease in anxiety contributes to pregnancy, then psychologic intervention might decrease anxiety and enhance the potential for spontaneous conception.

There has been a paucity of controlled research in this area; most reports are based on clinical experiences. In one report, five women were assessed for nine weekly 2-hour sessions with a registered nurse. The main themes discussed were how to get through the infertility workup, coping with feelings of guilt and inadequacy, preventing frustration from being taken out on husbands, and coping with the feeling that husbands lacked sufficient understanding. At the end of the five sessions the members felt better, with improved insight into their own situation and an increased sense of well-being. Three years later the investigators found that three of the five members had become pregnant. One refused to have tubal reconstructive surgery and one was lost to follow-up. A similar study investigated infertile couples who had attended six sessions of couples' therapy. All of them showed significant decreases in depression and anger.

Significant psychologic improvement has also been reported among infertile women who met in group sessions for 4 to 6 weeks. The average duration of infertility was 3 to 4 years, and all had completed their workup and terminated treatment. A 21% conception rate was achieved within 3 months of completing the group sessions.

Despite these encouraging results, there is only one study with a randomized design. In that report of 14 women with unexplained infertility, the patients were randomized into two groups. Seven women in the control group received no psychologic or behavioral intervention. The remaining seven made up the experimental group who attended 16 individual anxiety-management training sessions twice a week for 8 weeks. The sessions included relaxation training, cognitive restructuring, and self-instructional management, three basic components of a behavioral treatment package. Four of the seven experimental patients became pregnant by the end of treatment, whereas none of the control patients did. These data, though few, represent an interesting connection between behavioral medicine and fertility.

Together with Dr. Machelle Seibel, we initiated a formal study of women with unexplained infertility in an effort to elucidate a possible connection between stress and reproduction. The intent was to study 50 women who had completed a workup that revealed no cause for their infertility. Half of them would be randomized into the control group and half into the experimental group who would be taught to elicit the relaxation response. We were to follow them for a year and compare their outcomes.

The first three women were randomized into the control group. At the initial meeting they were simply handed some forms, tested, and asked to return in 6 months. What should have been 20- or 30-minute testing sessions turned into 3-hour sessions because they were crying too hard to be tested. Watching these women cry as they were going through our protocol made us realize that we were uncomfortable

TABLE 35.1. Mind Body program for infertility.

1 Physiology of the fight-or-flight response; introduction to the relaxation response
2 Diaphragmatic breathing; mini-relaxation exercises
3 How to be good to yourself; how to have fun
4 Half-day session: yoga, exercise, nutrition mindfulness
5 Cognitive restructuring
6 Challenging automatic negative thoughts
7 How to cope with emotions; emotional release
8 Anger
9 All-day Sunday session: yoga; using humor to approach stress management; mindful walk; couples exercise
10 Assertiveness; reintroducing spontaneity into your sex life; summary; review

doing a multiple-year research project. Therefore we decided to cancel the project and start a clinical program.

The first Mind/Body Program for Infertility was started in September 1987. As of this time more than 150 women have gone through the program which consists of 10 weeks of group behavioral treatment sessions (Table 35.1). Eight sessions begin with an unstructured half-hour of optional mutual support, followed by a 20-minute group relaxation response exercise. Participants then pair up to discuss their experiences with the relaxation response. A group discussion concerning questions and problems eliciting the relaxation response follows. An introduction and a brief lecture on the daily theme is given. People are then paired up, and do an exercise on the daily theme, and return as a group to discuss it. Homework is assigned on how to practice the exercise over the course of the week. Each session ends with 5 minutes of relaxation response. The husbands participate in two of the 10 sessions. At this time we do not have a separate program for husbands.

In session 1 the physiology of stress and the relaxation response is presented as well as the effects of stress on the reproductive system. In session 2 diaphragmatic breathing and mini-relaxation exercises are introduced. Initially, we were using session 3 to concentrate on cognitive restructure and affirmations. This involves challenging negative thought patterns. It is extremely difficult for infertile couples because they have one dominant negative thought: "I will never get pregnant, I will always be infertile." That is an extremely difficult thought to change. Therefore, it was pushed back to session 5.

In session 3 we talk about having empathy for oneself, learning how to be good to oneself, and learning how to have fun. A valuable component is that people brainstorm about what they can do to be good to themselves. They pair up to discuss their ideas and then the whole group writes some of them on the board. Examples include hiring a cleaning lady for a day, going for a walk, taking a mental health day from work, and many other little things that are not necessarily expensive. Playfulness and creativity to keep the spark of romance alive are encouraged.

Session 4 is scheduled on a Friday and lasts for a half-day. A catered vegetarian lunch is served. Participants perform about an hour and a half of yoga stretching exercises. We talk about nutrition and the benefits of moderate exercise, and introduce them to the concept of mindfulness, that is, being in the moment. This is taught by handing out an orange to everybody in the group and asking them to peel and eat it with an acute awareness of the smell, sound, and taste of the food. Living in the present, taking pleasure in immediate sensory experiences, provides a possible balance for the negative weight of infertility.

In session 6 we continue to talk about the mind and how to be in the moment. Patients challenge recurrent negative thoughts and explore a concept we call "awfulizing," in which people experience recurrent, negative, unclear thoughts.

In session 7 we talk about emotions: how to recognize them, how to accept them, and how to express or contain them. Many people may find they are able to express happy thoughts but not negative ones. This may be due to childhood experiences when they were not allowed to state their anger, but only nice feelings.

Session 8 includes a discussion of anger and forgiveness. We seldom have time to discuss forgiveness, however, as the entire 2 hours is usually spent talking about anger. We do not do this session earlier to allow people's anxiety levels to come down and so they may talk about anger without the anxiety that can overlie it.

Session 9 includes the husbands and lasts for an entire Sunday. We start out with the exercise on forgiveness followed by an hour and a half of yoga. We have a group discussion and relaxation exercise as well as couples exercises. We take a meditation walk along a river, followed by a pot luck lunch. The Sunday session is almost invariably the highlight of the program for the members. It is a way for each woman to spend an entire day with her spouse. The men usually arrive thinking the last thing in the world they want to do on a Sunday is sit around talking about infertility, and in effect we do not talk about infertility. We talk about the couples. It is a wonderful day.

Tha last session is a review. Information is provided on where couples can go for programs such as yoga and referrals to local psychotherapists. The concept of reintroducing spontaneity into their sex lives is discussed.

Patients are given a battery of psychologic tests before and after they enter the program. These tests include the Profile of Mood Scale, the Speilberger State-Trait Anxiety Inventory, and the Speilberger Anger Expression Scale. There were significant decreases in depression, anxiety, hostility, fatigue, and confusion, and increases in vigor (Table 35.2).

Patients take these tests between the first and second weeks of the program, when they already have some anticipatory improvement. They complete the second version several weeks after the program ends so they are not still in the "postprogram high." In our opinion, if patients were tested the first night and the tenth night we would have greater differences. Nevertheless, the levels of significance are impressive.

Despite the exciting improvements that they perceive, these women are also concerned with conception. The anticipated conception rate in this group is approximately 10–20%. In fact, after the first year of our program the pregnancy rate was 34%, and over the entire 2 years it was 32%. These women were infertile an average of 3.3 years. Most of them have completed treatment and some have been through in vitro fertilization (IVF). Although there seems to be an increase in conception rates, we cannot say conclusively it is because of the program. Infertility causes stress; however, we are less clear of the opposite.

The last thing in the world an infertile woman wants to hear is, "Just relax and you'll get pregnant." When we use the words relaxation and infertility together, people automatically think that is what we are saying. We are not talking about going on vacation, having a glass of wine, or quitting a job. We are talking about an intensive 10-week behavioral treatment program with at least once- or twice-daily elicitation of the relaxation response.

TABLE 35.2. Psychological test results of mind/body program participants ($N = 72$).

Test	Pre	Post	p
Profile of mood states			
Depression/dejection	14.93	8.62	<0.0001
Tension/anxiety	13.00	7.85	<0.0001
Anger/hostility	10.99	6.93	<0.0015
Vigor/activity	14.19	17.06	<0.0001
Fatigue/inertia	9.15	7.15	<0.0079
Confusion/bewilderment	7.92	5.89	<0.0001
Spielberger			
State	42.56	35.82	<0.0001
Trait	44.73	39.24	<0.0001
Anger expression	24.46	20.79	<0.0001

This includes intensive cognitive restructuring exercises, homework, nutrition, exercise changes, and group support.

Evidence exists that high levels of emotional tension can cause tubal spasm, problems with ovulation, the luteinized unruptured follicle syndrome, progesterone deficiencies, and decreases in sperm count. Those things in and of themselves can cause infertility. For couples experiencing infertility evaluation and treatment, even if their organic problem is treated, their emotional tension can be activated and may cause infertility. We assume at the outset that every patient we see has an organic problem. Our objective is to decrease any potential contribution of stress to infertility. Our program does result in a clinical decrease in psychologic symptomatology. We are less certain about conception rates. The answer to that question will require a controlled, randomized study. Until that time, we are unable to make any conclusive statements.

Questions and Answers

Question. I would like to comment on the statement that research methodology relies on the relevance of comparing idiopathic infertility with organic infertility. I think it is important to remember that idiopathic infer-

tility is by definition the inability to discover an organic problem. It does not mean there is not an organic problem, and in fact, the two groups may not be dissimilar. In addition, as was pointed out, women with organic infertility may have as well psychologic causes of infertility. Therefore, I suggest we stop thinking of this as a linear problem, and think more of an interactive model between infertility and stress. We must look at predictors of what would contribute to psychogenic infertility as well as how stress caused by infertility contributes to the maintenance of organic conditions.

Alice D. Domar. I agree. The problem with doing research is that it is difficult to separate organic and psychogenic causes. The literature from 25 or 30 years ago suggested idiopathic infertility defined 50% of infertile women. The figure is now only 5%. Not all problems lacking a specific diagnosis are idiopathic or psychogenic. Certainly stress is not an absolute cause of infertility, but an interactive effect may exist.

Suggested Reading

1. Benson H. The Relaxation Response. New York: Avon, 1976.
2. Benson H., Stuart E. The Wellness Book. New York: Birch Lane Press, 1992.
3. Brard H. Psychological stress and infertility. Part 2: Psychometric test data. Br J Med Psychol 1982;55:385–388.
4. Domar A, Seibel M, Benson H. The mind/body program for infertility: A new behavioral treatment approach for women with infertility. Fertil Steril 1990;53:246–249.
5. Domar AD, Seibel MM. Emotional aspects of infertility. In: Seibel MM, ed. Infertility: A Comprehensive Text. Norwalk, CT: Appleton & Lange, 1990.
6. Lukse M. The effect of group counseling on the frequency of grief reported by infertile couples. JOGNN 1985;14:67–70.

36
Psychotherapy with Infertile Couples

Susan Cooper

When crises occur, even strong marriages are shaken. Most crises that happen in the lives of a couple, however, affect one spouse more than the other, such as a job loss, an accident, serious illness, or death of a family member. In the best of circumstances the crisis is short-lived, the less affected person becomes a major source of support for his or her mate, and the couple, coping together, survive the storm, heal, and get on with their lives.

Infertility, however, is different in many ways from other crises. For many it is a prolonged ordeal usurping months and probably years from their lives. Its resolution is unclear and the end may not be in sight for a very long time. Furthermore, infertility is a crisis in which the usual order to life—marriage then children —is interrupted, and the universe feels out of sync. It makes people feel out of control—powerless. For the inability to bear a biological child touches feelings at the core of the self—feelings about one's masculinity, femininity, sexuality, and self-worth.

These omnipresent feelings and issues are the emotional reality for infertile men and women, forming the backdrop for their marriage, and leaving them minimal emotional resources with which to cope. Furthermore, the ways in which men and women experience the crisis tend to be different. Each person has his or her own point of reference for feelings, beliefs, and actions. Couples usually seek help when communication has broken down and neither partner can access the other's reference point.

In working with infertile couples, it is important to understand the ways in which men and women, in large part due to socialization,

deal differently with their emotions and with stress in their lives. Although men's and women's roles have changed enormously in the last 20 years, and will continue to do so, there are certain generalizations that can be made. Men grow up learning to be "strong" and "tough," caretakers of women—which tends to mean not expressing sadness or feelings of vulnerability. They learn to be independent, autonomous, to not need anyone else. Women, on the other hand, learn at a young age how to relate to other people and to form deep attachments. They learn that it is okay to express vulnerability and to reach out to and depend on others.

When a couple faces the crisis of infertility, these sex-related differences become more pronounced and can create a wedge between them. The process usually occurs in the following way. Men begin to feel helpless and frustrated about not being able to make their wives feel better. Nothing helps, certainly not the usual ways—presents, indulgence, reassurance, etc. It becomes intolerable to see their wives cry, to witness their pain and not be able to assuage it. Furthermore, they are burdened by their own sadness, often unacknowledged, but which makes them less emotionally available. As a result, they tend to withdraw, rather than express feelings of inadequacy or defeat. Sometimes, though perhaps unconsciously, they may feel angry with their wives for being "weak." In fact they are worried—afraid their wives will collapse emotionally, that their infertility will do them in.

Wives, on the other hand, feel increasingly disappointed in their husbands for their lack of comfort or concern. They feel angry for not getting the support and attention they crave. They believe that their mates just don't understand them and they feel rejected. Even worse, they may fear that their husbands are not particularly invested in having a child, that perhaps they will call it quits. Gradually both husband and wife become emotionally estranged from one another, each suffering from feelings of loneliness and isolation in addition to the pain of infertility.

In general, women feel the loss associated with infertility sooner than their husbands do. But while the wife experiences the emptiness and loss of not having a baby, her husband experiences the loss of not having a wife! Though she has not left him physically, he feels emotionally abandoned by his mate, who appears to be consumed with desire for a child and not for a husband. Each feels sad and lonely, yet these feelings have different roots.

Many couples who seek help during an infertility crisis feel that they previously had strong, healthy marriages in which they shared many values, beliefs, and interests, and in which their individual differences were allowed to flourish. The experience of infertility, however, is so fraught with loss that conflicts or differences feel like defects that threaten to tear them apart and leave each of them in a state of abandonment, without child, and without mate. In addition, any difficulties, even minor ones, that couples had in communication, style, or interpersonal dynamics, become exacerbated, as the tension, frustration, and pain of infertility make them less and less resilient.

Therapists working with infertile couples have a difficult job. They must be skilled at both crisis intervention and marital therapy, and be flexible enough to abandon either track when the infertility roller coaster indicates a different approach. They must educate the couples they treat about the process of infertility, in order to normalize their experience. They must help couples grieve the losses they face, make difficult decisions relative to their treatment or alternatives to their treatment, as well as work systemically with them in their couple relationship.

All infertile couples at one point or another experience the five stages of grieving first identified by Dr. Elisabeth Kubler-Ross—denial, anger, bargaining, depression, and finally acceptance. These stages are not experienced in a linear fashion, however, as they may be by someone who is dying or losing a loved one. The nature of the infertility roller coaster with its ups and downs of hope and despair preclude a smooth journey towards resolution of one's infertility. Rather, couples move in and out of the various stages depending on the time of the month, test results, new treatments being tried, or how many of their friends recently announced a pregnancy.

Therapists must be able to identify which stage of infertility a client is experiencing, so they can respond appropriately, with empathy and with helpful interventions. For example, in the bargaining phase patients typically look inward in an attempt to find a reason for their infertility. Often this introspection takes the form of guilt or self-blaming, for any explanation for their infertility—even if it is a punishment for 'bad' behavior—may feel better than no explanation at all. Thus clients in this stage may make statements to their therapist such as, "Maybe I deserve this; perhaps it's punishment for the abortion I had five years ago." Therapists need to engage their clients observing egos during this stage, while empathizing with their feelings of guilt and helplessness. The following statement might help, "I know how upsetting it must be to have no reasonable explanation for your infertility, but it is important to understand that it is not a punishment. Bad things do happen to good people." This intervention reflects an understanding of the patient's feeling state, attempts to stop the self-blaming, and injects a dose of reality to her irrational fears. Similarly, when clients are in a rage about the unfairness of infertility, and seem to be blaming everyone, including their doctor, it is important that we echo their feelings about the unfairness of it all, and the helplessness they feel. At the same time we can help our patients determine what gripes are legitimate and what they can do about them.

Couples who seek therapy in the midst of their infertility crisis may appear to be functioning at a lower level than they truly are. It is particularly important that therapists do a careful assessment of psychological functioning. Sometimes normally healthy, neurotic level clients appear to be more disturbed, especially if they present themselves in our office during an angry stage. Therapists must obtain some historical data from couples, assessing their past and present ego strengths, defense mechanisms, and ability to cope. Couples, or clients who would have been diagnosed as character disordered prior to their infertility experience, must be treated with this knowledge in mind. It is especially important to help identify when they are "splitting" or projecting, or using denial in an unhealthy way. We need to help them engage their observing ego and to make decisions in a careful, well thought out manner.

Couples who are in the throes of their infertility treatment can rarely see the light at the end of the tunnel. In fact, there *are* great differences in the timetables of infertile couples. Many couples feel they must leave no stone unturned before moving on to other alternatives; their process may be quite lengthy. Other couples decide to end treatment before exhausting all their options; they know they have had enough and must move on. Thus, in addition to determining what stage of grief a couple (or individual) is in, therapists must also help couples (and themselves) assess whether they are in the beginning, middle, or end of their infertility process. Depending on that determination, therapists can set specific goals with couples, including treatment timetables, and renegotiate as the process moves on and these goals are met.

The beginning phase of infertility is when couples acknowledge to each other that they have a problem, usually after 6 months to a year of attempting to conceive. They are probably in the care of a physician—hopefully a reproductive endocrinologist, and undergoing diagnostic tests in an effort to determine the scope of the problem. This phase usually lasts between 6 months and 2 years. Therapists can help couples set timetables, evaluate the medical care they are receiving, and help them establish a foundation for open dialogue, communication, and expression of feelings.

The middle phase of infertility is the period in which most of the treatment gets done. Clients are usually feeling their most intense emotions during this period, and it is usually in the middle phase of the crisis that they are most apt to seek help. In fact, due to differences in emotional timetables, couples are likely to seek the help of a therapist because they are fighting frequently, because they cannot seem to agree on decisions, or because they feel uncomfortably distant from each other. It is during this phase that they feel most out of sinc with one another.

In doing psychotherapy with infertile couples, it is important not only to educate them about the emotional aspects of the experience, but also to talk to them about the various stages that occur. Most couples probably have not had the opportunity to know many other infertile couples, which is why support groups can be so helpful during this time. They are thus unaware that their feelings, attitudes, conflicts, and interpersonal dynamics are normal in this situation.

Since their emotions tend to be so labile, husbands and wives frequently find themselves on diffferent emotional wavelengths, and may have difficulty connecting. Therapists can play an important role in teaching couples how to "tune in" to each other, to suspend their own feelings and judgments temporarily, and be empathic to their mate. And since infertile couples behave in their usual, though somewhat exaggerated fashion, during this crisis, therapists must point out the negative patterns or interactions which are most destructive to their relationship, and help couples find constructive ways of dealing with their differences and with their feelings, as they would with any couple in treatment.

As I mentioned earlier, wives tend to feel the losses associated with infertility sooner than their husbands do. Consequently, women tend to be ready to move on to more drastic treatments such as in vitro fertilization, or to alternatives such as donor insemination or adoption, when their mates are still hopeful of achieving an unassisted pregnancy. Therapists must help their clients understand how these differences in emotional experience influence their opinions relative to treatment and alternatives to treatment.

When one person is ready to move on before another, they can compromise. When one person wishes to move on and the other says "never," compromising is not possible. One cannot do half an IVF cycle, or adopt half a child. At this point therapists are faced with a more difficult task. We may need to spend up to several weeks helping both people express their feelings—including both sides of their ambivalence—about the choice in question. When couples disagree, rarely is one spouse 100% pro and the other 100% con. In exploring resistances to the other's point of view, often spouses become less emotionally wedded to their own, and are able to shift more towards the middle. At this point a decision can usually be made more easily, without either party feeling that he or she has won or lost really badly.

The end of the infertility crisis is usually characterized by a couple's intense desire to get on with their life and to put infertility behind them. Therapists sense that couples feel more in tune with each other and are experiencing greater intimacy. Differences no longer feel like a threat, for there is faith they can be resolved. Many couples realize that their primary desire is to have a child—not necessarily a biological one. Others realize that their lives are indeed rich, that they were happy before infertility set in, or that children are not the cure for mortality. Couples begin to think about adoption, or the advantages of a childfree life-style. They can envision a life—a good life—beyond infertility.

As therapists we begin to feel we are not needed anymore, and that is a good feeling.

Before concluding, I would like to mention that interspersed in the various phases and stages of infertility are the enormous losses experienced every step along the way. There are major losses such as the loss of the pregnancy/childbirth experience, the loss of a genetic connection to one's past and one's future through a biological child, the loss of the parenting experience, and, perhaps most profound, the loss of self-esteem which results from feelings of defectiveness, helplessness, and failure. In addition, there are other significant losses such as the loss of time when life is put on hold, the loss of money, which can add up to tens of thousands of dollars spent on treatment or alternatives, the loss of the ability to family plan, and the loss of sexual intimacy within the marital relationship. Therapists working with couples must help them grieve these losses and bear their intense effect, whether it be anger, fear, or grief. This is difficult work, and takes an enormous amount of energy, but the ability to grieve is probably the single most important determinant of the ability to move on. It is also empowering.

Couples who have survived the crisis of infertility usually find that their marriage has deepened. They understand each other better and have a renewed appreciation of their relationship. They have become closer because they have solved a difficult and painful problem together. It is the one benefit of infertility that is enduring, that we can offer to our clients.

37
Support Groups

Ellen Glazer

Infertility causes people to feel isolated, confused, frightened, and out of control. In an effort to cope with these upsetting feelings—and hopefully, to diminish them—many infertility patients join support groups. This chapter will look at the role of these groups as an adjunct to medical treatment, focussing on the following issues:

1. Curative factors in infertility support groups
2. Group composition
3. Potential pitfalls in infertility support groups
4. Termination

Curative Factors in Infertility Support Groups

Diminished Isolation

Although people come to infertility support groups with a range of interests and needs, I have found that what they want most is companionship. They report feeling isolated and alone in a world that is filled with pregnant women and babies. Although they know that infertility is common, they feel alone and different.

"I read in TIME magazine and see stories on TV about infertility. They all say that it is common—that as many as one in five or one in six couples is going through it. But all I can say is that I don't know them! Everyone that I know is in the other four or five. They're all fertile. They're all having babies. We seem to be the only ones who can't manage to join the giant club of parents."

Many people report feeling a sense of relief when they meet others who are struggling with infertility. Some express this at a first support group meeting, saying that it is comforting for them to see that there are other attractive and appealing people who are dealing with the problem.

"I don't know what I expected? A room full of freaks? People with the scarlet "I"? I know it sounds silly but it felt great to walk in the room and see other normal, nice looking people—people I immediately wanted to know."

Education

In addition to offering people much needed and longed for companionship, support groups provide another important function: education.

Most infertility patients become experts in their own treatment. They read extensively on infertility, focussing special attention on their own diagnosis and treatments. Their knowledge is often helpful in their treatment planning and decision making and it offers them some sense of participation and control. Nonetheless, this medical information can be confusing and at times overwelming. I have found that patients use support groups to sort it out.

"I learned a lot in my support group that helped me to deal with our unexplained infertility. Before I went there I simply wanted a diagnosis: after all, how could they 'fix' something if they didn't know what was 'broken'? Other members of the group helped me to accept some of the confusion inherent in my problem and to understand ways in which we could deal with it."

Groups usually include members who are well informed about local physicians and their practices. Although there are times when group members may become confused by the advice of member "experts," discussions about local opportunities for medical treatment are usually productive. In addition, members help each other with questions of insurance, offering advice on how to navigate through the confusing waters of medical treatment.

Decision Making

Closely related to the educational function of infertility support groups is their role in assisting members with decision making. Patients are often bewildered by the multitude of treatment options available to them and plagued by the question of "when is enough, enough?" Groups provide them with an arena in which to explore their choices and begin to distinguish among them. I feel that some of this comes from hearing other members speak about the decisions they are making.

"Before I went to the group I would not even say the word 'adoption'. I thought of it as a last chance solution.—as something that people turned to when they had failed at all else. At the same time, however, I was miserable going through infertility treatment and had a strong sense that I couldn't tolerate much more of it.

Then I found myself in a group with some terrific women who were considering adoption. One who was especially helpful to me had been adopted herself. She had grown up well adjusted and delightful. I felt so reassured in talking with her. I knew, for the first time that adoption would be an option for us".

"Reality Testing"

In the midst of infertility people sometimes fear that their judgment is impaired or worse still, that they are "going crazy." Support groups provide an important checkpoint: members hear what others are going through and gain some sense of what is "normal".

"Before I joined the support group I thought that there was something wrong with me for having so much difficulty with my friend's pregnancies. I could accept the fact that I did not want to attend baby showers and didn't hit myself over the head for avoiding them. However, I did think that there was something wrong with me for having such a hard

time learning that others—especially other infertile people—were pregnant. Why couldn't I be happy for them? Was I turning into a hard-hearted, mean-spirited person?

The group was a great comfort. I was surprised and relieved to find that everyone else there had trouble learning that friends were pregnant. I even learned that others also 'played detective', looking for any clues or signs that a pregnancy announcement was imminent."

People use groups as a forum for discussing the troubling comments and questions that come from family members and friends. "Was I being too sensitive when so-and-so said such-and-such?" "Was there something else that I could have said at my high school reunion when the thirtieth person asked if we had children?" "Was I overreacting when I went for my first visit with my new infertility specialist and saw that she was pregnant?"

Groups assist members with questions about their reactions to medications and treatments as well as to social and interpersonal situations. Some members are puzzled by the mood swings that they experience on clomid or on pergonal, wondering whether these are side effects of the medications or simply, the emotional sequelae of infertility treatment. Others find it helpful to check out how group members deal with the stresses and strains of high tech treatment—the frequent blood tests and ultrasounds, the precisely timed injections, the discomforts of egg retrieval.

"My doctor told me that the retrieval would not hurt. 'Just a little pressure', he had said. Then I went through it and felt excruciating pain. I thought that there was something wrong with me. That I was a wimp. That I was a coward. That maybe this meant that I should not be trying IVF. It was really helpful to hear that others had found it painful and to learn that some had even requested general anesthesia."

Humor

"When the going gets tough, the tough start laughing." This could be the motto of infertility support groups. The common fear that the group will be an assembly of weeping, angry, long suffering souls is rarely, if ever, well founded. Instead, new members are usually pleased to find that there is a refreshing expression of humor. They are also surprised to find that some of the worst insults and injuries of their infertility experience, can become high comedy in the right setting.

"My favorite story was that of a lawyer in my group who was going through donor insemination. She was in downtown Boston with a tank of frozen sperm that she had picked up at her doctor's office and had to drag to her car. On her way to the parking lot she ran into several colleagues from her law firm. None could help but spot the conspicuous tank that trailed her and each asked what it was. As she went along, she found herself piling one lie upon each other: the explanations for what she was transporting and why she was transporting it became more and more elaborate—and preposterous! I'm sure that it wasn't funny at the time but when she told the story in the group, she had some of us rolling on the floor."

I feel that the humor in infertility support groups is not diversionary: it is healing. Members learn through it that they can, indeed, make something good of a difficult and trying situation. They see that the other side of the loss of privacy and the intrusiveness is companionship and comraderie. They realize that there is a "silver lining" to even the dark of cloud of infertility.

"The laughter and the sharing that I experienced in the group will be with me for a long time. I met women there that I would never have known in my 'normal' life. We talked about things that were awkward and embarrassing but we did so with grace, compassion and lots of good humor. I know that many of us will not remain close over the long run but the experiences that we shared in the group were enriching and sustaining."

Group Composition

Much of the value of infertility support groups depends on group planning and composition. It does not work to bring together a random collection of people who are dealing with infertility: this could be a formula for disaster. Rather, I feel that there are certain guidelines that a leader should follow in putting a group together. They include:

Homogeneity vs. Heterogeneity

Infertilty support groups can include a delightful mix of people: physicians, plumbers, teachers and truck drivers can all relate to the common denominator of infertility. However, there are certain "mixes" that do not "mix well" in support groups.

Age

Since a woman's age is a major prognostic factor in infertility treatment, it is difficult to include women of widely varied ages in the same group. Older women tend to feel envious and resentful of their younger counterparts knowing that they have the advantages of time: younger women sense this resentment and feel that their own pain is neither acknowledged nor understood.

Sterility and Infertility

People who have definitive sterility, such as those who have had a hysterectomy, should not be included in a group of people who are pursuing medical treatment. They are likely to be frustrated and upset by the extensive talk about treatment and their reactions could inhibit others from discussing their medical experiences in detail.

Individuals with Serious Psychiatric Disorders

Although the majority of individuals seeking help in infertility support groups are stable and well functioning, there may be someone with a serious psychiatric disorder who seeks membership. Including him/her poses a serious threat to the group. Some members might make an erroneous association between infertility and mental illness, afraid that their medical problems could really drive them crazy. Others may simply be put off, wondering why they came to an infertility group to deal with serious emotional problems.

Gender

Most infertility support groups are composed of women or of couples. Men's groups are also available, through RESOLVE and through private practioners, but they tend to be less popular. The reason for this seems to be that women commonly feel a need to talk about their problems and men are often reluctant to do so.

Occasionally a woman will approach a group that is designated for couples and ask that she be able to come alone. This happens most often with "preadoptive" groups: those designated as a forum for discussing and exploring adoption. Sometimes the reason for her request is logistical: her husband's work or travel schedule makes it impossible for him to come. Other times her reasons have more to do with his reluctance to attend: she feels that if he will not participate in something she values, she will come alone.

Whatever the reasons, it makes no sense to have women come alone to groups that are designated for couples. To the extent that her request to come alone is related to marital tension, her group membership is only likely to increase her anger and resentment. To the extent that it is related to her husband's schedule, it is likely to prompt or fuel frustration, for him as well as for her. It is also unfair to other members who need and count on a balance of men and women in the group.

"At the first group meeting the leader asked if one woman could join the group on her own because her husband couldn't be there. 'Bull-shit' I thought to myself: If I had to be there than he did too. If my wife dragged me there than she could get him there. I surprised myself and spoke up in the group."

Primary and Secondary Infertility

Although they share much in common, people with primary infertility have a different experience than those with secondary infertility. While the first group is struggling with the pain of childlessness, the latter population focusses on many issues that involve their child: "can we live with an 'only' child," "what would being 'an only' mean to our child," "what about the difference in their ages if it takes several years to conceive," "could we possibly adopt after having a biological child," and so forth.

Mixing people with such different experiences is most often inadvisable. Those with primary infertility are likely to resent those who have succeeded in having a child, as well as to be baffled by why they are so upset. As a result, those with secondary infertility feel misunderstood and recognize that others cannot comprehend their pain.

"I wanted to join a support group and when there was no secondary group starting, I agreed to be placed with women who were experiencing primary infertility. At first I thought it would work out but as the weeks went on, I realized that the group was making me feel worse. I have a little boy whom I adore and each week I felt that I had to pretend he didn't exist."

Group Size

A small group is probably better than no group at all but as a rule, infertility support groups rely on size. As guidelines, I try to have ten or more members in a women's group and five or more couples in a couples group. Too many members is rarely, if ever, a problem but scanty membership can cause a group to fail.

There are several reasons why infertility support groups are so dependent upon numbers. First, there is the need to "cushion" for pregnancy: when a member becomes pregnant, the more nonpregnant members there are, the better. Numbers are especially important when there are two or more pregnancies in the group.

A second reason why a support group relies on a sizable membership relates to people's busy lives (and schedules made more complicated by infertility treatment). Groups tend to be self-selecting and to attract people who are active and involved. Consequently, members will have competing commitments and there will be times when they need to miss the group. Placing them in a small group would only put undo pressure on them to attend a meeting at a time when it was difficult.

Finally, there are the demands of infertility treatment. Egg retrievals and transfers can come at the most inconvenient times, including during regularly scheduled group meetings. A group that includes several members is not disrupted by these cancellations.

"When I first joined the group, I was surprised—and a bit put off—to see that there were so many members. I felt that I would never have a chance to speak, nor would I really be able to get to know people. There were fourteen women in the group and it felt more like a crowd scene than a comfortable discussion.

I am glad that I decided to stay with the group and didn't give up at the first meeting. What happened was that one woman dropped out and another promptly became pregnant. Then there were absences: someone always had a business trip or an anniversary or an egg retrieval. Meetings usually consisted of seven or eight members and that was fine."

Group Focus

Some infertility patients seek support groups for general purposes: they want to be with others who are going through infertility. Others come to a group with more specific needs. This latter group predicatably gets more out of joining a focussed group. The following are some of the "topics" that I have found provide an effective focus for a group:

When is enough, enough?
Younger women/couples dealing with infertility
Older women/couples dealing with infertility
Considering adoption
Preadoption (for those who have decided to adopt and seek support in the process)
IVF/GIFT (for those in the midst of high tech treatment)
Donor insemination
Donor egg
Surrogacy
Premature ovarian failure

Duration

Some infertility support groups are brief and time limited. Others are longer, but also time limited. Finally, there are long-term groups that are open ended. There are advantages and disadvantages to each format. They are:

Brief and Time Limited

The advantage to this type of group is that it is time and cost effective. Members can make a brief committment in time and money and still gain a great deal. Unfortunately, since infertility is rarely brief and time limited, members may feel that their groups have ended prematurely, leaving them stranded.

Longer, Time-Limited

A group that meets for several weeks but has a designated end point, has many of the advantages of a very brief group as well has the benefits that come from time spent together. Relationships begin to develop which can continue to grow after the group ends. Either as a whole group, or in some part, members may continue to meet, possibly changing the format to a more informal and social one.

"When our support group 'ended' none of us were the least bit ready to say good-bye. There was lots of 'unfinished business'—our infertility as well as our relationships with each other. We decided that we would continue together without our leader and that is what we have done for several months. At first we met weekly, now we're down to once a month. We've weathered the stresses of a few pregnancies, a miscarriage and an ectopic. Right now we're all swept up in the excitement of a recent adoption."

Long Term, Open Ended

The advantage of an open-ended group is that it remains there for members during what may well be a long, arduous course of infertility. This can be immensely helpful and satisfying. However, it also means that members must be prepared to deal with the pregnancies of other members (since these are much more likely to occur in a long-term group), to cope with members leaving because of pregnancy or adoption and with other changes in the group composition. Those that remain in the group for a long time may begin to feel that their experience there mirrors their experience in the rest of their lives: everyone else is moving on and they remain on hold.

"At first I was pleased that the group had no scheduled end point. I felt that I would need it for a long time and was glad to have it there. But as the months went by, people began to get pregnant or adopt. I started to feel like an old maid—they were all moving on and as usual, I was standing still."

Group Pitfalls

There are several potential problems that infertility support groups can encounter. Some are unavoidable but others can, with careful planning, be circumvented. They include:

Pregnancy

Everyone comes to an infertility support group wanting to be pregnant but no one comes prepared to deal with the pregnancies of others. A leader needs to address this paradox at the first meeting and to propose ways of handling pregnancies within the group. The following are some guidelines that I find useful:

1. Group members will be protected from learning about a pregnancy in the group.

   In the first session, the group leader instructs members to phone her if they are pregnant. She or he then phones all members to let them know the news, thereby giving them the chance to deal with it in privacy.
2. The pregnant member will not come to the first group meeting following her pregnancy test.

   Group members will have a chance to express their reactions to the pregnancy without worrying about the feelings of the pregnant member.
3. The group will decide whether pregnant members can stay in the group.

At the start of the group, members are instructed to make some clear policies about pregnancies. The goal here is to avoid a personality contest in which some pregnant members are encouraged to stay and others feel like they are being "booted out." Members should decide, at this time, whether those with histories of pregnancy loss will be treated differently than those who are not at increased risk for loss.

One pregnancy pitfall that cannot be avoided is that which occurs when several members become pregnant at the same time. Although it is unlikely, it can happen in a support group and when it does, the experience is devastating for other members. They feel that they sought the group to diminish the isolation that they feel and now they feel even more alone.

Problem Members

Support group leaders can try to avoid including problem members in a group, but even careful screening is not fool proof. I have found that some individuals with serious personality disorders do quite well in a focussed support group and conversely, some seemingly well functioning people are problematic participants in a group.

I think it helps for a leader to use the screening interview to gage a prospective members anger. Anger can reflect a normal and healthy response to infertility diagnosis and treatment but there are some people who are overcome with rage. An expression of the rage that they feel can be destructive in a group.

A leader should also try to get some sense of a prospective member's sense of humor. While admission to a group is not predicated on someone's ability to make others laugh, it does help to include members who can step back from the situation—at least briefly—and experience some amusement.

Imbalance

Support group leaders should feel comfortable including members with varied interests, backgrounds and diagnoses. However, it is important, in putting a group together, to attempt some balance. Since infertility is such an isolating experience, the leader needs to avoid promoting isolation in the group.

"I came to the group and was relieved to find several lovely women with whom I felt that I had much in common: I felt that these were people that I could be friends with even if we did not meet through infertility. Unfortunately, these feelings diminished when we began talking about our medical problems. It turned out that nearly all of them had endometriosis. They had it, they suffered from it, and they talked about it AD NAUSEUM. As much as I liked them as individuals, the discussions in the group became more and more frustrating."

Termination

Although infertility support groups have a formal end point, hopefully pre-determined, oftentimes support groups continue to meet, in some fashion, long after the "last" session. Some meet monthly, others have less frequent reunions. Some groups become more social, while others attempt to stay with a structured format.

As group members become parents, relationships change. This transition time can be a difficult one for many groups, especially as it often comes soon after they "end" with their leader. I encourage groups that I lead to feel free to call upon me for formal—or informal—consultation, should they hit rough spots in the months that follow our termination. This is a pleasure, as well as a responsibility, since one of the satisfactions of being a support group leader is seeing people move beyond their infertility and become parents through birth or adoption.

In this time of rapid and dramatic advances in reproductive medicine, support groups provide infertility patients with a valuable adjunct to medical treatment. In the company of others who travel the same uncharted roads, people are able to sort through complex questions and face bewildering decisions. As one man commented . . .

"I didn't want to be here. I didn't see what good it could do. I didn't even want to know anyone else who was infertile. I came only because my wife made me do so. Now I am glad that she did.

We don't have a baby. We don't have answers. But we have made some wonderful friends and together we have visited the issue."

38
Psychological Experience of Medical Professionals on the IVF Team

Judith Bernstein, Moderator

As health care professionals, we are constantly talking about the emotional health of our clients. The purpose of this panel is to focus on the emotional wellbeing of the in vitro fertilization (IVF) team, the effects of working in this very intense environment, and some of the things that we can and cannot do to improve the situation.

Most of us began in IVF or in infertility with tremendous enthusiasm. Some of us were drawn to it because of the love of the science, and others because of a real commitment to family building. Some of us entered the field as a result of our own infertility or experiences of others close to us. Some of us were just interested or eager for a new opportunity or challenge. Whatever the reason, we all started out with a great deal of enthusiasm and excitement.

Over time, however, something significant happened. A number of experienced people began leaving the field.

At a meeting of in vitro fertilization (IVF) nurse-coordinators we talked about care for the caregiver. One woman who had been an IVF Nurse for several years said, "Here I am helping other people have babies, which I am committed to, but I hardly ever see my child. When I am at home with my own family I have nothing left to give them. I am going to have to quit, as much as I love doing this."

This is burnout, and it is not a buzzword; it is a real phenomenon that is worth examining in terms of the specific, concrete conditions in which an IVF team works. Burnout is characterized by feeling trapped by the expectations, demands, and realities of the helping professions, unable to achieve a balance between meeting patients' needs and one's own personal needs. A person who is burned out works for obligation, not pleasure, going to work because he or she absolutely has to, and fearful of what might happen that day.

Some of the symptoms of burnout include chronic fatigue, susceptibility to illness, such as frequent colds, and, injury-prone behavior. Intellectual symptoms include indecisiveness, a cynical, negative attitude, empathy that turns into apathy, and blaming both patients and colleagues. The emotional symptoms can be anger, sometimes almost as much anger as our infertile patients exhibit to us, diffuse anxiety, depression, sleep disturbance, and weight change. Of great significance is failure to take care of oneself: too many days with no lunch, too many weeks with no exercise, and nothing done for personal pleasure.

The sources of burnout are many. Certainly they are prevalent among the helping professionals, but there are aspects that are specific to IVF teams. One of them is musical chairs. A lot of good people have switched from institution to institution, hoping to find in another job a better set of circumstances, only to realize that it is the occupation itself that creats some of the problems. We give too much bad news. We work in teams that operate by crisis management. There is too much dichotomy between what our patients expect of us and what we can realistically give.

The technology, although it is wonderful, contributes to a sense of depersonalization. We are overworked and overstimulated, and we have problems with interdependence in the team. There is little reserve energy. If one team member falls short, the burden falls to the others. Then the team, which can be a very positive helpful source of support, can turn into a negative drain. Certainly all of us have our moments of intense joy no matter how long we have worked in this job or how difficult it has been. However, if we do not pay attention to the vulnerability, the risk, the tendency for these things, burnout may occur.

Societal values have a great deal of influence. Much can be said about the altruism that is required of people in the medical profession, including mental health therapists. We are supposed to take care of people, yet we live in a society that is increasingly focused on the individual and the pursuit of individual happiness, with very little social reward or validation given for altruism.

Gender issues are also important in contributing to burnout among nurses. Most nurses are women. Women are socialized to help people, and helping is positive. When helping occurs in a context for which there is little validation, when it is just seen as what is expected of women, some real difficulties arise.

Social class stratification is another major contributor to burnout. Class is another way of talking about power, and two issues arise about power in medicine. One is the problem for those who have had it and are losing it, mainly physicians who in the past were the respected elders of the community, and are now being declassed and moving toward becoming employees (e.g., health maintenance organizations, institutions, etc.). They are often confronted with feelings of powerlessness, although many of them became physicians precisely so that they would never have to be in that situation, so that they could order their own day and control their own destiny as much as any of us can.

For nurses the problem is that they must participate as a team member and cannot be a medical director. As such, they have a great deal of responsibility with almost no authority, and that contributes to role strain. It is a major source of burnout.

Psychological makeup can lead to vulnerability and burnout. It has been estimated that approximately 70% of nurses, for example, come from dysfunctional families with a history of alcohol or substance abuse. Children in such families learn the roles of the martyr, the helper, and the rescuer. These are all phenomena having to do with codependence that have to be examined. The martyr in the IVF team stays late, does it all, and gets volcanically angry. The helper helps others at the expense of the self, and cannot sustain such a pattern. The rescuer tries to make all patients feel better, an impossible task.

Educational preparation also contributes to burnout. None of us are prepared for the roles that we must live up to, no matter what our discipline. Students in medical school are taught little or nothing about the emotional needs of patients. A publication from the American Board of Family Practice promotes the idea of a revolution in medical education because it is not meeting the needs of doctors or of society. One of the big issues was the importance of training physicians to cope with the emotional load of their patients, and their own emotional reactions to those patients.

As nurses we have no education at all for the specifics of our job. We learn very little about reproductive physiology in nursing school and must learn entirely "on the job." We are just beginning to develop some crash courses to help people pass specialty exams. Yet to be developed are mentorships and school resources that help people become specialists in reproductive endocrinology and infertility, and learn to cope with the flow of negative emotion that is part of the specialty.

The healthy individual interacts well with the environment, much the way a cell does. A cell has a boundary or membrane, and is intact. It has an identity. It has a receptor or a place on the outside where it is open to the world and can take in information. That information is brought to the central core, the nucleus. Information is brought back out into the cytoplasm where it is transformed, which is our processing of emotions, and the waste or excess products are brought back out of the cell again. In the healthy individual emotion is engendered by something that comes in from the environment, and that emotion has a place to go.

For many of the IVF team, this normal process is diverted. Emotion comes in, and we as professionals have no place to put it. We have no way of knowing what to do with it. So we wind up with discongruent communication, communication that does not reflect our emotions. Our behavior is not in keeping with our feelings, and that contributes to burnout.

In addition to communication problems, some commonly used coping mechanisms such as denial and detachment may work for the short run to protect medical professionals from a steady diet of negative emotions, but backfire if used continually or indiscriminately. Physicians and nurses are often taught that detachment is the appropriate professional response to patient emotion, but detachment is a two-edged sword. It is a difficult expectation to achieve in an intense setting like infertility, and if rigidly enforced, can interfere with patient needs for emotional support, empathy and validation. Detachment can also carry over into personal life, with negative consequences. When medical professionals compensate by attempting to protect patients from all bad outcomes, becoming indispensible, or over-identifying with patients' emotional pain, they are setting themselves up for burnout.

These dysfunctional coping behaviors go with the territory of infertility specialty, and most medical professionals develop them to some degree. One technique that seems to work well to combat these trends is reframing. Reframing is the ability to restate a problem less globally, and in a form that permits solution. If a nurse confronted by an angry patient can figure out what is behind the anger and feel some empathy for the patient, she may be able to facilitate some real communication and problem solving, and finish the encounter feeling satisfied instead of frustrated. In analysing factors that contribute to burnout, it helps to divide factors into internal and external.

External factors are related to self-preservation, protection from negative interactions. If that means that by the fifth call to report a negative pregnancy test, a person just cannot do one more, somebody else has to be available. We have to restrict role pressures, define our jobs, learn to set limits, and feel comfortable explaining to people why it is not realistic to expect us to be able to come through with this or that. Changing the environment, reducing the external sectors that promote vulnerability to burnout, requires a team approach.

The second set of solutions focuses on internal factors, our own emotional growth and development. These are the things that we know we can fix. We do not know if we can rewrite a job description, but we do know that we can work on ourselves. One of the issues for people working in this type of a stress environment is to learn to recognize repressed anger, and learn not to use denial and withdrawal.

We must validate ourselves. We are doing a superb job, whether anybody else tells us that or not. We also have to reframe our expectations. I have learned painfully through the years that I cannot help everybody have a baby. What I can help them do is move through the process so they come out the other side with some dignity. That has helped me enormously. Taking time for stress-reduction activities like eating lunch, running, and playing tennis, are important.

We can also reexamine our concept of normalcy. It is not normal to work 16 hours a day under pressure 7 days a week. When I first started in this field I worked 7 days a week. I came in every weekend to do procedures because nobody else would do them, and patients would lose the appropriate timing if I did not. I was indispensable. Then I stopped and I saw that I was losing too much. The patients were losing a lot, as well, because I did not have much left to bring to each encounter. It was also not optimal for the residents, whose avoidance of these procedures was reducing their own learning experience. Everyone benefited from changing this dysfunctional pattern. For all those years I thought working more than 60 hours a week was normal. Many of us think that incredibly high expectations of ourselves and other people are normal.

Just as important as redefining our expectations is learning new communication patterns. Techniques for expressing feelings in difficult situations can be taught and incorporated into a professional persona. One experience that helps here is to use "I feel" statements: not "He did" or "It happened," but in this situation, "I feel." When I began doing this with patients, I thought, "This isn't very professional. How can I do it?" Yet it turned out to be extremely useful. When a patient is very angry with me and is behaving in a way that is inappropriate, instead of criticizing her, what I say is, "When you say that I feel this way." That often is enough to defuse the situation and reframe it. It also works with co-workers.

Comments

Sandi Rufo. As a clinical coordinator, dealing with infertile couples is a challenge in many ways. Things they do or say can affect us in many ways, and we each have things that bother us most. For example, the patient who relies heavily on you to be available to do their treatment, to make sure their bloods are drawn on time, to make sure that nothing is missed and all things are covered. You work very hard to do this. You are there on Saturday mornings. You may even be there on Sunday afternoons, late in the evening, early in the morning to accommodate the woman's schedule, and you try not to upset her life any more than it already is.

Such a patient, unfortunately, may come to expect that her needs are of utmost importance in your life, and therefore, the things that you might need for yourself or the time you might want to put into your own life or your family come second. This is often very difficult for me, because I feel a strong relationship with my patients. It bothers me when a woman misses a cycle, misses a treatment day, or has problems at work with a boss who complains because she is arriving late or leaving early due to her infertility treatment. I try hard to be there for them.

When it is impossible, or when you reach the point that you feel there is something you must do for yourself or your family, this patient may become angry. She feels that you are cheating her of something that is rightfully hers. She is not considering you. Probably the hardest thing to do is to allow yourself to say, "No. I have to take time for myself because if I do not I cannot do my best for you." It is very difficult, but I think it is in our best interests to structure ourselves so we have the ability to say no at certain times.

Machelle M. Seibel. As the director of the program I have unique challenges. I must deal with difficult situations because the buck stops here. I try to make complicated decisions as a group. I utilize the entire team for their common sense and good judgment and also, sometimes, to support difficult decisions.

One particularly challenging circumstance is helping a patient stop treatment. We have given significant effort to helping people come to closure when it is appropriate. However, for many couples this remains a very difficult decision. I recall one individual who had been through no fewer than nine cycles and whom I told it was in her best interest to discontinue treatment. The team and I had discussed her case extensively, and we all agreed that it was time for her to stop.

The patient's response was both interesting and troublesome. I said, "You have been through nine times. We have looked at our statistics, and we know that if you do not become pregnant in four tries, the likelihood is great that you will not have a child through in vitro fertilization." She said, "I understand that, but I am willing to continue. It is not a financial hardship." I responded, "The last tries we have not been able to achieve really good ovarian stimulation." She said, "I know that, I have only been able to have an egg retrieved twice and I have only achieved fertilization once. But that is all I want: to get fertilization. Even if I don't have a child, I just want to get fertilization." We discussed the positive experience associated with fertilization and how having an embryo could be considered a union of man and wife. However, I emphasized again that it was extremely unlikely that she would achieve a pregnancy. Her response was, "It is my body. I understand the statistics. I appreciate all you are saying. Nevertheless, I am going to do another cycle." This type of interaction creates intense pressures that continue to be particularly stressful. To prevent this from happening our team has established guidelines for discontinuing treatment depending on one's age and diagnosis.

Heidi Mover. As one of the team technicians, I consider my job to be getting everything ready. I am one of the people who actually gets the cells together, and I want it to work. I want to be able to have something to pass on for the next step. I have to make sure medium is made and kept warm, that everybody knows where they have to be at what time, and that we will have coverage. Several aspects of this job make me feel stressed.

In a gamete intrafallopian transfer (GIFT) procedure it is necessary to process the sperm literally while the woman is on the table. Sometimes the man has had poor semen specimens before, and I just hope he will have enough sperm there when it is time to put them into the fallopian tube.

It makes me anxious when embryos from three people all have names that start with the same initial. Although we have many safeguards including color coding, using different incubators, etc, it continues to feel stressful. We have to be very detail-oriented, and we must be accurate. Regular lab meetings also help establish good communication.

Pat Hametz. An assistant coordinator, I have had trouble with patients who call and seem very cooperative and pleasant, but who use this as a way to lever one team member against another. He or she will call and say that somebody told them to do something, and call the next person and say I said do this. By the time it is sorted out, we realize that this patient created the whole treatment program as she wanted it to go. This puts me in the awkward situation of talking to the patient while having to sort out the facts. It can also create a sense of mistrust among the team and a potential for miscommunication. We now discuss these patients at team meeting and make certain that we know who might do this. It is only through communication following every interaction that we can avoid this type of manipulation and prevent mistrust among ourselves. We discuss

our plan and make sure that everything is very clear so that we can really work as a team with this patient.

Susan Levin. As director of mental health and as a social worker on the team, I wear many hats. I often share those hats with the IVF nurses. We sometimes share the responsibility of stepping back and letting the team talk about things, especially when one of us is more involved in a case than another.

One problem I deal with is helping the providers set limits. This includes discussing what is causing the problem, and seeing where limits are appropriate. I try to help them understand when they are acting out of anger and when their anger is inappropriate and when it is appropriate.

Sometimes I have not seen a particular patient, but I hear about her at our team meeting. It is interesting because I can learn a lot without specifically seeing her. I can hear how a particular patient appears to each member of the team, and it's not always the same. We then know we have a complicated and perhaps even difficult patient who needs our help. Also, we need the help of each other in managing her because she could split the team, which is a potential hazard. This maybe the forerunner to burnout in a team. If the team continually burns out, we cannot turn to each other for support.

I particularly have difficulties with patients who are referred for consultation prior to IVF but who do not want to see a therapist. It is difficult to sit with someone who does not want to be with you and does not want to talk to you. I have had people sit in my office and say they are there because it is required as part of their evaluation for IVF. I let them just sit there and grunt at me, and try to go through the interview. I would rather have them grunt at me, however, than not be there at all. It is a beginning.

Participant. You seem to have a lot of angry patients. What are they angry about?

Sandi Rufo. I think they are probably angry for a lot of reasons. They may be angry at each other, with their circumstances, or with the medical profession in general. They assume that if they go to a doctor he or she is going to cure them. When there is no cure, they are angry. Infertility makes people angry because they are so totally out of control in every aspect.

Machelle M. Seibel. I also see anger from other perspectives. Infertility is covered by insurance in Massachussetts. After that occured, people found that insurance did not cover everything, or that they had to switch doctors in order to obtain coverage. Furthermore, different insurers created their own restrictions and limitations on case. All of this added stress beyond the infertility per se.

Judith Bernstein. I find it helpful to remind myself that anger is healthy. The patient about whom I am really worried is the one who is passive and cannot get angry in her own defense. I may not enjoy patients' anger, but at least it is an honest expression of emotion and it does give some strength. Although one would hope that anger will be transformed into a more productive way of coping as time goes on, anger is a beginning for many people.

Participant. I am curious about the times when something has to be done and it is a weekend. It sounds like it is a situation that creates a lot of feeling on both sides. I wonder if there is any way to help everybody.

Sandi Rufo. I cannot remember the last time that I did not come in on a Sunday to do a treatment if it was the optimum time for a patient. I may feel strongly that I have to do it, but sometimes I am angry because it may really interfere with something that I had planned a long time for myself or my family. If I do it, the patient is very grateful. If the time ever comes when I cannot do it, that gratitude becomes anger and a feeling that I am denying them their chance. That is a problem.

Participant. Then why is the problem not addressed systematically so that people don't have to give up their time?

Judith Bernstein. Ideally, IVF teams would probably be larger than they normally are. I think we are overextended not only because of our own inner things, but also because of the difficulties of providing care 7 days per week.

Machelle M. Seibel. We have now worked out a system whereby nurses who work week-ends get planned time off during the week. So 7 days a week is not the absolute issue. No matter how many perfect cycles a person has had in the past, if it does not go as expected once, they may become angry. It took me approximately 5 years to not personalize this reaction. I realize how important it is to allow people to ventilate. That is all I can do, because no explanation is likely to make them feel better. They are angry at the system and their situation. The removal of personalization for circumstances one did not create is essential to prevent burnout. Problems can occur no matter how many backup systems are in place. For instance, the courrier transporting a specimen could have an accident. That is not our fault. One cannot plan for every possibility, but someone will be upset. This type of situation will occur and one cannot personalize it.

The focus is generally and traditionally on the patient, but we are turning the tables. In this discussion we are recounting what the infertility experience is like for the providers. In a referral practice such as ours, no more than 50% of the patients are going to become pregnant, depending on the etiology of their infertility. Some surgical or ovulation problems will do better, but other types of problems will not yield high success rates. Understanding and accurately explaining the potential for success is essential. However, understanding and accurately explaining the frustration and anger which may accompany failure is equally as essential.

On a daily basis one must face intelligent, high-power successful people who are accustomed to being in charge of their lives. With infertility treatment, and medical care in general, the patient is forced to give over control to their medical providers. Despite the best care possible, we know that many will not conceive. That is what is so difficult. We have to be happy and grateful and excited for each pregnancy. We must also be prepared each time a treatment fails.

Heidi Mover. When my husband and I were going through our adoption procedures, the breakthrough for me came when we were placed on a list. It took 4 years, but once it happened I knew I would be a parent eventually. That took the pressure off me. I have come into this with a more holistic view, and I think the whole team shares that view. IVF is one way to build a family, and we are in touch with a lot of our patients who have built families through agency, foreign, and private adoption. I consider that very much a success, and I know a lot of the members of the team do as well. I think if we can view it in that light it is one way to keep us on an even keel.

Participant. I am a clinical psychologist, and when I had my first referral of a couple who was diagnosed as infertile, my first thought was to remove all of the pictures of my daughter from my desk. My question is about your own guilt feelings about having a child and dealing with these couples. When I went through my infertility workup, I remember staring past the physician to his wall and the pictures of his children, and feeling anger and despair. Could you comment on your own feelings?

Judith Bernstein. I am glad you brought this up. It is a dammed if you do and dammed if you don't situation. If you have had infertility, that enables you to be quite empathetic with patients. It also means that every time someone else feels pain you are likely to be reminded of your own experiences. Sometimes it can make you more subjective and less able to be therapeutic. If you have not been through infertility, you can never say, "I know just what it was like," because you don't.

I came from a smaller community where I would frequently run into patients. I would be in the supermarket with three children, and I would almost feel like hiding them. I felt guilty having something so wonderful and precious when my patients were not able to achieve them and I had not been able to help them achieve it. I think those guilt feelings are emotions that we have to deal with to work in this specialty.

Susan Levin. I think the therapist has to be careful about that too. The patients don't know whether you have had infertility problems or not unless you reveal that to them. If you feel guilty about either having infertility problems or not having infertility problems you might try to help patients too much which can effect judgement.

Machelle M. Seibel. After I got married we had two children in a relatively short period of time. Although I never discussed this with any patient, it was certainly well known to my patients. It is impossible to have a totally private life outside of our patients because we are in the community, and people become aware we have children. I don't pull out my wallet and say, "Let me show you a picture of my kids." I think that would be insensitive, but I don't deny what is real. Some patients will ask me about my kids routinely, even if they are going through infertility. They want to know. What is essential is being comfortable with one's own history and not letting it interfere with patient care. Although some discomfort is understandable depending on one's past, each professional in the field has to process and understand his or her emotions in order to be effective with patients.

Sandi Rufo. I am not so sure the patients are angry that you have children. I think that they simply wish they had what you have. In most cases the patients who know I have children, have seen my children, or heard me talk to them, have never seemed to express anger.

Maureen Kearnan. I am a technologist on the Faulkner IVF team, and I was pregnant last year. When I was first pregnant, I was very concerned about the patients' feelings. I found myself hiding behind the operating room door, but I never experienced any hostility or anything from any patient at all. They would ask me how I was doing, when the baby was due, and even today a woman I haven't seen in a long time will ask me about the baby. I think they feel good for us, and I don't think anybody has to feel uncomfortable about their children or actually being pregnant in front of the patients.

Judith Bernstein. I agonized for a long time about a baby picture bulletin board. Was it right to put pictures up because some patients seemed to want that? Was it going to be uncomfortable? Most patients said they liked having the board of successes up there because it gave them something to feel good about and to hope for. I think we have to give most people credit for a lot of kindness and a lot of altruism, despite their infertility. They wish other people well.

Merle Bombadieri. I think that not only a pregnancy or adoption is success, but some people choose to remain child free and that is really the best decision for them. So, that can also be a success if they have help with grieving and they have really come to terms with it.

The comments about angry patients are parallel to what adoption workers say about the anger that they hear. What often happens is that the pain of infertility makes people see medical teams and adoption workers as paths to babies, not as human beings. They feel wronged by nature, and by others who have treated them, and now it is your job to make them parents.

Therapists have the luxury of not being in the position to provide the pregnancy or to provide the baby. We can talk to people, and they will listen to us. One of the things that I find really striking is the question of grief, when people have not dealt with the awareness this may never happen. They put all of their energy into being furious at the medical team or the adoption agency. But when they can get some help with dealing with their grief, they are better able to understand the realities of running an adoption agency or an IVF program, and begin more to see the people who work in these places as human beings who might disagree with them, but might actually have a valid reason for saying what they are saying rather than just being deprivers.

The other thing that therapists can do with clients is to teach them about assertiveness. We have to tell them that if they come on spewing anger, no one will listen to them. The medical team will become angry and frustrated, and the patients will not get their point across. If they want to change how people deal with them, they have to communicate it in a pleasant way. If they are spilling over with anger, they must do something else with it. They can talk about it in therapy, in Resolve support groups, with husbands and friends. They cannot put all of their fury over infertility onto a medical team or an adoption agency. It is only going to make things harder.

Judith Bernstein. I had two goals for this section, and I feel that they have been met. I was hoping that medical people working with infertile patients would realize that we all have similar experiences. All the difficulties described are par for the course.

I also hoped to provide mental health professionals who don't treat the medical aspects of infertility an appreciation for the kinds of constraints and stresses under which the team operates. The patient's description of her interaction with her medical team is subjective. It is always worth investigating a little further to see if perhaps there might have been some other circumstances.

39
When to Call It Quits

Merle Bombadieri

When medical people work with infertile couples, the best time to raise the question of when to say enough is right at the beginning. We must let people know that treatment may or may not be successful, although it may be awkward for either partner or the medical team to bring up the subject. It seems to work well if we say to the couple, "If at some point in treatment you are feeling tired of it, or you want a break, you are questioning it, please let me know. If, as we go along, the outlook does not look hopeful, you are welcome to bring up the possibility of taking a vacation, or beginning to look at stopping treatment."

So many times patients do not talk about stopping therapy because they think they might hurt the medical staff's feelings, that they would be representing the medical staff as incompetent rather than simply recognizing that therapy has not been effective. Physicians may also be afraid to suggest calling a halt. Nurses sometimes feel that treatment has been going on forever, and it does not look hopeful, but they are afraid to say something because they do not want to hurt the couple's feelings or discourage them when they are so hopeful. Therefore a ground rule must be established from the start: we will all be open with each other. If anybody feels that therapy is not working or perhaps needs to change, we can talk about it.

Acknowledging that enough is enough requires making decisions. The term is ironic, however; in fact, these are couples for whom decisions have not worked. They made a decision perhaps 2 years ago, perhaps 5 or even 10 years ago, to have a biologic child. They made a decision to do it in the ordinary way, but it

did not work. Now, after they have had years of therapy and hoping, we speak with them about stopping, and they feel they have no more alternatives. They have run out of good decisions and do not want to face the others. Moving on to donor insemination from medical treatment of male infertility does not feel like an alternative; moving on to donor eggs, adoption or child-free living does not feel like an alternative, at least not when people first begin to think about it.

Decision making is an eight-step process. The first step is to understand the process and the normal feelings that go into it, such as confusion, loss, and need for closure.

Step One: Accepting Confusion and Understanding the Decision-Making Process

Ambivalence is normal. These patients often feel as if they cannot make a decision because they are confused. They interpret their doubts to mean that they are not on the right track. A decision starts with ambivalence, a 60/40 state of mind, and it evolves with time, with talk, soul-searching, grieving, and values clarification. If these couples can understand that, they do not have to be so angry at themselves. So much decision-making energy is wasted because people are angry with themselves or their partners: "What is the matter with us? Why is this taking so long? This is our seventh year of infertility, and we are just beginning to think that enough is enough. We are just beginning to consider adoption. We know people who went through 2 years of infertility who are already adoptive parents. Why are we taking so long?"

People who have moved very quickly from infertility treatment to adoption may actually never have grieved or come to terms with the infertility, and may represent a lower level of emotional growth than the couple who are struggling with alternatives. Couples can feel reassured and empowered when they understand the decision-making process and accept it. A decision is not a neon sign that suddenly flashes. It is a blurred picture that comes a little more into focus every few days, every few weeks, every few months.

One of the incorrect assumptions that couples make in their desperation is that they are always going to be confused. They might say, "We just have to close our eyes and throw a dart, and get on with our lives." It is helpful to let these people know they do not have to stop the process prematurely. A little more time, a little more psychologic work, and possibly a little more medical work will make the difference. The best alternative will become clearer to them.

Fear of parenting can contribute to prolonged ambivalence. When people have gone through several years of infertility, they have had time to build up the idea that if they can only have a baby everything will be perfect and wonderful. It is quite common to make a bargain, often never verbalized even to oneself, with God. Typically it goes, "Look, God, so many people in this world are doing a lousy job of parenting. They didn't have any trouble getting pregnant. They are on their third child, their fourth child. We will be such good parents. If we never say anything negative about children now, and you reward us with a child, we won't have any negative feelings. We will be perfect parents."

When adoption proceedings are launched and it dawns that a real baby will arrive, they panic. They say, "We are crazy? What's going on here? Maybe we really haven't wanted a baby. Maybe we just got into a power struggle with Mother Nature, a contest that we have been determined to win, and maybe we don't even really want to be parents!"

People are surprised to run into negative feelings and the fear of ambivalence about parenting. They must be told that it is a normal thought right now. They are terrified. "If we adopt through one of these agencies that goes fairly quickly, we are not going to be able to go out to dinner without getting a babysitter. What is going to happen to the wife's career? Are we really going to be able to share roles equally? Are we going to slip back into the patterns of the lives our parents lived?" All of the things that people do not have to deal with when they are not parents now come to the forefront. Couples need to be reassured that it makes sense to be scared to become a parent.

The decision that enough is enough does not have to be simultaneous with a decision to pursue adoption, to be child free, or to move to some therapeutic alternative. Some couples do make these decisions simultaneously. Others do not. They say, "This is all we can take of the medical treatment. We are going to need some time off before we know what to do next."

It is also true that decisions involve loss. People often want to get on with their lives, want some closure, but cannot achieve it because decisions mean losing the other alternatives. The word decide comes from a Latin root meaning "to cut away from." Thus, decision making by its very definition involves loss. We have to give up one or more options while at the same time grasping another. By not deciding, we hold on to the illusion that we can have it both ways. By not deciding, the couple can enjoy all of their fantasies that the next cycle is going to bring a successful pregnancy. When they decide to stop trying for pregnancy, they are letting go of the opportunity for a biologic child. Moving toward adoption is different, in that the couple is not necessarily saying that they will never have a biologic child, but only that their first child is going to be adopted. It is understandable that this couple feels a sense of loss when they make the decision to stop treatment, to relinquish the biologic child of their fantasies.

A good decision also involves facing a fear of mortality. This comes out in different ways. When people try to hold on to all the options, they are dealing with the illusion that they can have it all. Making a decision to stop trying to achieve a pregnancy, to accept losses, is an acknowledgment that they are not going to live forever. They are at a certain age, they are at a certain point in their treatment, and if they want to be parents, they have to make that decision now.

Irwin Yalom, an existential psychotherapist, quoted a patient: "Decisions are so expensive because they cost you everything else. Not only not getting the pleasures and satisfactions of the other decisions, but really acknowledging that life is finite, that time and energy and resources are finite, and that you have got to make choices about where you are going to put those things."

Techniques for Assisting Couples with Resolving Ambivalence

Several things can be helpful in values clarification. These include meditation and fantasy, taking time to imagine what it would be like to stop trying, or what it would be like to have an adopted child, and talking to other people who have made the decision through support groups and informal networking. Therapists might be able to put them in touch with other people in similar circumstances. Physicians can introduce patients to others who have said enough is enough or decided to adopt.

Journal writing can be helpful. The idea is to write something spontaneously when people actually have thoughts, positive or negative, about continuing or discontinuing treatment, and suggest that people use two different-colored ink pens; green and red are popular because they suggest stop and go. So the people write in green the thoughts that represent a desire to keep going no matter what, and use red for the feelings that say, "This is all I can stand." What is especially helpful about this method is that one can see a decision evolving without even reading the content. If a woman does this over a few weeks or a couple of months, she can flip through, and see that one ink color begins to dominate over the other. When they see more of their writing in one color than another, they realize that they really are working their way into a decision, and this realization is good for self esteem.

Step Two: Taking Stock

Another step in decision making is to take stock, and this includes several different things. First, the couple must talk to each other about what they want to do. One couple continued treatment for a year more than they wanted to because each was sure that the other wanted to keep going, and neither wanted to hurt and disappoint the other. It is hard to over-emphasize the importance of thoughtful communication between the partners. It is also important to investigate the realities of therapy with the physicians and nurses and to be open with them. People often hesitate to do this to avoid hurting feelings or appearing to lack confidence in the medical team. That can lead couples to continue when it is not in their best interests. It is helpful to set up a special appointment for evaluation so that enough time is available to cover the ground completely, instead of trying to have this discussion tacked on to a procedure or treatment session.

This is also a time when some people find it helpful to get a second opinion. It helps to know that someone else who has not been working with their case for so long can evaluate their situation.

People who are leaning toward stopping therapy can be threatened at these meetings because they fear that the medical team will tell them 12 more things that can be done, and if they decide not to do them, they will be accused of giving up too easily. We have to emphasize that getting the information does not mean that they have to follow through. If 12 things can be done, the couple might decide to do one or two, or they might decide to do none.

Some couples actually reach the decision that enough is enough or set a deadline when they have these medical meetings. When they hear the 12 things that can be done, they feel they would like to try more, but 12 sounds like too much. Negotiating limits is particularly crucial if one spouse is dying to stop, wanted to stop 18 months ago, but is going on because the other spouse wants to continue for another year. Couples may be apprehensive about such a meeting, fearing that when they hear the things that can be done they will be angry with each other because one person does not want to do anything and the other person wants to do everything. The response of the medical team should be, "Go to the meeting and see what you can learn."

Providing an overview of the latest medical information can make a difference in how the couple understands options. The medical team also can be tremendously helpful with respect to the psychologic aspects of decision making, whether it is saying, "You two have seemed so tired for so long," or "I understand you are thinking of stopping, but this last cycle looked better than ever. I really would like to see you try another two cycles." Such psychologic input can be invaluable.

Step Three: Creating Space for Decision Making

The third step in decision making is to take a vacation from trying. This can mean skipping some Pergonal cycles, skipping the in vitro fertilization (IVF) and gamete intrafallopian transfer (GIFT) cycle, not going for husband insemination or intrauterine insemination, or not going for donor insemination. For some couples, it is using contraceptives for a month or two. That idea sounds outrageous at first to infertile couples, but those who can bring themselves to do it get even more relief during their vacation than the ones who do not. It gives them a chance to rediscover who they are and lets them identify themselves and each other as people who are not just halves of a disappointed baby-making team. It is a real opportunity to meet each other again as a couple, and it can sustain them whether or not they go back to trying for five more cycles.

Taking a vacation also gives people a taste of how wonderful it is going to feel when they are no longer trying to become pregnant. It gives them hope. Whether they continue trying or decide to take a permanent vacation, this

time off gives them a perspective for decision making that is invaluable.

Step Four: Setting Limits

Another thing that can help is to set a deadline for stopping, for example, three more cycles of Pergonal, one more GIFT or IVF. The idea of a deadline is that the partners are warning themselves, giving themselves time to try on the idea of stopping without actually doing so. Deadlines do not have to be adhered to strictly. A woman might decide to do four more cycles of Pergonal, or do one, and say enough. On the other hand, she might say she is only going to do one more cycle of Pergonal, but when she finds she responded better than ever before, she might decide to do two more.

The idea of a deadline is not for the couple to box themselves in. It is to consider the possibility of stopping, to reassure themselves that the tests and the injections and the appointments are not going to last forever, and to help them figure out when they want to stop. Thus a deadline might be wrong, but it might help the couple find out the right time to stop.

Some people cannot bring themselves to set a deadline. It sounds too final, and they do want to continue several more months of medical therapy. In such cases I recommend setting a time frame. This is looser than a deadline, but again, it is a message of the couple to each other that pain is not going to go on forever. With a time frame, the couple looks at whether or not they want to be actively trying to become pregnant by next Christmas or by a certain birthday. This can work well for people for whom deadlines sound too final.

Step Five: Grief Work

The fifth step in deciding enough is enough is working out grief. Couples must allow themselves to feel all of the appropriate anger and sadness about not producing a biologic child. One of the things that gets in the way of this is the idea that grieving might jinx the couple. If they dare to say that it may never happen, then it really will never happen. It can also be a feeling of great finality. In fact, we tell people it is common to do grief work and then unexpectedly have a successful pregnancy. I must emphasize, however, that we do not say that the reward for grieving is going to be a pregnancy.

Grieving releases the stress from all the cycles that did not work. If the couple has had 4 years of infertility, and the wife has 12 periods a year, they are grieving the 48 babies they did not have. If they have gone through IVF in which there were six embryos, they are grieving six children that were lost. Counting IVF and Pergonal, especially with IVF where there have been transfers, people can have 30 losses in addition to the monthly loss. This is powerful, but it validates to them that they have had losses, and they are not coddling themselves by being depressed.

Helping Couples Grieve

We try to make the loss of grief more tangible to these patients. We have them write down the month and year they started trying for pregnancy and to figure out how old their first child would be if they had conceived the first month they were trying. If they have had 5 years of infertility, they might have a 4-year-old and a 2-year-old, and if they had planned to have three children, they might currently be pregnant with their third child. This is a way of acknowledging to them that they have experienced major loss, and even if they went on to have three or four biologic children or three or four wonderful adopted children, they will never get back the children they would have had earlier in their lives.

We also ask couples to make a list of all their family, friends, neighbors, and co-workers who have given birth since they have been attempting pregnancy. Often they will name siblings or close friends who have had a second or even a third child during the time that they have been trying. Again, this is a real statement to them. They are not wallowing in misery, making much ado about nothing. They have been trying to have a baby for all these years, and they have had their noses rubbed into everybody else's babies. This list becomes tangible proof of their losses.

Often, in the beginning of infertility treatment couples do not feel overwhelmed when they receive birth announcements. They feel hopeful; "This treatment is going to work and we are going to be next." Recalling those announcements is usually not so poignant. Then comes the middle period during which it dawns on them that their infertility problems are major and are not going away. They are filled with anger and sadness then, but by the time they have reached the third stage they have become so numb that they do not remember how bad they felt. They are overwhelmed by disappointment. These lists help them reacquaint themselves with grief that they had touched on but lost.

People resist grief work because they fear it means they will go crazy. They feel as if they won't be able to go to work. Wives worry that they will cry constantly. Husbands worry that they will be so angry that they will be paralyzed. In 10 years of infertility work with couples, I know only a few people who have missed one or two days of work because of this process, and no one has had a psychiatric hospitalization or been unable to function for weeks on end. What people say is, if anyone could have told them ahead of time the relief they would feel from doing the grief work, they would have done it long ago. The energy that it takes to push down those grief feelings for all of those years was much greater than the energy required to breathe.

The major difficulty people have to face in grief work is that they deny that they have more grieving to do. They have pounded their fists, torn up baby announcements, cried, talked. They cannot believe that there is more to do. If they can feel the anger and sadness, however, they will actually have more control over their lives. Instead of losing control they will gain control because they can finally get on with their lives.

Step Six: Overcoming Obstacles

Step six is overcoming obstacles. One of these is belief in persistence, the idea that if a couple just keeps going long enough they will be successful. They must be helped to understand that success can take many forms, and sometimes that can be recognizing that something is not working, and moving on. Even the puritans gave up.

It is ironic that we often talk about the puritan ethics of nose to the grindstone for success. The puritans gave up life in England because they recognized that it wasn't working for them, and in order to have a successful economic and spiritual community they needed to go elsewhere. Examples like this are helpful to people who are obsessed with perseverance.

Another obstacle is incorporating imperfection into one's self-esteem. People are worthwhile even though they may have imperfect bodies. They have a right to be in this world even if they never produce a child. They can become good parents through adoption. Achieving the goal of pregnancy is not more important than their needs as human beings to have peace, to have a normal life, to have energy and feel good when they get up in the morning.

We have prepared a checklist to help people figure out whether or not they have grieved. A common sign of resolution of grief about infertility is that they can talk about the subject. There may be a few tears or some rage, but not heavy sobbing or an inability to mention it. Another is that they describe infertility primarily in the past tense: "That was a dark, dark time for us. Thank goodness it is over." The couple also can acknowledge the magnitude of their loss in not producing a biologic child. Awareness of other people's pregnancies may cause pain, but it is no longer overwhelming. The couple can enjoy other people's children as the individuals they are, rather than as symbols of children that they are not able to produce. An important item on the list is that the partners feel that life is moving on. They are glad to be alive again. An especially sensitive indicator of the degree to which people have completed grief work is their energy level. If they are exhausted, if they feel that they simply are going through motions and that they cannot expect much return, they still have more grief work to do. If they are involved in plans, new projects, and activities

and are no longer focused on infertility or adoption exclusively, they are basically finished. Barbara Menning said, "My infertility resides in my heart as an old friend. I do not hear from it for weeks at a time and then a moment of thought, a baby announcement, or some such thing, and I will feel the tug, maybe even be sadder, shed a few tears, and I think there is my old friend. It will always be a part of me."

People who have done their grief work can go through medical treatment with much more peace of mind when they no longer feel desperately that they must produce a biologic child. They are able to experience the treatment in a more positive and less loaded way. Completing the grief process is also good preparation for adoptive parenting. It means that they will be able to enjoy the child when they get it.

The final obstacle, but an important one, is raised on how to proceed. Most typically, the wife initiates trying for pregnancy. She is also the first to recognize a possible problem and suggest switching from a regular gynecologist to an infertility specialist. The husband often is lukewarm about that idea and prefers to go on as usual for another month or two. Once they switch to the infertility specialist, however, the woman seems to become pessimistic much more quickly and brings up the idea of adoption. The husband's response is, "How in the world can you be saying it won't work? How can you begin to think about adoption? We have just started treatment. We have been told our chances are very good. Of course medical science is going to work for us."

What has occurred here is that the wife has already begun to grieve the possibility that she will never have a biologic child. This is furthered by the fact that it is her body that is most directly involved. She knows whether she is pregnant or not. She knows what it feels like to get her period again. She has the physical reminders that her husband experiences second-hand.

Therefore, when couples talk about discontinuing treatment, it is usually the wife who brings it up. She is beginning to fantasize that an adopted baby would be wonderful and she wants to take the necessary steps to becoming a mother. She also feels that she would like to stop treatment. There is often a 4- to 6-month gap between what the wife is oriented toward and what her husband is oriented toward.

As professionals sometimes we panic when couples disagree. We might say, "You are either doing the treatment or not. You can't compromise on this. And you can't be an adoptive parent one year and not the next." Yet often just a few more weeks or a few more months is all that the more reluctant spouse needs to agree to say enough is enough or to agree to adopt.

When working with people who are disagreeing it helps to clarify where the disagreement lies. Perhaps the man is saying, "I am sort of willing to say enough is enough, but I don't want to adopt. If medical treatment doesn't work, I think we should be childless." The wife, however, is saying, "I really want to adopt." This couple has made an unconscious, unspoken pact that they are not going to discuss the matter because it is too frightening. They are afraid that they are going to end up divorced. Each one is afraid that the spouse is going to deny the other what he or she wants. Therefore they simply do not talk about it. Let's say the husband does not want to adopt and the wife does. He does have one positive thought about adoption, but he is not going to say it aloud, because he does not want his wife to say "On Tuesday, June 5, you said this positive thing about adoption, and that proves that you would be happy as an adoptive father." Conversely, say the couple visits friends who have three children under the age of 5. The children are unruly and undisciplined because the parents do not set limits for them. When the couple leaves, the wife walks out feeling, "Oh my God, that was awful. Maybe I don't want to be a mother." She is afraid to say that, however, because her husband is probably going to counter with, "See, you don't really want to be a parent either."

One of the things that these people have to be told is that they must say it aloud. It will not be written down, will not be tape-recorded, and it will not be held against them. Unless they give themselves the freedom to talk, however, they are not going to have a chance to work it out.

Frequently in this setting the partners become salespeople. The husband is trying to sell his wife on child-free living, and the wife is trying to sell her husband on adoption. They become marketing representatives instead of a couple working things out together. One vignette illustrates the dangers of this.

The wife said only positive things about adoption. She thought all of her problems would be over if the husband agreed to adopt. The couple visited friends who were newly adoptive parents, and the man absolutely fell in love with the adopted child. When leaving the friends' house, he turned to his wife and said, "Guess what. I have great news, I am ready to adopt. Let's call up the agency." Now the wife panics. She has spent the last 7 months selling her husband on adoption, and she has not had an opportunity to deal with her own terrors of motherhood in general and adoption in particular.

For such a couple it is important to encourage the partners not to remain entrenched in their polarized positions. They both have to understand what frightens them, what has to be worked out, and what appeals and what does not appeal about each option. The wife who favors adoption should read about child-free living, and talk to some couples who decided to remain child free after infertility. The husband who fears adoption should do some reading and visit couples who have adopted. Whatever they decide to do, it will be much more palatable if the spouse whose option was not chosen recognizes that the decision was reached based on well-informed perspectives.

Finally, the couple must be aware that there are no winners and losers. Whether one spouse talks the other into stopping before he or she is ready to stop, or into adoption, or whatever, they both are going to have to live with the consequences. Regardless of what their goal is with respect to becoming parents, another goal that cannot be set aside is their continuing, happy relationship.

Step Seven: Making a Decision About Simultaneous Pregnancy and Adoption

The seventh step in decision making is facing the possibility of pregnancy and adoption simultaneously, and deciding on it one way or the other. Some people pursue adoption too soon, as they have not finished grieving. They do not recognize that part of the anguish of infertility is not resolved by adopting a child. Adoption solves the childlessness problem, but it does not solve all the feelings of defectiveness, disappointment, and loss of fertility. Such couples are really using adoption as an insurance policy: if they cannot produce a child, at least they can adopt. In reality, they are not ready to adopt.

More frequently, however, couples who are in their late thirties to middle forties feel it is now or never for a child by either means. It used to be that adoption agencies across the board said a couple could not possibly be ready to adopt a baby if they were continuing medical treatment. This is no longer the case, although with some agencies the options become more limited over age 40. People who want to have two children and are afraid they are not even going to have one may especially feel the need to pursue both courses at the same time. It may make sense to start the adoption process and at the same time do one or two IVFs or GIFTs.

Many people who continue infertility treatment while applying for adoption will, if they adopt before they become pregnant, adopt a second child rather than go back to medical therapy. They looked at treatment as something that they had to do for their peace of mind before they closed the door to a biologic child altogether. It was a matter of peace of mind and a matter of one more way to pursue a child.

When I train adoption workers in this issue, I say that what you need to look for is, What is the insurance policy? Is the insurance policy for this couple adoption, and they really are dying for a biologic baby, or are they feeling at this point that they want to be parents in whatever way they can, and continuing with the medical program just in case that works faster than adoption does? The issue in such couples is where their energy is being expended. If 80 or 90% is going to adoption and 10 or 20% into medical treatment, they probably are ready to adopt.

People have to be aware of a few things if they are going to continue infertility treatment and apply for adoption. First, it causes high levels of stress to do both at the same time. Most couples going through infertility have two careers. Medical treatment is like one more full-time job, and pursuing adoption is another. Therefore, the couple should ease up in other areas. This is not the time to reciprocate on 6 months of dinner invitations. It is not the time to take on extra projects at work.

In the typical pattern, the wife assumes that if she becomes pregnant they will still want the baby the agency is preparing for them to adopt. The husband assumes that in such a case they will take their name off the agency's list. If his wife miscarries, they will return to adoption. It can be a shock if they thought their ideas were synchronized to find they are not. In fact, if they actually have different desires, they will not know what they will actually do if a pregnancy occurs. This points up the importance of communication. At least if they know that they disagree, and they have begun a dialogue, when pregnancy occurs they will have a basis for making a decision. Similarly, they must agree, or at least know that they disagree, on what they will do if they are offered a baby before they finish medical treatment.

As a rule, a couple sets a deadline of 3 or 4 more months of medical treatment before starting to put out feelers for an adoption. This makes sense; an adoption of any kind can take a year, if not two. It happens not infrequently, however, that they are offered an adopted child before they are finished with medical treatment. How do they deal with that? Do they take the child? Do they give themselves several months of being adoptive parents, and then come back to treatment? Do they take the child and continue treatment at the same time? Both partners must know their own and each their feelings openly they will be that much farther along in reaching a decision if the matter comes up.

Couples should be cautioned to avoid juxtaposition of medical and adoption activities. An adoption home study visit should not be scheduled for the same day as donor insemination or an ultrasound for IVF. Even if both partners have done 90% of their grieving and most of their energy is going into adoptive parenting, exciting medical news can be disorienting. Medical and adoption procedures should be separated at least by a day or two, if not by a week or two.

It is extremely important for people to seek an adoption agency that has a liberal policy about continuing infertility treatment and recognizes that these couples can be ready to adopt. These agencies are compassionate about people who are still trying and will ask, for example, how the GIFT cycle is going. If the GIFT cycle does not work, they can be supportive in the couple's disappointment.

Step Eight: Making the Decision

The kinds of decisions that couples have to make in deciding when enough is enough are traumatic; however, they do force couples to think about the meaning of life and death, and what they want to happen in their lives before they die that has not happened yet. It forces them to recognize that each one is a human being whose needs, interests, and timing may be different from those of the other. The kind of communication that is necessary to work all of this out, and the kind of soul searching that is necessary even in one's own decision making can really make for a wonderful marriage relationship and parenting experience.

Bibliography

1. Bombardieri M. The Baby Decision. New York: Rawson, Wade, 1981.
2. Rubin TI. Overcoming Indecisiveness: The Eight Stages of Effective Decision Making. New York: Harper & Row, 1985.
3. Yalom I. Existential Psychotherapy. New York: Basic Books, 1980:314–346.
4. Bombardieri M. Courage to mourn. Interview with Laurie Nee. Resolve Newsletter, June 1983.
5. Friedman R, Gradstian B. Surviving Pregnancy Loss. Boston: Little, Brown, 1982.
6. Menning B. Infertility: A Guide for the Childless Couple. Englewood Cliffs, NJ: Prentice Hall, 1988.
7. Panuthos C, Romeo C. Ended Beginnings. South Hadley, MA: Bergin and Garvery, 1984.
8. Sterns AK. Living Through Personal Crisis. IL: Thomas More, 1984.
9. Tatelbaum J. The Courage to Grieve. New York: Harper & Row, 1980.
10. Bombardieri M. Coping with the stress of infertility. Resolve publication.
11. The twenty minute rule. Free reprint sent out by Resolve as a sample newsletter page.
12. Bombardieri M. Tug-of-war or what to do when couples conflict. In: The Baby Decision. New York: Rawson, Wade, 1981.
13. Bower SA, Gordon H. Asserting Yourself. Reading, MA: Addison-Wesley, 1976.
14. Fisher R, Ury W. Getting to Yes. New York: Penguin, 1983.
15. Halas C. Why Can't a Woman Be More Like a Man? New York: Macmillan, 1981.
16. Mason MM. The Miracle Seekers. Fort Wayne, IN: Perspective Press, 1987.
17. Miller S, et al. Straight Talk: A New Way to Closeness with Others by Saying What You Really Mean. New York: N.A.K., 1982.
18. Naifeh S, Smith G. Why Can't Men Open Up? New York: Crown, 1984.
19. Rubin L. Intimate Strangers. New York: Harper & Row, 1983.
20. Childfree Decision Making. Resolve publication with specific guidelines for infertile couples.
21. Bombardieri M. Childfree living—the road not taken. Interview with Lynne Wood. Resolve Newsletter, September 1982.
22. Carter M, Carter J. Sweet Grapes: How to Stop Being Infertile and Start Living Again. Fort Wayne, IN: Perspectives Press, 1989.
23. Gilman L. The Adoption Resource Book. New York: Harper & Row, 1988.
24. Lasker JN, Borg S. In Search of Parenthood: Coping with Infertility and High-Tech Conception. Boston: Beacon Press, 1987.
25. Melina LR. Raising Adopted Children: A Manual for Adoptive Parents. New York: Harper & Row, 1986.
26. Menning B. Donor insemination—the psychosocial issues. Contemp OB Gyn 1981;18:155–172.
27. Plumez JH. Successful Adoption. How to and Decision Making About Adoption. Rev. ed. New York: Harmony Crown, 1987.
28. Schlaff W, Vercollone CF. Understanding Artificial Insemination: A Guide for Patients. Co-published by Resolve, Inc., and Zetek, Inc. National Resolve, 1987.

40
The Adoptee's Search: Who Are the Real Parents of Adopted Children?

Lyle L. Warner

Couples who have given up on infertility therapies often consider adoption as a last resort. Their wish for a biologic child to continue their family lines is relinquished. However, the longing to nurture a child remains, and adoption provides them that possibility.

It is important from the outset for medical providers to understand that in addition to the difficulties and strains of the adoption process, there are long-term challenges to adoptive parenting. One of the troubling uncertainties for prospective adoptive parents is whether the devotion, love, endless caring, and responsibility that they will commit to raising an adopted child will make them real parents and offer them an authentic experience of parenthood. Is it possible that the child will one day reject them and go in search of the mother who gave him or her birth? Will they lose the affections and loyalty of the child to whom they are devoted and to whom they will become as committed as they would have been if the child had come from their own bodies? They might wonder whether they will become mere surrogates when they view newspaper pictures depicting the excited meeting between a birth mother and the child she surrendered to the care of other parents. Will the adoptive parents be able to see a reflection of themselves in the child they have raised that is deeper than the color of the eyes or the shape of the body?

In the past the child's loss of his or her birth parents and the infertile couple's loss of a biologic child were denied. The loss endured by the birth parents also was dismissed. This is directly opposite to new models of open adoption which maintain the connection between children and their birth parents. Children formerly were not told they were adopted. Social workers placing children for adoption, following the advice of an eminent psychoanalyst[8], reversed this custom by insisting that adoptive parents pledge themselves to telling the truth. However, the full consequences of disclosure were not immediately understood. Children were told they were adopted, but the premise among professionals and parents was that the only significance was the way they entered the family. Many difficult questions followed: Who was my mother? Why did she give me away? Adoption professionals did not prepare parents to understand children's continuing search for the meaning of adoption. Questions about their original mother were discouraged, and children were left to wonder about the secrets of their birth and to hide fantasies about their lost parents. Adoptees changed our model in a profound way when they began to insist on searching for their original parents—lost but not forgotten.

Since the 1970s, adoptees have become increasingly interested in knowing their birth parents. Adults who were adopted as children coined the word "adoptee" to signify an identity and an experience of loss that lasts beyond childhood. In a parallel way, the term adoptive parents also distinguishes couples who adopt from birth parents, despite their years of immersion in the parenting role.

All of these social changes have raised the question, Who are the real parents of an adopted child? Does a severed blood relationship maintain primacy over the bonds of attachment which are created by years of loving and being there? From adoptees who have searched for their birth parents, we learn that the real parents, the parents whom they carry in their hearts and minds, who have become an essential part of themselves, are the adoptive parents.

Certainly from the child's point of view, the first importance of parents is security and love. Sadly, an adopted child has lost the security of the fantasy of an unbreakable connection between a child and the parents to whom he or she was born. The child's most fervent wish is that he or she had been born to the adoptive parents. Following childhood, the wish for an unbreakable connection may surface in a search for the birth parents. At the end of a search whose meaning has been fully explored, the loss of that fantasy of childhood will at last have been grieved.

Today the media often present stories of an adoptee's search as a romantic tale for his or her lost mother's mysterious past, and any clues that will connect the child to it. The story ends with a meeting of mother and child; the search has won its prize. One is left to imagine that they will live happily ever after. Loose ends, as in all romances and fairy tales, are unnoticed.

These media presentations depict the archetypal yearning to believe that a mother will love forever the child to whom she has given birth. There is also a common gratification in believing that a child's forgiveness for the mother who had abandoned him or her can become the basis of a relationship of exceptional fulfillment. Although the reunion is the end of the story in the sentimental version, this is not the case in reality.

A more complex quest emerges from an understanding of the roots and process of the child's search for the lost parents. Ultimately, the search is for the self.

"Who am I? To whom do I belong? Where did I come from?" These questions are asked when an adoptee begins a search. These are identity questions for everyone, but they are more difficult to answer when one is adopted. The answers cannot be found simply by reuniting with a stranger, even if the stranger is the birth mother.

When an adoptee sets out on a search, he or she often withdraws from adoptive relationships that appear to be a barrier to finding one's true self. Eventually, however, to know who they are, they must rediscover how their sense of self was influenced by their adoptive parents. When the birth parents become real people it is possible to disentangle and clarify the images of two sets of parents and to harmonize self-image conflicts.

In the best of circumstances, an adoptee can use the search to gain a feeling of wholeness that has been elusive. The mental images of two sets of parents warring for one's allegiance provide a conflictual basis for identity. A fully realized search can merge a harmonious sense of self with a coherent sense of one's psychologic roots.

Research Project

My view of the adoptee's search for the birth mother comes from a study that I completed in 1985[14]. I began with a notice in the newsletter of a local adoption organization, The Adoption Connection, which assists many adoptees and birth parents with searches. A voluntary sample of 30 woman was collected, 24 of whom had completed the search. With few exceptions, they had come to their adoptive parents by 6 months of age. When I met them, they ranged in age from 22 to 46 years (median 31 years).

When I began, women were in an overwhelming majority as searchers. There are no reliable figures, but a frequently quoted statistic was that 97% are women. The relative percentages have not changed much since then[12]. My findings rest solely on women's experiences, but the themes of loss in adoption are universal. Many of the most important conclusions reported can be expected to be significant for men as well as women.

I was afraid that my method of voluntary recruitment might bring me a skewed sample that would include only those whose experiences had been happy. What I might have known is that people volunteer for their own reasons. One woman could choose to be interviewed because she felt gratified by the events of her search and reunion and wanted to portray a positive view of the search to the social work and adoption community. Another might seek the opportunity of the interview because hers had been a painful experience and she longed for the opportunity to talk about it to someone who might listen with special understanding. Most of my informantion is from women who were still actively processing reunions, which had usually taken place within the last year.

I gathered my data in semistructured, life review interviews that lasted between 2 and $2\frac{1}{2}$ hours. I also used a psychologic instrument for a formal assessment of the level and content of the subjects' mental representations: how they perceived the separateness, integrity, and motivations of others.

Although adoptees also search for birth fathers, I soon discovered that it is the search for the birth mother that has the greatest meaning. Thus I chose to focus on this aspect.

Literature reviews typically list a number of different types of papers. None are academic psychologic studies that investigate the intrapsychic phenomena of the search. This study examined the experience itself in the context of these adoptees' memories of their adoptive relationships, particularly with respect to learning about the meaning of adoption. It included changes in the thinking, feelings, fantasies, and expectations of adoptees and in their self and mother images during four periods: deciding to search, during the search, meeting their mothers, and the postmeeting period, at the time of the interview.

I believe the adoptee's search is for the self: for a more positive, more integrated, more affectively stable sense of identity. An important task is grieving for the dissolution of the first connections and removing the stain of a spoiled adoptive identity. That search is successful when the sense of self and identity is enriched, when there is a firmer sense of the meaning of both one's adoptive and biologic connections.

My case studies have allowed the formation of a general model of adoptee development through their searching. For the adoptee the process of integrating her divided identity begins when she decides on a search. By claiming an adoptive identity, for the first time she is no longer denying the difference that adoption has made to her feelings about herself. Guided by her memories of childhood resistance to the idea of adoption, we can understand why she seemed to forget all about it after being told at the age of 4. She didn't want to know, and as an adult she may continue to believe that adoption has not affected her sense of self and that it has no meaning in her life. In searching, the issue comes up into consciousness, revealing itself like a hidden text. Claiming an adoptive identity and setting out to discover her first parents, the adoptee discovers a new narrative form for telling her story.

When did she first know that she was adopted? The question begins to peel back layers of experience. She was told early; she can hardly remember when she didn't know; perhaps she has rueful memories of her comforting chosen baby story; or she may have a memory of a momentous occasion of being told more than she could assimilate—that her mother had not given birth to her. Then silence. Elliptical answers to her questions about her other mother; confusing answers to the question of why she was given away. She learned that asking these questions made her parents sad. She hid the wonderings that threatened disloyalty, finding an unadmitted protection for her own fears. To whom did she really belong? She had retreated, keeping a part of herself hidden, unrelated.

Out of the experience with her adoptive mother she had created two mothers. Her images could be analogous to the sun and the moon. From the sun has come warmth, and the light that reveals the moon—a mysterious image, sometimes bright, sometimes in shadow. The sun, the center of her universe, is her adoptive mother—a steady presence in her life. Without her there would be no self. The moon, a reflection of the sun, is her birth mother.

Idealized fantasies about her birth mother fantasies that make her feel good about herself, have their roots in her infant experience with her adoptive mother. They may again be experienced upon meeting her birth mother. They contain hopes that her mother only wanted what she wanted and that she had the power to make all wishes come true.

In addition to her fantasies, she has attempted to imagine the separate reality of her birth mother's life and choices. For this endeavor she has very little information, and she is working against a longstanding impression that her adoptive mother holds a devalued view of her birth mother according to the needs that arise from her encounters with her adoptive mother and her emerging sense of self.

She might set aside her questions concerning her other mother, finding reassurance in the parents' conviction that the only difference made by adoption was how she had come into the family. Or the search for the meaning of adoption might be pursued secretly: fears about loss, about the fragility of the adoptive connections endured in lonely silence.

The secret fantasies of her other mother, which comforted her when she felt misunderstood or her wishes were denied, have been banished. Now they interfere with her search for truth. These fantasies became buried by her adolescent confrontations with the realities of sex and unwanted pregnancy, giving way to images of a bad mother and raising fears of a bad self.

Following childhood she moves from her adoptive home and begins a life of her own that leaves adoption behind. One day, however, the old questions are back, prompted perhaps by a loss, her won pregnancy, or the realization that something about her life feels stuck. A new way of thinking about her lost connections gives her courage to confront her past. From the back of her mind, the idea of searching for her birth parents emerges.

The bad image of her birth mother that settled in her mind in adolescence is subjected to an adult's considerations of the realities that force a woman to relinquish a child. The testimony of others who have searched before her awakens a new image of a woman who has been unfairly judged because of one long-past mistake. A more motherly image takes its

place. She has begun to forgive her mother and herself. Anger about the deception she suffered begins to liberate her wish to go back to her beginnings.

She separates her quest from her adoptive relationships. She tries to assure herself that this is not an abandonment of her adoptive parents. She believes they will be hurt and accuse her of disloyalty. Will she have to go forward without their blessing? Does she dare to risk the abandonment she fears if she tells them?

When the search begins, it releases enormous emotional turmoil and causes a reexamination of self feelings and their sources. Her conflicted images of two mothers create a divided sense of self. The image of her adoptive mother creates an unwanted feeling of separateness which causes her to disavow her identifications with her adoptive mother. The image of her birth mother feels like an undifferentiated part of her self-image. What earlier had felt like the bad part of herself now represents her hopes for the realization of her ideal self.

To find her birth mother she must follow a disconnected line of clues, breaking through the legal barriers that oppose her wish; often she will think she has come to a dead end. In addition, as her birth mother begins to emerge from her fantasies to assume the characteristics of a real person, a new question absorbs her: will her birth mother be receptive to a meeting?

She cannot share her search with her adoptive mother because of her fears of abandonment and because she needs distance from her. She would like to shed the imprint on her self-image of her adoptive mother's inevitable limitations and failures, of her real or imagined disappointments in her adopted daughter.

At the time of meeting her birth mother, the most crucial question arises, framing the wish to believe that her birth was meaningful, that in some sense she was wanted. It is a happy experience for the adoptee whose birth mother welcomes her with evidence that she has grieved her loss, that she had not been forgotten, that she was cared about at birth. All sorts of differences can be forgiven if she gains the belief that she was not rejected. That childhood fear had persisted despite an adult's knowledge of the realities of the surrender of children for adoption.

Meeting her mother, an adoptee may unknowingly recapitulate her first experiences with her adoptive mother. The relationship may begin like that first love affair, bringing the good feelings that come from a sense of oneness, of deep similarities and understanding. The fantasies of finding the perfect mother who could bring about the birth of the ideal self, until now not permitted into consciousness, may take over the reality. Eventually, however, the illusion of an inseparable union will have to be relinquished.

The meeting may occasionally lead to an enduring and evolving relationship or the relationship may soon fade, unincorporated into the adoptee's life, and limited to the exchange of greeting cards and birth announcements. In the best outcomes, regardless of how the relationship wears, the effects of meeting the birth mother have dynamic repercussions. As enhanced feelings about herself take hold, feelings about her adoptive parents begin to shift. Now her identifications with them are recognized, the mixture of learned and inherited characteristics can be explored, and the rewards and failures of these relationships can be viewed in a new light. It becomes clear that a parent is the person who has taken care.

Just as the image of the birth mother had been developed from the experience with the adoptive mother, it is now discoverable that the image of the adoptive mother may have borrowed some of its affective tone from the unassimilable fear of a primary rejection. Anger that derived from fears of an earlier rejection sometimes has been displaced onto the relationship with the adoptive mother. Could she ever have loved her enough to make up for the first rejection? Her feeling of belonging to her adoptive parents has been given new strength through her encounter with her birth mother and her uncovering of the meaning of her past. As once she had been chosen, now she can choose her parents.

But what if the search fails? Failure is the story of the unhappy reunion, of the mother who refuses to acknowledge her daughter or a daughter who finds a mother who is only disappointing, when the meeting becomes another rejection or the adoptee becomes the rejecter. The adoptee who lacks the capacity to disentangle her image of herself from her image of her birth mother, and who has a disastrous encounter with her, must feel that, like Lot's wife, she has looked back and has been punished beyond endurance. She has failed and the failure proves her own inferiority.

The fortunate adoptee was the one who had been prepared by good enough parenting to retrieve a good and even a more wholesome sense of self from a troubling search outcome. She could fall back on strength, on a mature view of otherness, in time creating a newly separate and loving image of herself, leaving behind the frailty and bitterness of the other, saving some glimmer of the positive qualities that had been visible even in a frustrating encounter. It took time to triumph over misery. In these circumstances some are able to realize the gains and some fail. That also can be true when the reunion outcome is pleasing. In either case, when the meeting outcome is satisfying or when it is disturbing, the eventual outcome for the preservation and enhancement of a good sense of self depends on psychologic maturity.

One can wonder whether the prevalent childhood fantasy of having been adopted lends extra resistance to our culture's doubts about the legitimacy of adoptive relationships. Both adoptees and adoptive parents describe tactless comments they have endured from people who simply cannot believe that the bonds of adoption are as real as those of biologically connected children and parents. The real story of the search, however, demonstrates the primary place of adoptive parents in their children's lives and loves. An adoptee, like many a fabled heroine, undertakes a quest that leads to a discovery of her true home.

The Role of the Professional

As professionals who become involved in helping infertile couples to sort out their desires and capacities with respect to the choice of adoption, it is important that we convey a positive conviction about the authenticity of adoptive parenting. Their most important tie with their adoptive children is the one that will provide the basic sources of security and identity. They need strong confirmation of their parenting roles so that they can give themselves wholeheartedly and empathically to their children.

A counterbalance to the culture's doubts must also be built in. Especially at this time when open adoption is putting emphasis on the ties to birth parents, adoptive parents must be assured of their privacy. We must hope that all the professionals they encounter before they become parents will view as a major part of their task to give them empowerment in the role they are undertaking: they will be the real parents.

Parents who feel confident of their importance will have a better chance of reading their children's needs and of knowing when the fact of the adoptive history makes them different. They will have less need to deny the differences that adoption makes, but they also will be less likely to blame adoption for the struggles their children will share with all children. They will see their children as children first of all, just as they see themselves as parents first of all, with adoption as an added circumstance that does not change the basic requirements. They will understand that their children's first need is for secure attachment, and they will not be persuaded to follow advice that might jeopardize that essential early confidence.

The parents will have to remain constant in their belief in the essential place of their love and caring when their children test their bonds. For example, as children weather the storms adolescence often brings for adoptive relationships, they must be assured that they will not be abandoned. When children ask questions about their separate origins, the parents will fall back on the conviction that they have established an irrevocable bond and they will not give way to their fears of competing allegiances to other parents. Freer to follow

their intuitive feelings, they will understand that these questions come from a child's search for self. Adoptive parents who feel secure in their role will enable their children to fall back on confidence in secure attachments.

In the context of the decision to search, adoptees emphasize childhood dissatisfactions with their adoptive parents; what felt bad, what they wished had been different. This is part of the process of separating their images of themselves from their images of their adoptive parents. They feel the necessity to justify an action that seems disloyal to parents and even to their own affections. The issues are attachment and separateness, the fear of not belonging, the fear that separateness can become a loss of connection, alienation.

In a culture that has declared the importance of roots and in which ever new discoveries are made of the influence of genetic factors, it is likely that the search for birth parents will continue to entice. The healthy and adaptive goal is to prepare a child to do a good search, one that will result in a more harmonious sense of self.

Preparation for a good search could be the title for a guide for adoptive parents. This begins at the time of adoption. Whether or not they meet the surrendering parents, anticipating their child's need to know about them, they will learn as much as they can about the birth parents and their circumstances.

The next preparation is to build a secure attachment, the developmental goal of the early years that takes precedence over other concerns. It is the imprint of our earliest, most gratifying relationships with our parents that creates our expectations of love. This is a prime requisite for a good search. Adoptees who do not have this experience, or do not have enough of it, will go forward lacking essential optimism.

Open recognition of losses is the adoptive parents' special responsibility. They must first remember the child's loss and the vulnerability to loss that will remain. Second comes acceptance of their own enduring feelings of loss. From this recognition can come empathy for the child's feelings of loss. As the child progresses toward creating a separate identity, the issue will make hers a more tangled passage to adulthood. This is the reason why separation issues acquire extra meaning in adoptive relationships.

Instead of denying the separateness of their beginnings, adoptive parents must be available to talk about the separateness of adoption and about the child's origins and feelings of loss on many occasions. In acknowledging the divided beginnings in an atmosphere of warmth and acceptance, new connections are built. Paradoxically, talk about the feelings that belong to separate origins can weave new feelings of connection. When feelings about separate origins are hidden, however, the feelings of alienation are increased.

The adoptive parents who feel themselves to be the real parents will have taken a step toward seeing their real child. That does not mean that the fact of adoption can be dismissed. Instead, the conviction of being the real parents must be a certainty that adoptive parenting, despite its special twists and turnings and vulnerability to further loss, has an equal legitimacy with all other parenting. It is real parenting and neither counterfeit nor less because it is different.

Bibliography

1. Brinich PM. Adoption from the inside out: A psychoanalytic perspective. In: Brodzinsky DM, Schechter MD, eds. The Psychology of Adoption. New York: Oxford University Press, 1990:42–61.
2. Burgess LC. Adoption: How It Works. Tilton, NH: Saint Bani Press, 1989.
3. Dunne JG. Quintana. In: Dunne JG. Quintana and Friends. New York: Pocket Books, 1980.
4. Erikson EH. Identity crisis in autobiographic perspective. In: Erikson EH. Life Crisis and the Historical Moment. New York: Norton, 1975.
5. Fraiberg S. The origins of human bonds. In: Fraiberg L, ed. Selected Writings of Selma Fraiberg. Columbus: Ohio State University Press, 1987:3–26.
6. Kirk D. Shared Fate. New York: Free Press, 1964.
7. Knight RP. Some problems involved in selecting and rearing adopted children. Bull Menn Clin 1941:65–74.
8. Krementz J. How it feels to be adopted. New York: Alfred A. Knopf, 1982.
9. Lifton BJ. Twice Born: Memoirs of an Adopted Daughter. New York: McGraw-Hill, 1975.
10. Nickman SL. Losses in adoption: The need for dialogue. In: Solnit A, Eissler R, Neubauer P, eds. The Psychoanalytic Study of the Child. New Haven: Yale University Press, 1985;40:365–398.
11. Pearson S. Phantasie. New York: Broadway Play Publishing, 1989.
12. Schecter MD, Bertocci D. The meaning of the search. In: Brodzinsky DM, Schecter MD, eds. The Psychology of Adoption. New York: Oxford University Press, 1990:62–90.
13. Warner LL. Adopted women's search for the biological mother: A developmental perspective. Unpublished doctoral dissertation, Smith College School for Social Work, Northampton, MA, 1985.
14. Jette SH. The adoption alternative. In: Seibel MM, ed. Infertility: A Comprehensive Text. Norwalk, CT: Appleton & Lange, 1990.

41
Parenting After Infertility

Ellen Glazer

When a child finally arrives, whether by birth or adoption, most parents who have experienced infertility are filled with delight. Not only do they have a child to be with and care for, but they have also been freed from the torment of their childlessness. Life is no longer on hold. They have a car seat in their car and diapers in their shopping cart. They have—at long last—joined the world of parents.

But parenting after infertility is different in some ways from parenting without this history. Some of these ways add to the pleasures of parenting: what are small events for other parents can feel like momentous occasions for those who waited so long to experience them. Similarly, things that are frustrating and upsetting to fertile parents often seem inconsequential to those who suffered the long-term pain and frustration of infertility treatments. Then there are the ways in which a history of infertility does not feel like a gift to parenting, ways in which it feels like a burden.

Absence of Family Planning

Soon after the arrival of their first child, infertile parents realize that while their lives feel full, their families are incomplete. Their fertile friends can relax and enjoy their first child, talking idly about timing and spacing a second. They, by contrast, must take a serious look, early on, at when and how they will expand their families.

Advances in the new reproductive technologies and changes in adoption practice make this all the more complicated. Some couples who adopt decide, especially in light of the new treatments, to make one more try at pregnancy. Others, who may finally have had a successful pregnancy, decide for many reasons to turn to adoption for their second.

Those who turn—or return—to the assisted reproductive technologies know that they may have a multiple birth resulting in more children than they are prepared to raise.

Not Quite in the "Club"

While they are in the midst of infertility treatments, most patients feel that they are excluded from a "club" of parents (especially one of mothers) and that they are noticeable for their nonmembership. Once they finally join the club, they take great pleasure in this long-awaited affiliation.

For example, the club meets in the pool at the Y during "Baby Swim and Gym." There is the infertile new mother, bouncing her baby in the water with the rest of them. "Smile," she tells herself, "you're a member." But she is not. Not quite. Once everyone is dry and clothed, the club reconvenes in the snack bar. The babies are asleep in their strollers and the mothers are busy talking about labor and delivery, about nursing, about timing and spacing a second. They are complaining about stretch marks and weight gain. The infertile mother feels like an outsider. If her baby was adopted, she may feel that the others are confirming the fact that she is not a "real" mother: their conversation implies that pregnancy, labor, and delivery are key criteria for motherhood.

Even the infertile mother who has had a successful pregnancy feels like an outsider. She doesn't care if her labor was long, not after a 7-year bout with infertility. She doesn't mind the stretch marks; they are a reminder of her pregnancy. And she can't talk about timing and spacing because she has learned that she will take her children as they come, when they come.

The Imprint of Childlessness

Fertile couples go from being child free to having children. Infertile couples, by contrast, have experienced a prolonged period of child-lessness which has left an indelible mark. They can remember it at a moment's notice. Many of their actions and reactions are governed by a fear that they will again be childless.

Because fertile couples have not been traumatized by childlessness, they maintain a comfortable reference point. Time away from their children, whether for work or for pleasure, is accepted, often celebrated. It is not attached to a threat of loss. They can nourish their relationship and replenish themselves without fearing punishment.

Infertile couples frequently find it painful to be away from their child, especially when they are away together. Infertility has taught them that things go wrong: that if a misfortune is going to happen to 1 in 100 or 1,000, it could happen to them. Infertility has instructed them to stand guard against loss. Because marriages, friendships, and careers require time spent away from children, infertile couples have to try to develop a child-free reference point. Most realize that their child needs them to do this: if they do not begin to separate now, they will have problems later on.

Difficulties with Discipline

The child that arrives after long-term infertility is often treated like a little crown prince or princess. Sometimes the parents find it difficult to discipline the child. They say to themselves, "What he is doing really isn't so bad. After all, look how special he is."

Parents who fail to discipline their children often come to regret it. The little prince becomes a growing tyrant. The little princess expects that the world is her due. Difficult as it may be initially, parents usually realize, fairly early on, that they will simply create new problems if they delay in establishing rules and setting limits with their child.

Privacy and Secrecy

Infertility forces couples to take the most private area of their lives out of the bedroom and into the doctor's office. Many, in fact, take it further: into an operating room and laboratory. Those who adopt agree to further intrusions on their privacy: they open their lives to the scrutiny of adoption agencies. When they finally become parents they find that decisions have to be made about privacy and about secrecy.

When parents go out with a baby, strangers feel they have license to make comments about the baby, even to ask questions. This can tap into the vulnerabilities of parents who have experienced infertility. This is especially true for adoptive parents who sometimes feel compelled to tell strangers that their child is adopted, for fear that withholding this information means they are being secretive (and hence ashamed of adoption). However, it is also true for others, especially those who have had multiple births after taking Pergonal. What do they say, for example, when a stranger asks them if twins run in the family?

I encourage parents to begin reclaiming their privacy early on. They would not normally reveal personal information to strangers they meet on the street, so there is no reason for them to tell people the details of their child's origins. When strangers comment that the child is pretty, they can say, "Thank you." When people ask where the child got his blond curls, they can say whatever they want, recognizing that they are not being secretive: they are simply establishing and maintaining the boundaries of their families.

Questions about privacy do not vanish with a child's infancy. Grade school applications often ask direct questions about pregnancy, labor, and delivery. Some ask questions about adoption. Others leave room for parents to volunteer information. Parents must continue to sort out for themselves what should be told and what they prefer to keep private. Most find that it is always best to err on the side of privacy, since they can always tell people more another time, but it is impossible to withdraw information once told.

The "Deal with the Devil"

Infertile couples, desperate for a child, make imaginary promises. "If we are ever able to have a child, I promise to be eternally grateful. If I am able to carry this pregnancy, I promise never to complain." And so it goes.

Now these earnest bargainers are parents. Now they are tired, deprived of free time, and perplexed by all the new challenges that they face on a daily basis. They realize, to their embarrassment and fear, that they have made promises they cannot keep. They begin to feel as if they have made a "deal with the devil."

At the same time that they recognize that they have entered into an impossible agreement and wonder if they might chance going back on their promises, parents who have suffered with infertility realize that their fertile friends face no such dilemma. Once again, they are different.

I encourage infertile parents to see their deal with the devil for what it is: an example of magical thinking. They have to try to put it aside, recognize that it has no real hold on them, and free themselves up to complain, feel disappointed, and acknowledge that parenthood is not always all it's cracked up to be. I encourage them also to stray from their definition of "perfect parents" and recognize that this will be beneficial for their children, as it will free them from any obligation to be "perfect children."

Being Older Parents

For a number of reasons having to do with the length of their infertility or with delayed parenting, infertile parents are often older.

Many are relieved to find that they still have a great deal of youthfulness in them and that fears of losing energy were unfounded. On the other hand, many also find that the arrival of their child coincides with other midlife events: friends are sick, parents are aging, other couples are going through divorce or trying to adjust to an empty nest.

Couples must learn to acknowledge that lost time is often the biggest and most enduring cost of infertility. True, they are parents; true, their lives are no longer on hold; but it is also true that other people's lives have been progressing at the same time. For grandparents the passage of time has taken a special toll.

Infertile parents are often deeply saddened to realize that their parents are unable to be the grandparents that they would have been 5 or 10 years earlier, had things gone as planned. This is especially painful if grandparents die or develop a serious illness, but it is also painful for those who are simply aging normally. The 40-year old mother may be delighted to find that she has as much stamina (and more patience) as she had at 30, but she may also be troubled to see how different her own mother is at 70 than she was at 60. A couple may look at their aging parents and realize that they probably will not live for milestones such as a bar mitzvah or high school graduation.

Other Losses

Beyond the loss of time and all that it involves, infertile parents are faced with other losses. There were the children never conceived, as well as those who were conceived but not carried to term. There were adoptions that never happened: birth mothers who changed their minds or political eruptions that interfered with international placements.

As they close the ranks of their families, I encourage them to say another good-bye to these "missing persons." The losses will remain with them, but it is important to try to get some closure so that they can truly celebrate the family that they do have. For some couples this means planting a tree or writing a poem. For others, it involves acknowledging that they had names for their unborn and never-adopted children and that these ones were indeed different from the ones that they chose for their real children. What is important is not how they acknowledge these losses, but rather that they find some means for establishing the boundaries of their families.

Although a legacy of infertility carries with it some extra burdens, many couples feel grateful to have infertility as a reference point. Recognizing that parenting is a difficult, often exhausting, and thankless job, they appreciate being able to call upon memories of childlessness. They know firsthand that it feels much better to get up to feed a baby several times in the middle of the night than it does to awaken, well rested, to the somber greeting of a thermometer. A toddler's worst tantrum pales by comparison to the frustration and despair that they felt each time a menstrual period demolished their hopes of pregnancy.

Suggested Reading

1. Andrews L. Between Strangers. New York: Harper & Row, 1989.
2. Glazer E, Cooper S. Without Child: Experiencing and Resolving Infertility. Lexington, MA: Lexington Books, 1990.
3. Glazer E. The Long-Awaited Stork: A Guide to Parenting After Infertility. Lexington, MA: Lexington Books, 1990.
4. Melina L. Making Sense of Adoption. New York: Harper & Row, 1989.
5. Noble E. Having Your Baby by Donor Insemination. Houghton Mifflin, 1987.
6. Smith J, Mirof F. You're Our Child. Washington, DC: University Press of America, 1981.

42
Public Policy and the New Technologies

Gary B. Ellis

Media representation of an issue is an important driver of public policy. Senators, congressmen, state legislators, and other political figures all receive as much information from the newspaper and electronic media as from any other single source. For this reason I maintained a 7-day surveillance watching for stories in the national media related to fertility and infertility. The information that came to my attention through my surveillance could reasonably be expected to come to the attention of policy makers. As it turns out, it was an unremarkable week for reproductive issues; I only picked up four items. First, the June issue of *Money* had a story on America's top 15 careers, one of which is infertility doctor. The article described infertility as a growing industry. The word industry has been used referring to the increase in office visits for infertility that occurred through the 1980s. I suspect that that single statistic is what impressed the editors at *Money* to proclaim infertility doctor as one of the 15 most promising careers. It included salary quotes, the number of patient visits that can be anticipated, the number of technologies that are proliferating, and some fundamental new technologies.

Second, the *Los Angeles Times* had two classified ads. The first said, "Give the gift of life, help a childless couple become a family through the in vitro fertilization process. Carry the biological child of an infertile couple. Previous childbirth required. Call attorney at [a Los Angeles area number]." The second ad on the same page said, "Be a surrogate mother. Help a childless couple."

Third, *U.S.A. Today*'s classified section had six ads under A for adoption. I don't imagine this issue of the paper is any different from any other day.

Finally, the *Wall Street Journal* has a column in which they run statistical items from time to time. I spotted a paragraph documenting that over 4 million babies were born in the United States in 1989, the most recorded since the baby boom ended in 1964 according to the National Center for Health Statistics.

Taken together, these four items picked up in a casual surveillance deliver a mixed message to policy makers. First, infertility is a serious problem, one that the medical profession is actively pursuing. Next, couples are seeking novel, sometimes desperate, solutions to their infertility. Yet the largest number of babies in 25 years was born in the United States in 1989. This last fact is so impressive that it might lead a policy maker to dismiss infertility as a matter of public concern. Therefore, the question really becomes whether or not we care about infertility as a public policy matter. If 100% of the population were infertile, this would be our highest priority. If we did not attend to it in a generation, we would all be gone. In fact, about 8.4% of couples in which the woman is aged 15 to 44 years are infertile; that is, about 1 in 12.

There is something unsatisfying or inappropriate in looking for a threshold of caring based on population statistics saying 8.4% of couples are infertile. Should we care or should we not care? We know that for an individual couple, resolving infertility is probably the highest priority in their lives. As a society, we ought to proceed with the finding that infertility is of sufficient importance to a sufficient number of people that action is warranted. That may sound sophomoric but if we cannot declare that a problem affects a sufficient number of people who are concerned at a sufficient level, then no policy action is going to be taken.

The authoritative source of data on which public policy related to infertility is based is the National Center for Health Statistics, which is part of the Department of Health and Human Services (DHHS). The center's National Survey of Family Growth reports all reproductive statistics, from contraceptive use, to family planning clinic visits, to number of infertile couples.

The survey was conducted in 1982 and 1988. Between January and June 1988 about 9,000 American women, a nationally projectable sample, were interviewed for 60 to 70 minutes. The data are now analyzed, and the number of couples who were infertile in 1988 is no different than it was in 1982. This is a significant fact. Interest in infertility has increased; the number of options available has increased; the number of office visits has increased; the amount of money has increased; media attention has increased. But the underlying phenomenon does not appear to have changed. The overall infertility rate does not appear to have changed between 1982 and 1988, or for 10 or 15 years prior to that through the 1970s.

Aside from collecting data, the federal government has acted on several fronts with respect to new reproductive technologies. The Ethics Advisory Board of the DHHS existed until the beginning of the 1980s. It was required to review research proposals that would involve human in vitro fertilization (IVF). Failure to reappoint the board falls on the heads of three administrations. The board expired in 1980 at the end of the Carter administration and no members were appointed to continue it. The whole Reagan administration passed with no board, and there was still no action during the Bush administration.

In 1986 Congress exerted its oversight over the DHHS. Congressman Ted Weiss of New York made the DHHS promise to revive the Ethics Advisory Board so that research related to human IVF could proceed. In September 1988 the DHHS published a charter in the Federal Register for a revived board. Public comments came in. The Reagan administration then ended, and no action was taken. As the matter stands now, the government has put out a proposed charter to revive the board but has not proceeded actually to do it.

The federal government still does not have the ability to support research that involves human IVF. This has dire consequences for couples who would avail themselves of this technology. I do not say that to denigrate the practitioners of IVF or the science that exists now, but I do suggest that the situation in the United States would be much further along if the federal research engine had been turned on since the 1980s.

What do the next 10 years hold with respect to federal support for IVF? I cannot be optimistic. We are talking about research that involves biologic material during the time from conception to birth, the 9 months that are absolutely the most politically sensitive time of human growth and development. It is a political football that no one will throw, and if someone were to throw it, no one would catch it. I do not believe that, either soon or in coming years, the government is going to resolve this issue of federal funding through the National Institutes of Health for research to support human IVF and all the spinoffs that would come from that sort of research. In contrast, the animal world has good funding, and excellent progress has been made with reproductive research and biology involving animals.

In August 1984 Congressman Albert Gore held hearings on human embryo transfer. This was in the wake of Baby Louise's birth 6 years earlier. At the beginning of the 1980s the Jones Institute in the United States had the first in vitro baby. In the summer of 1984 Congress focused on this with a hearing, an important landmark.

In 1985 Congress asked its in-house research office, the Office of Technology Assessment, to produce a report on reproductive technologies. The report came out in May 1988 and was followed by a flurry of activity in the Congress partly as a result of its findings and partly for other reasons.

The focus was on two aspects of infertility as a policy issue. First was the expression of success rates by the growing number of IVF clinics around the country. There was concern that as a result of shuffling numerators and denominators of the success rate or refusing to reveal all success rates, couples were not getting the best information, or at worst were being misled by some clinics.

Machelle Seibel wrote an important editorial about delivering a fraction of the truth that was very well received. Hearings were held by Congressman Ron Wyden about this issue, and his subcommittee conducted a survey that compelled the 150 or so IVF clinics in existence at that time to report to Congress their success rates in an identifying fashion; in other words, with the clinic name associated. This congressional effort broke the code of anonymity that had existed. Clinics were contributing their success rates on an anonymous basis to the American Fertility Society and the group data had been published, but that did not necessarily help a couple going to a particular clinic to know what that clinic's record was.

In May 1989 Congressman Wyden's subcommittee published a book with the responses from about 140 clinics listing their success rates. This effort will not be repeated, but perhaps it illustrates how congressional oversight is exerted in a positive way, because the American Fertility Society and its contractor will continue this effort and begin to publish success rates on an identifying basis.

The General Accounting Office, another research office within Congress, conducted a survey of human embryo laboratories and published its report in December 1989. It makes the point that common standards or a regularization of laboratory practices would probably be a good thing across the board in IVF laboratories. Congress may consider this issue in making that formal law in the near future. Congressman Wyden introduced a bill that would set up standards for human embryo

laboratories, and the House passed it in summer 1992.

Congresswoman Patricia Schroeder and Senator Tom Harkin have introduced identical bills that focus on basic research. The bills would direct the National Institutes of Health to set up five research centers, three on contraception research and two on infertility research. Some senior senators and congressmen and congresswomen have signed on as sponsors of these bills. Their seniority and their power may be enough to move this legislation along. It would be a dramatic event if Congress passed these laws and directed the National Institutes of Health to support this research, since for 10 years at least one subset of research involving human IVF has been blocked. We watch the fate of these bills very closely.

In December 1990 Congressman Weiss' subcommittee made certain findings in a report entitled "Infertility in America, Why Is the Federal Government Ignoring a Major Health Problem?" A brief discussion of the findings of the committee and its recommendations may provide clues as to where the government is going.

First, the staff and funding at the Centers for Disease Control for sexually transmitted diseases, an important cause of infertility, are inadequate. The committee found that increasing federal funds to study and control sexually transmitted disease would actually save money by decreasing the cost associated with infertility and other complications. It also noted that the DHHS commitment to Congress to appoint a new Ethics Advisory Board had not been kept.

Second, infertile American couples are paying more for ineffective services because of the lack of federally funded research on assisted conception techniques. In addition, research on male infertility has lagged behind that on female infertility. Federal funds are needed for more research on male infertility.

The committee recommended that Congress increase the Centers for Disease Control staff and funding relevant to sexually transmitted diseases, that the government appoint an

Ethics Advisory Board, and that the DHHS increase research efforts to study infertility. It went further, however, and this recommendation may give a clue to the future: the DHHS should fund a national data bank to include follow-up information on the offspring resulting from IVF, gamete intrafallopian transfer (GIFT), surrogacy procedures, and other assisted conception procedures, as well as the health of the women receiving infertility treatment. This perhaps falls in the category of recommendations that are somewhat debatable.

We have a tendency to think of the couple who avail themselves of a high-tech conception as perhaps requiring a high-tech pregnancy, and then a data bank for their children and themselves. It is difficult to know where intervention should logically cease. This committee at least is thinking of a national data bank for follow-up information for the children and the parents who use these technologies.

Whatever the results, policy through the next years will likely be driven, as it has in the past, by extraordinary events rather than by day-to-day information. If the 1980s were the decade of achieving conception in a dish, the 1990s may well be the decade of manipulating human embryos in that dish. Certainly, the manipulation of animal embryos is already well underway, which would suggest that this is going to be technically possible. Conferences are now being conducted to discuss preimplantation genetics. Preimplantation genetics means in vitro fertilization followed by removal of one cell for analysis of its genetic material. It is, in essence, a biopsy being performed on the embryo before implantation. This kind of procedure is going to fall into the category of extraordinary news.

In summary, it is difficult for public policy makers to discuss the sexual topics usually reserved for private conversation, but such frank and open discussion by legislators and by other leaders will be necessary and absolutely imperative if infertile couples are to be treated fairly and if research to help them is to proceed.

Suggested Reading

1. US Congress, Office of Technology Assessment. Infertility: Medical and Social Choices. Washington, DC: US Government Printing Office, 1988.
2. US House of Representatives, Committee on Small Business, Subcommittee on Regulation, Business Opportunities, and Energy. Consumer Protection Issues Involving In Vitro Fertilization Clinics, Serial 101–105. Washington, DC: US Government Printing Office, March 9, 1989.
3. US House of Representatives, Committee on Government Operations. Infertility In America: Why Is The Federal Government Ignoring a Major Health Problem? House Report 101–389. Washington, DC: US Government Printing Office, December 1, 1989.
4. Ellis GB. Revival of the ethics advisory board. Science 1988;242:168.
5. Seibel MM. In vitro fertilization success rates: A fraction of the truth. Obstet Gynecol 1988; 72:265–266.
6. Phillips DP, Kanter EJ, Bednarczyk, Tastad PL. Importance of the lay press in the transmission of medical knowledge to the scientific community. N Engl J Med 1991;325:1180–1183.

43
The Legal Response to the New Reproductive Technologies

Susan L. Crockin

Reproductive technology is changing the way we create families. In turn, the ways in which society, policy makers, and lawmakers view the family is changing. The explosion in reproductive technology since the birth of Louise Brown in England in 1978 has stretched the concept of procreation and the family far beyond both traditional expectations and established legal parameters. Long gone are the days of "Mom, dad, and baby makes three." A child born today may have as many as five "parents"—a biological father and mother, a gestational mother, and a rearing father and mother.

While assisted reproductive technologies have gripped the public's imagination, the realities of the children and the families they are capable of creating have set off novel issues and unique legal and policy challenges for the courts, lawmakers, medical providers, and society as a whole to grapple with. For the first time, conception has been taken out of a woman's body. With cryopreservation, gestation can literally be suspended, permitting conception and birth to be separated by years instead of months. Moreover, third parties are now actual participants and not merely assistants in procreation. Unique factors such as these are challenging the existing legal models and traditional legal analysis.

The public policy response in the United States to these medical developments is still evolving; to date, no comprehensive or coordinated plan exists. The federal government has declined to take the lead in either regulating or guiding these developments, or in funding research to improve the results of the applied technologies. The federal government's Ethics Advisory Board, first established in 1975 to review research proposals, fell victim to the politics of the abortion controversy and has never been staffed. For over a decade, federal funding for IVF and related research has been at a standstill. This is in contrast to Australia and Great Britain which established national commissions to develop guidelines for the assisted reproductive technologies. Recognizing the vacuum created by the federal government's failure to act, the American College of Obstetrics and Gynecology and the American Fertility Society announced in 1991 the proposed formation of a private body, the National Advisory Board on Ethics and Reproduction. The intent of this newly formed body is to establish standards for fetal tissue research and the new reproductive technologies.

In the absence of a comprehensive public policy, traditional legal approaches and laws governing families are now being applied to reproductive technology on a case-by-case and state-by-state basis. Because these were written long before any of the reproductive technologies were developed, the result is a patchwork of inconsistent legal decisions emanating from different courts and legislatures around the country. Practitioners and consumers of the assisted reproductive technologies cannot predict with confidence whether or not the families they create outside the bedroom today will end up in the courtroom tomorrow.

To examine some of the responses that courts and legislatures have produced applying traditional approaches when confronted by the new technologies, I will first review the legal perspective in general, and then focus on specific cases and controversies which have arisen involving donor insemination, surrogacy, cryopreservation, and access to the assisted reproductive technologies. In doing so, potential pitfalls for patients and their medical providers and the existing legal deficiencies will be highlighted. On this foundation I will discuss means for improving the present system.

The United States Constitution is the starting point for any legal analysis of procreation and the family. The United States Supreme Court has long recognized that the right to procreate is one of a very few "fundamental" rights and therefore deserving of the utmost protection and respect.[1] Consistent with that right, further regulation of families and children is usually left to the laws of individual states. The assisted reproductive technologies are now forcing courts and legislatures to explore both the outer dimensions and scope of this constitutional right and the appropriate application of traditional family laws to very nontraditional arrangements.

Donor Insemination

Donor insemination (DI) represents the oldest and simplest assisted reproductive technique, from both a technical and a legal perspective. The procedure introduces a male donor as a third party. His rights and responsibilities must be defined. Although differing in details, many states have laws that declare the donor to have no parental rights or obligations to a child conceived with his sperm. Such rights and obligations are assigned to the partner of the recipient. Nonetheless, litigation has arisen on a number of issues relating to donor insemination.

Courts across the country have been confronted with issues involving sperm donors who have sought, and by some courts received, parental status of DI children when the recipient was an unmarried woman.[2] Husbands in divorce disputes have argued that their children by DI were not entitled to child support, because the written consent requirement of the particular statute was not adhered to.[3] In New

York an ultimately unsuccessful challenge to a will was brought on the grounds that two of the testator's grandchildren were conceived through DI and therefore arguably not entitled to inherit from their paternal grandfather. A Virginia court approved a husband's adopting his twin children conceived through DI despite a state law that apparently made his parental status clear.[4] The court found that although the statute—which was similar to that in many states—clearly limited the sperm donor's status, it did not thereby protect the husband's status. That state's legislature has since amended the law in question.

These and other DI cases demonstrate the variety of issues and the varying results that can arise when third parties are introduced into the reproductive process and no consistent policy is articulated.

Surrogacy

Although surrogacy is in some respects the "mirror image" of donor insemination, it differs significantly in other respects. In a surrogacy arrangement, the third party participant is a woman. In a "traditional" surrogacy arrangement, the "surrogate" is inseminated and therefore provides both the egg and gestates the child. In a "gestational" or "embryo transfer" surrogacy arrangement, the surrogate receives an embryo from a couple and gestates a child who is not genetically related to her. In either form, a surrogate will necessarily have a much more involved relationship (both physical and temporal) with the child than a sperm donor.

In the relatively short time that surrogacy has been available it has been surrounded by controversy and fierce legal battles. Opponents of surrogacy argue that it amounts to slavery and baby selling and violates any decent view of motherhood. Its supporters argue equally strongly that surrogacy is and should remain a constitutionally protected right for those who choose to participate. Arguments have also been· raised that prohibiting surrogacy while allowing donor insemination amounts to blatant sex discrimination.

The application of existing laws to the issues raised by surrogacy has yielded varying and inconsistent results. One California court has ruled that a gestational surrogate is akin to a "foster mother" with no legal rights.[5] Another California court is currently trying to sort out a three-way custody battle between a "traditional" surrogate and the now separated couple for whom she conceived a child.[6] That court recognized the "traditional" surrogate as the legally protected mother vis-a-vis the preadoptive mother. The surrogate must now fight the biological father for custody of the child. Some courts have applied laws governing adoption and prohibiting baby selling to void prebirth surrogacy contracts while simultaneously ruling that it was in the best interest of the child to remain with the biological father and his wife.[7] In one court a surrogate was not allowed to execute adoption surrender documents which would permit adoption by the wife of the child's biological father unless she agreed to return her surrogacy fee.[8] Lawsuits filed by surrogates are also currently pending against doctors and lawyers who helped create these surrogacy arrangements.[5]

State legislatures around the country have been struggling to respond to surrogacy by considering and enacting various laws which prohibit, allow, or regulate surrogacy. Some prohibit payment altogether; others require a court accounting and approval of fees paid. Others focus on whether surrogacy should be guided by laws similar to those in adoption, where prebirth agreements to relinquish children are unenforceable or subject to a "cooling off" period after birth, Interestingly, two national legal associations took up the task of drafting model laws which, if enacted into law, could govern surrogacy arrangements. Both of those groups drafted proposed laws which, with numerous safeguards, would authorize and enforce paid surrogacy contracts.[9]

In the absence of any uniform guidance on the controversial subject of surrogacy, state by state enactments and court decisions are proceeding in a haphazard and largely unpredictable fashion. Unfortunately, this currently leaves any participants to a surrogacy arrangement vulnerable as to the enforce- ability of their agreement and the security of their family building efforts.

Cryopreservation

Cryopreservation allows conception and birth to be separated by much longer than the traditional 9 months. It also removes conception from the body. Both of these aspects raise unique legal problems. Many well-publicized legal battles have already occurred and many more are likely.

A now divorced Tennessee couple, Junior and Sue Davis, have fought over which of them had the right to "custody" of their cryopreserved embryos and to the decision whether or not the embryos would be donated and implanted in an anonymous couple or discarded.[10] The trial court originally found that the seven embryos were "children in vitro" and deserving of their best chance in life. The higher courts found that decision "abhorrent" and rejected suggestions that the embryos were either life or property. Recognizing instead that they were deserving of "special respect" as human tissue but not full human life, the court ruled that, in the absence of a pre-fertilization agreement, the right *not* to procreate overrode the right to procreate. The clinic was then ordered to follow its "usual procedure" in dealing with unused embryos, and presumably discard them.[1]

In contrast, *York V. Jones Institute*[11] pitched the clinic that had possession of an embryo against the couple who wanted to transfer their embryo to another clinic for implantation.[12] That court considered the embryo analogous to property and ruled that the couple were the owners of the "property" and therefore its legal custodian. Whether an embryo is seen as

---

[1] Ironically, since the clinic's usual practice was to anonymously donate unused embryos, which the court found unacceptable in light of the husband's objection, the ultimate fate of the embryos remains unclear (New York Times, June 4, 1992, Doctor's act on embryos Sends case back to court. by Ronald Smothers).

"life" or "property" apparently depends on where in the country, and before what judge or lawmaker, the disputing parties find themselves.

These two cases illustrate the need for comprehensive policies related to cryopreservation. In the absence of some guidance, the potential legal battles are limited only by imagination. For example, traditional estate law has long provided for the "after born" child—the child conceived but not born before its father's death. A child born to a father long deceased but whose embryos were frozen could be entitled to inherit from an estate intended only for children born or anticipated at the time of the man's death. Clinics utilizing cryopreservation will need to consider many legal issues. These include anticipating and resolving participants' intentions as to embryos that survive beyond their marriage or life, and whether or not the surviving spouse or partner should be permitted to control those embryos and have decision-making power over them.

Miscellaneous Issues

In addition to the controversies surrounding these particular procedures, the assisted reproductive technologies present other novel issues as well. An even newer area of uncharted legal territory involves donor eggs. Recent developments enable eggs produced by fertile women to be inseminated with the sperm of men whose partners cannot produce their own viable eggs. The embryos are then gestated by the intended mother. Cryopreservation may or may not be involved. Individual clinics around the country are currently developing their own guidelines involving screening of donors, criteria for selection, genetic testing, and information sharing between donors and recipients. In addition, issues of resource allocation and access to the technologies have been raised, as have issues of liability of providers who provide or deny these services.

Future Directions

The new reproductive technologies have introduced unique factors into the formation of families which need to be reflected in the public policy responses. The inclusion of third parties as participants in the procreative process requires a thoughtful approach to defining the rights and responsibilities of *all* of the participants. Furthermore, the fact that conception can occur outside the body of the child's mother and the embryo can be frozen indefinitely requires society to confront the status of that embryo and of those involved in the process.

All of these unique issues deserve to be analyzed in a manner that places a priority on defining and protecting the rights and responsibilities of the child and the family for whom these medical miracles were designed. Adopting guidelines and policies that recognize the unique features of these assisted reproductive technologies would make the tasks of the courts and legislatures easier, and the results more consistent and fair. Much like Cinderella's stepsisters trying to fit into the glass slipper, the new technologies simply cannot be forced to fit laws and approaches written and designed for a simpler time.

There are presently no clear or comprehensive policies shaping the reproductive technologies. What is clear is that progress in the reproductive technologies is not going to wait for society and lawmakers to catch up. Medical possibilities that were beyond the imagination only a few years ago are now commonplace. Newer techniques and permutations are inevitable. The question is, What do society, lawmakers, and policy makers intend to do in response to these new realities?

An opportunity is being created to help shape the new face of created families. Failing to seize that opportunity while continuing to respond in reactive and piecemeal fashion will do little to enhance and shape the new families. Rather, passiveness could do much to add to the uncertainty and confusion participants already confront. How society ultimately responds to these medical challenges will greatly impact the future of the American family and its children.

References

1. Skinner v. Oklahoma, 316 U.S. 535, 62 S.CT. 110 (1942). Eisenstadt v. Baird, 405 U.S., 92 S.Ct. 1029 (1972). Carey v. Population Services, Inc. 431 U.S. 678, 97 S.Ct. 2010 (1977).
2. McIntyre v. Crouch, 780 P.2d 239 (1989). C.M. v. C.C., 152 NJ Supp. 160, 377 A. 2d 831 (1977).
3. Anonymous v. Anonymous, NY Sup.Ct., New York (01/18/91).
4. Welborn v. Doe, (VA Ct. Apps., 1990).
5. Johnson v. Calvert, Cal. (Orange County) Sup.Ct., docket #63-31-90 (10/22/90) Appeal Pending.
6. Jordan v. Moschetta, et al. (pending Santa Ana, California) (4/91).
7. In the matter of Baby M, 109 NJ 396, 537 A.2d 1277 (N.J. 1988).
8. Matter of Adoption of Paul, 146 A2d 379, 550 N.Y. S. 2d815 (1990).
9. Uniform Status of Children of Assisted Conception Act, National Conference of Commissioners on Uniform State Laws and American Bar Association House of Delegates (1989). Model Surrogacy Act, American Bar Association (1988).
10. Davis v. Davis, Tenn Ct.App. (1990).
11. York v. Jones Institute of Reproductive Medicine, 717 F. Supp. 4217 (D.C. Va. 1989).
12. York v. Jones Institute of Reproductive Medicine, 717 F. Supp. 4217 (D.C. Va. 1989).

44

Diethylstilbestrol and Infertility: The Past, the Present, and the Revelance for the Future

Susan M. Fisher and Roberta J. Apfel

"It is difficult to call to mind any subject upon which more rubbish has been written than the sex hormones. This is very largely the result of the general public's desire for the maintenance of youth and all that it implies, together with the successful exploitation of this trait by commercial firms." In 1939, 5 years after making this remark, Charles Dodds was knighted for his key role in the synthesis of sex hormones. In 1932 he wrote that oestrin had been seriously recommended for all types of menstrual disorders, for every form of insanity, for the treatment of vascular disease in men, and for hemophilia. He commented that sex hormones were so popular that it was only the difficulty of obtaining them that prevented their use in every condition from simple hives to megalomania.

Patients, doctors, researchers, and drug companies all wanted a cheap, easily produced, standard form of synthetic estrogen. In 1938 Dodds and his co-workers sent a letter to the editor of *Nature* announcing that he and colleagues at the Courtauld Institute in London and at Oxford had successfully collaborated to produce what they called the "mother substance"—stilbestrol and related compounds. It was a relatively simple structure, easily and cheaply manufactured from coal tar. It was more potent than natural estrogen and it could be administered pure in oral form. Because diethylstilbestrol (DES) was discovered under a grant from the British Medical Research Council, whose policy it was that new discoveries be well publicized and not patented, it became widely available very quickly.

By the time Dodds gave the Cameron Prize lecture in 1941 he had become as enthusiastic about the clinical uses of DES as he had previously been cautious about natural estrogen. He said that DES heralded "a new era." By 1939 it was already popular in the United Kingdom, France, Germany, Sweden, and the United States, where it was used to treat menopausal complaints, amenorrhea, and genital underdevelopment, and to suppress lactation. It engendered enormous excitement. In the 3 years after its synthesis, 257 papers appeared in the medical and scientific literature describing various animal experiments with the drug and clinical uses for it.

Estrogenic substances had been implicated in the development of tumors as early as 1919, and between 1936 and 1940 numerous studies in mice and rats showed that DES increased tumor size, particularly neoplasms in genital and breast tissues. This body of animal research was largely ignored.

During World War II the hormone's use was extended to agriculture: DES-supplemented feed and implanted DES pellets decreased feeding costs and produced marbling in red meat, and juicer chickens and lambs. This use was later outlawed, but it remains covertly operational nonetheless.

In September 1941, after extensive review of the literature and positive testimony of 50 of 54 experts, the U.S. Food and Drug Administration (FDA) approved the safety of DES. Until the thalidomide disaster in 1962, proof of a drug's efficacy was not required. The requirement of safety was a reform introduced in 1938 by the Food, Drug, and Cosmetic Act, and DES was the first important substance to be considered under this act.

The agent was expressly licensed to treat vaginitis, gonorrhea, and menopausal symptoms, and to suppress lactation. An early concern, which in hindsight seems prescient, was that it would be used too generally and inappropriately. Usage did generalize quickly and was extended to the treatment of amenorrhea and dysmenorrhea, pregnancy problems including nausea and vomiting, infertility, toxemia, and diabetes. A low dosage was suggested by the FDA, and contraindications for use were issued based on the known risks from all estrogens. In retrospect it appears that given the groundswell of enthusiasm for DES, the quality of drug evaluation in 1940, the absence of efficacy as a criterion, and the interdependence of the parties (drug companies, researchers, and FDA officials all worked together to process the reams of letters, clinical anecdotes, and research reports), there was no way the review of DES could have come out differently. The few skeptical critics with a historical perspective were not heeded, including a 1939 editorial in *JAMA* passionately seeking restraint.

Between 1941 and 1947 two prominant Harvard scientists, Olive and George Smith, used DES for a variety of indications for which DES was not FDA approved. Their enthusiasm encouraged many other physicians to use DES for non-approved indications as well. In 1947 a supplementary new drug application was granted to permit its use during pregnancy and to allow the production of a 25-mg pill in addition to the 1-, 2-, and 5-mg pills previously approved. In 1952 the FDA declared that DES was safe and no longer required annual approval. The expansion of its usage to pregnancy, and the introduction of larger doses, were done by simple administrative fiat. No new research data or reviews were required, and the use of the compound was now exempted from official regulatory constraint.

It had been observed that progesterone levels dropped prior to the onset of toxemia. Estrogen and progesterone levels were noted to drop earlier in high-risk women with pre-

vious pregnancy losses than in those who did not have toxemia. From these findings it was postulated that DES could be given to stimulate the placenta to produce an increased quantity of natural hormones. A treatment regimen was launched based on the observation that specific dosages of DES at specific times in pregnancy altered the production of natural hormones, and that the alteration improved pregnancy outcome. In 1945, 119 obstetricians in the United States and Europe were enlisted to do clinical trials of DES in high-risk pregnancies. Between 1948 and 1954 seven papers reported data demonstrating that the agent had reduced pregnancy accidents and produced babies who were bigger than average.

None of these seven studies was blind. Three used no controls, four used inadequate controls. None of the control women were treated at the same time as the DES group or by the same methods and personnel, although they were roughly the same as the treatment group in other respects. On the basis of these studies, DES received enthusiastic endorsement, although it is impossible to conclude from any of them that it was the drug itself that made the difference. By 1948 the same British Medical Research Council that had sponsored the original research developed the technique for randomized clinical trials. The conviction of the effectiveness of DES for high-risk pregnancies was so great that none of its proponents thought to attempt such a blind control or randomized clinical trial, although the techniques were available.

The vast and complex literature shows the positive effect of almost any treatment involving special care and attention to high-risk mothers, by people who believe strongly in what they are doing and in the likelihood of an improved pregnancy outcome. Thus DES may actually have been of no more value than placebo.

Seven controlled studies of DES were conducted between 1950 and 1955. The largest and best-known of these trials compared the effects of DES and placebo given to 2,000 women during normal first pregnancies. Dieckmann did this study because he had noted that the drug was used increasingly in these women.

This shift from treating high-risk pregnancies to improving normal pregnancies was an extraordinary social event. The results showed routine use of DES to be ineffective in normal pregnancies, however, and later evaluation in England of his data proved the agent actually to be harmful.

Three smaller studies showed that DES did nothing to improve salvage rates in high risk-women. These results were ignored, however, and were not used as a basis for larger-scale studies, as one would have expected.

In spite of this research, usage slowed but remained high until 1970. Between 1950 and 1961 the *Physician's Desk Reference* never mentioned the negative findings of the seven controlled studies; rather it stated that DES was useful in preventing accidents of pregnancy. In 1960 the *Merck Index* stated that DES had formerly been used prophylactically, and the 1958 *Modern Drug Encyclopedia* and *Therapeutic Index*, unrelated to drug companies, mentioned no usefulness for the compound in pregnancy. By the late 1960s, six of seven leading obstetrics-gynecology textbooks concluded that the agent had no effect in preventing spontaneous abortions in any group of patients. It has been estimated, nevertheless, that as many as 100,000 pregnant women per year received it for at least 15 years after it was shown to be ineffective. Thomas Chalmers, then president of Mount Sinai Medical Center, in analyzing all the studies, cited DES as an example of the power of the anecdotal report and of the resistance of medical practice to the results of well-designed clinical drug research.

In 1970 almost unprecedented appearance of a very rare adenocarcinoma of the vagina was observed in eight women under 20 years of age. The neoplasm was rapidly linked to DES, and in 1971 the compound was banned by the FDA for use in preventing spontaneous abortion. By that time, however, in the years during which it was used routinely in pregnancy, at least 4 to 6 million mothers and children had been exposed.

Currently, 557 cases of clear cell adenocarcinoma are listed in the International Registry for Research on Hormonal Transplacental Carcinogenesis of the University of Chicago, with about 20 still under investigation. About 100 of these women are dead. Two-thirds have a positive history of in utero exposure to DES or a similar compound. Many of the remaining third were unable to ascertain if their mothers had taken the drug while pregnant. The range of age at diagnosis of cancer in the exposed women is 7 to 36 years, with the peak being 19.5 years. New cases are still being diagnosed. According to the most recent estimate, the risk of developing malignancy is less than 1 per 1,000 through age 34. Recurrences have developed in women who had been cancer free for as long as 20 years. At least 12 had recurrences after 12 years. The recurrences tend to be in distant organs and the patients have not done well. Four factors increase the risk of developing cancer: history of prior miscarriage in the mother, DES exposure early in gestation, fall season of birth, and prematurity. In light of some of the newer findings, it is the exposure early in gestation that is probably most significant.

Seventy percent to 90% of DES daughters have adenosis; that is, columnar cells instead of normal squamous cells in the vagina and cervix. Adenosis produces copious discharge and contributes to infection. Menstrual irregularities are common. A high frequency of cervical and vaginal dysplasia and carcinoma in situ were reported in DES daughters, although some studies did not find this. An increased risk of breast cancer in mothers who took DES also was cited, but again, not all studies demonstrated this. Reports of increased rates of urogenital tract abnormalities and testicular tumors in DES sons are somewhat controversial. Several studies suggest changes in the DES sons and daughters with regard to socialization patterns, psychiatric problems, and gender identity problems. Many of these studies are problematic in their design.

What is absolutely not controversial is the devastating effect of DES exposure on childbearing. Ninety percent of the women whose mothers took the drug have deformities of the uterus or cervix and changes in the fallopian tubes. Fifty percent to 60% have great difficulty maintaining a pregnancy beyond the second trimester and are at high risk for premature births. The follow-up of the Dieckmann cohort showed a risk of primary infertility of 33%, as opposed to 14% in their controls. The earlier the mothers took DES, the more likely the daughters are to be infertile.

The newest, and unexpected, addition to the list of sequelae is an increased occurrence of autoimmune disease among DES daughters, such as asthma, arthritis, lupus, diabetes, and high prolactin levels (a possible contributor to infertility). The hypothesis is that prenatal exposure leads to impaired immune system functioning. A relationship seems to exist between very early exposure and development of autoimmune disease. One could wonder about a connection between immuno-suppression and the development of clear cell adenocarcinoma.

The word that most captures the essence of the psychologic effects of DES exposure is trauma. The word comes from the Greek for wound or external assault. Psychologically, trauma is an event or experience that is un-expected and undesired, an event that disrupts, temporarily or permanently, the sense of bodily or psychologic integrity, producing a feeling of deep personal vulnerability. A trauma is the stroke of the hammer that cracks the previously intact crystal and so reveals the hidden structure, to use Freud's splendid metaphor, and with DES the hidden structure of many aspects of medicine was disclosed.

The whole gamut of experiences associated with trauma has been the aftermath of DES. The insults inflicted by it are social and personal, external and internal, public and private, sudden and enduring. Emotional responses ranging from total denial to mature reintegration can be seen among all those concerned: researchers, physicians, mothers, children, and the community at large.

The trauma produced by DES takes several forms. As a medication, DES is related to sexuality and fertility, to the past and the future. It touches on issues at the heart of the mother–child relationship. In all grieving, the childlike parts of us return, and we seek, literally and spiritually, the care of our mothers or of those who represent basic maternal care. But one of the most disturbing features of the DES experience is its isolating nature, because

the usual sources of help are the very sources of pain. It is the providers of early tender care who unwittingly have let down the DES daughters and sons: the mothers brought pain to their children, the physicians brought pain to their patients.

DES remains most powerfully connected with childbearing, which is both a profoundly private experience and a complex social event involving the extended family and the larger community. Childbirth taps a woman's deepest sense of her own body, intensifies her rela-tionships with her loved ones, and awakens fantasied communion with past figures who have been important to her. It involves the continuity of the generations, in her mind and in actuality. The trauma of DES sequelae follows from the violation of feelings and rela-tionships. The obstetrician, trained to deal with the simple, natural problems that can occur in pregnancy, hardly expects or is expected to be the source of disasters. The reproductive behavior of the mother is obviously not intended to poison the reproduc-tive capacity of her children. The quality of the experience surrounding DES exposure lies somewhere between a natural disaster and a bad dream in which safe relationships appear uncannily menacing. In the healthiest and happiest of persons and families, this combina-tion of external and internal components of the DES trauma reawakened distressing fantasies and long-buried constellations of conflicts and concerns that for most individuals had been solved quite satisfactorily in the course of development.

In general, women have dealt with their exposure as their characters permitted. Mothers and daughters who openly expressed their fears and anxieties did better than those who isolated themselves and repressed their feelings. Daughters tried to spare their mothers, mothers tried to spare their doctors, and everyone blamed the drug companies— not incorrectly.

Originally, DES was recommended for pregnant women who had been unable to bear children because of severe medical illness or diabetes, or those who had had repeated miscarriages. If, in fact, it helped these women bear healthy infants, even the small frequency of cancer observed in 1970 might have been considered by these women, their physicians, and the FDA as a risk worth taking. Its use however, was widely extended to women in whom risk was slight or who had no apparent problems at all. While it was cautioned that DES was "no panacea," it was treated by other physicians as just that, and given to "make normal pregnancies more normal." It became a routine part of the quality care that private practitioners gave their predominantly middle-class patients, including their own wives. Considered the best possible pregnancy enhancer, it was even included in vitamin tablets for pregnant women. The original rationale had been lost in the shuffle.

Our present understanding is that there is no consensus that the agent did anything for toxemia, but not everyone agrees about the available data. If babies were going to be premature because of the mother's underlying disease, DES increased their weight so that their chances of surviving early birth were improved. A tricky point here is that the Dieckmann studies suggested that in normal pregnancies DES increased the likelihood of prematurity itself. It may have contributed to the very conditions its weight-enhancing properties improved. But these results were derived from a healthy, not a high-risk, population. Had a low frequency of clear cell adenocarcinoma of the vagina been the only problem, and had the agent been surely effective in preventing pregnancy loss, a condition with a relatively high frequency, it might have been worthwhile to consider continuing its use in pregnancy in carefully selected cases. It is a fact, however, that most miscarriages are caused by problems of the fetus, not by maternal deficits, and DES was a treatment directed at improving the maternal milieu.

A number of dilemmas and considerations deriving from the DES experience are relevant.

Medical Competence: How Do Doctors Deal with Error?

Consider the implications of the reluctance of physicians to identify patients with unsatisfac-

tory outcomes, and their difficulty responding to the distress of their patients. This requires an understanding of the difficulty physicians have in coping with error, as well as of their vulnerabilities.

Unlike their patients, physicians seemed to have responded to the aftereffects of DES with little overt guilt or self-blame. Relatively few obstetricians complied with requests from the American College of Obstetricians and Gynecologists and the FDA to identify affected women, and this failure was responsible for the development of public health outreach programs in several states. Most patients learned about the situation through such efforts and the mass media. The responses of many physicians to such public interventions in their private domain ranged from indifference to resentment to active disapproval.

This apparent underreaction is puzzling and distressing, and not adequately explained by fear of lawsuits. In fact, not a single lawsuit has been brought against a physician who prescribed DES. In addition, DES-exposed families report being far more upset by their physicians' manifest nonchalance than by the exposure itself. They complain bitterly of superficial reassurance, authoritarian dismissal, and failure to offer a collaborative, supportive, relationship.

This nonchalance actually masks elaborate defenses against dealing with error. Medical training—to diagnose and treat illness—leaves physicians peculiarly unprepared to cope with iatrogenic illness where their image of themselves as healers of the sick is inverted, where they become the cause rather than the cure. The spectre of incompetence is not well tolerated in modern medicine.

Scientific medicine is accustomed to treatment regimens that are used for a while, fall into disfavor, and are replaced. Failed efforts, tragedy, and death are one thing. Error is another. The DES experience addresses the deepest fears of doctors: of facing their own mistakes; of failing in the eyes of peers and younger colleagues; of being criticized, regulated, and even used. It elicits feelings of powerlessness, helplessness, and paralysis in the face of uncertainty and chronic illness. The DES experience may stir unconscious and universal fears of sadism, maiming, and castration. The contrast between the original promise of DES, to create life, and its actual devastating effects suggests that practicing physicians may, like their patients, be responding to trauma.

Crucial experiences in training and early practice make it more possible to tolerate mistakes, to learn and grow from them. All beginning professionals make mistakes; that is why they need some modulating protection from excessive guilt, which could lead to an emotional withdrawal from patients and a reluctance to take necessary risks. Patients may perceive this cautious stance as indifference on the part of the doctor. If doctors have no defenses against the consequences of their own mistakes, they may develop a rationalizing, seemingly cavalier "we all make mistakes" attitude, which allows them to deny actual feelings of responsibility. Suppression of their own feelings seems to limit responsiveness to the feelings of their patients. Such physicians may increasingly regard patients in detached, even formulaic ways, in the service of maintaining self-esteem, which depends on being exemplars of competence.

Hippocrates Versus Prometheus: *Primum Non Nocere* Versus Therapeutic Zeal

The DES story unfolds in the context of the longstanding tension in medical history between public pressure for a cure and the philosophy that argues for the restraint that avoids harm. Indeed, the history of Western medicine can be seen in terms of a dialectic between the *primum non nocere* doctrine and the Promethean desire to know and to cure without limits. Both forces have been responsible for advances and setbacks in the healing arts. In general, the more extreme the therapy in either direction, the more problems eventuate. Only a fool would wish to maintain one side or the other of the dialectic.

Truly, DES was a bold treatment. It came to be used to prevent the possible problems of pregnancy and thus to alter the quality of life,

not merely to control or ameliorate specific diseases or defects. Its application in its time was a dramatic example of daring, of tampering with nature, and expecting to save and cure. Its popularity was untempered by information from studies suggesting that it would not succeed.

Even if thoroughly tested, no one could have anticipated a 20-year time bomb. Is it possible it will happen again? We all know about drugs, desperately sought, waiting to be available in the United States. No people, except perhaps the parents of a dying child, are more desperate than those yearning to conceive a child. In vitro fertilization (IVF), first developed for women with blocked tubes, is now almost routine for infertile couples, those with female factors, male factors, and unexplained infertility. As with DES, the guidelines for IVF have slowly shifted and expanded. At first there were rigid age limits, and only women with damaged tubes were to be involved and for a limited number of attempts with limited quantities of drugs. Now the age limit is expanding, the number of tries is increasing, and new drugs are used. Yet the evidence from DES keeps shouting at us that the earlier in prenatal life we intervene, the more serious are the long-term consequences. At how close to conception do we define the beginning of prenatal life and worry about the long-term effects of the drugs we prescribe to facilitate conception?

Can the DES tragedy be averted in the future? Many of the recent changes in the policies and institutional structure of medicine are clear improvements. The development of informed consent, the elaborate procedures for conducting randomized clinical trials, the emergence of public-interest investigative groups, the improvement in medical reporting by the popular media, and increasingly informed medical consumers all may lessen the probability that the more egregious mistakes associated with DES will be repeated. But we all know that informed consent has severe limitations. Desperate, frightened, or even habitually compliant people consent to activities they might question in other circumstances, and the very role of patient diminishes a person's independent judgment and lessens the very meaning of informed consent. Besides, looking at DES, who can give informed consent for events whose consequences are 20 years in the future and primarily affect someone else?

The development of sophisticated testing mechanisms is subject to the same problems. Who spends 20 years conducting an experiment before collecting and publishing the data? Research on the complexity of the diffusion of medical information suggests that procedures are frequently in use before the data are even finalized.

The size of the new medical research establishment has inevitably created a new special-interest group with its own needs and concerns. The improvement in medical reporting frequently means that a better-informed public demands access to new or experimental procedures before they are adequately tested or understood. All the continuing dialogues of general policy and of specific issues and developments are to the good—the consultative teams that discuss cases; the presence of ethicists, psychiatrists, and multidisciplinary panels to review procedures; the debates on risks and benefits.

Yet DES was extensively discussed from the 1930s until its approval by the FDA in 1941, and the participants in that dialogue were largely unaware of the degree to which their positions were governed by their special interests, the prevailing fashion, and their passions. Remember those carefully designed studies that no one attended to because they were caught up in the enthusiasm of the medical community and the public to bring DES into wide use. Of what value are excellent, refined, formal procedures if no one pays attention to their findings? Occasionally there are heroes like Frances Kelsey, who remembered the presence of limb deformation in preliminary reports on thalidomide in European journals and kept the drug out of the United States. But DES had no hero, no one to scream that the carcinogenicity in animals would somehow catch up with humans.

Technical Skills Versus Practical Virtue

New technical developments and improved institutional arrangements will not approach the problem. What is needed, rather, is a shift in the character of the participants. We already have an abundance of technical virtuosity and theoretical sophistication. Now we require a special kind of human excellence or, to use an old-fashioned word, virtue. In antiquity Aristotle called it prudence, or practical wisdom; in the eighteenth century Kant called it judgment; in the early twentieth century Alfred North Whitehead called it foresight. It refers to that developed human capacity to make independent, autonomous judgments about urgent practical matters for which there are no general rules.

With respect to this capacity, modern medicine may face its most striking dilemma. Most of its enormous power derives from the interplay between its technical capacities and its theoretical understanding. There is a synergy between them in that new technical developments make greater scientific understanding possible, and scientific understanding frequently leads to the creation of new techniques. In its fascination with these twin sources of its power, medicine is in danger of forgetting that our understanding is, and will always remain, profoundly limited, and that our technical abilities are always subject to profound misuse and error.

Take DES. Single daily doses were given that far exceed a woman's lifetime production of estrogen. Prudence suggests we should approach such dosages only with extreme caution. Prudence focuses not only on what we know and can do, but also on what we do not know and cannot do. We have to remember our ignorance and our clumsiness as well as our knowledge and our skill. We have to be aware of our zeal for truth and for healing, not only as sources of power but as passions that can lead to self-deception and errors of judgment. The consuming public, both as individual patients and as the politically organized community, must exercise the same moderation and prudence in the demands it makes on the medical profession.

These reflections can easily become platitudinous, but it is well to remember that the DES disaster derived precisely from the passion for truth and the desire to improve the quality of life—and from the passion to have what we want. The head of DES research at the University of Chicago said that the DES daughters who are trying to become pregnant do not seem to think about the implications of their exposure when they try a new drug or a new technology; that their cells were bathed in estrogens that well may sensitize them to future cancers; that they are the passive participants in a sorrowful tale; that perhaps for them caution is in order. When he asks them, it appears not to have crossed their minds. Another woman consulted a colleague about possibly adopting a child. She was entering her eighth IVF cycle. So there we are: hope, denial, stubbornness, passion, persistence, idealism, grandiosity, greed.

The story of DES, for all its modernity, bears many of the marks of classical tragedy. Everyone acted in good faith, with the best of intentions, and within the established norms of medical procedures of the day. Thus the consequences seem unavoidable. What we can learn from the story is not whom to blame or what technical procedure we can employ to avoid the errors of our predecessors, but that we are subject to the same stresses and temptations as the actors in the DES tragedy. The story is a sad one but it need not be futile if we can learn from it. In the words of Aeschylus, "From suffering comes wisdom."

Suggested Reading

1. American College of Obstetricians and Gynecologists. Newsletters of May 1973, January 1975, October, 1975, April 1977, and November 1978. Items on DES. Suite 300 East, 600 Maryland Ave. SW., Washington, DC 20024–2588.
2. Apfel RJ, Fisher SM. To Do No Harm: DES and the Dilemmas of Modern Medicine. New Haven and London: Yale University Press, 1984.
3. Barnes AB, Colton T, Gundersen J, Noller KL, Tilley BC, Strama T, Townsend DE, Hatab P, O'Brien P. Fertility and outcome of pregnancy in women exposed in utero to diethylstilbestrol. N Engl J Med 1980;302:609–613.
4. Becker HS, Gerr B, Hughes EC, Strauss AL. Boys in White: Student Culture in Medical School. Chicago: University of Chicago Press, 1961.
5. Beecher HK. Ethics and clinical research. N Engl J Med 1966;274:1354–1360.
6. Bell SE. A new model of medical technology development: A case study of DES. In: Roth J, Ruzek S, eds. Research in the Sociology of Health Care. Vol. 4. Greenwich, CT: JAI Press, 1984.
7. Beral V, Colwell L. Randomized trial of high doses of stilboestrol and ethisterone in pregnancy: Long-term follow-up of mothers. Br Med J 1980;281:1098–1101.
8. Belsky DE. DES daughters: Adaptation to bodily uncertainty. Unpublished manuscript based on independent investigation for degree of Master of Social Work, Smith College School for Social Work, 1978.
9. Bibbo M, Gill WB, Azizi F, Blough R, Fang VS, Rosenfeld RL, Schumacher GFB, Sleeper K, Sonek MG, Wied GL. Follow-up study of male and female offspring of DES-exposed mothers. Ob Gyn 1977;49:1–8.
10. Bibbo M, Haenszel WM, Wied GL, Hubby M, Herbst AL. A twenty-five year follow-up study of women exposed to diethylstilbestrol during pregnancy. N Engl J Med 1978;298:763–767.
11. Bichler J. DES Daughter: The Joyce Bichler Story. New York: Avon, 1981.
12. Bishop PMF, Boycott M, Zuckerman S. The oestrogenic properties of "stilboestrol" (diethylstilbestrol). Lancet 1939;1:5–11.
13. Bosk, C Forgive and Remember: Managing Medical Failure. Chicago: University of Chicago Press, 1979.
14. Brackbill Y, Berendes HW. Dangers of diethylstilboestrol: Review of a 1953 paper. Lancet 1978;2:520.
15. Brian DD, Tilley BC, Laberthé DR, O'Fallon WM, Noller KL, Kurland LT. Breast cancer in DES-exposed mothers: Absence of association. Mayo Clin Proc 1980;55:89–93.
16. Burke L, Antonioli D, Friedman EA. Evolution of diethylstilbestrol-associated genital tract lesions. Ob Gyn 1981;57:79–84.
17. Burke L, Apfel RJ, Fisher SM, Shaw JG. Observations on the psychological impact of diethylstilbestrol exposure and suggestions on management. J Reprod Med 1980;24:99–102.
18. Burroughs W, Culbertson CC, Kastelic J, Cheng E, Hale WH. The effects of trace amounts of diethylstilboestrol in rations of fattening steers. Science 1954;120:266–267.
19. Buxton CL, Engle ET. Effects of the therapeutic use of diethylstilboestrol. JAMA 1939;113:2318–2320.

20. Chalmers TC. The impact of controlled trials on the practice of medicine. Mt Sinai J Med 1974; 41:753 758.

21. Coleman J, Katz E, Menzel H. The diffusion of innovation among physicians. Sociometry 1957;20:253–270.

22. Cosgrove MD, Benton B, Henderson BE. Male genitourinary abnormalities and maternal diethylstilbestrol. J Urol 1977;117:220–222.

23. Crowder RE, Bills ES, Broadbent JS. The management of threatened abortion: A study of 100 cases. Am J Ob Gyn 1950;60:896–899.

24. Davis M. Variations in patients' compliance with doctors' advice: An empirical analysis of patterns of communication. Am J Pub Health 1978;58:274–288.

25. Davis ME, Fugo NW. Steroids in the treatment of early pregnancy complications. JAMA 1950;142:778–785.

26. DeCherney AH, Cholst I, Naftolin F. Structure and function of the Fallopian tube following exposure to diethylstilbestrol (DES) during gestation. Fertil Steril 1981;36:741–745.

27. DES Task Force. Summary report, 21 September, 1978. NIH pub. no. 82–1688. Reprinted October 1981. Available from US Department of Health and Human Services, National Institutes of Health, Rockville, MD 20014.

28. Dieckmann WJ, Davies ME, Rynkiewicz LM, Pottinger RE. Does the administration of diethylstilbestrol during pregnancy have therapeutic value? Am J Obstet Gyn 1953; 66:1062–1081.

29. Dodds EC. The bearing of recent research on the sex hormones on clinical obstetrics and gynecology. Proc Royal Soc Med 1932;25: 563–570.

30. Dodds EC. The practical outcome of recent research on hormones. Lancet 1934;2: 1318–1320.

31. Dodds EC. The new oestrogens. Edinb Med J 1941;48:1–13.

32. Dodds EC. Synthetic oestrogens. Brit Med Bull 1955;11:131–134.

33. Dodds EC, Goldberg L, Lawson W, Robinson R. Oestrogenic activity of certain synthetic compounds. Nature 1938;141:247–248.

34. Ehrhardt AA, Meyer-Bahlburg HFL. Effects of prenatal sex hormones on gender-related behavior. Science 1981;211:1312–1318.

35. Eichna LW. Medical school education, 1975–1979: A student's perspective. New Engl J Med 1980;303:727–734.

36. Ferguson JH. Effects of stilbestrol on pregnancy compared to the effect of a placebo. Am J Obstet Gyn 1953;65:592–601.

37. Francis V, Korsch BM, Morris MJ. Gaps in doctor-patient communication: Patients' response to medical advice. N Engl J Med 1969;280:535–540.

38. Geschickter CF. Mammary carcinoma in the rat with metastasis induced by estrogen. Science 1939;89:35–37.

39. Gill WB, Schumacher GFB, Bibbo M, Strauss FH, Schoenberg HW. Association of diethylstilbestrol exposure in utero with cryptorchidism, testicular hypoplasia and semen abnormalities. J Urol 1979;122:36–39.

40. Gitman L, Koplowitz A. Use diethylstilbestrol in complications of pregnancy. NY State J Med 1950;50:2823–2824.

41. Heinonen OP. Diethylstilbestrol in pregnancy: Frequency of exposure and usage patterns. Cancer 1973;31:573–577.

42. Henderson BE, Benton B, Jing J, Yu MC, Pike MC. Risk factors for cancer of the testis in young men. Int J Cancer 1979;23:598–602.

43. Herbst AL, Anderson S, Hubby M, Haenszel WM, Kaufman RH, Noller KL. Risk factors for the development of diethylstilbestrol-associated clear cell adenocarcinoma: A case-control study. Am J Obstet Gynecol 1986;154:814–822.

44. Herbst AL, Bern HA. Developmental Effects of Diethylstilbestrol-(DES) in Pregnancy New York: Thieme-Stratton, 1981.

45. Herbst AL, Scully RE. Adenocarcinoma of the vagina in adolescence: A report of 7 cases including 6 clear-cell carcinoma (so-called mesonephromas). Cancer 1970;25:745–757.

46. Herbst AL, Ulfelder H, Poskanzer DC. Adenocarcinoma of the vagina: Association of maternal stilbestrol therapy with tumor appearance in young women. N Engl J Med 1971;284:878–881.

47. Jacobson HN, Reid DE. High risk pregnancy: A pattern of comprehensive maternal and child care. N Engl J Med 1964;271:302–307.

48. Jordan EP. Modern Drug Encyclopedia and Therapeutic Index. 7th ed. New York: Drug Publications, 1958.

49. Estrogen-therapy—a warning. JAMA 1939; 113:2323–2324.

50. Contraindications to estrogen therapy. JAMA 1940;114:1560–1561.

51. Medical news: No DES for animal growth. JAMA 1979;242:1010.

52. Karnaky KJ. The use of stilbestrol for the treatment of threatened and habitual abortion and premature labor: A preliminary report. Southern Med J 1942;35:838–847.

53. Katz J. Experimentation with Human Beings. New York: Russell Sage, 1972.

54. Kaufman RH, Adam E, Binder GL, Gerthoffer E. Upper genital tract changes and pregnancy outcome in offspring exposed in utero to diethylstilbestrol. Am J Ob Gyn 1980;137: 299–308.

55. King AG. Threatened and repeated abortion: Present status of therapy. Ob Gyn 1953;1: 104–14.

56. Kurzrok R, Kitson L, Perloff WH. The action of diethylstilbestrol in gynecologic dysfunctions. Endocrinology 1940;26:581–586.

57. Loeb L, Burns EL, Suntzeff V, Moskop M. Carcinoma-like proliferations in vagina, cervix and the uterus of mouse treated with estrogenic hormones. Proc Soc Exp Biol Med 1936;35:320–322.

58. MacBride CM, Freedman H, Loeffel E. Studies on stilbestrol: Preliminary statement. JAMA 1939;113:2320–2323.

59. Melnick S, Cole P, Anderson D, Herbst A. Rates and risks of diethylstilbestrol-related clear-cell adenocarcinoma of the vagina and cervix: An update. N Engl J Med 1987;316:514–516.

60. Mink, Patsy Takemoto et al. v. University of Chicago et al. 1982. Depositions and transcripts of trial, no. 77 C 1431 before Judge John F. Grady in the United States District Court for the Northeastern District of Illinois, Eastern Division. 460 F Supp. 713 (N.D. ILL. 1978) and 27 F.R. Serv 2D. 739 (N.D. ILL. 1979).

61. Muckle CW. The suppression of lactation by stilbestrol. Am J Ob Gyn 1940;40:133–135.

62. Naftulin DH, Ware JE, Donnelly FA. The Doctor Fox lecture: A paradigm of educational seduction. J Med Educ 1973;48:630–635.

63. Newton M. Editorial about ACOG Technical Bulletin on DES, encouraging casefinding. ACOG Newsletter 1973;17(5):2.

64. Noller KL, Blair PB, O'Brien PC, Melton LJ, Offord JR, Kaufman RH, Colton T. Increased occurrence of autoimmune disease among women exposed in utero to diethylstilbestrol. Fertil Steril 1988;49:1080–1082.

65. Noller KL, Townsend DE, Kaufman BH, Barnes AB, Robboy SJ, Fish CR, Jeffries JA, Berstralh EJ, O'Brien PC, McGorray S, Scully R. Maturation of vaginal and cervical epithelium in women exposed in utero to diethylstilbestrol. DESAD project. Am J Ob Gyn 1983;146:279–285.

66. Payne FL, Muckle CW. Stilbestrol in the treatment of menopausal symptoms. Am J Ob Gyn 1940;40:135–139.

67. Peña EF. Prevention of abortion. Am J Surg 1954;87:95–96.

68. Plate WP. Diethylstilbestrol therapy in habitual abortion. Proc Int Cong Ob Gyn Geneva 1954;751–757.

69. Randall CL, Baetz RW, Hall DW, Birtch PK. Pregnancies observed in the likely-to-abort patient with or without hormone therapy before or after conception. Am J Ob Gyn 1955;69:643–656.

70. Reid DD. Use of hormones in the management of pregnancy in diabetes. Lancet 1955;2:833–836.

71. Richmond J. Physician advisory: Health effects of the pregnancy use of diethylstilbestrol. Surgeon-General's advisory sent to physicians, 4 October 1978. Published in Clin Toxicol 1979;14:313–318.

72. Robboy SJ, Noller KL, O'Brien P, Kaufman RH, Townsend D, Barnes AB, Gunderson J, Lawrence D, Bergstrahl E, McGorray S, Tilley BC, Anton J, Chazen G. Increased incidence of cervical and vaginal dysplasia in 3,980 diethylstilbestrol-exposed young women: Experience of the National Collaborative Diethylstilbestrol Adenosis Project. JAMA 1984;252:2979–2983.

73. Robinson D, Shettles LB. The use of diethylstilbestrol in threatened abortion. Am J Ob Gyn 1952;63:1330–1333.

74. Rosenberg L, Shapiro S, Kaufman DW, Slone D, Miettinen OS, Stolley PD. Patterns and determinants of conjugated estrogen use. Am J Epidemiol 1979;109:676–686.

75. Ross JW. Further report on the use of diethylstilbestrol in the treatment of threatened abortion. J Natl Med Assoc 1953;45:223ff.

76. Russ JS, Colins CG. The treatment of prepubertal vulvovaginitis with a new synthetic estrogen. JAMA 1940;114:2446–2450.

77. Schwartz RW, Stewart NB. Psychological effects of DES exposure. JAMA 1977;237:252–254.

78. Surgeon General seeks physicians' help in DES alert. Science 1979;203:159.

79. Senekjian EK, Potkul PK, Frey K, Herbst A. Infertility among daughters of either exposed or not exposed to diethylstilbestrol. Am J Obstet Gynecol 1988;158:493–498.

80. Sherman AI, Goldrath M, Berlin A, Vakhariya V, Banooni F, Michaels W, Goodman P, Brown J. Cervical-vaginal adenosis after in utero exposure to synthetic estrogens. Ob Gyn 1974;44:531–545.

81. Shimkin MB, Grady HG. Carcinogenic potency of stilbestrol and estrone in strain C3H mice. J NCI 1940;1:119–128.

82. Simmel E. The doctor-game, illness and the profession of medicine. Int J PsychoAnal 1926;7:470–483. Also in: Fliess R, ed. The Psycho-Analytic Reader. New York: International Universities Press, 1948:259–272.

83. Smith GV, Smith OW. Estrogen and progestin metabolism in pregnancy: The effect of hormone administration in pre-eclampsia. J Clin Endocrinol 1941;1:477–484.

84. Smith GV, Smith OW. The prophylactic use of diethylstilbestrol to prevent fetal loss from complications of late pregnancy. N Engl J Med 1949;241:410–412.

85. Smith GV, Smith OW. Prophylactic hormone therapy: Relation to complications of pregnancy. Ob Gyn 1954;4:129–141.

86. Swyer GIM, Law RG. An evaluation of the prophylactic antenatal use of stilboestrol: Preliminary report. J Endocrinol 1954;10:vi–vii.

87. Taussig HB. The evils of camouflage as illustrated by thalidomide. N Engl J Med 1963;269:92 24.
88. Turiel J, Wingard D. Immune response in DES-exposed women. Fertil Steril 1988;49:928.
89. Vesey MP, Fairweather DVJ, Norman-Smith R, Buckley J. A randomized double-blind controlled trial of the value of stilboestrol therapy in pregnancy: Long-term follow-up of mothers and their offspring. Br J Ob Gyn 1983;90:1007 1017
90. White P, Koshy P, Duckers J. The management of pregnancy complicating diabetes and of children of diabetic mothers. Med Clin N Amer 1953;37:1481–1496.
91. Wingard DL, Turiel J. Long-term effects of exposure to diethylstilbestrol. Western J Medicine 1988;149:551–554.

45
Ethics of the New Technologies: A Discussion of Case Histories

Machelle M. Seibel, Moderator, Rabbi Joseph Polak,
James O'Donohoe, George Annas, John D. Biggers,
Susan Crockin, Susan Levin, and Judith Bernstein

Advances in Reproductive technology have created the potential for a variety of ethical dilemas. To consider some of these issues, three composite cases are presented. A group of panelists will then introduce themselves and respond to the questions.

Three Composite Cases

Those of us involved in the care of infertile couples, or associated with them in any way, will recognize aspects of these people from our own personal experience.

Case No. 1: Oocyte Donation from a Known Donor

Molly and her husband Derek are requesting the in vitro fertilization (IVF) team to assist them in achieving a pregnancy using Molly's sister's oocyte and Derek's sperm (oocyte donation from a known donor). In this process Molly's sister will undergo gonadotropin therapy to induce superovulation and will be monitored as if she were undergoing IVF, with daily ultrasounds and serum estradiol measurements. Just before ovulation, her oocyte will be retrieved by ultrasound needle aspiration and fertilized in the laboratory. The resultant embryo will be transferred into Molly's uterus 2 days after fertilization. The medical risks are relatively small.

Molly is 43 years old, and has been married for 10 years to Derek, who is 45. They have received extensive unsuccessful treatment for infertility. No specific cause has been identified for their inability to conceive, but Molly has respondeed poorly in her IVF cycles, and despite six attempts has never reached the stage of oocyte retrieval. Her age is thought to be a significant factor in her inability to produce matuve oocytes. Prior to their marriage Molly became pregnant by Derek; however, the couple chose to terminate the pregnancy because they felt they were neither emotionally nor financially ready for parenthood. Adoption is not an option for them. Their desire is for either a biologic child or none. Derek seems to be more ambivalent than Molly about parenthood at this time in his life, but "wants to make his wife happy." The marriage has been stormy at times but is currently stable. The couple are college-educated professionals. Who are financially secure.

Molly's sister June, age 36, has been asked to donate her oocytes so Molly and Derek can have a child. June is divorced with two children, ages 3 and 5. She states that she has finished her family and desires no more children. She expresses delight in being able to help her sister. She lives 150 miles away, however, and will have to accept the inconvenience of staying with Molly and Derek for several weeks while preparing for the procedure. Her children will come to stay also.

There are several areas of potential conflict:

1. Disagreement over the issue of secrecy. June believes the entire family should know about the procedure and that the child should be told about June's contribution to its genetic heritage. Molly and Derek want the donation to be a closely held secret with no one else knowing.
2. The necessity for amniocentesis. June wants to be sure that any child she is partly responsible for bringing into the world is healthy, whereas Molly does not think she wants to know about problems, and is sure she could not go through an abortion if abnormalities were discovered. Derek agrees with June.
3. June and Molly's relationship. Molly denies any concerns about this. She feels that her

425

sister owes her this help, since "June got all the good eggs."

Despite these possible complications, all three parties state strongly that they wish to go ahead with the oocyte donation and believe that any problems that might occur can be solved. All three appear to be emotionally stable.

Case No. 2: Difficulty with Closure

Madeleine is 33 years old and has never been pregnant. She is a teacher of learning-disabled children, and has received several awards for her work. She is in her second marriage, to Robert, an engineer, who is 45. Robert has two grown children by a previous marriage. Madeleine reports that her first marriage ended because of her infertility. Her first husband has remarried and now has two young children.

Madeleine has severe endometriosis and has undergone repeated surgeries to remove scar tissue and endometrial growths (endometriomas) on her ovaries. The disease also involves the bowel, and Madeleine had an episode of rectal bleeding that required hospitalization. Dysmenorrhea is a significant problem, and she misses at least 2 days of school a month. The suggested treatment for her condition is hysterectomy and removal of both ovaries. If she were able to conceive, however, pregnancy might improve her endometriosis, and hysterectomy might not be necessary. She has discussed the donor oocyte program and is not interested, saying, "I want to make my own system work."

In the past 3 years Madeleine has had eight IVF attempts, five at another hospital and three in her current setting. Each time oocytes were obtained, fertilized, and transferred back, but none of the fertilized eggs implanted. Madeleine has met with the counselor in both settings and discussed her obsessive drive to become pregnant. She did not wish to continue in therapy in either program. During the intake interview in the present program, Madeleine's husband stated that he was happy to go along with her desire to have children, but he already had his family and had no desire to adopt. In her last consultation with her current physician, Madeleine expressed the desire to try "just one more" cycle. The physician explained that it was extremely unlikely that she would ever become pregnant, and that continuing on was not in her best medical interest. Madeleine's response was, "If you don't do this for me, I'll never have a child. I know I

could be a good mother, better than the ones I see all the time around me who yell at their kids in the supermarket. Why don't you give me a fair chance? Don't I have rights?" Faced with this responce, her physician did not know what should be done.

Case No. 3: Single Woman Requesting Donor Insemination

Barbara is a 37-year-old physician who has had two serious long-term relationships but has never married. She is financially comfortable, owns her own home, and has a circle of close friends. She has discussed with her mother and father her desire to be a parent without waiting for marriage. Her parents say that they understand her feelings and will be as helpful as they can. She has also talked to two male friends who have expressed their willingness to be role models for her child—spend time, do sports, and so on. All her life she has seen herself as a mother, viewing parenthood as an important part of her core identity, and does not want to keep waiting for the "right man to come along." She hopes that she may marry some day, but would not enter into any relationship with someone who had negative feelings toward a child conceived by artificial insemination. Right now her goal of getting married comes second to her goal of becoming a mother, and she finds it difficult to focus energy on meeting new men or deepening existing relationships with those she is dating. She has been in therapy to understand these issues, and feels that she has resolved them and is now ready to begin artificial insemination. Barbara is requesting a donor source where she will be able to learn about the donor's beliefs, value systems, physical characteristics, hobbies, and family composition as well as his medical history, although she does not want any identifying information.

The Panelists

George Annas

I am a lawyer. I teach at Boston University School of Medicine, School of Public Health, and direct a program called the Law-Medicine Ethics Program. My interest in infertility started about 20 years ago when I did a legal analysis on the major infertility program in Boston. I have been interested in this area ever since.

I do not think there is a difference between the legal and social issues that confronted us in the past and those which will continue to do so in the 1990s. One of these issues will be to determine what position to take as a society in terms of the new reproductive technologies. We tend to think of the procedures one by one rather than looking at their overarching issues; however, the social policy issues are really not related to specific techniques, whether it is artificial insemination by donor, surrogate motherhood, IVF, or surrogate embryo transfer using frozen embryos. Rather, the social policy issues they cut across are the potential use of reproductive technology for noninfertility use, protection of the human embryo, identification of the mother, identification of the father, donor screening, donor anonymity, and opportunities for commercialization.

IVF is the least problematic of all the techniques from a social policy point of view, at least if the gametes are those of the mother and father. There are really only two issues. One is advertising. *Advertising Age* identified IVF as one of the most overhyped and misleadingly advertised commodities of any kind in the United States in the early 1990s. The other issue is the status of the extracorporeal embryo —whether or not it has the status of a human being and how to protect it.

Artificial insemination by donor (AID), has been performed for some time, and egg donation is beginning to be used more widely. One big issue is, as shown in case No. 3, how much the recipient should know about the donor of eggs or sperm. One of the California sperm banks has a chart listing all of the characteristics of its donors. The woman in case No. 3 would appreciate this, as she could learn everything about the man from athletics, to IQ, to impacted wisdom teeth.

Another issue is whether the recipient or the child has a right to know the identity of the donor at some point. A glaring example is that of Dr. Graham, who runs the Nobel Prize sperm bank. This type of concept raises the issue of a woman purposely choosing a specific individual in an attempt to increase her childs genetic potential or make better babies. Much more practical aspects of this issue are the potential social and legal ramifications created for all parties by removing anonymity.

Surrogate motherhood involves no new technology, but it raises significant questions of law as the law applies to the rights of the couple who contract with a surrogate. The use of the word surrogate, even abbreviating the term from surrogate mother, is an attempt to dehumanize the woman. However, as the New Jersey Supreme Court pointed out in the case of Baby M, the woman who bears a child is the child's mother in every biologic, genetic, and legal sense of the word, and current adoption laws, termination of parental right laws, baby-selling laws, and custody laws all cover the surrogate mother arrangement. In no state in the United States are contracts that protect the rights of the couple enforceable if a surrogate mother changes her mind about giving up a child. They are technically legal, but they are not enforceable.

Frozen embryos appear to raise the ante, and the ramifications of the technique are just beginning to be addressed. The Davis case in Tennessee raised the question of the status of frozen embryos. The judge said that he had to decide whether embryos were furniture or children, and he decided they were children. Some people have tried to finesse this issue by calling frozen embryos preembryos. This seems like deception. Although frozen embryos may be living, human embryos are probably not children.

The combination of frozen embryos with surrogate motherhood means that a woman could be hired to gestate an embryo to which she is not genetically related. That has been done, and it raises the novel legal question for the first time in the history of our country as to whether the gestational mother or the genetic mother should be considered the legal mother with rearing rights and responsibilities. I would argue that the law should remain the way it is: that the woman who gives birth to the child should always be considered the legal mother for all purposes. That should be an irrebuttable presumption. She should be the only one who has the legal authority to give up rearing rights and responsibilities with that child.

In all of these cases we must consider opportunities for commercialization, donor screening, donor anonymity, identification of the donor mother or father for the child, and steps that are taken to protect the human embryo. Although it is not a child, it is not furniture either, and it deserves proper respect. In the next 10 years these issues are going to become much more complex, since through the human genome initiative we will learn the sequence of the entire human genome. The issues we have confronted already with cystic fibrosis are going to look trivial in the future, when perhaps hundreds and even thousands of genetic conditions may be teased out and diagnosed at the embryo level. It is possible that every woman will routinely flush out her embryos before she continues a pregnancy and have them genetically diagnosed and replaced only if they are healthy. There is no doubt that this is going to lead to many issues that we have not even begun to think about such as what is genetically normal: should we try to increase the height, intelligence, eye color, hair color, or other characteristics of individual children; who should make those decisions; who should judge what is a normal child or an abnormal child, a normal embryo or an abnormal embryo; and what role should the law play in our future? It looks as though the future may involve attempting to define what are good, better, and best human characteristics.

Rabbi Joseph Polak

I am the Rabbi at Boston University and am associated with the Center for Health Law at Boston University. I would like to discuss counseling issues as they relate to these three cases.

In the first case we were told that prior to her marriage Molly became pregnant by Derek. The couple terminated the pregnancy because they felt they were neither emotionally nor financially ready for parenthood. At this point some big questions are raised about the couple. What are these people's values? The answer is that they themselves are where all things begin. Whether or not to have children is their decision. It is them. There are no outside factors or sets of values to which they appeal; only whether or not they want to make that

decision. Adoption is not an option for them. Their desire is for either a biologic child or none. That is a very interesting decision. I would like to understand their aversion to adopting a child, and from what context that value comes. It seems the only set of values that must be satisfied are those of these two people's feelings, their inclinations, and what they feel.

Derek seems to be more ambivalent than Molly. The most important thing is that he wants to make his wife happy. While it does tell us something about Derek, wanting to make her happy may not provide the best basis for making such an important decision.

Molly's younger sister June, we are told, has finished her family and desires no more children. At what point do we decide that our family is finished? In what context do we make that decision? We are tired; we would like to spend more time on the golf course; we feel we have suffered enough raising children. The carpools and everything get on our nerves, and it is time to finish having children. Is this where it comes from?

June also wants to be sure that any child she is partly responsible for bringing into the world is normal, because if it is not, it could require hours of time away from the pursuit of pleasure. One must question whether parenthood is the goal or if having a baby is seen exclusively as an acquisition.

The second case I find interesting. Madeleine is saying, "I stand a 0.005 chance of ever conceiving a biologic child; however, I have a million dollars to spend on becoming pregnant. Here is my $5,000. Let's do another workup and try one more time. If it doesn't work, I'll have to go to Miami for a while and relax. I will come back, and we will try again."

At what point do we say, "Hold it"? At what point do we say there are overarching, to use Mr. Annas's word, questions. I think people have to ask America to go beyond what the sociologists have called habits of the heart. I think people have to ask the fundamental questions: What are we doing in this world? Why are we here? What is life about? Are we really here just to get the most satisfaction and pleasure in the quickest amount of time, or are we here to do something to improve the world, make it a better place? Is there no shape, no structure to the universe? Is there not some higher power out of which comes certain kinds of moral demands? Why are we alive in this place and in this time? If we start to contemplate these questions, the pursuit of happiness becomes less significant. The question is no longer what we can do for ourselves or even what we can do for others, but rather what we ought to be doing all together.

The problem in a clinical setting, even with a wonderful hospital and a wonderful set of social workers and psychiatrists working with the infertility clinic, is that those people do not have to address those questions. Although the mental health team would like to, somehow the setting does not allow them to because they have to take a posture of nonjudgment. If somebody wants an infertility workup and she appears to be stable, there is nothing to hold back. This, it seems to me, is making no judgments; or it is taking absence of judgment much farther than anybody intended. I would suggest, for example, that any woman for whom the chances were very poor, who was pushing hard for an infertility workup should be required to talk with a clergyman or someone who is capable of forcing her to deal with transcendent values. I do not just mean doing a value structure setup asking, "What do you feel about this, what do you feel about that?" I mean asking those fundamental questions. What are you doing in this world? What is your understanding of God, and what is your understanding of the implications if there is no God, and if there is no God, what do you think your purpose is? Those questions have to be asked because if they are not, they will make us crazy. In the end we are going to have a generation of children whom they will make crazy.

John D. Biggers

I am a professor of physiology at Harvard Medical School. I noticed that the program lists me as a medical ethicist. I do not claim that at all. I am a scientist, a physiologist. I got involved in the ethics of reproductive technology the year following the birth of the first test-tube baby, Louise Brown. The former department of Health, Education, and Welfare had an ethical board review of this whole subject, and I was invited to be their chief scientific advisor. Since then, I have become involved in some of the political activities in this area. Politicians and members of the Right to Life movement have tried to invoke science to support their case. I found many of their arguments very misleading, so this is the area in which I focused.

I think the question that scientists face when working on these issues is what their role should be. Several roles are possible, and they fall into the area that philosophers call conceptual analysis. For example, we on this panel are concerned with making sure that the people who are not scientists understand what science is saying. All we have to do is listen to the public debates to realize that the misuse of the language of our subject is atrocious. In particular, we should be alert for what Professor Margaret Somerville in Australia called behavior-generating words, like the ones that are bandied about on television and in the other media. They are really no more than slogans dreamed up to present a case. I have been particularly interested in two words or phrases in the last 2 years. One is this phrase, "Life begins at conception." That seems innocuous and straightforward. If you know the biology, you soon discover that it is very complex, and when this statement is used as a slogan for discussions on television or even in sermons from the pulpit, it misleads people terribly. It is the role of a scientist to point out what the problems are.

The second is a new word that was introduced in 1986 in two places. One place was the United States, and the word was used in the report that the American Fertility Society produced on the guidelines of ethics that should underlie reproductive technologies. The other place was the United Kingdom, and the word was introduced quite independently by the voluntary licensing authority, the body that acted and put into practice the recommendations of the Wornik Report. Both of those bodies used the word "preembryo" to mean that stage of development from fertilization up to 14 days of age, suggesting that this is a separate part of development to which one can attribute separate moral values. It is used quite commonly by people who are not experts in the scientific field. In my view, the word should never have been invented, and I encourage all of my students to forget it.

The reason that scientists are concerned about those phrases is that at the turn of the century an important biologic concept was developed: the concept of the life cycle. The process of fertilization was finally discovered in 1879 and described as we know it today. In another 20 years the life cycle was discovered. It starts with fertilization, proceeds through puberty and to adulthood, and eventually ends in an individual's death. During the cycle, eggs and sperm are produced, which may be used to form new individuals. Normally we think of fertilization as the beginning of a new individual; that is, a sperm and egg fuse to make a zygote, which then cleaves, enters the uterus, and implants, which is the beginning of pregnancy.

Thus, the life cycle is split into phases by two events—meiosis and fertilization: the diploid phase of 46 chromosomes and the haploid phase with 23. People frequently say that we are genetically different individuals. That is perfectly true, but so are sperm and eggs all genetically different. They are just another part of human life, and if they disappear the whole cycle stops, and we become extinct. There is a cycle of life, and the sperm and egg are just as much a part of it as are the man and woman from whom they make a new individual.

When people say that life begins at conception, and they are prepared to discard the haploid-stage ovum and sperm, what they are doing is ascribing different moral values to the haploid sperm and egg and to the adult. It is not at all clear on what basis that judgment is made. It is not scientific. They have to produce a nonbiologic reason to justify that ethical point of view, and this is what they fail to do. They think they are making a scientific statement, which they are not.

This has terribly serious implications. If this were ever passed into law—and there was a proposal to amend the U.S. constitution to say that life begins at fertilization—this would almost certainly interfere with methods of contraception, IVF, and the treatment of infertility. This is not a trivial issue, and scientists must speak up and demand that if the Right to Life people want to say life begins at conception, they must produce convincing biologic reasons for saying so.

James O'Donohoe

I am a priest of the archdiocese of Boston. I teach ethics at Boston College, including the School of Nursing. I have a doctorate from the University of Louvain in Belgium both in church law and in what we call moral theology.

To begin with, I would like to clear up a major misconception. The church does not teach that life begins at conception. Some Right to Life people say that, but it is incorrect. On the contrary, the basic teaching is that life is to be respected from the first moment of conception, which is different.

Ethics is primarily concerned with humanization. It may therefore be described as a disciplined inquiry into what contributes to or distracts from the humanization process. Technology, too, is concerned with the humanization process. Ethics replies, "We know that you can do it, but we wonder if you should."

Ethics tends to urge the promotion of what is truly humanizing. We call those values. Ethics tends to discourage the promotion of that which is truly dehumanizing, and we call those disvalues. Where does one look to discover humanizing values and dehumanizing disvalues? Herein lies the distinction between what we call philosophic and theologic ethics. Philosophic ethics seeks values and disvalues through the use of human reason alone. You will find this in Aristotle and Plato.

When you become a believer you do not check your reason at the door of the church. Theologic ethics seeks values and disvalues through the use of human reason enlightened by, informed by, supplemented by, complemented by a religious faith that is a positive and affirmative acceptance of some sort of a divine revelation. You will find this in Muslim, Jewish, and Christian ethics.

It is important to note that neither kind of ethics can promote humanizing on its own. Reason of itself is quite fallible and often it can be reduced to rationalism. True faith cannot contradict reason, in spite of what you will hear from many people who are believers; otherwise, it deteriorates into fundamentalism. In the twelfth-century definition, theology is always faith seeking understanding.

The society in which we live is pluralist, and it grows more and more complicated. It has an officially accepted system of philosophic ethics but not one of theologic ethics. As a consequence, there is a plurality of ethical systems. This can have its advantages because many dimensions of the issue are exposed, but it also can have disadvantages because one can be tempted to say a plague on all your houses and do one's own thing. Both of these are tragic.

Parenthetically, it might be observed that average Americans ask neither philosophic nor theologic questions, although they may be believers or philosophers. The average American asks only the pragmatic question, "will it work?" Efficiency alone is the measure of what our society values and disvalues. This is, I think, something that we have to face up to.

Reproductive technology has made tremendous advances, as you know better than I. However, like every other human discipline, including theology, it must be challenged vis-a-vis its potential for humanization. That is precisely the task of the ethicist: to be the platonic gadfly, that annoying thing that buzzes around asking provoking questions and not providing answers.

The specific matter addressed here is the ethical dimensions of contemporary reproductive technology. How humanizing are such things as egg and sperm donation, surrogate motherhood, IVF, embryo transplants, and so on? It seems to me, and this has been indicated already, that there are two extreme assessments of the situation, both of which are misleading.

The first extreme adopts as a moral standard the biologic integrity of the marital sexual act, which may not be tampered with for any reason. This can be found in the Vatican declaration. It states that love making and baby making can never be separated. Any technology that interferes with the biologic integrity of the marital act is immoral.

The other extreme focuses solely on the individual's desire for a child. It holds that any adult should be able to engage in any alternative reproductive procedure that technology can provide. This is evident in some of the case reports. The essential ethical issues here are individual liberty, reproductive privacy, and reproductive rights. If these are protected, any inference in the reproductive function is quite moral and should be pursued.

Neither of these assessments is adequate to determine an ethic of reproductive technology and perhaps enlighten us with regard to our respective beliefs. Dialogue is an overused word. Nevertheless, it is necessary for people to speak with one another because no one has a fullness of the truth, and we are all working to try to find it as much as possible in our fallible way.

Machelle M. Seibel. The perspectives of the panelists are varied and interesting, and demonstrate the complexities of trying to make sense of what we must consider when an infertile couple comes into our office. We realize suddenly that the medical circumstances with which we are faced are only part of a much broader picture, and we must consider the impact of what we are doing beyond medicine per se.

The panelists will now be asked to comment on the dilemma presented in case No. 1: Oocyte Donation from a Known Donor.

George Annas. This case seems to be highly problematic. It is unclear who wants to be the mother and why. Who wants to control the pregnancy? Who wants to control rearing this child? I think a lot more talking has to be done before this case approaches resolution.

Judith Bernstein. This brings up the position of the gatekeeper, which generally is considered to be passive: a position of taking no action, making no judgment, taking no ethical stand. For me, however, it is a strong and positive ethical position of commitment, of faith that the average human being is capable of examining the issues and coming to a decision that I may not agree with, but that I have to respect. I have a great deal of difficulty with this particular case. I would certainly like to see all of these individuals engaged in serious therapy to work out some of the things that they are not now apparently aware of as potential problems, but I do not see myself at this point in my life declaring that I know enough to determine that something should be denied someone because that person's set of values is different from mine.

Rabbi Joseph Polak. I have a similar problem, but I would come at it a slightly different way. I think people can be wrong, and I think they can be told that they are wrong. Not everybody is right because they make a judgment. My sense is that it is unfortunate that the medical profession sometimes winds up being the gatekeeper. It is hard for them to do anything but ask, "Have you thought it through"? I also feel that a psychiatrist, social worker or other mental health professional cannot deal with these questions. If they can it is not due to any skills that they have learned. In fact, it is not a matter of skills, but it comes out of the capacity to understand values and to focus on them in a much broader sense than therapists are typically taught during their training. That is the problem with the first case. It is not clear to me that the medical profession has an understanding of those broader questions.

Susan Levin. I would only restate what Judith has said. In addition, however, I would recommend therapy for this couple or these three people, plus the children from the previous marriage. They also have a stake in the outcome of this procedure. Therapy as most of us know takes a long time for some of these issues to be resolved, and it is not the answer to everything. This case is familiar to me because I have worked with people who are facing many of the same difficulties. They talk about it, and they think about it, and they still want to go through with the procedure. It is not my role as their therapist to tell them that they should not do that. At least, I don't think it is.

John D. Biggers. I do not think a physician would be wrong refusing to take part in the treatment as it presently stands. There are too many problems that will affect the family later. The sister's need to interfere with a pregnant woman and tell her what to do—whether or not she can have amniocentesis—is going to cause endless trouble. Interference by the oocyte donor could go on for several years, affecting major issues such as how that child is brought up. It seems to me the potential for disruption of the family is enormous. I think it would be probably best, until things are sorted out, not to treat under these circumstances.

Father James O'Donohoe. I am very uncomfortable with this case. Molly's problem is something she feels deeply. She is not embarrassed. She is uncomfortable with her infertility. Derek seems to be totally ambivalent. He wants to make his wife happy, but that is hardly an ethical reason to bend to her wishes. At times the couple has a stormy union; in addition, Molly says that her sister "owes" her help. She may indeed, but I do not know if this is the type of help that is owed. When you use the word "owe" you are talking about what is due. You are speaking rights language, and rights language is always concerned with essential needs. I wonder whether Molly has an essential need? Perhaps she will not be a fully realized person without this experience. The attitude of these people, however, admits to no ethical dimension, at least such was not mentioned.

Machelle M. Seibel. These cases reflect a composite of every gamete-donation couple. Teams who work with them must be a cohesive unit in making decisions. Sometimes that is difficult to accomplish because team members have different personal, religious, and ethical beliefs. In addition, most team members have a commitment to doing what is best for the patient. For these reasons, IVF teams are a study in group dynamics. With effort, patients receive the best care and team members broaden their perspectives. However, it is a slow and ongoing process.

Judith Bernstein. I have great concerns about the manipulation implicit in this arrangement and also about some of the ambivalence. We do not as a society require couples who achieve parenthood without our intervention to pass certain tests to prove their ability or their lack of ambivalence about having a child, or their stability. Why should we require these things of the couples who come to us for assisted reproductive techniques?

Audience. I practice both gynecology and psychiatry, and I have worked with a lot of people with infertility. The problem as I see it is down the road later on when the divorce comes: Who gets custody of the child? The sister June will want custody because she will say the child is really hers. I have been impressed, having followed pregnancies from infertility workup until the child is 10 years old, at how badly things can go. I have also been aware that most of the warning signs are there at the start of the infertility workup. I cannot tell the number of times when a workup is successful but the woman comes in the next week and asks for an abortion because the marriage is falling apart. I do not feel any satisfaction in helping someone become pregnant just so she can have an abortion because she is going to be divorced. I would rather work preventably before that happens.

Rabbi Joseph Polak. I always joke around when people ask me what is going to happen. I tell them that I am trained as a rabbi and not yet as a prophet. The medical profession is also being asked, "Well, if you offer assisted reproduction for a couple, what is going to happen?" From another side, when a couple comes to you and wants treatment, do you have to treat them any differently than a couple that does not come to you for treatment? That is to say, if the couple with no infertility problem wants to have a baby they go ahead and they have one. They do not ask anybody. So, should you make a different judgment regarding the couple who does come to you? Once people ask you whether you can help them to have children, you are forced into a situation where you have to make a moral decision. We are talking here about two areas in which physicians have to make decisions: that is, about the physical health and mental health of the people who come for assistance.

I would ask you another question, about the spiritual health of those people. Somehow that

is no longer a category in American thinking. The fact is that it matters. You have to listen to a couple and tell them the implications for a greater society if you perform these kinds of procedures. Just to focus on this hypothetical couple, it is likely that there is going to be a disaster eventually, and not making a moral decision about them implicates you as a party to that disaster.

Susan Crockin. People who could do this at home would do it at home.

Machelle M. Seibel. That is a possibility. For instance, one could buy sperm themselves for donor insemination. But many people do not feel comfortable doing that. There are circumstances when people could do it themselves but choose not to.

Susan Crockin. What I am getting at is people without infertility problems can create their family without intervention and related judgments. It seems to me the issue in case No. 1 is that the physician is required to give the treatment specifically requested. The infertility team is required legally to assist in the exercise of the constitutional right to procreate. They must also have an obligation to assist a couple to have a child, but not necessarily the child the couple and their donor are contemplating.

Machelle M. Seibel. One could refer the couple to another program. But the same circumstances exist for that team, wherever they are, to come to the decision—I can or I cannot.

Susan Crockin. That is an easy answer too. What if 10 programs made the decision not to offer this treatment. Would one of those 10 physicians have to reverse the decision and agree to offer it? I would suggest no, because what you are being asked to do is to help create a family in a particular way that is not, in your professional judgment, appropriate. But you are not denying the infertile couple treatment for infertility. You might well recommend a gamete donor who is not related.

Rabbi Joseph Polak. What is the difference between a hospital and a department store? A man comes into a department store and says he wants a large screen television set for $5,000. The department store checks his credit, and it is barely all right. Everybody at the store knows that if this man buys the set it is going to be repossessed within one and a half years. The man's credit rating will go down. The store will lose money. Everybody will suffer except the people who charge a lot of interest. Should the department store sell the man the television set?

Along comes a couple to the hospital. They say, "I know we have a certain number of liabilities, but we are going to work really hard to keep this baby healthy, happy, and all that kind of thing." What right does the hospital have to let them down? Is the hospital a place that is available to consumers, or is it a very different kind of place with a different perspective on the world? A hospital is not a department store. To me, That is the concept we are discussing.

Charlotte Richards. I have done ovum donation, and I have seen how happy the women are when they have a baby as a result. This is true even in cases where we use their sister's gametes. I think that if you take too strict an attitude toward who will and will not be allowed to do ovum donation, all you are doing is encouraging couples and patients to lie. If this couple had not been so frank about their feelings, they would have been allowed to sail through this. If you are judgmental and controlling in your attitude it only encourages people to present a beautiful façade that in fact does not exist. I find myself often starting to make judgments on patients, and then realizing that probably what they are telling me is not exactly the way things are. I think that they need a lot of counseling, and our couples come for that several times. I think the suggestion that they seek help from their rabbi, priest, or minister is appropriate.

Finally, I do not agree with the notion of having a perfect life. No matter what anyone does, people are just going to live their lives. I have worked hard to help couples become pregnant, only to have them come back and say they do not want the pregnancy. I would have had no way of knowing that. Life is not perfect, so we have to treat people the best way we can. I do not think we can be judgmental all of the time.

Carol Frost-Vercollone. The only thing that I have not heard said here is what concerns me

the most, and that is the concept of informed consent. If I was counseling this couple I would be overwhelmed, but I would look for some internal consistency in all of the parties involved. The reason for counseling is not that these people are mentally ill. They seem to be having a normal reaction in an unusual situation. They are not consistent in their reactions, though, and they need help to be guided to talk them through. Therefore you do not have informed consent at this point. One person wants anonymity, another wants secrecy, we are not sure the husband wants to proceed at all. There is not equally informed consent. I find that the way out of this dilemma that medicine so often does not take is the counseling referral. The presumption is that with some further discussion, people might be able to reach that sort of faith and acceptance of one path or the other. It is really the wise way out so that they do come to some kind of internal decision. This is what adoption agencies do, by the way. It is not a matter of saying that you can do this or you cannot do this, you can cope with this or you cannot, but that you need more time to think about what you are coping with.

Audience. In general, I do try to respect a patient's reasonable request. For the panelists who feel we should go along with the requests of the patient, why do you provide psychologic counseling at all?

Machelle M. Seibel. There does not appear to be uniform agreement that we should provide what patients want because they want it. Unfortunately, our current screening methods do not always allow us to determine whom we should or should not treat. Often, we never find out if we made the correct choice. It is further complicated by the fact that no two situations are identical.

John D. Biggers. The main concern to me is the donor sister wanting to tell the recipient what to do. For example, you must have amniocentesis, and if the child is abnormal, have an abortion. That is a pretty serious thing to require. I am not saying that it may be fully unjustified to have the abortion, but for the donor to make that as a requirement tells me that big danger is ahead. There could be a lot of further interference. What is wrong with making an alternative suggestion and telling these people that donation by the sister is not appropriate? I feel it would be far better to have an unknown ovum donor.

Machelle M. Seibel. The issue of known ovum donation is complex. This is due in part to the fact that it is a relatively new procedure with little follow-up information available. Because most centers do not perform known sperm donation, correlative data is lacking as well. However, because it is relatively difficult to identify anonymous women who are phenotypically similar to the recipient and who are willing to undergo ovulation induction and oocyte retrieval just to be oocyte donors, known ovum donors do provide a distinct advantage. It also typically eliminates any exchange of money to the donor for the inconvenience of providing her eggs. Most known donors do not ask to be compensated for their time and inconvenience.

However, whether a donor is known or anonymous, one point has not been raised: ovum donors are not patients, they are volunteers. As a result, ovulation induction and oocyte retrieval is an end, not a means. Most oocyte donors are substantially more anxious than most infertility patients because they have not evolved through a progression of earlier treatments and they have no vision of a child to focus on. For this reason, ovum donors require special consideration and treatment.

We will now have the panelists' comments on case No. 2: Difficulty with Closure.

Father James O'Donohoe. What strikes me is the second to the last sentence: "Don't I have rights?" American society is very litigious, and we speak about "rights" when often we are really talking about "wants." I wonder if Madeleine has a right in the properly understood sense of the word—a rationally demonstrable claim to continue treatment.

John D. Biggers. I agree about the use of the word rights. I do not think she has a right. If it is impossible for her to get pregnant, this notion is ridiculous. I do not find anything wrong with a physician refusing to treat this woman. After all, when you do the treatment

there is a risk to the patient, so what you are doing is exposing her to risk knowing full well that she is not going to benefit from it. It is a very small chance like winning the lottery. In addition, you are expending a lot of medical resources that could be of use for other people, which I think is an important issue.

In hearing this case I noticed that the husband has a family and has no desire to adopt. It seems to me that someone should work on the husband and tell him maybe he should adopt.

Susan Levin. Obviously, this couple should be referred for counseling. Some couples refer themselves and say, "We can't stop. We really need help stopping infertility treatment." Those are the kind of couples we can work with. However, this couple will seek counseling only if required. They wish they were not there, and in fact they really are not there, except physically. They answer questions, and they say basically, "We really do not need counseling; we need another infertility treatment, another cycle of IVF. If this doctor won't do it, we will find one that will." And they will.

As a counselor, it is hard to do other than ask questions, try to stir something up, try to find some tension that I can engage and get something going with the couple. Then they may come back if they have gone through enough defeats. Other than that, I am not sure what the role of the therapist can be except to advise, support, and counsel the doctor.

Rabbi Joseph Polak. Let us say a couple came to me with this question, a Jewish couple, with some respect for the Jewish tradition. The issue is not what I think, but what does the Jewish tradition think. Judaism has a body of law that would deal with this question. I would make a decision one way or the other. That decision would involve risk–benefit ratios, and it certainly would recall a 2,000-year-old legal apparatus.

I do not know how I would decide this particular case, however, because I do not have enough information. I think, though, that it strongly highlights the question of whether a hospital is a department store. I do not think it is; it does not have to give its customers everything that they demand. I think that if in the end people do come to us, and we are put in the unfortunate situation of having to make judgments about their lives, we have to do so. We have to do so with a great deal of responsibility, but not with the notion that we completely know and understand the people. Although we must never forget that aspect, we do have greater wisdom. We should not choose for them, however. We should make them aware. We should try to help them to understand the wisdom that we have gleaned through our years of counseling, and medical experience; wisdom that they simply do not have. If a couple comes to us closed, our task is to open them up and persuade them to talk about the issues.

Judith Bernstein. The nurse often receives an enormous amount of anger when limits are set for couples. The physician is not going to get that anger because the woman is still harboring hopes that maybe he or she will have a change of mind. The therapist is not going to get that anger because the woman is trying to put her best foot forward and look as stable as she can. The anger comes to the nurse and is difficult to deal with. However, receiving the anger is necessary because I do tend to agree with Dr. Biggers that if there is not a reasonable chance for success, it is not worth the risk to the patient.

Susan Crockin. The really angry people come to me. At some point it is certainly correct for medical professionals to make a judgment call that it is not appropriate for patients to continue in a particular program. It is fascinating to hear how far we have come in infertility treatment. It was not very many years ago that one would never discuss the issue of giving patients an equal voice, and it would have been automatic that the professional judgment was asserted and applied. I think it points up the serious problem we have today of knowing when enough is enough.

Machelle M. Seibel. I will now ask the panelists for comments on case No. 3: Single Women Requesting Donor Insemination.

Father James O'Donohoe. Given my tradition, and this probably includes the Jewish tradition as well, I have great difficulty with a single woman requesting a child. It creates all sorts of problems and difficulties: doing harm, doing good. We do not resolve this. We rather attack it through a cost–benefit analysis, and no one is comfortable with it. I cannot sit back and say that the decision I reach as a physician not to do this is the right one, but it is the one that I, in my conscience, have to follow, while respecting the conscience of the other individual. I think that is what we have to clarify here. So, I would have great problems in my own tradition. One cannot say this is a bad woman. On the contrary, I think I would have to ask in doing this, am I doing her harm? Am I doing her good? What is her right in this matter?

John D. Biggers. Of the three cases I find this the most difficult on which to give a clear answer. In my case, ethical views are largely influenced by the way I was brought up, which was in the Church of England in a strict religious family. In the society that I was raised in, children without marriage were forbidden. That thought keeps coming through when I read this case. On the other hand, in this day and age I know very well that single parenthood is being condoned by society more and more, and when I think about the pros and cons I do not really see much harm in it. I would like to give a clear answer saying either no or yes, but I cannot.

Susan Levin. This woman says that she has had therapy, and I think I must believe that that is so and that she is making a self-informed decision about what she wants. I cannot see any reason to deny her this, although I was also raised that children without marriage are forbidden. That would not mean if I were providing therapy I would think that her wish meant she was abnormal or something was wrong with her. Many single women provide good families for babies as a result of adoption, artificial insemination, or divorce. There are many reasons why women are single mothers, and I would have a hard time arguing against doing this procedure.

Rabbi Joseph Polak. Once again, the Jewish tradition is fairly clear that we do not have sex outside of marriage, and as a result we do not have children outside of marriage. A woman came to me with some questions (but she came to me after the fact). She lived in a suburb in a communal home. She had been divorced. She had two grown children, but she was young. She was a wonderful mother and raised delightful children. She then decided to have another child, so she made an arrangement with one of the men in the communal home where she was living. They agreed that he would father a child, but would not formally be its father. He would not have any child-raising requirements or have to be a role model. She asked no one and went ahead and had the baby. The baby is wonderful; it is now about 5, a happy, solid, well-nurtured child. The woman came to me with questions: "What do you think of all this? Are you mad at me? Do you think I am a terrible person?" I do not think she is a terrible person; I think that she violated our tradition. I think she violated our Torah, but there are ways for her to deal with that if she wants to, and I can help her. But my sense is that this is the wrong time for hellfire and brimstone, and that we have to be respectful of the choice even if we do not agree with it. If she is interested in getting my approval it means that she is having some questions about her decision. I want to pursue those questions. I want to tell her what the tradition has to say about them.

Judith Bernstein. I have no trouble with this case, partly because I had a 10-year experience as director of an artificial insemination program that was open to single women. I felt extremely good about the kinds of families that I was helping to build because of the seriousness and integrity of the women with whom I was working. That has given me some concrete and practical reassurance. One has to remember that fully 50% of the children who are conceived without our help will grow up in homes in which the biologic father will be absent. Given that, do we have any right to deny a single woman the chance at motherhood?

Susan Crockin. I think the woman deserves to receive artificial insemination. Physicians or a unit that refuses to treat her make this group of potential parents extremely vulnerable. Single women who do not receive artificial insemination must use people they know. They are then vulnerable to medical problems because the donors have not been screened properly for AIDS and undergone genetic testing. They also are vulnerable because they have been made to resort to known donors. The constitutional right to procreate is an individual right. Pushed to the wall, we may see a case in which a single woman succeeds in suing a sperm bank for not accepting her, or a physician who refuses to treat her.

Meryl Bombadieri. For the last 6 years I have been working with these women and I am impressed with them. They are conscientious and do a lot of soul searching. If they have any question at all that they are not quite ready to be a mother, they are much more rigorous in working out psychologic issues before they become pregnant than any couples I have seen. They are mentally healthy women who are simply at an age where it is now or never for motherhood. Maybe they will be married 10 years from now, maybe never, but they are doing a wonderful job as mothers. Society is supporting 14-year-olds keeping their babies. How can they tell me at 40, established in my career, mentally healthy, with family and friends as a wonderful support system, that I am not capable of raising a child?

Audience. I would like to offer another interpretation of the role of the therapist in evaluating these three couples and one that I am most comfortable with as a psychologist. It is our duty to warn them of potential harm. I think that is all that we can do. The rabbi said he was not trained in being a prophet. Psychologists are not trained in being prophets either, but I hope that we have done research, and have worked in this field for a while and seen the benefits as well as the harm that has been done in similar kinds of situations. In the first case, what troubled me the most was Molly's comment that her sister got all the good eggs and owed her this. I would want to explore that with her more, and warn her of the potential difficulties in their relationship and the kinds of family problems that might ensue as a result. In the third case, I would want to talk with the woman about the potential disadvantages of being a child who has just one parent. I probably would have the least problems with the second case because I do not think harm is really being done to anybody by this woman pursuing a pregnancy so vigorously. I would suggest to her that she meet with a therapist and work through her grief, because she is not dealing with it.

In summary, the only role that I can feel comfortable with is advising people what might happen. We do not know. We have no way of knowing, but we can predict what the possibilities are. The couples have to go back and search their souls, and decide whether they feel comfortable with the potential effects down the road.

Machelle M. Seibel. We presented three cases that were complicated and not easily handled. We are in a technologic time when many things are possible, but the answers are still evolving. In fact, the questions are still evolving. We hope we have had an opportunity to provide useful perspectives on some of the issues that we all face.

Index